Master Robert Bruce has been one of my spiritual inspirations for over fifty years now. I read his biography in the late 1960s, and then went through such of his sermons as were then in print. I always longed for more, and now my good friend, David Searle, has fulfilled that desire in his diligent work on Bruce's Sermons on Hebrews 11! David has done a superb job in rendering into very clear English the old Braid Scots that Bruce originally used to communicate with his congregation. David demonstrates Bruce's strong command of the Biblical languages, and in his translation (with its valuable notes), we find evidence of the deep pastoral insight that Bruce used to the benefit of his people, one of the qualities noted about him in the biography. Bruce's understanding of the struggles of the as yet imperfectly sanctified believer, always leaves us with hope, and greater zeal to follow the Lord more fully. Read this excellent work, and you will find it will build your faith, and draw you closer to Christ. Your reading and meditation will more than compensate David Searle for the immense effort he has put in to this translation.

DOUGLAS F. KELLY
Professor Emeritus, Reformed Theological Seminary,
Charlotte, North Carolina

Robert Bruce was a highly significant figure in the post-Reformation Scottish church, not least owing to his strained relationship with James VI. Yet, for too long, his twenty-eight sermons on Hebrews 11 have been preserved only in a set of handwritten manuscripts, impenetrable to most readers. In this volume, David Searle has performed a most valuable service in both transcribing and translating these materials, thus making them accessible to a contemporary audience. The publication of this work will do much to enhance our appreciation of Bruce as a distinguished preacher, scholar and spiritual leader of his time.

DAVID FERGUSSON
Professor of Divinity, University of Edinburgh, Scotland

In presenting these sermons for the first time to the modern reader David Searle has worked from the coalface of Bruce's own handwriting – hence it is truly manuscript work. He has then not only transliterated but 'translated' after the manner of TF Torrance's *Bruce's Sermons on the Sacraments*. The author and editor's shared connection to the Larbert-Airth area is a meaningful one. Out of his own ministerial experience Searle knows this heartland of Reformed piety and theology and he provides a useful, comprehensive account of Bruce's Life, with a digest of Shaw (General Assembly Acts), McCrie and Calderwood. More than this there is a thematic introduction to the work, all the better to help the sermons to speak. What we have allows the force of Bruce's theology, whose training in rhetoric and scholastic organisation of material allows for a prose that is compelling as it is nourishing, to come right through. There is a light amount of annotation, for the purposes of (e.g.) what is meant by frugality, secondary causes, attitude to witchcraft and many other topics. What we have is a detailed Reformed treatment of a seminal biblical text brought to light, with the graveclothes of old language and antiquarian topics gently taken away.

MARK ELLIOTT
Professor of Historical and Biblical Theology,
University of St Andrews, Scotland

What kind of preaching is needed in the churches? Today, as at all times, it is surely preaching which is direct, clear, truthful and appropriately simple. All these qualities are present in the preaching of Robert Bruce whose sincerity and passion break down the walls of the centuries separating our day from his, impressing on us both the nature and glory of faith. Nowhere does Robert Bruce speak to us more urgently than in his constant emphasis on conscience which is effective not just as a faculty permanently residing within us but as the immediate voice of God addressing us. The phrase 'labour of love' is familiar and overworked, but this is what David Searle has undertaken in bringing to the light of day Bruce's sermons on Hebrews 11: truly a labour in research and translation and obviously undertaken in love for God, church and pulpit. We owe much to David Searle; more to Robert Bruce and most to the Lord whose word to his people comes through so clearly in these pages.

STEPHEN N. WILLIAMS
Honorary Professor of Theology, Queen's University, Belfast

David Searle has provided a very valuable resource for the church today through his painstaking project of editing significant numbers of Robert Bruce's sermons. Valuable, that is, for studious preachers, who will be reminded again, in preaching, of application after exposition. The 'lessons' Bruce brings out from the text, appear to be relevant, courageous and specific for his original hearers. Valuable, also, for earnest Christians, who are eager to learn of and live out the enduring principles of faith expounded in Bruce's searching sermons.

MARTIN ALLEN
Retired minister of Chryston Church of Scotland
and former chairman of The Crieff Ministers' Fellowship

David Searle, in this living translation of Robert Bruce' sermons on the letter to the Hebrews, enables us to enter the world of 16th century Scotland. Robert Bruce, as he expounds the scriptures for his parish, relates the text with an earthy and practical tone. We get a feel of the unstable social and political context in which he spoke. Robert Bruce, therefore, was no abstract theologian. He knew the pastoral and missional context of his people and is not afraid to apply the Word of God to their real and felt needs. What is even more striking is how relevant his applications are to us in the 21st century.

TREVOR W. J. MORROW
Minister Emeritus, Lucan Presbyterian Church, Dublin

We are indebted to David Searle for making these sermons of Bruce available in modern English. This will open up the profound preaching of that man of God to a new generation. This has been a huge labour of love for David and we are the beneficiaries. Bruce's sermons are deeply theological, expounding among other themes the nature of faith and justification. At the same time, they are direct and personal, with amazing pastoral insight, graphic illustration and pithy application. Bruce often demonstrates the depth and riches of the love and compassion of God for sinners, while also speaking boldly to the leaders of both church and state, telling them to stand fast for justice and righteousness. Studying these sermons ought to make us better Christians.

A. T. B. MCGOWAN
Director, The Rutherford Centre for Reformed Theology

David Searle has done us a great service: making available a rich Biblical resource of potent evangelical conviction and powerful pastoral instruction which otherwise would have remained for ever illusive and inaccessible to the ordinary person.

Frank Sellar

Former Moderator of the
General Assembly of the Presbyterian Church in Ireland

Translated and Edited By

David Searle

Preaching Without Fear or Favour

Previously Unpublished Sermons on Hebrews 11

by Robert Bruce

CHRISTIAN HERITAGE

ISBN: 978-1-5271-0363-4
First published in 2019
in the
Christian Heritage Imprint
by
Christian Focus Publications Ltd,
Geanies House, Fearn, Ross-shire,
IV20 1TW, Great Britain.
www.christianfocus.com

Cover design by Daniel Van Straaten

Printed and bound by Bell & Bain, Glasgow

FSC www.fsc.org MIX Paper from responsible sources FSC® C007785

Contents

Dedicated to

My beloved sisters

Mary, Priscilla & Liz

and in memory of

Our dearest Lily who already knows

that to be with Christ is far better

Foreword

It was over five years ago during a telephone conversation with Iain Murray that I mentioned to him I was engaged in translating and editing Bruce's sermons on Isaiah 38. He immediately said that there was a more demanding project waiting for someone—the transliteration of Robert Bruce's sermons on Hebrews 11 from the scripts held in the Special Collections of New College Library. Once they were put into the English alphabet, they could then be translated from the Braid Scots.

And so, having completed the Isaiah 38 sermons, in November 2015 I embarked on a new challenge: transliterating three hundred and forty pages of neat, regular handwriting that had been done using the old Scots lettering, and then translating and editing what has proved to be a truly remarkable example of sixteenth-century post-reformation preaching in the Great Kirk of St Giles, situated in the heart of Scotland's capital.

I am indebted to various friends who have helped me on my way. First are Anne Burnett who efficiently photographed three hundred pages of the sermons, then Nathan Bircham and Stuart Irvin who in the later stages photographed the remaining documents. New College Library stipulates that only a hundred pages may be copied at one time, therefore several visits to Edinburgh were required. The Library staff have always been most helpful and courteous.

Next, my thanks are due to Dr Bruce Durie who kindly translated the first two pages for me, his help enabling me to master the mediaeval alphabet that the preacher used. Other academics have assisted me in tracking down some of Bruce's more obscure citations and thus I am indebted to Professor David Fergusson along with members of his faculty, and also to Professors Jane Dawson, Mark Elliot and John

R. McIntosh. My long-time friend and colleague, the Rev. Alasdair B. Gordon, a lawyer as well as a theologian, enlightened me on several of the more obscure legal terms used by Bruce. My friend from Larbert days, Albert Calder, has checked over the text of each sermon, identifying an average of a dozen typos in each chapter, as well as indicating an occasional awkward sentence; however, any remaining traces of bad grammar are my fault alone.

Finally, it would be remiss of me not to acknowledge my wife Lorna's loving patience (too often sorely tried far beyond acceptable limits) as, in my obsessive zeal for the task, I have constantly procrastinated over scores of husbandly responsibilities, resulting in innumerable ongoing sins of omission!

My thanks also must go to Rosanna Burton and the staff at Christian Focus Publications for their helpfulness and efficiency in the production of this book. I know they will share with me the prayer that it may be of some usefulness and value as an instrument in the Lord's hands towards his Kirk's calling of extending his Kingdom. *Soli deo gloria*.

David C Searle
The Grange, Errol
January 2019

Introduction

Master Robert Bruce, Minister of Edinburgh

I had bought and read MacNicol's biography of Bruce in 1965, but my interest was greatly quickened when ten years later I became minister of the Old Parish Kirk in Larbert, Stirlingshire. There in the vestry hung Bruce's portrait, along with that of John Bonar and Robert Murray M'Cheyne. I then found his gravestone in the old cemetery about twenty yards from the Larbert Kirk's entrance. The remains of the alms house can still be seen, but after the present church building had been erected in 1820, the original Kirk that had stood for some 300 years or more had been demolished in order to extend the burial ground. However, because Bruce's mortal remains had been laid at the foot of the pulpit where he had preached for the last few years of life (*c.* 1625–31), it is possible to determine the site of the original kirk.

My intention in this Introduction is first to give sufficient historical background of Bruce's twelve years as Minister of Edinburgh for readers to appreciate his relationship to the king and his court. Second, to elucidate the preacher's understanding of, and relationship with, 'the living God' (as he constantly refers to him), who was essentially the Triune God. Third, to bring out some of biblical teaching that was particularly dear to him, for it had guided and moulded his own calling and lifestyle. Fourth, to try and enable readers to gain some understanding of the godly character of this remarkable man whose gospel labours were in the context of a society still emerging from its pre-reformation superstition and widespread lawlessness. For Bruce's Scotland was constantly bedevilled by bribery and corruption in high places and the murderous brutality of powerful apostate barons. The leaven of sound biblical theology still had much more to do in transforming the nation.

Early years

Bruce was born (*c.* 1554) in Airth Castle, now a luxury five-star hotel. The second son of Sir Alexander Bruce, he was endowed by his father with the barony of Kinnaird, and although the original Kinnaird House was demolished and rebuilt by Robert Orr in 1895, the original (renovated) stabling still stands at the rear of the property. Bruce's father anticipated that Robert would become a senator in the College of Justice, and so he studied law at the University of St Andrews. Thereafter, he was sent for further study to France, and then to Louvain, the capital of the Province of Flemish Brabant.[1] Perhaps his parents had become aware of the influence upon him in St Andrews of the reformed faith, which may have been why they sent him to Louvain, an area noted for its strong adherence to Roman Catholicism.

However, after a profound experience of God one night in 1581, young Bruce turned his back on earthly prestige and wealth, and decided to enter the ministry of the Kirk of Scotland. We cannot doubt but that his parents were distressed by his decision. His mother, Janet Livingstone of Callendar House (her sister had been a lady-in-waiting to Mary Queen of Scots), a great-granddaughter of James I, was a devout Roman Catholic, and, opposing such a vocation, she insisted that he renounce his right to his barony with its substantial income and lands before he should return to St Andrews to study for the ministry.

Two years later, his father became reconciled to his son's calling, and significantly we find his name recorded as a commissioner at the Kirk's General Assembly in 1590. Along with John Erskine, Earl of Mar, and Alexander Seton, laird of Gargunnock, Sir Alexander Bruce of Airth attended the Assembly as an elder of the Presbytery of Stirling. Four Stirlingshire ministers were commissioners, but none of the four were from Larbert;[2] however William Cowper, minister of Bothkennar, was

[1] Both France and Flanders are mentioned in Sermon 24 and by implication in Sermon 28.

[2] I could find no mention of the Larbert Kirk in the General Assembly Minutes of 1587–1618, but we know that when Bruce was at last permitted to return to his home in Kinnaird House (*c.* 1625), he repaired the derelict Larbert Kirk at his own expense. However, in the May 1586 Assembly's inventory of all charges in the land, twenty-three charges are listed in the Presbytery of Stirling, including Larbert and its neighbouring parishes of Dunipace, Bothkennar and Airth, all of which are viable congregations today. (Shaw, p. 800.)

at the Assembly and was probably Sir Alexander's own pastor, for Airth Castle is only about three miles from Bothkennar Kirk.

In St Andrews, Andrew Melville had been installed as Principal of the New College (St Mary's), and his nephew, James Melville had begun to teach the Hebrew classes. Both men were to become key figures in the Kirk in the years after Knox's death. James, though a year younger than Bruce, became a significant influence on him. By the time Bruce had reached the age of thirty, he was preaching with great acceptance in the town.

In 1587 James Melville took Robert with him to Edinburgh to the General Assembly. While there, commissioners for the town of Edinburgh voted for him to become minister of the Great Kirk of St Giles.[3] He immediately declined, for he was extremely reluctant to leave his pulpit in St Andrews where he had recently been invited to become minister, and so set off back to Fife. Nor did he relish the prospect of being so closely involved with the court. 'And surely I liked better to go to St Andrews,' he wrote, 'for I had no taste for preaching before the court. For well I knew that the Court and we could never agree.'[4] However, commissioners from Great St Giles pursued him across the Firth of Forth and he finally agreed to return with them. He wrote, 'I advised with my God, and thought it meet to obey.' The fact that the very next year he was elected as Moderator of the Assembly was a clear indication of the extraordinarily high regard in which he was already held throughout the Kirk.

For a time he was a favourite of James VI who appointed him a Privy Councillor in 1589. When James crossed the North Sea to bring back his bride from Denmark, he regularly wrote lengthy letters to Bruce, some of which are still extant. The following year Bruce anointed Anne of Denmark at her coronation as James' Queen. However, as the Hebrews sermons make clear, Bruce's relationship with the king was difficult at times, and as the years passed, that relationship became increasingly problematic.

[3] At this time the building was divided into four parts: The Great Kirk, the College Kirk, the Upper Tolbooth, and the East or Little Kirk, and so accommodated four distinct congregations. The preacher in the Great Kirk ranked as the senior minister in Edinburgh. (Quoted from Murray, p. 68, note 12.)

[4] MacNicol, p. 40. This sentence is quoted from Bruce's Narrative in Cald. IV, p. 637.

Conflict with the king

For the first three or four years of his ministry in St Giles, he was often elected by the General Assembly to take in person their concerns to the king.[5] The ambivalence of James towards the Kirk has been fully documented by many historians, for one third of his subjects continued to give their allegiance to Rome and he did not want to lose their favour. But on occasion he could persuade the Presbyterians of his loyalty to the reformed faith. For example, during the 1590 Assembly in Edinburgh, he spoke saying, 'As for our neighbouring Kirk in England, it is an evil said Mass in English … I charge you my good people, ministers, doctors, elders, nobles, gentlemen, and barons, to stand to your purity, and to exhort the people to do the same; and I forsooth, so long as I brook my life and crown, shall maintain the same …'. The Assembly so rejoiced that there was nothing but loud praising of God and praying for the king for quarter of an hour.[6]

However, it was well-known that the king's lifestyle was often loose and inappropriate. He consorted with members of the nobility who were profane and unscrupulous men. His incompetence and impotence in ruling was displayed in the notorious murder of the Protestant Earl of Moray at Donibristle in Fife, where he was domiciled at James' injunction. The Earl of Huntly, the leading Catholic baron who was a sworn enemy of the popular Moray, plotted with Thirlestane the Lord Chancellor to murder the young Earl of Argyle and his guardian Campbell of Cawdor, along with Moray who was a kinsman of Argyle. Thirlestane was to receive a slice of Stirlingshire as his share of Argyle's estate.

The murder of Moray in 1592 shocked and appalled the nation. Many believed that James was complicit in the deed, not least because Huntly was briefly imprisoned in Blackness Castle and then released without any genuine trial taking place. Further, the king's leniency towards the rascally Bothwell was scandalous. (Bothwell's father was an illegitimate son of James V, and his mother was a sister of Mary Stewart's Bothwell, hence the leniency showed towards a scoundrel who defied all the first principles of civil order.[7]) James' reputation fell to an all-time low!

[5] 1590, 1591, 1593 (Shaw, pp. 914, 928, 938).

[6] Shaw, p. 915. He is quoting Calderwood.

[7] On Bothwell's misdemeanors see Hume Brown, Vol.2, pp. 165-66.

I cite one single incident to cast some light on Bruce's many reprimands and exhortations to the king in his Sermons on Hebrews 11. Three times in Sermon 11 he directly appeals to James, and the final two sentences summarise the burden on his heart:

> The Lord in his mercy grant (if it please him) that I may yet see during my lifetime, and before I die, some order restored over these confusions, for beyond all doubt, sooner than you may think, Sire, they will cause your throne to totter unless discipline is established. Therefore, not only for the sake of stability for the throne of Jesus Christ, but for your own throne's stability, and for the common well-being of your subjects, let order be reinstated. Then shall our mouths be opened to thank and glorify God for you, and to crave his blessing upon you and your queen from the hands of Jesus Christ (p. 188).

In Sermon 17 he refers to some disgraceful incident involving the king that had taken place that week in public, but then hastens to say that the root cause of the disgrace lay in the nation's sin (p. 300). In the next sermon he refers to 'the dangers that have beset both our Kirk and the common folk on account of the evil company our king enjoys' (p. 328). In Sermon 26, alluding to the Council's failure to enforce the law on those who despise it, he warns that it will be the magistrates' fault if the outcome is that the king is robbed of 'his office, honour and status, and then those who ought to be serving him become his masters' (p. 510). In the penultimate sermon he says, 'This time and place is not appropriate for him to hear this exhortation … If he was present among us he might see that his own attitudes towards good and evil ought to be changed.' He then adds, 'No doubt it is our own sins that are responsible for this negligence in the prince's person' (pp. 525-26). In the final sermon, warning of impending trouble that will be visited upon the nation, he says, 'This applies to all, from the highest to the lowest, from prince to people …' (p. 548).

These few citations from sermons Bruce was preaching in St Giles make it obvious that his pulpit references to the king's failures will most certainly have got back to the royal residence, and will have initiated the change in James' feelings towards this forthright minister. Indeed, six or seven years later, James was recorded as saying of Bruce, 'I hate him more than I hate Bothwell!'[8]

[8] Shaw, p. 1158.

Three significant incidents between Bruce and the king

There are three other incidents that make it clear that the minister of the Great Kirk of St Giles had become a thorn in James' side. The first arose from a false allegation that a tumult which had arisen in Edinburgh on 17 December 1596 had been stirred up by certain ministers, Bruce being one of them, when in fact Bruce had sought to calm the people.[9] The court issued dire threats against four Edinburgh ministers, Bruce being one them, and on the advice of their friends the four men fled, Bruce crossing the Border and going as far as Yorkshire for safety. A few months later the king did ask him to return to his pulpit and admitted it was as well he had fled, otherwise he might have taken action against Bruce that he would later have regretted.

The second incident was foreshadowed by James drawing up fifty-five questions, which he put to the Kirk for their consideration at a special Assembly appointed by him to be convened in Perth the last day of February 1597. Although the occasion for this was not ostensibly his increasing dislike of Bruce, probably it was, for Question 6 was clearly directed at the Minister of Edinburgh: 'Is he a lawful pastor who wants *impositionem manuum*' (ordination by laying on of hands)? The next three questions challenged the right of ministers in their sermons to criticise magistrates, accusing them of vices, in such a manner that the congregations could recognise those to whom the minister was referring.

Readers of the Sermons on Hebrews 11 will find frequent references to the court's councillors, to James' companions, to magistrates and judges, and to some of their vices, such as perverting the course of justice by accepting bribes and dealing leniently with their friends and relatives.[10]

Bruce had never been ordained by the laying on of hands. The king persuaded a number of the ministers to insist that this ordinance be performed. Bruce agreed to submit to their demand, but only on condition that it was made clear it was done without prejudice to his previous ten years of ministry. It was for him a most trying time as he firmly insisted that, though he would obey the Kirk's instruction, his ordination must be understood to be a confirmation of his past

[9] See M'Crie, Vol. I, pp. 407-12; Vol. II, pp. 2-8.

[10] See e.g. Sermons 25, 28.

ministry, not a denial of his years of fruitful labour. However, the form of words to be used during the laying on of hands was firmly disputed by Bruce, for the king made it abundantly clear that he wanted the ceremony to signal the beginning of a lawful ministry, thus by implication discrediting his preaching of the previous decade. The wearisome dispute lasted some five weeks from 14 April to 19 May 1598. At last Bruce submitted to ordination as a *confirmation* of his ministry, and without prejudice to his appointment by the General Assembly eleven years earlier. Without doubt it was an intensely trying experience for him and must have increased the king's antipathy to him.[11]

The third incident occurred in 1599. The year began ominously with the Edinburgh ministers finding fault with the king for reinstating James Beaton as bishop of Glasgow. Thereupon, James began the process of seeking to take from Bruce his pension from the abbacy of Arbroath, a lifelong income for which he had full documentary authorisation. Bruce agreed to surrender the pension but only if it was to be used entirely for the Kirk's maintenance or for the king himself; he would not deny his sovereign anything he asked from him.

However, when it emerged that the king was proposing to transfer Bruce's income to one of his favourites, a Catholic priest, James found himself being resisted both by the council and the Assembly. He was enraged. It was recorded that the king declared that 'if it were not for shame, if he had a dirk, he would cast it in his [Robert's] face'. For a full fifteen weeks the king harassed Bruce by sending messengers every week with various accusations deliberately intended to disturb and terrify him.

So public and heated was James' anger against Bruce, that the synod of Angus petitioned the king to make peace with Mr Robert Bruce for the sake of the Kirk and of the kingdom. The king responded that he was the only minister of the Kirk who would obey neither man nor God (by 'God' meaning no doubt himself, for he aspired to be head of the Church as Henry VIII had been). James was resolved to cut off Bruce's means, 'thereby to disable him from living in Edinburgh; or if he insisted, to put not only himself in danger, but also all his friends that loved him, as well as advocates, as lords of the session'.[12] In March

[11] Shaw, pp. 1139-50.

[12] Shaw, pp. 1153-59.

1595, the question of Bruce's income had come before the Assembly in Montrose, and Bruce had submitted his pension to the will of the Assembly and surrendered part of it to the Kirk for the maintenance of another (Andrew Lamb, minister of Arbroath); what remained was unanimously assigned to him by the Assembly for his lifetime. But now the king summarily annulled the Assembly's decision, and maliciously reduced Bruce's income to poverty level.

The murder of the Earl of Gowrie

The final blow came in 1600 on 5 August and was occasioned by the murder of one of the most outstanding Protestant nobleman, John, the Earl of Gowrie and his brother Andrew, Master of Ruthven. The twenty-two year old earl had only recently returned from Geneva, and was a quiet, meditative man, given to learning; he was seen by many as a future leader in the Reformation. The problem with understanding exactly what happened is that the only account of the incident was that given by James himself. The day after the double murder, James sent a letter to Edinburgh, in which he ordered that the ministers should go to the kirk, convene the people, ring bells and give praise to God that his life had been preserved and the murderers had received their just deserts. The Assembly's record states that when the ministers went to the east kirk to confer, they could not say there had been an act of treason [on the part of the earl and his brother] as the king's instructions had made no mention of treason.[13]

However, the upshot was that ultimately most of the ministers, apart from Bruce and a few others, agreed to do as the king demanded, but the minister of the Great Kirk of St Giles found he could not believe that the earl had been guilty of treason, nor James' account of his attempted murder.[14] Once again Bruce stood almost alone, supported only by four ministerial colleagues, James Balfour, William Watson, Walter Balcanquhal and John Hall. It appears that while he was ready

[13] Shaw, p. 1224.

[14] A full record of a sermon preached by Mr Patrick Galloway to the people of Edinburgh on 11 August containing the full report James had made of the attempted murder can be found in Shaw, pp. 1225-31. Hume Brown comments: 'The singular story which James gave to the world … was received with a smile of incredulity alike in Scotland, England and on the Continent.' Vol. II, p. 183. The king's own account is given in Appendix IV.

to give thanks for the king's preservation, he could not be sure in his conscience that the Earl of Gowrie could have been the perpetrator of such murderous treason. Being uncertain, therefore, he could not fulfil the king's instructions to the letter. All five ministers were forbidden to preach, under pain of death, throughout all the king's dominions, and were charged to leave Edinburgh and not come within ten miles of the capital, under pain of death.

Over the next few weeks, the other four ministers who had stood with Bruce, regained the king's favour and were reinstated in their congregations. James asked them to seek to persuade Mr Robert to do likewise, but though they wrote graciously to him he stood firmly by his conscience. It seems that the general populace of Edinburgh did not believe Gowrie had attempted to murder the king, and when a fellow minister visited Bruce at Airth where he was temporally living, he told him that the Earl of Mar was of the opinion that if he would rebuke from the pulpit 'the people, and reprove them for their rash and lewd opinion they publish of a prince, without sound and solid ground', Mar considered that would bring about the reconciliation of Bruce and the king.

However, James remained implacable. As Bruce was making final preparations to leave Scotland, he wrote to James seeking clemency and assuring him of his willingness 'to show conformity with the rest of my brethren of the ministry', and stating he would stir up his people to join him in giving thanks for his majesty's deliverance on that fateful day of 5 August. He ended his letter, 'awaiting for your highness's answer, in all humility I take my leave'.[15] No answer came, until on his journey to Queensferry he received a message from two ministers that unless he left the country within twenty hours he would be charged with treason. So on 3 November he embarked in a ship lying at anchor and set sail for France.

What I have written is only a brief account of Robert Bruce's tempestuous relationship with a duplicitous and double-dealing monarch, who was unworthy of the loyalty and devotion shown to him throughout his finest subject's twelve years of service as Minister of Edinburgh.

[15] Shaw, p. 1254.

The state of Scotland during Bruce's ministry

Reading these sermons, one might be tempted to think that Bruce had an extremely pessimistic temperament, always assuming the state of the nation was far worse than it really was. In his final sermon on Hebrews 11 we hear him speaking regarding the impending confusion about to erupt upon the nation:

> Regarding our own land, unworthy as we are, it does not appear that we have yet reached the lowest depths of worthlessness, though we are moving in that direction. Yet because some of our godly men are spared and not withdrawn, even though there are not many of them, I do not anticipate we will be smitten with an unexpected state of chaos. But undoubtedly if the Lord withdrew even a few of his servants to the extent that our unworthiness deserves, we could expect a terrible confusion to envelop our whole nation (p. 552).

Nor was this untypical. He was convinced that divine judgment was imminent on account of the lawlessness and widespread rejection of the evangel. He was not, however, exaggerating, for the minutes of the Kirk's General Assembly portray the same foreboding over the deplorable state of the nation. The minutes of the Assembly in Edinburgh in August 1590 record that 'great scandal lies on the Kirk through manifold murders, notorious adulteries and incest, and the parties being brought under process often elude the Kirk, by moving from place to place … and all the time the scandal continues and increases into odious and horrible crimes.' Again during the Assembly in Edinburgh in July 1591, it was recorded that there were 'violent invaders of ministers by striking them and shedding their blood … and murderers and blood shedders overflow the land'.[16]

Five years later during the Assembly in Edinburgh in March 1596, distressing reports were recorded, including the deterioration of godly practices among the king's household: he seldom attended Sunday worship, there were no prayers offered, no grace before or after meals, and his majesty was tarnished by cursing and swearing, also common in his courtiers whose example he was following.

> The flood of bloodshed and deadly feuds was caused by lack of training in godliness and virtue in the people's homes; there were

[16] Shaw, pp. 919-20, 927-28.

> adulteries, fornications, incest, unlawful marriages, and children from such marriages declared to be lawful. Heavy drinking and gluttony among the nobility, wearing of vain, expensive clothing, and filthy, bawdy speeches. There was increasing sacrilege in all estates without any conscience, to the undoing of the Kirk and the prevention of the planting of the gospel. Cruel oppression of poor tenants, whereby all the commoners in the country are utterly wracked by extremely expensive rentals, and impoverished workers suffer through unfair dealing on their corn. Added to which is oppression under the pretext of the law and unscrupulous interest rates being charged.[17]

These are not occasional complaints made in the Kirk's courts. Because they frequently crop up, they reflect badly upon the king's government of the nation, for he took little heed of his people's woes, preferring rather to spend his days in hunting with godless barons. Thus Bruce's constant sorrowing in his preaching over the moral decline and near anarchy in Scotland must not be passed over lightly. At times he expresses exasperation that after so many years of the evangel being proclaimed without hindrance, the land was still wracked with such widespread wickedness.

Another aspect of the widespread spiritual need in Scotland at this time was the dereliction of many kirk buildings and manses. Several times, he urges the wealthy nobles in the congregation to contribute to the restoration of tumbledown church buildings (e.g. p. 257). We know that when at last after James' death in 1625, Charles I gave him permission to return to Kinnaird, the Larbert Kirk was in dire need of repair and had been without a minister for some time. Bruce used his own resources to have the building restored, and subsequently preached there himself. Significantly, a new manse was completed just four years after his death and remains the oldest inhabited dwelling in Stirlingshire; it is tempting to surmise that this was evidence of renewed spiritual life in the Larbert parish through his own brief ministry there.

[17] Shaw, pp. 1029, 1031-32.

Bruce's theology

His doctrine of God

Readers of these sermons may be surprised to find that, in stark contrast to much preaching today, Bruce does not often speak of God's love for us. I shall give you every single reference to this with the pages in parenthesis.

[Chastisement] 'comes from his *love*, learn to accept it as given in *love*, thanking God that he has prepared you for it' (p. 107). 'There is no doubt that Abraham had come to know God through his mercy and *love* … Now that he knows the divine mercy, *love* and favour, he commits into God's hands his soul, life, body and all future provisions for himself and his family … Have you at any time in the past had experience of the *love* of God towards you, some deliverance he has brought you when you were in some trial? so that you may say to yourself, "This God has always *loved* me and been merciful to me, therefore I commit to him my life … Because I am assured that he *loves* me and will be merciful to me, I will obey him." Thus you see that the greatest spur we have for obeying God is our previous experiences of his *love* and mercy' (pp. 126-27). '[The Lord] will give you just the measure of it that he considers sufficient for your heart and soul to be drawn into the experience of God's *love* … strive now to obtain faith in your hearts and minds together with the *love* of God and Christ Jesus … Just as God surpasses princes in *love*, so also he surpasses them in humility and kindness … The Lord expresses his *love* and condescension in naming himself after his servants by saying that he is their God …' (pp. 197, 204). 'Once we have recognised his *love*, no chastening of God would be visited upon us without our bowing before him … The Lord expresses his *love* and condescension in naming himself after his servants by saying that he is their God … so that your affections will turn increasingly towards the *love* of God' (p. 326) '[I]t was his *love* that drew us into this life of suffering, he has promised us a free reward, and freely will he fulfil his promise' (p. 396). '[T]he God who had shown such *love* for them would bring them safely through the waters across to dry land … such is the concern and deep *love* he has for his Kirk' (p 437). 'For when we hate what God hates and love what he *loves*, we are at one with him, and if we are at one with Him then we are partakers of his nature and his Holy Spirit.' 'How does a man experience heavenly joy? Only by love, for *God is love*' (pp. 524, 533). Only twenty times is the love of God mentioned in over 220,000 words!

Indeed, God's love for us is not mentioned at all in nineteen of the twenty-eight sermons. However, our love for God occurs much more often, well over fifty times, as well as love for others in Christ, love for the things of God and the prospect of his heavenly kingdom. He speaks too of family love, and of course, by contrast, of the misplaced love of worldly things.

How can it be that so fine a theologian can dwell so seldom upon the great doctrine that 'God is love'? It would be a futile exercise to try and count the number of times that Bruce speaks to his people of the kindness, mercy, grace and favour of God. Every sermon is saturated with the sense of an utterly holy, awesome God who nevertheless extends his lavish kindness and grace to undeserving sinners.

The answer will occur to the thinking reader of this book. Bruce preached of a trinitarian God. Judgment is balanced by mercy, wrath by loving-kindness, chastisement by grace. He was unquestionably a man with a passion for the God of the Scriptures. The balance of the triune God, the Father, the exalted Lord and Saviour, and the blessed Holy Spirit is unsurpassed in any of the sermons I have ever studied. When he speaks of 'the living God', as he does countless times, it is this triune God to whom he is referring.

The face of God

As I translated and edited these powerful sermons, I came across another unusual expression of Bruce's concept of God. He constantly refers to the privilege of believers whose consciences are purified and who are so enabled to look upon the 'face of God'. Sometimes he speaks of our not being able to see God's face, because some sin or love for this fleeting world has clouded our spiritual vision. He apparently contradicts himself on this, for on one occasion he states that only in heaven will we be able with unalloyed joy to look fully upon the Lord's countenance; but nonetheless, we should constantly strive for that vision of God's face here and now in this life; for, as he asserts, our experience of heaven ought to begin here on earth.

As we read our way through these sermons, we soon recognise that Bruce's concept of God is grounded upon the Psalms, for in them the 'face of God' and 'his countenance' form an essential aspect of the nature of the Almighty, both in his inviolable holiness and in his merciful tenderness. Dozens of times the Psalmist prays that he may be granted the smile of God's face. (The following few examples are from the AV, which is the nearest version in use today to Bruce's Geneva Bible.) 'How long wilt thou hide thy face from me?' (Psalm 13:1). 'When thou saidst, Seek ye my face; my heart said unto thee, Thy face, LORD, will I seek. Hide not thy face far from me; put not thy servant away in anger …' (27:8-9). 'Make thy face to shine upon thy servant …' (31:16). 'Hide thy face from my sins …' (51:9) 'Seek the LORD and his strength: seek his face evermore' (105:4).

As in the Psalms, with their inspired balance between, on the one hand, the burning holiness and wrath of God against all profanity, vanity and rebellion against himself, and, on the other hand, his lavish grace, forgiveness and compassion towards humanity, so it is in Bruce's concept of God. It is for me a source of personal sorrow that so much preaching today either neglects, or is ignorant of, this aspect of the self-revelation of God through his word. May those who read Bruce's sermons catch something of his faithfulness to Scripture in his truly biblical depiction of the nature of the Almighty.

He also speaks much of divine providence. Repeatedly, he says, 'It pleased the Lord …', whether he is referring to some chastisement, or blessing, or judgment or whatever. God is in control, and nothing in our lives occurs that does not have his purposes and will stamped on it. '[A]ll that takes place flows from his gracious providence … neither would there be any mercy bestowed upon the Kirk that would not bring tears to our eyes and melt our hearts in thankfulness' (p. 326).

The Lord Jesus Christ

As we would expect from sermons on Hebrews 11, the emphasis on Christ is on his meritorious sacrifice for sin. Virtually every time Bruce preached, he appealed to his hearers to cast themselves wholly upon the mercy of God offered through his beloved Son Jesus Christ. His blood, his cross, his grace, his forgiveness—all are at the centre of every expression of gospel truth. He speaks too of the grace that enables the believer to see Christ's face. Thus the doctrine of justification, which he fully expounds in terms of Christ's righteousness being imputed to us through faith, is clearly set forth.

The Holy Spirit

Irresponsible writers have sometimes claimed that it has taken the twentieth-century Charismatic Movement to (re)discover the Holy Spirit. Clearly, those who make that kind of wild statement have never read the sermons of the Reformers. Again and again, Bruce insists that unless the Holy Spirit 'concurs' (his expression) with the preaching of the word of God, it will have no effect in the hearts of his hearers. Likewise, the Spirit must 'concur' in the celebration and participation of the sacraments. He also writes, 'Consider the power by which Christ overcame the devil. That is the power that must turn my soul to God, and cause me to detest my sins and repent truly.' Further, 'When you feel the chastening hand of God upon either your body or your soul, you ought to pray, "Lord, sanctify to me this affliction, this experience you have sent, this delay of your relief to me; may your Holy Spirit do his work inwardly in me, as plainly as your word is heard outwardly, that my heart may be converted to obey you"' (p. 108).

Again, 'The only afflictions that are able to work for our sanctification are those wherewith the power of the Holy Spirit concurs' (p. 134). When we pray, we should 'always start with the enlightening of our minds by craving that the Lord would illuminate our spiritual eye with his heavenly light …' (p. 168). Again, 'That [Abraham] was able to withstand harassment by powerful chieftains lets us see how greatly he was assisted by the power of the Holy Spirit, who clothed him with supernatural strength from above … he was constantly upheld by the Holy Spirit' (p. 174).

The Holy Spirit will be at work throughout the whole of the believer's life. Preaching on Moses, he says, 'We have seen how the Lord constantly cared and provided for him, both at his birth and in his education. Now he watches over him as he reaches his adult years, graciously inclining him to obey his calling, and sending his Holy Spirit to bend his will, mortify his heart and illumine the darkness of his mind. That was how it came about that Moses recognised his effectual call and gladly responded by his obedience … Yes, [the Lord] watches over every aspect of our lives, from infancy, through childhood and on into maturity' (p. 376).

Fallen humanity

It will hardly be surprising that those who read these sermons will find the preacher exposing the problem of the human heart and soul. 'Such is the corruption in human nature since we fell away from God that our intelligence, which is the best part of us, has made us enemies of God' (p. 390). We are swayed in our judgment by outward appearances, and mistake mere show and shadow for those things that really matter. Corruption loves corruption, so that an evil environment will influence adversely the best souls that ever lived. If we are not able to resist the intruder (he means the tempter), when he has only one foot in the door, we will scarcely be able to eject him when he has occupied the whole dwelling (our hearts and souls).

He often emphasizes that even when our inner corruption has been mortified, what we thought had been put to death finds new strength, and 'our passions which seemed to have become a tamed lamb now rage like a tiger. They become like the roar of a lion awakening from its restful composure.' He urges his hearers to search their hearts to uncover that one thing that is their dearest idol, and to which their whole souls long to yield. And yet there can be victory over it, and although it tortures us day and night, if we resist and pray for grace to conquer it, little by little our consciences will be able to say, 'I thank God that what I once loved, now through the power of Christ in me I abhor it.'

Bruce indulges in what could be called 'exordia'. He expands on the evils of a hard heart in a single 'exordium' of 1,560 words (Sermon 22), before he returns to the main subject of his text. In Sermon 17 there is an 'exordium' on pastoral visitation, especially for those who are sick, and he continues to urge his people to care for such in a digression of nearly 700 words. His most lengthy 'exordium' is in the twenty-first sermon in which he deals with various aspects of banishment in some 2,100 words; banishment was to become a most painful experience for himself, though at the time he was indirectly referring to several of his colleagues who had fled from King James to find refuge across the border in Berwick.

Roman Catholicism

Errors

In passing, he occasionally pauses to deal briefly with what the reformers understood to be errors in the Roman Catholic Church. Because Roman Catholics have failed to understand the biblical teaching on justification by faith, they have no assurance of salvation. The Church teaches that 'satisfactions' are required, over and above the full and free pardon of Christ's grace. It was error to teach we could obtain grace through 'supererogation', that is, through the performance of acts which go beyond the acceptable duty required in order to gain further benefits of grace; obviously this doctrine implied earning divine approval through human works. Bruce himself had witnessed 'self-flagellation' while he was studying law in France, but nowhere in Scripture are we taught to do such a thing. He exposes from Scripture the error of veneration of relics, quoting Pope Gregory of the Great who forbade such a practice.

The doctrine of transubstantiation is not taught in the word of God:

> Consider how some say that in the sacrament Christ is physically present in his bodily flesh: that is not an article of my faith. I am not bound to believe it because it is not taught in the word of God, and all the articles of my faith are based firmly on his word. Because such a belief is condemned in God's word, I cannot hold to it. When we say that our faith looks to things that are not seen, that only applies to what is taught in the word of God and is declared therein as being not seen … we believe the word when it says that the sacramental elements are the body and blood of Christ. You have been taught this regarding the Lord's Supper so that your faith and soul may be assured that his body and blood are represented by the bread and wine (p. 39).

Heretics

He deals with this subject in an unexpected manner. Across the border, during her short reign Queen Mary had burned over three hundred Protestants. Queen Elizabeth had also engaged in the defence of her kingdom by torturing, burning or beheading dozens of Catholic plotters against her. Bruce, however, roundly condemns any kind of pain or torture being inflicted on a fellow human being (p. 543). When Jesuits were found to be defying the Protestant laws of Scotland which forbade celebration of the mass, they should be banished to some other country where they would be free to engage lawfully in their idolatrous practices (p. 494). There is only one recorded martyrdom in Scotland (the Jesuit Ogilvie) in the decades after the Reformation.

The Kirk

The Kirk prior to Christ's incarnation

The Kirk was founded in Adam and Eve, but Cain who slew his brother, was outside the true body of believers. The Fathers all believed God's word and that included the promise of the incarnation of the Son of God who would bruise the head of the serpent (Genesis 3:15). The promise also included the Land which was understood by the Fathers as a type of heaven and eternal life there for all who have faith. By faith the Fathers were all freely justified. This simple theological framework underpins all that Bruce says regarding those who lived and died before Christ was manifested in the flesh.

Sacrament of the Lord's Supper

Bruce reminds his congregation that he has already spoken to them at length regarding the Lord's Supper, and so he deals with it briefly. His main concern is to urge his people to come to the Table and partake of the bread and wine. Not to do so is disobedience and that will grieve the Lord who commanded his followers to draw near to him in this manner. To those who hesitate through doubts about their worthiness, he addresses his words very pointedly and graciously:

> Someone wonders, but what if I find myself burdened with my sins, great as they are and constantly committed? Shall I then abstain from the Supper? For certainly, whenever I search my heart I find within my soul an unclean midden[18] of evil desires and wrong motives. How then could I ever come to the Lord's Table? I even find within myself an inexplicable rebellion against God's commandments, and I cannot subdue my will to his will. How

[18] Bruce uses this Scots word; it is still in use, especially among gardeners, farmers and country folk; it means a heap of dung, manure or rotting vegetation.

then could I ever draw near? How could I ever approach his Table with such a proud and stubborn heart?

I answer, 'Yes, come with your stubborn, hard heart!' And I will tell you why you must come. I agree, you do have an evil disposition, and it would be far better if your heart was cleaner and softer, and your will more subdued to his holy will. It is good that you acknowledge your condition, for every heart that recognises its great need is in a very good spiritual state. It is evidence that the Lord himself has been at work within you to show you your great need of him. And that means you are already on your way to his Table, there to find his healing touch. He says, 'I love the one that comes with the knowledge of his need far more than the person who comes imagining that his heart is clean and upright.' I myself never come to the Table thinking that I am clean and just—that would be foolishness. Rather, I draw near to confess my failure in godliness and grace, to acknowledge my sin, to open my unclean heart before Christ that I may be cleansed. So I draw near for healing of the diseases of my soul and my body (p. 42).

The quotation above is from Sermon 3 where his fullest comments are found on the sacrament. In Sermon 5 there is a confirmation of what he has already said to his people in the previous sermon concerning doubt: '[I]t is better to doubt than to despair. For where there are doubts there is also faith; doubts cling to the pillars of faith. How can it be possible for anyone not to doubt when each of us is weighed down with such a load of sins ...?' (p. 73). It should be obvious that this skilled 'surgeon of the soul' (as I like to call him) often brings consolation and encouragement to his hearers, as well as faithful rebukes, and nowhere is this so evident as in his teaching on the Lord's Supper.

Bruce uses the crossing of the Red Sea (as does the apostle Paul) to lay down principles of the sacrament of baptism. He says that in our baptism the symbol of water and the word concur with the invisible grace. Likewise 'these three elements—water, the word and grace—also concurred in the people's passing through the Red Sea' (pp. 443).

A definition of the Kirk

The Kirk is the bride of Christ and is nothing more than 'a company of penitent sinners'. If we come across a religion that practises cruelty [as the English Church was presently doing in its brutal executions of heretics], 'you will know it is from the devil and flows out of hell and human corruption, for it is a godless world that delights in such viciousness'. Bruce also was aware of the biblical meaning of 'worship' as 'the pledge of total obedience in service'. In this quotation from Sermon 24, he uses the two words, 'worship' and 'service', as synonyms: 'It is not possible that an unclean heart can offer clean *service* to the living God, for pure religion and righteous *worship* acceptable to God can only proceed from faith.'

However, we learn that right from the time of Abel and Cain the Kirk was impure. Ever since it has always contained the evil mingled with the good, cunning men who invent mischief and who practise nastiness towards the godly. 'It will always be so until the Lord makes that full and final restoration.' (p. 45)

The Kirk's ministry

It is often evident that other ministers at times came to worship at St Giles. When dealing with the necessity of having a clear call from God to serve in a particular parish, Bruce addresses himself to his fellow-ministers present. He speaks of the initial call to the ministry as 'the general' but the specific call to a parish as 'the particular'. The same applies to the decisions of the Kirk's General Assembly:

> If we in the ministry had been guided by this principle and only proceeded according to God's counsel, following his directions in the particulars as well as in the generalities, then our service for him would have had far better outcomes. But having had the warrant of God for the general, but failing to seek his warrant for the particulars, we have taken the wrong courses of action and failed to reach the right outcomes (p. 278).

In Sermon 18 he warns that ministers can temporarily lose the grace necessary for effective preaching. God may allow that to happen so that 'the world might see the difference between a man left to himself, and those who are furnished with God's grace. It is the difference between nature and grace: there is nothing but confusion in the one, while in the other is displayed holiness and divinity.' Therefore, he warns congregations 'not to gaze upon the Lord's servants, but set your eyes on him who sent them forth' (p. 341). Moreover, every minister must have a warrant from God, without which he will never effectively fulfil his ministry.

The anointing of the Holy Spirit must be upon the preacher. Talking of the presence of the ark of the covenant at the fall of Jericho, he says,

> The ark of God, so to speak, must be present in the heart of the preacher and in the hearts of the hearers, otherwise the trumpet blast will avail us nothing. What I mean is that Jesus Christ must be in the preacher's heart, that is, he must be endued with the Holy Spirit, and likewise those who are listening must be possessed by Christ's Spirit (p. 458).

Bruce also emphasises that obedience to God must always have priority over civil obedience.

> Be certain, therefore, that this calling of ours will never be rightly exercised unless the living God sends forth pastors who will not preach their own ideas, but those who will accept the burden of God's commission. Yea, the living God who sends a man forth with this burden will always be with him; he will not suffer him to withhold any part of the message that has been entrusted to him, for as he commissions him and sends him forth on his journey, he will be with him; he will give him a heart to obey and a mouth to speak the words that have been committed to him (p. 412).

Alas, there were always kirk ministers willing to please King James and to silence their consciences in doing so. During his final three years in St Giles, Bruce was often deserted by his colleagues who were unwilling to take their stand on conscience as he courageously did.

The Christian life

The meaning of faith

In the first sermon, we have his introduction to the great biblical theme of faith. Faith has two 'properties', assurance and evidence. There are three essentials for true faith, knowledge of the truth, an obedient will and assurance; yet obedience is an 'effect' of faith, as is repentance. It is by faith that we believe in creation. In the next sermon, it is also by faith that we are able to see the spiritual:

> Using only his natural intelligence, the wise man is as blind as a mole, because he refuses to accept spiritual insight. He does not see that true wisdom is by faith alone. Only the faithful [i.e. those with faith] are truly wise and divinely blessed (p. 34).

Ordinarily, the engendering and begetting of faith comes primarily through hearing the preaching of the word. But in extraordinary times when the word is not being preached, hearing the word through truthful reports is able to engender and work faith in the hearts of those who hear, even in the heart of an idolatrous Canaanite who was not a member of God's chosen people (Rahab, Sermon 24). However, miracles (and signs) were never intended to produce faith, only to confirm and establish what God has already begun.

Several times in these sermons, Bruce insists that faith is absolutely essential for those who partake of the Lord's Supper, for in the sacrament there is always a command and a promise: 'the command demands our obedience, and the promise requires our faith' (p. 413). As far as the assurance of faith is concerned, we must be certain that our eternal felicity depends only on the blood and righteous merits of Jesus Christ (Sermon 16). Another benefit of faith is that 'Jesus Christ counts as his own all the crosses, injuries and trials that we sustain through no fault of our own, but for the cause of righteousness and for his sake. I mean he counts them as done to himself' (p. 394).

'Real faith is always accompanied by wisdom, and wisdom with faith prevents a man from doing what is foolish or rash' (p. 359). When our faith is guided by godly wisdom we will not despise the most mundane methods, but will employ all legitimate and everyday means that the law of God permits. However, in itself faith is weak, and in the best of us is mingled with incredulity, so where faith believes one hour, the next two hours faith is beset by doubts. Rather, faith relies upon the power of him to whom it looks and on him on whom it fixes its sight.

Justification is by faith:

> There never ever was, nor ever will be, any persons perfectly just before God on their own account. Every one of us is sinful and an abomination; would to God that everyone recognised that! Therefore, the righteousness we have is loaned to us and imputed to

> us as if it were our very own. Of this righteousness we are only assured by faith in Jesus Christ, that for his sake God forgives us our sins and unrighteousness, and accounts us as justified as if we had attained this ourselves (p. 70).

The gift of true faith is one that God never revokes. To whom faith is given, it is given for ever. That is why Jude says that those 'who are called are kept for Jesus Christ, and he is able to keep us and present us to God'.

Tribulations and trials

Living in this lost and evil world is essential for all believers, so that they may yearn for God's heavenly kingdom, even though for those who have faith, heaven begins here and now in this life. Yet believers will invariably have trials and tribulations as may please the Lord to send upon them, at times to chasten them, also to refine and purify their faith, but mainly to bring them to yearn for the eternal happiness and joy of their home in heaven.

Every believer must bear the cross. We must not deceive ourselves 'with ideas of repose, or think that being in Christ's Kirk means entering a state of ease, earthly peace and security. The Lord has never promised any such thing, rather he warns us that we must daily bear the cross' (p. 68). Indeed, the cross is inseparable from faith:

> [T]here cannot be genuine, justifying faith without some trial. Neither is it possible that the Kirk can stand firm without troubles and persecution. It is impossible that true faith can be in a man without temptation [trial]. Be assured, then, that if the faith you have has been begotten by the Spirit of God, the same God shall make your faith known to the world through your trial; and whoever cannot endure that trial makes it clear that he is a hypocrite. On the other hand, if a man does endure the trial, then it becomes apparent that he is not chaff, but good corn that is appointed for life everlasting (p. 221-222).

However, there is another facet to trials: '… as faith inevitably faces trials, so these same trials are sent to bestow honour upon us, to reward us and to raise us in the esteem of both God and men. For the Lord tries none but those whom he loves, and whom he loves he will honour' (p. 233).

The prospect of peril was ever present, for Scotland was often a dangerous place in which to live. Moreover, the possibility of a further attempted Spanish invasion was ever present.

Repentance

Repentance is impossible without faith, for indeed repentance is an 'effect' of faith. However, suppose a man cannot at first sever himself from everything that is carnal, if he resolves to deal with his sins little by little, and he constantly prays for strength, asking the Lord to impart more and yet more of his grace, then, by the effectual working of his Holy Spirit, the Lord will enable him at length to make a complete break from what he knew what was wrong.

Prayer

Believers must continually seek God in prayer. First, they must believe that *he is* (general revelation), but secondly God must illumine our blind understanding, that we may be enabled to believe that he does hear and will answer our prayers. For without doubt, those who seek will find. Moreover, prayer is the only antidote to the Lord's severe chastening:

> When you feel the chastening hand of God upon either your body or your soul, you ought to pray, 'Lord, sanctify to me this affliction, this experience you have sent, this delay of your relief to me; may your Holy Spirit do his work inwardly in me, as plainly as your word is heard outwardly, that my heart may be converted to obey you.' Not just once, but as often as you recognise the hand of God upon you, you ought to pray, 'Lord, make this visitation a blessing to me …' (p. 108).

We should also constantly beseech the living God that he would pour down upon us 'more drops of grace and mercy, so that our regeneration may progress and daily take us forward in our spiritual lives' (p. 119). We must ever 'flee to the place of prayer that the Lord in his mercy would sanctify adversity to us.' In our prayers, we must always 'start with the enlightening of our minds by craving that the Lord would illuminate our spiritual eye with his heavenly light'. It is only through prayer that we will attain to the gracious sight of the Lord's countenance.

Perseverance in prayer is needed: 'if the Lord has promised then it is not wrong for us by prayer and tears to beg for him to act, as in faith and expectation we await his fulfilment … in due time he will certainly accomplish his word' (p. 332).

Mortification

The mortification of our flesh must be one goal of our praying, for 'without mortification we will never see the face of Jesus Christ'. Bruce defines mortification thus:

> [This is] the way of the mortification of my sinful lusts, and of the denying of myself and own will. As soon as we begin to subdue our stubborn, selfish will to the will of Jesus Christ, and start preferring God's will to our own wills, we then enter the narrow way. This mortification is only brought about by a daily cross which the Lord sanctifies, enabling it to subdue our fleshly desires. Therefore, I consider the way for a Christian to be the way of the cross and trials (p. 183).

However, never think that mortification is a once and for all exercise, for 'the mortified corruption that you thought had been slain will get new strength' (p. 363). Again, '[Y]our steadfast aim should be to mortify and subdue your fleshly lusts, because the devil is never idle and our inner corruption is never barren' (p. 245).

The wide scope of these sermons

It is impossible to cover in an Introduction all the theological ground that Bruce covers. For example, he repeatedly defines the death of believers as the departure of the soul to God, while their mortal remains await the final resurrection and new heavenly bodies. He writes at length about dying 'a good death'; indeed in Sermon 17, there is an 'exordium' of over 1,110 words on this theme. He persistently emphasizes the need of right stewardship of the believers' material possessions, and challenges his hearers as to whether they have acquired their possessions honestly. Those who listened to Bruce would have known that in order for him to obey the Lord's call into ministry of the word, he had given up his wealth and beautiful manor house; thus they would have recognized in him a living embodiment of what he preached.

One of the many problems facing the Kirk in his day was derelict buildings, both kirks and manses. The patrimonies that ought to have gone to the Kirk at the Reformation had been seized by noblemen and landed gentry, and other incomes had been retained by former prelates. General Assembly minutes constantly record this widespread dereliction of properties. So Bruce appeals passionately to the wealthy in his congregation to apply their resources to the restoration of kirks and manses, as well as to the supplementation of stipends (pp. 255-56).[19]

Another issue that disturbed the Assembly was the admission to the Lord's Table of those whose understanding of its meaning was still clouded by the superstition of the former unreformed church. One of the Kirk's finest theologians, John Craig, had written a new catechism, and during Bruce's second tenure of the Moderator's role, the Assembly requested Craig to shorten his catechism. The following Assembly, the revised catechism was approved and the Assembly instructed it to be published and made widely available throughout the Kirk. Needless to say, Bruce brought up this topic in his sermon probably preached around that time (pp. 276-77).[20]

The fearless preacher of Great St Giles did not shrink from severe reprimands on the nobility, judges and magistrates. On occasion, he all but named one corrupt councillor. No doubt it was these courageous reprimands that caused the angry king to include Question 7 in his infamous document 'Fifty-five Questions' submitted for resolution to the convention of the estates and General Assembly in Perth 1597:

> Is it lawful for pastors to express particular names, councillors, or magistrates in the pulpit, or to so vividly describe them, that the people may understand whom they mean, without notoriously declared vices and private admonitions preceding?

Of course, Bruce was not the only pastor to engage in such pulpit declarations against corruption in high places. But if in his sermons several years earlier he had been rebuking magistrates and judges as he did in these sermons, we can hardly have expected him to have

[19] For some examples of the assembly's concern over derelict buildings, see the following pages in Shaw: 833, 841-43, 853, 883, 919, 961.

[20] See Sermon 16, note 16, for comment on John Knox's attitude to examination prior to Communion. See also Sermon 15, note 28.

moderated his language as the problem increased during James' reign, owing to the king's gross mismanagement of the nation's government.

Here is a quotation from Sermon 26 in which he rebukes particular judges. Bear in mind that we must not forget Bruce spoke not only as a pastor, but as one who also was himself a highly qualified lawyer.

> The judges are not present today, but the part they play in this issue is hugely important, and the widespread complaints throughout our land must indicate there have been miscarriages of justice. I admonished them to some extent last week, for I dare not neglect my commission, and I only addressed them to correct them for their benefit. I am ever mindful that I must deliver myself from their blood, and, if it is at all possible, turn them to God. I only say what is in accordance with my commission, not from malice but out of love. If necessity did not constrain me, I would never take it upon myself to admonish them, but because the matter is so urgent, I have admonished them and will continue to do. If I was in full possession of the facts concerning some municipal case corruptly administered, I would publicly reprove what had been done. Let them be assured (I am not referring to our king whom I always reverence in God), that I stand in awe of none of them, but I dare to reprove them to their faces (p. 513).

Bruce's preaching

His view of Scripture

In his sermons he deplored the paucity of knowledge of the Christian Scriptures. They were read by only a few, and the general understanding of them was scandalously low. Yet they were 'Spirit-inspired'. Indeed, they could only be understood through the illumination of the Holy Spirit. Failure to comprehend rightly the Bible's teaching will always lead to error. The ongoing unfolding of the nature of God in the Scriptures reveals a God who brings low those who outwardly appear to be high, and who raises up high those who in men's estimation appear to be low. More, these sacred records themselves bear witness to their integrity, for unlike the hagiographies which pass over godly men's failings, the biblical records truthfully recount their faults as well as their faith; 'the Holy Spirit is a true and faithful historian'. Supremely, the Scriptures bear witness to God in Christ Jesus.

His sermon structure

His method of interpretation should also be noted. Significantly, he sees the Old and New Testaments as adhering together in harmonious unity. We could accurately describe his view of the Bible as being 'two Testaments, but one Bible'. His method of exposition is as follows. He first fully explains the 'history' of the Old Testament passage to which the apostle is referring in Hebrews 11; he then extrapolates the teaching that emerges into the New Testament's teaching on the same theme. Of course the unity he finds between the Old and the New is found in the manifestation of Christ in the flesh. Further, he elucidates what he regards in the passage as 'the general' and then proceeds to 'the particulars'. Finally, he forcefully drives home the application to his hearers. This whole process is repeated several times over in each sermon, so that contemporary lessons permeate his whole discourse.

Homely language

Bruce's style often uses very earthy language which instantly paints word-pictures in his hearers' minds. (Jesus did the same in his teaching.) For example, 'God did not need a lathe or loom or any other tools …' to do his work (p. 38). Nor does 'God threaten us as if he were a mouse.' Abraham held fast to the authority of God's word, 'grasping it as the guiding light and rudder'. 'But [the Lord] does not just let them off, so to speak, but he will appoint them to follow some course of instruction, in order that they might learn the lesson of obedience. Undoubtedly, the Lord's "school" will administer extremely severe discipline.' (All quotations in Sermon 8.)

One other quotation, this time from Sermon 11:

> You ought to think of this life as a pilgrimage, or as a voyage to another life. Just as the time we spend in our mother's womb prepares us for our lives on earth, so during our time here in this world we ought to be preparing for that life in heaven. Likewise, just as our time in the womb is temporary, so we who are in this world ought to be making ready to cast off our garments of uncleanness so that we might attain to that heavenly company … remember that this life is a voyage and the final mooring place is death. We are like a boat that is subject to the weather, often sailing close to the wind; so whether the mariner be eating, drinking, sleeping

or whatever he chooses, the boat continues on towards the port. Should we not labour to be certain that we are on course towards the right port?' (p. 186).

Readers of the sermons will come across scores of examples of such homely, down-to-earth language, for it pulls us up sharp and focuses our thoughts.

Bruce's scholarship

Bruce's knowledge of both biblical languages indirectly seeps out at times. For example, though he does not actually use the Greek word *hupostasis* in Sermon 1, he carefully defines its meaning in that context, pointing out its other occurrences in the epistle. Similarly, with the Hebrew word for the 'head' of Jacob's staff, he indicates how a misunderstanding has occurred on account of the absence of the 'points' (vowels) in the original Hebrew text (pp. 320-21). There is an interesting point about his quotation from 2 Corinthians 4:8. He departs from the Geneva Bible's (mis) translation of the Greek word ἀπορέω as *in pouertie, but not ouercome of pouertie*. Here the Geneva Bible probably follows Calvin's translation. But Bruce has *We doubt alwayis bot we dispair not* (Sermon 9, note 27). ESV translates as 'perplexed, but not driven to despair'.[21] It appears that Bruce's translation is more accurate than Calvin's.

Bruce also appears to have been familiar with a notable work by Gregory the Great, the one Pope regarding whom Calvin comments favourably (p. 322, note 18). The work is *Moralia in Job*, and the quotation comes from Book 7. It is an impressive exposition by Pope Gregory, and Bruce's allusion to it reflects something of the breadth of his learning.[22] He was also familiar with Tertullian's writings.[23]

Further, like Samuel Rutherford in *Lex Rex*,[24] from time to time Bruce uses syllogistic reasoning.[25] It seems to come naturally to him, and he could well have become familiar with this Aristotelian method during his studies on the continent. We get no hints that he had read

[22] See Sermon 18, notes 18 & 23.

[23] Sermon 26, note 19.

[24] Syllogistic reasoning was a feature of Rutherford's monumental refutation of Charles I's belief in the 'Divine Right of Kings', a subject on which King James also wrote in his *True Law*, and which consequently his perfidious son learned from his father.

Anselm, Duns Scotus or others of the scholastic school, who were also masters of the syllogism, but his style is characterised by rigorous conceptual analysis and the careful drawing of distinctions. Knowing that I was translating and editing his sermons for twenty-first-century readers gave me no encouragement to preserve his methodical, inexorable (and apparently repetitive) reasoning. I am sure congregations today would soon become bored if ministers constantly preached in Bruce's intellectually combative style.

Bruce the lawyer

Readers of his sermons will find footnotes in which I attempt to give the meaning and significance of the many legal terms he employs. A couple of examples of the influence of his legal training are worth mentioning. In his treatment of Jephthah's negotiations with Ammonite king, Bruce points out that Jephthah's third ground for Israel's rightful occupation of her territory was the argument of 'prescription of time'.[26] A second example of his legal mind patently at work is seen in the answer he gave to the question, 'Did Samson take his own life?' His careful refutation of the charge of suicide implicit in the question displays the meticulous arguments that one would expect from a trained lawyer.

Bruce the man

Without question, Bruce had a strong, gracious and resolute personality. We know he was tall for his generation.[27] Reading through the minutes of the General Assemblies from 1587 to 1600, the picture we get is of a man highly respected from the start, regularly entrusted with attempting to liaise with King James. He was honoured for his wisdom, learning and almost unique family history, so important to Scots. His generosity in willingly sharing with the minister Andrew Lamb his income from the abbacy of Arbroath, apparently embarrassed many of his fellow-ministers, for the Assembly minute states that as this was agreed, some of the ministers were silently 'looking through their own fingers'.[28]

His respect for, and obedience to the king was unimpeachable, but his respect for, and obedience to God was far higher. No amount of persuasion, threats or false calumnies could ever move this man from

[26] Sermon 26, notes 17 & 19.

[27] See the unusual evidence for his height, Sermon 18, note 49.

[28] Shaw, p. 1187

his steadfast guardianship of his conscience before the face of his Lord and God. When he was under immense pressure over refusing 'laying on of hands' in order to fulfil James' aim of declaring his past decade of ministry to have been unlawful, we find him departing from Edinburgh, simply to be alone and breathe in the country air, and meditate in the quietness of the rural lanes.

Apparently there were also times when he felt inadequate for the task. Those who listen carefully to ministers' sermons will learn a great deal about the preachers themselves, for when someone preaches from the heart, he unintentionally opens up more than he intends about his own soul, trials and failings. Although much application of spiritual truths to the hearers is drawn from the preacher's observation and experience of the society in which he lives, there is inevitably much that is also drawn from his own inner life. Bruce's telling sentence is revealing: 'For my own part, my own emotions, cogitations and perturbations can be my cross' (p. 549).

It is not difficult to see how Bruce empathises with Abraham's call to leave behind all he knew and loved, and to step out in faith, 'not knowing where he was going'. Likewise, he empathises with Moses who turned his back on wealth and honour (bear in mind that Bruce belonged to one of the nation's most respected families), but he chose rather to identify with a humble race whose future and fulfilment was in God alone. Thus constantly he warns his people 'not to rely on uncertain riches, neither upon their unstable honours, nor upon the fleeting affluence they can bring' (p. 335).

The date of the sermons

It is possible to date these twenty-eight sermons fairly accurately as having been preaching from late 1590 to 1592. It is doubtful if they were all preached consecutively, as Bruce will have had other duties imposed on him by the Assembly of visiting presbyteries furth of Edinburgh. At times, he does say in his introduction to a sermon that they will remember what they learned 'yisternicht' (a term which I have translated as either 'last time' or 'last Lord's Day'). On one occasion, he implies that the previous sermon in the series had been preached in 'the other place', possibly meaning in 'the east kirk' (see note 3 above). I have set down in Appendix I the full evidence for the date.

Conclusion

If I was to choose one passage of Scripture to sum up the experience of this outstanding minister of the Scottish Kirk, it would be from 2 Corinthians 4:1-12. The apostle begins,

> Therefore, having received this ministry by the mercy of God, we do not lose heart. But we have renounced disgraceful, underhanded ways. We refuse to practise cunning or to tamper with God's word, but by the open statement of the truth we would commend ourselves to everyone's conscience in the sight of God.

Paul goes on to write—and this was so true of Robert Bruce—

> But we have this treasure in jars of clay, to show that the surpassing power belongs to God and not to us. We are afflicted in every way, but not crushed; perplexed, but not driven to despair; persecuted, but not forsaken; struck down, but not destroyed; always carrying in the body the death of Jesus, so that the life of Jesus may be also be manifested in our bodies.

My sincere hope and prayer is that those who read these sermons will be challenged, enlightened and encouraged to press on towards the prize of the high calling in Christ Jesus, and to begin afresh to love, yearn and pray for the Lord's return in glory and power.

Abbreviations

Baldwin	*Haggai, Zechariah, Malachi*, Joyce G Baldwin, (Tyndale, London, 1972).
Brown	*Dictionary of the Bible*, Vols I & II, John Brown (Blackie, Edinburgh, 1866).
Cald.	*Historie of the Kirk of Scotland*, David Calderwood (Wodrow Soc. Edin., 1842).
Catherwood	*The Christian in Industrial Society*, H.R.F. Catherwood (Tyndale, London, 1964).
Donne	*Devotions Upon Emergent Occasions*, John Donne (OUP Oxford 1987).
DSL	*Dictionary of Scots Language* www.dsl.ac.uk
ESV	*English Standard Version*
Findlay	*Expositor's Greek Testament*, G.G. Findlay (Hodder, London 1904).
Foxe	*Foxe's Book of Martyrs* (Religious Tract & Book Soc., Edin. 1883).
Gibbon	*History of the Decline and Fall of the Roman Empire*, Edmund Gibbon (1776).
GenB*	*Geneva Bible* (1560) Bruce's personal edition, OT (1562) NT (1561).
GNB	*Good News Bible*
Grimm-Thayer	*Greek-English Lexicon of the NT* (T&T Clark, Edinburgh, 1908).
Hewison	*The Covenanters* (2 vols), J. King Hewison, (J Smith & Son, Glasgow, 1913).

* Still in the keeping of his descendent, Lord Elgin, Earl of Elgin.

Hodge	*The First Epistle to the Corinthians*, Charles Hodge (BofT, London, 1959).
Hume Brown	*History of Scotland* (3 Vols) P. Hume Brown (CUP 1911).
Hume	*Scotland before 1700*, P. Hume Brown (David Douglas, Edinburgh, 1893).
IBD	*Illustrated Bible Dictionary*, (IVP, Leicester, 1980).
Inst.	*Institutes of Christian Religion*, John Calvin, ed. John T. McNeill (WP 1960).
Isa. 38	*The Way to True Peace and Rest*, Robert Bruce, trans., David C Searle (BofT, 2017).
Josephus	*Antiquities of the Jews*, trans. William Whiston (Routledge, London, 1892).
Joseph	*Joseph: His Arms Were Made Strong*, D. C. Searle (BofT, Edinburgh, 2012).
JB	*Jerusalem Bible*
Knox	*Works of John Knox* (ed. David Laing, Wodrow Society, Edin. 1848).
Lindsey	*Divorced, Beheaded, Survived*, Karen Lindsey (Addison-Wesley, Reading, MA, USA, 1995).
LXX	*Septuagint*, Hebrew OT Scriptures translated into Greek.
Leupold	*Exposition of Genesis*, H.C. Leupold (EP, London, 1942).
M'Cheyne	*The Seven Churches of Asia*, R. Murray M'Cheyne (N. Adshead & Son, Glasgow, 1958).
MacKay	*Haggai, Zechariah, Malachi*, John L Mackay (CFP, 1994).
MacNicol	*Robert Bruce, Minister in the Kirk of Edinburgh*, D.C. MacNicol (BofT, 1961).
Maclean	*The Counter-Reformation in Scotland, 1560-1930*, Donald Maclean (Jas Clark, London 1931).
Murray	*Scottish Christian Heritage*, Iain H. Murray (BofT, Edinburgh, 2006).

NEB	*New English Bible*
NKJV	*New King James Version*
ODCC	*Oxford Dictionary of the Christian Church* 3rd edition (OUP 2005).
ODNB	*Oxford Dictionary of National Biography*, 1993 ed.
Rutherford	*Letters of Samuel Rutherford*, ed. Andrew Bonar (Oliphants, Edinburgh, 1848).
Shaw	*Acts of General Assemblies 1583–1618* ed. Duncan Shaw (Scot. Records Soc., Edin. 2004).
Sibbes	*Expositions of St Paul*, Richard Sibbes (BofT, Edinburgh, 1977).
Skinner	*Genesis, ICC Commentary*, John Skinner (T&T Clark, Edinburgh, 1956).
WCF	*Westminster Confession of Faith* (Edinburgh 1647).

Chapter One

Hebrews Chapter 11 verse 1

[1] Now faith is the grounde of things which are hoped for, and the euidence of things which are not sene.

The apostle, for those espoused to Christ Jesus, is exhorting his brothers to constancy, that they might persevere to the end in their profession. For endurance is most commendable and heartily to be praised, not least when a man perseveres to the end. But notice that, because he is speaking of a perseverance sorely tried and tested with all manner of troubles, both from within and from without, he is encouraging his hearers to endure and earnestly exhorting them to patient constancy. Such perseverance is not like some common plant found by a wayside stream! No, it must spring forth from the true fount of faith, having its roots in Christ; this is the only genuine, living faith that will endure.

Therefore, the apostle now proceeds to describe such faith, praising and commending it, so that many may drink more deeply of the one and only fount from which all the heroes of faith, of whom he will tell us, have themselves drunk. In vain shall anyone, destitute of genuine faith, be exhorted to have patience in his trials. Those who waste their time in empty follies will find themselves disillusioned by the very pleasures they have been seeking; they will even come to detest them. That is why their impatience erupts into frustration when in their troubles they think of turning to Christ, but end up far away from him.

True faith alone enables us to endure

Therefore, I repeat: however great a man's trials might be, true faith will enable him to endure, because true, unfeigned faith fixes one's eyes upon God alone, and upon his bounteous mercy and grace. It does not look to Christ and God with worldly eyes, hoping to gain prosperity, comfort and wealth in this life. Rather, faith looks to God and Christ for heavenly wealth, spiritual comfort, future prosperity and eternal life. Thus, though troubles arise and storms blow never so vehemently, this faith shall hold fast, garrisoning the heart; nor shall it be disappointed in its expectation of heavenly rest, for God himself is that rest. Oftentimes here and now in this life faith will receive from God that blessed comfort from his presence.

Whoever stands firmly with a loving faith endures his trials with patience, unlike those who think to gain from Christ some immediate, earthly gain, such as ease, honour and possessions; those persons always find themselves disappointed and deprived of what they impatiently sought, so separating themselves off entirely from Christ. How can they continue in him when what they most long for is not to be found in him?

Think of many—indeed think of all—who come to Christ. Not all come in the same way. There are many who come after much thought, and come only after calculating what the benefits might be of coming to Christ. If that is your attitude, then your first consideration ought to be about Christ himself, and the rigours he endured while he was here on earth; clearly, worldly ease, prosperity and honour are not to be found in him. I have commented on this before in a previous sermon. Secondly, you must weigh up the cost of following him every day of your life. This is what he calls us to do, for he never deceives us. Thirdly, you must understand and accept that coming to Christ is not about entering God's kingdom and partaking in its glory without walking in his way, and treading in the same steps in which his own Son trod as he endured many trials and afflictions. Now as this is what the Holy Spirit tells us, it behoves us all with careful consideration to come to Christ in order to enter the kingdom of heaven.

I repeat, before you seek to enter God's kingdom, you must carefully consider and accept the implications of following Christ. Do not doubt that trials will afflict you, and that then you must depend wholly on God to grasp all that he offers to you.

The cost of following Christ

As I have said, there are those who come hoping for worldly advancement, but then when the pathway turns out to be fraught with difficulties, they react angrily and end up departing from Christ's way. Would you seek to continue in the right way and fix your affections on the true foundation? Then be prepared for the way to lead you through many hardships in this world. However, suppose that on occasion you are blessed with peace and a time of tranquillity, bear in mind that the promises of Christ are indeed yours; yet never forget that worldly comforts are not your reason for following him, rather it is that heavenly rest and glory that is your goal.

Further, be resolved that storms and trials shall not shake you, but that you shall cleave to Christ. Genuine, unfeigned faith must pass through trials, however tempestuous the storms of affliction might be; you may even feel you are not going to survive, and that death will swallow you up. Then secretly, as it were, your soul will overcome by means of that faith, your spirit will be quickened and you will know the encouragement of peace wrought by courage.

The importance of faith

Hear again what is accomplished through the agency of faith. Although human powers decay, decline and succumb to old age, not so with faith. As you undergo afflictions, by faith you live through them, by faith you can be steadfast, by faith you must engage in the conflict and by faith you will receive the crown. This is why the apostle insists on developing his discourse on faith; indeed, he cannot desist from writing on it, and so he composes this eleventh chapter with the commendation of faith as its theme. And surely, true faith could never be commended too much! Such faith is perhaps the foremost gift God ever gave to man, and as the apostle honours it in this passage, so ought we also to honour it.

Faith gladdens the heart of both God and man. It unites people who are completely different and who previously held contrary opinions; the things they enjoyed and loved were often very different. Thus justifying faith breaks down barriers, because all who have it are reconciled both to God and to each other. For as God first breathed into our bodies making us living souls, so now our souls have been quickened by justifying faith. As the body without any soul is merely like an empty carriage lacking all of the five human senses, so the soul without genuine faith is like an empty carriage without any heavenly and spiritual senses. Thus it is that by justifying faith the soul begins to live the life of the eternal God, and by faith the Son of God makes his dwelling in men's hearts.

Further, faith is the only means whereby God blesses men, both in body and in soul. Faith blesses not only the body and soul, but also the heart and mind. Without this faith it is impossible either to please God or to serve him; it was always by faith that God was pleased and truly served. Range right through the Bible. Even though in the time of Moses God gave the law, and commanded his people to obey and practise these ceremonies, he was never pleased by mere outward observance; rather he was always pleased with faith and the obedience of faith. Thus faith is the only way to please God and to make our service acceptable to him.

Our purpose in living

I do not need to speak further about this commendation of faith, except in this regard: always remember why the Lord has put you in this world, and why he brought you here to live for a few fleeting years. Never forget but always call to mind that you were not brought here to live on earth to have the use of material things for ever. But the Lord has granted you a loan of a few years of life, so that during your sojourn here you may tread the pathway to heaven, and to that everlasting life that is found in God alone and will never end. This life is to be a preparation for that eternal happiness and bliss.

That blessed life cannot be earned or bought or obtained. It can only become ours through God's heavenly and perfect justice. And this divine justice can only be grasped by genuine, living faith. Therefore, whoever hopes to live eternally with God must seek this genuine, living faith. The Scriptures declare that it is the only instrument and means appointed by God whereby we may grasp hold of Christ Jesus, who alone can be our righteousness, imparted by the Father and received through faith. The only arm that can reach out and lay hold on the righteousness of God does so by this same true and living faith. Therefore, the commendation of this faith cannot be praised enough, nor can its properties be described sufficiently. That is why I have prepared this introduction before I move on to describe faith more fully. However, before I come to that, I must first analyse and lay out more clearly faith's properties as they can be found in the Scriptures.

Different meanings in Scripture of the word 'faith'

The phrase 'the faith' is sometimes used to refer to the doctrine of the evangel whereby faith is begotten and engendered in the soul of man. We find it in this sense in 1 Timothy 1:19, *Hauing faith and a good conscience, which some have put away, and as concerning faith haue made shipwracke.*[1] Therefore, we are exhorted to keep faith and a good conscience (see verse 3 of the same chapter). We find it again in the same epistle: *Now ye Spirit speaking euidently, that in ye latter times some shal depart from the faith.*[2] (See also Galatians 1:22.) As well as this use of the word 'faith', secondly, the Scriptures speak also of one historical faith, which Paul calls 'the faith concerning the mysteries of God' (1 Timothy 3:9). However, a faith that is merely historical can be the same as a dead faith.[3] Again, the Scriptures make mention of a temporary faith as in Luke 8:13.[4] Thirdly, the word of God also mentions faith inspired by miracles; certainly, there is a gift and calling to work miracles.[5] Fourthly, the Scriptures frequently speak of justifying faith, whereby men are accounted righteous in the presence of God. Regarding of all these, I will expand on them only briefly because I have often preached on them to you from this pulpit.

Therefore, here is a little more about the historical but dead faith. At first it does seem to be based on God's word. However, it arises from

[1] ESV: '... holding faith and a good conscience. By rejecting this, some have made shipwreck of their faith.'

[2] ESV: 'Now the Spirit expressly says that in later times some will depart from the faith...'

[3] No Scripture reference is given, but the allusion may be to passages such as 2 Corinthians 3:6, 'the letter kills', and 14, 15, 'But their minds were hardened ... For to this day whenever Moses is read a veil lies over their hearts'.

[4] Luke 8:13, 'And the ones [where the seed fell] on the rock are those who, when they hear the word, receive it with joy. But these have no root; they believe for a while, and in time of testing fall away.'

[5] Romans 12:3, '... each according to the measure of faith that God has assigned.' 1 Corinthians 12:7, 9, 'To each is given the manifestation of the Spirit for the common good ... to another faith by the same Spirit'.

concentrating upon a certain truth that it finds repeated throughout the whole Bible. It delights to get to know this particular doctrine, but goes no further than mere head knowledge. The doctrine it studies never leads this person to a living and active faith. That is why it is a dead faith.

By contrast, the temporary faith is different in that it does go farther than the dead faith. It accepts the truth of God's word and starts by believing its promises. At the very first hearing, it realises what God is saying and what he asks of us. But it only fixes on the promise of mercy in Christ, at which it rejoices as it tastes of his grace. But though those with temporary faith '*receiue the worde with joye*', it is only temporary. The ground has not been prepared; it has not been made ready to receive the seed, but is still full of stones, or else overgrown with briars and other rubbish that make real growth impossible. (I speak now of both the rocky ground and the ground overgrown with weeds.) The result is that the young shoots are choked, or when trials come they wither. At first, the seed growing in the stony ground looks just the same as that growing in the good ground; there seems to be no difference in the early stages. But there is an important difference: the seed growing in the rocky ground speaks of a temporary faith.

What of the third kind of faith that arises from miracles? It is inspired by witnessing God's power, and has its source in that demonstration of power; at the occurrence of the miracle it appears to believe. But it depends entirely on some extraordinary event that it witnesses. But some phenomenon does not implant real faith in a man's heart; such faith cannot see beyond the miracle. It has no other foundation on which it leans except this seeming supernatural occurrence.

That brings us last of all to justifying faith. This faith does not only depend on the truth of God in the same way as the historical faith does; neither is it only inspired by some miracle it witnesses; nor does it solely hope for the blessing of God's promise. Rather, it reposes on all of these—God's truth, his power, his promises of mercy and kindness—with the result that it issues in obedience to Christ. It is not a faith that quickly springs up and then evaporates. It is proven to be justifying faith in that it for ever is grounded on God's grace in Christ Jesus. It is this enduring faith that is the theme of the writer of the Epistle to the Hebrews.

I hope to preach on faith and open up for us all its various attributes, as the apostle describes it, in so far as God may grant me understanding. In this introductory verse of the letter, the apostle writes of two aspects of this justifying faith. (Next he will proceed to speak of the beginnings of faith, that of the fathers and of the creation of the universe by the word of God.) Therefore we shall begin by thinking about the two attributes of faith here in verse 1.

The first property of faith

The first property of faith is that it is substantial or of subsistence.[6] This word is used in a slightly different sense in two other places in Hebrews. In his epistle at 1:3, it is used of a person, where it is said that *his Sonne … who being the brightnes of the glorie, and ingraued forme of his persone* …'.[7] Here is he saying that the Son of God is the exact imprint of his Father's nature or person. Again, the same word is used in 3:14, where it means a sure persuasion and steadfast confidence: 'For we are made partakers of Christ, *if we kepe sure vnto the end the beginning* …'.[8] He means, 'Do not cast away your first confidence.' These two instances of the same word in the original language [Greek] used in our text, (*Now faith … is the euidence of things which are not sene*),[9] draw out for us something of the significance of what the apostle is saying. I take the second of these two occurrences of the word to be the meaning of our text for us: 'a steadfast assurance and confidence'; that is why he speaks of 'the substance of things that are hoped for'. Therefore, because he calls faith the substance of things hoped for, that must mean that faith is not yet come into its own essence—has not as yet come to completion—but rests only in the promises of God. This substance has no existence apart from God's promises, and it rests only on the certainty that those promises will yet be fulfilled.

6 Bruce is referring to the Greek word *hupostasis*, meaning: 'substructure, foundation, that which has actual existence, a real being'. (Grimm-Thayer.) As well as its occurrence in this text, he will cite two other occurrences of the word in Hebrews: 1:3; 3:14.

7 ESV: '… his Son … He is the radiance of the glory of God and the exact imprint of his *nature*' (1:2-3). The word in italics translate the Greek *hupostasis*.

8 ESV: 'For we share in Christ, if indeed we hold our original confidence firm to the end' (3:14).

9 ESV: 'Now faith … is the assurance of things hoped for …' (11:1).

But what is faith, you may ask, if these promises and this assurance have no reality in and of themselves? But that is what real faith is: it makes this assurance that does not as yet have any substance, to have substance! Already the promises have substance (reality) in the believer's heart and mind. You may ask how this can be? Faith brings to your heart and mind with an unshakeable certainty the assurance that these promises shall come to pass. Indeed, so firm is that confidence that you believe the promises are being fulfilled before your eyes, and that they are already a reality. So firm is the assurance in the believer's heart that it earnestly waits upon God for his answer.[10] In other words, we hold in our hearts his promises, as if they were already fulfilled, and as if the reality is there beside us. Creditors dealing with other men will try to obtain what is their due so that they can pay off their own debts. Faith is a little like that: it fervently holds God to his word, believing it will surely come to pass, as if the thing promised was already fully paid and in our hand.

In respect of this firm assurance that faith has of things to come, faith is said to be the substance and essence of things that as yet have no substance. Nonetheless, by faith they have a reality of their own. This may be difficult to grasp, and the Holy Spirit must give you understanding; we can only make sense of these things when we have a genuine experience of faith in our hearts. Therefore, there is no point in trying to apply logic or human reasoning to the rhetoric of these words; rather you must strive for hearts and minds that are filled with faith, until by the eye of faith you accept the promises of God to be as real as the shining of the sun. It is when faith is truly present in my heart and mind that what I hope for in God becomes a reality. Thus, when faith has its dwelling in my heart and mind, this assurance is termed a substance, so that we believe that things not yet present will become reality when and as God's promises are fulfilled. Thus far for the first property.

The second property of faith

Here is the second property that the apostle ascribes to faith: he calls it a demonstration or *evidence* [ESV, 'conviction'] of things not yet seen. He means it is a kind of declaration of what will come fully into view.

[10] The phrase Bruce uses is not easily translated: 'it makis us corrupt the promeis of god payment'. The last two sentences in this paragraph explain the use of the unexpected verb 'corrupt'.

The nature of it is that what cannot be clearly seen with our human eyes, can be seen, as it were, by the eye of our soul. Indeed, by faith the evidence is seen even more clearly than if it was corporeal, and able to be experienced by the human senses. Thus faith is said to be a display or demonstration of 'things not seen', because it manifests these things to my heart and mind and soul.

So we have it: the first property of faith is the assurance or substance of things hoped for, and the second property of faith is the evidence or the manifestation of things that are invisible to human sight. Is this not a spiritual mystery?[11] From this the apostle teaches us that faith has these two forms—'substance' and 'evidence'. These two words must be the most remarkable words among men. You will realise that faith—I mean a true living faith—is nothing to do with doubt, or fanciful ideas, or superstitions that border on the incredible; rather this faith is characterised by a certain, steadfast persuasion of the reality of God's mercy in Christ.

This is more certain, sure and substantial than anything you might investigate and perceive with your physical senses; it brings clearer and more perfect knowledge than can any visual or empirical explanation of some natural phenomenon. This—not something you can see with your eyes—is the one thing in life that you can trust completely. That is why faith does not give rise to doubts or uncertain theories; faith gives birth only to a sure, steadfast persuasion.

Serious error in the Roman Catholic teaching

This shows an important difference between ourselves and those in the Roman Catholic Church. They do not know of the substance and evidence, for they are never completely certain of the mercy and favour of God; their priests denigrate this kind of faith of which the apostle is writing. They make the accusation that the faith we profess and embrace is of our own invention, without warrant in the word of God; they allege it is devised by our own deluded minds like some imported homemade artefact. They deny it is the faith the ancient Fathers knew, and insist they had they never heard of it. Yet, I shall show you how their teaching completely misunderstands the New Testament, and you will see how they contradict themselves.

[11] The phrase Bruce uses that I have translated 'a spiritual mystery' is 'a strainge nature'.

Roman Catholic doctrine does not deny that men ought to hope for eternal life and entry into the glory of the heavenly kingdom. But I want to know how they can hope for the kingdom of heaven without being sure that their sins—which are the reason for death and hell—are forgiven. How can any man be sure of everlasting life unless his sin is taken away, when the punishment for sin is eternal death? It stands to reason that if a priest would rightly teach his people to hope for heaven, he must also teach them that all their sins can be blotted out, and sin's condemnation be taken away. Do you see, therefore, how self-contradictory their doctrine is, when full and free pardon for sin is not taught?

Here then is the foundation of the doctrine that we teach: the Lord will be merciful to us for Christ's sake, and will cast all our sins behind his back, for the sake of the satisfaction accomplished by his Son; this is the only means by which we can partake of that immortal glory. This is the faith we proclaim that teaches you how to live and how to die. This is the faith of which you must have experience, not merely a faith that gives mental assent, but a faith that believes in your hearts that you will die as Christians when the Lord chooses to call you to himself. Strive to be sure that your sins have been forgiven, for without this assurance, you cannot be certain of heaven. But strive first of all to be reconciled to God and to be at peace with him, and then you will have the confidence of eternal life in your heart.

Guarding conscience

How can a man be sure of that mercy of God? By guarding, and taking heed to, his conscience.[12] Be watchful each day regarding how you live. Also be fully aware of the things that prick your conscience and those that please it; in other words, learn what gives pleasure to God and what grieves him. For whoever disregards his conscience should neither expect to inherit eternal life, nor hope for mercy on that awesome day. I say all this quite deliberately that you may all be warned not to hurt your consciences, especially those of you who daily live and mix with people who practise idolatry or come from countries such as Spain where popish idolatry holds sway. No one can share in that kind of false worship without grievous hurt to his conscience.

[12] For an outline of Bruce's emphasis on, and understanding of, conscience, see the Appendix in his sermons on Isa. 38.

If this applies to any of you listening today, unless you change your course and repent, you have already violated your consciences and can expect no mercy on the Day of Judgment. Those of you already embarked on such courses of action[13] should be deeply concerned, for now you have set up barriers between yourselves and the face of Christ. Your consciences should already be warning you that even though you were cautioned that you have been violating your consciences, you have continued to subject yourselves to the righteous judgment of the God against whom you have offended. You should be saying, 'I have mocked my conscience and disobeyed its promptings.' The time will come when you crave mercy, but mercy will mock you.

Before you leave this place, I warn all who mock God and religion that you may expect no mercy from the hand of God, and that applies to you in the hour when you die. However, if you change the course of your lives, as the Lord God lives, you may still experience his grace in your souls. I say this to you all irrespective of what your station in life might be, because anyone—both you who are high-born and those of you who are of working stock—can find yourselves targets of the devil, whether he comes at us through this world's allurements or by working upon our fallen inner desires. Therefore everyone, whatever your social standing or calling may be, should carefully guard his steps, and watch out for whatever it be that angers God and robs you of peace and brings sorrow to your heart. However much a man is captivated by something in this life, he must shake himself free from it, and embrace only what he may enjoy along with God's eternal blessing, for with that will come inner peace. Such calm within one's heart will bring the assurance of the Lord's mercy, forgiveness and citizenship of his kingdom.

Surely such blessings must have the effect of encouraging us to seek God's constant blessing, and to pray that he would wean us from everything that draws us away from him, and goes against our consciences. Our desire must be that he would only bless us with such things as bring lasting benefit, because they nourish peace and serenity in our hearts; pray, therefore, that neither our flesh nor our wills will be able to rob us of these blessings. Pray also that by the Lord's enabling we will persevere in eschewing all that blinds us so that we lose sight of

[13] I have translated Bruce's word 'voyages' as 'courses of action'.

the face of God. Ask him only for those things that will bring enduring blessings to our souls.

I do not know of any petition in God's holy book more necessary than this: 'Sever us, O Lord, from all that separates us from you, and bless us only with whatever will keep us secure in your favour, and will enable your everlasting grace to grow and abound within us.' For all who hear but do not obey these admonitions, the condemnation will be all the greater. Therefore, examine your ways; likewise, study to set them right.

Scriptural illustrations of true faith

Back to our subject: faith constantly makes things that 'are not', to be real to us. I will illustrate this. Was Jesus Christ incarnate in the days of Abraham? The Scriptures make it clear that he was not. Indeed, it was more than two thousand years later before he was manifested in the flesh. Yet in John's Gospel the Scriptures assure us that Abraham saw Christ's day;[14] he grasped him and tasted of him. That is an example of faith causing something that in and of itself 'was not', to be truly present in Abraham's heart. That example that comes from the lips of our Master lets us see that faith made the incarnate Christ a living reality in his servant's heart.

Another example is Stephen, who by the eye of faith saw the heavens open and Christ Jesus sitting on the right hand of the Father.[15] What was invisible to human eyes was clearer to this man than anything material that he could see around him that day. Thus faith brings before a man the clear and unmistakable reality of things that 'are not', in and of themselves. This absolute certainty cannot be engendered by someone telling us about it, nor even by some angel's voice bringing a message; it can only be wrought in the heart by the hearing of the word of God. I'm not talking about that 'historical faith'—a mental assent to some doctrine—of which we thought earlier. Rather I mean by hearing that special word of promise (not just *any* promise, for there are many promises in Scripture), the promise of mercy, that is, the glad tidings of salvation in and through Jesus Christ. By the Holy Spirit working *inwardly*, and by the hearing of the word of promise *outwardly*, faith is engendered

[14] John 8:56.
[15] Acts 7:55.

in the human heart. This faith is not a precious stone quarried from the earth, nor a flower growing by the wayside; neither is it something already there within our natures. Rather is it a gift bestowed on us by Christ and wrought in us by the Holy Spirit; it is not given to everyone, but just to those whom the Lord has chosen to receive eternal life; it will remain within your soul for ever.

Can this faith be taken from a man?

This certainty of mercy and that your sins are forgiven shall never be completely taken from you. However, since we still have sinful natures, and constantly provoke God to anger by committing heinous sins, is it possible that we can still retain this assurance? Just say an upright man tells a lie, is he still assured of mercy? Yes, notwithstanding our failures, the Holy Spirit and the Son of God who has saved you will still have mercy on you; for he has appointed the gift of repentance for your deceitfulness and wrongdoing. If you do sin and fall away from him, his gift to you of repentance will call you back to him, so that by unfeigned repentance the full assurance of mercy, that you lost and discarded by your evil backsliding, will be renewed within your heart.

Just as it was God who first created faith in your heart, it is by his mercy that your faith perseveres, and it is by his mercy that your faith will finally be brought to perfection. The Lord himself begins, continues and completes the work for his own glory and for our eternal salvation. So much, then, regarding the properties of faith.

The first object of faith

The apostle now continues with two kinds of object: the first is, *things which are hoped for*. (The second is, *things which are not sene*.) Let us consider the first object. Strictly speaking, according to the Scriptures, no 'thing' can be the object of faith; the 'actual things promised' are the object of hope, not faith. As to faith and belief, the object is, in a word, 'the word of promise'. Do you ask why? Because the only thing in the whole world I can have faith in is God's promise. If someone orders me to do something, I am asked to obey the command, not believe in it. But if someone makes a promise to me, I must either believe that promise or distrust it. So promises are to be believed, but commands to be obeyed. We conclude that the object of faith is 'the word of promise'.

In short, faith looks to the *promise* given in the word, whereas hope looks to the *things* promised that seem to be hidden from us. Therefore the apostle writes that *faith is the grounde of things which are hoped for*; *by grounde*[16] he means reality or substance. What is promised by faith becomes an actuality. An illustration from the Lord's Supper: in his promise Christ is present really and bodily to the eye of faith.

I return then to my exposition. The only thing that can be believed is a promise. And we have seen that the word of God names here those things that are promised as the objects of faith, first, *things that are hoped for*, and second, *things that are not seen.* Now we must ask, 'What does he mean by *things* hoped for?'

The apostle is referring to certain things that are not as yet a reality, apart, that is, from our hope; for it is hope that waits expectantly for things that as yet are in the future. For as soon as these things become a reality, we cease to hope for them. It is therefore obvious that as long as they are only hoped for, they are not yet present.

You may ask what then are these objects of hope? An example is the full redemption of our bodies, as Paul shows when he writes about *the resurrection of our bodie* (Romans 8:23). I hope for the resurrection of both my soul and my body, and for the perfect sanctification of both. He compares that redemption to a bride *not hauing spot or wrinkle, or any suche thing … but holie and without blame.*[17] We can only hope for this to become a reality. Another example of hope is that I believe the Lord has forgiven my sin, yet I look forward in hope that on that great day he will finally show to all the world that I am truly forgiven, as my own conscience in some measure already tells me. Further, I also believe that the Lord, for Christ's sake, will then give me that crown of everlasting glory; I believe this now, yet in hope I look to him to grant me this when I am with him forever.

The second object of faith

The second object is of things that *are*, but as yet *are not sene*. Although such things are, having their own essence, yet they are invisible to the eye of man. Everything must have a reality, for if it does not it cannot

[16] ESV, assurance; see note 6 above.

[17] Ephesians 5:27: '… without spot or wrinkle or any such thing … holy and without blemish' (ESV).

exist. So if a thing is real, either it will be visible to the human eye, or only visible to the mind's eye. If it is something outward and corporeal, our human senses will be aware of it. But if it is something spiritual, it will not be visible to our human senses. I mean, either something is natural or supernatural. If it is the former, then by human reasoning it will be discernible and we will be able to evaluate it. But if it is something heavenly, spiritual and invisible to human sight, then there must be faith, and only by faith can we reach out and lay hold of it, in order to evaluate and meditate upon something that is both spiritual and heavenly.

Then must earthly reasoning and worldly thinking cease, as faith comes into her own, for only faith perceives what is spiritual and supernatural. An example is that we sinners, on the one hand, cannot yet enter into the holy of holies, whence our great High Priest has gone before us to prepare a place for us. On the other hand, we now are free to enter in, for Christ by his death and shed blood has procured for us liberty to enter. Suppose that because we are pilgrims here on earth, and as sojourners we may not yet enter the holy of holies, nevertheless, we have already been granted the freedom to draw near. This liberty cannot be seen by physical sight, nor grasped by our human logic, it can only be seen by the spiritual eye of faith. Therefore, though not seen, it is a reality.

This is why we speak of our effectual calling, and of our justification and sanctification: they *are*, yet are not seen. The natural man cannot discern them. Therefore, faith has these two objects on which it fixes its sight: first, things that are hoped for but not as yet present, and second, things that are in themselves but not yet discerned by the imagination or eye of man.

Three things essential for true faith

Regarding this explanation of faith to which you have been listening, the Spirit of God must inspire your hearing so that you can grasp its meaning, for real faith is comprised of three things: knowledge, an obedient will and assurance. Consider each of these. First, by knowledge I mean that you must *know* God in Christ, believing in him, *knowing* him to be a merciful God who is rich in mercy and will pardon your sins for Christ's sake. Second, as well as knowledge, you must also have an *obedient will* in order to receive mercy when it is offered to you. When your mind acknowledges the abundance of mercy that is available from the hands of God for Christ's sake, so your *will* must be bent and your heart inclined to seek after that mercy for Christ's sake. What good is it for you to *know* that there is a wealth of mercy in God, if it does not yet belong to you? Mere *knowledge* is not enough. You must also thirst for God's mercy and study to make what you have learned about in your mind the genuine experience of your heart.

Third, faith will bring you the firm *assurance*, and you will be certain that the Lord will not only be merciful, but already has had mercy upon you. For of what avail would it be for you to yearn and seek for something that you did not believe could ever be yours? A man may seek something and long to have it, and yet despair of ever obtaining it, so that he ultimately ceases to search for it and turns his affections to something else. Therefore, seeking and longing for mercy in itself is not enough; the Lord must impart assurance to your conscience, not just that God is merciful, but also that he has already been merciful, and in the future on that day fully and finally will make declaration of his mercy towards you.

Does Scripture teach that these three facets of faith are necessary?

Now when there is the knowledge of his mercy, plus an obedient will that thirsts for mercy, and thirdly the persuasion and assurance that you have been granted mercy, then there is true faith. Without all these three things, the faith is lacking and not yet genuine. You may ask what warrant there is for defining faith in terms of these three things. First, as for *knowledge*, it is implied in the word *evidence*, meaning demonstration; for when something is demonstrated I get knowledge of it. Second, where do I find in Scripture this *obedient will* that earnestly desires? It is there in the word *hope*, for hope longs for good things just as fear dreads evil things. Where there is hope of good things, there is bound to be the thirst and desire to possess them. Therefore, I understand the word *hope* to imply real thirst, desire and the strong will of the heart to partake of that mercy that it can see in its mind's eye. Third, regarding the *assurance* that the Lord will be merciful, it is present in the word *ground*[18] or substance; assurance is experiencing God's mercy.

[18] Bruce, of course, is quoting from the Geneva Bible, as in his text at the heading of this chapter. ESV translates as 'assurance'. Again, see note 6 above.

What was seen in my mind's eye is now felt, not by my outward human senses, but inwardly.

However, let me warn you, that even if your mind's eye rightly perceives the mercy of God, if your conscience is for ever distressing and accusing you, you cannot have full assurance of mercy; therefore you need to take heed to your conscience. For you must have that peace that passes all understanding to pacify your conscience and firmly believe in the Lord's mercy, so that the distress of your conscience may be taken away and you may be fully assured of his mercy.

What of the tormented conscience?

By contrast, the knowledge of the coming judgment, and of hell and its torments, should warn the conscience of everlasting damnation. If only men realized the reason for their consciences being tormented, and the trial to which the Lord will one day summon their consciences, and the folly of doing nothing about their troubled consciences, they would take more heed of its voice and change their ways. Consider how the lords and magistrates of our country take such little notice of their consciences. They do not banish from our land God's enemies, but tolerate Jesuits and heretics. Neither has anything been done, nor is likely to be done regarding this, in spite of all the promises they have made.

I warn them that as sure as night follows day, and the Lord lives, all that they have on their consciences will be laid bare, except they repent. If the evils deep down in their consciences were about to be opened up for all to see, how quickly would they become anxious to please God, and how swiftly would their feelings constrain them to obey him. But just now, because the window into their conscience is shuttered and barred, they do not think about the coming pangs of death, and for the want of this knowledge, every man studies to please himself, and none of them labour to please God.

Therefore, it is incumbent on us all to pray that the Lord in his mercy would awaken these men, and reveal to them the torment of their own consciences. It is complete folly for anyone to think he can serve God without knowing how essential Christ is to each of us. So this is an urgent prayer regarding our magistrates: that the Lord would awaken them, and in his mercy disturb their consciences, that by a foretaste of hell they may flee from that everlasting torment.

Yes, regarding those of you listening to me, unless the Lord awakens your consciences also, and gives you the awareness of the reality of hell, you will never flee from its flames. Therefore, I beseech the living God to make this prayer effectual in every one of you. May you see that the life of God cannot be attained but by the knowledge and awareness of hell. So may the Lord make every one of you aware of the distress that sin inflicts upon your consciences, so that you too may flee swiftly to Christ for mercy. The way to heaven must take us right past the very gates and bars[19] of hell, for there is no way to joy but by pain. I grant that the thought of souls in torment is sore, especially to our frail flesh.

But what of the anguish of our sinful natures, our souls and consciences, all committed to a fierce and consuming fate? Imagine all your sins that now lie concealed, rising up and staring you in the face, dragged up from your memories, and there is no escape from them. Alright then, there may not be any mention just now of your past sins, but when the Lord awakens your consciences, every single sin will be brought to mind, and with it the horror of what you did. Yea, the burning of human flesh in a hot fire is nothing compared to the anguish of a guilty conscience. And yet, this is the suffering towards which you are heading, and, unless you yourselves prevent it, you will too late discover that my preaching was not mere fables. The only safeguard against your impending anguish is the mercy offered by Jesus Christ. Therefore, may the Lord impart a deeper understanding in you, that you may avoid the everlasting torments of hell; this will be your lot if you persist in following the wrong paths.

Much more could be said, but because my time has gone I shall finish here. Only grasp this: faith depends on knowledge and assurance, and if you sever that assurance from your faith, it is not genuine faith at all. Knowledge in your minds and assurance in your hearts: such faith blesses the whole man, the knowledge blesses and sanctifies the mind and the assurance blesses the heart. Then justifying faith, by grace, blesses with everlasting blessings the whole man—body, soul, heart and mind. When we speak of mercy and judgment, we know we eschew the latter but attain the former.

[19] Bruce's phrase is 'the yetis of hell'; a 'yett' was a gate or grill made of latticed iron bars used at the entrances of castles and tower-houses.

In short, these things come by that knowledge of which we have spoken, and when your thirst has been satisfied, then you will have understanding in your heart, and you must nourish this understanding so that each day you may increasingly be assured of the Lord's mercy towards you for Christ's sake. Yet only the Spirit can make this word effectual in you unto everlasting life through the merits of Christ, to whom be, with the Father and the Holy Ghost, all honour, praise and glory now and for evermore.

Chapter Two

Hebrews Chapter 11 verses 2-3

---

[2] Ffor by it our elderis war weill reported of. [3] Through faith we vnderstand that the worlde was ordained by ye worde of God so that the things which we se, are not made of things which did appeare.

Recap of the first sermon

I will proceed, brethren, with the text we thought about last time— not that I will go over everything I said—but just to remind you of some of what we learned. You will recall that faith was described in terms of two properties, and, in turn, they were described in terms of two objects.

The first property of faith is that it is substantial or of subsistence, the *grounde of things which are hoped for*, that is, that are not in themselves nor are they in very deed, but are only in hope in the promise of the living God; they 'are' in God himself. The reason why faith is called the substance of things is that faith makes them substantial in our hearts, that is, realities in our hearts and minds. It is as if we already had them in full fruition in our hands; this is on account of the great assurance that accompanies faith. I mean that faith imparts this assurance to our hearts of those things God has promised, in such a way as if the fulfilment of his promises was already firmly[1] in our possession.

Secondly, this is why faith is called *the euidence* (substance) *of things which are not sene*, the evidence of things that are invisible to our physical sight; for faith brings an inward, illuminating light to the mind in such a way that by the eye of faith the mind can perceive clearly these spiritual things as if they were actually corporeal, and could be seen by

[1] Bruce's vivid word is 'gripid', i.e. 'gripped'.

our physical eyes. Regarding this clear sight in the mind that accompanies faith, it is also called a demonstration or declaration of things which are not seen.

Though faith be weak, God's love is irrevocable

The instruction here for us is that we must learn that each of these two properties of genuine, living faith produce a certain and steadfast persuasion of the mercy of God. Faith has nothing to do with personal opinions or conjectures or dubious superstitions. Rather, wherever this genuine faith is present, it works in us a clear sight, a solid and certain persuasion of the mercy of God in Christ. Certainly, though the conviction of God's mercy is a reality in our hearts, it is not always in quite the same state or condition.[2] Sometimes a person's faith in the divine mercy is extremely strong; at other times doubts may lurk in the soul.

The reason for such variations is that at times the firmness of our faith can be impaired by our sin. For even the very elect vessels[3] of God in Christ, the most holy and upright of believers, can and do fall seven times a day. That is why the condition of a person's faith is never always absolutely constant, but can be sometimes a little greater, but sometimes a little weaker; yet at other times it can fully possess that person's heart. Nevertheless, whatever the strength or weakness of your faith, be persuaded of this: the fact that you have living faith is a sure guarantee of your election. Indeed, your very experience of faith being tossed to and fro with sundry doubts is in itself a pledge that you are truly a child of God. It is God's election that is unchangeable, and however weak, feeble and fragile your faith may be, his love for you is irrevocable.

All those who have Christ Jesus, as well as this faith that is given us as the pledge of our salvation, also have the word of God assuring us of his mercy. Further, we all have some experience of the mercy and favour of God and of his protection in times of danger. Such experiences should be called to memory. The promise of mercy found in God's word should also be called to memory, and thereby the faith in our hearts should be nourished. Then, when our assurance is attacked by the devil, we may cast ourselves back upon God.

[2] This last phrase was not easy to translate; Bruce has 'is not ay in ane estait'.

[3] The Scots word 'veschell', meaning 'a household container, a pot or pan', is used figuratively in the sense of 'a person viewed as a receptacle of good or evil, chiefly in a religious context' (DSL). See also 2 Timothy 2:20-21.

This then is the first lesson we must learn. Even when our assurance is weak, it still remains a sure guarantee of our eternal salvation. Even though there are many other gifts from God as well as this gift of faith, yet it is not the same kind of gift as them. For when God gives us faith, he never takes it from us, he never changes his mind about it, so that he never removes it from the heart where he has placed it. Rather than revoke it or diminish it, he actually will increase it, for it may begin as very small.

Faith begins with conviction of sin

There are terms attached to Christ's gift of faith. Even though very weak and small, nevertheless it is alive and imparts life to the soul of the one in whom it lives; I do not mean it imparts physical life, rather it brings spiritual and heavenly life. Even though it is as tiny as a grain of mustard seed, and as feeble as a smoking flax that emits neither warmth nor flame, but only the tiniest spark giving off a wisp of smoke within your soul, and cannot even be seen, yet the Lord will never extinguish it, but will rather tend it, and in his own time cause it to bring forth the flame of unfeigned repentance. When faith is in this fragile state, it is subject to many temptations, doubts, vacillations and fears; it may even cause doubts about salvation.

All this partly stems from the insight a man gets of himself when it pleases God to open his eyes to his conscience, so that he sees himself as he really is, and the depth of miseries into which his own sins are casting him. It pleases the Lord to let him look into the depths of the pit of his innumerable sins, iniquity upon iniquity. Little wonder his soul quakes and his heart faints, and doubts flood his mind. Apart from the sight of the unfathomable depths of the riches and mercies of the ever-living God, no one ever glimpsed such a depth as that of the sinful heart! Imagine you lived as long as Methuselah, and then tried to measure how deep was your sinful heart, you could never plumb its depths.

So when the Lord opens the eyes of our minds and gives us just a glimpse of the wretchedness that is in us, little wonder that we foster doubts. Again, when it pleases the Lord to lay his heavy hand upon our souls and we realise his hatred of sin, and when he presents himself to us as a consuming fire, little wonder that we then may have doubts, and our souls begin to tremble greatly. Yet here is guidance for comfort for our doubting, wavering and fears, however great and many they may be: it is that the Lord will forgive them. He will never lay them to our charge, for in his mercy he will have been preparing us, by the sight of our sins, future as well as past, to live more vigilantly.

Faith needs continual restoration, growth and increase

Again, at times our faith is in a very different condition, in that this genuine and living faith possesses the souls of the faithful so mightily, and the assurance fills them so completely, that there is not so much as a single stirring of doubt. We have ourselves heard someone, who has now passed on, testifying that he was so fully persuaded of eternal life and mercy that there was not so much as a single motion of doubting in his soul. Again, we have heard another say that he was so certain of his election, that even supposing every creature in earth and heaven were to declare him reprobate, he would still be assured of his salvation. I myself have heard this. See, then, whether in these two persons their faith has not been in great measure, and whether also there has not been a fulsome persuasion in their souls of God's mercy. It is evident, therefore, that God's grace is not always in the same measure within us, for there are times when it is more potent and more plenteous than at other times.[4] And when this grace of God is more potent and fulsome than at other times, we are not only withheld from doing wrong, but we are also stirred up to every good work.

On the other hand, there are times when our faith is weak and we are living in our own strength, and then in its feebleness our faith does not stir us up to good works; that is when we fall, yes, sometimes into great and heinous sins. Yet as faith is a gift that is never revoked, however weak it might be, nevertheless it still continues to be living and genuine. Therefore, faith is a gift that is never perfected in this life, but it needs continual restoration, growth and increase. That is why the apostles in Luke 17:5 prayed earnestly that the Lord would increase their faith. Paul in Ephesians 1:17 records a very noteworthy prayer for the increase of the Ephesians' faith. This prayer of Paul's should teach us that if the apostle felt a lack in the believers' faith, and knew about it from his own experience of them, little wonder that we poor wretches

[4] The context makes it clear that Bruce is speaking about our awareness or consciousness of God's grace, for his subject is assurance.

sometimes have great doubts. Surely then, we too have to pray constantly that the living God should not abandon that tiny spark in us, but that in his great mercy he will tend it by his Holy Spirit, causing it more and more to burn brightly, and so bring us in unfeigned repentance to himself.

Faith requires knowledge and earnest desire

But let me tell you more. In faith there must always be three things. First, there must be clear knowledge; we find that in our text in the word 'evidence'. Second, there must be a thirst or earnest desire; that is shown in the word 'hope'. If you have no spiritual thirst, it cannot be faith, for in everyone who has true faith there must be some real desire for the assurance of God's mercy. When this yearning for assurance is weak, then without doubt the faith is also weak, and when the knowledge is dim and hazy, then faith is going to be very feeble, small and weak. For some people, the thirst is greater than the knowledge; in others it can be the other way, and the knowledge is greater than the thirst. (We will come to the third aspect of faith later; it concerns faith's 'objects'.)

I will illustrate what I mean. Think how certain our senses of sight and touch make us sure about physical things; we depend on these two senses to be sure about so much around us. We read how the Master gave Thomas the opportunity to use both these senses of sight and touch to be persuaded that he had truly risen. The same senses are used by all of us for anything outward and material. But far more convincingly should our faith assure us of spiritual things. So faith should convey to us both feeling and sight: the feeling in our heart[5] and the sight in our mind. These two will assure me that there is a store of mercy in Christ. When either knowledge or feeling (thirst) decline, the power of faith also will decline. In the past there have been many who put more emphasis on feelings than knowledge; in our times, it has been the other way round—greater emphasis on knowledge than on feelings.

We read in Acts 10 of Cornelius, a man of Caesarea who was a centurion in the Roman army. Before ever he heard Peter preach of the ministry of Christ, whereby he should ordinarily have been enlightened,

[5] See note 12 below.

he was nevertheless counted as a man that feared God. He was a good man who gave alms to the poor, and was constant in prayer to God. Yet he still did not have clear knowledge before he heard Peter's account of Jesus Christ. Yet he had such a strong desire and feeling in his conscience that he engaged assiduously in charitable deeds just as if he already had knowledge through the preaching of the word. Therefore we see that it has happened on occasion that a man has had strong feelings and the best of consciences before ever having knowledge of the truth in his mind.

Many are neglecting their consciences

But now the complete contrary is the case with us; our head knowledge is increasing, but our feelings are decreasing. The more that happens, experience teaches us that our consciences are neglected. Is it not strange that when we have so much more knowledge that ought to stimulate our consciences, that does not happen and our consciences are increasingly polluted by evil things? This suggests that men's hearts are more stubborn than they used to be, and that the rebellion in us is more obdurate than it ever was in the hearts of our forefathers. For now by the thraldom of our sins we deliberately hide the light and knowledge that we have in Christ Jesus. The apostle calls this thraldom 'the bonds of unrighteousness'.[6] Our sin is like a plague of lice in us that infests and defiles our knowledge. Without question our condemnation is bound to be great, for it seems perfectly clear that this knowledge of the truth has been given to our generation to render it all the more inexcusable.

Therefore it is high time for us to attend to our consciences and to let them guide us back into the knowledge of God. For when we sin against our consciences and neglect the truth, we take the highway to damnation. That is to tread the broad road that lures a man into the sin against the Holy Spirit. Therefore I urge you to reform your consciences in accordance with your knowledge of the truth. However, should you find that you do sin unwittingly against the truth, and realise that the stubbornness of your heart is so insidious that it seduces you to sin against the truth, you must have recourse to fasting and

[6] The allusion is probably to Romans 6:13, 'Neither giue ye your membres as weapons of vnrighteousnes vnto sinne' (GenB).

sobriety. Then through the mercy of God, your heart and mind may come together and lead you to follow steadfastly that knowledge that has been imparted to you.

Faith must look to the spiritual, not to the outward

Thirdly, we saw last time that faith was described as having two 'objects'. The first object of faith was 'things which are hoped for', that is, things that 'are', but not of themselves, but are only covertly contained[7] in the promises; they 'are', but only in hope and expectation of God. There is one other 'object' of faith; it is 'things that are not seen'. He means, things that cannot be seen by using our physical eyes, nor can they be seen outwardly. In short, he means by these 'objects of faith' such things that cannot be reached or touched by natural means, far less by the eye of reason. Not only can these 'objects of faith' not be seen by nature, neither can our physical eyes see them.

Faith is quite contrary to the usual laws of nature. It does not look to outward things that we all can see. Rather it casts its eyes solely upon the things that are not seen, for 'the things which are seen are temporal', as the apostle says,[8] and no temporal thing can be the object of faith. Rather faith reposes upon those things that are spiritual and eternal, and they are not seen. Strictly speaking, of course, only the living God is eternal, therefore in the final analysis, it is upon God that faith reposes; only in him is that perfect rest. It is true that faith reposes upon Christ, but then Christ is both a man and God.

Think about the Lord's Supper. In that sacrament, faith looks to the body of Christ, to his flesh and to his blood. Now the flesh of Christ is a carnal thing, and likewise his blood is an outward thing. While it cannot be denied that faith looks to these things, it not only looks to the human Christ, but chiefly to the divine Christ. In other words, faith looks to the true God who took upon himself the nature of man. The reason why faith looks to the flesh and blood of Christ is not as to something carnal, because in the sacrament his flesh and blood are no longer to us merely outward, but are now heavenly and spiritual. Do you ask why we call his body in the sacrament *spiritual*? It is because by it a spiritual and heavenly life is begotten in me, and nourishes me

[7] Bruce has 'lurking in the promeis'.
[8] 2 Corinthians 4:18.

in that life. If Christ's flesh and blood begat in us a temporal life, they might justifiably be called *temporal* in themselves. But his flesh and blood beget in us a spiritual life, for in the sacrament they are spiritual, no longer earthly and carnal.

In John 6:63 our Master leads his disciples to put their confidence in him as God when he says, 'It is the Spirit that quickeneth: the flesh profiteth nothing: the words that I speak unto you, are spirit and life.' Thus Christ was drawing them to put their confidence in him, the Mediator who is both God and man, but especially in him as God. It is true that outward things have been used in religion, for God has given many carnal things as signs.[9] As both the sacraments as outward things are signs and seals, yet they are not given to us that we should rest and repose our faith in them. Rather their purpose is that by outward symbols we might be led to spiritual things, whereon we might rest our faith. So we see that we have not only an earthly, carnal nature, but there is also by the grace of God a spiritual nature available to us. By the mercy of God we are able to be participants in that spiritual nature.

Now our earthly natures need to be guided, encouraged and helped on account of our great infirmity. It was because of our infirmity that the sacraments were appointed, that by them we might be led to the thing they signify. In that way our faith is enabled to rest upon the spiritual, indeed, upon the living God who alone is eternal. Reposing upon him is the only bulwark of our faith; for when God is present, there can be nothing absent. It is through faith that God is present with us, and then there is no trial or adversity that can destroy us.

Exhortation

So to return to the exhortation with which I concluded in my previous sermon. Suppose you die, are taken from us and your body is now dead to this world; by faith you will live. Why? Because through faith God's presence is with you, Christ Jesus is with you, and when God in Christ is with you, you lack nothing. Do you long for support or consolation? Find it in God. Do you need strength? Take it from him. Do you want armour for the fight? Receive it from him. Whatever you may lack, having God present with you, you can find it in him.

[9] Probably the reference is to the sacrificial ritual of the Old Testament.

There can be no question about it: it has been the presence of the living God that has enabled all his servants to triumph in their trials. Had they not recognised that God was with them they would never have had such great courage. It was the presence of God and Christ in their hearts that made them so enraptured that they were victorious and conquerors in the greatest calamities that could ever afflict their mortal bodies. In some trials in which his servants lost their lives, they actually won their cause and conquered; so the apostle pronounces them victors! In whatever way it was that they died, though from a human point of view they were defeated, yet by the mighty presence of God, even though their earthly bodies lay in their graves, their souls were transported immediately to heaven. Even though their bodies were buried, their cause was not buried, for experience teaches us that their cause was strengthened by their martyrdom.

The death of martyrs has been the propagation and confirmation of Christ's cause, but only because Christ himself was present in their hearts. It was his presence alone that made them victorious. The apostle says that we are 'more than conquerors' (Romans 8:37), and I take this to be in respect of their glory. For in the worst extremities that could overtake them, and in the greatest trials that the devil laid upon their mortal bodies, they gloried, rejoiced and praised God. It was their steadfast confidence that struck fear into their enemies, making them wonder in perplexity. Yea, they marvelled more than if there had been twenty thousand harquebusiers[10] accompanying God's servants. You can read in Acts 4 that after John and Peter were arrested, and after they had been imprisoned overnight, then tried and threatened, they continued to speak the word of God with boldness and confidence, and continued to praise God with joy in their hearts. The whole council marvelled, and were more baffled than if they had been confronted by a large army. Therefore this inward confidence that God's servants knew by the presence of Christ in their hearts made them more than victorious in the greatest troubles that could befall them.

[10] Harquebusiers were cavalrymen who carried a carbine with them in a leather holster fixed to their saddles. As they galloped towards enemy lines, they first discharged their carbines at the enemy before drawing their swords to engage in the fight.

While we have some leisure and calm, now is our opportunity to make our acquaintance with God, and to draw near to the throne of grace, that we may remove all barriers that come between us and the face of the living God. Then in the sight of his countenance we may obtain sure confidence, boldness and rejoicing to gainsay whatever foes confront us. Then we shall accept whatever trial it shall please the Lord in his mercy to lay upon us; and this confidence will remain with you throughout your whole lives. This should be your whole concern: to cast off the burden of sin that weighs you down and clings so closely, for by making your way straight you may get a clear sight of God in Christ.

We cannot be at all sure when Christ shall be concerned to be active in a country. It is possible that his quarrel with us may be nearer than many think. For beyond question this peace and apparent calm has lasted a long time, and it may well end unexpectedly. Now is the opportune moment to acquaint yourselves with God, that, in the event our form of religion be suppressed and the liberties we have enjoyed be taken from us, you may share the countenance of God in your hearts, and with boldness may resist and shame the enemy, who, seeing your rejoicing faces, your constancy and boldness, may question his actions and turn away from his intentions. Therefore, while you have the opportunity, examine your hearts according to the teaching in the law of God, and see in what ways you are hurting your consciences. Maybe you have offended a neighbour, or even sinned against yourself. So let every one of you search your consciences that with holy hearts you may draw near to God and his Christ, and looking into his face, find comfort, courage and strength to endure whatever trial may come upon you.

Our text for today

Ffor by it our elderis war weill reported of.
We turn now to our text, first, verse 2 of Hebrews chapter 11. As the apostle gives us a fuller description of this genuine and living faith, he demonstrates how real it is. He proceeds to cite certain effects, the first of which is that this faith brings us into acceptance with God, as it did our elders.[11] Second, its reality is proved in that it endows us (as it endowed our forefathers) with heavenly understanding and spiritual

[11] ESV: 'the people of old'.

light in our minds; this also is an effect of genuine faith. Thirdly, as is made clear throughout the whole chapter, by this faith both our elders and we are justified. Further, we discover in verse 2 how excellent his description of faith is both by the effect and the experience our forebears felt and found in their hearts and minds.[12] '*By it,*' he says, '*our elderis were wel reported of.*'[13] He means that by their faith they received commendation from the living God; the God of heaven and earth gave them a good report, praise and commendation.

Divine commendation

I ask you, from whom did they receive such praise and commendation? Did you notice? Not from some common, worldly person, but from a Prince, and that is of great importance! Not just from some earthly prince, rather their commendation came from the only Prince, the King of kings and Lord of lords; in his hands is immortality; he dwells in light inaccessible, upon whom no human being can ever look and live. It was from this same living God that our forefathers obtained everlasting praise and commendation. To obtain such praise and commendation from him is something beyond our understanding. For someone may praise you, yet you will never thereby have any benefit; a neighbour may praise you, but his praise will still not benefit you; yet when the living God praises someone, it cannot be but that such praise will greatly benefit him. That is why the apostle says, 'He that commends himself receives no credit, but he whom God commends finds acceptance.'[14]

Therefore, seeing that they were commended by a prince, indeed by the only Prince, the living God, there can be no question that our forefathers were worthy of his praise. Would you too have such praise and commendation from God? Study therefore to be holy, to present yourselves to God, and to have access to his face, for without holiness no one can see God. Let all you who would receive commendation from God strive after holiness, and wash from your souls those dark

[12] This constant emphasis in Bruce's preaching on 'feelings' is found also in some of the Puritans' writings, for example Sibbes, 'A Fountain Sealed', *Works*, Vol. 5, pp. 413-55.

[13] ESV, 'For by it the people of old received their commendation.'

[14] The allusion may be to 2 Corinthians 3:1, 5; 5:12, as well, of course, to Hebrews 11:2 .

blots, whose stains are so deep. 'Wash' from your body all evil habits, for by cleansing both soul and body you shall gain access to the living God and he shall crown you with immortal praise. So all of you study to present yourselves to the living God.

Through faith alone is God's commendation given

Set down for us is the means through which our forefathers obtained commendation from God: it was by faith. It is clear that it was not through their own works, but it was through faith alone that God's praise of them was given. Consider this with regard to an earthly prince. All of you would use every means in your power to win the approval of the king. Even though he be nothing more than a human being, you would rather lose your life than be bereft of the means of gaining the ear of your earthly prince. But access to the Prince of princes is only through the gift of faith; it is faith that makes his ear always open to your requests. Therefore you should embrace faith and guard it with the Holy Spirit's help. Because our faith can only be protected by the Spirit, we must study to maintain his presence, for he will watch over our faith and shall bring to us God's praise and commendation.

Faith must be watched over lest you be robbed of the privilege [liberty] it bestows. For faith has its own particular liberty of giving us access to the ear of the Prince of princes, who is constantly willing to listen. There is nothing that the Spirit inspires you to ask of him that you will not receive. Therefore, if some arise to challenge the liberties of the gospel, the Lord in his righteous judgment could well chastise this city of Edinburgh by allowing our liberty to be despoiled. Therefore, we must take our stand lest we be bereft of the favour of our access to the Prince's presence. We must see to it that none of us lose this privileged status [liberty] in which the Lord has placed us.

Take upon yourselves no other yoke but the yoke of Christ that the Lord God has laid upon you. If you are pressed to accept any other yoke, do not take it; resist such pressure even unto death. Hold fast to this liberty even though it costs you your life, so that your soul may live eternally. You must seek the strength of his presence to stand firm, so that by cleaving to this spiritual liberty you may confound and astonish the enemies of the gospel. By faith, then, and not by works, our godly forefathers received from the living God credit and commendation.

The example of our forefathers

You all know how superstitious men are addicted to their forebears, and are moved with such ridiculous feelings towards them, that they will go as far as to follow their example even in practising their vices and all manner of evils in which they engaged. This being so, how much more ought they to follow their godly forefathers in good things and in the kind of behaviour that will bring to them the approval of both God and men. Yet it is not in our own power to follow godly men in their godliness, rather it comes naturally to us to follow evil men in their vices. To pursue our godly forefathers' graces, virtues and love of heavenly things is not possible for the unregenerate. Therefore, we must take heed to their examples of the grace and mercy that motivated and empowered them, else we will never be able to follow them in well-doing. For their manner of living cannot be ours by human effort, but is bestowed freely for Christ's sake in order to lead us into obedience to him.

Therefore, let us now crave this grace, so that it would please the Lord to enable us to have the assurance of his mercy at work in our hearts, whereby we may be so drawn from this world and the love of it, that we may thirst for the world to come. It is foolish to think that you will ever be content to die without having come to love the heavenly world. You will have no contentment unless and until the Holy Spirit enables you both to see and taste of that better world. Therefore we have to beseech the Lord in his mercy to reveal that better world to us. He must touch us so that we begin to yearn for it as by faith our holy forefathers did; that is why they were well reported of.

The third verse

We come now to the third verse. *Through faith we vnderstand that the worlde was ordained by ye worde of God so that the things which we se, are not made of things which did appeare.* In this verse, the apostle moves on to another effect. We now see that genuine, justifying faith works a heavenly wisdom in the mind, an understanding of the supernatural. So another benefit for us of this faith, as well as for our forefathers, is to understand that this world was created out of nothing; not only the world, but everything in the world: all the fullness that the Lord God placed in both the heavens and the earth, is made from nothing. We understand this by the benefit of faith, by that clear light of the Holy

Spirit wrought in us through faith. Neither nature itself, nor the light of nature, can grasp such depths of knowledge.

Even the wisest of the Ethnics—heathen philosophers, for so they are called—because they were constantly lost and befuddled in their own futile vanities, were not able to see either how, or from what, this world has been made; although their natural reasoning may be robust and bold, in all spiritual and heavenly things it is as blind as a mole. The Ethnic, though his reasoning may be robust, is nonetheless ignorant, for the natural man cannot ever discern spiritual things. However daring and bold his logic, he never attains true understanding. That is why it is foolishness for him by his human wit to devise rubrics to measure God's handiwork. How God has made the worlds can only be perceived by the eye of faith.

Therefore, for the government of the household of faith and all your service for him, seek his wisdom, because by faith we attain the understanding that nature cannot ever grasp. By faith we see clearly by means of the word of God. Only through faith is the mind's eye enlightened. However, unless the cataract is removed from our mind's eyes, the word remains a closed book to us. But when the light of faith comes in and removes that obstruction from our sight so that we can now discern what God's word is saying, then we see Christ in the word; we see there is life and there is death, and a resurrection and judgment to come. But we only see all this by faith, not by any human insight.

We read how Justin Martyr sought by his native wit to come to the knowledge of God, and how, when he had learned all that Plato had to teach him regarding this, he thought he now had sufficient knowledge. Yet it pleased the Lord to put his finger on Justin Martyr's heart.[15] How

[15] Justin the Martyr was born *c.* AD 100 of pagan Greek parents. He studied philosophy in Alexandria and Ephesus, before joining himself first to the Stoics, then to Pythagoreanism and then to Platonism, always searching for answers to his questions. While in Ephesus he was impressed by the steadfastness of Christian martyrs, and by the personality of an aged Christian man he met while walking along the seashore. Justin was overwhelmed as his companion told him of Jesus and how he fulfilled the prophecies of the Jewish Scriptures. He wrote, 'Straightaway a fire was kindled in my soul, and a love of the prophets and those who are friends of Christ possessed me.' He spent the rest of his life engaging in debate with non-Christians, but was ultimately arrested on the charge of practising an unauthorised religion. He was martyred *c.* 167. Several of his written works have been preserved. (justus.anglican.org/resources/bio/175.html)

then can the likes of us think that we can come to the knowledge of the living God who perpetually dwells in light inaccessible, other than by this gift of faith? So note carefully that in faith alone is true wisdom; the man of faith is the only one wise, happy and blessed.

What shall we say about happiness? Can there be any happiness if you are going to hell? Even though you have all the riches of the world, it is only the one that is faithful who is truly happy and wise. Therefore, take heed and learn now, while the Lord offers himself to you, to obtain from him faith so that you can become wise in God and in faith. Then by that faith you will see clearly that everlasting life belongs to you.

By faith we vnderstand that the worldis wir maid.[16] I deliberately read the word in the plural number, *worldis*, for I take it that the apostle is referring to Hebrews 1:2, *Quhome he hed maid heir of all thingis, by quhome also he maid the worldis.* The apostle in this letter frequently contrasts this present world with the world to come, and when he speaks of them together, he makes the word 'world' plural. Again, these two worlds are implied in the same chapter at verse 8 in the words *evir and evir: Thy throne, O God, is for evir and evir.* And at the end of chapter 13, verse 21: *To quhome be prais for evir and evir.* This is his common custom, so whenever you read this, this present world and the world to come are to be understood. Again, when the apostle wants to distinguish between the two worlds, he calls this world 'this present world' (Galatians 1:4;[17] see also Ephesians 1:21). Likewise, as in Hebrews 2:5, he calls that other world 'the world to come'.

Therefore, remember that in this word *worldis*, he is referring to this world that will one day reach its end and in which is all manner of good and evil, but he is also referring to that other world, which is open only to the godly and in which the wicked can have no part; this other world to come is the dwelling place specially for the blessed saints and angels of God. It is he who made both these worlds, and we are assured by faith—not by our fallen minds—that he is the Creator of both. So

[16] Bruce is deliberately changing the translation of the Geneva Bible, which has the singular '*worlde*'. He is evidently using a Greek NT, which has the plural 'aionas'; ESV translates, 'By faith we understand that the universe was created'. The plural 'aionas' is also used in Hebrews 1:2, as Bruce points out.

[17] ESV: 'the present evil age'.

grasp this truth that by everlasting mercy you may be granted entrance to the world to come, and there have your place.

Exhortation

It would have been a thousand times better that you had never learned of this eternal world if you are ultimately denied a place there. Therefore, for Christ's sake, while there is still time, grieve and weep over your iniquities. Pierce through the thick clouds of your darkened minds, throw aside the sins of your filthy hearts and cast out your infidelities. For it is impossible that you will ever see God or the world to come, unless you first repent of your sins and throw off the faithlessness that cleaves too closely to your hearts. Only then shall you be granted sight of the world to come, and be touched with a love for it. Then, when the day comes that the Lord chaps you on your shoulder, you will say, 'Yes Lord, I am ready.' Otherwise, if you have neither a vision of that other world nor a desire for it, it cannot be that you are ready to depart from this present world.

Here I must finish for today and leave the rest until the next time. Meantime, do not let these words slip away from you; do not let them be spoken merely to the walls of this place, but let them be effectual in your hearts. For indeed our text speaks of a future world that is prepared only for the godly and for the blessed saints. Therefore pray that you may be numbered with them, and seek mercy and grace in time. Pray too that you may cast out of your hearts all those sins that will prevent you from ever seeing God through Christ.

May you obtain from the Lord by his infinite mercy entrance to that blessed and eternal life, through the righteous merits of Christ Jesus, to whom with the Father and the Holy Ghost be all praise and glory now and for ever. Amen.

Chapter Three

Hebrews Chapter 11 verse 4

4 By faith Abell offered vnto God a greater sacrifice then Caan, by the quhilk he obtained witness that he was richteous, gif testifeing of his giftis, by the quhilk faith also he being dead yit speakis.

Well-beloved in Christ Jesus, in the sermon you heard yesterday,[1] the apostle undertook to demonstrate that the faith he was describing is genuine, living faith. He showed this by the various effects that this true faith brings forth in the hearts of believers. First, he showed us that it is the only means whereby a person is brought into the commendation of God; it bestows on a person the approval of the one and only true Prince, bringing him into the grace and favour of his divine countenance. It was through this same faith that our godly forefathers were well reported of before the God of heaven.

The apostle went on to speak of another effect, namely, that this faith brings with it a heavenly wisdom; the apostle means a supernatural light, that is, a spiritual and renewed understanding, whereby, just as by our physical sight we can observe material things, so we may now clearly perceive the truth of heavenly and spiritual things. By this light that faith brings we understand that both this present world and the world to come were created out of nothing. Consider all the beauties of nature and the wonder of the skies: by the light of faith we understand that all that we can see has been brought into being out of nothing by the Lord God. There is no natural understanding, however

[1] His word is 'yisternicht' which means 'the previous night' (DSL). However, 'yisternicht' can also be used in a proverbial sense and therefore does not necessarily imply there had been an evening gathering, just a meeting 'the previous day'.

brilliant, that is able to comprehend how everything was created from nothing; only the spiritual perception endowed by faith can attain to this knowledge. The futile imaginings of worldly wisdom simply disappear like the mist, because none of those sagacious unbelievers is able to grasp the truth of creation out of nothing. Even though they immerse themselves in a multitude of learned books, the truth evades them. Yet, without any harassing hours of study that exhausts both mind and body, faith lets the believer clearly understand.

The same holds true regarding all that appertains to our salvation and the kingdom of heaven. Using only his natural intelligence, the wise man is as blind as a mole, because he refuses to accept spiritual insight. He does not see that true wisdom is by faith alone. Only the faithful are truly wise and divinely blessed. Therefore you must esteem the blessing of faith as the highest; no other blessing from God is granted without it. Indeed, all other blessings, whether spiritual or temporal, will end up despoiled unless you have faith, the foremost blessing of all. Therefore, I urge upon you again, seek after faith; do not be content with naked knowledge. It is only when your mind has been illuminated by God's work deep within you, piercing your heart, and your affections have been mortified and truly subdued, that his work within you will bless you with enduring faith, and the Holy Spirit will enter your cleansed heart.

Creation by God's word

All this I have already said to you last time, and so I will not continue any further on this subject. There remains only this: the manner in which the Lord created this world. In verse 3, we are told that by his word God made the world. The apostle clearly means that God did not need a lathe or loom or any other tools, neither did he use any materials or a mould, or any other substance; rather he used only the power of his word, and by his voice the world came into being. For things that 'are not' the Lord calls into being, and as soon as he speaks, lo, it is done. In fashioning these worlds, all that was needed was the voice of God. So unutterably powerful is the word of the mighty living God, that when he spoke everything instantly appeared.

To take up the subject of this world, implied in it are three or four things. First, this world had a beginning when the living God brought it into being. Second, we learn that it was made out of nothing. Third, he created it by his word alone. And finally, note carefully that these three can only be perceived by the eye of faith, for only faith can see those things that are not seen by our physical sight. As the apostle says in 2 Corinthians 4:4, unbelievers cannot perceive spiritual things. Only faith perceives what our physical eyes cannot see, because the things unseen by unbelievers are spiritual and eternal; faith pays careful heed to them. Therefore we should beware of putting our faith in temporal things. Before you put your faith in anything, ensure that it is taught by, and grounded upon, the word of God. It is not sufficient to think that because I cannot see something by my physical eyes, I can therefore believe in it and make it an article of faith. No, it must be taught in God's word and grounded upon it before ever I accept it and perceive it by faith.

Sola Scriptura

Consider how some say that in the sacrament Christ is physically present in his bodily flesh: that is not an article of my faith. I am not bound to believe it because it is not taught in the word of God, and all the articles of my faith are based firmly on his word. Because such a belief is condemned in God's word, I cannot hold to it. When we say that our faith looks to things that are not seen, that only applies to what is taught in the word of God and is declared therein as being not seen. So our faith must always look to, and be grounded upon, his word; such teaching alone must form the articles of our faith that we are bound to believe.

That is why we believe the word when it says that the sacramental elements are the body and blood of Christ. You have been taught this regarding the Lord's Supper so that your faith and soul may be assured that his body and blood are represented by the bread and wine. When you truly partake, your soul is truly fed upon the body and blood of Christ spiritually and for life eternal. Just as bread feeds and nourishes our bodies and wine relieves our thirst, so Christ's blood relieves the soul's thirst, cleanses the inner man of a stained conscience, and makes you a member of Christ's body. This we are bound to believe because the word of the living God teaches it. And these elements are called Christ's body and blood to assure our faith that his body and blood is given us, not as physical nourishment, but as spiritual nourishment for the heavenly and everlasting life.

The outward and inward in the Lord's Supper

I have had occasion today to speak a little about the sacrament, but as I have often addressed this subject in the other Kirk building,[2] I will not dwell on it just now. I will simply add this: during the Lord's Supper, notice what the minister does outwardly, listen carefully to what you are asked to do outwardly, respond to what he invites you to do outwardly in partaking of the bread and wine, so that your soul may benefit inwardly, and your faith may inwardly receive Christ's flesh and blood. For in this sacrament there are two kinds of elements: there are outward things that can be seen by our senses of sight and touch; there are also spiritual things that cannot be discerned by our outward senses, but only by the eye of faith. The outward things are bread and wine; the inward things are the body and blood of Christ. The whole Christ is the spiritual content of the sacrament. Why do I call him 'spiritual'? I do so because he begets spiritual life in me, and nourishes me to everlasting life.

As well as all this, there are in the sacrament two other actions—the outward action of the body, and the inward action of the soul. The first of these is done by the minister who gives the bread and wine to whoever is receiving it; the second is done by God himself whom the minister represents—God himself is the true minister of the spiritual; it is also done by the faithful soul who receives what God gives. So when you see the minister giving you the bread, look rather to the living God who is giving you his Son. For just as the minister passes over to you that bread, so the Lord is imparting Christ to you, provided you have the faith to receive him. As you watch what the minister does, look for the real meaning. When he breaks the bread, think of the passion of Christ and the grief he underwent for you. In the gift of the bread, he is forgiving you, so have your soul ready to receive him as you eat. Think on the wine and the blood of Christ that was shed for your sins, for 'eating of Christ', when we partake in faith, symbolises in part that his blood was shed for our forgiveness.

Further, as it applies particularly to our souls, and just as we believe that his blood was shed to change us, his body also was tormented

[2] See Murray, p. 68, note 12.

to relieve us from eternal torments. Therefore, recognise that, what is being enacted outwardly, it is God who is doing that in your soul inwardly. When you accept the bread into your hand, remember to accept Christ, and as you eat remember that assuredly Christ died for you. Preserve this meaning in your heart, and take heed to the relationship that arises from the interaction of the outward and the inward, and, treasuring that in your soul, you shall not easily go wrong in the matter of the Lord's Supper.

Preparation for the Lord's Supper

There ought properly to be preparation before something as important as this sacrament. I will give you four reasons. First, preparation for coming to the Table of so great a Prince demands due consideration. Each of us should consider how we have profited by (or declined in) our knowledge of Christ. Then as we find what is lacking in ourselves, our backsliding and the barrenness of our ignorant souls and the lack of heavenly grace, then we will acknowledge that there is reason for us to lament and grieve before ever we draw near. Second, with this knowledge of your unworthiness, you must come with your soul persuaded to seek mercy from the hand of God for the sake of Christ. Consider the depth of your faith: is it effectual? For the measure of blessing will be according to the measure of your faith. So as you come forward, draw near with full assurance of mercy, notwithstanding the spiritual poverty of your heart.

Thirdly, draw near with a penitent heart, not just on account of former sins of the past, but for those ever present sins that daily befall you. For you do not slip up just once each day, but you invariably find yourself with a handful of other sins. Therefore a penitent heart will repent afresh for those recent sins that you daily commit. Fourth, bring to the Table with you love, peace and concord with your neighbour; without that, you ought not to draw near. Especially be at peace with your brothers and sisters in Christ Jesus; if you are not, then do not come. All you should carry in your hearts as you come to partake is the awareness of your own sins, your sorrowful repentance and your love for others.

You may feel unworthy to partake

Someone wonders, but what if I find myself burdened with my sins, great as they are and constantly committed? Shall I then abstain from the Supper? For certainly, whenever I search my heart I find within my soul an unclean midden[3] of evil desires and wrong motives. How then could I ever come to the Lord's Table? I even find within myself an inexplicable rebellion against God's commandments, and I cannot subdue my will to his will. How then could I ever draw near? How could I ever approach his Table with such a proud and stubborn heart?

I answer, 'Yes, come with your stubborn, hard heart!' And I will tell you why you must come. I agree, you do have an evil disposition, and it would be far better if your heart was cleaner and softer, and your will more subdued to his holy will. It is good that you acknowledge your condition, for every heart that recognises its great need is in a very good spiritual state. It is evidence that the Lord himself has been at work within you to show you your great need of him. And that means you are already on your way to his Table, there to find his healing touch. He says, 'I love the one that comes with the knowledge of his need far more than the person who comes imagining that his heart is clean and upright.' I myself never come to the Table thinking that I am clean and just—that would be foolishness. Rather, I draw near to confess my failure in godliness and grace, to acknowledge my sin, to open my unclean heart before Christ that I may be cleansed. So I draw near for healing of the diseases of my soul and my body.

You may ask, 'Is there some warrant for me to receive the body and blood of Christ in the bread and wine, and be judged worthy to be a guest of the Son of God, even though my heart and soul are sinful and unclean?' I answer, 'Yes, there is warrant.' In Matthew 15:24, the Lord says that he came to the lost sheep of the house of Israel. Therefore, if you find yourself lost, oppressed with a hard, rebellious heart, you are the one whom he will accept.[4] Therefore go to him. Christ says in John 9:41 that if the people had acknowledged they were blind, they would not have had guilt, but because they claimed they could see, their guilt

[3] Bruce uses this Scots word; it is still in use, especially among gardeners, farmers and country folk; it means a heap of dung, manure or rotting vegetation.

[4] Bruce's phrase is 'thou art he quhome with he will mell'; the verb 'mell' carries the meaning of 'have dealings with' or 'consort with'.

remained. (This was at the conclusion of a conversation he had with the Pharisees.)

Therefore come away, though you feel rebellion, wickedness and uncleanness filling your heart, and blindness obscuring your mind; do not shrink from the Lord's Table. Rather come, acknowledging and confessing your sins, and seek restoration. You say, 'But my faith is weak, the consciousness of my sins sorely presses upon me, so that I have lost my assurance, and now I can hardly believe I shall find mercy and am beset by doubts.' I answer, 'Do not turn away from the Table!' For where there is doubt, there is also faith. Do you find yourself weak? Then pray earnestly; crave the help of Almighty God, crave also that your faith be strengthened. You answer, 'But I cannot pray.' Then seek the support of other believers and loving friends, so that they may together lift you up in prayer before God. Therefore, whatever temptations the devil may afflict you with, do not turn away from Christ's Table.

This is as far as I am going with the subject of Preparation. I return now to the text.

Verse 4

By faith Abell offered vnto God a greater sacrifice then Caan, by the quhilk he obtained witness that he was richteous, gif testifeing of his giftis, by the quhilk faith also he being dead yit speakis.

In this verse, the apostle points us to Abel as an example of the true, living faith described in the first verse. He shows his faith was genuine by another effect that he has not yet mentioned, namely, that Abel's justification was through faith. The apostle will go on to add other examples that also prove we are justified by faith. He had already shown us, you will remember, that by faith our forefathers received their commendation from God; also that it is through faith we are given heavenly intelligence and understanding. Now he proceeds to show that, although there was never ever anyone wholly just before God, by faith we are truly justified in his presence. After beginning with Abel, he will parade before us many others who were justified by faith alone.

Why the apostle begins with Abel

So why does he begin with Abel? First, because he was the first just man we read of in the Scriptures. The Master tells us that in Matthew 23:35 when he says, from the blood of Abel the righteous,[5] implying that he was the first spoken of in the Scriptures who was counted as righteous. Therefore, chronologically the apostle was quite right to begin with him. Second, his blood was shed on account of his righteousness; he was slain because of his faith. Third, he begins with Abel so that the Hebrew believers to whom he was writing would be encouraged to have patience in their trials, and remain in good heart in spite of their persecution by other Jews. Fourth, he was urging them to uphold their persecuted fellow believers by the example of Abel who likewise was killed by his own brother.

I do not doubt that Abel's father Adam repented of his defection and regretted it all the days of his life; he too, I believe, would have been justified by faith for I am sure he believed the promise God gave him that the woman's seed would tread upon the head of the serpent.[6] So I do not think we can doubt that Adam was justified by faith and was granted everlasting life.

Why then did the apostle not begin with Adam? I take the reason to be this that Adam forever is characterised by shame. Whenever he is mentioned in the Scriptures, it is because of his grievous fault; a dark stain of infamy marks him out; sin entered into the world through him, therefore in a sense he is the author of all calamity; his story shows him as the tool of the devil, that deceiver. Therefore, as often as the Scriptures speak of him, it is as the father of iniquity, not of righteousness. We read in Romans that death reigned from Adam to Moses, and that by one man sin came into the world (5:12, 14). He is also referred to in 1 Corinthians 15:21-22, where it says that by him death entered the world whereas by Christ there came the resurrection of the dead: *As in Adam all dye, eun so in Christ shal all be made aliue.* Because the Scriptures always mark him out as the author of sin, in our text the apostle will not place him first in the pageant of those justified by faith. Rather he puts first Adam's son Abel, just as our Master called him 'Abel the righteous'.

[5] ESV: *from the blood of innocent Abel.* The Greek is literally 'Abel *tou dikaiou*', so Bruce's Geneva Bible is accurate. See also NKJV.

[6] Genesis 3:15.

Abel and Cain

In our verse are two names. Although the apostle's discourse centres on Abel, his brother also is mentioned: alongside Abel there is Cain. The Spirit of God intentionally inspired both to be spoken of, so that the condemnation of the one could be contrasted with the justification of the other. There are many notable points to be learned in this contrast, but before I come to them, observe first that each of them offered a sacrifice to the living God. This indicates that right at the beginning of human history, the Lord already had a visible kirk, in which he had ordained a visible kind of worship through an outward sacrifice, in order to testify to the inward devotion of the heart, along with faith and thankfulness. In the same way this lets us see that in the visible kirk, right from its inception, there have been hypocrites.

An impure church

Even though there were at the beginning very few in the kirk, nevertheless, one was a hypocrite. So today, in the kirk, the evil will always be there among the good; this will always be so until the Lord of heaven himself makes that full and final restoration. Learn then that within the kirk there will always be cunning men, harassing the godly, inventing mischief, perpetually busy with some kind or other of nastiness against the faithful.

Beside all this, the hypocrites evidently also offered sacrifices just as did the godly. We are told that Cain, as well as Abel, offered an outward sacrifice. You might have thought that such an outward sacrifice would have been acceptable to God and that he would have been pleased with Cain. But God was not pleased with him. Therefore it becomes clear that an outward sacrifice, in and of itself, does not necessarily please the Lord. It is not your lip service nor your outward act of attending the kirk that will please God, rather is it a reformed heart, made right by faith, that is pleasing to the living God. When the affections have been mortified and the will subdued to the living God, then our worship is pleasing to him.

Faith cannot exist alone in a person's heart. Faith must be active in offering obedience to God. It stands as a clear principle, that when there is constant rebellion against his laws, there is no real faith in his promises. Genuine faith will be marked by physical obedience; I mean a total obedience that brings the body's actions into subjection to the outward law of God.

Abel's sacrifice

Now I turn to the example itself of which I have already spoken. As I expand on this, I shall follow this order. First, I shall comment on Abel's action that was done in faith. Next, I shall look at the testimony and commendation that came to Abel through his faith. Third, I shall explain that after this mortal life, he was granted a better life, one that included this immortal, glorious memory recorded here. These points I find in the verse itself, along with the commendation of his person and work, and that blessing of life everlasting with the immortal memory: '*He being deadyit speakis*.'

As to his action, we read of it at the beginning of the verse, where it says he offered a more excellent sacrifice than Cain, thus acknowledging that both brothers did make offerings. The account in Genesis 4 also tells us that Cain's offering was from the fruit of the ground and Abel's offering was from the firstborn of his flock. We cannot doubt that Cain offered the very best that he had, for hypocrites assume that all that is required is some outward action.

We also read that Abel was a shepherd and kept flocks, while Cain was a husbandman who tilled the ground; these were usual occupations of men in those ancient times. We find that the patriarchs were herdsmen, keeping sheep and cattle; so Joseph told Pharaoh.[7] On the other hand, Cain and his descendants appear to have worked on the land and built cities.[8] But the patriarchs were nomads, living in tents and shepherding their flocks. It would appear, therefore, that the implication is that Cain and his posterity invested all their energies and resources in the earth, without having any hope of a future other than in this world. By contrast, Abel's posterity was always on the move, suggesting that they looked forward to a better kind of city, for their hope was directed towards a heavenly city.[9]

I return to my subject that Cain's offering was from the fruits of the ground, but Abel's was from the best of his flock. The account in

[7] Genesis 47:1-3.
[8] Genesis 4:17.
[9] See Hebrews 11:9-10, 16.

Genesis 4 does not suggest that there was any intrinsic difference outwardly between these two offerings. Yet the God-breathed words of our text clearly indicate that there was a significant difference, in that Abel's sacrifice was offered in faith. Because Cain's sacrifice was a mere ritual, and not offered in faith, it came from a profane heart that harboured evil.[10] Consequently, Abel's sacrifice was offered acceptably, but Cain's sacrifice, offered from an unrepentant heart, was not accepted. Thus faith sanctifies a man's words, actions and deeds; on the other hand, unbelief defiles all words, actions and deeds. There can be no service well-seasoned that is not seasoned with the salt of faith, and by 'service' I mean 'rituals, ceremonies and outward exercises of worship'.

Abel's commendation

We turn now to the testimonial given to Abel. We find first that he himself is commended for his faith, and second that what he did is also commended. First, then, as to the personal commendation he was given, *he obtained witness that he was richteous.* Second, as to the commendation for his offering, we read, *gif testifeing of his giftis*,[11] that is, the Lord accepted his gifts. I do not want to enter into too prolonged a discussion as to whether or not these two commendations were either visible or invisible. But we can be sure that Abel's heart and conscience were assured by God's Spirit that he had been accounted by God as righteous.

As to the second commendation regarding Abel's offering, it must have been conveyed by some visible means, for Cain took offence at it, and from that commendation grew his hatred and anger. Had the Lord's acceptance of his gift not been made apparent in some way, Cain would not have conceived a grudge. In other words, the Lord must have made it clear that Abel's sacrifice was given divine approbation, and that was why such hatred was kindled in Cain's heart that he never rested until he had murdered his brother. Even though God remonstrated with him, when he was angry that his offering had not been accepted, nothing would satisfy him until his brother's blood had been

[10] Bruce seems to be alluding to the Lord's rebuke to Cain in Genesis 4:7b.

[11] ESV: 'He was commended as righteous, God commending him by accepting his gifts.' Bruce interprets the Geneva Bible *gif testifeing his giftis* by his added phrase, 'the Lord allowit of it', that is 'the Lord accepted his gifts'.

shed. Therefore, we conclude that the first commendation must have been secret and personal in Abel's conscience, and the second commendation must have been visible.

Moses gives us the order in which the commendations were given, first to Abel and then to his offering.[12] We should note this carefully. First, God justifies the person of Abel by his faith. Then, proceeding from this justified man, is the acceptance of his service. Therefore, we see clearly that the good work does not convey grace and justification to the man, but rather that the justification of the man is the ground of the commendation of his work. Learn then this lesson: first the person receives God's favour and is justified before him; only then is the work that person offers granted commendation and is counted as worthy. Self-evidently, there are many people who abound in good works, yet they themselves are evil, and hypocritically they consider their works as good as any others; yet they do not receive God's commendation and their service is not even counted as good works because what they do does not flow from a fountain of goodness.

Therefore, before ever your works can be commended by God, you yourselves must first be justified. First you must examine yourselves to enquire what God is saying to your hearts and consciences. When you are assured that God has forgiven your sins and so approves of you, then you may conclude that he will accept your work for him, whatever it may be that you are doing. But if you do not yet have his divine approbation, then neither will your works be accepted by him. Your first concern must be to receive his mercy; only then will the good tree bring forth good fruit.

Let me put this another way. The apostle is not saying that Abel was given his testimonial from God by his good work, that is, because his offering was good, even extremely good. Rather, in our text, he expressly states his offering to God was by faith. Faith versus works: I mean justification by faith and justification by works, are plainly incompatible. We are only granted the justification of our works when we believe God to be righteous for Christ's sake. Thus the apostle is letting us see that, right from the very beginning of time, justification has always been by faith.

[12] The reference is to Genesis 4:4b: 'And the LORD had regard for Abel and his offering' (ESV).

Though Abel died, he still speaks

We now come to the last part of verse 4. Added to all the apostle has said about Abel, he now adds that he was also granted everlasting life together with a blessed and eternal memory proclaimed for all to hear. For, even though slain by his brother, notwithstanding by faith he still speaks. In these words, *yit speakis*, I take it that we are to understand he is eternally alive. Even though his body is dead, his soul lives and speaks; for speaking is the action of someone who is alive, hence the clear implication of eternal life. And if he lives, it is because the life of God is within him. Even though his body was slain, the cause of his faith is not slain. Though his tongue was silenced, his cause and his faith still speak. It is as the apostle Paul says: though he was bound in chains, the word of God was not bound (2 Timothy 2:9). Therefore tyrants gain nothing by slaughtering the bodies of God's servants, for the Lord so blesses their bodies that he turns their deaths to the advantage of their cause.

The apostle Paul declared that his imprisonment and chains did not hinder the cause of the gospel; rather, they advanced it so that in Nero's court the evangel became better known than it would have been if Paul had had his freedom (Philippians 1:12-18). So the world gains nothing by persecuting God's servants. Indeed, the world's opposition is a means the Lord has sanctified, and whereby he not only makes his servants to be well known, but also enlarges their cause. Thus, in death they get life, in bondage they have liberty, and in dying they triumph and rejoice. Likewise Abel, though dead, yet speaks. Yes, he speaks by his faith, he speaks because of his cause, he speaks through his everlasting memorial, and he speaks on account of his godly example. Some have suggested that he also speaks by his blood, but I prefer rather to take it that he speaks because he now lives in the presence of the eternal God.

Faith and unbelief run towards different goals

There is yet one other point that we should notice, and I will not weary you much longer. I perceive that here faith and unbelief have two diverse courses and two diverse ends. The faithful man's course is set towards God, but the unfaithful man is focused on this world. Believing men such as Abel go from grace to grace, increasing in all spiritual and heavenly graces, and so they constantly grow in favour with God. Unbelievers go on from mischief to misbehaviour, and then further on into sin. That was how Cain went from hatred to murder, and from murder to contempt for the living God; likewise, unbelievers multiply their sins and every day harden in their hatred of God and contempt for him. Believers will be hated by the world, held in contempt and persecuted; if they do not share their family's religion, they might end up being killed by a relative.

Unbelievers look for the world's favours and acceptance. Believers, on the other hand, live entirely for God's praise and blessing and to be at peace with him. Therefore, when their physical bodies die, God takes their souls to be with himself, and they are seated with Christ and endowed with the highest graces. As for the wicked, when they die their souls are damned, and both their bodies and souls enter upon an eternity of pain and torment.

Therefore take careful note of these two very different courses of the believer and the unbeliever, that is, the pathway of love for God contrasted with the broad road of loving the world. Be aware of the treatment the faithful will receive from this world, and be prepared for persecution. Do not be deceived by the world's promises of a life of ease. All that Christ promises is trustworthy, but remember that he never promised following him would be easy; do not be deceived, for he warned us that we would receive persecution from the world, and not have an easy time. The course of his kirk in every generation has been trials and oppression; yet the kirk has known God's protection and mercy.

Pray for those who persecute you

Finally, we who are believers must ourselves abstain from oppressing others. Remember the sin of Cain, who shed innocent blood. Do not spill men's blood, least of all the blood of your kinsmen. For even when a man's tongue is silenced, his blood still continues to cry out until the land is cleansed and just reparation made. There must be many in our land whose blood is loudly crying out. Yet who hears, even though those cries demand to be heard? It seems everyone sleeps. Certainly, our magistrates do not hear. Therefore, since pleading does not avail, nor admonition, nor reproof, it may be that the sword of justice will be drawn. But for us as Christ's followers, the only remedy I know is prayer; we must all close in with God and beseech the Lord to arm the heart of our king with such courage that he banishes from our nation all those descendants of Cain; or else he must firmly administer the law.

On the other hand, strive to follow Abel in sincerity and meekness, in patience and sobriety. For in this way shall we receive the praise and commendation of the King of all kings. So shall you be blessed in both life and death. May the Lord grant us all grace, so that we may live in him and die in him, to whom be all praise for ever and ever! Amen.

Chapter Four

Hebrews Chapter 11 verse 5

---

5 By faith Enoche was takin away that he sould not sei death, nather was he found for God had takin him away; for befeir he was takin away, he was reported of that he haid pleased God.

Recap of the previous sermon

A British poet has written at some length in praise and commendation of faith, this precious jewel of a genuine, living faith.[1] You have already heard, first of all, of the benefit this faith bestows, namely, that by it we have the assurance in our hearts of things that 'are not', things that are only hoped for, and are yet to come; indeed, we are ever sure of them, as if they were present now and visible to our bodily eyes. Secondly, you have also already heard that by means of this faith we are enabled to see clearly and distinctly things that are spiritual, heavenly and eternal. Thirdly, you have heard, that by benefit of this faith, our forefathers, and we and our posterity, are enabled to come into the

[1] There is no hint as to which poet Bruce is referring. One possible candidate might be Anne Askew (1520–1546), a sincere Protestant who became a 'gospeller' or preacher in London. A diligent Bible student, through her study of Scripture she became convinced of the doctrines of the reformation. Arrested and thrown into prison, so severe were her injuries from torture that she had to be carried to Smithfield to be burned at the stake. While in Newgate she wrote a poem on Faith. See Appendix for the full poem, which begins with the two following stanzas:

> Like as the armed knight appointed to the field,
> With this world will I fight, and Faith shall be my shield.
>
> Faith is that weapon strong, which will not fail at need.
> My foes, therefore, among herewith will I proceed.

favourable esteem of the living God. Such acceptance by God has only ever been granted to any person through this faith with which he had been imbued.

Fourthly, you have heard that by means of this true, living faith we are granted such an understanding of the supernatural, that by the eye of faith we may see clearly what is happening in heaven, as clearly as we can see with our physical sight what is happening here on earth. Faith therefore enables us to lift our hearts to God so that we are able to communicate, not with the cesspit of earthly society, but with heaven where the blessed dwell, along with Christ Jesus our Master. Lastly, you have heard that, although we are vile in ourselves, full of wickedness and uncleanness, nevertheless by faith the Lord declares us happy, blessed and righteous. It was in taking up this fifth effect of faith that the apostle begins to demonstrate it by citing many examples.

Because our Master began with Abel,[2] the apostle also begins with him. By faith Abel was the first man counted as righteous; he was also the first who died for his faith, slain for righteousness' sake. The apostle also began with him because his example was very poignant for the Jews to whom he was writing; he was exhorting them to be patient in their suffering, for Abel too had suffered a cruel death at the hands of his own blood-brother. Thus the apostle makes it clear that Abel was justified by faith alone. This teaching I have so far given you I most strongly urge you hold in your memories, for every single portion of God's Book is provided for you; however, there is much more to be considered than the little with which I exercised your minds in my previous sermon. Let us then proceed.

Two brothers, Cain and Abel

First, I remind you of the two brothers referred to in verse 4, Abel and Cain, born of the same parents, the same flesh and blood, the same upbringing. Yet see how different they were in their behaviour and spiritual state; there could hardly have been two alive at that time more different than these two. All of you learn this lesson: having the same parents, the same family and the same upbringing does not mean that two people will therefore exhibit the same standards and spiritual state. Second, we learn from these two brothers that the difference between

[2] Matthew 23:35.

them can only be attributed to divine grace and mercy; it cannot be attributed to human nature or a privileged birth, for had that been so, Cain would have shared the righteousness of Abel. After all, he was the elder and had the privilege of the birthright, yet notwithstanding that, it was the younger brother who was in a right spiritual state. Clearly, it is grace that makes the difference, for grace separates off a person and divides where nature conjoins. Therefore, seek after grace that you may follow God, that you may imitate Christ and that you may be like Abel, and not like Cain, even though he was the privileged older brother.

Thirdly, I see that arising from faith is the fount of all spiritual blessing, and that all the benedictions granted to both body and soul in this life, also arise from faith. On the other hand, I see that unbelief is the fount and spring of all the woes and maledictions that befall a man. Likewise, the cause of every misery that afflicts body and soul stems from unbelief. Fourthly, I see that those who are endowed with this grace in their souls will grow in grace, and, progressing from grace unto grace, will ultimately have on his brow the crown of everlasting life. Again, I see that there is none that persists in incredulity and unbelief, but he progresses from sin to sin, from mischief to mischief, until his soul be ultimately lost and sunk into eternal damnation, so that there is no hope for him; those who continue in their wickedness are bound to indulge in more and more sin. It is as the apostle truly declares in Romans 6:16 that a man is a slave of whomever he obeys: on the one hand, the unfaithful go from one sin to another sin; on the other hand, those who obey go from grace to grace.

Look beyond the brothers to two Kirks

We see this clearly in the two brothers. But look beyond them to two Kirks, one militant and the other malignant; in Abel see the Kirk that is militant under the cross, whereas in Cain see the synagogue of Satan that lives according to the flesh. That the faithful do progress from grace to grace is clearly proven in Abel, whose sacrifice, offered in faith, though perhaps less worthy and valuable than Cain's, in God's sight was counted of greater value and worth. However, Cain's offering in men's estimation could have been of more intrinsic value than Abel's, but in God's sight it was counted as an abomination on account of his unbelief.

Consider also Abel's human nature: he was as sinful as his brother, for in him the seed of all wrongdoing was lurking, just as it was in Cain. Notwithstanding Abel's sinful nature, he was nevertheless justified by faith. For by reason of his faith in God's promises, and in spite of his inherent sinfulness, the Lord declared him to be righteous, because he believed that God's word was true. Although Cain's nature was just as sinful as was Abel's, yet because of his infidelity and unbelief, refusing to accept the truth of God's word, he remained in that sinful state in which he was conceived and born,[3] and his wickedness increased until it heaped upon his head eternal damnation; his condemnation was that he refused to believe.

It was, therefore, only by faith that Abel was justified, for by some visible token from heaven his offering was accepted and approved. Yet Cain's offering was refused and rejected, for no fire from heaven came down to consume them to show to him that God did not want his gifts on account of his infidelity. By faith as soon as Abel's soul departed from his body he was welcomed into the heavenly tabernacles. By unbelief as soon as Cain's soul departed from his body he entered into eternal torment. By faith Abel still speaks to his honour and praise, his memory has become famous within God's Book, and he is recorded there to his eternal honour. Cain also still speaks, but not the way Abel does; it is his unbelief that speaks and says, 'I am justly condemned because it is by my unbelief that I am debarred from God's presence and cast out of his sight; justly my memory is covered in shame, and my name stinks for ever upon the face of the earth.' So it is undeniable: the faithful increase in grace and in favour and in the love of Almighty God; the unbelieving increase in their sinfulness, therefore God's wrath and judgment multiply upon them.

Abel's cruel death was blessed

Someone may object, 'But Abel was murdered most cruelly! What kind of benefit do you call that? Was that a blessing? Did he not encounter the kind of violent and bloody death that no one would ever consider a blessing? How then can you say that he was happy, when in most people's view he died so miserably?'

[3] Psalm 51:5.

I answer, Spiritual things are quite independent of public opinion. When it comes to matters concerning the salvation and life of the soul, pay no attention to men's judgments, but rather take heed to the judgment of God. Consider what God's judgment was concerning the death of Cain, and on the other hand concerning the death of Abel. Then you shall find that in the righteous decision of God the death of the latter was blessed, whereas the death of the former was not blessed. Take no account of the manner of Abel's death; rather see how it was sanctified in the righteous judgment of God, but Cain's death was cursed for ever.

Some may ask from whence proceeds this judgment of God, yet God's sentence is never pronounced unjustly? The righteous Judge of all the earth never errs in his judgment. So how come that such a gruesome death as Abel's is counted happy? His blessedness proceeds entirely from the reason that caused him to be killed. So think about why it was he died, and you will then understand why his death was blessed; it was the reason for his death that caused it to be sanctified. Therefore, however any man dies, whether in combat or working in a field, if he loses in his life in some good cause, his death is then both blessed and happy. But whether he dies in his bed or while he was thought well of by others, if his demise happened as a result of some evil deed, then his death is not pronounced blessed but accursed by the mouth of the great God.

We see then that it was the reason behind the murder of Abel that sanctified it in the sight of God; it was the honourable reason for his death that made it a fragrant sacrifice to God. An honourable, godly cause signifies a good conscience, and one who dies with a good conscience dies well. Beware of tolerating an evil conscience that nags away unheeded; listen to its dire warnings; for if you purge it of everything that defiles you, then you shall die well.

So men should take heed to any charge brought against them, and have regard for their cause, lest they needlessly endanger their lives over some secondary issue. Before you hazard your life, see how it would be with your conscience if you were to be put to death, and how you would stand before God in the event of your losing your case in the court and giving way under pressure. Examine, then, your conscience to see if it bears a good testimony, for whether you live or die, you die or live before God. But if a man does not feel his conscience is calling him to stand his ground, then I would not wish him to engage in a controversy that might endanger his life.

Sharing Christ's reproach

However, among all the accusations that you will find among men, there is one contention that brings blessing upon both body and soul, and will bestow serenity both here on earth and in the hereafter; I speak of the reproach of Christ Jesus. When a man stands accused of sharing that reproach, and is willing to hazard his body and life, there is a blessed accusation indeed! It must make a man's conscience rejoice that in his final hour of life he will be snatched away and transported heavenwards. For there is no question but that if we have experienced the sweetness of Christ we would say, as does the apostle, *For Christ is to me bothe in life and in death advantage* (Philippians 1:21).[4] Therefore, if ever his reproach shall confront us, or his cause be challenged (as I suspect may soon happen)—for it is neither possible for faith to be without testing, nor the Kirk to be without persecution—be assured that the pearl of great value[5] will never be lodged in a human heart without being sorely tried.

Therefore, if ever Christ's cause should come into question, stand fast in your faith and be on your guard, awaiting the devil's challenge and persecution, prepared to undergo the trial of your love for him. That being so, now is the time to seek the strength of the living God, for without his enabling Christ's cause cannot be supported or maintained; beseech God to uphold you lest his Son's cause be dishonoured. Add to this prayer the request that you will eschew that complacency that blinds you to the danger. Be assured, there is no lack of danger, but too often there is our failure to see it. Therefore, stir up the spark of faith and hold fast to the gifts within you, lest they be quenched by your inner corruption, and that Christ may dwell more fully in you and by his strength preserve you from bringing shame upon him. Alas, the best of us would dishonour him unless he by his own strength enables us to honour his cause.

[4] These words in Latin are inscribed on Bruce's gravestone, now lodged in Larbert Old Church, just yards from where he was buried in 1631: 'Christvs vita et in morte lvcrum'.

[5] Matthew 13:46.

True faith is always blessed

You will find in every example given to us that faith is always honoured with spiritual advancement. Every single person endued with this living, true faith always received the praise and approval of the living God, and at his end was transported to the life to come. Yet, every faithful man also receives God's praise in the here and now; the Holy Spirit bears witness to his spirit that he is approved, this in addition to the testimony of his own conscience, which is affirmed by the Spirit who dwells in light inaccessible. No mortal being has ever seen, nor will ever see him as he is. Yet the King himself shall give you a wreath to wear, you—wretched creature that you are, whose wickedness, if it spilled out, would cover the whole land—our only Prince and immortal King will treat you so kindly that he will praise and commend you, lift you up and record your name on his roll of honour for all eternity.

It is only on account of our lack of understanding, insight and knowledge that the praise of the living God is not earnestly sought, and that the advancement he can bestow is not preferred to the praise and approval of earthly princes. Those who are ignorant do not recognise that earthly princes are no better than the worst of men; because they do not realise there is another Prince who is not of this world, they assume that the praise of earthly princes is most to be sought. Oh that they had eyes to see the difference there is in the praise that God can give; no tongue can express what it is to receive his approval. In respect of human commendation, the apostle shows us that some praise themselves whether or not they are worthy, others may be praised by neighbours, but only the commendation of the living God is of value (1 Corinthians 4:3-5; 2 Corinthians 4:2). For when God praises a person it is because he is worthy of his commendation, it is because it is the Lord's work in that man that has made him who he is.

We see, therefore, that it is out of ignorance that so many strive after the praise and approval of men, while they hardly bother to seek for the commendation and blessing of God. Because it is clear that God's approval may be attained, and the means to gain it are set out for us, how unhappy are those who never seek it! Was it not for praise that the famous Ethnics[6] wanted to be considered wise and so wrote

[6] By 'Ethnics' Bruce here means the Greek philosophers. Elsewhere it simply means 'pagans' or sometimes those outside Christendom.

many remarkable books, yet their works were but stones. Any who have a spark of spiritual life in them will be constantly seeking after God's praise. Indeed, though your earthly pilgrimage lasts as long as that of Methuselah, if you finally attain the approval of God, you may consider you have a great recompense for all your years of searching! But I depart from this now and proceed to the apostle's next point.

The apostle's deliberate repetition

In our text he turns from Abel to Enoch and then from Enoch to Noah, and from Noah to Abraham, and so on, telling us the same thing about each of the Fathers, that all of them were justified by faith. Because it is the mighty God who speaks and the Spirit of the living God who inspires,[7] the apostle does not tire of saying the same thing again and again. There is not a single person here who would not tire of hearing the same thing said a second time. But when the Holy Spirit keeps on repeating the same thing, we must take heed to it. It is noteworthy, for there is some importance in the point being made, some principle of our religion that cannot be over-emphasised.

This constant repetition is intended to ensure that we learn the lesson well; but if you find it annoying, the annoyance is caused by the writer. Paul says as much in Philippians 3:1: *It grieveth me not to write the same things to you.*[8] In other words, it is good for those who are listening to be told the same truths often. And when the Spirit of God does not tire, for the Lord's sake, we should not tire either. And because he does not weary in telling us over and over again that we are justified by faith, earnestly seek after faith that you may be justified thereby.

You all know what pleasure human nature can find in worthless things, for example, in hearing stupid, lewd songs, no matter however often they have been heard before. Therefore, it is obvious that if fallen sinners delight in foul things, those who now have heavenly natures will take pleasure in heavenly things; then ensure you are possessed of that heavenly nature. Earthly natures cannot enjoy any pleasures except those that are earthly. So sanctify your nature that it may be heavenly so that you may be able to delight in all that pertains to heaven. Because it is by faith that our earthly natures are transformed into heavenly

[7] Bruce's Scots word is 'dytis', literally meaning 'dictates'.

[8] ESV: 'To write the same things to you is no trouble to me.'

natures, do not weary in hearing about faith, but seek with all your heart and soul that your natures may be made heavenly, for a heavenly heart will take pleasure in heavenly things. In short, never tire of hearing that we are justified by faith.

So why does the apostle move on from Abel to Enoch, and omit any mention of Seth? The reason is that we find no particularly honourable mention of Seth or his descendants, until we reach Enoch. That is obviously why the apostle skips over them, without saying whether or not they were justified by faith, but stops at this holy man of whom the most honourable mention is now made.[9] Indeed, the Holy Spirit twice tells us that *Henoch walked with God continoullie*. Clearly, Enoch must have been a notable and singular person. This Enoch was also a prophet, as Jude tells us,[10] for his book was still extant in the days of Jude, though since then his writings have been lost or have perished.

More said about Enoch than about Abel

However, this honourable mention of him, by the one who judges all men, indicates that he was a singular instrument in God's hands. The same form of words is used of Enoch as of Abel: 'by faith … he was commended'. However, he now says something different about Enoch, not said about Abel, namely that his faith was rewarded by his being translated, that is, taken up from this world by the mighty hand of God and brought into the world that is to come; thus he did not see death. What does this mean, 'he did not see death'?

Here we have a special outward sense for a special inward sense, that is, seeing for feeling. Temporal death that comes to all men naturally is nothing more but a sudden separation of the soul from the body, a violent tearing asunder of these two which the Lord (if sin had not intervened) intended should be together for ever.[11] Enoch did not experience this; for his soul and body were never separated, as both were caught up to heaven. There he differed from Abel, for only his soul went to heaven, whereas both Enoch's soul and body went to heaven, as had never before happened to anyone. It is true that a law has been made

[9] Genesis 5:22, 24.

[10] Jude 14-15.

[11] This is a statement Bruce used elsewhere: 'Death is a violent twinning [tearing] and rugging sundrie of that quhilk the Lord hath appointed to bide together, to wit, the soul and the bodie' (Sermon 206).

by God, as you heard already expounded in the epistle, that every man should die once,[12] yet, notwithstanding that law, Enoch was exempted from this sentence of death and by a special privilege of the mighty God was caught up to heaven in both soul and body. For God who made that law is not under the law, nor is he restricted by it; therefore he is free to work in extraordinary ways.

Nevertheless, there is no one on earth who by trickery can devise some means of escaping from the compass of that law. The case of Enoch is intentionally recorded to let the Fathers see from earliest times, that there is something else to be looked for apart from the curse pronounced on Adam. For the faithful the curse of death is transformed into a singular blessing, in that it is now clear that temporary death was sanctified for Enoch. But now our deaths have been sanctified by Christ's death. By faith the Fathers saw this in Enoch's translation, for now the very thing that was a curse, by faith in the promise of God had become a singular blessing.

Our limited intelligence cannot comprehend eternal life, nor can our reasoning grasp its meaning. Therefore, to provide humanity with clear evidence, and to seal more securely in the hearts of his people the truth of this article of religion, the Lord in the earliest days of human history caught up to heaven one particular man. He wanted to assure us by this outward, physical act, just as our souls are assured by his inward, unseen work in us, that both body and soul shall ultimately live for ever.

History's three eras

Human history is divided into three eras. There is the era before the law, the era under the law, and the era after the law. In the first era, God took up Enoch to heaven to assure his people that soul and body would at last live eternally. Under the law, he took up Elijah, and in the third era after the law, he took up Jesus Christ, visibly in the sight of his disciples. In fact, all of these were taken up visibly to assure us that our bodies and souls would live for ever. Nevertheless, many do not believe; even when some witnessed it and in their hearts they at first believed, yet then they doubted, as do the majority of men. Happy were those who saw it, and blessed would we be if we ourselves were granted to

[12] Hebrews 9:27.

see it. God does not lift up into heaven his Son every day, nor Enoch or Elijah. Even if every day he did lift someone to heaven, without the dew of his Spirit we would never believe; it is because men have not had that sight of heavenly life, that they fix all their desires here on earth.

Therefore, for Christ's own sake, remember that both Enoch and Elijah were both lifted up to heaven; but especially remember Christ himself, 'the first begotten from the dead',[13] the first whom death yielded up, he who was raised from the grave, and who ascended to heaven before the very eyes of his disciples. Of course, unlike Christ, Elijah and Enoch did not die, but by an extraordinary privilege they were caught up to heaven before Christ's ascension. We can be assured that even though these two men's bodies did not experience death, beyond question they were changed, even though soul and body were never torn apart; they must have undergone the same change that we shall undergo when we die and are raised from the dead. It is the transformation we shall know when we meet Christ. For, blessed be his name, all who truly believe shall be caught up to meet him in the clouds.[14] Therefore, we conclude that although they did not die as we shall, yet they were changed in just the same way as we shall be changed when we die and are raised from the grave.

We shall be changed

In death, you and I lay down aspects of our humanity that must be left behind such as mortality and corruption, and we are changed as we take on new aspects of life that are prepared for us. We shall one day undergo this change that Enoch experienced instead of natural death. His translation was granted him to confirm the faith of the Fathers; they needed the assurance that although their mortal bodies would die and their souls be worn out, leaving them lying as lifeless corpses which would soon be reduced to powder, yet these ashes would be quickened by the Spirit of God who would remember them and come to them. Is this not wonderful that the Spirit of the living God should visit our ashes, after our bodies and flesh have become mere powder, and will not allow our ashes to be mingled with the ashes of others buried near us, whether man or beast, but shall keep those remains safe and ready to

[13] Revelation 1:5.
[14] 1 Thessalonians 4:17.

be raised by the power of the Spirit. Yes, our bodies shall be quickened by the same power of the mighty Spirit, the same Spirit of Christ that made his dwelling in our souls during our mortal lives here on earth.

We can be assured that our souls are taken to heaven when they depart from our bodies. The Holy Spirit keeps watch over our ashes until the time when our resurrected bodies will again be united with our souls. This is not some natural union, nor is there any external second cause for it. This is the work alone of the Spirit of the mighty God, that is, the Spirit of our Saviour Jesus Christ. It is the gift of being begotten, conveyed to us by the work of the Holy Ghost, so that the power whereby Christ overcame and was raised from the dead works in us, making our souls to be infused with heavenly life, I mean wholly sanctifying us so that we are made completely spotless and perfect. The same Spirit also works upon the ashes of our bodies that are sown in dishonour, endowing them with new qualities, and bringing both soul and body to heaven, there to live for ever.[15]

I have spoken enough on this, but sufficient for you to remember that believers will live forever. This should be a spur to us to order our lives aright. Unbelief virtually murders the soul, unless faith intervenes and assures you of the reality of eternal life. It is not so much a man's sinfulness and evil deeds that condemn him, rather it is unbelief. As the apostle says in Hebrews 3:19, *So we sie that they colde not enter in because of vnbelief.* He says nothing of the way they tested God, nor of the sin of Dathan, Korah and Abiram, but only of unbelief.[16] So the one thing on earth that destroys the soul of man is unbelief. How can this be? The devil has infused our natures with unbelief, and we cannot ever have our souls purged of it; we are always ready to doubt the truth of God, even a thousand times more willing to believe some worldly man, rather than embrace those things that come from God. Unbelief is injected[17] into us by the devil, but under the righteous judgment of God, whereas faith is injected into our souls by the Spirit of God, through the righteous merits of Christ Jesus.

[15] Bruce's doctrine of the immortality of the soul and the resurrection of the body closely follows Calvin's teaching. *Inst.* 1.5.5; esp. 3:25.3-8.

[16] Exodus 17:1-7; Numbers 16.

[17] Bruce's verb is 'spout' which means 'to discharge a liquid forcefully and copiously'.

I began with praise of faith and I conclude with it. By faith we are both blessed and happy, for by it both our souls and bodies are for ever blessed. No tongue can tell the spiritual progress we shall make if we have but a spark of true faith; on the other hand, no tongue can tell the unhappiness of that soul that has no measure whatsoever of true faith. Terrible is the life and even more terrible is the death of those who do not die in faith. Therefore, for the sake of Christ Jesus, let not these things be spoken in vain, as if spoken to stones! Rather, strive after the Spirit, seek after the gift of faith which alone will bring you into happiness and blessedness. Even if you have to sell all that you possess in order to buy this precious pearl, is it not worth such a price? Then how shall I pray or exhort you, how is it possible to move you? I think prayer for you is the best way. Therefore I shall be seeking the living God that he might search out those who do not believe, and are in the devil's thrall; I pray that he will pour faith into all your hearts, that you may all be partakers of his everlasting glory. The Lord grant this through the righteous merits of Christ, to whom with the Father and the Holy Ghost be all honour, praise and glory, now and forevermore. Amen.

CHAPTER FIVE

Hebrews Chapter 11 verse 6

[6] Bot without faith it is impossible to pleas him: for he that cumis vnto God man believe that God is, and that he is a rewairder of them that seik him.

Remember, brothers, I beseech you, some of the observations that time allowed and God gave us the grace to hear; please take note of them from the last time we met.[1] For I am sure that if even a quarter of the doctrine that was expounded was well observed and digested, it would serve us well. But as far as what benefits you, more doctrine is often taught than you can take in. That is because the teaching is not thoroughly dug into the soil of your hearts, so that the main points of the doctrine are not inculcated in the way the Spirit of God intends them to be.

By faith alone

So recall firstly, when we looked at Abel, we saw that the spring and fountain of all blessing and spiritual grace, both for our body and soul, are by faith alone. Neither in this life nor in the life to come can there be any blessing without faith. Indeed, the best blessings can become the worst curses for those who are devoid of faith.

Therefore, as I emphasised, just as faith is the fount of all blessing, so Cain's unbelief became the spring of all the curses and maledictions that fell upon his body and soul. Just as unbelief is planted in our fallen natures by the devil, so the gift of faith is poured into our hearts from God for Christ's sake in order to renew our natures. Labour therefore

[1] See Sermon Three above, note 1.

to cast out unbelief, for by nature we are constantly prone to mistrust God's promises and care for us. None of us by nature render him the trust that is his due. Therefore, because our natures are poisoned with the root of unbelief, our chief concern should be to seek cleansing by that gift of faith. Only then will we in heart, mind and conscience repose upon God alone.

Growth is from grace to grace

Recall also how, secondly, I showed you from the example of Abel, that good and faithful man, that none can attain to maturity in an instant, but that each grows from grace to grace, and progresses from blessing to blessing, until finally he will be crowned with that everlasting, immortal blessing. On the other hand, I showed you from the example of unhappy Cain, that the unfaithful who defect from God do not have some fixed spiritual abode or remain in the same spiritual condition, but they continually sink from one sin to another, until both body and soul are submerged in everlasting despair without any hope of deliverance.

We must all daily bear the cross

Thirdly, I asked you to perceive in faithful Abel the state of the militant church so long as she is present here on earth, for the condition of the church, like that of Abel, is still to be subject to all manner of persecutions. Do not deceive yourselves with ideas of repose, or think that being in Christ's Kirk means entering a state of ease, earthly peace and security. The Lord has never promised any such thing, rather he warns us that we must daily bear the cross. Therefore, from the example of Abel, Christ's Kirk must constantly expect hostility, just as Abel was maliciously hated by his brother Cain. So let no member of the church be surprised when we meet animosity, malice and every device this world can invent to stain and shame us, whether physically or in some other way, until finally we are summoned to martyrdom as was Abel. Each of us has a choice: we must either be prepared to die in the cause of Christ, or else to drink to the dregs with Cain the poison of eternal condemnation.

Martyrdom is a blessed death

The final point of which I would remind you from yesterday is that you should never consider the martyrdom of the Lord's saints as a curse, even though they died a violent, bloody death. It is not appropriate for us to pay undue heed to the manner and means of someone's death, but rather carefully to consider the cause for which a person has died. I pressed upon you that it is the reason for an untimely death that renders it either a blessed or a cursed demise. Whatever the time or place, whether in the person's own home or somewhere in the open country, or on land or sea, if the cause for which he dies is good, then his death is blessed; for it is the cause that sanctifies the death. By contrast if a man dies for some wickedness he has done, then his death cannot be considered blessed. An ill cause arises from an ill conscience; it makes no difference if that death is in a bed with satin covers.

Therefore, the means and manner of death are of no importance, it is the reason for martyrdom that matters. To be killed for the sake of Christ and his gospel is undoubtedly the most felicitous and blessed death that anyone could die. For the death of those who die in the Lord, whatever the circumstances, is counted as forever precious in his sight. So pray for the cause of Christ; pray for the liberty of his gospel of grace that we have now enjoyed in our land for more than thirty years. Pray that this freedom may continue for many years to come, for should we lose it, it would leave this sanctuary destitute and no longer would you come here to listen to the word of God.

Indeed, in years to come such could be the result of the devil's craftiness and the malice of certain men, who are already scheming to rob us of the evangel's liberty, that, after these three decades of freedom [since 1560[2]] this place in which we gather could be doomed. If the Lord should permit this to happen and the Kirk be overthrown, then first and foremost all of us must be prepared—and may this word of God do his work of grace in you—to lose this liberty we have been granted, and to be ready to partake of his everlasting life. We will count it a joy to lose the liberty we have in this earthly life and to enter the heavenly life—that is, if we have the eye of faith to see the riches and joy that awaits us in Christ. How could we be disappointed to lose our freedom, life and possessions in exchange for such a prospect?

Our dearly bought religious liberty could be overthrown

In the past the Lord God has often warned our country, but he is warning us now more than he ever has done before. It seems that our hopes

[2] 1560 was the beginning of the Scottish Reformation.

and expectations are failing us, for we sense the devil's malice as incessantly as it ever was; increasingly each day we recognise it among us. Therefore, it becomes me to equip you that are the Lord's people, in case your sins bring upon you that harsh judgment of losing body and soul. No, you must be prepared here and now, so that you will be ready to be on your guard, as I have often said to you. The cause of the living God can be defended by his strength alone. No man, however valiant he may be, is able stand firm either on his own behalf or that of his neighbour; only by the strength of Christ can he defend the cause of Christ. Therefore seek the strength of the living God to hold you true to his cause; embrace the feeling of having this liberty wherein you stand; seek to possess the comfort that it brings, that finding it you may hold on to it.

I say all this only by way of cautioning and preparing you in case (the Lord forbid!) our precious liberties are assaulted. For it is my responsibility to give you this warning before the storm clouds break. Now back to our text in Hebrews chapter 11.

Enoch was also justified by faith

After writing about Abel and Cain, we saw how the apostle moved on to Enoch, and how he had been justified in the same way as Abel was justified. He will show how Noah and Abraham also were similarly justified by faith, as were all the other examples he will give us as he proceeds through the chapter. There never was, nor ever will be, any persons perfectly just before God on their own account. Every one of us is sinful and an abomination; would to God that everyone recognised that! Therefore, the righteousness we have is loaned to us and imputed to us as if it were our very own. Of this righteousness we are only assured by faith in Jesus Christ, that for his sake God forgives us our sins and unrighteousness, and accounts us as justified as if we had attained this ourselves.

This was the faith by which our forefathers were justified, by which we also are justified, and also by which our posterity after us will be justified. That is why we must depend upon Christ alone. Therefore, do not trust in yourselves or in your own strength, but learn that in your human nature is only what must be grieved and sorrowed over. But when you lift up your eyes to heaven you will learn to repose upon that rich mercy which is constantly being communicated to us for Christ's sake. Those who are strong in God's mercy are truly strong, but those who think they are strong in themselves have no strength at all. A good opinion of ourselves prevents us from imploring God to impart to us his strength; that is indeed a sorry state to be in. That is why the awareness of our own weakness makes us forsake all trust in ourselves, so that we rather cast ourselves upon divine mercy.

The faithful gain the praise and commendation of God

In the example of Enoch, I pointed out to you that every faithful man not only obtained his praise and commendation from God, but, as well as this, he also gained in stature and spiritual progress[3] both in this life and in the life to come. There was never from the beginning of time someone with genuine faith of heart and mind who could not bear witness that at some point in his life the Spirit of God commended and approved of him for taking his stand in defending the Lord's cause, even in the face of the devil's opposition. In his heart the very Spirit of God testified to his spirit that he was pleasing to the Lord. More, such men were granted the assurance of their standing before God and his blessing upon them both spiritually and physically, and ultimately of the crown of glory. It is absolutely certain that those who engage righteously in this spiritual conflict shall be commended in this life, and in the hereafter shall be crowned with everlasting glory. Thus we see that faith will be rewarded with the Lord's praise and commendation.

Therefore, what benefit was granted to Enoch on account of his faith? The apostle now tells us: namely, that the God of heaven translated him out of this world into the world to come to those blessed mansions where the Father dwells. Because Enoch was living in a very corrupt age, as wicked a generation as could vex any upright man, God deliberately removed him from that scene of time. Seeing him so often and so long grieved over the wickedness of those around him, the Lord saw fit to remove him long before he should reach his father's years. He only reached the age of three hundred and sixty-five, a much shorter life

[3] Bruce's phrase is 'he gat honoure and advancement'. He speaks often of this 'advancement' of the godly, but I am quite sure that the context makes it clear he means 'growth in spiritual stature and progress', as I have translated it.

than those of former generations.[4] So the Lord shortened his days and took him up visibly in body and soul to heaven.

Soul and body

The text says, *By faith Enoche was taken away that he shulde not se death: neither was he fovnde.*[5] He was not to taste the separation that by nature all must taste, by which the soul is severed from the body. Soul and body would never have been parted had we not sinned; it was on account of sin that the Lord pronounced the curse of this separation. I grant that by the death of Christ Jesus this curse has now been overturned, for in him death has now been sanctified—nevertheless it still remains a curse. However, for Enoch there was no severance, for both soul and body were borne up to heaven. There was a reason: as I explained to you the last time we met, God did this specially that the Fathers of that age might not only see inwardly by faith, but that also outwardly it might be documented that after this earthly life, both body and soul would live for ever. They were being assured by outward evidence, as well as by the inward assurance of faith, that both soul and body would continue in the life to come.

'Translations' in all three ages of biblical history

In each age of human history by such events as men being taken up to heaven the Lord gave clear testimony to convince the world of a life in the hereafter. By 'each age of human history' I mean this: there are three distinct ages. First, there is the age before the law and that was when Enoch was translated. Second, there was the age under the law and that was when Elijah was translated. Third, there is the age after the law when Christ, the firstborn from the dead, by divine strength was raised body and soul. All this was to assure us of the life everlasting, lest despondence and unbelief should alarm us. After the command is given forth on the last day, by the same power whereby Christ was raised from the dead, we are appointed to be caught up to meet him in the clouds. However, the reprobate shall not be caught up, but will remain on earth from whence they shall be assigned to ferocious elements in

[4] See Genesis 5.

[5] 'By faith Enoch was taken up so that he should not see death, and he was not found' (ESV).

the place of their damnation. Having met Christ in the clouds, the godly shall gather before his throne, and shall hear the judgment given on the unrighteous, but they themselves shall be declared to be recipients of divine favour.

Thus, we learn from Enoch, Elijah and lastly from Christ Jesus, that on that final day the whole elect people of God shall be gathered up to meet Christ and shall encircle his throne. (Not so unbelievers!) Therefore, seeing that there are so many blessings given through faith, we must pray that here on earth the Lord would enable us to ensure that we do indeed believe, and that he would bestow on us the firm assurance in our hearts and minds that we are not lacking that most notable benefit that makes both soul and body so blessed both here and hence.

Believers' doubts

They have real reason to doubt who consider the vanities of their own natures and the wickedness of their own souls; yet it is better to doubt than to despair. For where there are doubts there is also faith; doubts cling to the pillars of faith. How can it be possible for anyone not to doubt when all of us are weighed down with such a load of sins, and are constantly enticed towards some deviation or other.

Yet the Lord will not permit doubting to go so far as to drive us to complete despair; where a man's faith is mingled with doubts, the Lord will see and know his human frailty, and will accept him according to the small measure of that man's experience of grace; he will not rebuke him that his grasp on grace is not stronger. The Lord looks in each of us for the desire and the resolve to turn away from evil, and when there is that desire he will bless it, and cause it to come to fruition in due time.

So pray to the Lord that in his mercy he will help your unbelief and support you in it, so that in due season, by virtue of Christ's death, you may have the assurance of that great blessing. Then you shall know that on the final day you will be raised to meet Christ in the clouds, and will gather with the throng around his throne.

Why Enoch's faith was commended

Having explained how it was that Enoch received these benefits, the apostle then went on to tell us why the godly man was commended by God before he was translated. We find it in the last phrase of verse

5 and then in verse 6. Verse 5 first: *because the Lord liked weill of him.*[6] There can be no doubt that this was why the Lord conferred on Enoch this inestimable benefit. Also, a second reason for this immense blessing is found is verse 6: *becaus he soucht God continuallie.*[7] God desires us always to seek him throughout our whole lifetime, for those who seek always find, even more and more. Therefore, because Enoch diligently sought God, yearning to go to be with him, he did go and he found him! That was why it pleased the Lord to bless him in this extraordinary manner.

But you may ask, 'What has this to do with faith? Surely the apostle's purpose is to commend Enoch's justifying faith. Yet when he says that God took him, there is not a single word about faith.' When we throw this question at him, he neatly catches it, for in the 6th verse he shows that Enoch's translation has everything to do with his faith. To please God, to approach him, to seek and find—all these are the effect and work of faith. Therefore notice the first phrase in the verse that *without faith* (says he) *it is impossibill to pleas God.* Of necessity, this blessed man pleased God, sought and found him, only through his true and justifying faith. The import of the verse make that abundantly clear.

So what do you lack over and above faith? Even though you bring all the works of this world, they cannot either please God or be acceptable to him unless they are brought in faith. Only what is done in faith is acceptable and pleasing before God; it is by faith alone that we are justified. How can this be? The reason is that faith affects the whole person: it reforms the heart and the mind, it slays the heart's worldly affections, and it sanctifies the will to the obedience of the living God. Regarding this reformation of faith in the soul, once faith has truly begun its work, God is pleased, and that person is justified.

Out of all the multitude of things here on earth, faith is the chief thing that brings to God his rightful praise, glory and commendation. For where faith resides in the heart of a man, it enables him from the heart to affirm the pure goodness of God. John in his first epistle speaks of those who please God and says that the Lord seals in them his

[6] GenB: 'Before he was taken away, he was reported of, that he had pleased God.'
[7] GenB: 'He is a rewarder of them that seke him.'

goodness, truth and mercy, all by faith.[8] There is nothing in any of us that will bring us of our own volition to ascribe to God his truth, might and omnipotence; it is only through faith that God reveals these to us, along with his mercy, and that is why faith pleases him. Through faith we discover the essence of his goodness in that he performs his gracious promises as freely as he has given them to us; hence through faith we acknowledge him to be all-powerful and omnipotent. Neither the devil nor the world can set up barriers to hinder God fulfilling his promises; the Lord has endless means of performing his promises on behalf of his servants. Therefore faith acknowledges that power of the living God. Repose upon him and render to him the praise due to the only true, almighty and gracious God.

'Works' can never be meritorious

As to 'works', I grant that they are needed in this world and are the outcome of your salvation, but in no way are they necessary for your justification; every good work that you do flows from faith. On the other hand, if you try to offer God good works as evidence that you deserve your salvation, he regards that as an abomination before him. The only works that are acceptable to him are those that flow from faith, and faith flows from his mercy, for we are justified in the very instant that we lay hold on Christ and are assured of God's mercy.

Our salvation is different in that it is not instantly completed, as is our justification. Salvation is not finally accomplished until first the soul is severed from the body, and so loosed from sin's fetters; thereafter at the second resurrection, when body and soul are reunited and both go to the Lord's heavenly dwelling-place, then our salvation is finally accomplished. That is why, after we are justified by faith, the good works that flow from godly living are an essential part of our salvation. It stands to reason that there must be a pathway along which we travel towards heaven; if we have no good works we cannot be following that pathway, if heaven is to be our destination. In Ephesians 2:10 the apostle plainly declares that the Lord has prepared us and created us in Christ Jesus for works that we should walk in them.[9] Consider how

[8] The allusion seems to be to 1 John 3, verses 23-24. See also the whole chapter; Cain is mentioned in verse 12.

[9] 'For we are his workmanship, created in Christ Jesus for good works, which

important it is for someone on a journey to be travelling along the right road if he is to arrive safely. In the same way our daily walk must be good works if we are to reach heaven.

The error of Catholic teaching on 'Satisfactions'[10]

If this teaching had been carefully heeded, all the confusion and misunderstanding about justification would not have caused so much trouble in the Kirk as it has done. It is quite clear that good works must flow from a transformed soul and heart; nevertheless, good works (I mean obedience) cannot ever be the cause of our justification; it is only by our gripping hold of Christ—the moment we grip Christ—that we are justified. So it is that by the fruits of our faith we follow the road that will lead to the end of life's journey, that is, to life everlasting. There is no way to please God other than through the faith that clings to Christ alone.

You see therefore why the apostle constantly reiterates his theme of faith. This note sounds all the time because it is a string on which he never stops strumming. He cannot get away from it! Without justifying faith there is no reforming of our souls, or the bestowal of the blessing of reuniting body and soul in heaven. Justifying faith is so absolutely necessary that even if it were being incessantly repeated, you would do well constantly to hear it. So do not grow weary listening to it being often told, rather earnestly crave of the Lord that he would sanctify your soul that you will delight in hearing it, since faith is the only means of salvation.

Genesis 5 does not say that Enoch received God's commendation

I must move on, for next it may be asked what warrant the apostle has for claiming that Enoch received God's commendation: *for befeir he was takin away, he was reported of that he haid pleased God.* But where does it say in the Old Testament that Enoch pleased God? The words the apostle uses are not found in Genesis 5. I answer that the substance of the apostle's words are there in Genesis 5:22, 24, where he is twice given

God prepared beforehand, that we should walk in them' (Ephesians 2:10).

[10] In Catholic teaching 'satisfaction' is thought to be a necessary element of the virtue and sacrament of Penance; it is reparation made for sin by fasting, almsgiving and other good works. Though Bruce does not use this term, it is what he is referring to in this section of his sermon.

this praise that *Enoche walked with God*. Notwithstanding the widespread corruption of his generation, he constantly walked with God; those who shun all other company to walk with God must surely take delight in their fellowship with God, and therefore it follows that God takes pleasure in them. How could Enoch have walked with God unless he had both sought and found him? Therefore the apostle's conclusion that Enoch walked with God is obviously correct.

The implication of the verb 'walked' in Genesis 5:22, 24 is that this man *continuallie* walked with God. That word *continuallie* suggests something very unusual: that a man should live so piously and in such holiness that his gaze should be perpetually upon the Lord. That surely is remarkable.[11] Genesis chapter 6 makes it clear that when Enoch lived, society had become exceedingly corrupt, and the worship of God had been utterly profaned. This indicates that without doubt Enoch had become a truly holy man. For it to be twice said of him that he walked with God means nothing less than he did not follow the world's way, nor tread in its footsteps, nor yield to its allurements and corrupt practices, but constantly followed and worshipped God with a clear conscience.

The powerful influence of public example in a corrupt society

Every one of us knows that in our age, similar in some ways to Enoch's, we have witnessed how influential public example can be, and how, when the nobility and the powerful are wicked and evil, they can cause many others to join them in their godlessness. Again, every one of us also knows the strong influence of something that becomes accepted as normal; even though some vice appeared odious when someone first started to practise it, people gradually became accustomed to it, until what at first had shocked them ultimately became enjoyable and commonplace. Thus it comes about that men see all around them examples of evil practices, and observe society to be constantly engaged in wickedness generation after generation. Just as a flood can sweep away a pebble, so common practices can take on the force of law, so that throughout society men begin to justify their actions, however wrong they might be.

For a man to live in such corrupt times and yet stand firm and

[11] Bruce's phrase is, *that is a strainge mater*.

true is as an unusual occurrence of which I have ever read. The Spirit of the mighty God must have been strengthening this man that he was able to stand firm with God, and keep his eyes fixed upon him during such public confusion. Unhappily our own experience teaches us that, although we should be the light and stars of this world, when we ought to be people that others follow, on account of the evil influence of so-called great men, instead we follow them; we should be the salt seasoning their behaviour, but instead their rottenness is putrefying and infecting us. This is happening entirely on account of the powerful influence of their daily practices on our communal and national thinking; consequently we too are deceived.

I am emphasising this state of affairs in our land in order to let you see that Enoch is rightly praised, when in the midst of public corruption he was enabled to stand firm with God. When I say this man perpetually had his gaze upon God, I mean that he looked continually to the will of God. It was not that God was physically visible to him, for he did not look upon God in bodily form. Rather, when it says of him that he walked with God, it means he lived in obedience to his laws, he had his heart set upon his will and that he made no move that was not according to the instruction of God's will. For a man who was living in the midst of a corrupt society to do all this so unswervingly that he should have the approval of God in all that he did—this was commendation indeed. Enoch never turned aside, nor was enticed by either the allurement of the world, the flesh, or the evil example of others; steadfastly his gaze remained fixed upon the will of God.

You and I are in a similar situation, except that our times are not as corrupt as were Enoch's times. For throughout the whole of human history, there has never been as great human depravity as there was in Enoch's day. Consequently, we are forewarned, so that the evil examples and customs that are prevalent among us and are either acceptable or ignored, do not entice us nor lead us astray. Our only recourse is to learn to flee as far as we can from every opportunity to engage in any evil, and on the other hand constantly to be watchful in prayer, that the Lord would not allow our personal, private enemies (I mean our own fleshly desires), nor our outward enemies, so to overcome us that we bring shame upon his gospel. There is no help to be found but in prayer.

The worldly are so blind that they think if some activity becomes habitual it must be acceptable, no matter how evil it might be; they also consider anyone who criticises what has become accepted as customary behaviour to be puffed up with arrogance. Therefore we must arm ourselves by being employed in prayer, so that we are not carried away by the evil example and practices of this age and nation among whom we live.

Seeking God diligently

My final point here is that it says in verse 6 that Enoch came to the God who rewards those who seek him diligently. We need to understand clearly first, what is meant by 'coming to God' and second, what a man must believe who comes to God. Take heed then to these two things. As to the first, the apostle says in chapter 4 verse 16, *Latis ws go boldie to the throne of God.*[12] We do not approach God physically, for God is not corporeal, nor to be found in some particular location; God is a Spirit and therefore to come to him you must draw near in your heart and your spirit. To come rightly you must come with assurance and trust in your heart, for those who would come may not have their hearts set upon this earth, fixed upon earthly things. Rather, those who come to God must lift up their hearts from the earth to heaven, and to the consideration of spiritual things. In effect, to go to God means to raise our minds upward by lifting our thoughts from earth and setting them in the heavenly places where Christ and the Father dwell.

Earnestly seek him confessing our sin

However, there are two important points[13] regarding this approach to God. To be borne up above to within the sight of God, first we must bow down in humble confession of our sins. It is not only our fallen sinfulness that we confess, but also any particular sins of which we are aware; however, because our memories are unreliable, we may simply make just a general confession. This applies especially to those occasions when we come to the Lord's Table; search your consciences for ways in which you may have offended against God's eternal majesty.

[12] 'Let us then with confidence draw near to the throne of grace' (ESV).

[13] Bruce's word that I have translated 'points' is 'sert', literally meaning 'merits'; but the context makes it clear that he speaking about two essential points to bear in mind as we draw near to God, and not about something meritorious in us.

This confession is not to be made publicly, but only privately between you and God.

An example of confession is when Nathan came to king David (2 Samuel 12). In Psalm 32 we read of David's remorse as he confesses to both adultery and murder; he could find no peace for his conscience, but just a constant inner gnawing and torment.[14] We only find peace for our consciences when the glories of God are restored by our confession. Therefore, to find rest for a troubled conscience, resolve to confess without delay the particular sins that testify before God against you, and plead his mercy. In Luke 15:21 we read of the distraught son falling down before his father and confessing how he had sinned both against God and against his father; his was both a general and a particular confession—'against heaven and before you'. Thus we see that we begin our approach to God with a humble confession of our sins.

Seeking God diligently also means that we must pray for God's mercy with earnest pleading. We must be urgent in this prayer, and not dally, vaguely hoping for his mercy. No one has ever genuinely made confession to God seeking for his mercy, and not been blessed with the assurance that God has heard and answered. However, this earnest seeking for mercy can only be engaged in truly through God's Spirit at work in our hearts. This applies to any prayer we offer: we must have the Holy Spirit within us. The apostle tells us in Romans 8:26 that the Spirit in our hearts inspires deep sighs and groans. If you know of someone who has offended God and is craving for his mercy, and he is groaning and weeping, you can be sure that his confession is sincere and earnest.

The Spirit's presence in our hearts is not something temporary that lasts for a day or a week; he continues to be within us all that year and beyond, right through our whole lives. Consequently, the grief we have over any sins we commit will always cause us to deplore what we have done, when the Lord has been so gracious and merciful towards us. This, then, is the second point: we come to God in humility and repentance, seeking his mercy because our faith is grounded upon the free promises of God. Seek him diligently in these two ways: first, come

[14] Psalm 32:3-4: 'When I kept silent, my bones wasted away through my groaning all day long. For day and night your hand was heavy upon me; my strength was dried up as by the heat of summer.' (ESV)

boldly to his throne of grace; second, come believing, that is, come in faith in his gracious promises. You will find him; he will accept you.

I have already said that God desires only what will show forth his glory, and his glory is revealed when we confess our sins. Genuine confession condemns all the excuses of our arguments and reasoning, for these are not wrought by the Holy Spirit. False penitence may deceive the visible church and buy you time, but it will never deceive the all-seeing gaze of the living God, who searches our hearts, knows our thoughts and is never content with mere shadows. He looks for unfeigned remorse, even with tears, therefore those whose repentance is feigned most certainly aggravate their own condemnation. For they do not acknowledge God's glory, but mock him to his face, and so earn for themselves even more severe judgment. It is better to delay confessing your sins if you are not truly repenting in your heart. No, what you do must be done in all sincerity, that, just as you bow low physically before God, so in your soul you also prostrate yourself in all humility. You may easily deceive us, but you can never deceive God.

To seek God diligently we must also believe that he is

So much then for how we must draw near to God. The second point regarding coming to God that we must consider is what we must believe when we come to God. If we are to draw near to God in the right way, we must of necessity know who it is that we are approaching. As well as believing that 'God is', we must also be aware of what we learned about him, and that he is our God.

Even though what we know about him might be termed 'general knowledge',[15] this world does not even acknowledge him. The world may admit there is a God, but they will declare that he is only one God among many gods, that is, he is just one of many idols; that is the world's conception of him. From the beginning the world has been possessed by such foolishness; they say in their hearts that there is no God: '*The foole hathe said in his heart, There is no God.*'[16] Therefore, the apostle quotes from Psalm 14 in Romans 3:11 as witnessing to us that throughout every generation the world has never truly known God. The world imagines that they have some knowledge of God by the spark [of God's

[15] The context suggests that Bruce here is referring to 'general revelation'.
[16] Psalm 14:1.

image] remaining in their nature.[17] Yet this faint light and knowledge is so fettered (as the apostle says) in the bonds of unrighteousness, that their knowledge can never fully grow or attain the assurance that there is indeed a God. Their evil passions and wilful rebellion have caused their knowledge to decrease, gradually extinguishing its light, so that the older a society becomes, the more ignorant are they of the knowledge of the living God.

The same holds true of the Ethnics,[18] who, though they have that spark [of God's image], it is suppressed by their wickedness. It is even more so with us, to whom has been given the means of knowing God through his word being preached, for he can be seen in his word as in a mirror. If men despise the means [of knowing God] that they have been given, it is inevitable the world will languish, because all men's nature has is that faint spark of light. But upon us [possessing the word of God] who despise the spiritual light, there descends on the soul's sight a terrible blindness, resulting in such wicked living, that there was never a pagan as degenerate as an evil Christian.

You may examine the lifestyles of supposed Christians and you will find such condemnation has resulted from the despising of the light of his word, that God has completely deprived them of both the spiritual light they refused and the natural light which the pagans have already rejected. Consequently, our commonwealth is confused and abominations are rife among us such as have never been heard of among Gentiles; yet we legalise these evil practices. It has never been heard of before that a man who is manifestly God's enemy, excommunicated and outlawed by God,[19] shall then be welcomed, openly entertained and given free passage from one place to another; no one appears able to distinguish him from genuine Christians.

Surely you can see that it is contempt for the light [of God's word] that has brought such evils upon us. Beyond all question I see no future for us but that our land must be burned with fire; yea, it must spew out its inhabitants for the wickedness of our whole generation is so great.

[17] Calvin elaborates on this 'light' in his commentary in John 1:5.

[18] See above, Sermon Four, note 6.

[19] Bruce's phrase is 'at the horne of God': a horn was used in proclaiming an outlaw, three blasts being blown by the king's messenger. Thus the phrase 'put to the horne' means 'to outlaw'.

Former generations did not escape the hand of God, even though they did not have the spiritual light [of God's word]. Therefore we must be dealt with more severely than the pagans on account of our negligence and contempt of the spiritual light that is offered to our generation.

We come back, then, to what we must know in order to approach God: we must first know that there is a God. If the world never knew this nor shall ever know it, how shall we know God? Because he is a Spirit, he can only be known by a spiritual light. Therefore pray to him that he will enliven your dull senses, and illuminate your blind understanding, that by the entrance of spiritual light you may come to the understanding of his word; it is by that understanding of the word that you shall see God. Unless the Spirit of the living God is present within you, you will never rightly know him. The world has not the Spirit of God, therefore does not know him. The spirit the world has produces a very different kind of knowledge. So as I minister the word to you outwardly, seek the inward ministry of the Spirit to confirm to you God's word as I utter it.

The second thing you must be sure of if you would draw near to God is that God is your God; that is to say that you know he will be merciful to you for the sake of Jesus Christ: *he is a rewairder of them that seke him*. The reward of God consists in the mercy he gives a sinful creature. As we come to him, believing that he is, God shows mercy to us as we seek it diligently from his hand. Nevertheless, the great prerequisite in seeking God's mercy is that we know that we are utterly lost and deeply tainted in ourselves. When the Lord gives a man a true insight of his miserable condition so that he recognises there is nothing in himself except abomination, then his only recourse is to seek him, abandon himself, renounce all and run to Christ. For it is in Christ alone that we can be made anew. Whoever diligently seeks God by turning his back upon himself, must flee from his miserable state that he may turn and run to Christ for mercy. He must lay aside all supposed meritorious works that some erroneously think God will reward,[20] for those who truly seek him must have an inner conviction that they can only obtain mercy though Christ.

[20] A clear allusion to Paul's words: 'I have suffered the loss of all things and count them as rubbish that I may gain Christ' (Philippians 3:8).

Our God does 'reward'

Our text says that *God is a rewairder*, and he is a 'rewarder' indeed! You may ask, 'Why?' His promise to reward is only on account of his mercy, yet the reward is never for anything of worth in what we may have done; he only accepts the works I offer to him on account of his mercy and the faith from which my service for him proceeds. In God's sight, only Christ is meritorious. His merits become our merits, for because they are imputed to us, we participate in Christ's meritorious righteousness. It is for Christ's sake that God accepts our faith and all our works of faith, and this because of his mercy. Therefore, our Kirk takes no account of so-called works of merit; rather, in this building we point you to Christ alone, that for his sake you may seek and find mercy. If you have any awareness at all of your dire need, then make your way towards some awareness of his free mercy.

Those who seek him shall find him

The last lesson under this second point is this: 'Seek and you shall find.' You must each realise that you may not always obtain the thing you ask for, even though you seek it diligently. There are times when the answer may be delayed. Do not then assume that you have been cast off, rather assure yourself that your prayer has been heard; the Lord will not let you despair. We must understand that when someone seeks the Lord, he responds in one of two possible ways: either, if he sought in the right way, the Lord grants his request, or else he imparts to the petitioner the strength to continue in his pleading.[21] Those who continue in their pleas are not repulsed, rather God has vigorously exercised them, so that when the blessing is ultimately given, they may value it even more greatly because it has cost them such travail. Things that are lightly won may be lightly held, whereas what is gained through great travail will be more greatly valued.

So continue to bring your plea before him, for he is worth all the travail of your soul. All who truly seek him shall find grace multiplied to them, and little by little they shall see more of his face. It is never possible in this life fully to gaze upon the countenance of God, even though you continue to seek him steadfastly for all those years that

[21] Bruce uses a legal word, 'suting', meaning 'to have recourse to court action'; hence my translation 'pleading'.

Methuselah lived! Nevertheless, you will find that your soul is satisfied by his ever-nearer presence. When you do behold, even dimly, his countenance, on account of the delays he has imposed on you, it will be all the sweeter. When the Lord admits you into his presence, then doubts are banished, your old sins are cast away, and for Christ's sake he will bless you with the ineffable joy that is in his smile.

To him be all praise, honour and glory, now and for ever and ever. Amen.

Chapter Six

Hebrews Chapter 11 verse 7

> 7 *By faith Noah being warned of God of thingis which war not as yet sein, moved with reverence, prepaired the ark to the saving of his household, throw the quhilk ark he condemned the world and was maid here of richteousnes quhilk is by faith.*

Reminder of what we learned in the previous sermon

You have already heard, well-beloved in Christ Jesus, that Abel is not only counted as the first righteous man by Christ our Master, but also by his apostle here in this chapter. He is counted as the first to be justified by faith, followed next by Enoch who was also justified by faith. Although Enoch was in the seventh generation after Adam and sixth after Abel, he is the second recorded as having been justified by faith. There is no honourable mention, either of their deeds or their faith, of those who lived in the intervening generations; thus the apostle skips over them and comes straight to Enoch, a prophet of the living God. We noted also how his prophetic writings were referred to by Jude,[1] but these prophecies are apparently no longer extant, having been lost over the passage of time.

Enoch continually walked with God

Enoch is greatly praised in the Scriptures which twice tell us that he *walked continuallie with God*, this in spite of the habitual degeneracy and wickedness of the age in which he lived. We too are called to walk continually with God, notwithstanding the corruption of our times.

[1] Jude verses 14-15.

We must not defect from God as most of society is doing, but must keep our eyes upon him and his holy will, so that we direct our living according to his commandments. We must neither squint,[2] nor turn aside to the world by copying others whose earthly passions succumb to the enticements of the devil's agents. Rather we must hold to a straight course, having our mind's eye constantly fixed on God and his will, so that we obey all that his word commands. This is what 'walking with God' means, not least for us who live in such corrupt days when wickedness is habitually condoned; walking with God in such an environment is worthy of praise and commendation.

Called to be the salt of the earth

We who are called to be examples to others should profit by imitating Enoch's example, so that the powerful allurement of the present prevalent corruption in our nation should not entrap us, but rather that, through the mercy, grace and help of God's Spirit, we may be able to influence others to join us. For are we not appointed by God to act as salt in a society governed by earthly princes and worldly men? (Is this not why we are called to be 'the salt of the earth'?) Yet unfortunately experience shows us that we tend to be drawn after the crowd, rather than others being drawn to follow us. Many of those who should have been stars giving light to the world have fallen and their light no longer shines; this is not only to their own condemnation, but now their evil conduct is waylaying others.

Therefore, since we have been appointed to be as salt to 'season' the world, we are to stir up others by our good example. Notwithstanding the weaknesses we have in common with those around us, and also that we are deeply aware of our faults, negatively our aim should be both to eschew this world's evil and any events that expose us to such evil. On the other hand, positively we must aim at waiting continually upon God in prayer and meditation, so that our souls may thereby be sanctified. Then the world will only see in us such things as may provoke some to honour God; then in the world to come the testimony of our lives shall condemn those who have rejected the Lord.

[2] Bruce's verb is 'gley', an old Scots word still occasionally used.

Enoch specially favoured by God

Because Enoch held to a straight course, the God of heaven greatly favoured him, so much so that he had compassion on him, living as he did in the midst of such manifold evils that constantly grieved his righteous soul. For that reason God did not require of him to live as long as his fathers; indeed, Enoch did not even reach half the age of his own father. Rewarding his godly service and faith, God cut short his days by taking him up, body and soul, to his eternal deliverance. No doubt this was to teach the Fathers who were born later—and indeed to teach the invisible kirk—that there was a better life to come; God was thereby instructing them that there was more than this earthly life, and that there was another life they should aim for. He wanted them to see, not only that death was a terrible curse upon a reprobate world, but that he, the living God, has sanctified death to them, in that the separation of their souls from their bodies would actually be a passageway to a far better life that would last forever. Even though Enoch benefitted by being translated, I do not doubt but that his experience was specially directed to the Fathers, that through this visible sign their outward senses would assure their inward souls of the life in the hereafter; if they walked with God as Enoch did, they too would go to that eternal life.

Enoch was carried off[3] before his time, as was Elijah, for neither of them experienced the kind of death all mortals must die. Christ also was caught up to heaven after he had tasted our natural death. These three were all caught up so that we might be assured that if we follow in their steps, we also will be taken up to heaven in that moment when it pleases the Lord to come to judge the world. Regarding the final judgment, I cry to God that you might be more certain than you presently are; that day will come according to his will—it draws ever nearer—when at the second resurrection, we shall stand before the Lamb, even Christ Jesus. It may happen before we face natural death as with Enoch and Elijah. But as Christ was caught up, so many shall also be caught up in body and soul to meet him in the clouds. The apostle assures of this is 1 Thessalonians 4:13-18.

[3] The verb Bruce twice uses of both Enoch and Elijah is 'revisched'; it literally means 'to be ravished'; no doubt Bruce was seeking to convey a wonderful spiritual experience that we might describe as 'being snatched away' or 'swept upwards'.

You may marvel and be astonished to hear that Enoch was caught up to heaven, and all of you who have a heart would want to share such a blessing. Well, believe, and you shall share it and be visibly caught up to meet him in the clouds. Resist that unbelief that poisons and permeates the whole of your soul, labour to cast it out, and seek God's grace and strength that your soul may be set free from unbelief; then trust yourself to the Lord and accept his word. For just as they were caught up, so shall you be caught up in body and soul in the clouds to meet him, the righteous Judge, in the air.[4] May the Lord increase your faith!

God only pleased by faith

The apostle was not content with what he has written so far as in verse 6 he adds this wonderful sentence: *But without faith it is vmpossible to please him.* Leave aside just now Enoch, Noah and the others, for this is a sentence on which we must ponder. Present yourselves to God as acceptably as you are able, your posture composed, your eyes looking upwards, your gestures refined—all this is an abomination before the Lord. By faith alone and nothing else (a faith that issues in godliness[5]) is the Lord pleased. In the same moment that faith quickens the soul and lays hold on the promise of mercy for Christ's sake, you are justified for ever. How then can it ever be possible that God can be pleased without faith, seeing that only by faith do we acknowledge God to be true? Faith seals up his truth, his goodness, his power, his mercy and his kindness towards us for Christ's sake. Only through faith do we come to know and trust him, and acknowledge that he alone can overcome those mountains of obstacles that the world and the devil devise to try and nullify our salvation.

Every single one of us must be sealed by faith (as we are told in John 3:16), otherwise we will never please God. With all your hearts you must put your signature to this, and then you shall both please the Lord and he shall become all in all to you. You must learn to sanctify your memories, so that you can store in your minds these doctrines, for I cannot always be reminding you of them.

[4] Bruce is clearly alluding to 1 Thessalonians 4:17.

[5] The context makes it clear that in the parenthetical comment there is an allusion to James 2:22.

Three lessons regarding the resurrection of the body

Regarding these same verses 4-6, as well as the teaching from it that I have given you, there are other lessons that must be digested for your edification. First of all in the example of Enoch, who in body as well as soul was translated, there is the lesson of the resurrection of the body, a truth that transcends our natural understanding: the bodies of the saints shall not perish, even though now they may be asleep in the graves and their bones be reduced to dust.[6] Christ's Spirit who was in the soul of someone during his life and who received his soul when in death it parted from his body, still watches over the grave with its dust and ashes, until the moment when those remains are raised as a body to be united again with the soul, so that both soul and body are caught up to heaven where Christ is seated at the right hand of the Father.

Learn then that your bodies shall not die, but they shall live for ever, providing that now in this life you believe in Christ. Job knew of this resurrection and notably spoke of it: *For I am sure that my Redemer liueth, and that he shall stand the last on the earth. And thogh after my skin wormes destroy this bodie, yet I shal se God in my flesh.*[7] In Hebrews 11 at verse 19 the apostle clearly states the same doctrine. Thus we see that the ancient Fathers were taught by such accounts committed to writing that, contrary to what men naturally think, the bodies of the saints shall not perish.

Here is the second lesson from these verses: I perceive in the accounts of Abel and Enoch that the Lord is not restricted to just one mode of deliverance. He does not always employ the same means of delivering his own servants, for the storehouse of his methods of working is never empty; according to his good pleasure, one time he uses one means and

[6] It may be of interest to readers to know that, with Lord Elgin's permission, in order preserve Bruce's gravestone from further corrosion, I had it removed from Larbert kirkyard where he had been buried at the foot of the pulpit of the original church building, and installed into the present Larbert Church (built in 1820). I found his remains lying on the earth's surface under the gravestone. I conducted a brief service of re-interment, before Caithness flagstones were carefully laid over the place where his bones still lay; marking the burial site stands a memorial stone engraved with details of his life, and probably erected about the end of the nineteenth century. Having seen this great man's mortal remains, I can state without fear of contradiction that he was a tall man, probably nearly 6 feet in height.

[7] Job 19:25-26 (GenB).

at another time a different means. Thus whenever there is a faithful man he may be sure God will deliver him. Abel's soul was delivered by death, Enoch's body and soul were delivered by life. As for Noah, he was delivered but all others were drowned. God's methods are sometimes very ordinary, at other times they are extraordinary; nonetheless, be sure that the faithful will be delivered. We can be certain of this just as we can be certain of what daily we see around us.

The third lesson I find here is that Enoch was translated long before his allotted span appeared to be completed. God took him prematurely in order that his soul should not be grieved constantly by the wickedness of his generation. Therefore, I perceive that the Lord may shorten the sad days of his elect to save them from being continually grieved with the extreme wickedness of this fallen world, surrounded by which we are bound to live while here on earth. His faithful elect who boldly battle against the evil, courageously resisting the devil, he sometimes rescues by bringing them to their eternal dwelling.

Therefore learn from Enoch that faith makes provision for our bodies' future as well as for the future of our souls. Whoever has faith will never lack God's provision, for even if the stones need to be turned into bread, provision will be made. The Lord's servant may sometimes need special insight to discern how the caring eye of God's providence is looking after him. There is no doubt about it, that if we look with care for the divine providence, we shall find good cause to acknowledge our debt to God for his provision. There are times when we fail to recognise his care for us, and then he may use our lack of faith as a means of chastening us. But if we would only repose wholly upon him, the very stones would become a source of sustenance for our need. Thus both blessed and happy are those who possess the jewel of faith that is the channel of the provision for both our bodies and souls.

Seek insight from God

There is nothing on earth to make a man determined in some quest, more than his desire for possessions and financial profit; day and night he will do without rest in order to acquire them. Now faith offers great gain and profit in this life, that is a thousand times more excellent than material things; yet it is rare for men to embark on the quest to obtain this faith. Why should this be so? Undoubtedly, the reason is that the commodities of faith are spiritual, and cannot be seen outwardly by our physical eye; that is why hardly anyone strives for faith and its rewards. What the eye of faith discerns seems like poison to flesh and blood, for the glories of faith are within and are only perceived spiritually. What the natural man sees is affliction and hardship and, because they appear to be enemies to flesh and blood, few seek faith.

So where does this leave us? Seek insight from God, that you may be able to see faith's spiritual and sublime blessings. And as our Master says towards the end of Matthew 16[8] where he contrasts earthly, temporary possessions with the spiritual blessings of faith, we find that the latter far exceed and outlast the former. Therefore strive after the illumination given through the spiritual mind's eye. Without delay, crave Christ that by his Spirit he would bestow his light on your eyes, and that he would forgive you for shading your sight from his light, even for refusing his light and turning from it. Pray also that it would please Christ to open your hard hearts, that you may see clearly that everlasting light that can never fade, and that you may come to love and be guided by that light. With all your energy you should strive to enter eternal life, yet that life and its blessings are only gained through faith.

It is almost as if the apostle is wearying himself in constantly setting out the riches that flow from faith, as he seeks to allure us to strive to have faith; for it is only by faith that we are reconciled to God and our sins are forgiven. Writes Peter, *By faith onlie oure hairtis ar purgit* (1 Peter 1:5[9]). Every day that we have gathered here in this place it has only been to unfold the necessity and blessing of faith, that we all might have our hearts filled with the great aim to seek this precious pearl.

Noah as an example of faith

The apostle now comes to the subject of Noah to let us see that regarding faith, this man deserves honourable mention just as much as Abel

[8] Matthew 16:25-27, 'Then Jesus told his disciples, "If anyone would come after me, let him deny himself and take up his cross and follow me. For whoever would save his life will lose it, but whoever loses his life for my sake will find it. For what will it profit a man if he gains the whole world and forfeits his soul? Or what shall a man give in return for his soul? For the Son of Man is going to come with his angels in the glory of his Father, and then he will repay each person according to what he has done"' (ESV).

[9] 1 Peter 1:5 'through faith for a salvation …' (ESV).

and Enoch. He lived in a generation far worse than the other two. Yet the Spirit of God says of him that *he was vpricht and just in his generatioune*[10] and certainly that was praiseworthy, for it would be less worthy of note for a man to be upright and just in a righteous and holy generation. In the midst of corruption and wickedness, Noah practised godliness and did not conform to his generation, but held to a straight course in his walk with the living God. Therefore God held in high esteem this last righteous man before the Flood, as Genesis 6:9 tells us. However, it was without regard to his works, but on account of his faith alone and because he believed God's warning concerning the impending destruction of the world, that he and his household were saved, when the rest of the world perished. This is the purport of what we are taught in this long seventh verse of Hebrews 11.

The destruction of the visible kirk

Also set down here is the way in which Noah and those with him were preserved. However, Noah's situation will become much clearer if we understand first the circumstances of the destruction of the rest of the visible kirk. By the 'visible kirk', of course, we mean the posterity of Adam; they had become by that time wicked people who were in one sense already lost. Set out in Genesis 6 are two reasons why this extraordinary judgment fell upon them. The first is this: as humanity multiplied, society became greater in wealth, power and government; it also developed many skills and gifts that ought to have served the people well. But they did not seek God and his kingdom, but abused the resources he had given them, using them for filthy pleasures and to satisfy their own lusts.

Furthermore, those who were descended from Adam's posterity, had not yet openly consorted with Cain's posterity, but still claimed to be within the bosom of the visible kirk. They observed the wealth and ingenuity of the society around them, and saw the beauty of their women and all the rest of those lovely, pleasant, temporal things that

[10] In his handwritten sermon script Bruce always neatly prints Scripture quotations in lower case English script (as distinct from his joined-up writing throughout the Braid script of the sermon). But here his intended quotation from Genesis 6:9 is slightly altered; in the Geneva Bible it reads, *Noah was a iuste and vpricht man in his tyme.* The apostle Paul also sometimes altered slightly his quotations from the LXX without detracting in any way from the meaning.

men enjoyed. The sight of all this enticed the children of the visible kirk into sharing in such follies and drew them into adopting their lifestyles. This was the first reason for their destruction: they joined themselves together with apostates who had been cast out of the kirk of God.

The second reason is made clear: evil company led to evil desires. The beauty of society's women brought God's people to lust after them and, without regard to these women being unbelievers, to enter into marriages with them. So, ignoring their religion's strictures, and with contempt for God himself, they rushed headlong into alienation from him. That was the sum total of it and these were the two reasons for the destruction of the early generations of Adam's posterity and the visible kirk: evil company kindled evil desires.

The relevance of this for the visible kirk today

The same holds true today. Those who are lost are either lost through evil company, or else through evil desires—or a combination of both. These are the snares of the devil that lead to a man's destruction. What was true of the old world has not changed: by these two things the Lord's anger is kindled and his righteousness is offended. This is why he spoke to Noah and said, *An end of all flesche is come befor me: for the earth is filled with cruelty through them*. 'Even though I created this world,' he said, 'I will destroy it, for these people are ignorant of me and do not know me.' He could have executed this judgment immediately, but his own mercy intervened and moved him to mitigate his justice, for mercy pled[11] for a delay and craved that a preacher of righteousness be sent who would constantly proclaim the message, in season and out of season. So a delay of six score years was given,[12] to see if the world would repent. They could not have been sent a better preacher of righteousness than Noah, but there was no preaching that would do them any good, for they remained unmoved until the day came when the Lord in his righteous judgment sent the Flood and destroyed them, men and beasts, apart from those preserved in the ark.

[11] Bruce, originally a lawyer, often uses legal terms; the word I have translated as 'pled' is 'impetratis': 'impetrate' means 'to obtain by petition or formal application to a constituted authority'; hence 'to induce and prevail upon'.

[12] The figure of 120 years comes from a combination of Genesis 6:3 and 1 Peter 3:20; the latter verse also states: 'God's patience waited in the days of Noah, while the ark was being prepared' (ESV).

A remnant saved

Notwithstanding this wholesale destruction, the Lord was not unmindful of his own people, but in the midst of the flood he wonderfully preserved them, as we shall see shortly. The Scripture is silent regarding the obedience and repentance that the Flood produced in the remnant of the visible kirk. Christian charity would have us guess that such heavy judgment would draw repentance from them, so that their souls were kept secure from eternal punishment. We understand Peter to imply this when he says they were brought safely through the water. However, we need to consider the relevance of this for ourselves and the times in which we live. For Peter shows in his second epistle (3:5-7) that, just as the earth was at one time destroyed by water, so ultimately will it be destroyed by fire.

Therefore, this tells us that the appearance of the heavens as we now see them will change: they will be folded up and pass away with a loud noise: *the heaues shall passé away with a noyce.*[13] Do not delay in seeking faith to believe God's word! Fire will consume the elements, the earth and all that is in it. This our Master assures us of through Peter, that this time the earth shall not be destroyed by water, as the old world was, but by fire. I do not know what kind of fire is spoken of, but as we search for the signs and circumstances described in the Scriptures, we can see that the end is always imminent, just as it was in the days before the Flood. We dare not presume to suggest a time to the living God, for it is hidden in his secret counsels. It simply becomes us to wait with reverence.

Signs of the Lord's Coming

Our Master does not tell us the day or the hour in Matthew 24 where we read, *As it was in the dayis of Noa, so sall it be befoir the cuming of the Sone of man; as in these dayis befoir the flude, they eat, they drank, miried and gaue in marriage, and did follow the lustis of their flesche.*[14] In those days, men were ignorant and unaware of the coming destruction, but now in our day we are even more ignorant, licentious and wicked than they were. That makes me wonder if the final day is not far off. It is

[13] 'The heavens will pass away with a roar' (ESV 2 Peter 3:10).

[14] Matthew 24:37-8 (GenB). The last phrase 'and did follow the lustis of their flesche' is not in modern English translations.

hardly possible for iniquity to increase beyond the level it is presently at just now.

There is another sign of the imminence of the last day: the evangel that had to be spread across the whole earth has long since watered every land, and will—I do not doubt—already to some extent have watered the new continents more recently discovered.[15] Therefore the evidence suggests that the signs we have been given of the imminence of the final destruction have all been fulfilled, and because our generation is even worse than Noah's generation, what should we do? As at every proclamation and warning of judgment Noah feared and trembled, so should we. We also have to grieve that our hearts are so hard that no biblical instruction moves us. We have to crave that the Lord in his mercy would not impute to us those sins that harden our hearts, but that he would forgive those sins just as he forgives all our shortcomings.

I must move on. I ask how it can be that the face of the visible kirk, both in our country and in neighbouring lands—indeed, right across the world—is so defiled with violence and uncleanness?[16] Should we look for some causes other than those recorded in Genesis 6? No, there can be no other causes than consorting in evil company and yielding to wicked fleshly lusts; to be enslaved to one's lusts is the worst slavery of all. This is the reason for the foul defection that is rampant in our generation. Are there any here whose consciences accuse you of consorting with apostates? There are two renowned apostates, both of whom are noblemen.[17] Do any of you consort with them, ignoring the fact that before God in heaven they have been declared our opponents?[18] These dignitaries are accepted and entertained as if they were at peace with the living God and at peace with the king. Whatever has happened to our people's consciences? Is it any wonder that the Lord is hastening his judgment upon the visible kirk?

[15] Calvin occasionally also suggests that the gospel has now spread across the whole world.

[16] Bruce considers the so-called 'Christendom' of his day to comprise the visible church.

[17] The word Bruce uses can also mean 'a prominent citizen, burgess or magistrate'. The two robbers could have been the Earls of Huntly and Errol.

[18] Most probably those referred to were known to be hostile to the reformed kirk and faith, and still hankering after Roman Catholicism.

Pray that divine judgment may be moderated

Abel accepted his final hour as the Lord pleased to bring it upon him. Our particular judgment is not being ignored but is advancing swiftly towards us; it will overtake us to our shame if the Lord chooses to take up arms against us. Therefore we have to crave the Lord so to fortify us that the cause of Christ be not dishonoured in our fragile lands. So what is the likely cause that could bring ruin to this country? It will be that every citizen is found following his own desires and every aristocrat is satisfying his own appetites without respect for either God or man; they all prefer to fulfil their own foul desires, rather than obey the living God for the salvation of their souls and bodies. For if I put my salvation on one side of the weighing scales, and my lusts on the other side of the scales, and I choose my lusts, then am I justly condemned? Shall not my own conscience admit it? What would God have to say about it, other than to ratify the judgment of my own conscience?

Take heed to this: following our own desires will inevitably bring the judgment of the eternal God upon the visible kirk. Iniquity has come to such a pass that each of us must choose the right way, that the Lord may withhold his punishment. We can be quite sure that the Lord God is tempering his judgment in the meantime, for the Lord has not raised up just one Noah, but many preachers of righteousness who are summoning us all to repent. On the other hand, we can also be sure that in men's hearts there reigns even greater contempt and mockery than in the days of Noah. What will be the result of this? Shall the Lord be constantly reviled? Will he not weary in receiving such insults? There would be neither justice nor impartiality in God if he did not take issue with these affronts from our country. Because our magistrates permit all this, there can be no doubt that the Lord in his justice will take issue with us.

As for me, I will beseech the Lord that his actions against us will be moderated, for I am afraid that because our impiety and wickedness is exceedingly great, that his judgment will therefore be exceedingly terrible. Therefore we must all pray that the Lord will so administer his justice, that however severe it shall be towards the wicked, it might be used for our sanctification; that is, that his justice may be to us as a fatherly visitation, to draw us into the kingdom of heaven. Would to God that we would all urgently plead that his visitation upon us might have such consequences.

What effect has all the preaching of the word had upon your lives? What of all these signs that God has displayed in the heavens, in the seas and in all the elements? And what of the wonderful act of God in delivering and bringing safely home your prince?[19] So what have these various divine acts achieved, striking as they are, partly upon private individuals, partly upon public persons, partly within and partly outside our city, and even now continuing to affect others? Are any moved? Are there any who lament the state of our country? Are there any who yearn and grieve for mercy from God's hand? Therefore shall not all these things bring accusations against the visible kirk; there can be no disputing of it.

Now I draw to a close. No one can doubt that we must lament the miserable state of this country in which we live. Nevertheless, the teaching I have brought to you will not remain with you unless your hearts are softened, as was the heart of Noah; your great desire should be that your hearts also should be opened to the word. The Lord's sending out of his messengers so that his word has kept on ringing in your ears must be a portent of some particular judgment drawing near. None of us will be able to stand in that hour, unless the Lord visits us with his mercy. Should you not bow your knees and cry out most urgently that the Lord would from the riches of his grace cast out your sins from your hearts, and for Christ's sake cast them out of his own memory? Then in your own souls you may be assured of his mercy, and your sins shall never again rise up to condemn you. You must also earnestly pray for this absolute assurance that the Lord in his mercy will also cast out of your souls your own memories of your sins.

Should that judgment of God come, whether specifically for us or generally upon our nation, you should not cease constantly to ask God

[19] A suitable marriage was necessary to reinforce the monarchy of James VI, and the choice had fallen on fourteen-year-old Anne of Denmark, younger daughter of Protestant Frederick II. Shortly after a proxy marriage in Copenhagen in August 1589, Anne had sailed for Scotland but was forced by storms on to the coast of Norway. James had sailed from Leith on hearing that the crossing had been abandoned, taking with him a three hundred-strong retinue to fetch Anne personally. The couple were married formally at the Bishop's Palace in Oslo on 23 November and returned to Scotland on 1 May 1590, after short stays at Elsinore and Copenhagen. Robert Bruce had been appointed by James himself to be a member of the Council of State, sharing in governing the nation during the king's absence in Norway.

to continue his work in your hearts that you may be sanctified. But do not only pray for yourselves and your own salvation, also earnestly seek God for his mercy upon our prince and our country. May the Lord graciously be with every one of us, and grant to us the spirit of prayer, that we may call upon him for all these things, for the sake of Christ his Son. To whom with the Father and the Holy Spirit be all honour, praise and glory, now and for ever. Amen.

Chapter Seven

Hebrews Chapter 11 verse 7

> 7 *By faith Noah being warned of God of thingis which war not seine as yit, moved with reverence, prepaired the ark to the saveing of his household, throuch the whiche ark he condemned the world and was maid here of richteousnes whiche is by faith.*[1]

We began the last time we met,[2] brethren, as the Lord gave me grace, to see the chief causes that brought destruction upon the First World.[3] Set down in Genesis chapter 6 is the destruction of both the visible kirk and the rest of the unbelieving world. We noted that there were two causes for this, namely, evil company and wicked lusts. These two causes together were the reason for the Flood that swept away the entire visible kirk, excepting only the handful of those who were in the ark.

It was not that the Lord was hasty in executing this judgment, for he gave them a hundred and twenty years to repent, tempering his justice in this manner: he sent them a preacher of righteousness to warn them; along with the preacher, he gave them in the ark a clear sign of their condemnation, unless they repented. Yet neither word, nor sign, nor example nor anything else was able to move them, for they persisted in their mockery right up to the moment that the flood came upon them.

The indebtedness of the Kirk to God in our apostate generation

As I unfolded the teaching here, I pointed out that there was no nation or visible kirk in all the world that was more indebted to God by the

[1] Readers may notice that the Bible verse in this second sermon on Hebrews 11:7 is spelt slightly differently from that in the previous sermon.

[2] See Chapter 3, Note 1 above.

[3] 'First World' is sometimes referred to by Bruce as the 'Old World'.

multitude of his blessings. The same applies to us today. Consider all the various kirks that have been planted in the world since the gospel began to be preached, there has never been a kirk more indebted for the freedom given to it than we ourselves. Yet, notwithstanding, wicked lust has so prevailed among us that every man prefers his own desires and affections rather than to God and his service.[4]

What I mean is this: suppose men hear that, on the one hand the kingdom of heaven is offered to them with infinite joy and everlasting felicity, and on the other hand set before them are temporal lusts and desires with their fleeting pleasures ending only in bitterness, all of them prefer their temporal lusts rather than eternal joy and the kingdom of heaven. Everyone prefers his own inclinations rather than the living God, so each follows his own desires. Are we surprised that God is angry? The greater men's contempt, the greater his wrath! And the greater men's lusts, the greater their contempt! Why should we be surprised if he delays no longer, but hastens his visitation?

The imminent judgment God

Nevertheless, he does not always hasten his wrath. For as he sent Noah to preach to the First World, now to us he has sent thousands of preachers to various lands at sundry times, to warn the whole world that if they persist in their degeneracy all shall perish together. He has sent us his message, for his word speaks to us plainly. In fact it comes to us so often that our minds become inured to it, such is the corruption of our fallen natures. He has sent us signs in the elements, in the earth, in the air, in the waters, all testifying to his wrath and indignation provoked in him by our sins.

He has warned us through the sad spectacle of our neighbours, upon whom the avenging hand of God has often fallen; likewise, there has been the spectacle of prominent personages both in our own land and in other lands. Has any of this moved us? But no one thinks his just deserts will follow, even though judgment has been clearly threatened. No matter how often we are warned, men's hearts can never be

[4] It is most probable that here 'service' refers to the kirk's worship; see Exodus 20:5, 'Thou shalt not bowe down to them [graue image, verse 4], nor serue them' (GenB).

induced to render him service.[5] Upon such hardness of heart, doubtless the judgment of God is bound to come.

I am not referring to the final judgment day. But assuming I do not witness any change of heart in us shortly, it is inevitable that some particular judgment must be visited upon our heads. There are some—not all that many—who for their failures have been chastised. But what effect does such chastisement have other than a phoney repentance? If we took it upon ourselves to discipline some until they genuinely repented, probably only two would repent in any year.

Of course the kirk's discipline should be the normal means of evoking unfeigned repentance, yet it produces nothing in the common people other than phoney repentance. Will God be mocked in this way? Is there nothing that will be effective, whether discipline, convictions, warnings, signs in the earth and in the air? Then of necessity, judgment must fall! Weigh carefully all these matters, consider them, and since they are true, rather believe and fear with Noah than perish with a reprobate world. This far we proceeded last time.

Unbelief among us today

Now I come to the causes of all this, that neither word nor sign, national examples either of private or public personages, nor discipline, nor chastening[6] in body or in soul, nor anything else can move us. Similarly, nothing could move the Old World on account of the unbelief in them; the same unbelief is present among us. The devil has spewed unbelief so deeply into the fabric of our souls that we cannot get rid of it; indeed, we are so infected by it that it increases constantly rather than diminishing. So what effect has this unbelief on us? It causes us neither to believe God nor in the words that he speaks, whether in mercy or in anger. This unbelief is the cause of our chastening[7] in both body and soul.

Because Noah believed God's warnings, he and his family were kept safe, but the rest of the visible kirk perished because they mocked God and his word. Our whole nation partly mocks the word, partly mocks

[5] See Note 4 above.

[6] I have translated the word 'croce' meaning 'cross' as 'chastening', as I assume Bruce has in mind 'a thorn in the flesh'.

[7] The word translated 'chastening' is here 'wraik' which means literally 'retribution'.

our ministers and partly mocks God's judgments, so that we end up in the same spiritual state as pertained in the days of Noah; yea, for us the situation is even worse because the older this world grows, the more intransigent our unbelief becomes. Therefore, without any doubt, unless you adopt a different attitude and treat these things far more seriously, the hand of God will fall without warning upon our nation. I repeat: the cause of all our evil is our unbelief, that we neither believe God nor his word but mock both, therefore his judgment is bound to overtake us unawares.

Several profitable considerations

To help us in this situation are many profitable considerations, though none of them can be effective without the concurrence of the Holy Spirit. The first of these is for us to consider the nature of God, for there we will find that he has been just from the very beginning. Second, compare that with our own natures and we will find that we have been evil from the very beginning. Must he not therefore punish us? Think also about his word: there is nothing false in any word that he utters. Whatever warnings are pronounced in his Law, never has one jot of them ever fallen to the ground. In the light of this, return to the consideration of ourselves. Shall we perpetually break his law and not be punished? Self-evidently not!

Thirdly, think again about human experience since the beginning of time. Was there ever a single person who indulged himself in sin and escaped punishment? There are countless examples of this in the Scriptures of God: without exception all who delighted in sin were punished. Come to the present day and we find examples of God's wrath being meted out on members of our community who have engaged in wickedness, for God's divine nature does not change.

To sum up, it is not possible for us to escape unless we change course and are saved by grace. These three considerations are very profitable, but also necessary, in that they are appointed outward means to bring us to faith. But what else shall I say other than that nothing is effectual unless the Lord bless these appointed means with the concurrence of his Holy Spirit?

A God-given determination is needed

Alas, the devil comes to us to blind our minds, harden our hearts and persuade us to think that the Spirit's light will never shine upon us, even if it shines on everyone else. So your earnest desire should be (and I keep on telling you this) for the Spirit's light to shine upon you. Whatever may befall you—none of you is irrevocably blind—whoever thinks his blindness is worse than anyone else's is clearly most aware of the Lord's anger over his sin; he realises that it is his own evil that has caused God's hand to be heavy upon him. Therefore he must learn through his distress that if he deliberately continues in his sin, God will deal severely with him.

As society is at present, it is a great repentance for anyone to be resolved to turn away from all wickedness, determined to choose a far better path. The thing is that the Lord will not turn a blind eye to what is wrong, but will pursue us to fulfil his own purposes. Therefore, any of you who may be unbelievers, determine to believe; any who are unrepentant, determine to repent. And wherever such determination is found in someone, it is God himself who has imparted it, and he will bless that determination and save both soul and body for ever.

To continue with the account of Noah, you have heard how the earth was covered in water, and how Noah and his family were saved. Briefly, it was like this: Noah was given notice by the living God of the flood that was going to come. When he heard, Noah was afraid and trembled as if this calamitous act of judgment was imminent. Therefore his reverent fear motivated him to obey God, and it was through his obedience that he was saved. The rest of humanity were also warned, but they rebelled and disregarded the message, thereby provoking God to anger; consequently they were destroyed. The manner of Noah's salvation is set down in this verse 7 in its essential details, so we shall now follow the order in which it is given as I seek to open it up to you.

God's forewarning given to Noah

First, as I perceive in this verse, we have the effect that this information given to him had upon Noah. Second, we shall notice his obedience. Third, I see in this verse to what use and profit this obedience served. Finally, I find the commendation given to Noah, the reward of his faith and recompense of his belief. I shall deal briefly with each of these as God grants me grace and that will complete today's study.

First, then, comes the forewarning of Noah. God committed to him a weighty[8] secret that no angel or human being could have known about. This forewarning came long before the actual time of the event. The texts in Genesis 6, Hebrews 11:7 and 1 Peter 3:20[9] make it clear that Noah's responsibility was to warn others to render them inexcusable, but also to preserve and save his own household.

Before I proceed, I want to make two further points. The first is that there is no secret so deep, so lofty or so great that the Lord will not share it with his servants. He shares with them those secrets concerning both salvation and that final condemnation. Did he not say of Abraham, *Is their anie thing that I sould conceal from Abraham* seeing that I know him so intimately?[10] That applies to all his faithful servants: there are no secrets that God will hide from them, however deep or lofty those secrets may be.

My second point is that we learn that before God strikes, he does not land a blow upon any man (as we say) by coming upon him unawares. He gives to all his laws, so forewarning them in order that his wrath may be turned away. He forewarned Noah, and Noah warned the rest of humanity, but when they refused to repent, then God struck. Do we not read in Amos 3, *The Lord will do nothing vnto the tyme that he first tell his servantis, that they may tell the people*?[11] The Lord invariably forewarns before ever he acts in judgment, leaving us inexcusable.

Obedience and reverence

Then what will be the good we may derive from God's forewarnings? If you pay careful attention to such pronouncements, if indeed they have been given by God, you shall reap great benefits. Consider the obedience and reverence they wrought in Noah who did carefully heed them. God's warnings of impending judgment upon our country ought to produce similar obedience and reverence in us all; if they do then we

[8] Bruce's word is 'heich', literally meaning 'lofty' or 'elevated to a great height', hence 'weighty' or 'of great importance'.

[9] Hebrews 11:7 '…by this he condemned the world'; 1 Peter 3:20 '…when God's patience waited in the days of Noah' (ESV).

[10] Genesis 18:17.

[11] This is an allusion to Amos 3:7 which reads: 'Surely the Lord God wil do nothing, but he reueileth his secret vnto his seruants the Prophetes' (GenB).

are bound to be moved with fear and take his word to heart.

I am referring now to the most holy forewarnings that you could have heard during some particularly sacred time. Otherwise, if you are merely masquerading as his vessels,[12] his warnings will be ignored and simply bypass you. As a result, without any doubt, those sins that increase in spite of his word to you, shall be dealt with in direct proportion to their enormity: the greater the sin, the more severe the punishment! They are far more serious than sins committed in ignorance. Therefore do not ignore those warnings that come to you day after day! It behoves you all to be alert and prepared to bear the Lord's stroke, whatever its nature or form may take, so that in some measure God's Spirit may enable you to learn from it.

Beseech the Lord to sanctify this word to you, that when he sends some chastisement such as he may choose, you may be his submissive children, accepting patiently the discipline his hand administers, and looking from his merciful hands for the way out. His forewarning of his people is a token of God's favour. Therefore, as it comes from his love, learn to accept it as given in love, thanking God that he has prepared you for it.

The patience and benignity of God

We are told that when God forewarned Noah it was *of thingis which war not seine as yit*. He would learn what those events would be at the time God had appointed, namely, he would inform him then of the coming flood and the destruction that would be wrought upon the earth. This was not as yet known; indeed it would not happen for a hundred and twenty years. What does this delay of six score years teach us? Why, when humanity had become so depraved and were clearly deserving of punishment, did God delay for so long? The delay was through the patience and benignity of God, to allure and provoke men to repentance, if at all possible. This patience is extended to us also; how reluctant is the Lord to lose any of us, if by any means in this world we could be won to him.

Learn then this lesson: there is no delay, even if it took ten thousand years, let alone a mere six score of years, no patience or benignity, that could win those who had everything this world can offer to satisfy

[12] See above, Chapter Two, note 3.

them. Even if you preached constantly, there could be no exhortation, admonition or threatening, no torment in body or soul that could ever win such persons. You ask, 'So what could win them?' Oh, be quite sure that no outward attempts will ever achieve even a tiny change in the human heart. It is only when the Lord himself sanctifies your efforts and they concur with the inward working of his Holy Spirit, to bless inwardly the outward means you use, that there can be a change in human hearts. Otherwise no attempts made to win a person will achieve anything. Some judgment falling so heavily upon man that his soul is all but paralysed may produce a superficial temporary repentance, but the only power on earth or in heaven that is able to transform him is that unction that flows from the death of Christ.

The power of the Holy Spirit

Consider the power by which Christ overcame the devil. That is the power that must turn my soul to God, and cause me to detest my sins and repent truly. Then learn this lesson: when you feel the chastening hand of God upon either your body or your soul, you ought to pray, 'Lord, sanctify to me this affliction, this experience you have sent, this delay of your relief to me; may your Holy Spirit do his work inwardly in me, as plainly as your word is heard outwardly, that my heart may be converted to obey you.' Not just once, but as often as you recognise the hand of God upon you, you ought to pray, 'Lord, make this visitation a blessing to me; however it may be that I have brought this malediction upon myself on account of my sinful actions, for Christ's sake use as the means whereby your Holy Spirit applies your correction inwardly in my heart.' In short, there is nothing that can soften a hard heart except the Lord's concurrence with his inward power. So much then for that inward work of the Holy Spirit.

Faith was the first effect of God's forewarning

The apostle now proceeds to let us see two effects that this warning[13] from God brought about in Noah. The first was faith. If Noah had received this information from some other source, it would not have greatly concerned him. But we read that *by faith he was moved with rev-*

[13] Bruce's word is 'adverteisment', which in 16th century Scots means either 'warning' or simply 'information'.

erence.[14] As soon as he heard that God was going to destroy the world, even though it would not be for another six score years, he was moved by fear and great reverence as if the destruction was just about to take place. As for the rest of the people, they scorned and mocked, and considered him nothing but a fool. Nevertheless, his heart feared and trembled at the prospect.

Thus we see the effect that God's word has when it is sanctified and delivered to anyone with his blessing: it will always result in reverent fear. This is true especially of his warnings that are intended to restrain our corruption. For if there is neither fear nor reverence of God, a man would run headlong driven by his own desires, but this fear acts as a bridle upon our sinful natures, holding us back from many a wrong turning into which our fallen natures would entice us.[15] Therefore God's threatening is his sovereign medicine to treat our inward corruption.

The effect that the word of God produces in a man's heart is quite wonderful, not least in Noah: seeing that the coming judgment was still so far off, yet this man feared as if it was actually taking place. Here is an example of one the chief properties of justifying faith—being sure of things that are not seen, as if they are present and able to be seen by our physical sight; you heard it described in the first verse: *the euidence of things which are not sene*. Can you see how Noah is putting into practice this property of faith? He grasped what the judgment meant as surely as if he was witnessing it being enacted. Although it was only present in his mind, his apprehension found expression in his obedience; therefore, *moved with reverence he makis and prepared the Arke*. His outward obedience flowed from his inward reverence.

Obedience is the second effect of God's forewarning

When we consider carefully the circumstances, it was a massive task that he had to undertake to build the ark at such a time, and it was a singular testimony to this man's obedience. One hundred years is some length of time for the task, and it must at times have been wearisome.

[14] Hebrews 11:7, 'By faith Noah… in reverent fear…' (ESV).

[15] There appears to be an echo of Calvin here in his Second Use of the Law: 'The second function of the law is this: at least by fear of punishment to restrain certain men… not because their inner mind is stirred or affected, but because, being bridled, so to speak, they keep their hands from outward activity, and hold inside the depravity that otherwise they would have wantonly indulged.' *Inst.* 2.7.10.

But it behoved it to be wearisome, because the whole populace was scorning and laughing at him and thinking his mind must be confused. But those who mocked him did not know, nor could they know, the secret purposes of God. That was why they considered him the greatest of fools. Yet he held fast to his own opinions although no one else shared them; indeed, the whole world contradicted what he said. Yet, notwithstanding their mockery, he adhered steadfastly to his plans and continued with his building work. Over all these years, he persevered until he completed his task.

Think, was his not a strong faith? And was not construction of the ark a singular demonstration of his obedience? So what do we learn from this? We learn that unless Noah had believed the word that was spoken to him, he could never have embarked on this task he had been given. Clearly then, his obedience was completely dependent upon his faith. Do you believe God's word? If you do, you are bound to obey him. How is belief gotten? Well, how did Noah get such faith? He got it through hearing the word of God.

Third, the use and profit his obedience served

The third point in this verse is, to what end Noah's obedience served him? What advantage or profit did he gain through obeying God? His obedience served him in three different ways. First, his obedience in building the ark confirmed his doctrine, in that what he taught by word of mouth he confirmed by what he did. Just as by his words he assured the people and warned them of the destruction that was to come, so by his actions he also warned them in that he was preparing a means of safety for himself. Thus his first profit in making the ark was that it affirmed his doctrine.

Here is a lesson for those who are teachers: we must teach by what we do as well as by what we say, otherwise our teaching is worthless. This applies to us all. If your actions do not concur with your words, then you discredit more by what you do than what you build up by your words. Therefore, just as Noah, the preacher of righteousness, taught the people by both deed and word, so all our pastors ought to ensure that their words are confirmed by their actions. They themselves must have good testimonies, and God's approval in their consciences. However others may try to slander them, pastors should never give any cause for slander. Indeed, ultimately our actions speak far louder than our words.

The second advantage to Noah in building the ark was that it served as the means of saving his household from the flood. In other words, obedience brings salvation. Of necessity, obedience must come before salvation. For first we must do the will of God, and afterwards we shall receive his promises. You have already heard this in Hebrews 10:36: *For ye haue need of pacience, that after ye haue done the wil of God, ye might receiue the promes.* Well-doing must precede salvation.

Peter tells us how many persons there were in his family; there were only eight souls in his entire household, and one of the eight was a worthless fellow, Ham by name. Notwithstanding, he too was safe in the ark because he was in the company of Noah. See, then, the benefit of being in the company of a good and holy man. In such company we partake of both temporal and spiritual blessings.

We must notice also that there were only eight persons in the ark, which is a type of the kirk of God.[16] What do we learn from this? It lets us see that the number of true believers is not many; nonetheless, we cannot ever know the exact number of the invisible kirk, nor must we try to find out. You may ask, 'Does this teach us then that there are only eight elect believers?' Certainly not! Rather, we learn that large numbers are never a mark of the invisible kirk, and that we cannot know the true kirk by its outward appearance, strength, power or nobility, but only by its faith and holiness. So she must be holy, as God himself is holy, in all her conduct and behaviour. The ark, then, was built for the safety[17] of Noah's household. Pay heed, therefore, to the objective of faith: by faith we believe unto salvation through the blood of Jesus Christ. So our salvation is one of the special objectives of faith; Noah believed and was saved. When you also believe you will be saved. So much, then, for the second use whereunto the building of the ark served Noah.

There is yet a third use that is given in this same verse 7: *By the quhilk ark* (says the apostle) *he condemned the world.* That means that by constructing the ark he rendered the world inexcusable. For when the populace saw him preparing for the flood, if anything could have

[16] 1 Peter 3:20-21.

[17] In the context, Bruce's word 'saiftie' could have been translated as 'salvation'. See the next few sentences.

moved them, this should have done. He was so resolute in this task, they ought to have recognised that in his heart Noah was totally convinced. Over the years he continued steadfastly in the building work. It was his unwavering purpose that made them inexcusable.

For us, the point is this: the upright living of godly persons ought to bring the godless to glorify our Father in heaven,[18] otherwise it only serves to condemn them. Therefore, do not ignore the upright living of others around you, rather strive to imitate their example that you may be like them,[19] in so far as God grants you grace. Do not imitate the wicked of this world, for then the upright behaviour of the children of God shall condemn you. So much for the third use.

The recompense of faith

In the final part of the verse we have set down the recompense that Noah received, when it says that *he was maid here of that richteosnes quhilk is by faith.*[20] There can be no doubt that Noah had as great a faith of any of the Fathers who lived before him. For first he had the whole world opposed to him, and surely that must have been a sore trial. He was engaged in building the ark day after day, year after year, while the rest of humanity were idly pleasing themselves; therefore, when the worldwide catastrophe came, he and his whole family were saved. Then second, the strength of his faith can be seen in that he was to be saved in such an extraordinary manner, buried in the ark, as it were, in a kind of grave. Consequently, the benefit bestowed on him as recompense was that *he was maid here of that richteosnes quhilk is by faith.*

There is one kind of justification that comes through works, but another kind that comes through faith. The former is unattainable because not one of us is righteous in or of ourselves; therefore it is only through faith that we can be justified. The justification by faith is gratuitously given; by it Noah entered the kingdom of heaven. Justification by works causes a man to glory in himself, as if he had succeeded in achieving complete righteousness. The justification by faith causes me to deplore myself, because in me is no righteousness. Because righteousness is found only in God through Christ, I myself am humbled

[18] Matthew 5:16.
[19] 2 Thessalonians 3:7, 9; Hebrews 13:7.
[20] '[He] became an heir of the righteousness that comes by faith' (ESV).

and brought low, thus henceforth I am able to rejoice in the everlasting God. This all flows from Christ's righteousness, wrought during his earthly life, and it is his righteousness that is imputed to us and counted as ours. I believe that his righteousness shall clothe me, so that, covered by his righteousness, I shall be counted as righteous.

Just as Noah was saved and counted righteous, so every one of you must receive this gift of faith, whereby you may have the assurance in your hearts that you also are covered by the righteousness of Christ. On that final Day, will you be justified by your works and merits? By no means! Any works that are not of faith, and come under the scrutiny of God's justice, will be found to stink,[21] whereas the works that arise from faith are accepted by the Lord through his mercy. Then accuse your own merits of their worthlessness, despair of your self-righteousness and seek only Christ's righteousness. Strive after faith that you may believe, and have the assurance that God will impute Christ's righteousness to you. The only assurance of justification is in Jesus Christ.

Assurance comes through faith, so that our souls know that when we stand before him, through his holiness we shall be counted holy. Therefore, this must be the great aim of every Christian. All those who long to do what is right, to mend their behaviour and yearn to enter the kingdom of heaven, they shall be blessed with faith. But those who do no good, nor have any desire to do good, they are children of the devil and remain his slaves. Those who hunger and thirst after righteousness, their souls shall be satisfied. So examine your hearts that you may be persuaded of Christ's righteousness, assuming, that is, that the desire is there. If you do have that desire, but do not yet have the assurance that is the second stage of the righteousness by faith, but have only reached the first stage of believing, the Lord himself will nourish your faith, and you must earnestly look to him to do that for you.[22]

[21] Isaiah 64:6, 'But we haue all bene as an vncleane thig & all our richteousnes is as filthy cloutes' (GenB).

[22] What Bruce has been saying here in 1591 anticipates the teaching of the Westminster Confession of Faith, finalized in 1647, Chapter XIV, *Of Saving Faith*, paragraph III: 'This faith is different in degrees, weak or strong… growing up in many ways of a full assurance through Christ.' Assurance is not explicitly dealt with until Chapter XVIII, *Of Assurance of Grace and Salvation*.

Conclusion

From this whole verse, I want finally to gather up four brief lessons. The first is that the Lord judges no man until first he has been called and has heard the call. The second is that the calling of God to sinners is not effectual in all who hear, for it has one effect on some and another effect on others; on some greater, but on others less. In Noah, God's call brought forth reverence and obedience; but in the world, it brought forth only mockery and contempt. What is the cause of this? It is not that God purposes it this way. It is that the corruption of human nature produces the mockery and contempt. Paul tells us that God's calling is for some *the savour of lyfe vnto lyfe*, but for others it is the *savour of death vnto death*.[23]

The third point is this: every Christian, whether a working man or someone of high rank, ought to be a clear witness before the whole world by both his deeds and his words; he ought to communicate the message by the way he lives and by what he says. My fourth point is that all those who cast in their lot with Christ shall at the end be partakers of his righteousness. Therefore, so this may be your experience, pledge yourselves now to live that new life and repent of all your past sins. The Lord in his mercy do his work within you, and may his Holy Spirit concur to make these words of mine effectual in every one of you, for the sake of Christ Jesus, his Son. To whom with the Father and the Holy Ghost be all honour, praise and glory now and for ever. Amen.

[23] 2 Corinthians 2:16.

Chapter Eight

Hebrews Chapter 11 verse 8

> [8] *By faith Abrahame quhen he was called obeyed God to go out into ane place whiche he sould afterward receave for ane inheritance, and he went out not knowing whither he went.*

You have already heard—as God gave me grace—brethren, well-beloved in Christ Jesus, of the faith of some who lived before the Flood, examples of the most notable of the Fathers. There was Abel, then Enoch and then Noah; you heard how each of these by faith alone came into repute and esteem with the Prince of all princes and the living God. While they lived on earth, each of them was praised and commended, and on account of their faith were blessed and rewarded both in this life and in the life to come.

Reminder of the four points regarding Noah

The last of the Fathers before the Flood was Noah, and those who were present should remember his example. We noted four points regarding him. (Your memories ought to be sanctified for these studies so that I should not have to keep repeating myself!) First, there was the announcement that came as a forewarning that the God of heaven would destroy the earth. Second, there was Noah's obedience to this message he received from the Lord. Third, we noted how his obedience benefited him. Finally, we saw the reward of Noah's faith and obedience.

First, the forewarning given to Noah

Consider again the forewarning. Before ever the Lord caused that great Flood to cover the whole earth, he first revealed his intention to Noah, so that Noah would warn others. Thus God's severity was in no way comprised when, before he acted, men were given due notice of his purpose. This is always what he does, for before ever the Lord strikes a particular person, nation, country or even the world, he gives due warning, thus leaving that person, city or country without excuse. No one ever perishes without the Lord of heaven first warning him through his conscience, thus rendering him inexcusable.

Therefore, we must all take heed, for the Lord has many different kinds of 'preachers' to warn us. He does not always use the spoken word, nor does he always use some human agency to awaken us to our need. He may use either animate or inanimate means to act as his servants, but in some way or other your conscience will convict you before ever his judgment falls. Therefore have the insight to perceive what comes as a messenger to you from the living God, and have faith to believe and obedience to respond.

When he does forewarn us, he is not hasty. (I want to dwell again on this.) In Noah's day he gave the world six score years' respite for repentance. He sent men to warn them; he declared his word to them; he gave the instructions for the building of the ark as a way of admonishing them. Today, he may give us a visible example of his judgment by striking down someone who is a neighbour, or more publicly, an eminent citizen, but never without in some way first forewarning them. Yet when his 'messenger' warns them, what do they do but scorn, deride and mock his impending judgment? Yet his hand will strike them before they see it coming.

There is no outward warning that renders a man wise. No, there is not any outward judgment on body or soul, nor affliction of flesh, nor torment of conscience, that can make any of us wise, unless the Lord of heaven sanctifies to our hearts the trouble, affliction or admonition, and by the power of his Holy Spirit works in us reverence and obedience. Otherwise, all his chastening is in vain, and the more he afflicts us the harder our hearts become. A man may be temporarily bewildered by the Lord's affliction visited upon him, but there can be no genuine contrition in his heart if the Holy Spirit has not concurred with the chastening.

Everyone of us at times experiences God's hand heavily upon us in a manner we cannot avoid; then we must either follow God and accept the cross he lays upon us, or else we will follow the devil's path to even greater suffering. Therefore, seeing that afflictions are common to us all, crave the living God that he would sanctify them (not everyone experiences the Lord's hand in that way), for that is a very special blessing from our merciful God through Christ. Then your heart will be turned to praise and magnify his holy name.

Second, Noah's obedience

Noah obeyed God because he believed him. He recognised that God does not threaten us as if he were a mouse![1] He believed the warnings were genuine, and in that faith he obeyed God and made preparations for his family and himself. What leads to such obedience? Nothing but faith, for if you do not accept his word, you will not obey him. So how does anyone come to have such faith? Noah heard what God was saying, and hearing, he feared God and obeyed him. Therefore, faith comes by hearing.[2] That is the normal way by which faith is engendered in us.

Third, the outcome of obedience

My third point last time was how Noah's obedience benefited him. We saw that there were three outcomes[3] from the scores of years that it took to build the ark. First, building the ark served to provide safety for both his family and himself. Not only did he obtain by his obedience immunity for himself from the flood, but also for his entire household. Happy is that home that has a good head, and blessed is the household whose master is godly, for such a master will cause the entire family to be partakers of both temporal and spiritual blessings. Those of you present who are heads of your home take heed that you sanctify yourselves and your families.

Second, this outcome of the construction of the ark also served to affirm Noah's teaching of his children. As by his words he taught them that the flood would come, so by his building work he also assured

[1] This rather unexpected simile, 'woud not threat in mous' was used figuratively of weak, ineffective words or actions.

[2] Romans 10:17, 'So faith comes from hearing, and hearing through the word of Christ.'

[3] Bruce constantly uses the word 'vse' i.e. 'use', which in Scots generally means 'purpose', 'aim' or 'outcome'.

them that what he said was true. Then note carefully that those who teach should do so not only by their words, but also by their actions. Our doctrine must be confirmed by our deeds, for since our message renders our hearers without excuse, so our lives should also convict the consciences of those who hear us.

The third outcome of Noah's obedience in building the ark was that it served to render the entire world inexcusable, for it condemned their unbelief. They had six score of years to witness his prolonged work of construction, and during that time they ought to have prepared themselves for the coming disaster as they watched Noah preparing for it. Therefore, seeing that they procrastinated and prevaricated over so many years, they were justly declared to be inexcusable.

Fourth, the reward of obedience

My fourth point last time[4] was the reward of Noah's faith and obedience. That reward was that the Lord of heaven made him a partaker of the righteousness and justification of Jesus Christ. It surely is a great benefit for a wicked man, a sinful creature defiled with iniquity and unrighteousness in himself, to be made partaker in Christ's righteousness. It was on account of his obedience that issued from his faith, that he was justified by the high and heavenly righteousness of Christ Jesus. It was not on account of his works, but only on account of his faith. He believed God to be true, merciful, good and mighty, and so was justified by faith, not by his deeds. No human being can, nor ever will, partake of that heavenly justice by what he does.

There are two justifications. There is a perfect righteousness procured by fulfilling the whole law, as if it were ever possible for anyone to do that! If perchance someone did flawlessly attain that standard of perfection, then that person would have every reason to glory in their flesh. But since our fallen natures are incurably corrupt, it is obvious that no person can ever reach that standard of perfection. Thus there only remains the second justification, one that is procured only by faith; there is no other way to be declared righteous. Believe in the promises of mercy and salvation, and you shall be righteous by Christ's righteousness; it is a perfect and heavenly righteousness, indeed, it is the very righteousness of God.

[4] Again he says 'yisternicht'. See Chapter 3, Note 1 above.

Suppose you submit the justice of the mighty God to a legal investigation,[5] you will find its perfection incontrovertible. Put this the other way round: no human righteousness can ever be found guiltless before the investigation of the Mighty God; the divine righteousness stands unimpeachable, however meticulously you examine the case. It is of necessity by faith alone in this impeccable divine righteousness that a person is made a partaker in his justice to the end of attaining everlasting life. Does this fourth outcome of the reward of obedience not commend faith more than sufficiently?

What more do I need to say to commend to you the faith that leads to heavenly righteousness? Only this: surely you should pray more and more every day so that, by one means or another, you can declare to the world that this precious jewel of faith has its dwelling and lodging in your soul. Together with this prayer we should also constantly beseech the living God that he would pour down upon us more drops of grace and mercy, so that our regeneration may progress and daily take us forward in our spiritual lives.

The Fathers after the Flood

Having done with the Fathers before the Flood, the apostle now proceeds logically to those Fathers who lived after the Flood. He will deal with four very special men whose names bespeak gravitas and authority. They all lived before the Law was given: Abraham, Isaac, Jacob and Joseph. These notable men are the Fathers of the Jews, and although the first three are common to both Jew and Gentile, they may properly be regarded as chief among the Jews.

Abraham the father of the faithful

The apostle begins with Abraham, and with good reason. In the Scriptures, God gives this honour to Abraham that he is counted as 'the father of the faithful',[6] and set forth as a mirror of faith, a pattern and example. We find Moses set forth as a mirror of meekness,[7] David as a mirror of magnanimity[8] which is desirable in kings, and Job as a mirror

[5] As a trained lawyer, Bruce loves to draw his imagery from the practices of the highest courts of law in the land.

[6] Romans 4:16; Galatians 3:7, 9.

[7] Numbers 12:3.

[8] 2 Samuel 9:1-11.

of patience.[9] So now we have Abraham set forth as a mirror of faith to all believers who come after him. Why is he given this pre-eminent position? Because in his deeds and works is displayed the whole nature of faith; there is no other mortal in Scripture who exhibits faith as Abraham does, in so many ways and to such great effect.

Lastly, the Jews themselves made great boast of him, glorying in him; they would have him known as their Father, and nothing less than this satisfied them. Therefore the apostle puts him first and gives more space to him than to any other of the Fathers, perhaps to see if his readers were worthy to be called Abraham's sons. So much, then, for the order of these four who lived before the Law was given.

I do not now intend to go through all the verses that I have just read.[10] Rather I think that today it will be sufficient for me by God's grace to deal only with verse 8. However, in each verse that we read together, we find Abraham praised and commended to us on account of three noteworthy effects of his faith. First, he is praised because of his ready obedience to respond to the calling of the living God; we have that in verse 8: *By faith Abrahame quhen he was called obeyed God.* Next, we have him commended for staying in the land to which he been called. Thirdly, he is commended on account of the lifestyle he adopted as he lived in that land. Notice also that in verse 8 is added the reason why he continued to sojourn in that land.

The circumstances of Abraham's call

We shall now begin by dealing with the commendation of his ready obedience to the call of the living God—indeed, from the very first time that God called him. So that we may perceive how great his faith was in his obedience, we shall note the circumstances of the occasion when he was called. I am referring to his condition when God called him, and the nature of the command that came to him. It is implied that by religion he was an idolater, begotten and born of idolaters, living in an idolatrous country without any knowledge of God. As the biblical account tells us, his age at this time was three score years and

[9] James 5:11, 'Ye haue heard of the paciéce of Job' (GenB).

[10] The obvious implication, hinted at a moment later, is that he had read verses 8 to 19.

fifteen,[11] he was already married though he had no children, and apparently his own plan had been to stay with his parents and friends for the rest of his life. So much for his circumstances.

However, in comes the living God with his command, notwithstanding that at that time he was immersed in idolatry, had been married for many years and was quite content to live out his life where he had been born and brought up. But now God bids him arise and move towards a different calling and lifestyle, and for an altogether different occupation[12] to that to which he had been accustomed. The command must have appeared very demanding; beyond question, it was difficult to both flesh and blood. It is all there in the Book of Genesis: the Lord commands him to leave first his own land and native soil; secondly to leave his father's house, his family and friends; thirdly he commands him to take a long, long journey.[13]

God's call to Abraham

Now think! What can be sweeter to any earthly man, to flesh and blood, than all these things, notwithstanding the Lord's command to leave everything? 'Go out' (says he), 'and leave your own land.' It is as if the Lord is saying that he knows when Abraham reflects upon his own land that the prospect of leaving it will be extremely painful; nevertheless, leave it he must! God is saying, 'I know that when you think about your own people and country, the devil will cast it up to stop you from obeying me; your father's house and your family, they too will be obsta-

[11] Genesis 12:4; see also 16:3, 16.

[12] The word I have translated 'occupation' is *exerceis*; it also can have the connotation of 'family worship', and it is probable that Bruce wants to imply that as well as just 'occupation', the religion to which Abraham is being called would include his entire life, that is, the God he was to serve as well as the way he was to maintain his wife and family.

[13] The whole of the next section is, in my view, coloured by Bruce's own experience when in 1581 he resolved to study theology and prepare for Christian ministry at St Andrews University. His mother, a devout Roman Catholic, opposed his decision and insisted he give up his considerable annual income 'from some lands I was infeft in [heritable property with which he had been endowed]'. MacNicol, p. 28. However, Sir Alexander Bruce of Airth's name is recorded in the 'sederunt' of the General Assembly of August 1590 as a commissioner for the Presbytery of Stirling (Shaw, p. 904). Evidently, Bruce's father had become resigned to his son's calling.

cles to your obedience. Yet leave everything, and do as I command!'

There is more. Where he is to go the Lord never says, not a single word regarding the country or the place; he merely says, 'Go to the place that I shall show you.' God leaves this man in great uncertainty concerning the place, and the various particulars that natural reason would crave to know and would have sought out. He simply says, 'Wait upon me, go to the place I shall show you.' It is as if he is saying, 'Do not demand an indenture[14] from me; in due course you will find all your questions answered.'

Notwithstanding the hardness of this command, the great uncertainty as to the destination and the provision for his needs when he arrived there—and this is the cardinal factor in it all—Abraham did leave his own country, not knowing where in the world he was going! He depended entirely upon the guidance of the living God, that he would lead him in this journey as he considered most meet for his glory. Because he went forth trusting in the protection[15] of God is why his peregrination is so highly praised. Even though there have been many pilgrimages in the world since Abraham made his, yet there has never been a single one as renowned as his, for no other pilgrimage arose from such a command, or led to such a blessed outcome.

There was never yet anyone who instituted some expedition, knowing neither why nor where he was going. Travellers usually have some idea of their destination and the accommodation that will be available when they arrive; they also have some idea why it is they are going. Moreover, most travellers go looking for physical benefit and enjoyment, or else to learn something about the country they are going to in the hopes of being able to acquire some wealth they can take back home with them. Others may set out to avoid the punishment of the law of their own land, or else to escape some problem or other. But there was never a man set out on a journey to another country who was not motivated by one or other of such reasons.

Not so with Abraham. He was not moved by any of these reasons,

[14] Bruce constantly uses this kind of legal terminology; an 'indenture' was a comprehensive binding 'contract that bound an apprentice to a master craftsman'.

[15] Bruce's word is 'warrand' and, as well as meaning 'protection' or 'security', it can also have the connotation of 'authorization' or 'authority'; in other contexts it can simply mean 'warrant'.

nor was he driven by any such ambitions. He went looking only to the living God and, depending entirely upon his word, he committed all the particulars to him. So much, then, for the explanation of the first action taken by Abraham.

Three points regarding Abraham's call

I now come in this discourse to the three points I am asking you to mark. The first is the mercy of God in calling him, the second is his ready obedience to that call in spite of all the impediments, and the third is the nature of the faith that holds fast to the authority of God's word, grasping it as the guiding light and steering rudder before ever a single step is taken.

First, the mercy of God towards Abraham

With very good reason we now consider the mercy of God, so that you all may apply that same mercy to yourselves. For the calling of God to Abraham did not come to a righteous or holy man, but to someone immersed in idolatry, guilty both in particular and in general of all the curses upon soul and body contained in the whole law. Yet, notwithstanding, God intervened with his undeserved mercy and grace, for this man who was heading straight towards damnation was snatched away from this pestiferous[16] course, and led into the way that leads to life everlasting. He was guided and directed by the merciful hand of God along the pathway that leads to life. He saw the nature of mercy more clearly: the wonder of mercy expanded in his heart and the experience of mercy ravished him, so that the loss of all temporal things was as nothing.

What moved God to call him? Was it anything in Abraham? No! What could an idolater ever deserve? Therefore, the Lord was moved to call him out of his mercy, for out of his mercy whom he wills he saves, and out of his justice whom he wills he hardens.[17] Then thank God for your calling. Take careful note and remember when it was that in his mercy it pleased him to call you, and make you aware of your sin. Note the date when he spoke to you and you will realise that the Lord's

[16] Bruce's word 'pestiferous' (uncommon though still in use today) means 'corrupting', or 'causing some contagious illness'.

[17] Exodus 9:12; 10:1; Romans 9:14-18.

calling found you neither holy nor righteous, but of all his creatures most detestable, following some pathway or other of wickedness. Then praise the mercy of God for your calling, and by doing good seek to adorn it.

We return again to Abraham's ready obedience. When he was called by grace, you can see how hard the call must have been, and how difficult was God's command. If he had debated rationally with himself, or sought the opinion of his father or mother or any of his family, what decision do you think he would have reached?[18] No doubt his own reasoning would have dissuaded him from undertaking such a perilous journey, and likewise his father, mother and the rest of the family would have persuaded him not to go.

Then what is the lesson for us? When God calls, do not consult flesh and blood. When God bids you to redirect your life, that is no time to apply human reasoning to his command, and I will tell you why. Although in one way you appear to be self-contained as a person, there are nonetheless two separate aspects to your personality: there is the Spirit in you, but there is also the flesh. Let me explain what I mean. Now that he has called you, the living God has changed you by the work of his Holy Spirit; his Spirit is now within you. However, still within you are the remnants of that foul slime you have had since your birth, for you are a child of Adam; those remnants I call the 'flesh'. Will you then seek the advice of the flesh? Even though it is God who is calling you to step out at his command, the flesh will seek to persuade to stay where you are. Just as the flesh will want its own glory, ease and comfort, so the Spirit will seek God's glory and the bounties of his kingdom. In other words, the Spirit will give you sound counsel.

However, all too often the Spirit is weaker[19] than the flesh, so that the flesh prevails. Even in the regenerate man the counsel of the flesh is very often followed. If it was the other way round and the flesh was weaker, then the Spirit of God would undoubtedly prevail and persuade that man. When the corrupt praise of men prevails, it has a much

[18] When God's call came to Bruce, his mother adamantly refused her approval, and it appears his father was against him also, though ultimately he gave reluctant approval. See note 13 above.

[19] The Spirit is 'weaker' inasmuch as the flesh often dominates a person's cognition, emotions and volition.

stronger influence in a man's heart than the influence of the Spirit. That is why whenever I hear that a person whom God is calling sought the counsel of flesh and blood, it is always the same—the flesh persuaded that person to disobey God. And to disobey him will always bring some tangible judgment upon the body in this life, and after death the eternal damnation of both soul and body.

Further, I grant that the Lord may work in extraordinary ways, for if such persons repent and beg restoration to the Lord's calling, in his mercy he does preserve them. But he does not just let them off, so to speak, but he will appoint them to follow some course of instruction, in order that they might learn the lesson of obedience. Undoubtedly, the Lord's 'school' will administer extremely severe discipline. It will reduce a man to a kind of death, and he may find himself dangled over the flames of hell, until at last he is subdued and is ready truly to say, 'Lord, here I am!' This principle, therefore, is true: following the desires and dictates of the flesh will either bring upon a person the Lord's mercy in some painful chastening, or else it will lead to eternal loss. For as, on the one hand, obedience pleases the Lord, so, on the other hand, disobedience has inescapable consequences.

Jonah, an example of disobedience

I shall now give you an example of this principle in the person of Jonah. As you have heard in the account from Scripture, Jonah was given the difficult commission of going to Nineveh. Not following the example of Abraham, what did he do? He considered within himself, with his own wit and reason (I have termed this 'with flesh and blood'). What did his reason say to him? 'Have you not seen that God has been gracious in a matter far greater than this—his patience and longsuffering towards the Israelites themselves? If he was merciful to them, how much more will he be merciful to these untaught people, who have never been afforded the opportunity to embrace his promise of mercy?' His reasoning persuaded him that God would end up shaming him, making him appear to be a liar, and so would cause him great embarrassment.

Once persuaded of this in himself, he boarded the ship, thinking he could escape God's hand on his life, and so avoid the difficult commission. But meanwhile, there was something worrying away at the back of his mind, and he was anxious to try and forget his rebellion and get it right out of his system. Then you recall how he sought refuge in sleep, no doubt to rid his memory of disobedience to God. Therefore, you young men, take heed when you attempt to rid yourselves of some unwelcome memory, that you do not find an inward accuser lurking in your bosom. If you sin, respond to the biting sensation in your conscience, that urges you to awaken and return Jesus Christ. Cry out to him, 'peccavi',[20] and amend your life.

To come to my purpose, Jonah was sleeping, doubtless to forget the pain of his remorse. But the Lord had no intention of losing him and so he pursued him, and sent two 'messengers' to arouse him, the storm and his conscience; together these two awakened him from his sleep. Then the Lord arranged for the lot to be taken, causing it to fall on him, and in this way he cornered him. No doubt at this, Jonah's conscience was in as great a rage as the sea. He recognised that the hand of God was heavily upon him, and so he burst out into his confession, and admitted that he was sinning by fleeing from God. The result was that he was cast out of the ship, and by this death the Lord brought him to life.

I bring you this example to let you see what it is to follow the counsel of flesh and blood, bringing with it, as it does, the high price of death. Yet the Lord delivered him from death in the sea and brought him to the shore, and there he commissioned him for the second time. And what he would not do the first time, now that he had been disciplined in God's 'school', he willingly obeyed. No longer did he consult with his own reason as he did before, but like Abraham, he pressed forward without questioning. When the Lord commands so forcibly, then a man must obey.

Here is the lesson for us: those who have been called of God, when God's word comes to you bidding you to make some change in your life, make sure you do not fall back upon your own wisdom. Do not turn to a friend for advice, unless he has the Spirit of God in some measure, and will encourage you to follow the calling of the living God; otherwise, seek no counsel elsewhere. But as Abraham by faith overcame all impediments that flesh and blood can cast before a man, so too you shall find the way through. There is no doubt that Abraham had come to know God through his mercy and love, otherwise he would never have so unconditionally trusted himself to him, nor travelled (as

[20] Latin for 'I have sinned'.

we say) so far from home.[21] Now that he knows the divine mercy, love and favour, he commits into God's hands his soul, life, body and all future provisions for himself and his family.

What will bring men to obey and trust God? Nothing but the experience of his mercy. Have you at any time in the past had experience of the love of God towards you, some deliverance he has brought you when you were in some trial? Carefully register that experience in your mind, so that you may say to yourself, 'This God has always loved me and been merciful to me, therefore I commit to him my life and all my future needs both now and for the life to come. Because I am assured that he loves me and will be merciful to me, I will obey him.' Thus you see that the greatest spur we have for obeying God is our previous experiences of his love and mercy.

Second, Abraham's obedience

The second point that is worthy of note in this account of Abraham is his obedience. We find him refusing to do three things: first, he sought no counsel from flesh and blood; second, he did not ask God for an indenture,[22] that is, he did not demand from God an explanation of all the particulars as he faced great uncertainty regarding his future; third, nor did he say to God, 'What is there in this for me?' We do not find him questioning God either about the nature of the place he was going to, or the customs of the people there, or his provisions for the journey, or some place to live when he arrived there. If his dealings had been with some man, it would have been folly not to have asked all these questions. But because Abraham had to do with the living God, he was satisfied with the general instructions, and left all the particular details to his merciful and fatherly providence, which by now he had experienced.

Here is a most important lesson. When God asks you to do an about turn, do not try to enter into an indenture[23] with him, so that

[21] At this point, Bruce adds in parentheses ('as we say'). The words that I have translated 'so far from home' are 'bruntlie afeild'; while 'afield' means 'away from home', I could not track down any meaning for the word 'bruntlie'. It would appear, therefore, that 'bruntlie afeild' was some colloquial expression, hence his interjection ('as we say').

[22] See note 14 above.

[23] See note 14 above.

you have a full account of every detail. He has already told you, *Seik me kingdome first* (that is, obey me) *and all vther thingis sall be cast in to thee.*[24] So when some command comes from the Father, put your trust in him and leave all the details to his merciful providence. The more trust you put in God, the better shall be his provision for you. Whereas if you do not wholly trust him, but try to prise from him answers to your various questions, the further will you lag behind him, and the less blessing shall you have. Learn, then, to follow the call of God while trusting implicitly and unquestioningly upon his providence, as Abraham did.

Third, faith depends wholly upon the word of God

Before I dismiss you, there remains the third point about the call of Abraham. Notwithstanding that this man was ready and willing to set out on this journey, yet he did not obey mindlessly, but before he took one single step, he had been given the authorisation out of the very mouth of God. That meant that he had the living word like a lantern shining before him and shedding light upon his pathway.

I have already told you that when God bids you redirect your way, all difficulties will ultimately be overcome. I would not want you ever to be so rash as to embark on some enterprise until God so instructs you. Faith leans upon the word of God, therefore it will do nothing until out of his own mouth faith is given the warrant to begin. No, not out of the mouth of some ruler, prince or even an angel, only out of the mouth of God. So from the moment a man is given that warrant,[25] no impediment can stand in his way, all obstacles will be surmounted, and he will direct his way as he has been commanded.

A great enterprise must have a very clear warrant.[26] Though Abraham's command might have appeared far-fetched and unbelievable to flesh and blood, we likewise must always have the clear authorisation that he had, so that there may be no questioning in our consciences, nor any doubts, that the Lord will bless us. So only act when your conscience is clear that God's written word is bidding you make some move. Of course, at times our consciences may be ill-informed, and the

[24] Matthew 6:33 (GenB).
[25] See note 15 above.
[26] See note 15 above.

flesh in us may be strong and the Spirit weak; then the devil can cast before us a hundred delusions, and so blind our mind's eyes. Therefore in some important matter, we ought always to test our warrant, until our consciences are satisfied by God's word; we must be able to say, 'Even though this is absurd and incredible to the world, yet I have all the warrant I need'. This is not only the prayer of us who are ministers, who have been given in the mercy of God this commission to bring his word to you, but it is a warning to all, whoever you may be, not to meddle in any great matter without an equally clear warrant. A warrant, authorised by God's word, will commission both the one to whom it is given and the work to be undertaken.

Here I rest my case, and in concluding I remind you of the three points. Remember that the calling of God comes to us when we are unclean, unrighteous and doing ill; therefore thank God for his calling and strive to adorn it with good works. Next, when God bids you make some important change in your life, do not seek counsel from flesh and blood, do not demand an indenture from him so you can be satisfied with every particular, but commit all to his gracious providence and step forward. Thirdly, embark upon no great work without a great warrant, so that your warrant may sustain you. Learn these three lessons and your daily study of them shall not prove unprofitable. The Lord in his mercy concur by his Holy Spirit so that this word I have delivered may profit you to his everlasting glory and our everlasting salvation, through the righteous merits of Christ. To whom with the Father and the Holy Ghost be all honour, praise and glory, now and evermore. Amen.

Chapter Nine

Hebrews Chapter 11 verses 11-12

[11] Through faith Sara also received strength to conceave seid, and was delivered of ane child when sche was past age, because sche judged him faithfull quho had promised. [12] And theirfoir sprang their of ane, even of ane who was dead, so manie as the staris of the sky in multitude and as the sand of the sea schoire quhilk is innumberable.

Brethren and well-beloved, you have already heard that the apostle, for two specific reasons, praised the faith of Abraham. First, he praised his faith because of his willing obedience to respond to an extremely difficult calling; second, he praised his faith on account of his receiving and embracing an extremely hard promise.

Three Points about Abraham's calling

As to the calling, the Lord told him to leave absolutely everything and all that is appealing to flesh and blood—his native land, his parents, his friends and his kindred. Yet, notwithstanding the severity of such a command, he did not ask for other people's opinions. Had he turned to those who seemed older and wiser than himself, without doubt they would have sought to dissuade him. Moreover, he did not seek to question God nor to indent[1] him concerning the particulars of this call but, from the start, the Spirit of God being so mighty, he yielded willing obedience.

Second, we saw his faith was praised by the apostle because Abraham accepted and embraced such a hard promise: he was to receive the

[1] 'Indent' is a legal term, frequently used by Bruce, meaning 'entering into a contract, whose terms would be recorded in an indenture'. See Chapter 8, note 14 above.

heritable 'title deeds' that would endow him with the land of Canaan as his family's inheritance,[2] even though the actual possession of the land would be deferred for more than four hundred years. In fact, he and his descendants would for generations be isolated in the land. Nevertheless, he steadfastly trusted God's promise, allured in his own heart by the firm conviction that one day his descendants would take possession of their heritage.

I must add that the apostle's commendation of Abraham's faith extended to more than his acceptance of the promise of the Land, for his hope was also fixed upon a heavenly, eternal inheritance: Canaan was given to him simply as a pledge and binding agreement[3] of this heavenly inheritance. It was his faith in this spiritual inheritance, as well as in the promise of a temporal one, that the apostle commends. From the moment that Abraham received God's effectual call, it pleased the Lord by his Spirit to give him insight into heavenly matters; he was granted a vision of that heavenly city and country to which God had called him.

Thus from that time, he never took his eyes off his true destination, always keeping in his heart that vision of heaven, so much so that it increasingly filled his horizon. Consequently, because he had set his mind on things above, he took little interest in life's temporal things. Indeed, we read that he was constantly looking forward to that enduring city that has unshakeable foundations, whose builder and maker is the living God. So what effect on him had this heavenly vision upon which his eye was constantly fixed? It made him steadfast in his calling; it caused him to overcome all kinds of troubles, irritations and difficulties that confronted him during his pilgrimage.

Third, it caused him to steward his earthly possessions wisely. Even though his worldly wealth greatly increased, he used it in such a way as helped to further him on his heavenly journey.[4] Moreover, he witnessed

[2] More frequently than usual in this chapter, Bruce's earlier training as a lawyer is apparent in the legal terms he employs.

[3] A 'binding agreement' is my translation of another legal term Bruce uses, *ingadge*, 'an agreement to fulfil some specified undertaking'. (DSL)

[4] This is an interesting and important aspect of Calvinistic thinking which developed early in Scottish Presbyterianism. For example, see Calvin's *Commentary on Psalms*, at Psalm 23:1, 5, where he insists that those blessed with riches are bound to observe moderation; by nature we are all inclined to excess, but

to his yearning for that heavenly life both by dwelling in a tent and by his words and deeds; his life-style made it clear that he was just a humble servant of God, whose destination was a heavenly city; he was a sojourner here on earth. In Scripture, he is called 'the father of the faithful', and we may be sure that he was worthy of such a title. Therefore, whenever you read and hear of Abraham, resolve to learn from his example, for you will profit by stewarding your earthly possessions in the same way as he did.

First, fix your sight on the vision of everlasting life

The first lesson I want you to learn from today's sermon is that the only way any of you will become constant in the godly pathway of our heavenly calling is to keep before you the vision of everlasting life.[5] When you meditate upon that life, keeping its vision before you, no subtle difficulties shall divert you away from your onward course, for the only joy and consolation in adversities will come from the vision of the immortal crown. However great and grievous some afflictions may be—even those laid upon us by the Lord himself, whether in mind or body—nothing can be so painful and sorrowful to your hearts as the loss of your sight of the heavenly life.

If by some fault your eye is turned away from the prospect of your eternal inheritance—I mean by some folly that you dabble with—then you have erected a partition between yourself and the face of God, in whose countenance alone the joys of heaven shine. Therefore, in the

God's bounty to some is never to nourish them in this disease. The German Social Historian, Max Weber, in his *The Protestant Ethic and the Spirit of Capitalism* (1904), points out that regarding the prosperity of Presbyterians one of their ethical tenets was a hard 'frugality'; 'the restraints which were made upon the consumption of wealth' made possible 'the productive investment of capital'. Moreover, their conduct must always serve to increase the glory of God. Quoted by Catherwood, pp. 114-115. Also quoted by Catherwood: 'Calvin insisted on the virtues of thrift and diligence, duty and responsibility, without ever going back on the great watchword "by faith alone", the characteristic theme for the Calvinist Christian is that he lives by faith, for the honour and service of God in a world the whole life of which must be brought from sinful chaos into the ordered liberty of the children of God.' Prof. E.G. Rupp in an article in *The Times* on the anniversary of Calvin's death in 1964.

[5] This emphasis reflects the prayers with which Calvin concluded his lectures, for he almost invariably prayed for constancy in his hearers' journey towards everlasting life.

midst of some adversity that is afflicting you, should you find no way of escape or means of consolation—for true help can be found only in the countenance of God—then flee to the place of prayer and there crave that the Lord in his mercy would so sanctify that adversity to you, that through it the partition you have erected might be torn down, and your free access to his face might be restored.

The only afflictions that are able to work for our sanctification are those wherewith the power of the Holy Spirit concurs. Troubles are experienced by everyone, but sanctifying troubles belong only to the children of God. Therefore whenever you are cast down, grieve over whatever sins may have come between you and the Lord, and pray to him that your grief may be sanctified and become the means of you being granted a fresh vision of his glorious face.

Second, right stewardship of material possessions

The second lesson from Abraham's example is that we must neither set our hearts on temporal things, nor seek to acquire and rate them as the main way of attaining happiness.[6] Rather learn from the patriarch to use them as helps that can further you in your journey towards that higher heavenly felicity. For if you set your hearts upon riches, and hope for happiness from them, then be sure that your only reward will be here on earth. What more can we ask of the living God than to be granted our heart's desire? So if your desires are for the things of this world, and the Lord were to satisfy those longings, what more would there be for you to ask, when you have already got what you wanted? Therefore beware of what you thirst for and set your hearts upon; if you long for earthly things, take heed and mend your ways 'ere it be too late. Correct your thirst and desires and learn now to yearn for that heavenly life and inheritance.

We must not expect to be fully satisfied in the here and now, but must wait until at length we enter into that fullness of life and enjoy its fruition. If your thirst be for things that are above, you are blessed, for 'Blessed are those who thus thirst'. But for those who have set their hearts upon this world, once you have got what you wanted, there is nothing else; you have had the only reward you will ever get. Therefore I say, learn to use this world's earthly possessions simply to carry you

[6] See note 4 above.

forward towards your eternal destination; do not make these things your aim in life, but make the eternal inheritance your target. Use every means that God has afforded you as blessings that will further your heart's spiritual desires.

Third, here on earth we have no permanent dwelling

Before I move on, there is a third lesson for us to learn. Abraham ordered his life by living in a tent and wherever he was in the land, by all he said and did, he professed himself to be a stranger and sojourner; so he considered this world to be a continuous banishment, not only from his true home in the heavenly country, but also from his Lord and Master Jesus Christ and from his Father. Let us follow his example so that by our words and actions we may bear witness that here we have no permanent dwelling, for we regard that heavenly heritage as our true inheritance; until we reach heaven we are at present banished from our true home. Therefore, let your words and actions be seasoned with grace and salt, so that whatever you say and do may bear witness to all whom you meet, to the end that they too will acknowledge that you have set your minds on things that are above. It is time now that I move on.

The example of Sarah's faith

The apostle now goes from the husband to the wife as he proceeds to the example of Sarah's faith, this godly and honest mother. Even though there are many godly and faithful women well-reported of in Scripture, none of them have a place in the apostle's list as being a princess of God. Sarah is the only woman he specifically mentions. Her example is fitting for all godly and honest women, who have not besmirched their womanhood. Even though they may be 'the weaker vessels',[7] yet the Lord has made them capable of faith, and he has a special mercy and regard for them.

Further on in the chapter the apostle quotes the example of Rahab the harlot who had faith, no doubt to bring comfort and consolation to all penitent harlots, and to other lost, debauched women, whereas

[7] A clear allusion to 1 Peter 3:6-7, where godly women are said to be Sarah's children, though they must be honoured by their husbands as 'weaker vessels', for they are heirs with them of the grace of life.

Sarah's example is cited for the comfort and encouragement of faithful and chaste women. As God gives me grace, I want to consider now the aspects of Sarah's example that moved the apostle to bring her to our attention. I think there are several points to notice.

Four points why the apostle draws our attention to Sarah

First, as well as the great faith of both wife and husband, it was the singular work of God wrought upon the wife that is one reason why the writer wants it to be seen by us more clearly. That God's dealings with her and the pair's combined faith may be more manifest, he must include her in his account. It is not unusual for an old man to father a child, but it is very unusual for an old woman to give birth to a son. Second, I have no doubt that he cites Sarah because the child was begotten within the lawful relationship of marriage.

Third, he makes mention of her faith in order to strengthen and console all women, because the merciful Lord, notwithstanding the sin of Eve, has made them just as capable as men of exercising faith. It is true that when women think of Eve they have every reason to regret and grieve over her defection, but that should be no cause for despair, since the Lord gave Eve the promise of mercy and everlasting life before he gave it to Adam.[8]

Finally, he includes Sarah in his list to instruct husbands, by the example of Abraham, to share their faith and spiritual gifts with their wives. As they have become one flesh in body, and share together their temporal gifts and graces, so should they share together their spiritual and heavenly graces. Where there is such harmony in body and soul between a man and his wife, there can be no question but that such harmony in their relationship will be blessed. Therefore, the apostle's purpose in bringing before us the example of Sarah whose husband was her teacher, is to instruct all husbands concerning their duty towards their wives, as well as towards the rest of their households over which they are the head.

Four further points to note regarding Sarah

If I may be permitted, I want to mention four further points regarding this woman and the way in which her faith is praised, just as her

[8] Genesis 3:16-17.

husband's faith has already been praised. You have heard how her husband was praised for embracing and receiving a most difficult promise, indeed, a promise that was impossible to flesh and blood. In the same way, his wife's faith is commended in that she embraced just as difficult a promise as that given to her husband, namely concerning the heir to be begotten by him and borne by her. Surely this was a harder promise than any they had been given previously. From this heir would come such a numerous posterity that it would be comparable to the stars in the sky or the grains of sand on the seashore. Receiving these promises, both of them believed and rested upon them. It was because she embraced this difficult promise, humanly speaking quite impossible, that her faith is here commended.

As we consider what I shall now seek to lay out before you, by God's grace may you more clearly understand Sarah's faith.

First, she must believe she would be able to conceive

First, I set before you the person of the woman upon whom we will reflect. Consider according to the Scriptural account both the frailty of her nature and her advanced years. We are told that she had been barren all her days; further, at this time she was four score years and ten, therefore her natural female routine had ceased. Clearly she was by now considered to be of barren stock. Yet notwithstanding, she is promised that she will be enabled to retain her husband's seed and conceive. As to her husband, he too was by now also far beyond the age when he would be able to beget children as he had done earlier in life.[9] Being about a hundred years old and on account of his infirmity, he was also reckoned to be as good as dead.

These considerations of this woman let you see the problem with God's promise, if it was evaluated in terms of mortal flesh and blood. For Sarah had to begin by believing that the Lord's power and ability reached far above her human nature, and was able to give her the strength to conceive a child.

Second, she must believe God would care for the foetus in her womb

She must also believe that the same God by whose power she would be able to conceive, would then preserve the child in her womb, and

[9] Genesis 25:1-6.

enable the foetus to grow until the right time for him to be born a perfectly formed baby. Otherwise, she might have suspected that she would be able to conceive, but that then she would miscarry and the child be lost.

Third, she must believe she would have a safe delivery

Further, she must believe that when the full term was 'completed', the baby would be safely delivered and both she and her son would be safe and well. Otherwise, she might have kept the baby in her womb for the full nine months, but then at her delivery the baby be lost. Again, the same God must be trusted—right from her conception, throughout the pregnancy and up to the safe delivery of her son—so that his mighty power would bring her and the child safely through it all.

Reflect, then, upon her womanly nature, her age and her husband's age, for humanly speaking the prospect of a child was out of the question, a series of impossibilities according to the expectations of flesh and blood; yet, notwithstanding, she believed in spite of all this. It was through the power and virtue[10] of her faith, all came to pass.

Fourth, the great delay used by God

There was one other thing that tried her patience and therefore conveys to us the strength of her faith, just as much as the other three points I have made: it was the great delay that God used[11] before he gave her this son, the long neglect—as it must have seemed to her—of his promise. For at the time when she and her husband came out of Ur, the Lord made this promise of a son to them both; yet he deferred the fulfilment of his promise until they were stricken with old age. Therefore, by this lengthy delay he exercised the patience of both of them. Because there was no consolation to be found in any natural means of conceiving, they could only have been sustained in their faith and upheld by God's Spirit. It was the Lord who gave them patience, a patience that maintained their faith, and thus it was faith that enabled them to have confidence that nothing was impossible for the living God. That conviction

[10] Bruce frequently uses the word 'vertew' in respect of the godly; its meaning in reference to human beings was 'moral valour or excellence'; used in respect of God and Christ its meaning was 'supernatural, divine power'.

[11] When Bruce speaks about God 'using' a delay, he always has in mind that in his providence he has a hidden purpose.

did not have its source in human reasoning nor in any second cause.[12]

In the verse from Hebrews 11 that I read to you, the apostle confirms this. He tells us why she believed God's promise; it was *because sche judged him faithfull quho had promised.* The apostle does not attribute her belief in the promise as having flowed from natural reasoning or means, but from the supernatural power of the Spirit of God, and through the virtue[13] of her living and justifying faith. It was this faith that enabled her to believe God's promises, even though they were contrary to human nature, because she judged and counted him faithful. The implication in the apostle's words is that had Sarah not counted God faithful, she would never have believed his promise. It was only because she knew him to be a faithful God that, relying upon his power and strength, she was enabled to rest upon his word. Having often experienced God's goodness, mercy and kindness towards herself, she knew his word to be true, and that he would not fall short by a single jot of anything he had promised her.

I repeat: Sarah knew God was so strong and furnished with such extraordinary power, that there was no impediment which nature could raise up to hinder him; she knew that he could override any and every obstacle in order to fulfil his purposes. Therefore, knowing him to be gracious and merciful towards her, and knowing him also to be true and omnipotent, she reposed upon and trusted in his promises. God is said to be faithful when he fulfils his promises made freely to us; we are said to be faithful when we assent to his promises, and believe in full assurance that he will perform what he has promised, however hard that may seem to be to flesh and blood or to nature.

Two lessons from Sarah

Therefore learn two lessons from this woman. One is this: before you can believe God's promises you must first know him. It is the knowl-

[12] Secondary Causation is the philosophical proposition that all material and corporeal objects, having been created by God with their own intrinsic potentialities, are subsequently empowered to evolve independently in accordance with natural law; it was a primary theme of Scholasticism, and is found, for example, in Aquinas. Calvin, though not using the terminology of 'second causes', deals with God's uses of natural means: *Inst.* I.16.7. See also *WCF*, 5.2-3. Bruce's point is that the birth of Sarah's son was entirely and directly by the will and action of God, who is, of course, the First Cause.

[13] See Note 10 above.

edge of God himself that is the prerequisite for faith in what he promises. If you do not know him to be true, merciful and gracious to you, nor know him to be omnipotent, you will never believe his promises. It was her faith in God and her knowledge of him that enabled Sarah to trust his word, and that same knowledge of him in terms of his mercy and strength, and not least his omnipotence, is the only way we are able to put our faith wholly in his promises. If you know someone to be untruthful, trivial and inconsistent, it does not matter what assurances that person gives or however attractive they may seem to be, you will not put much faith in his word. On the other hand, if you know some other person to be reliable, honest and consistent, completely trustworthy in all his dealings, the integrity of such a person will incline you to believe what he says.

So it is with God: when you know of his grace, mercy and might, then in your heart you are able to rest in him. We must strive to know God as our friend whose mercy is extended to us; we must know too that through his Son we are reconciled to him. Being thus assured of his mercy, grace and reconciliation, there is no promise he will make, however impossible it may appear to be, that we will not believe.

However, if your conscience, doubting his mercy, is filled with guilt that testifies you have not been forgiven, no matter what God promises you will not be able to believe him. So if any of you have troubled consciences, and your assurance of God's grace is wavering, deal with your faltering and crave to be reconciled to him. Enquire of yourselves how it is that you have turned aside from the Lord's favour. Have you indulged in some fleshly pursuit, or run after some worldly fancy, or forsaken some truth of the gospel? Whatever it is that is troubling your conscience, cast it from you, and seek again the assurance of God's gracious favour. Had you from the start obeyed the Lord's word, it would already have been the means of your salvation; otherwise while it blesses other souls, it judges you. I must move on.

Assuming we do believe the promises of God because we know and trust him, consider what it means for faith to look to God; I mean, what the principal objectives of faith must be. Faith looks principally to the goodness of God. Genuine justifying faith is different from the various counterfeit faiths we find all around us. True justifying faith is not the same as 'historical faith' that is only concerned with theoretical religion; neither is it the same as 'faith in the miraculous', that is all taken up with the supernatural; nor is it the same as 'temporary faith', that declines and disappears when it is swamped by worldliness and the cares of this life.[14] Rather, faith that is steadfastly focused on God's mercy alone will bless you and your soul. Thus faith's principal objective in looking to God is that grace and mercy that has been his word to men for the sake of Jesus Christ

The second lesson from Sarah is that her faith looked to the power of God. Of what avail is that word of mercy unless the Lord has the power to accomplish his promise within us? As we contemplate the Lord's power, however impossible something is by natural means, faith knows that there is nothing impossible to God. So faith rests on these two, God's power and his mercy; this is what enabled this woman to count him faithful. Likewise for each of us: these two, his mercy and power, enable us also to consider the living God faithful.

A question regarding Sarah's faith

Someone may ask how it could be that this woman is praised by the apostle so highly for her faith. When we read the account of the promise in Genesis 15, there is no mention at all of Sarah's faith, not so much as a single footprint within the story. Indeed, moving on to chapter 16, we see clearly definite marks of doubting, infidelity and weakness in this woman;[15] it is manifestly extremely difficult to argue that she was a woman of faith when she acted as she did. Coming to chapter 18, I find that when the promise was renewed to Abraham, the text tells us, as she listened hidden in her tent, *that sche laith within hirself*[16] and that this laughter flowed not from faith, but from doubt, mistrust and unbelief. The Lord himself testified this in righteous discernment, while her own behaviour also had born witness of her failure to believe.[17]

[14] In Chapter One, Bruce has already mentioned these same three kinds of faith that are ineffective, and has distinguished them from justifying faith; see pp. 5-6 above.

[15] A clear allusion to Genesis 16:1-2, where we are told that in the seeming failure of God to give Sarah a son, she arranged to obtain a son by natural means by using Hagar as a surrogate mother.

[16] Genesis 18:12, 'So Sarah laughed to herself, saying, "After I am worn out, and my lord is old, shall I have pleasure?"'

[17] Genesis 16:1-2.

Moreover, the Lord also distinguished between Sarah's laughter and that of her husband.[18] While both of them laughed, their laughter flowed from very different attitudes, one from faith and the other from distrust. The 'natural man' considering the two laughs, Abraham's and Sarah's, would not discern any difference between them.[19] But the gaze of the living God, who knows the heart and its inner thoughts, saw that one flowed from faith and the other from unbelief.

Consider the case of good works. Just as it was hard to discern the fountain from whence flowed Sarah's laughter, today it is the same with good works. If you do not know the inner source of so-called 'good works', the outward appearance of them is meaningless, even if they seem to be meritorious. If they do not flow from faith, they are an abomination before God,[20] for in them is no desire for God's glory but only for personal ostentation.

To come to the point, the Lord by his righteous judgment testified that her laughter flowed from distrust. How can we say that? Because he reproved her for it. Moreover, by her own actions she admitted it, for when she was reproved by the Lord, she lied to him and denied that she had laughed. On the other hand, had her laughter flowed from faith, no doubt she would have welcomed the light that the Lord was shining upon her, and she would then have again avowed her trust in him; but because that was not so, by her denial she blatantly lied to God.

The footprint of Sarah's faith

So what is the point I want to make? Yes, here so far we find only the marks of her unbelief, but as yet no hint of any faith. Yet, when we read this chapter with its account of all this, there may be perceived a single footprint of Sarah's faith, and I want now to consider this faint footprint with you. In spite of the fact that she made that denial and lied to God, in his dealings with her, the Lord did not let her off with her

[18] Compare Genesis 17:17 with Romans 4:18-22.

[19] An allusion to 1 Corinthians 2:14-15.

[20] Such strong language makes it highly probable that there is an implied reference here to 'works of supererogation'; these are 'in RC moral theology, acts which are not enjoined as of strict obligation, and therefore are not simply good as opposed to bad, but better as opposed to good.' This teaching was repudiated by the Reformers and in the Thirty-Nine Articles (XIV). See article 'Supererogation' in *ODCC*, p. 1570. See also note 10 on 'satisfactions' in Chapter 5, above.

denial, but insisted that she had laughed: *It is not so: for thou laughedst.*[21] By his repeated affirmation a fear was wrought within her (it says, *she was afraied*); this fear I take to be a footprint and evidence of her nascent faith. It was as if God said to her something like this, 'I know what you are thinking: because your laugh was hidden in your gut[22] you assumed I didn't know you that had laughed, but I assure you I was aware of that silent laughter as plainly as if it had burst out volubly, and everyone had heard and witnessed it.'

Because of God's insistent assertion, Sarah was afraid. But why? Because she realised that it was not a mere man who was dealing with her, even though the Lord appeared to her in human form; neither was it an angel, for angels cannot see into our innermost thoughts. Therefore, at once it dawned upon her that this 'man' speaking to her was the living God; it was at that point she knew that nothing was impossible to such a God.[23]

However, suppose at first I doubt the promise of God because I do not know the source of that promise, when I do discover it is from the Lord himself, then I will no longer doubt, for I will know that he who promised is faithful. So it was with Sarah: God let her know who he was, and so I take it that by this knowledge he imparted to her, having had a blessed effect upon her, her faith was awakened, and she turned away from her doubts. As long as she did not know who it was who was making this promise, but considered only the impossibility of it because, humanly speaking, she herself was incapable of experiencing its fulfilment, she doubted it just as any other person would have done. But once the Lord awakened her and she knew it came from his voice, then, turning her eyes to him, her doubts were put behind her. She now knew that nothing was impossible to God, and she believed!

Lessons for today

Here are the lessons for us. First, I ask, why do men doubt when the promises of mercy and grace from the living God are offered to them?

[21] Genesis 18:15 (GenB).

[22] Bruce's word is 'stomak'.

[23] Calvin interprets Sarah's laugh of unbelief differently, saying that God gave her 'a friendly reprehension… hence we perceive with what tender indulgence he sometimes regards his own people… he freely forgives her all, and still chooses that she should remain the mother of the Church.' *Comm. in loc.*

It is because they examine and consider them by their own intelligence and human standards. Anyone who uses such criteria will think the divine promises can never be fulfilled. Therefore, when it comes to heavenly and spiritual matters and all other issues of faith, do not consider them by applying human reasoning. Rather consider them by the mind, word and power of God; I mean, take full account of the nature of God and, having meditated on him, you will find a steadfast faith.

Second, I perceive here that because the faith of this poor woman was mingled with doubts, consequently it became subject to weakness and temptations, and to strange hesitations, even though her faith was ultimately so highly praised. That leads me to believe that doubts and faith can both lodge in a person's soul—doubts when we look to ourselves, but then faith when we fix our mind's eye straight upon God and his mercy. The faith of the Lord's best servants of whom we read have been subject to such wavering, and to great weaknesses and manifold doubts. So that when the Lord set before them the most difficult promises, we find some of his servants asking for a sign that they might believe them.

When King Hezekiah was lying in his bed dangerously ill, immediately after Isaiah had prophesied, before ever he reached the palace's outer court, he received from God the command to return to the king with happier news, and to assure him of the prolongation of his days.[24] So the prophet came through into the bedchamber and gave the promise to the king that the Lord would spare his life for some time and give him another fifteen years to live. The king believed and with tears he expressed in faith his great joy.

However, the king saw that the two prophetic pronouncements were opposed to each other:[25] the first in which Isaiah had told him to make preparations for his death by setting his house in order was almost immediately contradicted by the second with the promise of his healing that had come before the prophet had even reached the outer court of the palace. Because these two messages conflicted with each other, Hezekiah begged for a sign that would assure him that the second pronouncement was the one he must believe. This lets you see that the faith of the best of God's servants was often subject to weakness

[24] 2 Kings 20:4-6.

[25] 2 Kings 20:1 & 6.

and faltering—hence this seeking for some extraordinary sign to confirm their faith. Similarly we read of Gideon also asking for a sign.[26]

Now the point is this: the faith of the best of God's servants has often been subjected to doubts, wavering, wrestling and great weakness. *We doubt alwayis* (says the apostle) *bot we dispair not*,[27] therefore we see that in both the apostle and in the elect vessels of God there have been doubts. Therefore, while doubting may occur in a faithful soul, despair is totally banished.

Third, in this woman I perceive the great mercy and loving-kindness of our God.[28] Even though her faith was exceedingly weak, we find that he did not reject it, but accepted and cherished it; he even constrained the apostle's pen to record in our text lengthy praise of it as if it had been faith in the highest degree. What is this to our comfort? The Lord does not reject us even if we come to him with the merest spark of faith, as small as a single mustard seed, and as feeble as a smoking flax that has neither heat nor flame. However weak it may be, if it be true faith, the Lord accepts it, even to the extent of rewarding and praising it. Then mark well the wonderful mercy and goodness of God, that if our faith deserves to be classed as mingled with doubt, even then he accepts it. This teaches us that faith is not so easily wrought in the human heart as many suppose; it is as easy to fulfil the whole Law as it is to produce faith in a man's heart. Invariably, however small faith may be, the Lord never rejects it.

Fourth, I perceive here that as soon as Sarah is reproved she becomes afraid. I take it that in the Genesis account, this is the explanation we need, in that it was her fear that caused her to shake off her doubting,

[26] Judges 6:36-40.

[27] 2 Corinthians 4:8b: *We doubt alwayis bot we dispair not.* When Bruce quotes directly from his Geneva Bible, he always changes the script he uses. (I invariably indicate this by using italics.) However, the 1560 edition of the Geneva Bible does not here translate Paul as Bruce does but has *in pouertie, but not ouercome of pouertie.* Yet Paul's verb, ἀπορέω, translated by ESV as 'to be perplexed' often has the connotation of 'to be in doubt' as in John 13:22; Acts 25:20; 2 Corinthians 1:8. No modern translation gives a rendering of 'doubt' to this verb in these verses I have cited, but Grimm-Thayer's *Greek Lexicon* gives its meaning as 'to be in doubt', or 'to be in straits not knowing which way to turn'. It would appear that the 1560 Geneva Bible has followed Calvin, who translated verse 4b as, *oppressed with poverty, yet not into destitution* (*Comm. in loc.*)

[28] See Note 23 above.

and at once, pulling herself together, she recognised who it was that had spoken to her. Here is the lesson from this: suppose you show contempt, suppose you laugh, suppose you mock and doubt God's word to you, not realising who it is that is speaking to you, in spite of all that the Lord does not reprove you. But as soon as he opens his holy mouth to tell you that it is he who is speaking, you should at once withdraw your contempt, and bow down in awe. Half of the floods and disasters that have struck our land would never have burst forth upon us if the warnings of God had been feared. But because of our contempt for those warnings from above, I expect that there will be no end to these troubles and terrible disorders until we come to our senses.

Finally, also mark the reason why this woman is praised, and see what it was that brought her into such high esteem with the living God, so that he caused commendation of her to be recorded for all generations, right to the end of the age. It was not her beauty, even supposing she was very beautiful,[29] nor was it her outward apparel; rather, what brought her into favour with the living God was the hidden clothing of her inward person. It was, as Peter writes of holy women, *ane quyit and meik spirit becumis wemen*,[30] that is, a heart arrayed in a true and living faith, that brought her into such esteem with God. Thus all who would have God's true praise and commendation should pay earnest heed to the inward decorum and clothing of the hidden person of the heart, and not to the outward adorning of the body.

You first heard the praise of her husband, and now you are hearing her praises. The combined praise of both by God, first of the man and then of the woman, lets us see that the estate of marriage is blessed by him. And the account of their lives, both husband and wife, also lets us see that this estate of marriage does not (as many suppose) produce a cause for sinning, worry and anxiety, so much as it provides room for faith, love, patience and all spiritual virtues. So there is nothing that the living God blesses more than this estate, if it is entered into for the right reasons, that is, to further us on the way to everlasting life.

In addition, it is clear that children are God's gift, when begotten

[29] Genesis 12:11: [Abraham] said to his wife, 'I know that you are a woman beautiful in appearance' (ESV).

[30] 1 Peter 3:3-5. Bruce's words here, purporting to be a biblical quote, are probably his own paraphrase of 1 Peter 3.

by faith that comes from his own hand, and born by means of their parents' prayers. Faith accepted[31] Isaac as a precious gift from the hands of the living God; the prayer of faith obtained him. So then, God's blessing did not come through the normal human procreative means, for nature had failed to give them a son.

Those who yearn for a similar blessing ought to have recourse to the spiritual power of faith and prayer, so that what nature by its normal means has denied them may be procured and obtained. This should be the course of action for those who are in lofty positions, whose continued posterity could be a blessing for other nations, as well as preserving in their own lands good relations with respectful obedience. Where the natural means is not blessed for princes, for whom an heir is important, by faith and prayer they may obtain what nature alone has refused.[32] Truly it is a duty to turn to God that in his mercy he would make the marriage bed of our prince fruitful, so that through his offspring's continuance, our country, and others to which he has a claim,[33] may continue in peace and harmony. This particular exhortation, because it concerns our king, I will leave until I next have the opportunity of speaking to him.

For you, well-beloved, consider a child a gift from the living God, and count faith and prayer as the means of obtaining that blessing. I am certain that many who are unworthy are deprived of this blessing;[34]

[31] I have translated Bruce's word 'borowis' as 'accepted as a precious gift'; DSL defines 'borow' as 'to take something on pledge or security', or 'to become surety for someone'; some readers may prefer as the translation, 'Faith accepted Isaac on loan from the living God', or, 'Through their faith the living God entrusted Isaac to them'. However, note that grammatically, 'faith' is the subject of the whole sentence.

[32] This is a bold word directed to King James VI, for at the time Bruce was preaching this sermon (1591?), Queen Anne had miscarried several times. However, Henry Frederick, Prince of Wales, was born 19 February 1594 (d. November 1612); Elizabeth was born 19 August 1596 (d. February 1662), and Charles was born 19 November 1600; he succeeded his father as King in 1625 (beheaded January 1649), but, alas, contrary to Bruce's earnest desire and expectation, Charles brought neither unity nor obedience to his realm.

[33] Bruce's words are 'as he hes richt to'. This is probably an oblique reference to Queen Elizabeth's failure to marry and produce an heir to the English throne, leaving James VI as strong claimant to succeed her.

[34] Bruce's word 'vnworthelie' is used very often of partaking of the Lord's Supper in an unworthy manner; the implication here, therefore, is most likely to be

I mean that their marriages have not been bonded in the right way. Indeed, in my opinion there are many marriages that are little better than adultery; that is why this blessing is denied them.[35] Therefore whoever enters that sacred union must fully respect its chief end, for when God is brought into the marriage right from the start, he will richly bless the husband and wife. There is nothing too hard in this world, or out of it, that faith cannot attain. It was by faith that Abraham got a son, and by faith his posterity grew to the number spoken of in those two similes.[36] So there is nothing too hard for faith to bring it to pass.

Now to come to the point. There is one huge promise to us in Christ's kingdom (his kingdom has already been inaugurated), and infinite blessings are there set forth. Without question, doubt and unbelief present an obstacle, for if we only had faith to believe those promises already available in the kingdom of Christ, we should experience them, whether they are spiritual or temporal. But because our land has treated the calling of the living God with rebellion, stubbornness and obstinacy, instead of blessings, we see maledictions and curses present in our nation, and these are likely to bring upon us even greater ruin and retribution. Consequently, when the time comes that the Lord withdraws the light from us, in my judgment, because of our contempt and rejection of lawful warnings, it will be useless to hope that the flame of godliness will be rekindled.

In conclusion, the only way to partake in the blessings that the kingdom of Christ can bestow is to have faith in Christ. Trust in him! For it is by trust and faith that we can be set free from the spiritual evils of the devil, and from earthly physical maladies, whether they be illnesses or poverty. It is by faith that we can see the face of Christ wherein is perfect joy. By faith the soul can be sustained in joyful vigour. What else can I say of faith? All that we have previously been speaking about these many Sundays has been solely to extol faith.

the charge of unspiritual living, or more particularly, as will emerge a few sentences later, of a spiritually deficient union.

[35] This is hardly a felicitous statement and unfortunately, owing to the absence in the 16th century of contemporary medical knowledge on infertility, may well have brought considerable anguish into many childless marriages.

[36] The two similes were: 'I will multiply your offspring as the stars of heavens and as the sand that is on the seashore' (Genesis 22:17; and of course the text of the sermon, Hebrews 11:12).

But just say the devil has spewed unbelief so deeply into your nature that he is able constantly by his efforts to cause you to distrust God and rob you of any trace of faith, and just say that your former sins have erected a partition between you and the living God, then tear down that partition, pray for those past sins to be banished from your heart and the memory of them to be erased. Then little by little clear out those old sins from your heart, and by prayer cast out your unbelief, that at last you may come to the vision of the face of Jesus Christ, in whose smile you shall realise that your pilgrimage has ended in a great victory. Then you shall experience contentment, now and for ever. Amen.

Chapter Ten

Hebrews Chapter 11 verse 13

> *13 All these dyed in fayth and receaved not the promisis bot saw them afar af, and believed them, and receaved them thankfullie, and confesed that they war straingeris and pilgrimis on earth.*

We have heard, brethren and well-beloved in Jesus Christ our Saviour, the praise and commendation of the faith of Abraham and of his wife Sarah. Both were praised, first, on account of their ready minds and obedience to a very hard calling; their obedience sprang from their faith. Second, they were praised because they embraced very hard promises of things invariably impossible to flesh and blood. One promise they embraced concerned the heritage of the land of Canaan; indeed, they steadfastly leaned upon God's promise even though its fulfilment was put to one side, and was to be deferred for four hundred years. They looked forward to the day when their descendants would enter into[1] the promised inheritance, and they were praised because they also embraced the promise that their heir would also enter into[2] his inheritance.

Reminder of the four points regarding Sarah's faith

First, their heir was to be begotten by Abraham and borne by Sarah, even though the fulfilment of this promise was clearly impossible, humanly speaking. By this time Sarah's age was four score and ten years, she was barren and past the age of bearing a child; in her earlier years

[1] Bruce's verb is 'bruik', a legal term meaning to take possession of, and enjoy, some land or property.

[2] Again, the word 'bruik'. See Note 1 above.

she had continued barren. As to Abraham, because he was now entering his one hundredth year, it was obvious that according to nature his vigour and virility were spent. However, in spite of all this, Sarah still embraced the Lord's promise concerning the heir, notwithstanding the self-evident impossibility of her being able to bear a child; being certain that God had promised, and not considering her own frailty, she constantly reposed upon God and his truth. It was on account of her great and strong faith that you heard she was praised.

The reason why Sarah accepted God's promise is set down at the end of verse 11; it was simply that she believed God: *sche judged him faithfull quho had promised.* Knowing God for herself, she embraced his promise and believed his word. Had she not been acquainted with God and had had no experience of his favour, she would never have believed what he promised. But, as her own experience testified, she knew that he was merciful and had always been favourable towards her, therefore, the same mercy that she had found in him enabled her to repose upon his promise. Likewise, she knew him to be true and that he would not fail to fulfil a single jot of what he had said. Last of all, she knew him to be almighty, and therefore nothing was impossible for him; he was able to work above nature, and what it might deny, the Lord could perform. Thus knowing God and being acquainted with him, she believed his promise.

Here we remarked that it is our knowledge of a person that enables us to believe his promise. No one will entrust himself to the promise of someone he does not know. But if you do know someone's fidelity, ability and integrity you will trust his promise. In other words, it is knowing a person and his good reputation that enables you to believe what he says.

Next we asked, 'What is it that faith looks to in God, and to what in particular does the eye of faith direct its gaze?' The eye of faith looks first to the mercy and grace of God given utterance in Jesus Christ; it also looks to the power and omnipotence of God who is able to accomplish whatsoever he has promised. But it is to the first of these two things that faith specially directs its gaze—to the mercy and promise of God's grace for the sake of Jesus Christ his Son. If we merely believe that there is a God we will never trust him, but if we know him in our hearts and taste[3] his mercy in our consciences, and have the hope that his mercy will be extended to us, then the taste and hope of mercy will enable us to repose upon him. Thus in times of special anxieties and hardships the Christian should labour to know how the Lord regards him and what his relationship is with God. You must labour to examine your conscience, and ask whether you have the assurance of his mercy for that great Day.

The diligent investigation into the enquiry as to our standing before God (this is the most vital exercise[4] any man can engage in during his entire life) must be in order always to retain the certainty in our consciences that on that great Day God will be specially merciful towards us. Therefore I commend to you the examination of your consciences, that if you find any wavering in your heart or doubt in your conscience, suggesting you are uncertain of the mercy and favour of God, then, if it is within your ability to put right what is wrong, do whatever you must, but if you are unable to do anything yourself about your concern, lay it on the shoulders[5] of Jesus Christ who has already obtained satisfaction for all our failures; then constantly labour in prayer yourself to gain the peace of Christ that passes all understanding. It is only by that inward peace that wounded consciences are healed and we are able steadfastly to repose upon the mercy of God in Christ Jesus.

Until we have that peace, our consciences remain adrift and are

[3] 'The taist of godis mercie' is a favourite theme in Bruce's preaching; DSL quotes it as a characteristic of his sermons. By 'taist' (taste) he means sensation, flavour or feeling of the divine grace offered in Christ. 'Feillingis' (feelings) are constantly linked to his mention of this 'taist' of mercy in one's conscience. A possible comparison might be made to John Wesley's comment in his diary, 'I felt my heart strangely warmed' as during the Aldersgate Street meeting Luther's preface to the *Epistle to the Romans* was being read. See also Chapter 2, Note 12, above. For an example of Calvin's comments on feelings, see his *Comm.* on 2 Corinthians 7:1-11, also *Inst.* III.8.9.n.7.

[4] The phrases 'diligent investigation' and 'vital exercise' are my translation of the word 'studie' which Bruce constantly uses; 'studie' means for him 'significant thought to investigate or consider some spiritual issue'.

[5] In his phrase 'on the shoulders of Jesus Christ', Bruce probably had in mind the shoulder pieces in the High Priest's ephod, with the two onyx stones set into them; the stones were engraved with the names of the twelve tribes, six names on each stone. (Exodus 28:6-14) The symbolism of course was that the High Priest would carry the people's burdens on his shoulders as he prayed for them in the Holy Place. See Calvin's *Commentary on Exodus, in loc.*

tossed about by doubts. So while you have the opportunity and time, and I am still afforded freedom to admonish you,[6] attend now to your faults, mend your way of life, and root out the wickedness and hardness from your heart. If there are matters you have no power to deal with, be constant in prayer until you obtain the peace of Jesus Christ for his sake.

Third, I told you that the Lord does not despise even the smallest, weakest faith if the trust you bring to him is genuine, even though it may be as faint as the smoking flax that has neither heat nor glow; even though it be as tiny as a mustard seed, yet if it is true and directed towards God's glory, he does not despise it. He will not break the bruised reed nor quench the smoking flax;[7] rather will he tend it and fan it into a flame, and strengthen it where it is bruised.[8] Therefore, however weak your faith may be, do not despair or flee from God, rather run to him. Seek his help to strengthen your frail and feeble faith. As he thus helps us, he utters his wonderful mercy towards us. Just say we have many different means and ways to strengthen our faith but have neglected them, so that we have not grown in faith as we ought to have done, what then? The Lord is so merciful that he will not despise even the weakest mite of faith, but, however small, he accepts and nourishes it; never does he quench it.

Fourthly, we saw how this woman's faith was mixed with great incredulity, and was subject to many errors and blatant faults, for she lied in the presence of the living God. Notwithstanding, the Lord did not distain her, but after he had awakened her by his own rebuke, we read that she feared and confessed, being convicted in her conscience and touched[9] with pangs of remorse for her fault. It was when her con-

[6] Here is one of Bruce's frequent hints that sinister forces are secretly conspiring to overthrow the work of the Scottish Reformation. At this time the 'counter reformation' was very active in Scotland. (Maclean.)

[7] Isaiah 42:3; Matthew 12:20.

[8] Robert Murray M'Cheyne makes the same point in his sermon on the Church in Ephesus (Revelation 2:1-7): '[I]f you were to be kind to a stranger, you may have in doing so but one grain of love to Christ, and a hundred grains of other feelings... But Christ sprinkles the other grains with his own blood, and treasures up the one grain of love to himself, and says to you, "I know thy works, and thy labour, and thy patience."' M'Cheyne, p. 8.

[9] The Scots word is 'twitchit'; this verb can have a forensic connotation of legalizing a document by touching it; it can also mean 'to pluck the strings of an

science was smitten and wounded in penitence that the Lord accepted her.

Suppose you hear God speaking to you through his word to admonish your conscience, do not expect that that in itself will produce a godly fear that leads you to submit to him; it will not happen until the Lord by his power awakens your dead conscience. When it pleases the Lord to concur with his word, so that he arouses your conscience to see and feel that what he is saying is the truth, only then will your conscience become aware of his power, and you will begin to fear, to tremble, to accuse yourself and to bow down before him.[10]

Further, I perceive that Sarah was neither convicted nor willing to submit to the Lord at his first reproof, even though it was God who was speaking to her. Initially, she was not humbled at all, but hindered by her faults in that she even lied in his presence. Though she tried to defend herself, the Lord persevered with her until she learned godly fear and admitted she had been wrong.

We see, then, that it is not one or two sermons that will move men to surrender, for even God did not move this godly woman straightaway. How much less will we who are so much more feeble and sluggish in godly reverence be moved by the first sermon we hear. It may not be the preaching of a whole year, or two years, or even thirty years that will arouse a dead heart. There is such a lingering death in the human heart that it is always impossible to awaken it, unless and until the mighty power of the living God intervenes. Therefore you must earnestly crave the quickening virtue of Jesus Christ, so that, however ardently you drink in the word with your outward ears, you will become equally ardent in having your inward senses awakened. Then in his kindness you may discern wherein you have offended against him, and by his mercy may find your refuge in the blood of Christ.

Today's text

Now I come to the reading from Hebrews 11:13. While the apostle has

---

instrument'; but its most likely meaning here and elsewhere in this sermon is 'to touch with painful consequences', hence my translation 'touched with pangs of remorse'.

[10] See 2 Corinthians 7:11, 'For see what earnestness this godly grief has produced in you, but also what eagerness to clear yourselves, what indignation, what fear, what longing, what zeal…' (ESV).

praised both Abraham and Sarah individually, he also reminds us that in verse 9 he had mentioned Abraham's posterity, Isaac and Jacob, *heires with him of the same promes*. Later he will also praise each of them individually with their own particular commendations,[11] including some notable and singular trials of their faith, in which they were different from their travelling companions. The apostle has done this respectively as he has written of each of these princes of God, the patriarchs, so in verse 13 he praises them all together: *All these died in faith and receaved not the promisis bot saw them afar af, and believed them...* As they were all given the same promises, shared the same faith and were subject to the same temptations, he conjoins them in affording them praise and honour.

Four aspects of the Fathers' faith

No longer is he concerned with the particular trials of faith each of them endured individually, rather he turns to certain aspects of their faith that they had in common. First he praises them for their constancy—they all persevered in their calling. Second, he praises them for their self-denial, *they war straingeris and pilgrimis on earth*. Third, he praises them for their confession and the nature of it, whereby they bore witness to their faith throughout their lives. Having thus praised them in verse 13, in verses 14 and 15 he shares with us the implications of their confession, as fourthly he shows us the nature of the country that they sought, and (at the end of verse 16) the reward with which the Lord would bless them: their immediate citizenship[12] of the heavenly country. I shall take these four themes, and as time allows shall speak on each of them, as the Lord grants me grace.

Perseverance in faith

First of all, then, the apostle praises them all for their perseverance, that the three Fathers, Abraham, Isaac and Jacob, remained constant in their profession and steadfast in their faith to their very last breath. Notwithstanding the difficulties they had to endure, whether from their homesteads among alien princes, or the privations brought on by

[11] Hebrews 11:20-21.

[12] Bruce's word is 'sute', a legal term again, meaning 'attendance required at a superior court or assembly'.

famines, they overcame all, constantly persevering right to the end. *All these* (says he) *dyed in faith.*[13] It is as if he wants to say, 'From the time it pleased God to give them faith, to call them effectually in their hearts and minds, they kept that faith, stuck to it, tended and honoured it, never defected from it nor backslid either in conduct nor religion, but persevered constant in that faith to their final breath—even to their very last gasp.'

We read in the Bible's account that not one of these three ever defected from his faith, nor did any of them bring dishonour upon that faith either in their conduct or religion. Indeed, each grew in their religion, both in their inward holiness and their outward godly profession. We find not one deviation in any of them either in their manner of living or in their doctrine. They were truly notable patriarchs!

Warnings against defection

There are many who go astray in their living and thereby stain their profession with serious sins; notwithstanding such failures they do not depart completely from the root of faith; yet, however grievously they have allowed filth to defile their lives, the Lord in his own appointed time will reawaken their consciences. (If he did not awaken each of us we would sleep on into death!) He will let them see that in the days when they fully believed, their defilement was buried by God; he will also let them see that they are fresh in his memory; he will stir up again those flickering sparks of faith that they have smothered by their corrupt acts; he will remove that corruption and cause the glimmer of faith, that lay almost extinguished under their sins, to break out once again into the clear light of unfeigned repentance. Then in shame they will lament, shedding pitiful tears, and they will confess and detest[14] those past sins that caused their departure from the Lord. Consequently, their repentance from their defection will bring even greater blessing to the Kirk, and God's glory will be advanced even more than if they

[13] On a point of antiquarian interest, Bruce's own Bible (Geneva 1561) has, *All these dyed in fayth*. Indeed, frequently his carefully written out biblical quotations using the English alphabet (as opposed to his normal Braid Scots alphabet) from a Geneva Bible he was using, differ in the spelling of his own 1561 edition which is still in the possession of his descendent, Lord Elgin. (See Chapter 9, note 27 above.

[14] See note 10 above.

had never fallen away.

All this comes about by the merciful working of the living God who will not suffer us to be lost, even though we have proved false by making a covenant with the devil to our own perdition. So I say again, many have taken wrong steps in their lives, and have wandered far from the grace of God and defected from the grace of faith. Yet in the Lord's own time they have retraced their steps and sincerely returned to him.

Nevertheless, I have only read of a few who slipped away from religion, committed apostasy against their knowledge of the truth so violating their consciences, but have returned to the faith and mercy of God. Hymenaeus and Philetus made one turning from the truth, but then continued along that path until ultimately they denied the resurrection of the body, and consequently the immortality of the soul.[15] Every departure from the right way and especially from true doctrine is to be avoided at all costs and firmly eschewed, for these are defections against the Spirit of God. When you deviate from sound doctrine you sin against the Spirit who first shone the light of that knowledge upon you.

These various defections come dangerously near to that one terrible sin, that few if any ever recover from.[16] Therefore, as experience teaches us today, there is no hope for those apostates who have been excommunicated on account of their departure from the acknowledged truth. The Lord sees that in their consciences they have deserted the truth, and so, according to his righteous judgment, they are now going from worse to worse—as the apostle has it 'from hardness to hardness'—until the time when the full cup of his wrath will be poured upon them.[17] That is why it is a waste of time to tolerate[18] them in the vain hope that they will be restored, for when at first they were possessed by one devil, by their defection he has taken the opportunity to return with another seven devils worse than himself.[19] All these devils now have such power over the man's soul that they will never allow him to believe anything

[15] 1 Timothy 1:19-20; 2 Timothy 2:17-18.

[16] The whole paragraph implies that the 'one terrible sin' was to return to Roman Catholicism.

[17] The allusions are to Romans 2:5 and Revelation 16:19, *et al.*

[18] Bruce's word is 'enterteine' and could possibly be translated as 'cultivate' or 'consort with'.

[19] Matthew 12:43-45 = Luke 11:24-26.

except lies and error, just as Satan himself is a liar. That is why we have various Laws and Acts drawn up to oppose them, and it is now high time to have them enacted.

Religious turmoil

I have heard myself that his majesty does want to ratify these Laws, so that they are on the Statute Book, but he has complained that he cannot get any support or executors to enable him to bring our Laws into full agreement with the will of God, as well as with his own will as king. It would appear that there is not a single legislator to be found in the land with sufficient zeal for the truth to execute these laws that are agreeable to God's will as well as to the king's will.[20] These laws are to guard against the king's enemies.[21] But this we must lament and grieve that there are those ready to enact laws to oppose the king's will, laws that will ignore our cause. It is clear that at this time the devil would be

[20] In February 1588, the Kirk's General Assembly had urged King James to take more strenuous action against Papists, many of whom they unflinchingly named. James reluctantly consented, probably because of the impending threat of the Spanish Armada. But when a year later there was a failed uprising of a number of Catholic nobles, the king treated them very lightly, for his policy was to hold the balance between the Reformed and the Roman Churches as evenly as public opinion would permit. Roman Catholics comprised about a third of Scotland's population at this time. Although in 1560 death and confiscation of goods had been the penalty for celebrating and hearing mass, 'the crown of martyrdom was only awarded' to one Catholic, the Jesuit Ogilvie (Hume Brown's words). It is probably this unwillingness of James to act firmly that Bruce is here lamenting. Alas, those accused of witchcraft were treated very differently; hundreds of supposed witches were strangled and burnt at the stake during this period and right until capital punishment for witchcraft was abolished in 1736. In spite of the king's personal obsession with witches, significantly there is a deafening silence in Bruce's sermons on this subject, and for what it is worth my own opinion is that he did not approve of the rooting out of so-called witches, torturing and burning them.

[21] At this time Popish plots abounded; leading enemies of James VI were the Earl of Huntly and the 5th Earl of Bothwell (a first cousin of James VI, and nephew of the 4th Earl of Bothwell who was Mary Queen of Scots' third husband). The 'Blanks Plot' in which Huntly was implicated was an alleged pro-Spanish Catholic conspiracy in Scotland, discovered in late 1592. A number of letters to Spain were discovered, which included blank sheets signed by prominent nobles. It is possible, but unlikely, that there is a reference here to this as this sermon was most probably preached several months earlier.

sooner obeyed than God, and an evil spirit has greater power to drive men to wickedness than a good spirit[22] has the power to move them towards godliness.

I am sorry, but I foresaw that judgment was going to have to begin at the House of the Lord.[23] At this time we will restrain ourselves, but certainly the truth of God will not be suppressed. By God's grace I shall continue to be safe from incarceration,[24] while you must prepare yourselves by putting on that armour whereby you may take your stand, and by showing your colours[25] and doctrine that has for so long has been freely taught you. Whoever it is that has been influencing the king is an enemy of God and a disgrace to his nobility,[26] as the outcome will make clear. For beyond question he will be seen as a visible example of judgment, unless, that is, the Lord in his infinite mercy obstructs him. So far as I know, the king's inclinations would not be to act in this way, but this enemy has sought to influence him.

However, we must always let God do his work, and allow the truth to be truth, and so long as not all are given over to the spirit of error, there will still be those who will testify that truth is truth, that error is error, that a right course is a right course and that a wrong course is a wrong course. Now is the hour when we must seek to don the armour of God, and every one of you must run to him for refuge. In confessing those sins by which you may have offended him, you must obtain from him such strength and courage that you may boldly make your profession before the world. Each of you, according to your social rank, must take your stand upon the faith of that gospel, which your consciences are persuaded is the one true evangel that brings salvation.

Back to the patriarchs

You have heard how the Fathers persevered to the last breath in the steadfast profession of the truth, right from the time they were first called. We must follow in their footsteps. So at this time, we have chiefly to seek the gift of perseverance and constancy, and because this gift

[22] The word 'spirit' here means a 'good disposition', and certainly not the Holy Spirit.

[23] 1 Peter 4:17

[24] See note 6 above.

[25] The word is 'cuide' which is literally 'a chrism-cloth'. (DSL)

[26] Bruce's word is 'estait'; he alludes to this unnamed nobleman in a later sermon.

does not grow naturally in us, we ought so much the more to seek it from the hands of the living God. Because there are none at present who openly oppose us during these unsettled days, we should not be content with easy constancy and perseverance. Rather, when it shall please the Lord to try our faith and religion, as he tried the patriarchs, and the storm clouds arise more threatening than ever, then it will become us to bear witness to our faith powerfully and courageously, and we must be willing to speak more boldly than we do during times of tranquillity.

Therefore you must take heed to the faith that dwells in your hearts, and ensure that it is firmly grounded upon the right foundation stone, that corner-stone, the sure infallible rock, Jesus Christ and his cross. Every departure from true religion, every defection from the truth, all occur for this one reason: heart and faith were not grounded upon the right foundation stone. Had those who deserted taken heed to their hearts and to their faith, they would not have been shaken by any of the storms upon earth that arise. But because they stand on shaky ground, depending on the favours of men, or upon the authority of princes, or upon the riches and plaudits of the world, the storm rises and their faith cannot help them. Yet when the anchor of our faith has fastened upon that solid rock Christ Jesus, in the greatest of storms we have the greatest of faith, and in the greatest of troubles we have the greatest of foretastes of the heavenly Jerusalem. Therefore, if your foundation has been built wrongly and rests on men or things of this world, change it now while there is time, repair your whole building, and re-lay your faith's foundations upon Jesus Christ and his righteous merits.

The urgency of the gospel

There is one particular thing that you must aware of, and I pray that you will take heed of it—indeed, I pray that I also may take heed of it. It concerns the day of grace, which the apostle calls *the acceptabill day and tyme*;[27] there is also the state of grace with God in Christ Jesus. This day of grace wherein grace, mercy and peace have been offered to you, has continued for many years now in our land, and chiefly in this town; it has continued uninterrupted in liberty and calmness. It has been greatly blessed with abundant fruitfulness. Therefore, many who see this relative peace lightly regard the prosperous affluence of the gospel;

[27] 2 Corinthians 6:2.

consequently they do not bother to examine their consciences as they ought to do. Without any searching of themselves, they assume that they are in a state of grace; nor do they consider it necessary to subject themselves to searching examination of their consciences. They seem to believe that what others think of them is sufficient evidence of their being in a state of grace.

As I have said previously, by nature we are all born dead and our souls are dead in sin and trespasses, as the apostle has said.[28] By nature there is such a sinful false sense of security within our souls that this deadness of our hearts causes us to satisfy ourselves with a superficial profession of the truth. It never permits us to engage in testing whether or not we truly stand in the faith of Jesus Christ, whether or not we are grounded upon the right foundation and whether or not we give evidence of the fruit of the Spirit, and so we content ourselves with nodding assent to gospel truths. In this way we deceive ourselves.

The need for self-examination

Therefore, you ought not only to examine yourselves by comparison with your neighbours, to see if you live as good and careful lives as they do. Rather, you must enquire whether or not by the laws and in the estimation of the living God you are in a state of grace.[29] This enquiry may take a whole lifetime, and it is only obtained by earnest calling upon God, praying that in his mercy the Lord would quicken your dead hearts and raise there some inward response that you may be smitten[30] in your consciences with sorrow over your sins that have grieved him, and then be touched[31] by the awareness of his mercy, offered so bounteously in Jesus Christ. Then in your minds you will clearly see the great store of mercy that is in Christ, just as there was previously a store of misery in your own souls.

Here are the markers that will guide you to judge rightly whether or not you are in a state of grace. These markers are not innate, nor do they grow naturally within us, but are freely given in response to earnest and diligent prayer. The right way to begin this personal enquiry must be by

[28] Ephesians 2:1.

[29] 2 Peter 1:10, 'Therefore, be all the more diligent to make your calling and election sure, for if you practise these qualities you will never fall' (ESV).

[30] See note 9 above.

[31] See note 9 above.

prayer: beseech God that he may concur with his word by the working of his Holy Spirit to make it effectual in all of your hearts. Then the Spirit must convict you of your condemnation, and then he must guide you to your eternal salvation, leaving behind that condemnation. So let us ever pray that the Lord, who is well able, will hammer down that rebellion that is within you, so that your souls may be turned around towards everlasting salvation.

Dying a 'good death'

All these dyed in fayth: they died as they lived, and they lived in faith according to the rule of faith and the controlling guidance of the Holy Spirit. Yea, they lived well and they died well. For a good death always follows upon a good life.[32] Likewise an evil death invariably follows upon an evil life, though its demise might not be what one expected, notwithstanding a past evil life. Choosing to live wickedly is the surest way to provoke God and to deceive oneself, for the life of an evil man cannot but lead to an unhappy end. It is true that God works entirely as he chooses, and he is not restricted in his choice of the day or hour. Some are called in the morning, some at noontide, others in the evening. But whenever, an ill life usually ends in an ill death, but a good life will end in a happier, calmer and better death.

An exhortation to both old and young

As for the patriarchs, they all lived good and godly lives, therefore they were granted good deaths, for they died in the Lord; to die in faith is nothing else but to die in the Lord[33]. Therefore, seeing that a good life leads to a blessed death, do not delay in improving your life. You who are elderly, hasten in the time you have left to mend your living, set your hearts no longer upon vain things, but constantly dwell in your thoughts during every hour of your lives that you are continually under warning, and you never know when the Lord will chap[34] you.

[32] 'Dying a good death' became a frequently taught aspect of Christianity during the 16th and 17th centuries.

[33] Romans 14:8.

[34] 'Chap' is an old Scots word, still used in some areas, and means either 'to knock on a door' or 'to touch someone lightly'. Elsewhere, Bruce uses of God's final summons to us to die the expression, 'He will chap you on your shoulder'.

You who are young, do not delay your repentance to your old age; do not say in your heart along with the fool, 'I will indulge myself in pleasures as there are yet many years ahead of me, and there will be plenty of time left to repent when I am older.' While you are still young you must remember that the gift of repentance does not lie in your hands, it is not nascent in your bosoms, that you may take it up whenever you may please. Remember too that the hour of your death is not in your hands either. Who can promise you one more hour of life, let alone one more year? Therefore, since neither the gift of regeneration is in your power, nor can you know when you will die, while your time here on earth continues, every single day should admonish you to take heed to yourselves, especially when it is still possible for your passions to get the better of you and cause you to do something evil.

While you are still young, make it your chief aim to turn to the Lord and strive after godliness. If you learn now to abstain from follies, you will find you are better able to practise self-control as you grow older. Those who do not discipline themselves in their youth but give free rein to their desires, find it much more difficult[35] to live wisely during the rest of their lifetime. Therefore, take control of your habits now while the devil is at his most active in harassing you; resist him and he will flee from you.[36] Crave from Jesus Christ the strength to mortify your passions and to expose the ways in which they deceive you by their false promises;[37] then you will discern the ugly truth about your corrupt desires. Until their falseness is unmasked, they appear to offer sweet pleasures, so you must pray that you may be given an awareness of the bitterness of sin; then you may willingly and wholeheartedly desist from it.

Without doubt, all would like a good passing from this life. Indeed, when someone dies the most common question that men ask is, 'How did he die?' If he passed away peacefully, even though his life had been marred by wrong-doing, a tranquil death covers the shame of a bad life. You all want a peaceful demise, especially if it is undeserved after many evil years, because you hope a quiet death will mitigate the memory of

[35] My phrase, 'find it much more difficult' translates Bruce's rather quaint, 'he hes ane stron turne to do'.

[36] James 4:7.

[37] Possibly an allusion to Paul's phrase 'deceitful desires' (Ephesians 4:22).

your shameful past. That being so, should you not strive to lead a good life and conform your living to God's laws, and ought you not to turn away from evil desires? Suffer the loss of your sinful passions rather than the loss of your souls. Though you enter the kingdom of heaven blind, bent and lame because you have cut off so many sinful affections, you will have heeded the words of our Master who said we should lose all rather than lose our souls.[38] Fight then against the power of the devil and against all your fleshly desires that are your spiritual enemies; slay them all, otherwise they will slay your soul for ever.

Living in expectation

All these dyed in fayth. The apostle further expands upon the patriarchs' perseverance by telling us that they all died without either obtaining the blessings that were promised or entering into possession of their inheritance. It does not matter whether by 'their inheritance' you mean the Land of Canaan, or the revelation of Jesus Christ their Messiah, or the full enjoyment of the heavenly destination. The point is that they died in the faith of those promises before ever they came to full fruition or were granted possession of them. You see, had they obtained the things promised, they then would no longer have needed to have faith in those promises. When you and I get something that has been promised, we then live by it, and no longer do we hope for it. But until we receive something, we live in expectancy of what it is that God has promised us. That is why he wants us in this world to live by faith, and why, sustaining us by hope, he gives us endurance to overcome all difficulties.

Sight and foretaste

Thus it was that Abraham was praised, for notwithstanding the temporal promises that were delayed in being fulfilled until his one hundredth year, he lived all that time in the land, waiting patiently without any sign of God's word coming to pass. I find set down for us two things that chiefly upheld his faith and inspired him to perseverance and patience. The Spirit of God says of the promises, *bot saw them afar af.* In effect the apostle is saying, 'Even though he did not come to the full fruition of the promises, the Lord gave him an eye in his mind, as

[38] Matthew 16:24-26 = Mark 8:35-37.

it were, whereby he saw clearly that God would do what he had said, so assuring him the promises would be kept.' That was why he persevered and patiently held fast to God's word.

The second thing that chiefly sustained him was an awareness of the blessings that had been promised to him through the foretaste[39] of the promises that God gave him in his conscience and heart. Just as he was assured through the eye in his mind that God gave him, his assurance was further confirmed by the foretaste of the promises in his heart and conscience that God would perform all that he had said. These, then, were the two supports that upheld him—Sight and Foretaste. As for 'sight', he saw the promises of God, as it were, *afar af*; he saw that after his soul was parted from his mortal body, his soul would inherit the kingdom of heaven. He also saw that the fulfilment of the temporal aspect of the promise regarding his posterity would be fulfilled after a long delay. This 'sight' upheld him. As to the 'foretaste', it enabled him to rejoice and likewise upheld him.

This is confirmed by our Master who spoke of Abraham being enlightened by an inward, spiritual sight, for we read in John 8:56, *Your father Abrahame reioyced to se my day, and he sawe it and was glad*. Now obviously he could not see either Christ or his days with his bodily eye, but only by the illumination in his mind imparted to him through the Spirit's power. And as he saw our Lord's day he rejoiced. Whence came this joy? Joy is an emotion within the heart, and Abraham's joy flowed from the foretaste in his conscience. Without that foretaste neither his heart nor conscience could have rejoiced, therefore his joy makes it plain that, as he saw in his mind, so he experienced the foretaste in his heart. Indeed, the joy in his heart bore witness to this foretaste, for when the heart is deeply moved by some emotion, that emotion prevails,[40] to the extent that our bodies cannot help but express that emotion. Thus when joy fills someone's heart to overflowing, it can hardly contain itself but will be evident in gestures and smiles.

We see, therefore, that Abraham had the spiritual eye to see clearly

[39] The connotation of Bruce's word 'taist' is complex; 'taist' combines the meaning 'test' or 'prove' with the meaning 'touch' or 'feel'. Sometimes 'foretaste' is a suitable translation, but other times 'taist' is better translated as 'put to the proof', or 'perceive by the taste', or simply 'experience'.

[40] By 'prevaillis' Bruce may mean 'overflows' as the context suggests; see Psalm 23:5, '... my cup overflows'.

the promises, and in his heart he had the foretaste that experienced the reality of these promised blessing. But, you may ask, what brings about this inward sight and experience in the heart? It arises from a steadfast and wholehearted faith within the soul. The inward sight allures the mind by the promises, and the experience of the foretaste brings assurance to the heart, and that is why the soul wholly believes that whatever God says will be accomplished. So faith rises up from spiritual sight in the mind and from the proof the foretaste brings to the heart.

A forthright profession leads to an open confession

However, it must be added that sight and foretaste alone are not enough. Added to them both must be constancy and the perseverance to endure and overcome all difficulties. And what more? These two, sight and foretaste, which inspire constancy in faith will also break out into a forthright profession in his life that will be consistent with the promises of the gospel. From this profession an open confession also breaks forth. 'I can see,' says the patriarch, 'and I confess that I am not here permanently, for I am a stranger and pilgrim on the earth. I know that my life here is but a journey to another country. I see that this earth is a kind of banishment for me. I see that my proper home is in heaven, for my only Master dwells there, and as long as I am here I am absent from his face.' That is what I mean by his confession 'breaking forth' from his inward sight and heartfelt foretaste.

Three lessons

I think time will not allow me to explain the following three verses, so I shall have to be content to stay with verse 13. Now that you have had the words opened up to you, I shall pass on to you briefly the application[41] as God gives me grace. First of all, from this sermon, what kind of eye is it whereby the promises of God in Christ Jesus are perceived? We find that just as Abraham could not see them by his physical eye, no more can you understand and perceive them by your physical sight. Because the promises that are set down in the gospel are spiritual, so they must be perceived by the eye of faith, and through a heavenly light from above; it must be through the Spirit of grace that we see the

[41] Although Bruce uses the word 'doctrine', the context suggests that he means 'the application' or 'use' of the verse's teaching.

promises of grace.

Therefore, let this be your constant prayer whenever you read these words, or as often as you come to hear them, or whenever you meditate upon them: always start with the enlightening of your minds by craving that the Lord would illuminate your spiritual eye with his heavenly light. Only then will you have true insight into the word of God, and understand what the Holy Spirit is saying by his own prompting. Only then will the promises of God be perceived by the eye of faith through the Spirit of grace.

Secondly, I learn that without this sight and feeling[42] there can be no faith or perseverance in religion. Neither will we endure in our trials unless we have a sight of heaven, and the Lord in his mercy gives us a foretaste[43] of it in our hearts. Unless he does this for us, we will not in our own natural strength be able to endure, and when we face afflictions we will not persevere or stand firm in the faith. If we do not have this spiritual eye (or if we lose it), then it can only be that some sin—or, for that matter, maybe many sins—have come between us and the face of God. Now there is a barrier separating you from the sight of the face of God, in whom alone our only happiness and well-being can be found.

Therefore, seeing that there can be no perseverance, faith or constancy without the vision of his face, and you no longer have that vision, most earnestly must you address yourself thus: 'I have separated myself from the Lord's countenance by my sins. I must repent again, and return to those things in which I used to delight. I must also go on the offensive against the sins of my heart to clear them out. Sadly, I recall the pleasure I found in wrong-doing; I must now despise and reject those pleasures, and pursue only what is good and godly.' Yes, by a sincere confession and an earnest plea[44] for mercy, you may again have that 'eye in the mind' by which you will have sight of the face of God, and will know that there is a life after this earthly one. Then you will have such a joy in your heart that you will disdain those trials of this world that torment and trouble both body and soul, for the sight and foretaste of the future life will swallow up all the pain.

[42] Though he uses here the word 'feilling', he is referring back to 'sicht and taist'; on 'taist' see above Note 39.

[43] He now uses the word 'fortaist' as a synonym for 'taist'.

[44] Bruce's word is 'sute'; see Note 12 above.

Therefore now, while you have the opportunity, be diligent in seeking the sight of this life that, having once obtained it, you may firmly stand, defended against all the temptations of the world. In this land of ours we have to lament that not only have we lost this vision, but we have even banished it. Nature brought us forth blind, and before we were called into that heavenly company our blindness increased. But when we were called it pleased the Lord to shine into our minds and in some measure to enlighten our understanding, so that in our hearts we knew we were sinful creatures and were persuaded that Jesus Christ was the only Saviour of the world. Yet all of us have returned again to the mire like the sow and like the dog to its vomit,[45] for we have gone back to offending the living God by the self-same sins that he had already forgiven. By the force of our conflicting emotions we have banished the knowledge of God from our minds and the feelings of sinfulness from our consciences.

There is someone that has never brought forth any fruits of repentance, for since ever the gospel was preached he has been a banisher of the light and a denier of the Holy Spirit; therefore this rebellious man must receive a heavier judgment than if he had never seen nor heard of the light.[46]

That apart, there have never been any of us, whether speaker or hearer, who to some extent are not guilty of the same fault. Every single one of us has at some time turned away from the knowledge that the Lord has imparted to us; we have not nourished it as we ought to have done but have thrust it from us. I know of only one remedy for this. For I assure you that if in his naked justice the Lord were to strike us, no tongue could describe the dreadful anguish that would come upon us, even though at the present we may be deluded into thinking that there is no higher tribunal, nor any future judgment awaiting us. However, the opposite is the truth. You yourselves have witnessed those who are in anguish as they cry out, 'We are all under condemnation!' From the moment that realisation comes upon them, the dark clouds of their iniquity have cut them off from any sight of mercy. Therefore

[45] 2 Peter 2:22.

[46] I found this paragraph rather obscure. Bruce may be referring back to the enemy of the reformed faith he mentioned earlier in the sermon; see the context of Notes 20 and 21 above.

the only remedy for those who have aggravated their defection by banishing the light and defying and denying their consciences is to confess and acknowledge their guilt, and then constantly and daily to crave of the Lord that he would turn their grief into godly sorrow.

All of you who have offended so gracious a God should in sorrow pray that the Holy Spirit will so work in your hearts that these words you hear should not appear to you as mere fables. By no means are they fables; they are far more momentous than fables. These words shall reduce you to molten terror on that Great Day of your condemnation. *We haue piped vnto you & ye haue not danced, we haue mourned vnto you and ye haue not lamented.*[47] So shall these words increase the gravity of your damnation. Therefore, I beseech the living God by the compassion of his Son Christ Jesus to illuminate your minds. Only then you will be able to see his righteous grace to which you have so freely been called these many years.

Thirdly, the last thing we learn is that faith must inevitably express what we are. I mean that when faith resides in the heart and mind, it is impossible for it not to burst forth into good works and an open confession to the glory of God. For as by faith you are justified in your heart, so with your lips you must confess to your salvation.[48] Thus while faith in your heart is necessary for justification, the words of your mouth and the works of your hands are necessary for salvation. Faith is essential for our justification. For the moment you apprehend faith (beware of thinking your apprehension is a work!), in that very instant you are justified through the merits of Jesus Christ. Such faith, when it is genuine, must express itself in confession.

Conclusion

So we have it here: the Fathers confessed that they were strangers and pilgrims in this world. They confessed that this world was for them a banishment, and that their gaze was fixed upon the heavenly life to come, and that they never considered themselves truly to be at home in the land they had been given to possess. We must apply this to ourselves and all that we possess. This confession of faith ought today to be the confession of the Kirk of God and every one of its members. All

[47] Matthew 11:17 (GenB).

[48] Romans 10:10.

of us in our hearts, minds and with our mouths must confess that we are sojourners here on earth, and that we are looking for the city that has foundations, looking to find mercy at the hands of Jesus Christ on that Great Day.

If you do not find this within your hearts—and I fear that there are but few who do—if your heart cannot say that you consider yourself to be a pilgrim here, then your spiritual state is not good and you do not have a sure foundation. Therefore all of you take heed to yourselves, for many who do make this confession make it only with their lips, it does not come from their hearts. Therefore I leave to each of you the ploughing and tilling[49] of your hearts. All of you must labour hard over this, you must take pains that unbelief be banished from your hearts, that your habitual sins be purged away. Thus may you confess with the patriarchs that you are strangers and pilgrims here, and that you are seeking as your country the kingdom of heaven, where the Lord in the mercy of his Son Jesus Christ and for his sake shall bring us. To whom with the Father and the Holy Ghost be all honour, praise and glory now and for ever. Amen.

[49] Bruce's word is 'manureing', by which he means the cultivation of ground that has been ploughed and broken up.

Chapter Eleven

Hebrews Chapter 11 verses 13-14

> [13] *All these died in fayth and receaved not the promis, bot saw them afar aff and believed them, and receaved them thankfullie and confessed that they wer straingeris on the earth.* [14] *For they that say such thingis declair plainlie that they seik ane cuntrie.*

Led by the Spirit of Jesus Christ, the apostle here jointly praises the patriarchs, Abraham, Isaac and Jacob, although earlier you heard each of them praised individually. Therefore, by God's grace, I intend to mark out from these two verses certain effects of their faith that were common to all three. For example, he praises them for their invincible constancy, notwithstanding the manifold difficulties they sustained both at home and further afield, and also the long delay lasting all their days of the fulfilment of the promise made to them. Nevertheless, they held fast to the promise, believing that it would most surely come to fruition for their descendants, even though that was denied to themselves. So they lived in faith and died in faith, they lived well[1] and they died well.[2] For a good life properly brings a good end, but an ill life properly brings an ill end.

In unusual circumstances the Lord, in the riches of his grace, may at times intervene in a person's life in the final hour of his death, but ordinarily an ill life must lead to an ill end. Therefore, how terrible and bitter is death for those who live according to the flesh. On the other

[1] The Scots word 'weill' is used several times in this sermon (as elsewhere throughout Bruce's preaching). Although I have translated it as 'well', it has a far fuller meaning: 'weill' includes 'happiness, acting fittingly, properly, suitably' (DSL).

[2] See Chapter 10, note 32 above.

hand, how comforting is death for those who have taken a heavenly course during this life, and have prepared themselves for that country which now we too ought to seek in conscience and in faith.

The unremitting constancy of the patriarchs

Thus the patriarchs are praised for their invincible constancy, whereby they overcame all trials, not only domestic ones such as Abraham had with Lot his brother's son and also troubles within his own family, but even foreign trials involving great princes. That he was able to withstand harassment by powerful chieftains lets us see us see how greatly he was assisted by the power of the Holy Spirit, who clothed him with supernatural strength from above. We know that it is not normal for a man to gainsay the will of royalty, particularly a prince in his own country. It is accepted that before a monarch men must give way, and that they will flatter or lie to their king. But when we find a man with the courage to withstand a prince's authority, we may be sure that this is not by his own strength, but by a power bestowed on him by God's Spirit. The patriarch's unremitting perseverance in all his troubles, not least when confronted by princes, makes it clear that he was constantly upheld by the Holy Spirit.

What we have to learn is this: we see that the gift of steadfast perseverance to the end is conjoined with the gift of true and justifying faith. It follows that whosoever has genuine faith in the blood of Jesus Christ is also given the grace of steadfast perseverance right to the end. Abraham's example is set before us to be followed and imitated, so that we in this present corrupt generation will defect neither in our conduct nor in our religion. For, surrounded as we are by multitudinous examples of iniquity, it is very hard for us to continue to stand true; easy it is to be swept along by the conduct of the majority into defecting either in our living or our religion. Therefore, so much the more ought you to watch and pray that the spirit of the multitude may not overwhelm you.

The first aid to constancy is mutual exhortation

Among the various helps that the Holy Spirit has set down in Scripture to enable a man to remain standing on his feet, preserved constant in his faith, I recall one in particular: it is mutual exhortation. In Hebrews 3:13, after the apostle has exhorted his readers to 'Take care lest there be in any of you an evil, unbelieving heart, leading you to fall away from the living God' [ESV], he adds another exhortation in the following verse, *Exhort everie ane another quhill it is the day, that your hairtis be not hardned throwch the decept of sin, and be the craft of Sathan who is working in it.*[3] Therefore, to keep us steadfast in our faith, there is not a more necessary means or method than for us to be diligent in mutual exhortation. It is our duty to stir up one another by mutual admonition, encouragement, comfort[4] and consolation; in this way 'the faith in me and the faith in thee'[5] may be jointly edified.

The neglect of this duty is to me an indication that your love for others is growing cold. Such negligence cannot help but weaken your faith. If you were as diligent in mutual exhortation as you are in such things as backbiting, scurrilous gossip and frequent maligning of each other, then doubtless the fruits and effects of it would be far more evident than they presently are. Those who aspire to be constant must engage in this duty by graciously admonishing others, and, within the bounds of their calling, lovingly stirring up others in their faith.

The second aid is to lay hold of his promises

Secondly, in this verse I perceive that, even though the Lord delays for a long time the fulfilment of his word, yet he never forgets the performance of his promise. His delays are deliberate, that in the meantime we may be exercised in prayer, constantly laying his word before him, in the knowledge that what he has truly promised he will in his own time complete. For the Lord knows our natural dispositions and the strength of the depravity that lurks within us. As often as he grants us some blessing or fulfils some promise he has made to us, such is the

[3] These words in italics are always carefully scripted in the original sermon notes in Bruce's handwriting indicating a direct quotation from Scripture; but here the final clause, *and be the craft of Sathan who is working in it*, is not in verse 13, nor in another verse in Scripture. It is possibly an amalgam of several NT phrases: 'that Satan may not tempt you' (1 Cor. 7:5); 'Satan disguises himself as an angel of light' (2 Cor. 11:14); 'the activity of Satan with all power and false signs' (2 Thess. 2:9); 'Be sober, be watchful. Your adversary the devil prowls around like a roaring lion, seeking someone to devour' (1 Peter 5:8), and others.

[4] I suspect that Bruce's word 'comfort' is not a synonym for 'consolation', but was used here in its original sense of 'imparting strength' or 'giving aid' (from Latin, 'cum', with 'fortis' strong).

[5] Bruce's actual phrase.

influence of our inward corruption, that we begin to misuse his kindness to satisfy our dissolute and sinful flesh. When God's goodness to us should cause us to thank and glorify him, our wantonness draws us away from him by abusing his kindness in satisfying our sinful desires. Therefore, the Lord purposely delays over his promise, yet he always carefully keeps in mind the timing of his plan for its fulfilment.[6] However, the main point for us here is this: however long the Lord may delay performing what he has promised, we must be assured that he never ever forgets it.

An appeal to King James

Regarding delays, I must take the opportunity to remind your majesty of your promise; even though you have not yet fulfilled it, nevertheless do not forget it! Because of your promise, you have put yourself under the obligation to your people to banish Jesuits and to do likewise with those who have been excommunicated.[7] Your promise also obliges you to confirm the establishment of our religion in this land through the appropriate legislation, and we await the fulfilment by your majesty of your commitment to undertake this.[8] Therefore, do not let it slip your mind.

And you, my lords who work for the community, regarding this particular task consider how diligent you are in those things that affect you personally. With that same diligence you must attend to what needs to be done for the community, so that God's glory may once again shine among us, and his majesty may be helped to perform this task that God has laid upon him; then shall the burden of it be removed from him. (I only say these things because my text offers me the opportunity.)

[6] The second clause of this sentence is difficult to translate (as are many others!): 'Theirfoir purposelie the lord delayis his promeis, alwayis he keipis in gude mynd the article of tyme in the quhilk he hes appoyntit to performe it.

[7] During Bruce's ministry in Edinburgh, the Counter Reformation was extremely active in Scotland, with specially trained Jesuits brought in clandestinely from Seminaries established in Europe with the specific purpose of educating them sufficiently well to engage in theological debate with the so-called 'apostles of Geneva', that is the Presbyterian Ministers.

[8] These two promises, first to banish Jesuits and those already excommunicated, and second to confirm the establishment of the reformed faith in Scotland, are referred to twice later in the sermon in a second and third direct appeal to King James and his lords. See Notes 15 and 40 below.

The importance of 'sight' and 'foretaste' in maintaining constancy

I come to the next thing I mark in the text. During the promise's long delay, there were two things that upheld the Fathers, without which it would have been impossible for them to have maintained their constancy. Along with the 'sight' of the promised kingdom God conjoined a 'feeling' of it; here the apostle calls that feeling 'a taste'[9] of the heavenly promises. You all know that there are two physical senses which are foremost in bringing to us certainty of anything. This was how Christ assured Thomas who questioned whether he was a real body or just a phantasy; he told him to look (sight) and touch (feeling). Because these two outward senses cannot be doubted, so certainty is communicated by these two inward senses, the spiritual and heavenly sight of the truth of the promises, and the spiritual and heavenly assurance[10] of God's truth. These two spiritual senses enable both heart and mind to be assured of what the Lord has promised. The inward sight assures the mind and the feeling in the heart assures the heart; then mind and heart assure the soul.

Therefore, by sight and the felt assurance, the Fathers stood firm, notwithstanding the difficulties that confronted them on their pilgrim way. Likewise, the vision and foretaste of that future heavenly life empowers us also to surmount all barriers in our pathway, and constantly to repose upon the promise. It was this vision and foretaste that enabled them to lead lives agreeable to the evangelical promise, that, having the heavenly life in their minds and the taste of it their hearts, they modelled their manner of living according to what by faith they already saw and felt. As they glimpsed afar off that other country, they confessed with the mouths that here on this earth they were pilgrims and strangers. I must move on.

Only through justifying faith we have sight and taste

What is faith? There is a mental assent that I call 'historical faith', but there is faith in the heart and that I call 'justifying faith'. So which leads to perseverance and despising the things of this world? Only that vision

[9] See above Chapter 10, note 3 on this distinctive theme in Bruce's sermons, 'the taist of godis mercie'.

[10] Bruce again uses the word 'feilling' which here is best understood as 'assurance'.

of heaven and the foretaste of eternal things. Consider how sublimely superior are these heavenly things compared to the pleasures that may be had in earthly things. This means that when you have both the sight and taste of heaven, you cannot but lightly regard any earthly pleasures and count them as worthless.[11] Those who invest everything they have in things of this world, assuming they will never leave it, clearly never had the vision of heaven nor the foretaste of the felicity of heavenly things.

It follows that for want of that sight and taste of the blessed future joys, we shall all perish, both pasture[12] and people. For should it please the Lord in his mercy to illuminate the eyes of your minds, that you might see the truth of these heavenly things, and to enable you to mortify the vileness of your sinful desires and soften the hardness of your hearts, so that you would fall in love with the promised blessed future felicity, then without fear of contradiction those dreadful flagrancies among us would not occur.

Stinging rebuke to the nobility

No, my lords, brutal murders would not take place at your hands, nor would adulteries abound and all manner of filthiness in your households. You would not pollute both body and soul with such things as burning oppression and the terrible confusions of which it is quite terrible to hear.[13] If only the Lord in his mercy would give you this inward sight and feeling, you would then abhor the devil and eschew these sins that bind you as the devil's slaves. Happy would you be, yea doubly happy, all you of lordly rank, if with this outward calling the Lord should concur through his Holy Spirit and bring to you his inward calling.

[11] An allusion to Philippians 3:7-9.

[12] Bruce does have 'both pasture and people', but I wonder if the context implies he has accidentally used the wrong word and meant 'both pastors and people'. He was frequently deeply grieved by the unfaithfulness of many pastors who were (in Milton's words) 'blind mouths': 'Blind mouths! that scarce themselves know how to hold a sheep-hook.' *Lycidas.*

[13] General Assembly of 1590: Minutes for Session 14 state: 'Because great scandal lies on the Kirk through manifold murders, notorious adulteries and incest, and the parties being [brought] under pressure, oft times eluded the kirk, and shift from place to place, whereby the process cannot be brought to a final sentence…' (Shaw, pp. 919-20).

It cannot be doubted that the deep feelings of these spiritual things would so influence you that you would not behave as you do; those who are magistrates would not act corruptly, but when dealing with the guilty, they would administer the law justly without respect of persons, while those of you in high positions of authority would acquit yourselves far better. Alas, we[14] have to lament that the impact of these words of my outward ministry is lost, for in his righteous judgment the Lord has hardened the hearts of those who hear. May the Lord in his mercy so illuminate your minds with the sight of that life to come, and with a foretaste of it in your hearts, that you may look for a better life after your time here on earth is ended. Therefore take heed to this exhortation, for it is brought to you most lovingly, and take action over the atrocious events that you see being daily multiplied.

The second appeal to King James

Sire, even though it may appear there is no one to support you, yet count it an honour to hazard both your crown and your life in banishing sin from our land, especially such horrible sins that cry to the heavens for vengeance; may the Lord strengthen your hand. And you, my lords, support your prince! And while there is time take heed to yourselves, and would to God that you had some awareness of the great examination that one day you are all to undergo. Then, without question, you would either resign your office, or else with greater alacrity and willingness you would discharge at least some of what you should be doing. I constantly look to the mercy of God, that both these things that have been overlooked[15] shall be put right by you, Sire, and that you also, my lords, will concur with your prince better than you have done so far.

The implications of being strangers and pilgrims

Back to the patriarchs. We have seen that this inward sight and feeling enabled them to say wherever they went that they were pilgrims and strangers on the earth, not only when they were in Ur and in Gerar[16] under Abimelech, but also in the land of Canaan, which the Lord had

[14] This may be a royal 'we', as we say; it is probable that he means 'I have to lament' for he then says 'my outward ministry'.

[15] See note 7 above.

[16] Genesis 11:31; 20:1; 26:6.

given them as a free inheritance. So Abraham speaks of himself in Genesis 23,[17] so Isaac lives a sojourner, Genesis 26,[18] and so Jacob says before Pharaoh in Genesis 47.[19] All three continually lived as sojourners in the land. Also in Genesis 26 the Lord spoke to Isaac and told him to be obedient as a sojourner as his father Abraham had been.[20] After saying that they acknowledged they were strangers on the earth, the apostle proceeds in verse 14 to explain what the Fathers meant by this. It is obvious what such a confession implied.

First of all, they were declaring plainly that they claimed no property or kinship[21] to this earth, but they claimed their kinship and property to be in the kingdom of heaven. From the time the Lord called Abraham out of Ur and its idolatry, he kept his gaze fixed upon that kingdom, and, professing himself to be a pilgrim on earth, he confessed in effect that he had the right to arrive at the heavenly kingdom. For pilgrims never claim any holdings or kinship[22] in the land of their sojourning. Thus in effect the patriarchs made it clear that they were not to remain here on earth and so would not put down their roots in the land,[23] for they were journeying to their own country.[24] You will all know how a traveller is glad to leave a stopping place in order to continue towards his intended destination. Likewise the patriarchs were glad to leave

[17] Genesis 23:4, 'And Abraham said to the Hittites, "I am a sojourner and foreigner among you...."'

[18] No specific reference, but the whole chapter bears witness to his obedience to God's command to him to 'Sojourn in this land, and I will be with you and bless you...' (verse 3).

[19] Genesis 47:9, 'The days of the years of my sojourning are 130 years.'

[20] Verses 1-5.

[21] Bruce's word that I have translated as 'kinship' is the Scots word 'kyndnes', a legal term meaning 'the native right of one to his holding or to the lands of his landlord'; hence his preposition is 'to'—'kyndnes *to* this earth'.

[22] See Note 21 above.

[23] Bruce's phrase is that they would not 'fix their staik heir', a 'staik' being 'a post or boundary marker'.

[24] Readers may question the validity of this statement for when Sarah died Abraham bought a cave as a family burial place (Genesis 23). However, Calvin comments on verse 8 that the text 'is more minute in this matter, to raise our minds to the hope of the resurrection. [Abraham] saw the half of himself taken away; and because he was certain that his wife was not exiled from the kingdom of God, he hides her dead body in the tomb, until he and she should be gathered together.' *Comm. in loc.*

their temporary camping sites[25] and to go forward on their journey at the commandment of the living God. As travellers keep in mind their intended destination, so the patriarchs fixed their sights steadfastly upon one particular country towards which they were journeying.

A further point: every pilgrim must patiently bear with any injuries he sustains along the way, and endure the various hardships that he encounters such as foul weather. Similarly, the patriarchs, as they moved from one place to another, had to cope with all the difficulties and hindrances that they met on their journey to the kingdom of heaven. Thus the apostle says, *They that say such thingis declair plainlie that they seik ane cuntrie*, and obviously that other country could not be here on earth, but must have been in heaven, towards which all their desires and daily living were directed.

As for us, we are so worldly-minded that all our considerations savour only of this earth as if we are to remain here for ever. I say our dispositions are so earth-bound, that hardly once in a year can we lift our thoughts to consider that there is a heaven after death; but there is also a place of torment! Yea, only once a year is but a small matter, so if you would drag your thoughts from this world to the contemplation of heavenly things that are here set before you so plainly, then perhaps such consideration might bring you nearer to salvation. For being continually occupied with, and desiring only, earthly things, causes you to be as blind as moles in the understanding of heavenly things.

The narrow way

Therefore lift up your thought once a day to ponder that you must appear[26] before the living God; then in your hearts resolve to reform your lives, and to set out for that city and heavenly country. Resolve upon a change of direction, that is, set out to seek the kingdom of heaven. Yet not all who seek come to the city of God. There is, on the one hand, a seeking that is in vain; on the other hand, there is a seeking that comes to fruition. In Luke 13:24 our Master commands us to enter in through the narrow door; he also says to enter in time, for many

[25] Bruce's word is 'tabernaclis' which in this context means 'the earthly body as the dwelling place of the soul' (DSL).

[26] The word used is 'compeir' and those familiar with Kirk Session minutes of the 18th and 19th centuries will recognize this legal term, meaning 'to appear in a formal act before some court of justice, or before someone in authority' (DSL).

will seek to enter but will not be able. The seeking that is in vain is when men try to enter 'out of time'; the right kind of seeking is when men seek 'in due[27] time'. This right way of seeking I call 'the narrow way'; 'the due time' I call the time of the preaching of the gospel, and it is called by our Master and his prophets, *the day*. For the Lord in his mercy has so ordered times that he has given every nation their own particular day, that is, their own time for the evangel. So the evangel has come to us, having passed through the rest of the world, and soon will go to The Indies also, so that every nation will have had its own day.

This is why David has said, *Today quhill ye heir his voice harden not your hairtis.*[28] And our Master says to Jerusalem, in Luke 19 verse 42, *O Jerusalem happie hade thou in this thy day*. And the apostle in Hebrews chapter 3 exhorts us to admonish one another, *quhill it is called the day.*[29] Therefore, by 'the day' we understand the preaching of the gospel whereby grace, mercy and peace are offered to the world. To underline this point, the right way is the narrow way, and the due time is the time of the gospel.

There are many narrow ways, but they do not lead to heaven. The priests of Baal imposed upon themselves a narrow way, and when they and Elijah the prophet confronted one another, they cut into their flesh and slashed their bodies to try and draw down fire by a superstition of their own invention.[30] Then there were the Pharisees who devised for themselves a narrow way, appointing a certain number of weekly fasts. Next come the Papists after them, with their vestments, hoods and other such things. All of these forged for themselves their own narrow way, thinking that by their particular inventions they would merit heaven. But, as the apostle writes in Romans 10:3, human flesh is ignorant: they do not know Christ who is the righteousness of God, and going about to establish their own righteousness, in the end they are robbed[31] of both.

[27] The word 'due' translates the Scots word 'dew', meaning 'acting as one ought' or 'as required by conditions' (DSL).

[28] Psalm 95:8.

[29] Hebrews 3:13.

[30] 1 Kings 18:25-29.

[31] Bruce's vivid Scots word is 'spuilyeit' which literally means 'plundered'; 'robbed of both' means 'robbed of both Christ and God's justifying righteousness'.

Carrying the cross means mortification and self-denial

The narrow way that leads to heaven is the way that Jesus Christ has set down in his gospel. It is called narrow, not because it is strait in itself, but in respect of flesh and blood and our corruption. For the yoke of Christ is sweet and light in itself, though to flesh and blood it appears narrow. That is why our Master says, *none can cum to me except my father draw him.*[32] This is the way that Christ has set before us in the gospel and is called 'narrow'. Why 'narrow' you ask. Because it is the way of the mortification of my sinful lusts, and of the denying of myself and own will. As soon as we begin to subdue our stubborn, selfish will to the will of Jesus Christ, and start preferring God's will to our own wills, we then enter the narrow way.

This mortification is only brought about by a daily cross which the Lord sanctifies, enabling it to subdue our fleshly desires. Therefore, I consider the way for a Christian to be the way of the cross and trials. *It behoveth us* (says the apostle) *by manie trubillis to enter in the kingdome of hevine.*[33] For by tribulations we are purged[34] of that dross with which by nature we were conceived and born; we are purged from those sins by which our souls are defiled, and which have raised up a barrier between us and the living God. That is why I reckon the narrow way is the way of tribulation and the daily cross that our Master commanded us to take up in order to follow him.[35]

Now you who would fain enter the kingdom of heaven must seek it in the right way, that is, you must patiently accept any cross that Christ lays upon you. Do not think that the 'flesh' of anyone can somehow escape the tribulations that will come. No, those who choose to side with the devil will have the heaviest cross, for the cross that is laid upon a Christian is very light, compared to the calamities that will befall the wicked. So go in whichever way you choose, whether in the broad way of your sinful desires, or in the narrow way of converted reason, and every day you will be subjected to some cross or other. Is it not, then, best to walk in the pathway of transformed reasoning? For the trials that you will endure without doubt will work towards the mortification

[32] Matthew 11:29; John 6:44.

[33] Acts 14:22.

[34] Bruce's word is 'scourit' which means 'washed clean by some cleansing agent'.

[35] Mark 8:34.

of your sinful flesh and the subduing of your will; then you shall be of the same mind as Christ, and will love what he loves, and hate what he hates.

Therefore, seeing that no one can win an exemption from trials, it is your duty to crave from the hand of the living God the sanctification of your tribulations by the power of the Holy Spirit, for then you will attain to the gracious sight of the Lord's countenance, to whose face you must flee, because only in his smile upon you is there life. Do this while you have time, for, as our Master has said, the night is coming when it will not be possible for you to work (John 9:4). When that night comes neither will it be possible to receive the virtue[36] that must attend his saving work of transforming your human affections. I have never heard of the gospel continuing so long in one nation as it has done among us. Therefore if, as could happen, this continuance were to draw to a close, it would make me think that the 'night' of which Christ spoke was at hand.

The impending day of judgment

However, it is not the continued freedom of the gospel among us that causes me to ask if that night is now imminent, rather is it the contempt, the extraordinary confusion and the enormities that are prevalent among us, in spite of the widespread preaching of the gospel. It is these things that make me think that the night of darkness draws near. Therefore, be careful to redeem the time before our day of grace comes to an end. Each of you must be assured in your hearts that you stand in God's favour, that the Lord has forgiven your sins and does not lay them to your charge. Every one of you, while it is still day, do this! For I must assure you of one thing, it is that there is a deadness of heart—we are all conceived and born with this deadness—that causes men to assume that all the Lord requires of them is an easy and light profession. That is because the Lord has not wakened their consciences so that they can see the pitiful misery of their own souls; not yet has he awakened their hearts to let them see the oceans of mercy that are available in Christ Jesus. Consequently, they continue as they were born in the same deadness of heart that would deceive us all.

When the great day of trial comes, the Day of the Lord, they will

[36] On 'virtue' see above Chapter 9, note 10.

cry upon the mountains to fall upon them,[37] all because they did not examine their consciences in time, while grace and mercy was being offered to them. Therefore, beware of this deadness and false sense of security that lurks in the souls of every one of you. May all of you resolve to examine yourselves.[38] It is in examining yourselves here and now, and acknowledging you are under condemnation, that the Lord may be able to justify you on that Great Day. For you can be sure of this, your conscience will be awakened, and the verdict shall go before the judgment seat of God. No one shall be condemned except those whose consciences have already pronounced condemnation; on the other hand, no one shall be justified other than those whose consciences have already been justified. This is why I urge you to pay heed and beware of this deadness of heart and false sense of security, in order that you are not disbarred from that heavenly country. I say again, every one of you engage in a deeper examination of yourselves while you still have the opportunity.

The third appeal to King James

It lies in your hands, Sire, as the Lord's chosen instrument, to ensure that this day of grace continues among us. We know that there are two means whereby it may continue. The first is the removal of false religion, for it is appalling[39] that those who are enemies of Christ Jesus should have been tolerated for so long in a Christian land. It is a foul and horrible thing! Therefore take it on your heart to deal decisively in this, even if you yourself in person have to arrest those who are openly opposing Jesus Christ. Be assured that you will have done great service for God. These enemies of the truth have been accepted these past seven or eight years, and they have been better tolerated as if the sentences passed against them had never been ratified. (They themselves bear witness to that by the way they are behaving.) Therefore, once you agree to attend to this matter, let us see your majesty acting as diligently in this as in the past you have been in other matters.

[37] Luke 23:30; Revelation 6:15-17.

[38] 1 Corinthians 11:28, 'Let a person examine himself…'. Bruce's powerful sermon on this text is available in *The Mystery of the Lord's Supper*, trans. T.F. Torrance (James Clarke, London, 1958), The Fourth Sermon. Reprinted CFP 2005. Part of this sermon forms Appendix 1 in *Isa.* 38. pp. 189-203.

[39] Bruce's word is 'beastlie'.

The second means[40] involves you, my lords, for you must be as decisive in this as you often are in other things. Do not delay, for when this malaise has been dealt with, in the hour of your death your consciences will bear witness that you have done some good to the commendation of your souls and the praise of God. The penalty for neglecting this is condemnation.[41] Therefore, I desire that God will add his power to his word, that it may make a deep impression on your hearts, and that you may never rest until you see this matter dealt with.

Before I conclude this discourse, I must add another note. Again, I pray that you will consider this and ponder this in your hearts. The evangel is not some fable; it has the power of Jesus Christ conjoined with it, and it is able to pierce through both bone and marrow and penetrate into the most secret thoughts,[42] and so convict of sin. But the man[43] who comes to this place and is faithful to his calling, he will be endowed with the power of the word, so that you shall then be amazed and converted to your salvation in Jesus Christ.

We do not know when the call may come

The last point I make is this. You ought to think of this life as a pilgrimage, or as a voyage to another life. Just as the time we spend in our mother's womb prepares us for our lives on earth, so during our time here in this world we ought to be preparing for that life in heaven. Likewise, just as our time in the womb is temporary, so we who are in this world ought to be making ready to cast off our garments of uncleanness so that we might attain to that heavenly company. Well then, remember that you are pilgrims here, and that is the same as saying that you have been given notice to depart, but you do not know at what hour the living God will chap[44] on you. Therefore, remember to be assured of his mercy, and be diligent in craving it, as if he were just about to

[40] The ratification of laws establishing the reformed faith as the religion of Scotland. See note 8 above.

[41] 'Condemnatioun' simply means condemnation as opposed to 'damnatioun', eternal damnation (DSL).

[42] Hebrews 4:12.

[43] Bruce may here be referring obliquely to himself, unless the building they were in lacked a minister at that time. It is possible that they were in another of the four sanctuaries in St Giles. See Introduction, note 3.

[44] See above Chapter 10, note 34.

chap upon you.

However, if you crave mercy with your mouth while your heart is still reluctant, remember, *he that incallis on the name of the lord sall be saved.*[45] This is a clear promise to all of us, for we are at times burdened with our personal sins. Then let us not be ashamed constantly to crave mercy from the hands of the living God. If you are resolved to be a pilgrim, never think that you are going to remain here on earth, do not put down your roots[46] here, and always remember that you are on your journey under notice, not knowing when the call[47] may come. Likewise, remembering that there are many trials and obstacles on this journey, be prepared to bear them with patience. And because patience is a gift from the living God, ask him to give it to you.

The course of our lives is like a voyage

Last of all, remember that this life is a voyage and the final mooring place is death, for as soon as we enter this world we begin our journey to leave it. Remember that your voyage is not the same as the usual journey of a pilgrim, for he may stop for a while on his travels and remain in the same place for a few days, even for a year or more as he pleases. But from the moment we enter this life there is no rest for us, we simply must continue our voyage, each hour leading us nearer to our death. Whenever I ponder upon the course of our lives, I find I cannot compare it to anything better than to a voyage. We are like a boat that is subject to the weather, often sailing close to the wind; so whether the mariner be eating, drinking, sleeping or whatever he chooses, the boat continues on towards the port. That is how it is with the course of our lives: do what we like, sleep or be up and about, life is incessantly moving onwards.

This being so, should we not labour to be certain that we are on course towards the right port? We must ask ourselves, 'Shall I be subjected to troubles in both body and soul during my life, and, after all that, shall I then enter into everlasting death? What is said and written about the second death, is it true or is it false? Are these things only fables, or are they the oracles of the living God? If they are true then our

[45] Romans 10:13 (Acts 2:21).

[46] See note 23 above.

[47] See note 44 above.

death must either be an entrance into eternal life, or else into eternal death and being plunged into hell with its everlasting torments. Seeing it is certain that you must die, for God has appointed death for us all, and your conscience assures you that is so, should you then not strive to die well?

I pray God that this exhortation has come with power to both speaker and hearers! Seeing that although your life continues you must ultimately die, and that you do not know when that knock[48] will come on your door, those present who are now hearing the Lord's call, unburden yourselves of the sins of your public and private lives, accept this discharge of the guilt on your conscience through the full forgiveness of all your iniquities, so that in death you shall have life.

The Lord in his mercy grant (if it please him) that I may yet see during my lifetime, and before I die, some order restored over these confusions, for beyond all doubt, sooner than you may think, Sire, they will cause your throne to totter unless discipline is established. Therefore, not only for the sake of stability for the throne of Jesus Christ, but for your own throne's stability, and for the common well-being of your subjects, let order be reinstated. Then shall our mouths be opened to thank and glorify God for you, and to crave his blessing upon you and your queen from the hands of Jesus Christ. To whom with the Father and the Holy Ghost be all honour, praise and glory both now and evermore. Amen.

[48] See note 44 above.

Chapter Twelve

Hebrews Chapter 11 verses 15-16

15 And gif they hade bein mindfull of that cuntrie from whence they cam they hade leasour to haue returned. 16 Bot now they desyre a better that is ane heavinlie, whairfore god is not aschamed of them to be called thair god, for he hes prepairit for them ane citie.

Reminder of the previous sermon

You have heard the apostle's praise of the three patriarchs, Abraham, Isaac and Jacob, and how it pleased the Lord to call them inwardly and effectually to have the vision of that heavenly life and community. From that time it also pleased the God of heaven to open their hearts and to implant in them a love for himself and his heavenly abode, so that they had a single desire to join that spiritual community. From then on they so guarded both the vision and foretaste of heaven that neither were ever impaired. What I mean is that the spiritual light within them never left them, nor did the foretaste of heaven ever diminish in their hearts, for they cared for the inward light and cherished the spiritual vision. In this way, they maintained a steadfast course in their onward journey, unwaveringly trusting in the ultimate accomplishment of God's promise. The presence of this 'eye'[1] in their souls enabled them to remain constant throughout the troubles that came upon them.

This same 'eye' enabled faith to grow in their souls, and fortified them with patience in their many afflictions; thus they were enabled to adopt a manner of living agreeable to the evangel and to the heaven

[1] By the phrase 'eye in their saullis' Bruce means both the 'sight' and 'foretaste' of heaven that he had expanded on in the previous sermon.

that they had glimpsed in the promise of God in Jesus Christ. Thus they were able to confess with their mouths and openly declare that they took no delight in earthly things; even though they had material possessions as others had, they reckoned all to be of no value now they had been given the vision of that better, heavenly city and the New Jerusalem. But the important point to notice is that from the time that the Lord enlightened their minds with that spiritual insight, and imparted to them the foretaste of that future joy, they never departed from it nor was it diminished in their hearts. I mean that their faith was never lessened, far less extinguished, by defection in either their life or their religion.

The relevance of this for the nation and the reformed faith

Before I go any further I must apply this to our land today. Had we been able to say that in our country during these thirty years in which the Lord has offered his light to us,[2] we had welcomed and guarded it, neither impairing nor diminishing it by evil living or by falling back into false religion, I am certain of this—however evil we may have been by nature or as a nation—we would have become the happiest and most blessed of peoples. All kinds of benefits, both temporal and spiritual, attend the kingdom of God as can be seen in those commonwealths where the kingdom of Christ Jesus has been established. So for us there would have been the blessings that accompany his kingdom and we ourselves would have experienced these blessings, both temporal and spiritual.

But by our failures in the way we live, by our evil customs and our false religion, we have not merely ignored this light, but have turned from it, quenched it and shut it out of our minds and souls. This is why these blessings we could have had as a nation have become a plague upon us, and the eternal curse is now imminent—I mean the eternal judgment of God. It is because we have so long abused the day of grace that the darkness of the Lord's dreadful judgment is drawing near. Surely I do not need to tell you this. You can all see the shocking events that occur day after day, because there is respect neither for the law nor for the king. The law protects no one, nor does the person of

[2] This detail suggests the date of these sermons was about 1590-92 as the Reformation in Scotland took place in 1560. See also Chapter 5, p. 69.

the king offer any defence, yet in him the image of God should shine. That God himself speaks out from this building, yet his word provides security for no one, is clear evidence that men have blotted out the light which has been offered to them. Thirty years ago it appeared that they were embracing the truth, but now total darkness has taken the place of the light. The consciences of these men[3] have lost all fear of God and they have cast off all semblance of godliness; now they take delight in sampling all kinds of wickedness and the most heinous sins that can be committed.[4]

You must see the point we have reached, and the outcome that is inevitable for our land and its inhabitants. According to the limited insight God has given me,[5] all that I can see for our future is that divine judgment shall surely come and that it will continue until it reaches into the king's own chambers. So shall this threatened universal confusion continue until the daylight fades and the night of awesome judgment envelopes us for ever in the gloom of its total darkness.[6] This is all extremely frightening! Would to God that you could grasp just how frightening it is. But for want of any inner spiritual sensitivity you are not moved by these things, the reason being that your consciences are so hardened you are inured to such a terrible prospect. But the judgment of God does not vacillate, it will surely strike and the night and darkness will overtake us.

Therefore I say, by the singular mercy of God you are not all cast in the same spiritual mould, and I doubt not that the Lord will have regard for some of you. Thus it behoves you to take heed to this, and, while you still have the opportunity, to rekindle the light which you have quenched by your evil ways. For there is no one among us whose consciences do not accuse us of failing to strengthen[7] the light[8] as we

[3] Presumably some in the congregation were aware of the persons referred to.

[4] See Chapter 11, note 13 above.

[5] This phrase suggests that Bruce himself was already conscious of a gift he had of 'Seeing Visions and Dreaming Dreams', as chapter 19 is entitled in MacNicol, pp. 185-192.

[6] Was Bruce anticipating the persecution of the reformed church during the period of the Covenanters?

[7] Bruce's verb is 'augmentis' and in this context could also be translated either as 'intensify' or 'extend'.

[8] Unquestionably, here by the 'licht' Bruce means the cause of the reformed faith.

ought to have done, as in my preaching I have been repeatedly pleading for you to do. Yet we have continually been neglecting it, preferring to satisfy our own desires than to act in the service of this light and of Jesus Christ who is offered in this light. All of our consciences (and I include myself) challenge us regarding this.

Before the light dies out completely, and the final few embers be wholly extinguished, it is now time that the remaining faint glow be tended, that the flame may be re-ignited and that we may turn to Jesus Christ to crave his forgiveness. For as to the entire country, it is clear that even though it has the name of being alive, the truth is that it is dead. There are hardly any who have sought to revive the tiny flame,[9] that even now is on the point of dying out, unless the light is soon re-ignited. Take far more seriously to heart this matter than you have done until now. For however hardened your hearts have become through your habitual evil ways, nevertheless the day is approaching when the reins of your hearts and its most secret thoughts will be brought to trial. Therefore, while there is still time, bring yourselves to trial and pass sentence of your own guilt!

Do not think that some trivial profession of faith in Christ and his gospel will be able to withstand the scrutiny of that perfect tribunal, or appear genuine before the Lamb who shall come in burning fire and whose gaze shall uncover the truth about you and whether or not you are in the faith. He will see if your faith is merely mental assent, or if it is truly in your hearts where he has his seat and holds the reins of your most secret thoughts. He will know if your love is sincere and evidenced by sacrificial work for him. Is this what you find when you bring yourself to trial?

Notwithstanding that you have smothered the light until now, the Lord will yet have pity upon you. But if after you bring yourself to trial you find there is one idol[10] that you prefer to Jesus Christ, be sure that your state is not good, for your god is whatever you love the most. If it be some human invention, turn away from it, otherwise both you and it shall perish together. Take heed to this, for the deceitfulness of our cravings[11] can be astonishing, for unless we are constantly on our guard,

[9] See above on note 8.

[10] Most probably a reference to leaning towards Papist ritual.

[11] An allusion to Ephesians 4:22-23, where Paul urges the believers to 'put off

the devil, who has a foothold in our affections, will continually deceive us. I had rather endure anguish in my emotions than being deceived by them, for any hardship that ensues from self-denial is far easier to deal with than the grief brought when I am deceived. Therefore, you should always ask God to save you from the deception of your lusts and cravings.

Four lessons from the patriarchs

Back to the patriarchs. They professed themselves to be pilgrims and strangers on the earth, and they took a lengthy journey, regarding the whole earth as their place of pilgrimage. I have already told you (as God gave me the grace in the other kirk[12]) what they understood by this profession: they chiefly meant four things.

First, even though they had earthly possessions as did other men (for the heritable title of the land of Canaan had been given to them), yet they would never lay claim to it as belonging to them; they would never assert their legal right[13] to it. The Lord had given them another heritable title to another land as well as the vision of that heavenly country, so the love of the one caused them to reject any love for the other. As pilgrims who lay no claim to any property in the country where they sojourn, so the patriarchs claimed nothing on this earth because they were simply pilgrims passing through it.

Second, their confession meant that they were not to remain in this world, for they were resolved not to fix their stakes on earth,[14] nor to settle down here; indeed, their confession clearly showed others that they had set out on their homeward journey. Consider how pilgrims rise each morning, glad to leave the inn where they lodged for the night and to continue onwards. In the same way the patriarchs would be glad to leave behind their earthly tabernacles of clay, whenever it should please the Lord to chap upon them.

Thirdly, they meant by this confession that they were in no doubt

your old self… *corrupt through deceitful desires*, and to be renewed in the spirit of your minds…'.

[12] See Chapter 11, note 43. Also Introduction, note 3.

[13] Bruce's word is 'kyndnes', kinship. See above Chapter 11, note 21 for the fuller meaning of this legal term.

[14] The phrase 'not to fix yr staik in this earth' means they would not mark out land as a possession for themselves.

whatsoever as to where they were going. They did not travel by clutching at some uncertainty in the way a blind person might have to do. They were convinced as to the identity of their true country, just as the archer is quite sure about the target at which he is aiming. Pilgrims know the land towards which they are heading, therefore they do not wander around or hang about; rather they follow a direct route.

Fourthly, by their confession they make it clear that they were prepared to endure any kind of trouble that might meet them. They were ready to overcome all difficulties and afflictions on their journey, be it from the weather or whatever hindrances man or devil might cast across their way. Yea, they made it plain that they were willing to drink every bitter cup, and to persevere to the end of their journey, for they steadfastly maintained in their minds their final destination. Thus we see their confession meant these four things.

Application

You ought to apply to yourselves every single word here, even though as I speak to you I may omit to do so for you. Every single member of Jesus Christ ought to resemble the patriarchs, for the resolve of all our hearts ought to answer to their resolve. Suppose the God of heaven has given all of you some property or material wealth here on earth, yet you must live in the knowledge that all is fleeting; you must live knowing that you could be called tomorrow morning and would have to leave everything behind. When you reflect on the laws and present government of this country, you must be aware that not one of us can be certain of a single hour on this earth! Therefore resolve to be but strangers here, and adopt the same course as the Fathers, always ready for the time when the Lord will summon you to leave everything behind.

However, the main point here is that by their confession they were pilgrims, they declared plainly that they sought another country that was not to be found on this earth, but was somewhere else entirely. This was the suit[15] for which they prepared themselves throughout their

[15] The word 'sute' is used 25 times in this sermon. In short, it means 'a summons to an obligatory attendance by a tenant at his lord's court'. DSL gives the following explanation of this legal term: 'As a condition of holding their fiefs, all the barons and freeholders within the sheriffdom had to give "suit", or "suit and presence", at three head courts annually, and at all other courts "set upon fifteen days' warning"; the suit-rolls containing their names making a practically complete list

entire lifetime. It is possible for someone either to seek in vain or else to seek effectively, and so I must show you the difference between these two kinds of seeking. Seeking effectively is seeking at the right time and in the right way. (There is a right time for everything, and also a right way and a wrong way.) As to the right time, it is with us just now, and (blessed be God!) it still continues, for the right time is this day of grace and peace and mercy which are now offered to the world.

Seeking God must involve the mortification of our carnal desires

This 'day' is still with us. We must slay our lusts and mortify our carnal desires, extinguishing them in our hearts. For unless we reverence the will of God and of Jesus Christ more than we have done hitherto, and prefer his will to our own wills and persevere in his way, we shall never see the face of God in his Son. Therefore, mortify your lusts and set out upon his right way. Subdue your wills, however stubborn and rebellious they are by nature. Because there is nothing so obdurate as the human will, crave Christ's help, for he is ready to give it; it is only by the power of his death that your will can be subdued. Only by the virtue[16] of his blood can your affections be mortified.

You must continue to crave the Lord's help in this, because even though for a time mortification can be painful, ultimately your prayer will be answered. This putting to death of sinful lusts can be so difficult for flesh and blood, that many are too afraid even to enter into it. The devil can impose blindness upon our minds and deception into our desires, so that we dare not attempt the way of mortification. Ignorance of the teaching of Scripture is the chief cause of this fear. There are so few who know the Scriptures, so that even when they hear them being read, or read them for themselves, they are not understood. Consequently they fail to deal with their passions, and the deceitfulness of

of the county gentry. The assizes were then formed by "calling" these rolls, and choosing, and then swearing in and admitting, a selection of the suitors.' I shall generally translate 'sute' as 'suit', but occasionally when appropriate, either as 'the final summons' or 'the great assize'; but readers will appreciate its meaning is to be understood as 'the summons our Lord gives to all his children to stand before him on the appointed Day of the final Judgment'. But as well as 'suit' being used in the passive sense of being summoned, Bruce also uses it in the active sense of the believer obeying the summons.

[16] On 'virtue', (Scots word 'vertew') see above Chapter 9 note 10.

certain pleasures blinds them so effectively that they try to follow a pathway of their own choosing.

It is because Christ speaks of his way as being strait[17] that they will not take his way, but try to invent a way for themselves. I have described to you what happens in France, where they use veils[18] and flagellations[19] to try and impose mortification upon themselves. Meanwhile, they entertain idols in their hearts, hoping to acquire merit; yet this idolatrous seeking of merit through self-flagellation is the greatest idol ever set over against the merits of Jesus Christ. I say again, it is ignorance of the Scripture that is at the root of this, for it is ignorance of that virtue that flows from the blood of Christ.

Beware of following the crowds who practise false religion

Those who from the moment they see that biblical mortification is a strait way, turn from it in despair and, following the example of the multitude, they look to the great men of their country, and to those they deem to be wise and learned. A great number of people look to important men, and so follow them in a way of life that does not offend their sensitivities; but they are choosing human authorities to guide them. This means that those who choose to follow the multitude end up preferring a false religion, and not the true faith that leads to heaven.

Alas, it seems that the spirit of error nowadays is more effective in deceiving men (this is in the righteous judgment of God), than is the Spirit of truth in conquering souls for Jesus Christ. That is why we see such crowds, along with great men, pursuing a false religion that is contrary to the teaching of Jesus Christ. These people think they are sufficiently equipped as long as they are on the same side as the multitude and the same side as kings, along with certain wise and learned men. Neither they nor this load[20] of people ever consult the Scriptures.

[17] Bruce constantly uses the (now) archaic 'streicte', strait, as does the Geneva Bible; it means 'narrow', 'difficult' or 'confined'. I have chosen to retain it throughout this translation. Readers familiar with the AV will know its meaning.

[18] Bruce's word is 'capuchis' which is literally 'a hood'.

[19] Bruce's word is 'batteris' which literally means 'cannons' or 'missiles'; the Scots had a phrase 'batteris to batteris'. His hyperbole must have caused many to smile. The word 'flagellation' is used in the next sentence.

[20] The word Bruce uses is 'draucht'; it has eight possible meanings among which are 'the load drawn by an ox-cart', and 'a receptacle for excrement'; it is clearly

These are the two stumbling blocks[21] that have caused the majority of the world to err since the beginning of time.

You must all take heed lest you be deceived with this false religion; rather look to see what Christ Jesus himself has said. He tells us plainly that the true way is strait, and few there be that enter upon it.[22] Then do not follow the multitude either in your manner of life or in your religion, but search the Scriptures as your Master commands you in John 5:39 (see also 6:45). You will find that true mortification can only be wrought by the virtue of Christ's death, and knowing this you should be continually in prayer. When he has given you an inward eye to see the power there is in his blood to cleanse your souls and mortify your affections, then in his infinite mercy it may please him to impart a portion of his virtue;[23] he will give you just the measure of it that he considers sufficient for your heart and soul to be drawn into the experience of God's love.

So again I say, do not be deceived by the example of the multitude's way of living and practice of religion, but crave the spirit of understanding that you may discern the right way. Finding it to be the way of mortification, crave the power of the death of Jesus Christ to purify your emotions and relationships, that he may then pour into your hearts a new love for God and of that heavenly glory that never dies, and so little by little your love shall draw you on towards heaven.

You are to be speedy despatch riders

The next instruction you must remember is this: never forget who you are and what this life is as long as you remain on the face of this earth. Do not forget either that in this world you always live in great uncertainty concerning your future and your material possessions, and that no matter what country you may live in, you are pilgrims. Never forget that this life of ours is but a journey or a voyage—at least it should be a voyage—to that joyful and blessed land. However you live, you are like

intentionally used in a highly derogatory sense.

[21] I take it that by 'the two stumbling blocks' Bruce means false religion as an easy alternative to the strait and narrow way, and willful ignorance of God's truth through blindly following the crowd.

[22] Matthew 7:13.

[23] See note 16 above.

a speedy despatch-rider journeying from post-station to post-station, either heading to heaven or to hell. This kind of rider's mission cannot ever be compared to the despatched message of any earthly rider. For the most urgent despatch rider must sometimes take a break to be refreshed, or to stay overnight in some hostelry.

We, however, are riding without any pause towards one or other of these two eternal destinations. Whatever we may be doing, whether sleeping, waking or eating, we continue to travel rapidly onwards. The course of our lives never takes even the briefest of stops to rest, but continues from the moment we are born until our final breath. The Lord of heaven has assigned to us our course and we can do no other than move inexorably onwards towards our final post-station. Therefore, seeing the course of our life moves so swiftly and continuously towards its end, should we not labour to be certain of a happy and good conclusion to life? I am quite sure that there is no one on this earth who does not desire a good end.

We can have a good end by being pilgrims who practise mortification

To change the figure slightly, we have all taken a post-chaise towards our termination, and the chaise cannot and will not ever stop until we reach the final post-station. Of the godly patriarchs it says that they all died in faith, that is, they reached a good end and died blessed deaths. Would you then have a good end? Then live in faith that it may said of every one of you, 'I heard that he died in faith!'. Even though there has been evil in your life, even scandal, a good end can bury and cover your various faults and errors of a sinful life. If you then would fain follow in the footsteps of the Fathers, seek heavenly things in time.

I doubt if any of you have thought deeply about this, far less resolved to seek things that are above. If that is true of you, hasten now to seek heaven, for constantly pursuing your suit during the right time will bring its reward, and this is the right time, the day of grace. Therefore, you who are still undecided, without delay resolve to take up this challenge and say, 'I will now lay everything else aside in order to seek heaven, no matter what difficulties may confront me as I set out along this way.' If that is your resolve, do not forget that the way you must go is that of mortification. If you sanctify your memories and hold fast to these two things,[24] you shall reach that heavenly country.

There remain still to be considered two further points. First, what was the nature of the country that the Fathers sought? Second, what was the outcome of their suit: what was the reward they received?

First, the nature of the country that the Fathers sought

There are two points I must make. Think first about the nature of the country they sought. (I am not going to go into detail on this, for it is a most important subject and there is not time to consider it fully just now.) Some might have objected that the country they were looking for was the one that they had already left. They had come from Mesopotamia and the land of Babylon and the Chaldeans, in particular, from the city of Ur. So were they actually intending to return to Ur?

The apostle forestalls this objection in verse 15 where he writes: *If they hade soucht that earthlie cuntrie quhair fra they cam, they hade leasure aneuch grantit to them to returne yarrto*. But they never did return there. Moreover, Abraham commanded Isaac and his servant, who went back to find a wife for Isaac, never to return there. *If sche will not cum with you, tak ye him not to hir*, he said.[25] That makes it clear to us that Abraham never ever had any intention of returning to Ur. Certainly Jacob returned, but it was of necessity, not because he wanted to, for he was fleeing from the wrath of his brother Esau whose birthright he had stolen. So you see the Fathers had no desire to return whence they had come, for their hearts were set upon another kind of country. This is why the apostle states in verse 15 that it must follow their desire was for a far better country.

In the next verse, the apostle uses the title 'a better country', but then adds another title, 'a heavenly country', making it clear that they chose the best. Before them stretched all the lands under the heavens, but they chose the best land of all. The Spirit of God says so: *they chused the better cuntrie*.[26] Would to God that we all had chosen as well as they did! No one who has the freedom to choose would not select the best. But our desires are so bound by sin that we mistake the worst for

[24] I take it that the 'two things' to be remembered are first that those who set out for heaven are to be pilgrims, and second that the pathway will necessarily be strait on account of the constant need of mortification.

[25] Genesis 24:5-6.

[26] The allusion is to the words in verse 15, 'they desire a better country'.

the best. The patriarchs made the right choice because they had been released from the bondage of their sins and, being set at liberty by the Spirit of Jesus Christ, they chose the best. Likewise, if we would only strive to have the shackles that enslave our desires broken, I have no doubt that sanctified affections would also choose the best. An illuminated mind and an enlightened understanding, that has attained to the vision of the heavenly life and what it is like to live there, would undoubtedly reason and resolve thus: 'This is the best life, and this is the way I shall follow.'

The reason why we prefer our stinking affections and filthy inanities to the heavenly life is that we have had neither a vision of heaven nor freedom granted to our souls. Whoever, except someone whose soul is both blind and deaf, would ever choose a vale of miseries—for what else is this world but a dark valley of grief—instead of that infinite felicity and eternal joy? Therefore, seeing that a better, heavenly country is being offered to you, strive now to have your wills set free, and to rid yourselves of those bestial desires that entangle themselves around your hearts, causing you to be bound[27] by this earthly life. Someone, seeing that he is so entwined, will strive hard to mortify completely his passions. By turning away from his carnal life, he may think that his mortification is now wholly accomplished; yet even when the dominion of sin is broken, there still will remain the dregs of sin in his heart.

What then? The problem is that none of us can attain to heaven unless our desires are in love with it, but our fallen natures simply cannot fall in love with heaven or spiritual things. Therefore all your meditation should be leading you to crave the living God so to transform your desires that he would enable you to love him just as passionately as you previously loved the things of this world. All your deepest desires must be realigned and changed before ever you experience the love of God. This is why the Scriptures repeatedly tell us that our minds should be renewed, that we must not be conformed to this world and

[27] Bruce twice here uses the verb 'twin' (from which we get the word 'twine'); his metaphor is of cords twisted together to fashion a rope. It is a powerful picture of earthly desires entwining the heart. Holman Hunt's painting, 'The Light of the World', shows Christ outside a door which cannot be opened on account of the rank growth of creepers and twisting weeds holding it fast shut. That is close to Bruce's intended imagery here.

to earthly things, but to God and heavenly things.[28] Thus we see how it was that the patriarchs chose and sought the better country.

The better country offers spiritual, divine and eternal rest

There is a second point to note regarding the nature of the country, kingdom and glory that is offered to you in the evangel of Jesus Christ. In the promises offered in Christ's gospel, even though these holy Fathers were far off in time from the incarnation of Jesus Christ, that is, his manifestation in the flesh, yet in his promises they saw a heavenly life offered to them in a spiritual kingdom and everlasting glory. They did not look in these promises for an earthly kingdom, temporal rest or happiness, but for a spiritual, divine and eternal blessedness. Therefore, the Fathers' example condemns their carnal children, both those who were alive while they were on earth, and we who live in later generations; I speak of those who think that in Christ and his promises they will obtain worldly, outward happiness. Yea, the day will come when the Fathers will rise up to condemn such carnality.

Some may ask, 'But what if we seek righteously the fulfilment of Christ's promises?' I answer that we must not seek from him outward, temporal rest and prosperity, nor any worldly glory or earthly kingdom; rather must we seek from him his spiritual kingdom and a heavenly glory unseen by human eyes that will not be made known until Christ shall appear in the clouds. Seek a spiritual rest, the inward peace of your consciences and the quietening of your hearts. For if you seek these blessings earnestly, assuredly you will receive them. But if you come to Christ hoping for earthly repose and prosperity, when worldly things do come to you they will soon lose their glamour; consequently what you thought you had gained from the hand of Christ shall disappoint you and so you will end up leaving the Master. Therefore I repeat, seek only spiritual and heavenly rest in him. Continue in your suit and you shall never be disappointed.

Ensure that you profit by this instruction. Because these spiritual, heavenly things are hidden (for our life is hid with Christ in God[29]), nevertheless, though unseen, they are infinitely more excellent and far sweeter to the taste. As there is no comparison between earthly joy and

[28] Romans 12:2; see also Ephesians 4:22-23.

[29] Colossians 3:3.

heavenly joy, so in the hope of obtaining these things that as yet you have neither clearly seen nor tasted, I beseech you to seek them with all your heart. Crave for that transforming virtue that flows from Christ and his death.

The better country must be the target at which your faith aims

Next I want you to think about the target of both your faith and your longings. From the moment faith was planted in your heart and mind, you will perceive how heaven became the target at which you were aiming; nor will your faith ever be fully satisfied until both soul and body arrive there. Although faith constantly aims at things spiritual, because your affections constantly aim at earthly things, they tend to drag your soul down from the heavenly places to this earth, so that your heart becomes taken up with worldly things or with some fleshly concern. Yet faith draws the soul upwards, and as we have been raised by faith with Christ, so it causes us to seek those things that are above, and to conform us to be holy as are the angelic beings. On the other hand, our affections draw us earthward, making us like mere swine and dogs.

So you see now the two different targets of faith and carnal affections. Because faith always chooses the best, as long as faith is offered to you season your souls with it. Without question faith is offered to all of you, and all may receive it unless unbelief stands in your way. When you do receive faith you will find that there is more than enough for you, so that you will have greater riches than if you owned the whole world. Seeing then that faith is freely available, after so many years of fruitless searching, strive now to obtain faith in your hearts and minds together with the love of God and Christ Jesus. I myself beseech the living God to do his work in your carnal hearts!

Compare the better country to this world

Next, we move on to think about this country the Fathers sought. Heaven is the proper home of the faithful, the place appointed for the saints of God for their everlasting joy and peace. On the other hand, our pilgrimage is here on earth where we meet with troubles, persecution and suffering. The reason for this is so that this world may become bitter and unpleasant for us. It is in his great mercy that God has ordained it this way so that our souls may learn to loath earthly things. Otherwise, if here on earth we were extremely wealthy, having all our hearts could desire, and if this affluent lifestyle continued without any interruption, we would then become so bound to this world that we would never have any wish to be changed. But the Lord has planned something better for us, in order that this world shall not be the place of our rest, but so long as we are here we shall be tested with some trouble or other in both body and soul. Nevertheless, as I have often said already, those who choose to follow the devil will have far greater troubles than any Christian, for whichever way men go there will always be hardships; no one has an exemption from difficulties.

Though troubles are common to all men, sanctified troubles are reserved for the few. Seeing that the Lord has appointed heaven as the place of our glory, and earth as the place of our sorrows and trials, ensure that your woes are all sanctified, either because you are suffering for the sake of righteousness, or for the cause of Jesus Christ, or simply because you are innocent; then, I do not doubt, you shall be blessed by spiritual peace. Even though you may be physically brought to the point of death, your soul shall grow ever stronger and its inner comfort and life shall continue to increase. Because heaven is the place of our rest, and earth the place of our difficulties, order your priorities to despise the latter, while aspiring to obtain the fruition of the former.

Second, the outcome and reward of the Fathers' suit

The second point we had to mark in verse 16 was the final outcome of the patriarchs' suit and its reward. As to the reward, it is set down in these terms, *Theirfoir the Lord was not aschamed to be callit thair god.* Here was the reward of their constant suit: the God of heaven gave himself to these godly patriarchs! The best reward that God can ever give is to give himself, and when he does he also gives a boundless store of spiritual joys and benefits, which nothing either in this world or out of it can ever match. The longer you gaze upon his face, the better are you satisfied with him, and the more is he satisfied with you. Thus the one who is omnipotent and all-sufficient gave himself to the godly Fathers. Yea, not only did he do this, but to their greater honour and commendation he took his very name from them, for when at the burning bush he commissioned Moses to appear before Pharaoh, he personally proclaimed as his title, *I am the god of Abrahame, Isaack and*

Jacob. So the apostle, meditating on Exodus 3:6, concludes that God was not ashamed to call himself by the names of his humble servants, however contemptible they may have been in the sight of this world's princes.

The king of heaven and earth, the God of glory whose majesty replenishes all that he has made, takes his title from these his servants. Is this not wonderful? Today princes would never take their names from their yeomen; indeed, if some noble took for himself the name of one of his servitors, he would be considered a most pathetic unmanly fellow. Though the apostle implies that even though this was never the custom and that the nobility would be ashamed to do so, yet he says that the God of heaven was not ashamed to call himself after his servants as *the god of Abrahame, Isaack and Jacob*. Just as God surpasses princes in love, so also he surpasses them in humility and kindness, and as his servants were not ashamed of him or his word during their lifetimes, he will not be ashamed of them after this life, but will acknowledge them before the world and all its princes.[30]

We must never be ashamed of our Lord

You can be sure of this: if we are not ashamed of God,[31] he will not be ashamed of us. Those who have eyes to see will know that God has far more reason to be ashamed of us than we have to be ashamed of him. Yet there are times when we are ashamed of him—indeed, it can happen every day! Flattering smiles can often cause us to defer to men rather than to God, and to be willing to take their side and not God's. That is because we cannot see God in the way we can see men. But when you get a glimpse of the Lord's infinite majesty, so that he is as precious and worthy to the eye of your mind as the majesty of any earthly potentate is to your bodily eye, without doubt you will then reverence him. Moreover you would then be as reluctant to intrude into his presence as you would be to intrude into the chamber of some earthly king. But when we lack inner spiritual sensitivity, we are ashamed of our Lord and rightly deserve his indignation. Alas, if we only knew that being ashamed of God incurs his displeasure, we would

30 Hebrews 2:11-12; see also 2 Timothy 1:8, 12; 2:8-13, especially verses 11-13; also Romans 1:16.

31 Romans 1:16; 2 Timothy 1:12.

then count as nothing the indignation of kings!

Just as the torment of the conscience greatly surpasses any pain inflicted on flesh and blood—for the spiritual is far above the physical—so our consciences are much more troubled by God's indignation than by any pain that mortal princes can visit upon our bodies. Then all of us who are resolved not to be ashamed of God whatever the cost, the Eternal One in his infinite majesty for his part will not be ashamed of us in whom there is nothing but cause for shame. Therefore let us crave strength while there is yet time, that insofar as it lies with us, come what may, we will be never be ashamed of him or of his word. So much for that point.

The all-sufficiency of God's goodness

The Lord expresses his love and condescension in naming himself after his servants by saying that he is their God. For a man to be like a god to his friend is the same as saying that that man is as good as perfect in his friend's eyes, for he would be willing to help him if he was in trouble, or avenge him if someone did him some wrong. Whoever has the Lord as his God has one who will likewise stand by him and ensure justice will be done if either prince or people inflict any injury upon him. Or to put it the other way round, may I count the Lord to be my God, and may I say in my heart and conscience that he is truly God to me?

It is pointless for you to say that God is good if you do not know that he is good to you. But can you honestly say in your heart with full assurance that God is good to you? I tell you the heart which can sincerely say that, has set within it the whole blessedness of God; he has become its defence,[32] the storehouse from which it will be provisioned and his means of protection in times of trouble or anxieties that may afflict body or soul. In short, without God a man who seems to have everything, in fact has nothing. But those who do have God constantly commune with him and depend entirely upon his providence; when in prison they consider themselves to be free, when in poverty they count themselves to be rich, in sickness, whether in mind or body, they count themselves to be healthy; God's presence is their sole joy and consolation.

Those who can say that God is indeed their God, if they need help

[32] Bruce has 'the armour of it'.

do not turn to man but to their Lord, if they have a troubled conscience they do not seek relief from man but only from him, or if they long for peace of heart it will be to him they will go; they need nothing other than their Lord and God. Even though all the kings of the earth offer them everything they could ever want, there is nothing they desire other than God, and what they need they will obtain only through godly means. Being assured of his presence, in him they have more than every comfort and delight that can be had from all creation.

How could this be? It is because God was already there before anything was created, and he was complete in himself before any earthly creature was made; having full perfection in himself, he did not need to borrow anything from what he himself had brought into being. That is why there is no joy to be found in created things that were not already present in God before anything was made. Therefore, whoever has God as his God and his presence in his soul, has all the delights that may be found in creation, because he already has the Creator who was there before anything was created. Thus nothing can be added to the presence of God in your soul; having that, nothing needful is lacking.

Because your consciences are so hardened with the pleasures of sin that you can only enjoy[33] evil and wickedness, you must labour to have a conscience that learns to enjoy the savour of God; strive then to purge your consciences that you may only enjoy that which is godly because it savours of him. Those who have him truly in their hearts and consciences can say that God is their God and upon him alone will they rest. They will have nothing without him, but in him they will have all they need.

How could God be the God of the Fathers when they were all already deceased?

However, we have yet to think of what we learn from the time factor in all of this. I will explain what I mean. When God spoke these words to Moses from the burning bush, he spoke long after Jacob had died, and obviously after both Isaac and Abraham had also died. We have to consider how God could say this one hundred and eight years after

[33] In this sentence Bruce has 'taist' three times; I have translated it as 'enjoy' and 'savour'; occasionally his use of the verb 'taist' has the obvious connotation of 'foretaste'.

Jacob's death. How could his divine majesty truly say that he was the God of these three who were so long deceased? This circumstance of time was referred to when our Master entered into a dispute with the Sadducees. You can read of it in Matthew 22:23ff. (Mark 12:18ff.; Luke 20:27ff.), where the subject is the doctrine of the resurrection. In these three passages our Master refers to this text from Exodus 3 where the Lord says that he is *the god of Abrahame, the god of Isaack and the god of Jacob*, as a proof of the resurrection. In his dispute with the Sadducees, our Master says that these words demonstrate that they were not dead but living; he says, for 'he is not the God of the dead but of the living, for all live to him' (verse 32). This is repeated in all three Gospels.

There are four points arising from this. First, after death his servants still serve him. Consider then whether any master can ever be called the master of such servants as are now dead and are no longer of any use to him. On the other hand, if he is their master they must still be able to serve him. Therefore God cannot be the God of Abraham, Isaac and Jacob unless they are still living and able to serve him. We must apply this teaching of Christ to ourselves. The Fathers' God is also our great God, and if we follow in their footsteps we may sure that, because he is our God, death shall not separate us from him. Death, the event that in the carnal judgment of the world appears to separate us from God, actually joins us to him far more closely than we were while we were still in this world. For just as Abraham, Isaac and Jacob who died to this world are now said to live unto God, so all those of true faith are not cut off from him by death, but joined more closely to him; for after death we live solely and exclusively to God without the distraction of this world.

Second, the deceased patriarchs now live to God in their souls. It is true that Abraham, Isaac and Jacob no longer lived in their earthly bodies. For as the apostle declares in the final verse of this chapter, 'All these … did not receive what was promised, since God had provided something better for us, that apart from us they should not be made perfect'.[34] Thus at this present time, the three patriarchs do not live to God in their bodies, but are said to live in the principal part of their persons, that is, in their souls. Their souls are in heaven and there they

[34] Hebrews 11:39-40; Bruce's citation of this Scripture text is not easily understood: *apart quhill we be perfected with them and sall not be perfected whill we be perfected also.*

live a perfect life, for they are living in the presence of God. However, seeing that God is the God of the whole person and not only of the soul, in the fullness of time he declares that as their God he will be God of their whole persons, that is, of their bodies as well as of their souls, for his salvation shall extend to our bodies as well as to our souls. Just as at death he took to himself their souls, so in due time their bodies shall take on the same perfection as has been imparted to their souls. The body that previously was subjected to sorrow and affliction during this earthly life, shall then live a heavenly life reunited with the soul.

It is foolish and vain to think that the eternal God who names himself after a man (as we have seen) would leave part of that man unredeemed. Otherwise, to desert his body and to perfect only his soul, would be an extremely weak favour to bestow on him; to suggest that would be to imply that God is weak, which would be totally absurd. Therefore, seeing that God will perfect the whole man, as the soul presently lives with him, so he shall in due time bring the body also to live with him. This why we speak of 'the immortality of the soul', for eternal life after this life is thus clearly proven.

Third, it has been demonstrated that death does not separate a man from God, but joins him even more closely with him, and this closer union is occasioned by death, the greatest curse upon humanity and a terrible experience for flesh and blood! O how bitter is death to those who live according to the flesh, but how sweet to those who die in the Lord! For it is this same death that brings a man into the closest union with his God. Therefore, that you may be partakers after death in this intimate union with God, now more than ever strive to live by faith as did Abraham, Isaac and Jacob.

It might appear that God who made so much of the patriarchs by calling himself by their names, placed them before the rest of his servants, but we must realise that to attribute that kind of favouritism to God is quite preposterous. Even though he called himself by their names, that does not mean he regarded them as worthy of such honour, for what he accepted in them were the gifts and graces wherewith he himself had blessed them. In other words, it was the very gift of faith with which he had endued them that he honoured. In the same way that he honoured them during their earthly lives, so he also crowned them in the heavenly life. It is faith that he honours in his saints, for without faith there is no honour given either in this life or in the next.

The outcome of patriarchs' suit

We come at last to the fourth point I have to make on the outcome. As you have heard of their reward, now at the end of the verse is set down the outcome of their suit: they sought a city and a heavenly country and they entered it, for the Lord had prepared it for them and welcomed them to it. Regarding this, note first that they did not build this city for themselves, it was the Lord who prepared it and gave it to them. So do we deserve it by any merit of ours? In Matthew 25:34 Christ our Master says, *he prepairit it befoir the foundatiounis of the world war laid*. Before we could engage in either good or evil, he prepared that city, and that lets us see that it did not come into being through any deserving of ours. Entirely of his own will the Lord established this place, without any merit of ours.

Also notice that we must seek this city diligently. Even though he has prepared it for you, still you must seek it. Seek it throughout your whole life. Continue in your suit, never ceasing until the final summons[35] comes at the end of your life. Some may make a quick attempt at something he would like, and then give up the quest,[36] but you must not be like that. You must constantly refresh your memories with reminders of the final summons, and when Satan tries to distract your thoughts away from heaven you must come to hear God's word, and pray that he would restore the vision of it in your memories. Crave pardon from the Lord that you have temporarily neglected your suit and have sought after other things. If you have completely forgotten your suit, pray that the Lord would stir it up in your memories, and enable you to stand firm in your suit to your life's end. For heaven is not gained without great anguish, and the harder it is to win, the better will it be. Things that are easily won are also easily lost. So do not grow faint-hearted in your suit, but crave that the Lord in his mercy would strengthen you in it, that when you forget about it he will cause you to recall and remember it.

[35] 'Sute' here translated as 'the final summons'; see note 15 above. The word 'sute' is used 17 times in this final part of the sermon.

[36] 'Sute' here translated as 'quest', since it is used in an active sense of something we must seek, rather than a summons to which we must respond. However, here Bruce is speaking about those whose faith is 'a flash in the pan' as we say.

I told you at the start, and I tell you again, that there was never anyone who was determined and constant in what he sought who did not attain it. There are some who fix their hearts on this world, hoping to find happiness and to get what they desire. But surely those whose suit is heaven and its blessed life will gladly part with the fleeting pleasures of this world in exchange for the fulfilment of their suit and will remain constant in their quest. Take heed, therefore, what suit you choose. For usually there is nothing a man sets his heart upon that he does not attain, but if it be something alien to God, it will not be blessed by him, but may end up being cursed.

Be warned, then, regarding what you seek, for it is the just judgment of God as to what you get when you ignore and bypass him. If you address your suit rightly, no matter how hard it may be, nor however long its fulfilment is delayed, be assured that ultimately you will be granted the blessing for which you suited. Do not expect to find the world in God, but suit after that better, heavenly country that is promised here. Set your heart on this and God will bless you. Resolve to strive after God alone. It matters not if I lose all my earthly wealth,[37] I know that I will never be satisfied until I reach that heavenly life. Make this your resolve, seek it without delay, and assuredly it shall be granted to you.

Those of you who have not entered upon this suit, but still have your hearts set upon this world, while there is still time, change your suit and turn away to seek the better, heavenly country. Wrestle with your desires that would cling to this world, for naturally all our hearts are inclined towards material things. Agonize over this, and little by little he will you give spiritual grace in your anguish; those desires that until now have been set on earthly things will be sanctified, so that your affections will turn increasingly towards the love of God. The Lord in his mercy so change your longings that they will seek the kingdom of heaven and that heavenly life that is in Jesus Christ, to whom with the Father and the Holy Ghost be all honour, praise and glory, now and for ever. Amen.

[37] As so often in his references to worldly wealth, Bruce is undoubtedly referring indirectly to his own experience; he had turned his back on great personal wealth to enter the ministry, and even sold his horse, so that to begin his studies for ordination he had to walk to St Andrews from his estate at Kinnaird, Larbert. (MacNicol, p. 24)

Chapter Thirteen

Hebrews Chapter 11 verses 17-19

> [17] *By faith Abrahame offered vp Isaack quhen he was tryed, and he that receaved the promisis offered his onlie begottin sone.* [18] *To quhom it was said in Isaack sall thy seid be called.* [19] *For he considdered that god was abill to raise him vp evin from the dead, from whence he receaved him also efter ane sort.*

You have heard, well-beloved in Jesus Christ, the kind of country these holy patriarchs, Abraham, Isaac and Jacob, were seeking, and you also heard the outcome of their suit,[1] and how they were rewarded for their diligent and earnest obedience to the Lord's summons. You also heard about the nature of the country that they sought, and that a heavenly country, as well as an earthly one, was promised to them. You heard too that even if they had had as pleasant a country as any other in the world that they could have returned to, these godly Fathers did not seek earthly things, for they had no interest in worldly glory or honour. Rather they sought heaven which God had graciously promised, a spiritual kingdom whose glory is everlasting; in respect of that, they counted this world and all that it offered as nothing, for they reckoned earthly glory to be mere vanity.

Seek spiritual and heavenly blessings

The first lesson for us was that we must take heed of what we seek in Jesus Christ, and what we seek in his religion and the promises of the evangel. Do not seek this earth with its worldly glory or honour. But turn your eyes upward and lift your minds heavenwards, to seek a

[1] On the word 'suit' see above, Ch. 12, note 15.

far better country than can be found here. So seek eternal rest in that spiritual and everlasting kingdom that is offered to you in Jesus Christ. For be sure of this, if you seek in Christ and his gospel anything other than what is to be found in him, he will not grant it to you, and you will end up disappointed in him. That is always the outcome for those who seek to find in Christ blessings he has never promised; his truthfulness has not been found wanting, but they have ended up with no religion and no Christ. On the other hand, those who seek what is to be found in him—rest for their souls, a spiritual kingdom and the eternal glories of heaven—whenever the day of his visitation comes upon them, they shall find the truth of his gospel to be vindicated.

No one who rightly seeks Christ's rest and his heavenly blessings, however weak in faith he may be, shall ever be disappointed, for the Lord will at once begin the work of his spiritual kingdom in that person's soul. We have been thinking about that suit—our obedient response to Lord's summons—and the initiation of his spiritual reign in a soul is a confirmation of that suit. For the very act of rightly seeking Christ indicates that the Spirit has begun his work in that person; that is, Christ by his Spirit has already entered the seeker's soul to reign there. This means that when it pleases God to bring Christ to someone with the realisation of the truth about him,[2] by the Spirit that person shall confess Christ with his mouth, and then the Spirit will strengthen him, furnish him with the words to say and enable him to persevere and so continue with him to perfect the work that Jesus Christ has begun in him. Then seek in Christ that spiritual rest and the heavenly country, and the Spirit will never let you be ashamed of him, but will help and uphold you, and bring you to the end of your journey.

Humility and faith

There was a second thing that I pointed out to you regarding the way the Fathers sought the heavenly country. In what way did they seek it rightly and at the apt time? We saw that their manner of seeking it rested chiefly upon these two virtues, humility and faith. Yea, it was by faith and humility that during their lifetime they ran the race towards

[2] I have translated Bruce's word 'religion' by the phrase 'the truth about him'; when he speaks of 'religion', the context invariably indicates that he means 'the reformed faith'. Occasionally he does spell out 'religion' as 'the reformed faith'.

the heavenly kingdom. Their humility arose from their knowledge of themselves and of their miserable state. For the more a person knows of himself and the more clearly he sees his own inward condition, the more lowly and humble he will be.

The Fathers were brought to realise their own inner wretchedness, and the more clearly they understood their spiritual state, the more they were humbled and acknowledged their shame. That was why, wherever they happened to be on their journey, they confessed themselves to be but pilgrims and strangers, men who found no fulfilment in this world, but would fain be in their true home. On their journey they were just as prepared and willing to experience all difficulties as any other pilgrim on earth might be. Thus it was the awareness and knowledge of themselves that begat and engendered humility in them.

However, they were raised up by the sight of God's mercy and kindness, and the assurance of his goodness in his promises to them brought their faith to birth. Just as the sight of themselves cast them down, so the assurance of God's grace that was extended to them lifted them up. In God they became strong, whereas in themselves they were low and weak; in God they rejoiced, whereas in themselves they mourned. Now take careful note. What is the way in which a Christian must be conveyed to heaven? The only way is through faith and humility; whoever has genuine faith, of necessity will be humble. Just as faith and humility go together, so pride and unbelief always go together. The person who knows neither God nor himself is bound to be proud. On the other hand, the one who knows both himself and God cannot but be lowly. So if you eschew pride and unbelief, you will also eschew the broad road. Choose the pathway lit by the sight of your sinful state and the merits of God, that is, the way lighted by humility and faith, and you will find that you are walking along that strait way.

We have to deplore the wickedness of many of the nobles of our country who have departed from the strait way, and have entered the devil's way, the way of pride. Their hearts and swords are inflamed with the desire to revenge themselves with the blood of others. God in his righteous judgment stirs up one against another, so that they have become executioners of each other, and all this because they have spurned the way, so long and freely offered to them, that could have led them to heaven. Their lawlessness and blood-letting can only be divine retribution upon them. Therefore, learn the lesson: the way to heaven is by faith and humility, through knowing the mercy and kindness of God, and, so far as lies with you, in the foretaste and assurance of it.

The blessings of the assurance of God's presence

Thirdly, the Fathers obtained the very things that they sought so urgently, for all their lives they pursued the Lord and his presence, and therefore God gave himself to them along with his own presence. What more could any man wish for when he has the presence of the eternal God? For the faithful soul is fully satisfied with God, and the more he feels the divine presence, the better he is for it. For as long as they lived, the Fathers were assured in their hearts and consciences that heaven was prepared and appointed for them. As often as the Lord spoke to them, he assured them of this, so when their lives on earth ended and they died in faith, their souls were immediately borne to heaven, where they found the full fruition of all that the Lord had promised them.

They sought God and his presence and were rewarded with both. So do you know that presence of God? Those who have the presence of God in their hearts, find that all he has created brings them joy; nothing he has created can ever bring pleasure in the way God's presence does. His presence can transform a foul prison cell into a delightful garden,[3] and can turn what could have been a bitter death into a sweet departure. So the presence of God can take what is hard for flesh and blood to endure and make it palatable and satisfying. The more aware we are of the Lord's presence, the more we find happiness in living. We learn this by the peace that he brings to our consciences and the rest he imparts to our souls; then the joy with which he fills our hearts increases the nearer we sense his presence with us.

Should not your suit be employed solely upon seeking God and his presence? For a contented and joyful heart should surely be our great desire, and seeing that it can only be obtained from the Lord and his

[3] Those familiar with *Letters of Samuel Rutherford* will be reminded of his descriptions of his prison cell in Aberdeen: 'How blind are my adversaries, who sent me to a banqueting-house, a house of wine, to the lovely feast of my lovely Lord Jesus, and not to a prison or place of exile.' LXXVI; 'I am well. My prison is a palace to me, and Christ's banqueting-house. My Lord Jesus is as kind as they call him.' LXXX. (Both of these letters were written in 1637, six years after Bruce's death.) Rutherford pp. 162 & 168.

presence, what else should you be striving for other than this? But we are bewitched by the corruption of our human natures, by the enticements of flesh and blood and this world and by the temptations of the devil. As a result we neither seek the right end, nor are we willing to begin seeking it. I fear that the consequences of this are imminent, even though we would not want what our nation has been pursuing for some years now.

Impending judgment

As our people have abandoned God in favour of the devil, preferring lies to the truth, the righteous God is now beginning to give the evil one power to deceive them, and in just retribution the spirit of error is being given free rein; so the throne of his Son is being removed from our land to be replaced by the throne of Satan. The hearts of men are not touched with compassion or sorrow for their own souls, far less for the poor souls of the miserable peasantry. The hearts of the earls, dukes and magistrates[4] remain unmoved, and their obduracy of heart and lack of any human affection is sure evidence the Lord has some swift judgment ready to pour out.

This is how far we reached in my last sermon.

Today's verses 17-19

In the verses that I have read, our apostle, having conjointly praised the patriarchs and the faith they shared, as now he begins to praise each of them individually,[5] first returns to Abraham. Having left him at verse 12, he takes up his story again in verse 17, where he praises the faith of this godly man, evidenced in the record of a most singular and notable act of obedience. Indeed, the remarkable record that I read does not have the like in the entire Scriptures of God. This was an action in which flesh and blood could have had no place, for it is evident at every stage of this event that it was only accomplished by the operation and control of the Spirit of God. The account of Abraham's act of obedience at God's command is recorded and described in these three verses that

[4] The phrase indirectly refers to the Second and Third Estates of the *Thre Estaitis*, loathed by the reformers; the First Estate was 'Prelates'.

[5] The writer of the Letter to the Hebrews did not in fact return to Isaac or Jacob; Bruce probably has in mind that Moses also is dealt with individually and more fully.

I have just read, and the apostle has set it down accurately to help us understand it.

First, we must note the circumstance of time when Abraham undertook this action. Secondly, the apostle deals with the deed itself, describing it and amplifying it according to the person of Abraham and his son. Third, from there he moves on to the fountain from where and of which it sprang, and he also amplifies this 'fountain' in order that we may see the greatness of Abraham's faith, not only on account of the deed, but also on account of certain effects of it.[6] These three points are all implied in the opening words in verse 17: *By faith Abrahame offered vp Isaack quhen he was tried* or tempted by God.

First, the events immediately preceding the sacrifice of Isaac

So we come to the first point, the circumstance of time. The record notes the time when this deed was done at God's command, namely when it actually came about that it pleased the living God to try his faith, his obedience, his profound reverence and love for him. We learn this from the history recorded in Genesis 22, the original record of this event. It came about immediately after the agreement and compact that Abraham made with Abimelech, king of Gerar. The Lord had done his servant this great honour in that he put it into the heart of Abimelech, a great and powerful chieftain, to request Abraham's alliance and favour, and not to be satisfied until he had a compact with the promise of friendship.[7] After he had moved this powerful prince to seek out Abraham and to beg for his favour, and lest this honour should have stirred up the heart of God's servant, or unduly raised his opinion of himself, making him proud or 'stuck up' (as we say[8]), the Lord immediately subjected him to this trial. Abraham had never been confronted by such a

[6] The English of this paragraph may seem stilted, but I have preserved as accurately as possible Bruce's order of words, to try and convey to the reader the way in which he handled the outline of what he will expound in the main part of this sermon.

[7] Genesis 21:22-24.

[8] I have translated Bruce's word 'guobit' as 'stuck-up'; 'guobit' seems to have been some colloquial slang expression meaning 'cocky'—hence his comment in parenthesis '(as we say)'. His fuller comment is 'least this work... should heisit him... and maid him proud and guobit (as we say)'.

sore trial as this, nor had he previously ever been so painfully tested or treated in this way.

So what is there here for us to learn? We must learn never to be beguiled by the riches or honours of this world. We must never repose or settle ourselves down upon worldly wealth or plaudits, for these things are unstable and can soon be lost. The Lord has mingled the lives of his servants with contrasting conditions, in that there can be bitter sorrow, but then a time of happiness, or there can be great prosperity but then it may be overtaken by adversity. That is why he commands us when all seems to be calm to watch out for the storm, and, when our affairs are prospering, to be constantly on our guard for we may be afflicted with some trial. Think about the life of this holy man, our father in the faith, and you will observe that throughout his whole life there were these contrasting conditions: sometimes honour but other times infamy, sometimes wealth but other times poverty, sometimes tranquillity but other times affliction. Thus the Lord orders these vicissitudes continually to alternate in the conditions of the lives of his servants.

Therefore profit by this lesson. Yes, at this time the Lord has blessed us with quietness, a measure of prosperity and calm compared to other lands that have been more worthy of it than we are. Then learn not to take such conditions for granted as if the peace in our country is to continue indefinitely. Rather, while the Lord gives us time and grants us the opportunity, let us watch out for a possible storm. Already gathering are dark clouds which could burst upon our country in great measure, for our peace and tranquillity already is being threatened, and our reformed faith endangered. Consequently I fear that this storm will be upon us sooner than we imagine.

Let us then, while the Lord continues to grant us a time of ease, seek to have hearts, that are contented to accept any conditions that it shall please our Sovereign God to place upon us, looking to him for strength. We need his help because in Christ's cause no one can be strong without his aid. So look to him, if for no other reason than that his evangel will not be disgraced by our foolish and weak actions. Be strong in the Lord, therefore, and put on the armour of God, that we may even welcome whatever impositions our Sovereign God may choose to impose upon us.[9] So much, then, for the circumstance of time.

[9] In my view, the context here does not suggest that by 'his majestie' Bruce is

Second, the trial of Abraham's faith through the command to sacrifice Isaac

It is recorded in Genesis that God tempted or tried Abraham. Now God is said to tempt, and man also is said to tempt. But we must start with the devil for he constantly tempts with evil. Sometimes in person he tempts profligately, at other times he tempts through his lieutenants or through the flesh or the world. Whether his temptations are moderate or immoderate, his aim is always to destroy us by deceiving us and then ensnaring us.

If it happens that the Lord intervenes and frustrates his purpose, causing his arrows to fall short of their intended target, yet he still does not give up. His malevolent aim remains the destruction of both our bodies and souls. Have you not heard how our Master said to Peter, *the devil heth desyrit to sift thee Peter* (Luke 22:31)? Yea, and he would sift you too, to destroy you both in body and soul as he desired to destroy Peter. Indeed, his intention is the same for every Christian, so he constantly prowls about, awaiting the opportunity to devour you.[10] But our Lord interposes his power and mercy, frustrating the devil's cruel schemes; sometimes swiftly, and other times after a delay, he snatches his children out of the devil's jaws, rescuing them from those evil conspirators who serve him all their lives.

Satan's assault upon our nation

Today before our very eyes there are many visible examples of this in our nation. It hardly matters whether the devil goes about covertly to establish his kingdom by infestations in men's hearts, or whether, as now, he goes about doing his work quite openly with his disguises cast aside. Thus overtly manifesting himself to the people, he causes many

referring to King James. Occasionally, he refers to God as 'his majestie' which I prefer to translate as 'our Sovereign God'. Readers who are familiar with the unreliable, slippery character of James VI, and are aware of his support for episcopacy and his intense dislike of many of the staunch Presbyterians, will not consider that Bruce here is actually referring to James. Nevertheless, like all Scots of his day, Bruce had a profound respect for the office of the king, and saw the monarchy as divinely appointed. However, it could be that I am mistaken and that Bruce is, in fact, referring to restrictive measures the king might yet impose upon the Kirk.

[10] The allusion is to 1 Peter 5:8.

to renounce God, and knowingly and willingly to renounce Christ and their baptism. No doubt his intention is that both their bodies and souls shall be his possession for ever.

In his mercy, I say, the Lord is frustrating him, as I do not doubt the devil shall be disappointed respecting some of those he has ensnared at this time. But because he is always evil, his purpose is certainly not to let these poor people slip from his grasp. But it will be through the virtue of the prayers of Jesus Christ that they are rescued, for it was through Christ's prayers that Peter was sustained and did not fall away. At the Last Supper, Peter had made an unexpected assertion.[11] Nevertheless, the power[12] of Christ's prayer upheld him so that he did not completely fall away. Just say there are deluded people who appear to have totally fallen away, and have lapsed in the same way as Peter, yet it may please the Lord to enlighten their minds, and to let us see that the virtue of Christ's prayers prevail and are as effectual for them as well as they were for Peter.

Brethren, you have to recognise that among all ranks and conditions of men we share a common nature with those miserable wretches with their broken bodies who have long been the devil's slaves. He has had such singular power over them that their sad condition cannot be attributed merely to nature or human influences. Yet the devil does not have as great control over you as he has over them, for there is a special grace of which you may be unaware, and it has never occurred to you to ponder on that grace that has protected you from his terrible slavery, even though you are in a better condition than those who have not been exempted from his power. When God has thus so generously dealt with you, because of your base ingratitude to him, you would justly deserve a mightier evil spirit to enter you; the stronger that spirit is and the more clandestinely he conceals himself within you, the harder would it be to expel him. Therefore pray for gratitude and that you may be touched with the sense of God's great mercy that has protected you from the devil's snare into which others, who were no different to you, have fallen. And when you see the tragic sight of those who have become the devil's slaves, ask God to enable you to learn from such a spectacle.

[11] Luke 22:33.
[12] 'vertew'.

The devil's purpose in temptation

Be sure of this, that in whatever way the Lord restricts the temptation and however he lessens its onslaught, yet the devil's purpose is always to destroy. So the Lord bridles him and holds him back as he rushes at you, for every temptation in this world is in the hands of God, and ultimately they all emanate from him.[13] A profitable lesson may always be learned from this consideration: whenever we are tempted, either directly by the devil, or by our own desires, by our neighbour or even by God himself, then let us constantly pray that he would not permit either the devil or the flesh to prevail, and that we will not give any place to the temptation. The point is this: the devil will always tempt you to evil. When it is a man tempting someone, it is in order to try to get further insight into that person and to find out what he intends. But when God tempts someone, it is not for further insight into him. The Lord was not ignorant of the condition of Abraham's heart, nor of the strength or greatness of his faith; what lay hidden in his servant was already known to God, for he had implanted all that was in him.

God's purpose in temptation

The reason why God tempted Abraham was that his faith might be known to the world, and so that the Kirk might see the greatness and strength of a faith that otherwise lay concealed within his heart. He chiefly tempted his servant for this purpose that his faith, fear and love towards the Almighty God might be seen to be engraved on his heart and so be made manifest to the whole world. For if the devil constantly tempts us for evil, the living God constantly tempts us for our good, and, after our temptations have been endured, that we may be crowned. For the crown is only given to those who have endured temptation and have fought lawfully. Says Christ, *You abaid with me in my tentatiounis,*[14] therefore I will give you a crown. The apostle says, 'I have fought a good fight,' therefore a crown awaits me.[15] So the pathway of temptation leads to a crown, but only those who fight lawfully and endure temptation will be crowned. If it is the Lord himself who tempts you, he will impart strength to you in your suffering; likewise, if

[13] Job 1:6-12.
[14] Luke 22:28.
[15] 2 Timothy 4:7-8.

it is the devil or some person through whom the temptation comes, he will also give you strength to resist. So every temptation—and they all come from God—is for your good.

The Lord also had another purpose in this tempting of Abraham. Everything that took place on this occasion (see in Romans 4)[16] was not done for his sake only, but also both for us and for all posterity to the end of the world. It was the same with the temptations of Jesus Christ and what he suffered at the hands of the devil—you can read about it in Matthew 4:1-11; it was also the same with the temptations of Job. These accounts are all set down as examples for us. Therefore profit by them and note by what armour they resisted and stood firm, so that you also may stand firm, defended by that same armour. Note also how these all employed prayer, and follow their prayers so that you may endure temptation.

Third, the Lord's final purpose in tempting us is to take away the false conception we have of ourselves. For beyond all question, so long as a man is not tempted, he thinks of himself as strong and worthy, and is puffed up with a very mistaken view of himself. But once it pleases the Lord to make him examine himself so that he might gain an insight into the condition of his fallen nature, immediately he changes his opinion. Whereas before he thought a lot of himself, now he sees his unworthiness. He begins to recognise that within his fallen nature is much that is grotesque and abominable. Thus the third purpose of the Lord in tempting us is that we might know our own infirmity, weakness and sinful corruption. In short, the Lord chooses for us what will be profitable and for our good.

It pleased the Lord at that time, therefore, to tempt and test his servant in a manner that in all possible ways was most difficult, grievous and burdensome for him. But before I embark upon the subject of this deed, there is a general point that must be noted, namely, that there cannot be genuine, justifying faith without some trial. Neither is it possible that the Kirk can stand firm without troubles and persecution. It is impossible that true faith can be in a man without temptation. Be assured, then, that if the faith you have has been begotten by the

[16] Though Bruce points his hearers to Romans 4, he does not actually quote verses 23-24 which read, 'But the words "It was counted to him" were not written for his sake alone, but for ours also.'

Spirit of God, the same God shall make your faith known to the world through your trial; and whoever cannot endure that trial makes it clear that he is a hypocrite. On the other hand, if a man does endure the trial, then it becomes apparent that he is not chaff, but good corn that is appointed for life everlasting.

Because faith can never exist without some trial, I am persuaded that faith in this land of ours must be very weak for it has been some time since we were visited by trials. The fact that trials of our faith are delayed does not mean that our weaknesses are being overlooked; no, in his own time the Lord will put our faith to the test. He will winnow[17] you, but the devil wants to sift you and will somehow find the opportunity to test whether or not you are in the faith. So examine yourselves to see whether you are mortifying your lusts and sinful desires. Then see what love you have for the Lord's kingdom, and whether you thirst to partake in that inheritance; but chiefly take heed to the mortification of your lives. When sin is beginning to lose its domination in someone's life and little by little is decaying, and where godliness is in some measure being embraced, faith has entered that person's soul. But if a man continues without any restraint in some sin or other, he is a hypocrite, and the Lord by some trial shall make that evident, for all faith must be tried and tested.

Third, the purpose of testing Abraham's obedience

Now I must move on to my third main point, the purpose of testing Abraham's obedience in offering up his son Isaac. In order that his obedience in this deed may be seen more clearly, we need to examine the nature of the command recorded in the Genesis account, therefore return with me to the twenty-second chapter. We need to consider the difficulty of this deed to human flesh and blood. God's command is first, 'Take your son, your only son Isaac, the son whom you love'. Then he is commanded to take him to the land of Moriah, and when he arrives there, to slay him by offering him as a sacrifice. This deed must be done upon one of the hills to which God would guide him and confirm to him as the appointed place.

In order that the greatness of Abraham's faith may be more clearly evident, let us consider the hardness and seeming callousness of this

[17] The obsolete agricultural process of separating chaff from the wheat by hand.

command. Can you see how each word is loaded with emotion and is like a sharp sword-thrust to pierce his heart? Each word is followed by another, making the pressure mount up to bring even more sorrow to the father's heart. Observe how in the natural flow of these words, each phrase is calculated to bring home to us its weight, enormity and grimness. They are so gravely spoken, so precisely uttered, that nothing could be more solemn.

It is possible that originally there had been a conversation between the Lord and Abraham, for the words are so carefully chosen that it seems as if they have been spoken to answer some objection that Abraham might have made. Indeed, there is so much significance within these words, that unless the reader is thoroughly sanctified (which none of us are), he will never understand them fully, not even a quarter of them, let alone their meaning in its entirety.

Four points regarding God's command

First, I shall try to let you see that there appears to be an intimate exchange between God and Abraham.[18] Then I shall let you see how each word in turn rises in gravitas above the word before, in order to pierce his heart. As to that mutual conversation, it may have occurred in this way. When God bade him take his son, he may have answered, 'But which of the two sons do you mean? I have one by Hagar and one by Sarah. They are each the only son each mother has borne.'

God then answers, 'I mean the son you love with all your heart' (for the words 'your only son whom you love' refer to a total and complete love), and then in case a further objection might be made, God condescends to name him, 'your son Isaac'. The phrases are so complete in themselves that each one appears to be an answer to an objection Abraham might have raised. As to the weight of the words, I repeat: each phrase rises degree by degree above the phrase preceding it. For was it not a most serious matter to command a man to take as a sacrifice his own son, from his own loins and of his own flesh and blood? Could there be anything more grim than this?

Second, the account proceeds. God commands him to take 'his only son'. When a man has many sons, it would be painful enough to lose just one of them, but losing an only son would be bound to bring

[18] Bruce's phrase is 'a mutual answering betuix god and abrahame'.

deepest sorrow to him. Isaac is called 'his only son', partly because Ishmael had been sent away and partly because Sarah had borne no other children, but chiefly because the promises applied only to him. Not only the various particulars of the covenantal promises regarding the land of Canaan were to be effectual in Isaac alone, but also the promises regarding the blessing upon Abraham's posterity were to be fulfilled through Isaac. That is why the Spirit of God deliberately names him as 'your only son'. Therefore, although to be told to 'take his son' would have wounded his heart, taking 'his only son' must have wounded his heart even more deeply.

Third, the Lord continues speaking of this son for whom Abraham has such a total and complete love. It is one thing for a man to have a son, an only son, whom he loathes on account of his wicked life, but it quite another thing, indeed, the bitterest of deeds, for a man to have to slay his only son whom he loves unreservedly.

Fourth, he names him. He was called Isaac because through him the Lord was to fulfil all his promises, both spiritual and temporal. In this God wounds him, causing great pain. Yet he does not only pierce his heart with the most deadly and bitter darts, but he commands him to take his son far away to the land of Moriah. As far as we know, this is where today Jerusalem is situated, and this was to be the place where Solomon would build the temple. It was three or four days' journey from where they lived.

Notwithstanding this place being quite unknown to Abraham, God commanded him to take his son there, to offer him as a sacrifice at that particular place, nowhere else. What is the significance of this journey? God deliberately wanted his sorrow to continue to weigh heavily upon his heart, and for that weight to press hard upon him for these three or four days without any relief. The only consolation he could possibly have had was from his faith. No other comfort was afforded him. This journey to the land of Moriah was also to make it clear to us and to Abraham's household, that since the deed was suspended for these several days, he was not acting rashly on a sudden impulse, but his actions flowed from godly fear and obedience to the Lord.

The 'fifth degree' of God's command

See how the command reaches its highest point to the fifth degree when they arrive at the place and God commands him there to slay his son and to offer him as burnt offering. The fifth degree came when God commanded Isaac to be a burnt offering. 'Must I be the executioner of my son? Is there no one else who could slay him except me, his father? I begat him by the gift of God, given to me in my old age, and now must I destroy him? What is the meaning of this? How can this stand beside the law of God "You shall not kill", and must it be I who does the deed? Is the Spirit of God contrary to his divine person? From whence comes this command?'

Can you see how Abraham had much to wrestle with? There was natural reason to contend with. Also, were these lies of the devil bringing the divine laws into disrepute? Further, he had God himself to wrestle with. (We shall deal with these observations on another occasion.) But always the word that comes is that he must offer his son as burnt offering. The burnt offering was the kind of sacrifice that was wholly consumed, leaving no part for the use of the priest or Levite; all had to be burned up before God. It was presented entirely to God and in the original language it is spoken of as ascending before him. It was a kind of ascension.

The reason for the chosen location

The final part of God's instructions was, 'Offer him on one the hills that I shall show you'. It is surely strange that God not only delayed the sacrifice for three or four days, but he also delayed showing to Abraham the place where the deed was to be done. Why was this? The reason was that Abraham might see that the Lord was not going to deliver him by flesh and blood, nor by his own ingenuity, but he would have all the details controlled and directed by the working of his Spirit; nothing must be done by human reasoning, so God must choose the place, not Abraham. Even though his servant was given the general outline of his plan, the exact details God kept to himself for Abraham could only receive them from the Lord's mouth through prayer. How Abraham knew where the place was to be is not told us in the sacred record; perhaps he met a man who was a great prophet and in touch with God, and to whom the location had been disclosed. However, there can be no doubt that in some way the Lord gave him insight in his heart, and revealed the place to him.

Application: God reveals the 'general' but the 'particulars' are given through prayer

We come now to the lesson here for us. It appears that the Lord withheld all the details from Abraham, not sharing them with him at first, but only communicating them to him as he prays. Why? Here is the importance of this: suppose someone knows that God's general calling for him is that he is to preach the Word and administer the sacraments, nevertheless the Lord keeps hidden in his own hands the 'particulars' of his calling. He guides events by his fatherly and gracious providence, until those details are revealed to his servant through his prayers and his earnest appeal for guidance: in what place and with what status he is to exercise his calling, when he should begin and when he should leave—all these and other 'particulars' he must beg from God's hands. He must be instant in prayer, and with very good reason he must depend upon God's providence.[19]

Therefore, brethren, learn never to enter upon any 'particulars' in your calling, without seeking guidance from God; always first seek his mind in prayer. Even though you know that the work to which you feel called is good, yet, because both the warrant and blessing must come from God, share it first with him and crave his guidance. In this way shall your conscience give you glorious testimony in the day of your visitation,[20] as well as at the time of your final breath. But if you neglect God in your choice of the 'particulars' and proceed to arrange and select them by your own preferences, the Lord shall in the end disappoint you, and what you have chosen for yourself shall become a plague upon you and a blight upon your work. Therefore let us cultivate the spirit

[19] From the earlier sentence in this paragraph beginning, 'Here is the importance of this…' all the personal pronouns throughout the rest of the paragraph are in the first person plural 'we', what is today called 'the royal we', for it is highly probable that Bruce is referring to his own experience. See Chapter 14, note 7 below.

[20] A 'visitation' in the post-Reformation Church was an inspection of the work of the minister by presbyters. According the *First Book of Discipline*, Superintendents were to be appointed whose role, along with elders, was to undertake pastoral care for ministers. *Knox*, Vol. II, 'The Fift Heid, Concerning the Provisioun for the Ministeris' I-III, pp. 201-208.

of prayer, and share everything with God before we ever embark upon any work for him. This far, then, for the opening up of the verses I have read.

The conflict between natural affections and spiritual affections

Because the time is marching on, I shall just note two further points and leave the rest for another occasion. The first remaining point in the command of God is that here we witness a strange and remarkable conflict between natural affections and spiritual affections—Abraham's love for his child and his love for God. On the one side are nature and the devil urging reasons for disobeying God. Nature says, 'You are his father, he is from your loins and is of your very substance; you cannot be his executioner!' The devil says, 'This is a deed contrary to the law of God, therefore it cannot be God who is commanding you to do this. It is some alien spirit that you are mistaking for God.' Further, the devil adds, 'Moreover, this is the Lord's promise, *In Isaack sall thy seid be called*, so all God's promises are to be fulfilled in Isaac; he cannot destroy his own promises and commandment.' Abraham answers back, 'Even though by my natural understanding I cannot see how this command of God can be compatible with his promises, by faith I know that God cannot contradict himself, and that his purpose is not to destroy his promise, but to confirm it.'

Furthermore, Abraham's reply to the devil can only have been this: 'Faith assures me that God is able to raise the dead. I know his power and his will, and that he shall raise my son again after he has been slain, so that all the promises of God shall be effectual in him.' Faith reasons unswervingly and rests strongly upon the Lord's promises and power. Because faith prevails is why Abraham obeyed God and attended to the thing that had to be done.

We are all subject to similar temptations as both fallen nature and the devil combine in their arguments to dissuade us from obeying God. But lest you cannot resist them when they reason with you, take care to be constant in prayer so that they do not prevail, for even though the appeal to your fallen nature is agonisingly painful to resist, only by prayer can faith overcome. Prayer, I say, is the Christian's only defence. Therefore follow the patriarch's example, and put on the same armour, the armour of God, that your faith may prevail.

Abraham's love and fear of God was being tested

The second remaining point to note is this. He was being tempted regarding his fear of God: did he love God more than he loved his only son? Which was the greater fear in his heart, to transgress against God or to transgress against his son? Even though this was the most horrendous trial, we see that his love for, and fear of God prevailed in his heart. He was more afraid to transgress against God than he was to slay every one of sons, however many he might have had.

These two—fear of God and love of him—should season the heart of every Christian. Holy fear of his divine majesty should be predominant in your hearts. Even though you have to do with a king or an emperor, do not let either love for, and fear of your king be stronger in your hearts than your reverence and love for your God. Fix your gaze upon God's majesty, and rather offend the king a thousand times than offend your God just once. Rather suffer the loss of your son, your wife and all your other children than fall by affronting God. Let the fearful spectacle of those who have transgressed against God be a warning to you against doing as they have done. When a man falls from God, where does he then find himself but in the hands of the devil! There can be no comparison between a soul that is filled with glory and is holy before God, and the torment of the poor souls whose bodies the devil has occupied; let that thought be a spur to you to resist the devil.

Therefore, learn to put loyalty to God before loyalty to the king. Give to each his rightful due: render to God what belongs to God and to Caesar what belongs to him. This way you will maintain a clear conscience that will not accuse you. There are torments of conscience and torments of body: even though princes subject your bodies to the most cruel pain possible, even to be thrown into an iron barrel of molten lead, having a clear conscience is preferable to being a tormented soul. So acknowledge that God must always have his own orb[21] and sceptre, and love whatever you love in him, preferring nothing above him. Any of you who have set your affections on this world, turn away from the

[21] Bruce's word is 'rowne', meaning 'a circular panel' or 'a sphere or globe'. It may be a spelling error (frequent misspellings occur in the Bruce's scripts) and he may have meant a 'crowne', which he sometimes spells as 'croun'. Therefore I have chosen to translate 'rowne' as 'orb' and have added 'sceptre' as these are twin symbols of royal power.

vain objects of your love and rather set your affections upon God. If you love your wife or children more than God, change your priorities and hold God first in your hearts, and then you will be able to love in God the families he has given to you in his mercy.

Should it come about that the Lord appoints a trial to test you, it will soon become apparent if you are setting your wife and children above him in your affections. Therefore, before any trial is visited upon you, give him the first place. For as God is a Spirit, so he must be served in the spirit with a love devoid of carnal affections of the heart. So love him above everything else, and then you shall not think your trial has been in vain. Because God is God, whatever you forsake for his cause he shall restore double to you, therefore in this life and in the life to come you will repose upon the mighty God. Crave from him an increase of your love, your fear of him and also your patience, but crave even more for his mercy and grace, all for the sake of Jesus Christ, to whom with the Father and the Holy Ghost be all honour, praise and glory both now and for ever. Amen.

Chapter Fourteen

Hebrews Chapter 11 verses 17-18

[17] By faith Abrahame offered vp Isaack quhen he was tryed, and he that receaved the promisis offered his onlie begottin sone. [18] To quhom it was said in Isaack sall thy seid be called.

As you have already heard, brethren and well-beloved in Jesus Christ, the apostle returned to the general praise and commendation of Abraham and his most notable deed, the like of which we will scarcely find in the entire Scriptures of God. On account of this deed, he commends the patriarch's faith and obedience for putting into action the command of the mighty God. In recounting this deed, the apostle sets it down in this order: first, he notes the timing of the event; next, he amplifies the action; thirdly, he goes to the fountain whence flowed this obedience. In this way, he unfolds the greatness of Abraham's faith, which is the purpose of his exposition.

The timing of this trial

First, regarding the circumstance of time when Abraham offered up his only begotten son, it was when it pleased the Lord to examine him, putting him, as it were, on 'the Blackstone' (as we say), to test his obedience.[1] However, the sacred record gives us a precise time when this

[1] Scotland's oldest universities all made use of a 'black stone' in the ritual of student examinations. Today an original 'Blackstone', a slab of black dolerite, is still in the possession of Glasgow University where it was used from its earliest days (1451). In the medieval Scottish Universities the candidate for the Master's degree took his seat on the stone while he was being publicly examined, and the practice continued until the introduction of written examinations in 1858. Above the stone was an hour-glass (still in the University's possession) to mark the time of examination. When all the sand had run through the glass, the examiner called

trial of faith occurred. It was shortly after the Lord had honoured his servant, making one of the kings of this world seek his friendship by entering into a covenant or league with him. God had caused him to reverence and highly esteem his servant Abraham.[2] It was immediately after this lofty distinction bestowed upon him that the Lord cast him into the furnace of this grievous trial. Imagine this coming upon him straight after such an exhilarating experience, divinely granted to him during a time of exceptional prosperity! Now, by this fiery trial he is brought low!

Thus we learned that we must not trust ourselves to the transient honours of this world, nor try to gain earthly riches, nor to have men's approval. For there is neither satisfaction nor contentment to be found in anything under the sun.[3] Rather, should we not lift up our hearts and raise our minds to look to him alone in whose face is perfect joy? No matter whatsoever state we may be in, look to God's appointed will, and look to his word; above all earthly things, crave of him a contented heart, so that you may be able to accept whatever changes in your circumstances he may choose for you. Ask him for patience to endure his will, even if his purpose is to humble you, when previously you were held by many in high esteem.

Passing from consideration of the godly, the wicked cannot be certain of anything here below, for there can be no rest or certainty apart from the mighty God. Therefore, while the opportunity is still open to you, crave contented hearts that you may be as willing to taste the bitter as you have been to taste the sweet, to endure adversity as the Lord in his mercy has granted you to enjoy tranquillity. This far then for the first instruction.

The apostle enlarges upon Abraham's obedience

Next, the apostle amplifies the action. As for the reasons and to what end God chose to try his servant, I already explained to you his purpose, how it was to show the world (had they the eyes to see) and

out, 'Fluxit', 'it has flowed' i.e. the sand had flowed through the glass! (The chair in which Glasgow University's original Blackstone is now set is of the late 18th century.)

[2] Genesis 21:22-34.

[3] Bruce's phrase is 'vnder the cluddis'; 'under the heavens' could have been an alternative translation.

also his kirk, how dearly Abraham loved him, and how great the reverence was that his servant had for him. Abraham revered God so much that God's command came before his own life and even his son's life. Indeed, his son's life was more precious to him than both his own and his wife's life, for their very existence was wrapped up in their son. Yet all this was but chaff compared to the command of God. It was in order that Abraham's love and reverence might be seen and known that the Lord subjected him to this ordeal. God's purpose was to use this trial not only to honour him, but also to confirm his faith in every promise that he had given him, both spiritual and temporal; consequently Abraham was richly rewarded.

In all of this there is a lesson for us. There cannot be faith without trials. (Such testing may be focused inwardly on our inherent corruption, or else outwardly through some objective circumstance.) Yet as faith inevitably faces trials, so these same trials are sent to bestow honour upon us, to reward us and to raise us in the esteem of both God and men. For the Lord tries none but those whom he loves, and whom he loves he will honour. If you have never been subjected to trials, that can only mean that you are not walking by faith with God, for without question there cannot have been in you any faith worthy of being tested and winnowed in the fan of God's purposes.

As a Kirk, we could have been tried in the same way as believers have been in other countries. But the Lord, seeing the weakness and infirmity of our faith, has laid no more on us than he has given us the strength to bear. If our sins far surpass in their gravity the sins of other nations, and if the Lord has shielded our Kirk from the great trials they have experienced, his merciful forbearance with us is that he might establish the hearts of his own elect, that he may reform us more thoroughly. Then in some measure he will endue us with sufficient faith that we may stand firm to his glory and to our benefit, by enduring whatsoever trial it shall please him to lay upon us.

On the other hand, it may be that his trial of our Kirk is being delayed. We are not being exempted, for it seems to me that every day and hour in the events all around us we are moving towards some trial. Thus we are being provoked, exhorted and warned to prepare ourselves for what could well befall us in the future.[4] But because we

[4] It would appear that Bruce rightly anticipated the coming trials of the 17th century with the persecution of the Covenanters.

are so inured in our sin, we have contracted such a habitual hardness of heart that neither self-evident arguments nor more subtle reasoning are able to awaken us. Therefore we must crave of God to delay his heavy judgment. For if you realised what it will be to stand before that highest Tribunal, and experience the difference there is between a human tribunal and the Tribunal of the infinite God, you would be more diligent to eschew the latter than presently you are. Therefore while there is still time, take heed to your manner of life and pray that the desire of your hearts will be to abide by the holy will of God. So we see then that God put the patriarch to trial to honour him.

The fountain from which Abraham's obedience flowed

Thirdly, we considered Abraham's act of obedience and how the Lord wanted the fountain from which it flowed to be known. I pointed out to you the nature and seeming harshness of the command, so that you would understand more clearly the greatness of his obedience. We saw how he was commanded to take his son, his only son, whom he loved so dearly, and go to the land of Moriah to the hill on which Jerusalem stands today, and there to slay him by his own hand, and there at God's appointed place to offer him as a sacrifice. This was a totally unique command directed only to Abraham; it was like a weapon sharp enough to pierce his heart. As a command directed to flesh and blood,[5] there were perfectly lawful reasons to act as impediments to such a command. Each successive phrase in God's words offer an increasingly strong argument against obedience than the previous phrase, building up to a virtually unanswerable case against compliance to the command.[6] Yet notwithstanding all the human arguments against obedience, they did not prevail, but faith prevailed and Abraham obeyed.

Was not even one of the arguments strong enough to sway him? Surely, 'Isaac', the name of his only son, begotten from his own loins and of his own flesh and blood, would have caused him to stay his hand. But God goes on: 'the son whom you love'. As to his other son by Hagar, some years earlier he had been sent away, so as there was

[5] Readers will have already gathered that 'flesche and blude' is Bruce's usual term for our frail human nature.

[6] Expanding on Genesis 22:2, 'Take your son, your only son Isaac, whom you love,' Bruce commented in the previous chapter: 'As to the weight of the words, I repeat: each phrase rises degree by degree above the phrase preceding it.' (p. 225.)

only Isaac left, he was 'his only son'. Would this not be an even more compelling reason to desist? But the trial continues inexorably, for it was not that he was to slay him there and then; that might have been more or less terrible, for the deed would have been over and done with.

No, he is instructed to take him on a three or four day journey to the land of Moriah, and to one particular hill there. So the grief in his heart, and the anguish in his soul, must increase to intensify the trial. For as he constantly looked at his son on the journey, as they ate and drank together and as he embraced him before they lay down to sleep each night, his heart must have bled for his beloved. Thus this delay during these days of journeying could only have increased the sorrow of the father's heart.

This was the Lord's will. He deliberately planned this delay that the world might see that Abraham's action was not undertaken rashly; he did not all of a sudden embark upon this enterprise which seemed so obviously to be directly against God's law and explicit commandments. His servant was not acting unadvisedly or upon some hasty impulse; rather was he acting upon a steadfast resolution, without which he could have been deflected from his intention over those three or four days' delay. No process of time could alter his intention.

Therefore, God used this delay to enable the world to see that what he did arose from an unshakeable tenacity, even if the result was an intensifying of his grief. Then, when he arrived in the land of Moriah after all the trauma of the three days' delay, the Lord still leaves him in uncertainty as to where the hill was that he must climb to offer the sacrifice—no doubt there were several hills. The particulars of the assignment still have not been revealed to him, ensuring that he will have to continue to depend wholly upon hearing God's word.

The 'particulars' of God's will as opposed to the 'general'

The lesson that I pointed out to you last time (even though this sermon is somewhat different to my previous one), was that everyone of you—whatever the rank and status may be that the Lord has given you—has at least some knowledge of the generalities that pertain to each of you in your various callings. The Lord has not left you destitute or ignorant of the knowledge of your duty, therefore you are all without excuse as to what he would have you do.

However, as for the various particulars of your individual callings, of these you may be quite ignorant, for the Lord deliberately leaves us without this knowledge, so that we will have to consult with him, and humble ourselves before him in the exercise of prayer. In this way, he ensures that we will be guided by his word, and not depend upon our own ideas or inclinations. So learn that in every decision you must seek God's mind and his counsel before ever you enter upon some new enterprise to do with your calling. Even though he has given you the generalities, he may have withheld the particulars.

Therefore, mark carefully how Abraham certainly sought guidance from the mouth of God concerning the direction he should take, the destination that he sought, the location of the place and the actual hill on which the deed should be done. In all these particulars he consulted with God. Likewise, each of you in your own special calling must not venture on any particular work until you have obtained the blessing of God upon it. Rely upon the word of God, and from his mouth receive confirmation that the move you are planning is in agreement with his will, and that it lies within the compass of that vocation to which the Lord has called you. If only you would get to know the Lord intimately and make yourselves more familiar with his word, then your next move and venture will be embarked upon with full assurance.[7]

Yet many depend upon their own wits and follow their own opinions, ignoring God and his counsel. Even though those whose those advice they seek may flatter them, the outcomes are invariably disappointing, for I have never known a man's plans to be blessed when God was not in the enterprise from the beginning. That is why I think that

[7] Readers may be puzzled by the distinction Bruce makes between 'the general' and 'the particulars'. It is very probable that this distinction is reflecting his own experience when in 1587 he was called to be minister of St Giles in Edinburgh. He declined because he had another call in his hands to be minister in St Andrews. 'And surely I liked better to go to St Andrews, for I had no taste for preaching before the Court. For well I knew that we and the Court could never agree.' MacNicol, p. 40, quoting Cald. iv, p. 637. So he went back across the Firth of Forth to St Andrews. But a formidable deputation from Edinburgh pursued him. 'Loath was I to go: they threatened me with authority. So I advysed with my God, and thought it meet to obey.' *Idem*. The word 'advyse' is used twice in the paragraph, where I have translated it as 'sought guidance' and 'consult'. DSL gives its meaning as, 'to deliberate upon (a matter); to give consideration to; esp. in legal use, to review or revise (a case).' See also Chapter 13, note 19 above.

this great project concerning new regulations in the kirk cannot expect to be blessed because God was not in it at the start, nor consulted[8] with before being initiated; in addition, the recordings of the instruments[9] were all wrong. All of us have been negligent in humbling ourselves before God, and seeking his eternal blessing. Yet because there has been no progress, and little or no prospect of any, urgently all of us should bow low and seek from the living God a blessed issue in this matter.[10]

Because he has men's hearts in his hand, we should pray that he would so dispose those in authority to guide them to such a conclusion as will ensure for our posterity a measure of the liberty that we ourselves have enjoyed over these past few years. Therefore, for your instruction always remember that before ever you undertake any work you must first consult with God and seek his counsel and blessing. So much, then, for this point.

Three possible impediments to Abraham's obedience

Now that you have seen how hard and difficult God's command was, we next considered how it was obeyed, and the action that followed. In the verses that I read, this act of obedience is amplified in this order: first, the circumstances at that time when Abraham had to slay the sac-

[8] I have again translated 'advysed' as 'consulted'. See DSL definition in note 7 above.

[9] 'Instrumentis': 'a formal and duly authenticated record of any proceeding or transaction drawn up by a notary public. In this precise sense only Scottish.' (DSL)

[10] I cannot be certain to what Bruce is here referring. However, it may be that he has in mind the 'Book of Policy' that was agreed by the General Assembly in *Session 10*, 8th August, 1590. It enjoined 'all office-bearers in the Kirk to subscribe the heads of discipline of the Kirk of this realm who were allowed by the Assembly in the book of policy, which was registered in the register of the Kirk.' These 'heads of discipline' were being controverted by the enemies of the discipline of the reformed Kirk of the realm. Failure to subscribe would lead to 'public rebuke in the face of the whole assembly'. In the next Assembly, 2nd July 1591, *Session 4*, it was recorded: 'Anent the subscription of the book of policy, enjoined in the last assembly: in respect that the greatest part of the presbyteries as yet has not satisfied the order of the Kirk...,' a fine of 40 shillings per presbytery was to be charged for continued default. (Shaw, pp. 916, 923.) If indeed it was this 'book of policy' to which Bruce is here referring, then that would date his sermon either as a short time after 8th August 1590, or perhaps after the July Assembly 1591, as he says that there was 'little or no prospect' of any progress, although it could have been evident some time earlier that there had been no progress.

rifice and make this offering; second, the deed was further amplified by the description of the son who was to be the sacrifice; third, the deed was also amplified by the nature of the promise that was made to that son. Then we shall go on to how the deed was amplified and enlarged upon by the father's willing and instant obedience: he acted without any delay whatsoever. Each of these points contained an impediment that would deflect him from obeying the command, had he taken the counsel of flesh and blood.

First, as to one who must do this deed, note that he is called by his name, *Abraham*. Next, he is called *he that receaved the promeis*. Third, he is further denoted as *To quhome it was said in Isaack sall thy seid be callit*. Each of these three amplifications could have been impediments to prevent him from obeying.

As to the first, who was it who must perform this act and put it into execution upon Isaac? It was Isaac's own father who loved him so well, that old man who had yearned and waited so long for a son, who had prayed for so many years that God would grant him an heir and who had received so many promises concerning him. He is to be the executioner of his own son whom he loved so dearly, yea, even better than his own life. Thus these details concerning the father make clear the amazing obedience shown towards God in this incident.

Second, the man called to do this deed is described as *he that receaved the promeis, In Isaack sall thy seid be called*. The promise was also given to Isaac. It was not given through a report, or what Abraham read in some historical document, rather it was a promise that he heard with his own ears. Having this promise and having believed every word of it, now he was commanded to slay his son. The promise was that through Isaac's posterity he would possess the land of Canaan, and also that through his son's seed all the nations of the earth would be blessed. Nevertheless, though having heard and received the promises and readily accepted them, still he obeyed God, although the command appeared to be contrary to them, even destroying them.

Human logic he cast behind his back, along with all the arguments that could have been cited from God's own Book, and so he obeyed God's command. Why? Because he knew that death could never be an obstacle to the fulfilment of God's promises and that no power of nature could annul them. Thus, knowing the power of God, he chose to obey him. We can never reconcile life with death, but God by his power is able to do so; he can draw out the former from the latter, even though it seems to us that the two are contrary to each other. That is why Abraham did not hesitate in his obedience. Yea, it was him who heard the promises regarding Isaac who did the deed.

Moreover, the one who must do this deed was also the one who particularly, specially and singularly, received the promise in which Isaac was named: *In Isaack sall thy seid be called.* Might not this part of the promise, supposing he wanted to review its general terms, have caused him to delay a day or even an hour, until he felt he had been more fully appraised of its implications? Yet without any delay or appraisal he proceeds at once to execute the divine command. (So you see yet again how his obedience is amplified by the way his own person is referred to, *thy seid.*)

His obedience is further amplified by the way in which the name of Isaac is used when the command was given. Who was it that his father should slay, and on whom should he lay his hand to do so? (Notice how every phrase raises an objection!) Who was it? None other than his own son! So came the first depiction,[11] 'take your son'; then the second depiction, 'your only son' (for the first son Ishmael had been sent away); then the third depiction as given in Genesis 22:2, 'whom you love', for he was the son whom Abraham dearly loved, a son so dear to his mother that she must have loved him more than she loved her own life; this same son must be slain by his father.

Without question, it would have been easier for both Abraham and his wife to die themselves in place of their son, for the greatest part of the sand in their glass[12] had now run, and both of them had only a few years remaining. They had by now experienced all the happiness as well as the sorrow that awaits each of us in this world; therefore after living for so long, they would have readily yielded up their own lives. Whereas before Isaac there were still most of his years—his youth, his middle-age and those more mature years; his posterity was yet to be born, and the

[11] Bruce's word 'styll' is used throughout this sermon. It is a legal term (both as noun and verb) used in drawing up court documents and can mean a 'designation'. Depending on the context, I have variously translated it as 'title', 'called', 'designated', 'denoted' or 'depicted/depiction'.

[12] The 'glass' was the 'hour glass'.

promises of God had yet to be fulfilled. Therefore it would have been far harder for them to witness Isaac's death than to die themselves, for the sacrifice to be slain was so precious to both his father and mother.

Further, this son was the one for whom Abraham had stored up great wealth—Isaac was to receive a large inheritance. For many years, earnest prayers had been offered for the gift of a son; before he was even born the Lord had reiterated for him many wonderful promises. When Abraham heard of his imminent birth he had laughed, hence his name, Isaac [meaning 'he laughs'], and he had rejoiced at such a name.[13] Is this the child who must now die? He loved this child so completely that the command brought to him must have broken his heart. Nonetheless, even though his son was so dear to him, from the moment God spoke to him of this boy as a sacrifice, Isaac's life together with his wife's life and his own, counted as nothing: God and his command was for him the supreme priority. Was this not an amazing proof of Abraham's obedience? Thus we see that this deed is amplified by the consideration of the person of the son.

Thirdly, the deed is amplified from the nature of God's promises, for he had not made a general promise confused with ambiguous terminology, but he had made promises in particular, special terms, yea, promises concerning one man in terms that could not have been clearer. However, the clear nature of these promises could well have provided him with sufficient impediment to have kept him from this deed. However, even though the promises were so particular and were set forth in clearly defined terms, Abraham at once began the implementation of the command.

His obedience, which we now see must be counted greater than ever, is the last way in which the deed is amplified, namely, that he was so ready and swift in the command's implementation. Calmly and with restraint, as soon as he received God's command, he proceeded to carry it out without saying a word about it to his wife, his son or his servants, but keeping it strictly to himself. He knew that if Sarah saw tears in his eyes that that would be yet another impediment for him. Therefore he locked up the matter in his heart, and kept quiet regarding God's counsel. Thus as dawn was breaking, he set out in obedience to the Lord.

[13] Genesis 17:17, 19.

Lessons from Abraham's obedience

You have now heard of his action that in some measure I have tried to amplify for you, and I have described some of the apparently lawful objections and impediments that might have hindered him. It now remains for us to learn some lessons from Abraham so that we might profit by them.

Obedience without murmuring or questioning

First, we must perceive and mark how this godly man, without murmuring—even though the command was exceedingly harsh—and without grumbling or complaining to the mighty God who ordered him to slay his son, was also bidden to believe, for the same mouth that had promised him a son had fulfilled that promise in the gift of Isaac. Second, even though he could have found objections both from nature and possibly from God's own word in the Scriptures, yet he would not argue or dispute with God, but he simply obeyed. Third, he might have acted as if he was simply curious, and so enquired about the justness of the command and how it corresponded to the divine nature, and if it was compatible with God's laws. But he avoided such curiosity and went straightaway to perform God's command, for he was certain that God could not deny himself. Therefore, he shook off all hindrances that could be thrown at him by the devil, and any objective obstacles or arguments, and proceeded to obey.

You yourselves know from your own experience how rarely we follow this example! For either we murmur against God if we see that his word is hard, strait and contrary to nature, or else we enter into a dispute with him, or else we become curious and ask impertinent questions. Take up any of these various reactions and it only needs one of them to hinder us from what we should be doing. We will not find upon this earth someone who, like Abraham, obeys God without murmuring, without disputing and without questioning. Even Peter himself, though he did not murmur or dispute, succumbed to the third error of curiosity. In John's Gospel, when he was commissioned by our Master and was appointed to follow a certain kind of life and come to a certain kind of end, he would not meekly accept what was assigned to him but became curious and questioned Christ, *Lord, quhat shal this man do?* Our Master answered, 'What has that to do with you? Do what is enjoined and follow me.'[14]

So you see how hard it is to find someone who does not fall into one or other of the three errors. That is why this man is set before us as the father of the faithful,[15] and his example recorded for us as worthy to be followed and imitated. Certainly, unless the Lord frees our will and looses those bonds that bind us and make us slaves of the devil and our own fleshly desires—unless, I say, he brings us into the freedom of the Spirit of Jesus Christ—we fall into that first error and begin murmuring; indeed we continue our murmuring right to the end of our lives; consequently we end up shaking off all obedience to God.

Therefore, we must crave of God that it may please him to enable us to do what he asks of us by giving us wills to obey him. Crave that he will set free your hearts, breaking those bonds of iniquity and unrighteousness that bind us in chains, that you may go to do what he has commanded. May the Lord in his mercy so work in the hearts of every one of you, that you may avoid that awesome wrath that is to come.

As it is said that Abraham obeyed God without murmuring, it is also clear that he obeyed willingly, without restraint or delay. He did not consult with his wife who had her own interests in what was to happen, nor did he go and discuss the matter with his son, far less with his servants. But without any consultation either with his own natural reasoning, or with any other person on earth, he went expeditiously to do as God had commanded. How well do we follow him in this? Who among us goes so willingly without delay to obey God? I cannot think off-hand of anyone who obeys God so readily. By nature we all delay and say, 'Next day, or some other time will be better for this,' and so we procrastinate day after day. Finally, we end up perishing as rebels before the wrath of God.

Excuses we make for not obeying God

The second lesson is that we must not delay in obeying God. Young people delay their repentance because of their age, older people neglect to obey until next morning, or until next year. So each of us seeks

[14] John 21:18-22.

[15] Romans 4:11, '... the father of all who believe'; Galatians 3:29, '... if you are Christ's, then you are Abraham's offspring.'

some reason for delaying, as if every moment was not appropriate for godliness and for drawing near to the Lord. The devil has bewitched our natures in such a way, that unless the Lord sends out his army to exhort, admonish and plead with us to be reconciled to him, we will not submit. Mark this, then, that the command of God demands a willing obedience. It is not time to delay when the Lord commands us to obey, for he will not surrender his word or his command to our reasoning, he will not permit us who are but clay to oppose him in any matter, nor will he have us prolong our hesitation. Therefore we have to crave the Lord for his mercy for our long negligence and contempt for his commands.

Certainly, if our hearts were not so hardened that we neither sorrow over our own souls, not even over the souls of those who are perishing—nobles, lords and the common people—we would lament over the awful plight of our unfortunate country. For by our contempt for the mercy of God, men's hearts have become so hardened that they have contracted deadness of soul, and, as if there were no life after this nor hell either, they are immersing themselves in all kinds of iniquity and are roaming from sin to sin without any remorse. Would that God might give them a glimpse into the great and awesome wrath that is yet to come, and that he might wound their hearts with just one aspect of that terrible and fearful examination to which their consciences will be subjected on that Great Day. I beseech you from my heart to pause and think upon this matter more deeply than you have done, and not suffer yourselves any longer to be deceived through the obduracy of your affections.

What are your sinful desires doing? They are either flattering you by deceit, or else tormenting you by pain. Those things that allure you by flattery and in which you take pleasure, shall become torments when the Lord awakens you; I mean those same desires in which you now delight shall then become your torturers. What now seems to be pleasure shall then become pain. When your conscience is radically challenged by being awakened, then all your desires and agitated[16] cogitations of your heart begin to torment you. While you have the

[16] The Scots word 'motioune' has many shades of meaning; sometimes it can mean 'mental disturbance' or 'an agitated condition'; but it can also be used in a good sense of 'inner spiritual promptings'. Bruce uses this word 'motioune' here in the pejorative sense, and in the next sentence the same word in the good sense.

opportunity, make those mental promptings[17] heavenly and your desires holy. Do not let your bodily feelings be set upon wickedness, nor let your inward heart lure you into evil; in time seek to make good, that you might not be subjected to the holy wrath of the living God. Would to God that you might become aware of his wrath and that some sense of the anguish of it might bring you to eschew sin, which is the cause of all the pain and anger in this world. So obey God without murmuring, willingly and without delay.

Hearts resolutely set upon obedience

Curiosity was the third error. Procrastination can be caused by curiosity. Abraham obeyed God wholeheartedly with resolution and steadfastness. His heart was set upon performing the command that the Lord had given him. If your mind is resolved and your heart determined to do what he requires of you, then be assured that the Lord will think well of you, as if you had already begun to act obediently. When Abraham was told to offer up his son, even before he had begun physically to obey, because his heart was set upon obeying, his mind resolved and his will determined to execute God's command, the Lord counted his resolution as the actual deed.

This principle applies not only to the resolve of a man to do the right thing, but also to a person whose mind is set upon some evil; in both instances, the very determination to act is counted by God as the deed done. We find that in Matthew 5:28.[18] As with adultery, the heart and mind that is set upon murder God counts as murder. Because Christ means a determined mind and purpose, when a man's heart is set upon some act, he counts it as the actual deed.

So what is a determined or fixed purpose? It is such a strong resolve in the soul that there is not even a faint stirring in the heart to oppose it, so whenever the occasion presents itself, you are ready to do it. Even if you are prevented from doing the intended evil by some circumstance that interrupts you, it is not thanks to you that you did not commit the sin, but is due to the interruption; therefore, it is the same as if you had actually done what you were about to do. Take heed, therefore, to your

[17] See Note 16 above.

[18] Matthew 5:28, 'I say to you that anyone who looks at a woman with lustful intent, has already committed adultery with her in his heart.'

hearts and to the secret intentions of your souls, and ensure that you are not resolved to do wrong, for the Lord considers you guilty even though you have ended up not carrying out your intention. As to the other side, seek to ensure that your hearts and minds are set upon doing good and upon the love of God. To this end, constantly strive to correct both your life and your lifestyle; no doubt the Lord shall then honour your strong desire,[19] resolution and purpose, and will count it as good, as if the righteous deed had been done.

However, it is not possible to have hearts always determined to live righteously unless first a death is died in your hearts.[20] As Abraham offered his son, so must we offer our hearts as a sacrifice to the living God, but unless we slay our foul lusts it is impossible for us to offer him our hearts. As long as the fountain of ungodliness remains, it will continue to distil evil thoughts and notions that are repugnant to God. Therefore, put to death the foul things in your hearts, those fleshly cogitations that hide there, for only then can you have a resolute mind and determined purpose to serve God.

Therefore, your steadfast aim should be to mortify and subdue your fleshly lusts,[21] because the devil is never idle and our inner corruption is never barren. Therefore keep watch over your carnal affections and deceitful impulses, resist them so that your heart will not be set upon some wrongdoing. Resist them before they become strong[22] and you no longer have the strength to overcome them; avoid the occasions and things that might kindle evil intentions. Rather bow in your heart before God, and when you lack will-power, ask him to strengthen you. Thus, by resisting the devil he will flee from you, and your fleshly

[19] Bruce's word here is 'thrist', that is 'thirst' as in Matthew 5:6.

[20] Bruce's vivid phrase is, 'except ye mak ane slauchter of your hairtis.' His thinking here is not his frequent theme of mortification, but rather entering spiritually into Christ's death as in Phil. 3:10, '[T]hat I may know him and the power of his resurrection, becoming like him in his death…'. See also Eph. 4:22-23, also obviously Mark 8:34-35, *et al.*

[21] A superficial reading of the previous paragraph might cause some mistakenly to assume that Bruce is teaching the eradication of the root of sin within the human heart. Not so, for now he follows up the crucifying of our old self with the need of ongoing, daily mortification; 'our inner corruption is never barren,' he is about to write.

[22] Bruce has, 'Resist it quhill it is grein,' his imagery being of tender green shoots, still with shallow roots, pushing up through the soil.

desire and thoughts will wither; then you will find the peace that passes understanding together with the calm and quietness that flows from the blood of Jesus Christ, stilling your soul and pacifying your conscience. So slaughter your old nature, and offer yourselves as sacrifices to God, then your wills shall be conformed to his will.

The age of Isaac at this time

The Scriptures make no mention as to how old Isaac was at the time when he was taken to be offered as a sacrifice, but it would appear that he could not have been of mature years. It has been suggested that he was thirty or forty years old and some have even thought he could have been fifty years of age. But if that had been so, then surely he would have been greatly commended, and it would have been recorded that he willingly offered himself as the sacrifice—indeed, he would have been even more praiseworthy than his father. But the Scriptures, which are never silent in attributing honour when it is due, make no mention at all here of Isaac's faith. Thus we must conclude that he had not reached adulthood nor years of discretion; in other words, he would not have been aware of what was about to happen.

Further, had Isaac reached manhood, his consent would have been needed so that he could prepare himself for such a significant work. But we are told of no such thing, just that the Lord revealed only to his father what was to be done. It is quite obvious that the boy was unaware of the offering to be made, for we read that on the journey he said to Abraham, 'Father, I see the wood, I see the fire, but where is the animal? Where is the sheep or the lamb that is to be sacrificed?' (Genesis 22:7) You can judge for yourselves whether such a enquiry pierced the father's heart![23] However, his question makes it clear that he was ignorant as to what his father was about to do to him. Abraham answered in a voice full of faith and firm persuasion, 'Son, the Lord will provide a sacrifice for himself.'

This exchange between father and son clearly shows that Isaac knew nothing of what was about to happen. When we add Abraham's binding of him and laying him upon the altar, it is abundantly obvious that

---

[23] It is interesting here to compare Calvin's comment on the same passage: '*My father*: God here produces a new instrument of torture, by which he may, more and more, torment the breast of Abraham, already pierced with so many wounds.'

he was still a boy and had not yet reached years of discretion. We should note one other point: after his enquiry regarding the whereabouts of the sheep for the sacrifice and before he could have experienced any apprehension or fear, when at length his father told him what was about to happen and bound him to the wood, and when he saw the knife in his father's hand, it appears that no protest came from his lips, but that he was as silent as a sheep would have been in the same circumstances. He was worthy of praise in that he was as silent as the ram that was caught by its horns in the thicket.

We learn, therefore, not only that Isaac had imbibed godliness as his mother suckled him, but also a deeper mystery. He was a type representing Christ Jesus, who held his peace when he was bound to the cross; as the Scriptures say, *he was dume befoir the schearer*.[24] It is worthy of praise in Isaac that he was so restrained when he saw with his own eyes that he was about to be sacrificed. But I must return to his father, for these comments regarding Isaac are only incidental.

The Lord must be first in our lives

As well as Abraham's willing and ready obedience, I perceive a fourth point about him, namely, that he puts the living God before everything else in the world—before his own life as well as before the lives of his son and his wife. Try to calculate what he lost on account of his obedience to God, yet he was able to recover double. According to the promise in Mark 10:28-30, whatever you lose for the Lord's sake, he will not only restore double in this life, but everlasting life in the age to come. Watch over your hearts, therefore, and ensure that your love is not fixed upon any earthly thing, but only upon God. Give to him the most important seat and room in your hearts, that there he may set down his throne; in everything that might challenge him, make sure he has the first place.

If you have to match God with your king, let him be honoured above the king; or if you have to match him with your own life, let him be obeyed above it; or if you have to match him with your child or the life of your wife, see to it that he be given first place. I fear that if we were brought to trial over this point, our own consciences would bear

[24] Isaiah 53:7. Though written in the elegant English script he always uses when quoting Scripture, Bruce's quotation of Isaiah's words seems to be from memory.

witness to an evil character; certainly, our trial could begin sooner than we expect. Therefore, it would be wise, while in God's mercy the opportunity is still afforded to us, for you to dislodge any idol concealed among us. By faith and through the Holy Spirit's power we must cast out that most pernicious idolatry that has continued so long among us; the more secret the idolatry and the more it lurks under a veil of hypocrisy, the harder will be the task of expelling it.[25] Therefore, examine your hearts and see what it is concealed there that robs God of your love, for whatever your heart loves most has become a god to you. Where you find your love lavished upon any other earthly creature, that is, upon anything less than God himself, if the object of your love be vile, seek to rid yourself of it, or if in itself it is honourable, then seek to assign it to its proper place in your life.

I urge you therefore to beseech the living God so to incline your soul that he may have all the love of your heart. It is not possible that this can be unless and until your hearts are seasonably prepared,[26] and the Holy Spirit has sanctified them. Not merely for one day, or even for one year, but every one of you crave continually for the whole of your lives that the Lord would so sanctify the desires of your hearts, that you may hate what he hates, and love what he loves. When your priorities are in agreement, you can be sure that the Lord will be with you in your time of sore trials. Indeed, his gracious presence shall so lavish your souls with his love, that even if you are incarcerated in the vilest, hellish prison, it will seem to you as the Lord's most fragrant garden.[27]

[25] Although 'the idolatry' most certainly must refer here to personal sins (see the next sentence), it is also clearly implied that 'the pernitious idolatrie quhilk hes continowed so long with ws', included celebration of the mass, prayers to deceased 'saints' and veneration of images and other papish practices. Bruce knew perfectly well that some of the nobles such as Huntly and Errol had priests hidden in their castles and houses, and that behind closed doors they were secretly practising the Roman Catholic religion. In an earlier sermon, he had exhorted the king to banish the Jesuits from Scotland, for at that time the counter-reformation was insidiously at work, along with post-Armada plots such as 'the Blanks' (see Introduction), devised to bring Scotland back into submission to the Pope. See above in Chapter 11 notes 6, 7 & 8, and Bruce's three appeals to King James.

[26] This homely metaphor depicts the Holy Spirit preparing the heart for love for God, as a skilful cook takes various unlikely ingredients and uses them to prepare a wholesome meal.

[27] As under Note 25 above, the allusion is most probably to the unsettled religious state of the nation, and to the possibility of the future domination of

We must be diligent in continually examining the motives of our hearts and minds, for they can easily go astray and slide from the mud into the peat ditch. On the other hand, if the inclinations of our souls have been renewed, our daily living will be focused on things above.[28] When we are in Christ's company, our conversation with him will be concerning the life to come and the pathway there. Always the first step to wholeness and a godly heart is to know our spiritual sickness and evil inclinations; striving and wrestling against our sinfulness is the best we can do in this life. What I mean is that we all must engage in this conflict, ever resolving little by little to increase the serenity of our consciences by casting out our sins. We must exercise our faith to be assured of every spiritual and temporal promise that the Lord has given us to guide us here on earth, that we may ultimately walk by sight hereafter.

A final amplification of Abraham's faith

Today I am not going to look at what the next verse tells us about the greatness of Abraham's obedience, but, before I conclude, as well as what I have already said on this subject, I shall mention one other point. The Word tells us of many men and women whose faith was tried as Abraham's was, but there were none whose faith matched his in every respect. There have been others who have slain their sons by offering them as sacrifices to the devil.[29] Yet such deeds have no commendation in the Word of God, only condemnation, for they were neither done in faith nor were they acts of obedience to his express command.

The essence of faith is never to lift a finger until one hears the voice of God. That is why so many actions were not commended—those doing them never had the lantern of God's word guiding them. Thus they did not emanate from faith (and without faith it is impossible to please God[30]), rather such actions flow from a false opinion of their own merits, and from a vain conceit that worldly honour will make their names famous here on earth. Even if these deeds had some measure of

Roman Catholicism with the subsequent persecution of those of the reformed faith. See also Note 3 in Chapter 13 above for references to similar statements in Rutherford's letters.

[28] The allusion is to Colossians 3:2, 'Set your minds on things that are above…'.

[29] Leviticus 18:21; Jeremiah 32:35 (NKJV); Ezekiel 16:20-21.

[30] Hebrews 11:6.

outward likeness to that of the patriarch, yet because they did not flow from the fountain of righteousness, the Lord could never commend them, only condemn them.

Self-flagellation is not commanded in the Word of God

As for Abraham, he would have been loath to undertake such a deed, had he not had an express command from the mouth of God. The reason why his faith is praised is that he had the light of God's word as a lantern to show him the way, and he followed that light. By contrast, the papists whose practices cannot be commended but only condemned, act without either the divine command or the light of the word, relying upon establishing their own merits. For example, they have invented their own form of mortification by beating themselves, wounding and demeaning their own bodies. (We have reliable reports of this being done.) There is no warrant in the Word of God for this, so how can it deserve any praise? Who asked them to do such a thing? as the prophet says.[31] The Spirit of God has not given them instructions to flay their backs.

True mortification that is inspired by the Holy Spirit leads us to direct all our actions to glorify God in our hearts and souls. But when they flatter themselves and exalt their own merits they defraud Christ of his glory, so leading them ever nearer to the lowest hell. Part of the glory of the Son of God is that by his death he has paid the price for the sins of the world. Let us then pursue the true mortification which can only be wrought in us by the Holy Spirit, whose power alone is able to put to death sin in our hearts and minds. Seek his power and seek also the sword of the Word that is sharp enough to slay our fleshly desires and to discern the inmost secret places[32] of our hearts. Then you will be genuinely mortified, and you will seek only to glorify God in all you do.

Finally, we see that faith reposes upon the power and mercy of God. For we cannot doubt that it was his mercy in his promises and his power in fulfilling them, that upheld Abraham's faith. Therefore, join power with mercy and lean upon these two, and you shall be enabled to persevere and overcome the obstacles that the devil and the world will use to try and obstruct your way. To this same power and mercy of God

[31] Jeremiah 32:35.

[32] Bruce's Braid Scots word is 'hirne' meaning a nook or cranny.

I commend every one of you, beseeching him in his grace to make this word effectual in your hearts, by working in you an unfeigned remorse for your sins, that here in this life you may begin already to experience heaven, and afterwards to enter into its full fruition. All this through the righteous merits of Christ, to whom with the Father and the Holy Ghost be all honour, praise and glory now and for ever. Amen.

Chapter Fifteen

Hebrews Chapter 11 verses 19-20

[19] For he considered that God was abill to rais him vp evin from the dead, from whence he received him also after ane sort. [20] By faith Isaack blissed Jacob and Esau concerning thingis to cum.

Well-beloved brethren in Jesus Christ, you have heard of Abraham's great obedience to a very hard and strait commission and command, and how it was recorded and amplified, firstly from the viewpoint of the one who was to slay the offering, even the father who was to be the executioner of his own son. The one who had received the promise concerning his son was now commanded to slay him, even though that unique and special promise had named his son Isaac as its recipient. Secondly, you heard how his obedience was amplified from the viewpoint of the one who was to be offered, in that it was his son, his beloved son, who must be offered; this only son, who was to have been the heir of all his father's possessions, was more precious to Abraham and his wife than their own lives. Unquestionably it would have been easier for them both to have died themselves than to witness the death of their son.

Thirdly, you also heard his obedience amplified from the viewpoint of the promise that had been made to Abraham. God's promises were neither unspecific nor vague, nor were they set down in ambiguous terms. Rather the promises were quite definite and particular, and were set down very clearly in terms that plainly confirmed them;[1] indeed,

[1] Bruce's phrase here is interesting: 'set doun and twitchit in as plaine termis as could be'; the equivalent today of 'twitchit' would be 'shaking hands to signify agreement on some matter that had been resolved'. (DSL)

those terms were so specific that Isaac's name was included in them. Yet, notwithstanding all of this, Abraham proceeds to the slaughter of his son. Fourthly, you heard of the readiness of his obedience, how he immediately began his preparations for this task, without consulting either his wife, his child or his servants. Shaking off all impediments, he rose early in the morning to start out on fulfilling God's command.

Five praiseworthy aspects of Abraham's obedience

(It cannot be denied that there are many other aspects of Abraham's obedience that are worthy of commendation and praise.)

Abraham acted without questioning God's command

The first of these was that he acted without murmuring or querying, without arguing against the command and without any questions regarding its justice. For example, what then would become of Isaac or what would happen thereafter to the promises to his son when he had been killed? Such obedience is surely worthy of great praise. There was no inquisition, he simply obeyed.

Remember the lesson that we learned: when God commands us to do something, it is not for us to enter into a dispute with him. Once his sacred mouth has spoken there is no way we can argue with him, for his command demands obedience. The Lord has not put us into a position to control either him or his word, but he has ordained that we should learn to obey him. Therefore, whenever you hear his command, resolve at once to obey. On this occasion, had human nature, flesh and blood or the devil prevailed, Abraham could not then have obeyed. But it is clear that his natural inclinations had been set aside, for the Spirit of the mighty God had set his will free; the Spirit's power had such dominion over him that he invariably ignored himself and even his son.

All of us have experienced how stubborn our human natures can be, and how active the devil is when God intervenes with his command; therefore if you would follow the patriarch's example you must learn to bid farewell both to Satan and to your fallen natures, and to give the first place in your hearts to the Holy Spirit's presence. You must learn to keep in step with the Spirit, else you will never have the will to do what God commands. May the Lord in his mercy work mightily in all your hearts so that this lesson might take root and grow within you; for unless nature is banished and the Holy Spirit sets his seal upon you, it will never be possible for you to follow or imitate Abraham in his ready obedience.

Abraham obeyed without delay

The second thing that is praiseworthy in this man is that, notwithstanding that the command was hard, he embarked upon obedience to it without any delay. He did not look for some way to avoid obeying, or some excuse to procrastinate. Rather he was immediately ready, without consulting or seeking advice, to undertake what the living God commanded, no matter how exceedingly hard it was to flesh and blood.

How prone are we to delay, and how easy it is for human nature to find some other alternative to avoid instant obedience, and so to put off acting until another day! Everyone of us in some way or another has experience of this. For there is no single person who does not have some sin or other that clings fast to his soul, or some delight or other that his heart's affections enjoy to such an extent, that at first he finds it impossible to part with them.[2] Consequently, he opts for a delay until another day, and so does a body swerve[3] round God's command. Therefore let us have recourse to prayer, and only to prayer, that the Lord would make us ready in heart and mind to obey when he commands. Abraham gives us the example: he at once willingly did what God commanded, and he acted without any delay.

I take occasion here to address you, my lords, who have any interest in this work of planting kirks. I urge you to do whatever lies within your power to follow Abraham's example in this point, that you may readily and without delay respond to the challenge which God has given you the grace and ability to undertake. I refer to derelict kirk buildings that need to be restored. Among some it is assumed that the impediment to this work is in us [pastors] and therefore is our fault. But I think I can answer for my fellow-ministers in this, and assure you that there will be no hindrance offered by ourselves. Rather we are ready to accept any proposals and programme concerning the re-establishment of kirks[4].

[2] Bruce's homely phrase here is 'to bid them gude nicht'.

[3] Literally, 'so shiftis god and cast af his obedience' which means 'finds an alternative to God's command'.

[4] During the General Assembly of 1588, when Robert Bruce himself was Moderator, the minutes of *Session 5* recorded that the king be informed of the Assem-

Without our own influence or the influence of those who come after us, whatever you can give would be most acceptable, even if you only finance such kirks as are near you.[5] That would give us the hope that when the Lord provides you with the opportunity, we may be able to expect further help from you. Therefore, my lords, as you will want to have a peaceful end to your lives, and a quiet conscience whenever the Lord shall call you, make provision for this work so that it will greet you in your final hour. Let your consciences minister comfort to you at your departure, that the Lord has blessed you by enabling you to be his instruments in some small measure by propagating sound doctrine to future generations.

Abraham's obedience was wholehearted

The third thing that is praiseworthy in Abraham was his hearty obedience. He obeyed the living God wholeheartedly and with a determined and resolute mind. This is clear evidence that he loved God more than he loved even his child. The living God came first in his life, before Isaac and before everything else that was dear to him. This could only

bly's 'regret for the decay of certain kirks which are ruinous and, without repair, are not able to be remedied (p.833). The minute of *Session 14* records 'a humble suit from the Kirk to the king,' the second point being concerned 'with the planting of kirks' and for the need for 'provision to be made.' (pp.841-843) The same minute recorded: 'It is grievously lamented in all parts of this realm, that the planting of kirks, and the flourishing of religion, are hindered by want of qualified ministers and teachers, and *lack of provision for the same*.' (p.853) The Assembly in March 1590 concluded with an injunction to Synods to help with burgh towns within their bounds that were '*not provided for* and not helped, and provide pastors thereto.' (p.883) Again, during the General Assembly of August 1590, the minutes of *Session 14* recorded, 'Forasmuch as it is considered that the patrimony of the Kirk has been wasted with such as are provided with benefices, which is the cause of the lack of provision to the ministry.' (p.919) Again, the Assembly of 1593 in *Session 9* lamented the lack of provision of a stipend, manse and glebe for the minister of Auchterarder, and the derelict condition of the kirk building. (p.961) The required resources were in the hands of both lords and prelates who held wealthy benefices and who were constantly being urged by successive Assemblies to contribute to the urgent need of kirk planting and repair of derelict kirk buildings. Hence Bruce's appeal! (All refs and quotations from Shaw.)

[5] Some of the realm's benefices were held by ministers, but others were held by wealthy men bearing no function whatsoever in the Kirk. The subject of benefices was often discussed in the Assemblies, for those holding benefices clearly had the resources for repairs and provision for ministry in their areas. (e.g., p.917, Shaw.)

have been so because he had already offered up his heart, yielded his will to obedience, and consecrated his soul to whatever service the Lord might ask of him. The one who has not died to self and offered to God his own heart will never whole-heartedly surrender anything to the Lord. The 'slaughter of the heart' is when we put to death our vile affections. The devil disguises our renunciation of our sinful desires as robbing us of our enjoyment of those deceitful allurements that appear to us just now to be pleasant. The truth is that they always turn out to be the cause of our greatest misery.[6]

Until you get the strength and power to cast out those vile affections and to slay those deceitful pleasures, and so offer your hearts to God, those same affections from which you now hope for happiness, shall in the end prove to be your executioner. For in that day when the Lord's wrath is revealed and his righteous judgment is manifested, then shall the deceit of sin be exposed, and those sins and evil desires in which we immersed ourselves for pleasure shall become our greatest tormenters. However pleasant they seem to be, unless you put them to death they will imprison you and bind you with fetters; yea, except you slay them, banish and renounce them, be sure that they will torture you in the life to come. Even though such slaughter of your sinful natures may bring you immense pain, endure that pain just now, so that you may enjoy calmness for ever in the life to come.[7]

However rebellious towards God our stubborn wills may be, they must be subdued, moulded to his obedience and conformed to his will, until you are able to say, 'God and his will are first in my life; the Lord comes before whatsoever is dearest to me on this earth'. I know that this total surrender cannot be attained instantly, and I know that we seem to have only just set out upon this course before our earthly lives draw to a close. Nevertheless, the great aim of the Christian should constantly be to resist sinful desires, and at the same time to guard against those desires resisting his will, even as he continues to seek to subdue it to the will of the mighty, living God.

The Lord considers a firm purpose to be the same as the deed

The fourth thing I mark is that I perceive the Lord considers a good

[6] Colossians 3:5-10.
[7] Romans 6:20-23.

will, a firm purpose and a resolute mind the same in his presence as the actual deed. Abraham did not slay his son, nor did he offer him as a sacrifice, even though he was commanded to do so. Yea, he resolved to do so and was steadfast in his resolution, and quite genuinely he was prepared to slay him. In the same way, God knows of your good will, your firm purpose and your resolute mind, and even though you do not come to the point of action, he counts this as if you had done the deed. You can read in the sacred record how he says to Abraham, *because thou hes done this, and hes not spaired, thy onlie sone*, and so his son was spared and not sacrificed. So the Lord counted a good, firm resolve the same as if the deed had been done. When there is no impediment in your soul, and should the time and occasion be offered and you were on the point of doing the deed, but were prevented by some unexpected interruption, the Lord accepts your good intention as if the action had been done.

This principle also applies to a wrong purpose or an evil deed. When a man's heart is set upon some sin, the Lord then counts his wicked intention to be the same as actually committing that sin. Just say a man's heart is set upon murder, then God counts that as murder, or if his heart is set upon adultery, he counts that as adultery.[8] This applies to every vice. Therefore, set your hearts upon good actions, especially on those that may advance the glory of God. On account of our fallen natures, all our hearts are inclined towards what is wrong, so that our imaginations, thoughts and desires are bent towards what is evil. Yet by the work of the Spirit of God our hearts can be transformed, so that we are enabled to aspire to the heavenly life, and are resolved to put right those things in our lives that are amiss.

My lords, at this time an opportunity is afforded you—a great opportunity—for you to have an excellent aim. Nor is there any impediment to delay this work. Therefore, do not let your good intentions remain as good intentions, but let your actions be extended to the full extent of the grace[9] with which God has endowed you, so that at this time your intentions find fulfilment in your actions.

[8] Bruce is undoubtedly alluding here to Christ's teaching on Anger and Lust in Matthew 5:21-30.

[9] The context suggests that by 'grace' Bruce means the wherewithal to repair derelict kirks and to provide for stipends. See Note 4 above.

The sacrifice of Isaac was one of the most notable deeds ever done

The fifth point about Abraham's deed of slaughtering his son as an offering that is recorded in God's Scriptures to his perpetual praise is that it was counted as a singular deed, one of the most notable deeds ever done, or intended by him to be done. It only came to pass because he did not follow some counsel of his own invention, nor the notion of a preposterous zeal, but rather he followed the light of God's command. Otherwise, had he himself initiated this deed through some blind zeal or a mistaken idea of something heroic he could do, of all the evil deeds done in this world it would have been considered the most monstrous, abominable, foul and unnatural parracide[10] that could be conceived.

However, he had the light of God's word and the most extraordinary warrant from the Lord's own mouth. Can you see, then, what the express warrant from the mouth of God does, along with the light of his word? Without that warrant, the deed is a detestable sin, an abomination that arises from within a man, via the devil. However, that same deed when it proceeds from God's will and his revealed word is wholly commendable and praiseworthy.

You can read of similar actions such as the spoiling of the Egyptians by the Israelites at their exodus from the land.[11] We also read of the slaughter of the man and woman by Phineas, who enacted judgment upon the pair.[12] All such acts as plundering and killing are condemned by God's laws; however, at times they are permitted in the Scriptures because they were sanctioned by God's will [and were divinely judicial]. That is why Abraham's action, otherwise expressly forbidden by the divine law, was praised because it arose from God's will and the warrant came from his mouth. There can be no sin in any deed which is executed under the divine warrant. If I have that warrant, God's will sanctifies my action and there can be no sin in it. So pay careful attention to the author and fountain from whence the action flows, for the action that comes from God is not sin, but if it is inspired by and flows from some other fountain, and not from God, it could well be sin. Thus this deed of the worthy patriarch, Abraham, not only commends his

[10] The murder of a near relative (*Concise Oxford Dictionary*).

[11] Exod. 12:36, 'The LORD had given the people favour in the sight of the Egyptians... Thus they plundered the Egyptians.'

[12] Numbers 25:1-13.

faith but also lets us see just how great it was, even had the apostle not enlarged upon it.

The sacrifice of Isaac pre-figures the death and resurrection of Christ

However, in the verses that I have read the apostle goes even further in his praise of Abraham's faith, partly on account of the patriarch's awareness and assurance of the mercy and power of God, and partly on account of the remarkable way in which the Lord rewarded his faith. It was because of his awareness and constant assurance of the divine mercy and power that he unwaveringly believed that the slaughter and death of Isaac could not be an impediment to the fulfilment of the promises God had made regarding the boy.

Now he was faced by this new crisis, his past experience of the Lord's favour and omnipotent power confirmed his faith as he steadfastly trusted upon God. He had witnessed God's secret power when this child had been conceived and when Sarah had been safely delivered of her son, so Isaac himself was testimony to the invisible virtue[13] of God. Therefore he is allured by the memory of his past experience, and his faith was assured that after the sacrifice had been offered his child would be raised up, and all the promises made concerning him, both temporal and spiritual, would be performed. He was not disappointed in his hope that his son would be restored to him alive and well.

Therefore verse 19 tells us that the Lord raised him in a certain manner: *God was abill to rais him vp evin from the dead, from whence he received him also after ane sort.* The apostle writes *after ane sort*[14] because the child did not actually die, but was, as it were, only slain in the father's heart. As far as Abraham was concerned, on account of his resolve to obey God's command, the boy was as good as dead. It was because of this that, speaking through an angel, the Lord raised him up and delivered him to his father, just as Abraham himself had already given him up and freely delivered him to God. For Abraham, the Lord's voice from heaven became the resurrection of his son, and therefore what he had hoped for became for him a reality.

Now there is a reason why this statement is added in the verse that it had pleased the Lord to raise up the child 'in a manner of speaking',

[13] 'Vertew' ('virtue') used of God refers to the unseen power that flows from him to remedy some human need. See Chapter 9, note 10 above.

[14] ESV translates, 'figuratively speaking'.

that is *after ane sort*. It was that this should be a type and figure of the resurrection of Jesus Christ. Thus implanted in Abraham's heart was an article of faith, namely, the resurrection. That is why the apostle wrote as he did. We read of these types in 1 Corinthians 10 verses 6, 11: *whatsoevir was done by the fatheris was done by them in figuris and in teipis, and ar set doun and writtin for our exhortatioun and admonitioun.*[15] His purpose was that his hearers should benefit from the Fathers' examples; therefore we too should profit from them. For both Abraham and Isaac in this event became types representing something else: Abraham represented God the Father offering up his only Son, and Isaac represented Christ Jesus who was offered up on the cross.[16]

I will show you in more detail the extent to which Isaac is a type of Christ. As Isaac was repeatedly promised before he was finally born, so Christ was often promised before he was at length manifested in the flesh. Then as Isaac carried the wood on which he was to be bound, so Christ bore his own cross on to which he was nailed, and as Isaac was silent as he was tied to the altar, so Christ also never opened his mouth when he too was fixed to his cross. Finally, as Isaac returned home safely to his father's house, so Christ returned safely to his Father's heavenly dwelling where he now sits on his Father's right hand; there, by his

[15] As Bruce does so often, he is here either paraphrasing or quoting from memory the verses to which he is alluding.

[16] Some readers may be interested to follow Calvin's commentary on the sacrifice of Isaac, both in Genesis 22:1-14 and in Hebrews 11:17-19. (It is highly likely that Bruce used Calvin on the Hebrews passage as there are striking similarities to Calvin's exposition.) In his commentary on Genesis, Calvin agrees that when the ram was substituted in place of Isaac, 'God shows us, as in a glass, what is the design of our mortification; namely, that by the Spirit of God dwelling within us, we, though dead, may yet be living sacrifices'. However, he adds, 'I am not ignorant that more subtle allegories may be elicited ; but I do not see on what foundation they rest.' In his commentary on Hebrews 11:18 and the impending sacrifice of Isaac, he writes: 'Isaac is not to be thought of as one of the common company of men, but as one who contained Christ in himself,' but that is as far as he is prepared to go. On verse 19, he writes: 'I admit that it is true, what some say, that an image of Christ is depicted in this sacrifice.' He continues, 'But I am now discussing what the apostle meant and not what could be said with truth.' (*Commentaries in loc.*) His mention of 'subtle allegories' is typical of his strict avoidance of the extreme allegorizing in which so many of the mediaeval divines indulged. Here, however, as this sermon proceeds, Bruce has no inhibitions about expanding on OT 'types' and 'figures' of what was promised in the gospel.

triumphal entry he has opened up the yetts[17] of heaven, so that those who trust in him may enter hereafter. So Isaac in various ways represents Christ, and chiefly in this event.

There is however a chief twofold difference between Isaac and Christ: where Isaac suffered only an imaginary death and was not actually slain, Christ Jesus suffered a real death and did die; similarly, where Isaac was not really raised from the dead, Jesus Christ by divine power genuinely arose from death. This is the great difference between the type of Christ and Christ Jesus himself.

Three points of application

There are three further points that I mark from these verses. First, I take up the following lesson: what should be your duty and to whom should you have recourse in the hour of temptation? In any time of trouble, when the Lord afflicts you either in body or in soul, run to the mercy and power of God as Abraham did. Call to remembrance your past experiences of God's grace and mercy and constantly lean upon his power. As he cannot deny himself, trust him and he will deliver you, for his power and mercy are the only bulwarks by which our faith can be sustained in the hours of trial.

Those who have no experience of his power and grace are deprived of faith, and will not be able to withstand afflictions. However, those of you who have been here for the past ten years are bound to have had experience of the mercy and power of God, assuming you have eyes to see and memories that you can recall.[18] Therefore if you need comfort[19] when you are under pressure (and very soon you will be put

[17] In Scotland a yett is a gate of latticed wrought iron bars used for defensive purposes in castles and tower houses. Unlike a portcullis, which is raised and lowered vertically by mechanical means, yetts are hinged like traditional gates. See Chapter 1, note 19 above.

[18] It is not possible to pin-point to what particular experience he is referring. However, if the sermon had been preached after May 1592 when the Black Acts were abolished, he would have been referring to the 1584 Acts passed by parliament which 'rendered James the absolute monarch of the bodies and souls of his subjects,' for these Acts 'declared the king head of the Church as well of the State.' Hume Brown, Vol.2, pp. 154, 158.

[19] The word 'comfort' as Bruce uses it has the connotation of aid being given; Latin *cum* 'with' + *fortis* 'strength'.

under such pressure[20]), mark diligently your past experiences of God's mercy and power, that as bulwarks they may uphold your faith in the day when it pleases the Lord[21] to try you in both body and soul.

The second point that I mark here is that whatsoever we look for in faith shall be granted to us. When faith looks and hopes for something from the hands of the mighty God, then faith and hope are rewarded. Abraham's faith looked to God for the restoration of his son, that he would be raised by his power, and according to his faith it was granted him. So we are assured that whenever it is faith that looks to God, if our warrant arises from our past experience of his mercy and power and we abide firmly in his gracious deliverance, our faith will be rewarded.

The third and last thing is this. Consider how God used Abraham's great trial and testing to benefit him. We too can profit from our trials. The outcome for Abraham was that he was rightly rewarded by the restoration of his son. Although he set out with him sad, they both returned home glad. So the mighty God lays trials upon us for our profit, and as a good example for our posterity for follow. Abraham's righteous reward includes the example he has become for us who are his descendants: in all our trials we are to lean upon the power and mercy of God as he did, and we are to look for as gracious an issue as Abraham had in his trials. Then doubtless our afflictions shall have the same happy ending as Abraham's had. This is as much as I shall say to you regarding the patriarch's faith in obeying God and being prepared to sacrifice his son.

In praise of faith

In his praise of faith the apostle cannot satisfy himself without setting down in this chapter its entire history, taking in almost the whole Bible—all in his admiration of this most worthy jewel. Certainly, all that has been taught in this kirk, right from the beginning of chapter 11, gives us many reasons why faith uniquely should be praised. Without it, what can be accomplished? 'For without faith it is impossible to please God' (verse 6). Therefore this praiseworthy faith is to be pursued

[20] Bruce had sombre forebodings of future persecution of those of the reformed faith; he was right, for ahead of the Scottish Church lay the trials of the covenanting period with its many hundreds of martyrs. See above, Ch. 14, Note 4.

[21] Bruce's view of the doctrine of Divine Providence inevitably meant that nothing could happen without God's permission. (See Job 1:6-12.)

and alone is to be embraced.

Through faith we are delivered from all dangers that threaten the soul, as has been proven in the life of Abraham. Also through faith we are delivered from dangers that threaten our bodies, as shall be seen at the final end. Through faith the whole law is fulfilled, for Abraham's faith was imputed to him as righteousness.[22] Through faith we are freed from the curse and condemnation of the law, for there is now no condemnation to them that are in Christ, and by faith we are in Christ.[23] By faith we have provision for these bodies, for those of us to whom the Lord has imparted faith, and who are still here on this earth, shall certainly be provided for and shall not want.[24] By faith we also have provision for our souls. Even before ever we are reduced to want, if we have faith these [proverbial] stones shall become nourishment to feed us.[25] Want of faith casts men into desperation and into many doubts regarding their provision.

Unquestionably, if we in faith would crave from the hands of God provision for the planting of the kirks, having respect to him only, it would be easy for him who holds the hearts of men in his hands to loosen their hearts and enable them to give as much as would meet the needs of the kirks. It is the lack of faith on our part that this work is not blessed and continually sees no success.[26] Therefore, in important challenges let us in faith have recourse to the mighty God who holds the hearts of men in his hands, for if we pray in faith the Lord shall answer our prayers and meet our expectations.

The faith of Isaac

Now from Abraham the apostle moves on to his son to bring before us the example of Isaac's faith. He lets us see that just as he was his father's heir of all temporal goods, gifts and benefits which it had pleased the Lord to bestow on Abraham, so also the Lord made him the heir of his spiritual graces and gifts, and not least of that remarkable faith that had dwelt first in his father's heart. For by the same faith that Abraham

[22] Genesis 15:6.

[23] Galatians 3:10-14; Romans 8:1.

[24] Matthew 6:28-33; Psalm 23:1.

[25] The allusion would appear to be the first temptation of Jesus recorded in Matthew 4:1-4.

[26] See above Notes 4 and 5.

saw, as it were, afar off the truth of the promises made to him, so Isaac also saw from afar off the truth of those heavenly promises. And just as Abraham had led a life agreeable to the promises and the evangel, so did Isaac: his lifestyle was entirely compatible with the evangelical promises to which he was heir; he also professed himself to be banished from this earth, and to be only a pilgrim living here as a stranger who was far from his true home. Hence both father and son led lives worthy of the gospel.

That brings us to verse 20: *By faith Isaack blissed Jacob and Esau concerning things to cum*. Here we see that in this blessing of his sons Isaac's faith was strong, for he promised *concerning things to cum* as if the deed was done and sealed. He could never have done this unless the substance and evidence of them[27] had been written in his mind and soul. Because by the eye of faith he saw them clearly written in his soul through the power of the Holy Spirit, he was able to enunciate them distinctly as if they were a present actuality. So Isaac's faith was similar to the faith of his father.

Notice that the act of blessing is added here because in this respect Isaac differed from his father. We do not read that at his departure Abraham blessed his children as Isaac did, even though in every other respect the faith of the two men was the same. That is why Isaac's faith is worthy of the same praise as Abraham's faith. Be that as it may, the apostle deliberately mentions the blessings Isaac gave, because in this he merits his own special commendation. To show forth the praise of Isaac, he chooses a rare event so that we may compare his faith to that of his father: before he blessed his sons, we read in the sacred record how he first tested them, but was deceived. After his botched testing, he proceeded to give his blessing, but it was not bestowed on Esau as he imagined it would be, and so did not achieve what he had intended, but was given according to the will and appointment of God.

Three lessons from Isaac's blessing

First, the act of blessing is sacred, therefore in considering it, we must realise that it requires proper preparation. Isaac proceeded to test Jacob, thinking that he was Esau, but we are intended to understand that this holy action should be administered impartially. As the apostle

[27] Here is an allusion to Hebrews 11:1.

teaches us, first there ought to be testing, and in this regard Isaac was praiseworthy. Today, we who are teachers ought to test whether those to whom we administer the 'blessing' are dogs or swine, before we offer to them what is holy.[28] However, in his trial Isaac errs when he assumes that Jacob is Esau, and he is deceived in his blessing; but the living God was not deceived, for the blessing was administered to the one for whom it had been appointed.[29]

Second, men may be deceived when they administer the sacraments and apply the Word, but God can never be deceived. Alongside Isaac's faith was a gross error to let us see that in this world no one's faith is perfect; we are all subject to mistakes. Errors and faltering have occurred in even the finest men that have ever lived, therefore do not despair of mercy even when your faith is mingled with manifold faults. Rather strive towards greater maturity and earnestly crave the help of the Holy Spirit.

Third, we see that the blessing was not applied according to Isaac's will, for if it had been then it would have been given instead to Esau; rather it was applied as the living God had appointed and decreed. Likewise, the will of the minister is not always effectual in applying God's grace through the Word and sacraments, rather is it the will of God that is unfailingly effectual. Whoever God curses is cursed indeed,

[28] Matthew 7:6, 'Do not give dogs what is holy, and do not throw your pearls before pigs.' A form of examination prior to communion had been prepared by John Craig, but in the minutes of the General Assembly of 21 July 1591 the following was recorded: 'Anent the form of the examination before communion, penned by their brother Mr Craig, the Assembly thought it meet to be imprinted, being by the author thereof contracted within some shorter bounds.' (Shaw p. 927) During the next Assembly of May 1592, Robert Bruce being Moderator for the second time, the following minute was recorded of Session 10, 30th May: 'For as much as, at the special desire of the Kirk, *An forme of examination before the communion* [Edin. 1592] was penned and formed by their brother Mr John Craig, which is now allowed and imprinted by the voice of the whole assembly: therefore it is thought needful that every pastor travail with his flock, that they may buy the same book, and read it in their families, that they may be the better instructed; and that the same be read and learned in lecture schools in the place of the little catechism' [John Craig, *A short symme of the whole catechism*. Edin. 1581]. (Shaw p. 931) Craig's 1592 catechism is available online: www.swrb.com/newslett/actualN-Ls/communca.htm. See also Chapter 16, Notes 15 & 16 below.

[29] Genesis 25:23.

but it may happen that someone whom the minister blesses is in fact already cursed. Therefore let us reverence the living God, knowing that any who are cursed are cursed by him, and that all who are blessed are blessed by him. His blessings and his cursing are immutable, whereas the blessing or cursing of mere men may serve no useful purpose.

The relationship between temporal and spiritual blessings

Finally, we see that within the blessing as it is recorded in Scripture[30] are three main points. First, there is the promise of temporal things, of grain and wine. Second, there is promised to Jacob lordship and dominion. Third, there is the promise of spiritual authority: *They sall be cursed that curs him and blised that blis him*. And so we see that in his blessing the Lord always conjoins the temporal with the spiritual. It is the same today for God gives his people sufficient temporal blessings to enable them to develop and use his spiritual blessings. The measure of his temporal blessings corresponds to the measure of his spiritual blessings, which in his time he imparts to us.[31]

Therefore, whether you have to do with temporal or spiritual things, seek the living God, depend upon no one else but him, casting your cares on him; then unquestionably the greater the acknowledgment you give him concerning your provision, the better shall you be provided for. But if instead of casting your cares upon him, you take God's office out of his hands and usurp his place, robbing him of his divine concern for your needs, then you commit the greatest sacrilege; for to do that is to rob God of what is proper to him, as if we were more competent than he is. Therefore depend upon God for your provision for temporal things, and pray only for as much of this world as you need in order to prepare yourself for the world to come. Pray also for enough of his spiritual gifts to enable you to have a clear light of heaven and insight into the heavenly life.

I close with a brief word to my fellow ministers who may be present: depend upon God concerning your daily provision, and no doubt you shall be enabled to see the way forward, and you will leave this place

[30] Genesis 27:26-29.

[31] The allusion could well be to Luke 12:48b, 'Everyone to whom much was given, of him much will be required,' and also to the Parable of the Talents (Matthew 25:14-30) and the Parable of the Ten Minas (Luke 19:11-27).

with a more relaxed heart and mind than you had when you came here. At this point I shall stop and leave the rest of the verse to another time.

It only remains for me to commit each of you to God's merciful provision and protection, that in all the various details of your lives you may have recourse to the living God. May the Lord so work in every one of your hearts through the righteous merits of Christ, to whom with the Father and the Holy Ghost be all honour, praise and glory now and for ever. Amen.

Chapter Sixteen

Hebrews Chapter 11 verse 20

[20] *By faith Isaack blised Jacob and Esaw concerning thingis to cum.*

Well-beloved in Jesus Christ our Lord, the apostle, after recording the example of Abraham, then moves on to bring before us the example of the son who was the father's only heir to all the earthly goods and possessions he had received in heritable title from God. This son was also heir to the spiritual graces and rare gifts that had been bestowed on his father during his lifetime. In other words, the same faith that had dwelt in the father took up residence in the son. As the father had seen from afar the truth of the promise that had been made to him by God, so the son saw the truth of the same promise; and as the father had felt the power of the world to come and had been given a foretaste of the promise that lodged in his heart and conscience, so the son sought the powers of the world to come and was also granted a foretaste in his heart and conscience of the felicity of same promises. As the father saw the day of Jesus Christ and was glad,[1] I have no doubt that the son also saw the day of Jesus Christ and rejoiced in it.

The blessing on Jacob was truly a spiritual blessing

Thus we see that this godly father had been given this godly son to succeed him. I say they were both godly because they were full of faith, and godliness only comes through faith. That the son Isaac was a faithful man, not only in word but in deed also, the apostle demonstrates in verse 20 by an outcome of his faith which he declares was peculiar to him and not shared by his father. Hence the commendation of it redounds only

[1] John 8:56.

to Isaac. That outcome of faith which the apostle wants to emphasize was the blessings he gave, long before his own death, to his two sons Jacob and Esau. First, that these blessings proceeded from and were the fruit of faith is apparent not only from certain statements within the blessings, but also by his own actions after he had given the blessings.

Regarding the principal blessing, note secondly that it contains a solemn prayer. Now prayer arises from[2] faith, so that the prayer within the blessing is an outcome of faith, for his blessing speaks clearly of things to come. Indeed, Jacob saw as clearly as if these things were already present and were being seen with his physical eyes; self-evidently, this is 'an effect' of genuine faith. For because faith (as you have already heard) is the ground and substance of things to come and hoped for,[3] this blessing must flow from faith.

Thirdly, Isaac's actions after the blessing testify plainly that it had been inspired by the Holy Spirit and from his own spirit. For after he had learned of his error when Esau came to him and he realised that he had mistaken Jacob for his brother, he would not recant or change his mind about what he had done. But he reiterated that he had 'blessed him, yes, and he shall be blessed.'[4] So he stood fast by what he had done, otherwise, had the blessing been from his own will and love for the one he assumed was his elder son, he would have withdrawn it from Jacob and transferred it to Esau.

However, the old man's recognition that God's will had been at work is evidence that he knew the Holy Spirit had spoken through him, and no doubt he then recalled to his mind the oracle that he seemed to have forgotten.[5] That is why when he saw plainly that the blessing was according to the divine will, he accepted it and said, *I have blised and he sall be blised*. Therefore the apostle is at pains to emphasize this notable outcome of his faith in order to prove that Isaac was possessed of genuine faith.

[2] Bruce's phrase is 'the effect of', and is used many times throughout this sermon. The word 'effect' tends to be used in opposition to 'word', in the sense that 'the word' is meaningless unless it results in some action, outcome, deed or 'effect'. His underlying point is the same as that in James' Epistle that 'faith without works is dead'. See James 2:14-17.

[3] Hebrews 11:1.

[4] Genesis 27:33; see also verse 37.

[5] Genesis 25:21-26.

Jacob's blessing was God's blessing and foreshadowed Christ

Here in verse 20, we have two main points to consider. The first is the person who pronounced the blessings, an aged man who was failing not only physically but also in his memory. A man may be said to bless, but God blesses in a different way, such as when in his mercy he blesses by bestowing particular goodness to his creatures, for the blessings of the living God are always effectual. His blessings are never in vain, for each pronouncement becomes an actuality.

A man may be said to bless when by prayer he craves from the mighty hand of God some good thing for himself or for someone else. When God blesses it is in his own name and by his own authority, whereas when a man blesses he does not bless either in his own name or by his authority, but in the name of God and by the name and authority of Jesus Christ. Isaac was a man who became the instrument of God's blessing and who blessed in God's name: 'May God give you of the dew of heaven….'

Secondly in this verse, the persons who were blessed were his own two sons, brothers conceived in the same womb, born at the same time and one by nature and substance. But these two were very different in terms of the mercy and grace of God. As we reflect upon them, we see that each blessing was very different. Heavenly and spiritual blessings were poured out upon the younger son, together with so many material blessings as would serve to be pledges of the spiritual promises, and as such would enable him to obtain and appreciate them. However, chiefly and specially was he blessed with heavenly gifts.[6]

By contrast the elder son was blessed only with material things, without any kind of heavenly or spiritual gifts. The same temporal blessings were granted to both sons, but the spiritual blessings were given only to Jacob. Why should this have been so? The reason was this: Jesus Christ, to whom the heavenly blessings properly appertain, according to the flesh, was already 'lurking' in the loins of Jacob, and he can never be divided. There is only one Mediator, not two, between God and man, the man Christ Jesus. Thus the promise made first to

[6] Calvin makes this point more fully than Bruce: '[A]lthough Isaac makes the temporal favours of God prominent, nothing is further from his mind than to confine the hope of his son to this world; he would raise him to the same elevation to which he himself aspired' (*Comm. in loc.)*.

Abraham and again to Isaac (and then through him to Jacob), was conceived in these terms, *In thy seid* (speaking of one) *sall all the natiounis of the earth be blised.* He does not say, 'in thy seeds' but uses the singular, as we read in Galatians 3, *in thy seed*, speaking of Christ Jesus who is one, not two.[7] The spiritual blessings appertain to Christ alone, to him as to the Head, and to us as to his members who are mystically united to and sustained by Christ our Head.

Esau, having nothing to do with either Christ or his members, could in no way be a recipient of his blessings, for he proved to be the enemy of both Jesus and all his members. Take heed to the oracle stated by Malachi, *I haue loved Jacob, bot I haue haited Esaw.*[8] Therefore the spiritual blessing could not be extended to Esau.

Briefly, would you too be partakers of the spiritual gifts and do you desire to be grafted into the body of Christ Jesus? Have you ever yearned to live with him for ever? Then now is the time for you to have the assurance that you are standing in the faith of Jesus Christ. Be certain that for your eternal felicity you are depending only on his blood and his righteous merits. Be absolutely assured in your conscience of this, otherwise there can be no spiritual or heavenly blessing that appertains to you. 'Why?' you may ask. Because all these spiritual blessings are but the fruit of the faith that reaches out and grasps hold on Christ; none of us can ever partake of them unless we are in his faith. Esau was not in this faith, which is why he could not receive the spiritual blessing. Therefore you must take heed and examine your consciences and change your ways, so that your hearts may have this assurance and your ways bear witness to the truth that you do have faith in Jesus Christ alone. Then the heavenly grace promised in Christ will also assuredly be extended to you.

When he blessed his two sons Isaac began first with Jacob, even though he was the younger of the two. Notice also that the apostle names him first in the text. He does not say, as we might expect, 'Esau and Jacob', but, *he blised Jacob and Esaw.* He names him first because

[7] Genesis 22:18; 26:4; Galatians 3:8, 16.

[8] Malachi 1:3. Some may find difficulty in this statement, mainly because our concept of hatred is contaminated by sinful human bitterness and malice. For helpful comments on Malachi 1:3, see Baldwin, *in loc.*, and Mackay, *in loc.* Calvin's exposition of Malachi 1:3 gives an extended exposition of this verse: *Comm. in loc.*

the principal, only real blessing (for in respect of our subject, Esau's blessing was not a genuine gospel blessing at all) was bestowed on Jacob, notwithstanding that he was the younger son.

The custom would have been for Esau, the elder son, to have been put in the first place. By right of birth, by the law of nature and by the law of God set down in his Word, the older brother ought to have been preferred to the younger brother. And had the father's own affectionate preference been followed—remember, Isaac was one of the patriarchs—then Esau would have been given the principal blessing. Nevertheless, by the ordinance of God, and according to the secret decree of the Lord's election, the younger was preferred before the elder.

God's favours in Christ are conferred upon the lowly in heart

What then do we learn from this? Here there is a notable instruction to us not to depend upon outward things, nor to glory in earthly titles and status, but rather to seek after the favour of God in Jesus Christ. We must have the assurance of his divine favour. Moreover, we must remember the words of Jesus who expressly says to us, that *that manie now quho ar last, sall be first in the kingdome of heavine, and manie quho appear to be first, sall be last.*[9] For the living God takes those who are despised in the judgment of men and raises them up, but those who are high in men's estimation he makes the lowest.

Therefore do not judge by outward appearances or by worldly prerogatives and inherited honours, rather look to the favour of the living God, before whose countenance all earthly possessions and privileges must be consecrated and sanctified for our use. Whatever title or inherited prerogative you may have, unless you have the favour of God, your privileges will lead you down into hell, whereas if you are blessed with honours and have God's favour, they should be as a ladder to conduct you into his divine presence. Thus the whole course of the Scriptures reveal a God who brings low those who outwardly appear to be high, and to raise up high those who in men's estimation appear to be low.

We see how he brings Cain low but lifts up Abel; he brings down Ishmael and lifts up Isaac; he chooses Jacob but turns from Esau; he raises up Joseph but casts down Reuben; he lifts up Ephraim but sidelines Manasseh. Therefore do not depend upon outward appearances

[9] This allusion is apparently a conflation of Matthew 19:30 and Mark 9:34-35.

unless they are seasoned with the countenance and favour of God. It is a mistake to say that the favourable smile of a king makes men great. No, it is only the countenance of God that imparts greatness. The final outcome shall reveal that whoever is destitute of the divine favour shall be cursed and maledictions shall be pronounced upon him, even in this life and before he enters eternity. So entrust yourselves only to the favour of God, and he shall truly make you great, both in this life and in the life to come. Thus our text tells us that in the secret decree of the living God the younger was preferred to the elder, overturning the natural order.

As we turn now to think further about Esau and Jacob, their lives and their behaviour, we will find the reasons why the elder was put to one side and the younger was put in his place. The description of the two is to be found in Genesis 26 and 28 where we discover that the lifestyle and behaviour of Esau made him unworthy of the spiritual benefits of a real blessing. On the other hand, Jacob was sanctified in both heart and mind, and showed reverence towards holy things, hence the spiritual blessings poured out upon him.

Esau

Consider, then, the kind of man that Esau was: he is depicted as being an evil and undisciplined[10] man who despised both God and his parents, a profane man who preferred this world and his belly to holy things and those singular privileges which were his by right of birth.[11] He is recorded as having been irreligious for he angered both God and his parents by his marriages to pagan women;[12] he was inconsistent in his supposed repentance and unstable in how he lived. So it is evident that he was possessed of an evil disposition. By contrast, the younger brother was a quiet man, dwelling in tents, and whose godly and upright behaviour made it evident that the Lord was with him. Therefore in common justice Jacob was preferred to his older brother whom God set aside.

[10] Bruce's word is 'barbarous'.

[11] Genesis 25:29-34.

[12] Genesis 26:34-35; 28:6-9.

Godly sorrow and repentance is needed in our land

I have already taught you that not everyone is willing to receive these spiritual things, and even though they may claim to have faith, they are unfaithful in their deeds, and are therefore unprepared to receive spiritual blessings. I ask you, how is it possible that when the gospel of Jesus Christ has sounded so long in this land, that our nation should be so barren of these spiritual blessings, promised, as they have been by both the prophets and the apostles, to be available in the kingdom of Christ? Had we been prepared in our souls and faithful in our deeds, we would have received them. Alas, it has not been possible. Yet, out of all the nations under the sun, our nation ought to have been the most flourishing in both government and spiritual graces; but in our living and actions we have not matched what we say. However, in the meaningless, empty profession of our words we have thrown in our lot with Esau and rejected the example of Jacob, which is why we have been deprived of the fruits of these spiritual blessings and graces that ought to have flourished among us.

Even if this is not true of some of us, there is real reason for complaints regarding those who have defected.[13] Therefore I beseech the living God that my voice may be accompanied by his power, that my words may work effectively in both speaker and hearer, to the end that every one of us may escape the wrath that is to come by fleeing to Christ. May we all be more vigilant than we have been in unfeigned remorse for our sins whereby we have offended against God, and so may we seek daily to practise godly sorrow throughout the rest of our days. We silently ignore those from among us who have fallen into heinous sins and grotesque backsliding, but they should cause us to weep and to pray for their repentance; but alas we regard them with indifference. It will not be merely the deadness of your hearts or the insecurity of your consciences that you will hold on to as if to hide from the wrath of God. No, that deadness will be swept away and the records engraved on your consciences will be exposed, and then you

[13] Probably he means some have been attending Mass in Huntly's castle, or in Megginch Castle whose scion, Edmund Hay, had trained in France as a Jesuit missionary and returned clandestinely to Scotland. But after referring to 'defectors' he proceeds to address those who have fallen into ungodly living, and whose consciences have become hardened.

shall have a sight of infinite wrath you shall not be able to abide, for it shall confound you for ever.

Therefore now while you have the opportunity, even if there is little or no stirring in your hearts towards repentance, nor even any desire to forsake your evil ways, yet let this small seed be sown in your consciences: 'Since my life bears constant witness against me, I shall crave the will of the living God to enable me to repent that I may seek a real change in my thinking.' I beseech you to crave the Lord to show this mercy towards you and give to you the desire to beg forgiveness for your past sins, that you may redeem the time that is left to you. I am not able to apply this to any particular person. It is up to each of you as your own consciences bear your records, to be in time for God's mercy to enable you to reform your lives.

Isaac, Jacob and Rebecca all had fallen, sinful natures

We turn now to consider the blessing given to the chosen son, Jacob, who was living worthily. In addition to the living God who was the Director in this entire event, there are three other persons who were involved in the blessing. There was the father who gave the blessing, the son who was blessed and the mother who was the persuader and who made the arrangements for her son. These three each deserve some particular praise, but also each of them had their own weaknesses and faults.

Isaac

We think first about the old man. He was certainly praiseworthy in that he would not admit Jacob—assuming him to be the elder—to the holy, spiritual blessing without testing him. So before he gave him the blessing he examined him to determine whether or not he was prepared and ready to be blessed. Last Sunday we touched on this lesson and how it applies especially to those of us who are teachers. We saw how we ought not to admit anyone casually to holy things, but that we ought first to examine them, to see whether or not they are in the faith of Jesus Christ, and so able to receive what is holy. (Each of us should try ourselves as the apostle commands us.[14]) Also those of us who are

[14] This is a subject on which Bruce preached powerfully in a sermon on 1 Corinthians 11:28-29. See Chapter 11, note 38 above.

pastors should also submit ourselves to be tried.[15] Some examination should always precede participation in holy things.[16]

But back to Isaac. He fails in his trial of his son, for he mistakes the person to whom the blessing properly appertained by the explicit appointment of God. Indeed, it would appear he was ignorant as to which of his sons the blessing should be given. Certainly he knew that one of them should receive the blessing, but he was unaware which son it should be. His uncertainty cannot be excused lightly, as far as the Lord enables me to perceive, for I do not doubt that his wife had reported to him the oracle that she had received from God. Its message had been spelt out plainly: it was that *the elder sould serve the younger*, and therefore the blessing had to be given to Jacob, for one of the terms of the blessing was, *be lord ouer thy brethre.*[17] She must have told Isaac of this, and either he forgot about it, or else he thought her account had not sufficient authority for him to depart from the usual custom; for, as we have seen, by both the law of nature and the law of God set down in his Word, the eldest son inherited the birthright.[18] We may also assume that because he himself did not receive this oracle directly from the mouth of God, it had little or no authority when it came through his

[15] The Buke of Discipline, under 'The Sevint Heid, of Ecclesiasticall Discipline,' Part III, states that 'subject [to discipline must be] the Preachearis thame selfis, asweill as the poorest in the Churche. And because the eye and mouth of the Churche aught to be most single and irreprehensibill, the life and conversatioun of the Ministeris aught most diligentlie to be tried.' The narrative proceeds into considerable detail on the examination of the Ministers: 'Yea, the Seniouris aught to tak heyde to the life, manneris, deligence, and studye of thair Ministeris…'. See also Chapter 13, note 20 above.

[16] Bruce does not define what he means by 'holie thingis', but most probably he is referring to the two sacraments as defined in the 1560 *The Buke of Discipline*. See 'The Secound Head, Of Sacramentis', where there is much on sacramental discipline under 'The Sevint Heid, of Ecclesiasticall Discipline' (see Note 15 above) and under 'The Nynt Heid, Concernyng the Policie of the Churche' where we read, for example, 'Such as be ignorant in the Articulis of thair Faith; understand not nor can rehearse the Commandimentis of God; knaw not how to pray; neathir whairinto thair richtuousnes consists, aught not to be admitted to the Lordis Tabill.' Under the 'The Fyft Heid' in the section on 'Schollis', I. The Necessitie of Schollis, it is laid down that children and youth should be instructed in [Calvin's] 'Catechism, as we have it now translaited in our Booke of Common Order, callit The Ordour of Geneva.' See also Chapter 15, note 28 above.

[17] Genesis 25:23.

[18] Deuteronomy 21:15-17. See Article on 'First-Born', *IBD* pp. 507-508.

wife. Further, no doubt because he knew her love was greater for Jacob than for Esau, he may have thought that she was speaking out of affection for her favourite son.

Where then does this leave us? In 'the general' Isaac was quite certain regarding the blessing that must be given, but in 'the particular'[19] he was wrong about which of his sons should receive it. Here there is again a lesson for us. The Lord never at any time revealed to the prophets who spoke in his name both the general and the particular of any action he directed them to take. Indeed, right since the beginning of time, he has concealed in his own counsel a great number of the particulars,[20] so that in our prayers we may be exercised in worship[21] as we seek the particulars from him, never deciding ourselves, but depending wholly upon the almighty God and his will.

A solemn warning to the Kirk

If we in the ministry had been guided by this principle and only proceeded according to God's counsel, following his directions in the particulars as well as in the generalities, then our service for him would have had far better outcomes. But having had the warrant of God for the general, but failing to seek his warrant for the particulars, we have taken the wrong courses of action and failed to reach the right outcomes.[22] Therefore my counsel—and it is God's own counsel—is this: because he conceals from us the particulars, we have to plead for them by prayer, fasting and spiritual exercises.

This applies to you all: before you embark upon any particular work, on your knees seek the counsel of God, and through the direction of his word and the conviction of his Holy Spirit, proceed step by step with the particulars; but do nothing without his warrant. Had the old man gotten his own way and been allowed to follow his own wishes, he would have blessed Esau, the enemy of God, one whom the Lord had explicitly stated that he had rejected.[23]

[19] Citing the 'general' and the 'particular' is one Bruce's favourite steps in developing his line of reasoning.

[20] He means 'the specific details'.

[21] Here he uses the word 'worship' in its most basic biblical meaning as 'submission before one's Lord'. See, e.g., Matthew 4:9 = Luke 4:7.

[22] See Chapter 14, Note 10 above, together with the paragraph to which it pertains.

[23] Bruce's word is 'haited', but in using the verb 'rejected', I am guided by the

This is a most important matter. You must recognise how great a peril it can be, and how dangerous it is for God's prophets, servants and ministers to follow their own feelings in dispensing spiritual things. You must see how hazardous it can be for someone who teaches God's word to be swayed by his own emotion. Therefore before ever we come to this place, let us earnestly present ourselves to the living God, craving fervently that our wills be may be sanctified and subdued according to his will.[24] Pray too that our sanctified desires may guide us to the holy purposes that the Lord intends, so that we may not be guided by our own wishes, but by his will. Pray also that the Holy Spirit may so rule over our affections that all we say may emanate, not from ourselves, but from the living God. If this be done, I have no doubt that the Lord will enable us to speak according to his purposes, and he will equip us to withstand any mortal man who rises up to promote himself and not Christ. On the other hand, if we are motivated by what we ourselves desire, then because the Lord has not granted us the enabling, neither will he uphold us. Therefore do not trust your own ideas or desires, but strive ever to present yourselves to God, that when it pleases him that we be opposed, he who motivates us may also sustain us.

Esau would have received the blessing, but it transpired that it was bestowed upon Jacob, a most reluctant recipient, who was given it quite contrary to his father's wishes and intentions. What does this teach us? Here is yet another important lesson. Because Jacob represents the whole elect of God, in this incident we learn that such is God's loving care towards his chosen ones, he uses what opposes his purposes to be his unwitting instruments; they unintentionally bless and benefit his people. This truth should cause us to depend less on men, and to rely solely upon the living God. Because he holds in his hands the hearts of all men, he can use them to bless his children, even though they are unaware of what they are doing.

This lesson is needed at this time, for doubtless if only we would bring our needs before the Lord, he would more than supply our necessities. This applies also to our country and to some of the judicial acts which appear to be opposed to us, for the Lord could use what we regard as the greatest of our enemies to be instruments of benefit to the

---

expositions of Baldwin and Mackay. See above note 8.

[24] See above note 21.

Kirk. But the fault[25] has been in ourselves, in that we have not sought help from God as we ought to have done, nor depended upon his gracious providence; this is why he has not yet tamed those acts of parliament[26] by taking action to deal with them, as we hope he will yet do. There is still time for us to seek God in this matter, and beseech him to draw forth from the parliamentary acts, however unyielding they may seem to be, some benefit for the Kirk. If we seek this earnestly from the Lord, I have no doubt that he will grant it.[27]

Jacob

This far then for the old man Isaac, and that takes us next to Jacob. In the part he played in securing the blessing it would appear that he was worthy of reproof over three things. The first is that it seems he was ambitious enough to strive after preferment. The second is that he actively inveigled himself into his brother's place. The third is that although he was destined to inherit the birthright, he gained it by underhand methods. In these three ways, it would appear that he erred.

Jacob's three apparent errors

To clear him of at least of two of these errors, we have to turn to Genesis

[25] Bruce's word is 'wyte' meaning 'blame, fault'; in a legal context it means 'responsibility for carrying out an illegal act'; therefore he is still referring to some judicial acts which opposed or restricted the Reformed Kirk.

[26] The word is again 'instrumentis' being used with its particular Scots' connotation (see Chapter 14, note 9 above), so I have translated it here as 'acts of parliament' (in the next sentence also), for the context makes it clear this is his concern here.

[27] Bruce may be referring to the 'Black Acts' of 1584, for he would have been fully aware of the past struggles of the Kirk to survive. By the 'Black Acts' the autonomy of the Kirk had been wiped out completely, leaving James and the prelates supreme in the land; the Act of Uniformity had followed later that year. 'As if by magic, the church had become the tool of Arran, Knox's unreformed brother-in-law, afterwards Chancellor of the realm.' But in 1587, Parliament had passed an Act (No.8) which secured all teinds, glebe and manses for the Kirk, but annexed to the Crown all temporalities of the prelates, meaning in effect that episcopacy was a spent force. (Hewison, pp. 119-120, 128.) However, it was not until 1592 that Parliament passed what became known as 'The Magna Charta of the Kirk', whereby all previous legislation in favour of the Reformed Church was ratified. (*Idem*, 133; also Hume Brown, II, 167.) It is quite possible that it was this Act of 1592 for which Bruce is here longing. Undoubtedly its enactment would have been seen as an answer to fervent prayer.

27, where the full account is recorded. We deal first with the accusation that he was ambitious for preferment, and recall what was written of him in chapter 25:27, *Jacob was a plaine man, and dwelt in tetes.* Then add to that the answer he gave to his mother when she began to persuade him to take his brother's place, and we find that he was neither ambitious nor seeking any preferment. It had not occurred to him to deceive his brother, for he answered her, *Behold, Esaw my brother is rough, and I am smothe.* 'If my father should take hold of me, immediately he will perceive it is me, and will think I am insulting him. Instead of blessing me, he will then curse me to ensure that I cannot take my brother's place.' Thus we see from what he said to his mother that Jacob was not seeking preferment.

The second supposed error was that he inveigled himself into his brother's place, trying to advance himself without any command from God to embark upon such an extraordinary action. It was indeed an astonishing thing to do, as if some ghost should materialise to impersonate Esau, and snatch away what was his right by birth. Jacob himself had not had any command from God to do such a thing, though there had been a word from the mouth of the living God to his mother regarding the birthright, recorded in Genesis 25:23, and it was she who persuaded him to undertake this deception. In that oracle the Lord had declared his will that the younger should be the master and the elder should serve him, in effect implying that the blessing appertained to Jacob upon whom it should be poured out.

It is probable that when his mother set herself to persuade Jacob that she used this oracle as her argument: 'My son, it is the will of the living God that you take the first place, for he has ordained that this blessing should be yours, therefore obey God and take the birthright.' The 'plain man' would never have been persuaded by the authority of a mere woman to accept the blessing, unless he had seen by the light of God's word the actual warrant from his mouth; such an extraordinary action would have required an extraordinary warrant. Clearly this most solemn matter was beset by many uncertainties, and doubtless Jacob knew he needed God's explicit warrant before ever he made a move to supplant his brother. Therefore, from the time he heard about the divine oracle and understood for the first time God's will for him, he now took it to heart and proceeded with his mother's plan.

There is a lesson for us here. In any important matter that is going against the normal custom and established order, be careful to look first to God, and get from him the needed extraordinary warrant, because what you are about to do is out of the ordinary. If you are not certain of this, the outcome will achieve nothing. But if, because you are attempting something contrary to the normal practice, with God's clear sanction the means you use will be sanctified, and the Lord will bring about a blessed result. Therefore in such matters you must keep your eyes upon God. Thus we must conclude that the means used by Jacob to obtain his father's blessing were sanctioned by the Holy Spirit and controlled by God for the scheme to secure its intended purpose.

Having said that, we see that Jacob rashly mismanaged the plans, and displayed his own sinful nature in twice saying to his father, 'I am Esau,' for that had all the characteristics of falsehood. As far as God gives me grace to understand, his intention was deception. Over against that, when the Holy Spirit is in charge, the sinfulness of the act is secondary.[28] However, as God gives me the discernment to see, I regard Jacob as failing and sinning by repeating his affirmation that he was his father's elder son. We men are not angels, and there is no one, not even the holiest person who ever lived, who does not have his own weaknesses lurking within him if we examine him closely. This far, then, for Jacob.

Rebecca's role

We come now to Isaac's wife, and no doubt she deserves some praise in this matter, for she proved to be a key instrument in bringing the blessing to the one for whom it was intended. The first point in which she is to be commended is that she kept the oracle locked up firmly in her mind, showing that her memory was more sanctified than that of her husband. So well did she guard it, that the content of the oracle was not lost through the passage of time. Second, she was persuaded in her heart and conscience of the truth of the oracle she had received from the mouth of God, that it would be effectual for her younger son. Consequently, she was neither negligent nor slothful, nor (as we say)

[28] I found this sentence difficult to translate: 'Bot quhen the holie spirit moderatis thir thingis, sin decayis.' DSL gives the meaning of 'decayis' as 'decline, or, impair'.

was she 'loathsomely amiable'.[29] Therefore, by all possible means she uses her wit and industry to accomplish God's purposes for her son.

Yet again, there is an important lesson for us. Just say God has bound[30] himself by his promise that he will do something good for us. And even if our faith is assured that what he has promised will not fail, but shall be fulfilled in his good time, nevertheless we must not be slothful or negligent, for in the meantime it becomes us to use all proper means that he has appointed whereby we may ultimately experience what he has pledged to give us. It becomes us to exercise ourselves in prayer, to engage in works inspired by love and so to strive with all our strength, diligence and activity, so that what the Lord has promised may be accomplished through us.

Do not, therefore, allow the mercy and grace of God to be wasted on the wantonness of your flesh. Do not allow yourselves to become negligent just because the Lord has pledged[31] himself and you know that his word cannot fail; you may not then presume to turn to pleasure or to pursue whatsoever you desire. That would be a devilish outcome! Rather learn from this woman to be careful and diligent, and use all the means that God has appointed. Be all the more thankful that the Lord has pledged himself, without any deserving on your part.

Back, then, to the means that Rebecca used: she persuaded Jacob to take upon himself the persona of another person, disguising his hands and neck and instructing him in what he must say. I cannot excuse her faults in doing this. But as I have already pointed out the weaknesses of Isaac and Jacob, so we have to admit that she too had her weaknesses evidenced in the means she adopted. Because she was persuaded that the blessing was most certainly destined by God for Jacob, surely she ought to have consulted with the Lord as to what means she ought to use, and not to have depended upon her own wits. Had she sought the Lord's mind on what she should do, she could well have been guided

[29] Bruce's phrase is 'nor is she foull fairand, as we speak'; 'foull' means 'loathsome, ugly' while 'fairand' means 'amiable, pleasant, good-looking' (DSL). This oxymoron means 'loathsomely amiable'. Another possible translation might be the contemporary Scottish expression 'a nippie-sweetie', or, 'so earthly minded as to be no heavenly use.' However, I have opted for a literal translation.

[30] The word 'oblist' is another of Bruce's legal terms and means 'bound by a contract'.

[31] See note 30 above.

rightly by the Holy Spirit. In this she failed.

What can I say? We cannot find any man or woman in this world who does not have weaknesses and faults. Even in the best work that we undertake, the devil will find some way to mar it, for he is always seeking to cause us to do it our way, or else to use it to gain personal credit, or causing us to do last what was most important and to do first what was least needful. He will even encourage us to be so busy that we have not time to use the means appointed by the Lord.

God's mercy overrules our frailties

Yet even though these three, Isaac, Jacob and Rebecca, clearly displayed their weaknesses and faults, nevertheless we must not so much dwell upon the frailties of these Fathers and other holy persons, as to look to the mercy of the living God, who in his rich and infinite grace overruled their errors. His purposes of grace were not impeded by their shortcomings, but his will was executed as easily and swiftly as if there had never been any hindrances on account of their sinfulness. We have to turn our eyes upon the riches of his mercy that covered the infirmities of his chosen ones in such a way that enabled what they did to accomplish his will. Let us, therefore, always have recourse to that same abundant mercy, and when we are not aware of the pitiful state of our own souls, let us ask God that in his compassion for us he would open our eyes to recognise our spiritual poverty, in order that we may render to him all the praise for what he had done. Only then will we confess that there is nothing in us but shame and ignominy, infirmity and weakness, and so we will ascribe all praise for the beginning, continuance and completion of the work to the merciful grace of the living God in Jesus Christ.

Esau's 'blessing'

Now from Jacob, the apostle moves on to Esau, for Isaac is compelled, as it were, to bless him also. Thus by his counterfeit tears and voluble complaints, Esau extracts a blessing from his father.[32] As to his blessing, earthly and temporal goods are promised him, and indeed all temporal and earthly benefits that flow from God's creation are in and of themselves real blessings. But when we look carefully at the language in which the blessing was couched, it is evident that they ceased to be

[32] Genesis 27:38-40.

blessings to Esau, but became the cause of his downfall.[33]

However, in spite of the temporal blessings promised, there are two significant things I have noted, as God has given me discernment. While in Jacob's blessing there is much mention of God, implicitly as well as explicitly, in Esau's blessing God is never mentioned. Further, notice how the word 'blessing' is not used either: he does not say, 'the fatness of the earth shall be your blessing,' but *'from the fatness of the earth shall be your dwelling'*. This was no oversight, but was the deliberate purpose of the Holy Spirit who inspired Isaac's words that God was not mentioned and the word 'blessing' was omitted.

Why was this so? It was because the Spirit of God saw clearly that Esau would never show any gratitude for anything he received; he would never thank the Lord that he had clothes on his back and a full belly, for the provision of such necessities he would ascribe to his own wit, devices and industry, being quite unaware of divine providence. That is why there is mention of neither God nor his blessings in Isaac's pronouncement. In short, Esau was a godless man.

Esau stands in contrast to those who reverence the Lord in their hearts, and have not imbibed the errors of godlessness; they are said always to be blessed, for they acknowledge every good thing that comes from God; thus they give thanks for the most inconsequential of the Lord's provisions. When they receive some benefit, they do not attribute it to either the means by which it came to them, or to the person who brought it, but to the God who moves in men's hearts. The Lord so deals with his own people that he lets them see with perfect clarity that every good thing they receive, whether it comes to them through some human instrument—man or woman—or in the course of nature by purely natural means, it is his own hand that is blessing them; this they learn from their experience of his provision.

The Lord let Abraham see clearly that it was neither by the course of nature, nor by his own virility, nor by his wife's ability to conceive, that he fathered a son; rather was it God himself that granted him a child when all natural means had failed. Similarly, the Lord let Joseph

[33] Implicit in these words are the phrases Isaac used, 'away from the dew of heaven… by your sword you shall live… when you grow restless… you shall break the yoke from your neck', though Bruce also has in mind Esau's exclusion from the covenant.

see that his preferment did not come either from the warp or the weft,[34] or by coincidence or good luck (as profane men of this world often say), but from the merciful and gracious providence of the ever living God. In the same way, he let the people of Israel see that neither their deliverance from Egypt, nor their return from exile in Babylon, came by natural means, but both emanated straight from the merciful hands of God. It was the same with David who recognised that his kingdom did not come from his keeping of sheep, or from his parentage, or from his own wit or endeavour, but directly from heaven and God's hand. This has always been the way in which the living God has blessed the faithful, and so they have acknowledged him in everything they have received and thanked him for the smallest of his blessings, even if it was only a drink of cold water.

However, there is no mention of God in the 'blessings' granted to the wicked, because they neither acknowledge him nor give thanks to him, but give all the credit to their own wit and industry. If you would declare yourselves to be the children of the living God, and thus those to whom Jacob's spiritual blessings appertain, take care that you acknowledge the Lord in everything, and that you see his image and fingerprints upon all your possessions. For there is nothing that God has created that does not bear his own stamp, and if in good conscience you possess something he has fashioned, your conscience will constrain you to give him thanks.

Warning against dishonesty

If something in your possession gives you a bad conscience, you will not be constrained to give him thanks, but your guilty conscience will torment you until you make amends; otherwise your heart will be hardened and your conscience will lose all sensitivity. Therefore ensure that all your possessions are obtained with a clear conscience. When your goods have been rightly obtained, give thanks to the living God who has guided you and given you good success in your endeavours. In that way, your acquisitions will be of benefit to your family and household.

[34] In Isaiah 38:12, Hezekiah had shown his familiarity with the home loom: 'like a weaver I have rolled up my life; he cuts me off from the loom'. In his sermon on this passage, Bruce shows he was also familiar with the weaver's work when he comments, 'He [Hezekiah] means "the throombs that go about the beam", that is, the unwoven ends of the warp threads.' *Isa.* 38, Sermon 4, Note 20, p. 94.

Would to God that all men had the eyes to see this. Because the Lord is long-suffering and delays administering his awesome justice, men assume that there is no such thing as his punishment. But do not doubt that it shall be manifested in your lifetime, or else in your children's lifetime; but most probably while you are still alive to witness his curse alighting on the dishonest either visibly or invisibly. Therefore, I exhort you, my brethren, ensure that all your wealth has been gained honourably and honestly. Put right anything that is wrong, and be thankful to God for all that is right.

There is a further point I want to make regarding the absence of the word 'blessing' when Isaac says, *In the fatnes of the earth sall be thy dwelling*. He seems to be saying, 'As long as you live on earth and have your dwelling here, the soil shall be fertile for you, yielding abundance of temporal goods to sustain this transient life.[35] But because you will not have the grace to thank God from whom these things come, nor will you even acknowledge that they flow from his hand, they shall never be a blessing to you. And because you will abuse his good gifts to the wantonness of your flesh, instead of blessing you, they will be a curse and will utter maledictions upon you.'

Gratitude to God incumbent upon us all

What you and I must learn is this. God desires all men and women in this world to bear witness to himself for all his goodness towards them. Without such acknowledgement, his bounties will rise up as a testimo-

[35] In verse 39, Geneva Bible has, 'Beholde, the fatnes of the earth shal be thy dwelling place, and *thou shalt haue* of the dewe of heauen from aboue'; AV, RV and NKJV have similar renderings: 'Behold, thy dwelling shall be the fatness of the earth, and of the dew of heaven from above.' But RSV (also NIV, ESV, GNB) have a significantly different translation: 'Behold, *away from* the fatness of the earth shall be your dwelling, and *away from* the dew of heaven on high,' suggesting that Esau and his progeny would be desert dwellers. See also Skinner, *in loc.*, who adopts the same translation as the later versions, 'Away from… away from…'. Baldwin comments on Esau's blessing: 'Esau was relegated to territory on the border of the desert, where farming was impossible and his highest hopes would lie in freedom fighting, and in throwing off his brother's domination' (*in loc.*). Calvin's comment on the blessing is summed up as '[Esau] chooses rather to have prosperity in the world, separated from the holy people… and voluntarily becomes an exile from the people of God' (*Commentary in loc.*). Whichever translation the reader opts for, Bruce's understanding of the text's spiritual meaning for the apostate elder son holds true.

ny against us and will accuse us of ingratitude. In effect, our ingratitude will mean that we have not in all conscience confessed to God's goodness, but can only say that we have wasted our time on earth by abusing his benefits to the wantonness of our flesh. After all, the Lord God gave us rain, he granted fruitful seasons to us as well as to our neighbours, he filled our mouths with more than sufficient corn and he caused our hearts to rejoice and be glad.[36] Yet have we been thankful towards him? Or have we paid him back with ingratitude, not recognising either him or his servant? The Lord, I say, sends all these temporal gifts to men, so that their own consciences may prepare them to stand before him on that great Day.

Therefore take heed to yourselves as to how you use these things God has created, and resolve to eschew wicked selfishness, for it is sin. Also resist the devil who does not want you ever to be thankful to God, but rather crave his grace that you will not abuse his benefits to the wantonness of your flesh, nor use them as a rope with which to hang yourselves. The provisions of his providence are blessings in and of themselves, so over and above them all, crave for that special blessing of being able to use well whatever it is that he has given you. For you will not be judged upon the plenitude of your goods, but upon the right stewardship of them.

Whoever uses well what God has given to him, according to the measure of God's grace, it shall be counted as his own. On the other hand, if your conscience testifies to you that you have abused his gifts, then it shall be your conscience that will condemn you. So whether it be temporal or spiritual blessings, ask God to grant you that other blessing of being able to redeem your past ingratitude, and from now on to steward everything you have to his glory, to the advancement of his Kirk and to the salvation of your souls.

All who have the blessed hope must purify themselves

My final point today is that Isaac blessed each son concerning things that were yet to come, not concerning things that were already physi-

[36] Every pronoun in this sentence is in the first person singular: 'me… my…' suggesting Bruce is deliberately putting words into his hearers' mouths; but as he reverts to the plural pronoun in the next sentence, I have rendered all the pronouns as plural: 'us… our…', as this flows more naturally for modern readers.

cally present; he was looking forward to what would be fulfilled after many generations. Jacob was blessed concerning the future in order that he and his descendants would depend upon God in the here and now, but also that they would by faith look and hope for the accomplishment of them in the Lord's own time. In the same way, today we have been blessed from heaven in having his gospel, therefore today while you hear his voice, do not harden your hearts.[37] I say that he has also blessed us through his ministers concerning things to come, that we too should depend upon God in the here and now, while by faith we look for the accomplishment of his blessings, waiting steadfastly in hope for their fulfilment.

As others before us constantly looked in faith for the first coming of Jesus Christ, so the Lord has appointed us in faith and hope to look for the second coming in glory of Jesus Christ, when he shall appear in the clouds accompanied by ministering angels. As our forebears looked for that Day when the Lord would make them in both soul and body partakers of his heavenly glory and award them the immortal crown that cannot not fade, so the Lord's will is that we too should look in faith and hope for eternal life in his everlasting kingdom.

Would to God that we might be able to say in our consciences, as the holy Fathers doubtless said, that our yearning is as great for his second coming as theirs was for him to be manifested in the flesh. There is no one among us whose conscience does not accuse him in this, that it rarely enters into our minds to long for Christ's second coming; we hardly think about it even once in a year, let alone earnestly yearn for it. I fear that men's consciences are disturbed and alarmed to hear tell of that coming Day. They are not at all like Jacob who looked earnestly to the future, because they have no desire to reform their ways, nor to redeem their wasted past.

Therefore, brethren, as I began so I now end. For the sake of Jesus Christ, learn to lament upon the state of your souls, to eschew the wrath to come that will be poured out on the last Day. Strive to increase your faith in the blood of Jesus Christ, and pray that the Lord would enlarge in you the hope of that eternal happiness, purchased through the righteous merits of Jesus Christ. Resist those enticements that arise within you, and seek strength from God to fight against the devil who

[37] Psalm 95:7-8.

insinuates himself into your affections, to draw you after murder, adultery and to many other sins.[38]

Seek strength from the living God to resist the devil, both inwardly worming his way into your desires and outwardly in the means he devises and uses. I lay this resolve before each of you: 'I will abstain from this ungodly act even though my heart draws me towards it, because if I yield and do it my conscience will ultimately bring the accusation against me. The evil that I did will rise up to condemn me before the tribunal of the living God.'

To make such a resolve will ensure that you have a peaceful passing from this life through God's mercy. Seek strength to resist the devil, because what may seem pleasurable to you now will in your final hour inflict upon you great pain. Whereas if your conscience says to you at your departure, 'By the grace of God I have been enabled to withstand the devil and his assaults,' then shall this witness of your conscience be a glorious testimony, and shall bring such great gladness to you that you will thank God a thousand times that he preserved you from doing wrong. And all this can only be through the righteous merits of Jesus Christ, to whom with the Father and the Holy Ghost be all honour, praise and glory now and for ever. Amen.

[38] Hewison writes: 'Scotland in 1588 was in a lamentably vicious condition, according to the indictments of the Church courts.... Many of the aristocracy were rude ruffians and irascible shedders of blood, attended by retainers barbarous to the verge of heathendom. Thirty years of the Gospel had done nothing more than illuminate the borders of darkest heathenism'. In 1592 Parliament's Act 12 sought to outlaw blood feuds being carried out in Kirk graveyards on Sundays, causing would-be worshippers to be so afraid that they stayed away from coming to hear the Gospel (p. 130). See also Chapter 11, note 13 above.

Chapter Seventeen

Hebrews Chapter 11 verse 21

[21] *By faith Jacob when he was a dieing blised both the sonis of Joseph and leaning on the end of his stafe worschip god.*

Well-beloved in Jesus Christ, from the example of Isaac and his faith, the apostle immediately proceeds to the example of Jacob and his faith. As Isaac had lived and died in faith, so Jacob also lived and died in faith. After expounding the example of the former, he adds on the example of the latter, lest we should think that the father's faith, blessings and works were sufficient to save his son Jacob. Rather, Jacob was justified through his own faith, not his father's. The just man must live by his own faith, therefore it is through my own faith that I must grasp[1] the righteousness of Christ. As to the virtues, gifts and graces of my forebears, if I myself am upright then no doubt they serve to add to my praise and commendation. But no virtues or gifts of my forebears can ever serve to aid me in my justification and salvation. Just as my father's good works cannot be the fruit of my faith, neither can his faith ever justify me. Only by my own personal faith can I be justified, and only my own good works are able to commend me before the living God.[2]

Ezekiel the prophet cites Daniel, Job and Noah to illustrate clearly this point, when he says 'they would deliver their own lives by their righteousness' (14:12-14). By their faith they would not be able to save the souls of anyone else, not even their sons or daughters. The prophet

[1] Bruce's word 'grip' is a strong word in Braid Scots and means 'seize hold of,' 'clutch' or 'take possession of' (DSL).

[2] Bruce's implication, of course, is that justifying faith will always be evidenced in good works. 'Faith without works is dead' (James 2:17).

then repeats three times that the faith of these holy men could not save the souls of others.[3] He wants us to understand that we cannot depend upon the merits of saints who have gone before us, nor lean upon their faith and works. Unless our souls are furnished with our own faith that is evidenced by good works, we shall perish without hope of redemption. The lesson he would teach us is that we must seek faith and the reformation of our souls in time, for it is faith that reforms the soul. You must begin now to send your good works to heaven, so that you will already have friends awaiting you there.[4]

The first evidence of Jacob's faith is in the effect of his blessing

So much, then, for the apostle's point that Jacob himself had faith and lived his entire life in that faith. He then goes on to demonstrate by two clear evidences that the patriarch also died in faith. His first proof is the effect of Jacob's blessing. As his father before his death had blessed him, so he blesses his sons before his own death. His father had blessed him, not concerning his life at that time, but prospectively concerning his future, so Jacob blessed his sons, not concerning their lives at that time, but also prospectively concerning events in the distant future.

Likewise, as his father's blessing had certainly offered clear evidence of his faith, so Jacob's blessings offered similar evidence of his faith. Both men by virtue of their faith pronounced blessings accurately predicting what would happen, though, if it were possible, Jacob's predictions were even more specific than his father's had been. For Jacob (like his father) only had received a simple promise from the living God regarding the heritable title of the land of Canaan—a simple promise, I say, but without actual possession of the land at that time.

At the time Jacob pronounced his blessings, he was an old man who had effectively been banished from the Land on account of famine; a serious illness had weakened his mortal body, now frail with sickness and his years of nomadic wanderings. If there was any stage in his life that his faith might have appeared to be weak, it was surely now. Yet against all expectations, in the hour of his death he gives efficacious expression to his faith with greater conviction and power than he appears to have had at any other time in his entire life. For even though

[3] Ezekiel 14:15-20.

[4] Bruce may be alluding to Luke 16:9.

he was ensconced in Egypt, far off from the land that had been promised to him and to his posterity, yet by the faith that most surely was at work in his heart, he proceeds boldly to allocate that land to his sons. He spoke as if he had been king of the land, seated on his lofty throne in Jerusalem. An undisputed monarch could not have divided out his land with more confidence than Jacob divided it among his sons.

To let you understand further the nature of his faith and the way in which it gave him the most unshakeable conviction, these lands as you already know were ultimately divided between the tribes of Israel by Joshua using lot[5] and cavil.[6] Yet now Jacob himself divides up the land, giving to each son the portion that was ultimately allotted by Joshua and the elders, as if he, Jacob, was actually seated in the council with them, seeing how the lot fell for each tribe. He did not fail in one single jot. Examine his death-bed pronouncements and compare them with the portions of the land finally allocated, and you will find that what transpired was exactly as he had spoken. Now there is nothing in this world that can be subject to greater error or hazard than making decisions by lot and cavel. Yet centuries before the division of the land took place, this holy man got the allocations absolutely right!

I say all this very deliberately that you may realise that faith is the most certain persuasion in the whole world. There is nothing on earth given to us by God that is able to engender in the human heart a more certain and firm assurance than genuine justifying faith. Therefore, if someone says that faith can only lead to unreliable and uncertain opinions, it is clear evidence that person has never experienced genuine faith. None of our human senses can bring us such assurance as the faith that springs from the surest, purest fountain there is in heaven or earth, for faith has its source in the Spirit and word of God. And what can be more reliable than the Holy Spirit and God's word?

Whoever doubts this argument proves that he has not yet become spiritual and that the true and living faith has yet to make its home

[5] Where ESV translates in Joshua 15:1; 16:1; 17:1, 'The allotment for…', GenB translates, 'This then was the lot of the children of Iudah…' and, 'And the lot fel to the children of Josephe…' and, 'This also was the lot of the tribe of Manasseh…'. Hence Bruce's statement that the land was divided 'by lot and cavel'.

[6] A 'cavell' was a piece of wood used for casting lots, and came to refer a portion of land that had been allocated by means of a cavell. (DSL 3.)

in his conscience. Therefore it is urgent that when men recognise the frailty of their personal assurance, they must pray for the entrance of the Spirit of God to multiply in them his grace and mercy. Only then by the mighty working of his Spirit will they come to the firm assurance of everlasting life through the remission of their sins, just as Jacob came to that resolute persuasion concerning the land of Canaan.

The second evidence of Jacob's faith was his worship of God as he was dying

We come now to the second evidence whereby the apostle proves that Jacob had true faith throughout his life. Shortly before he died, he worshipped God: by his outward act of bowing down he signified to his sons the great love and reverence for God that deeply lodged in his heart. Although this man was so close to death and was seriously ill, and even though he was weary and worn with great age and with the infirmity now afflicting his body, he prostrates himself as he takes on his lips the name of God to speak of his mercy and kindness,[7] that he had experienced throughout his life. The very recollection of God's goodness and mercy kindled such love within him, such a stirring within himself towards the Lord in heaven, that his emotions brought forth a veritable flame, causing his frail body to pull itself together, sit up in his bed, take hold of his staff and by the additional support of his bedhead, to kneel and bow low in prayer and worship of the One whom he loved and reverenced in his heart.

As by his blessing he expressed the great strength and power of his faith, so also by his rising from his bed and bowing down in reverence before God, he gave expression to the same faith. In this way he let his sons see how thankful he was to God, in that he must include his gratitude towards him in his rehearsal of his life's benefits. In this way he set them a good example, that whenever they should reflect upon the Lord's benefits, and upon his notable deliverances which they had experienced, they must not recall them with dry eyes, but must bow down and thank the living God for all his grace and goodness. May the Lord stir up everyone of us in our hearts, that we may never recall his benefits towards us without thanking him for them. And I pray that God will take away from us that natural deadness and hardness with which we

[7] Genesis 47:31; 48:11-12.

are born and that thrives and grows within us. I pray that God will so remove it that we will never think upon him and his mercies without our hearts melting before him.

Thus by these two evidences the apostle shows us not only that this patriarch died well,[8] having lived in faith as a godly man, but also that he passed away with an even greater faith and godliness than he had had while he lived. The Lord had taken his children from him and his wife, Rachael, whom he loved dearly; he took Joseph from him for many years, as well as the Land[9] that had been promised to him; for a time he took from him temporal blessings through famine; he then caused him to go down into Egypt, an idolatrous country; yet in his mercy, the Lord did not take his faith from him. But in spite of all the temporal things the Lord took from him, he left intact Jacob's 'Jewel of Faith'; indeed, the greater his loss of material possessions, the more this Jewel increased within him.

Now, banished as he was from his native Land and at the point of death, the Lord uses his faith to comfort him, and to grant him an even clearer vision of the heavenly city to which he was going. By faith he gave him both a sense and a foretaste of the powers of the world to come and of the joys of heaven. So through his faith the Lord upholds the heart of this poor old man in such a way that he finds more joy in the promises of faith than in all the things of this world. Yea, he has ten thousand times more joy in meditating upon these promises which the Lord held out before his faith, than he would have had if he had been given all the kingdoms on earth.

An exhortation to hold fast on faith

By faith the Lord comforted David when he was banished by Saul. By faith he sustained his servant Paul, so that he blessed the living God who does not leave his saints and servants destitute of the Jewel of Faith. Therefore, if you are deprived of temporal possessions, beware lest you be also deprived of faith. Those who have faith are never deprived of

[8] Readers will begin to realize that 'dying well' was a dominant theme in Bruce's thinking and preaching; 'a good death' is a prominent feature of this sermon. Over the following three centuries, 'dying well' became a regular subject in evangelical and reformed preaching.

[9] I am capitalizing 'Land' in this sermon as Bruce is using the word 'Land' with a particular eschatological emphasis.

consolation. Therefore strive to seek for this faith that brings so many benefits with it. For, as you have seen ever since this chapter began to be expounded to you, faith makes provision for both soul and body, delivering them from all perils. Faith brings both body and soul to that immortal kingdom, adorning both with the crown of glory. By faith we live, by faith we are righteous, and through faith we have all temporal and spiritual joys. So in whatever you do, ensure that you are never deprived of faith. The only way you may be despoiled of your faith is if you give over your body and soul to sin. Nevertheless, when we fight against sin and persevere in the battle to resist it, our faith will not be taken from us, for the plundering of our great felicity can only be done by sin.

Therefore, learn to reverence God. Guard your conscience, and be more alert to the dangers of sin than you have been until now. Abstain from all that is wrong so that you may be preserved from the despoliation of your faith; that can only happen when you turn aside into sinfulness.

Four details of the first effect of the blessing

We now return the first effect of Jacob's blessing, because there are four details regarding it that need to be considered. That takes us back to the sacred record of his blessing. First, there is the attendant fact of the one who blesses. Second, there are the details of the two young men who were brought to him to be blessed. Third, there is the significance of the time when the brothers were brought to Jacob. Fourthly, the cause and purpose for which they were brought to him must also be considered.

First, then, is the circumstance[10] as to the one who blesses. In his earlier life he was called Jacob, but thereafter his name became Israel,[11] because he had prevailed with the living God. This same man who confessed to Pharaoh, *Few and evill haue bene the dayis of my lyfe*,[12] and who was exhausted with his constant journeys and trials, that gave him little or no peace or leisure hardly to draw breath during his entire lifetime—this is the man who now blesses.

[10] Bruce's word 'circumstance' means 'detail' or 'attendant fact' or 'significance' which is how I have translated the four occurrences of it in the previous paragraph.

[11] Genesis 32:27-28.

[12] Genesis 47:9.

The second circumstance of Joseph's visit

Second, as to the two young men, we are told they are both Joseph's sons, brought to Jacob by their father. We read in Genesis 48 how Joseph while he was in court received a message that his father was sick. Without any hesitation or delay, he immediately went to visit his father, taking Manasseh and Ephraim with him. Most probably he took his sons with him because they had been born to him in Egypt, outwith the family and Kirk of God; also their mother was from an idolatrous family. Clearly, in order that Jacob might acknowledge them as two of his own descendants and of his own flesh and blood, he brought his sons to be accepted into the family which was then the visible Kirk. This indicates how godly a curator[13] Joseph was, for if he had been seeking worldly honour, preferment or riches for his sons—if this had been his plans for them—there would have been no need to leave his courtly surroundings, and to have gone to the humble dwelling where his father lay.

Doubtless at that time he would have had ample opportunity to arrange whatever advancement he wished for the young men; he had such power and influence with the king. But Joseph feared God, and being endued with godly wisdom in his heart, he considered it greater riches and esteemed it a thousand times more honour, for his family to be engrafted into the mystical body of Jesus Christ. He wanted his sons to be part of the family of the living God, members of the Kirk of God, rather than to be endowed with the dignities, honours and wealth of this world. Before a sceptre or throne, and before the fleeting attraction and riches of this world, Joseph preferred the blessing of his sons being counted faithful members of the people of God. This makes it clear that even though he had remained at court, he had not let its allurements ensnare his soul. It was truly amazing that his many years in a profane court had not changed his disposition nor corrupted his spirit. Even though he had been more than twenty years surrounded by idolatry, he had preserved in his heart a loving reverence and fear of God. We should note this carefully.

We see, then, the kind of man Joseph was. Immediately he heard

[13] A legal term meaning 'an administrator of another person's affairs either nominated in a will or otherwise, or appointed by the court. A curator to a minor, or to an idiot, is the equivalent of an English guardian.' (DSL)

his father was sick, without delay he went to him. He made no excuses as courtiers often do when they say, 'First I must ask the king's permission.' Nor did he say, 'Old men are often subject to illness; he will not die just yet.' Nothing caused him to postpone going to him. He recognised that God had laid his hand upon his father, therefore moved with love and reverence for him, he left the court to visit him. He was ready to leave the house of earthly pleasures and to go to the house of mourning to comfort his father.

The grace of visiting the sick and elderly

We read in Psalm 41:1 that those who visit the poor and weak in their illnesses are blessed by the Spirit of God. Indeed, when we comfort the sick, it is as if they are visited by the living God. Our Master plainly says so in his command to us in Matthew 25:31-40. Those who neglect the duty of visiting those who have been visited with sickness by God[14], on that Day shall be accused by Christ: *I was seik and ye visited me not.* Thus we ought to visit those who are sick.

Suppose you do not feel able to give them words of comfort, do not make that an excuse for staying away, for a sick man does not want to hear you talking, far less having to put up with you bringing him some message. Therefore, if you yourself have no word of comfort to offer, go to the sick person and find comfort from him, for often those who are unwell speak wise and perceptive words. Further, even if you feel you have nothing to say, your presence with him may well do him some good. The spirits of those who are ill are often afflicted by many temptations: they feel they can no longer be of any use in the world as they once were, or they imagine they have been rejected and no one cares for them any longer; so just by sitting with them you may comfort them. Therefore, when they are visited they are refreshed just by seeing a friend, and they recognise that God does care for them in sending them some company.

When any of your own friends, or fellow-members of Jesus Christ, are visited by him[15] either in soul or body, if you have the opportunity to call on them, go and comfort them with your presence. It does not

[14] The phrase 'visited with sickness by God' is a clear expression of Bruce's firm belief in the sovereign providences of God in every circumstance of life.

[15] See note 14 above.

matter what affliction falls upon someone, do not leave him on his own; whether it be an affliction of mind or body, do not neglect him, but go and visit him that he may be comforted. Not everyone is diseased in the same way, for the illnesses of some are not so serious as others who are very sick; but all ought to be visited.

Some illnesses are readily remedied, whereas others who have been ill for a long time have been seriously debilitated by their maladies. (I refer to maladies of both mind and body.) Indeed, because some have lost the use of their legs and have become bedridden, they have been compelled to send for medical help, which they neglected while they could still stand on their feet. Yet their case is not necessarily desperate, for they feel able to send for a physician.

A further occurrence of sickness is when a person has been bedridden for so long that he has been completely overwhelmed by his illness. Such persons have sunk into such a state of melancholy that they have not only lost the use of their legs, but they have also lost the use of both their senses and their memories. They are unable go to anyone for comfort, and are unwilling to admit anyone who wants to visit and comfort them. So serious is their sickness that they are in despair. If you are here today and are becoming unwell either in mind or body, do not neglect to seek help while there is time, for there are many cures available for both spiritual and bodily ailments.

All of us who hear of those who are ill must not neglect our responsibilities, even though we may not be sent for by the sick person. We must discharge our duty laid upon us both by nature and by the law of God. If it is quite impossible for you to visit a sick person on account of heavy commitments or work, then seek to be present with him in spirit, if not in body, by committing him and his sickness to the living God in your prayers.

A word of caution to courtiers

Joseph, then, does the part of the loving son. As soon as he sees his father, he testifies to the love and respect in his heart towards him, embracing him with his face upon his neck.[16] Yea, he pays him extraordinary reverence, as he removed his bonnet and embraced him; even though he was the most important courtier in the land, he surpassed

[16] The reference must be to Genesis 46:29, or possibly to 50:1.

the respect that his brothers gave to Jacob.

What can I say of courtiers? There are none who can give the respect and honour that is rightly due, either to God, or to the king, or to their kinsmen and friends, other than those who have the fear of God in their hearts. That is why kings should appoint godly courtiers, and ought to assure themselves that those they select do fear God, otherwise they may be sure they will be dishonoured by them. Think of those men who caused trouble in our streets this past week. Had they been indwelt with the fear of God, even with respect for men, would they have treated the king as they did, having no more regard for him than if he had been a private citizen who had no authority? How does such a thing happen? It came about partly because the king himself has been too familiar with them and so has deprived himself of his unique status, and partly because these courtiers have been educated so poorly, and have not been nurtured in the fear of God.[17]

What does this tell us? The admonishment of God is bearing down upon our prince, and if he does not take care, it will come and he will not be able to escape it. Therefore, because of the love and reverence I have for his majesty, it pertains to all of us to crave of God—I would that God would grant me such a desire—that in his mercy he would give our king eyes to see just how near to coming upon him are the Lord's rebukes; so I crave of the Lord that he will grant him extra grace now before it is too late to avoid them. It is surely a pity that his many gracious gifts are not being fully used. Therefore we must also pray that, as the Lord has already endued him with such graces (and he does know

[17] We cannot be certain what Bruce is referring to in this paragraph. It may be an incident recorded by Calderwood: 'On 7 Januar [1591] the king coming doun the street of Edinburgh from the Tolbuith, the Duke of Lennox, accompanied by Lord Hume, following a little space behind, pulled out their swords, and invaded the Laird of Logie. The king fled into a closse-head, and incontinent retired to a skinner's booth, where, it said, he fylled his breeches for fear. The querrell was, that Logie, a varlet of the king's chamber, would not ishe at the Duke's command, being chamberlane, till he was put out by force, whereupon he upbraided the duke. The Duke and Lord Hume were dischairged the court, but repaired again to it soone after.' Cald. vol. V, pp. 116-117. The same incident may be referred to when Hewison comments that the king was seen 'scuttling down shady alleys out of street brawls'. Vol. I p. 132. Some have suggested that unseemly street brawls involving the king were not uncommon, but this is the only one recorded by Calderwood that I have been able to find.

his royal responsibilities), so he would fructify these good graces within him, that he may carry out his responsibilities. Undoubtedly it is our sins that have brought this divine visitation upon him, and through him also upon us. Yet it is not his own sins so much as ours, and that is why it is we who must crave of the living God to spare him, body and soul, by granting him grace to eschew his admonishment.

The third circumstance of Joseph's visit

Thirdly, regarding the time of the visit of the courtier to his father, it also noted in this verse that it was *when he was a dieing* and was preparing to yield up his spirit, that Joseph came to him, bringing his two sons to visit their grandfather. They were both young men by this time, the younger being about eighteen or nineteen years of age. Jacob had lived seventeen years in Egypt, and they had been born there before he arrived. So he brought the two adolescents to their grandfather to see and hear him when their emotions were at their height and their manhood was beginning to blossom.

It was for their mortification and a lesson in humility[18] that they were brought to hear their grandfather. It is usual for someone's final spoken words to make a deep impression and to be long remembered, so their father wanted these two young men to have Jacob's dying words imprinted on their memories. Further, his intention was not only that they should be able to recall their grandfather's last words, but also that they should see in his face a portrait of death, so that, reflecting upon themselves and their own condition, they might realise there was no guarantee for them of a similar length of days.

They would also be warned that as the aged man was soon to leave them they could not know at what hour the living God would chap upon their shoulders. This consideration might engender in them some humility before the living God, and cause them to mortify those powerful lusts within themselves that could lead them into evil. We have a proverb, 'the lambs' skins come to the market as well as those of the old sheep'. Our sovereign Lord has determined that by the sight of some

[18] Bruce's word is 'humiliatioun', but I don't think 'humiliation' as we use the word today quite expresses his meaning. Its use in the 16th century may be understood from the following quotation: 'The sacramentis … war also ordanit for our humiliatioun' (Hamilton, Cat. 16/2).

disease in old men, and also by some sickness in young men, that we should constantly live aware of the tenuousness of our lives, and so in humility always be ready for his final call. No doubt this was one reason why Joseph brought his two sons to see their grandfather.

The fourth circumstance of Joseph's visit

Fourthly, consider Jacob sending for Joseph as soon as he fell ill, suspecting as he did that he was about to die. (He also sent for his other sons.) Because God was involved with Jacob, he also was involved with God. It was not that he was actually breathing his last, rather he was preparing for his departure, and making himself ready should the Lord chap upon him and summon him to depart. He had already made arrangements for his burial as we read in the preceding chapter,[19] therefore as soon as he realises this illness will be final, he reviews his testamentary provisions, disposes of his worldly possessions and says farewell to this earthly life. He speaks with each of his sons and bids them 'good night'. Then he yields up his soul to God, for his meditations, farewells and his final words were all inspired by the Spirit, and thus it was only heavenly and holy words that came from Jacob's dying lips.

What constitutes a 'good death'

Those of you who are stricken in years, take heed to all of this. The true wisdom within a man is apparent as he is dying. Count that person irresponsible, even foolish, who does not give evidence of wisdom in his final hour. The wisdom of which I speak can only be found in God's Book, and therefore knowledge of it is sought and found there. The reason why the way in which the Fathers died is recorded in God's Word is not so much for their praise, as for an example to commend to us dying in the fear of God. We are to follow them and so to learn to be ready, having prepared ourselves for death during the years of good health that the Lord has granted to us, just as Jacob prepared himself for death during the time when he was well.

Therefore, while the Lord grants you good health and you have ample opportunity, as it becomes you to follow the example of Jesus Christ, so prepare yourselves for the hour of your departure, and, like these holy men, meditate upon this matter. Surely you all are aware that

[19] Genesis 47:29-31.

foresight and preparation for any event—however irksome and difficult that may be—mitigates the outcome when the time comes. Being prepared to die makes the grim reaper welcome to us. But if he comes to chap on us completely unexpectedly and we are not prepared, then anguish, fear and gnashing of the soul seize us, and we are speechless. When faced with death, our trembling disturbs our memories, confuses our reasoning and robs us of our judgment. So the only wise course of action is clearly this: now, while the Lord affords you the opportunity and grants you good health, prepare yourselves for death and be ready for it when it comes.

What must we do to prepare ourselves for death? Death is the severing of the soul from the body; the soul returns to him who made it, while the body is left sleeping in the ground for a while. The affections[20] are in the soul and have their place in the heart of man. Now if your soul binds you to any earthly thing, to flesh and blood, to wife or children, to possessions or material goods, then undoubtedly death will be a most grief-stricken departure for you. For a man will be overcome by sorrow to be torn away from what he dearly loves. Therefore your preparation for your departure should concentrate mainly on whatever it is that your affection points to clearly. (This is a most important lesson, if you can succeed in putting it into practice.) So what is it that most possesses your soul? Are you addicted to some possession? Or does the love you have for your wife or children enslave you? Or is it worldly honours, riches or something else that entwines your heart? Then one day you shall perish and worldly honours and riches with you.

In order to sever your affections[21] from things that belong here in this world, you must crave the spirit of sanctification, that the desire of your heart may be love for God. So while here and now you have the opportunity, strive to direct your affections aright, that you may be able truly to say from your heart, 'I thank God that I am able to part amicably from anything that is in this world'. This would be a mighty confession if you could genuinely make it.

[20] Bruce often uses the word 'affectioun'; it has various connotations such as 'fondness', 'feelings', 'passions', 'affinity' and 'relationships'. I would suggest that here he intends it to include all five meanings, that is, the entire 'inner life' of a person.

[21] See Note 20 above.

Moreover, if the Lord grants us sanctified affections, so that we are willing to be parted from any earthly thing or person, then we may pray that whatever he takes away from us here on earth he will send up to heaven,[22] that we may find pleasure in the sight of his face. For however far down the love of earthly things may draw your souls, the love of heavenly things shall draw your souls just as far upwards. Thus death shall then be welcome to you, and you will be able to commit your wife and children to the providence of him who is taking your soul to heaven, and will be assured that he will provide for them even better than you could yourself.

Therefore, our one great aim and desire should be to wean our affections from fleshly things, that love for them might not prevent us from loving the living God. Labour then to sever your affections from this world, and even though at present your souls are constantly earth-bound and carnal, consider in your mind that your soul needs to be changed, for it ought to be spiritual.[23] Even though it is entirely our fault that we are so tied to earthly things, this new spirituality can only be granted to us through prayer. Therefore seek from God this change in your disposition until it becomes truly yours.[24]

Consider the persistence of Mary Magdalene who in her importunity came to the grave before John and Peter, and then remained there weeping long after they had left.[25] Her perseverance was rewarded by God who first sent two angels to her, and then later Jesus Christ himself appeared to her to comfort her.[26] Even if you find at first that your heart is constantly disposed towards carnal things, yet by persevering in constant prayer, you shall ultimately meet his angel sent to you, and after such a visitation you shall experience the comfort he will bring, and then you will be prepared when the final call comes to depart from this life.[27]

Learn therefore this lesson. Examine your hearts and consciences

[22] The allusion is most probably to Matthew 6:19-21, 25-33.

[23] There are constant echoes in these two paragraphs of Colossians 3:1-11.

[24] Galatians 5:16-26.

[25] John 20:1-11.

[26] Bruce has conflated two Gospel accounts: Luke 24:1-9 and John 20:11-18.

[27] Bruce here is echoing his own experience of a crucial meeting with God during the night of 31 August 1581. His account may be found in MacNicol, pp. 24-26.

and resist your carnal desires, severing yourselves from them for the sake of Jesus Christ. Rather set your affections on things that are above, lest both you and your fleshly lusts perish together.[28] So much then for the visitation of Joseph along with his sons to his father.

A final circumstance of Joseph's visit

The final circumstance concerns the reasons for which the two young men were summoned and why their father brought them, for there can be no doubting that Joseph had a specific purpose in mind. I have already mentioned that they had been born in Egypt and were so far outwith the visible Kirk. This was a dishonour to Joseph, even though the Egyptians will have considered it an honour for his sons to be born in their land. So, firstly, he brought them both to be received into Jacob's family, and thus to be made members of the visible Kirk.

This was the reason he had in mind, that his father Jacob might give them the right to be ranked along with the rest of his sons; Joseph wanted them to have their place with Reuben, Simeon and the others. By Jacob's adoption of them[29] they were to be received and made members of the visible church, for then they would not only be made inheritors of the heavenly Canaan, given freely in Jesus Christ by virtue of his work as our Mediator, but also would be heirs to the specific allotment of land in the earthly Canaan that the Lord had bequeathed to Jacob's progeny. That was the first reason why Joseph brought Ephraim and Manasseh to his father.

Secondly he brought them so that as well as this general blessing of adoption, Joseph's two sons might each also receive an individual blessing,[30] just as a blessing was bestowed on each of Jacob's sons.[31] However, before his pronouncement of their adoption, 'Ephraim and Manasseh shall be mine, as Reuben and Simeon are,' and prior to his words of blessing upon these two young men, Jacob laid down the foundation upon which stood all that he was about to utter. For the spring and fountain from whence flowed all he would say, including the blessings upon each of his twelve sons, was the covenant of grace and mercy

[28] Colossians 3:2, 6.
[29] Genesis 48:5.
[30] Genesis 48:15-16, 20.
[31] Genesis 49.

vouchsafed to his grandfather Abraham, thereafter to his father Isaac, and then finally confirmed with himself at Luz in the land of Canaan.[32] It was there, he said, that the Lord had appeared to him when this covenant of grace made with Abraham was confirmed to him, and on the ground of which his adoption of his two grandsons was declared, as well as the blessings that were to be bestowed on them and subsequently upon all his family.

We must learn this lesson that our adoption flows not from nature, nor from our deserving, but from the free promise of grace and mercy in Jesus Christ—and only through faith may we partake of it. It is the Lord himself who has made this promise freely, and who performs it freely, and it is from that free mercy arising from this freely covenanted promise[33] that our adoption comes, bringing us into the blessed progeny of Jesus Christ. This then was the sole ground of Jacob's faith, and on which he bases what he then says: 'In addition to the first confirmation of this covenant, the Lord gave me a fresh confirmation, for it pleased the Lord when I came out of Paddan-aram to renew the same confirmation and to appear to me. In that appearance he reminded me of his covenant and blessed me mightily; and so he comforted and encouraged my heart, so that all the memories of my sorrows were buried.'[34]

The believer will taste both the sweet and the bitter

It had pleased the Lord at that time to take his wife Rachel from him; thus these two events, the confirmation of the covenant and the death of his wife both occurred during the same journey. So as well as recounting the confirmation of the covenant he also tells Joseph of his bereavement: 'Your mother was taken from my arms, and I buried her on the road to Ephrath, a place that is now called Bethlehem, half a day's journey from that town.' He deliberately includes this detail during the course of his oration.

Take heed to Jacob's purpose. He mentions Rachel's death to teach Joseph what he himself had learned by experience, concerning the status and condition of God's children during this life. The Lord has

[32] Genesis 48:3-4; 35:6-15.

[33] Bruce has 'frie promeis contractit'.

[34] Jacob's reference is to the events recorded in Genesis 35:5-15.

not ordained that the lives of those who are appointed to the kingdom of heaven will be constantly the same, rather he would have their lives so seasoned and varied that at times he will mingle their endeavours with much sweat, even at other times with heartache; yet at other times he will strengthen and console them by his inner presence as he affirms to them the promise of his mercy. There will be times when he takes their 'Rachel' from their arms, even when he has just confirmed his promises to them; they have just tasted the sweet when he causes them to taste the bitter.

'Why should this be?' you may ask. It is so that you may forfeit the taste of this world and its attractions, and hold lightly[35] anything that belongs to what is beneath God's heaven, and thus that you may set your love so completely upon heaven that only the foretaste of it is truly sweet to you. This is why God mingles the lives of his children with the sour as well as with the sweet, that the things of this earth may become unsatisfying[36] to them, and only the taste of the free mercy of God in Christ Jesus should be pleasant. This is always the condition of the lives of God's servants, as you may witness in Jacob's life and in the way his successes are mingled with sorrows, the joy of the renewed covenantal promises being followed straight away by his bereavement.

Instructions regarding the burial of the godly

Jacob then speaks of the burial of Rachel,[37] wisely done by this holy man. Although he was only half a day's journey from the town, he buried her there by the wayside, and erected a pillar to mark the grave. Being such a short distance from the town, he could easily have carried her there, and, along with townsfolk gathered together, he could have buried her with greater solemnity. But he did not do that, for he did not want to bury her among the graves of the local inhabitants, but preferred the wayside where her remains would lie on their own. Rachel had been a godly and spiritual woman all her life, and she died as such, so he did not want to lay her to rest among faithless corpses.

[35] Bruce's verb is 'loth' from which our word 'loathe' is derived; but that meaning seems a little too strong here as the adjective 'loth' can mean 'reluctant' or 'unwilling'.

[36] Here Bruce's word 'taiste' has the connotation of 'offensive' or 'hostile' (DSL, *in loc.*, 1b), hence my translation of 'unsatisfying'.

[37] Genesis 48:7c.

He related this to Joseph to let him know, that although he thought so little of his own body, he did not want to be buried in Egypt. His remains were to be laid to rest in the land of promise. Surely this is the final honour we can pay to our friends, if during their life time they have been honest and godly men, by laying their remains among those of other honest men, and not among 'dogs and swine' as are the majority of people in this country. Therefore, remember that if you know your deceased friends were faithful and honest people, you must lay their remains among others who were faithful and honest. That is why Jacob wisely raises the issue of his own burial, that he may make his sons have respect to his wishes and do this final honour for his mortal remains.

Jacob's indebtedness to Joseph

Having related how his wife Rachel was not buried among the idolatrous people of Ephrath, Jacob then fulfilled his intentions, first by adopting his two grandsons and making them part of his own family. Jacob was obliged to do this, for not only was he guided by the Spirit of God and was thus fulfilling the divine will, but he was also extraordinarily indebted to Joseph. Not only was Joseph a son who had never angered him, but he had also sustained him in his old age along with his entire family; otherwise they would all possibly have perished of hunger. Yea, what else can I say? For Joseph had upheld the entire visible Kirk of God in the time of their greatest need and distress, and this for the space of seventeen or eighteen years. We see then that Jacob was more indebted to Joseph than to any of the rest of his sons.

You who have children know nature tells you that you owe it to them to fulfil your parental duties to them by making provision for them from the substance with which God has blessed you. It may be that you find yourself more indebted to one of your children than to the others, either by his particular help to you or on account of his exemplary actions. Of course it is possible that not one of your children deserves more from you than do the others. It is important in considering this that you are not influenced by blind affection, but that you see to it that your children are fairly given what each rightly deserves.

Jacob's second action after his adoption of Joseph's sons is worthy of note. He then proceeds to the individual blessing of each of his two grandsons, but in so doing, he scrutinises and examines them. His own father had sought to scrutinise him, but had failed in the attempt. Not so Jacob; for, upheld by the Spirit of God, as he subjected the two young men to his grandfatherly scrutiny, he fulfilled the holy will of God without making any mistake or being prejudiced by his special affection for one above the other. We read in the text that his eyes were dim with age so that he could not see.[38] Because of his impaired sight, we find him enquiring of Joseph as to who the young men were, for he wanted to be sure who each was.

Problems but also compensations of old age

This weakness of sight is common in old age, for as men increase in years their natural senses decay. It is true that we read of some who died before their senses began to fail. Moses lived to a great age, but his eyesight had not failed, for we read that he was 120 years old when he died, yet his sight was undimmed, and his vigour unabated.[39] Caleb likewise remained strong and vigorous in his old age.[40] Yet normally the course of nature causes men's strength and sight to fail as they advance in years. We read of this in 2 Samuel 19:32-35, where Barzillai tells David that in his old age he needed to stay at home. When the king was returning to Jerusalem after the rebellion of Absalom, this aged man went to a great deal of trouble to provide food to refresh the whole of David's company. Mindful of the loyal help he had received from the old man, the king urged Barzillai to accompany him to Jerusalem. But Barzillai answered, 'I cannot go with you, for my age is now past four score years, and my senses have failed. I can no longer distinguish between food that is savoury or plain, my deafness would hinder me from enjoying what you offer, and also my memory has gone. Because of this it would give me no pleasure to come with you, nor would my presence bring any pleasure to yourself. It is better that I stay at home and prepare myself for my death.' I remind you of this aged man to illustrate to you how in old age the senses fail.

Nevertheless, even though Jacob's physical senses had failed and his words now faltered, he was stronger in his inner senses than ever he

[38] Genesis 48:10.
[39] Deuteronomy 34:7.
[40] Joshua 14:10-11.

had been until this time. Now he saw more clearly the objectives of his faith than he had ever done before. He saw the Land that he was about to divide among his sons, and seeing also the kingdom of heaven, he knew that an angel was about to conduct his soul upwards—all this he perceived more clearly in his old age than he had in his earlier years when he was in full possession of all his faculties. Therefore, you who are old take heed that, even though on account of your advanced years your physical senses are waning, you may be able to say with Jacob, 'My inward senses have never been so fresh or green!' This is a lesson for the young as well as for the old, that as our outward faculties decay, our inward characters may grow. Then you will be able to depart from this world willingly, and be taken on to a better dwelling place.

The godly nurture of children

Back, then, to Joseph. He answers his father's question, 'Who are these?' and says, *Thir ar the childrein quhilk God gaue me quhill I was his servand.* In the Book of Ruth it is said that it is the living God who gives offspring.[41] Every faithful man and woman will agree that children are the gift of the living God, and are pledges of his favour and mercy towards them. Because we all acknowledge this, as soon as they reach the age when they are able to understand this truth, we ought to consecrate them to the living God and to his service. We also ought to be bringing them up in the fear of God,[42] and in the knowledge of their duty to God and to their king.

If you are negligent over your responsibility in this upbringing, and become unthankful to God, he will cause them to become a curse to you, a stick to beat your back. You have doubtless witnessed what a plague children can become to their parents, not least to their mothers. If she neglects her duties in raising her children, in the just chastening of God they can become a worse problem for her. So take heed, those of you who have children, that you train them carefully so that they grow up in the fear of the living God.

[41] Ruth 4:12.

[42] Bruce would never advocate that 'fear of God' is the cringing servile fear of a slave before a brutal master, but rather that 'the fear of God' is the loving filial fear and reverence of a dutiful son towards a loving father.

The unexpected order of preference in the blessings

After he had communed with his father, Joseph brought the two young men to his father and presented them to their grandfather, who embraced and blessed them, thus fulfilling the outward offices incumbent upon him. (I cannot disagree with such 'offices', for they are commendable when they are duly 'salted and seasoned', as they were in the case of Jacob.) After these introductions, Joseph took his sons and set them before his father in the order of his own preference and according to nature, the elder at Jacob's right hand and the younger at his left hand. He expected that his father would lay his left hand on Ephraim and his right hand on the older Manasseh. The right hand, as you all know, symbolises power and honour, for it is usually stronger than the left hand; no one takes your left hand to seal some promise just made. That he put Ephraim at his father's left hand indicates that Joseph was putting Manasseh before his younger brother, for it is common for the elder son to be favoured. In the case of Isaac, though there appeared to be nothing worthy of preference in Esau, yet he loved him better than Jacob. However, there is nothing here to suggest that Joseph actually loved Manasseh more than Ephraim, for I imagine that they had both been brought up well; nevertheless, to Joseph Manasseh clearly was preferred.

You will recall that when Samuel anointed David, his father Jesse apparently regarded all of his other sons to be better than David. When the prophet asked if there were any other sons, Jesse replied, *I have none bot ane that keipis scheip*.[43] So we see how he considered to be the least the very one whom God thought of most highly. This illustrates how parents tend to hold more affection for the eldest son than for the rest. But how did Jacob react? He did not move them over, but instead crossed his arms, so that his right hand rested on the head of the younger son, and his left hand on the head of the elder.

When Joseph saw that his father was not following what he himself had intended, thinking that the old man had unintentionally made a mistake or was acting out of misplaced affection, he began to correct him and tell him he was about to get the order wrong. But Jacob replied very firmly, *I knowe wel, my sonne, I knowe wel.* 'I am not acting out of

[43] 1 Samuel 16:11.

ignorance or affection, I know what I have done.' In this, Jacob indicated a much deeper faith than his father Isaac showed, for what he had done was according to the will of the God whose gifts are not given according to our natural abilities, but simply as he himself chooses. God is not bound by flesh and blood, but chooses the youngest when he pleases, or the eldest when he pleases.

Reverence God, therefore, in his actions, accept what he does as flowing from within himself and hold your peace. There are certain people who are unwilling to learn and who will not accept this lesson; they will not shut up when it is repeated to them, but grumble and complain, displaying their truculent, rebellious natures. It is better for us to accept the truth that is given to us here, and for us to acknowledge that God is not bound by nature, but that whatever he does is according to his own purpose and good will. It is according to his purposes of grace that he chooses to bestow his gifts on each one of his children.

The titles Jacob gives to God

First, note that when Jacob proceeds to give the blessing, he is not content simply to say, 'The Lord bless you,' rather he begins by using three different titles[44] for the Lord: *The Lord* (says he) *befoier quhom my foirbearis walkit, the god* (says he) *that sustained me all my lyfetyme, the great angell that preserved me from all evillis and dengeris of bodie and saull, bliss thir thy childrein*. Take note of these precise words and succinct sentences he uses in these three titles:[45] 'The Lord before whom I walked all my days, the God who fed me all my lifetime, the great angel who preserved me from all perils and dangers of both body and soul, this God bless these children!'

That he conjoins this 'Angel' with the living God makes it clear that the 'Angel' is no human being, for he ascribes to this Being divine attributes that he would never have used of any mortal. We must therefore conclude that this third title refers to a divine being, who must have been Jesus Christ, the Son of the living God. He deliberately makes this reference to *the great angell* as he pronounces the blessing, for Christ is the author of the reconciliation bound up in that blessed

[44] Bruce's word is from the law courts: 'styll' means 'a form or order of words acceptable in a court of law' (DSL).

[45] See Note 44 above.

seed. Therefore he correctly makes mention of the Angel in this covenantal blessing, for there is no blessing without Christ, and all blessings are to be found in him.[46]

Second, notice how he attributes to the living God all the good that he has ever experienced, as if he had never achieved any benefit by his own effort, as if he had been an idle fellow without any gifts at all, but whom God had found. However, in the sacred record we may perceive that he was the most hard-working man you could ever meet. For twenty years he served in Laban's house, not sparing his body in the intense heat of the day, nor caring for his personal comfort throughout the nights of bitter frost, and all this faithfully to serve his master Laban.[47] Yet when it came to the final reckoning, all this he counted as nothing,[48] but ascribed all his successes as coming from the hand of the living God, just as if he had received it direct from him.

Jacob knew well that whatever hard work we engage in, it is only when God blesses us in our work that our efforts become profitable. It was the same with all his travails: it was the Lord who had blessed him in them and so he also ascribed his trials to God as blessings. There is no one who struggles faithfully in his calling, all the while depending wholly upon God and attributing every trial to his providence, who will not experience God's blessing descending upon him, as if it came directly from his divine hand. So learn to discern God in his gifts and benefits, and as you receive them give him thanks for them.

Third, he does not simply say, 'the God who led me and before whom I walked', but 'and before whom my forebears walked'. It is an honour to have praiseworthy forebears, who themselves in body and spirit have been led and guided by the living God; therefore, when that is our experience, we must resolve to follow as they followed, and to persevere in walking in their steps. For us not to follow those who in

[46] Calvin also understands the 'Angel' as being the pre-incarnate Christ: 'Wherefore it is necessary that Christ should be here meant, who does not bear in vain the title of Angel, because he had become the perpetual Mediator. And Paul testifies that he had become the Leader and Guide of the journey of his ancient people (1 Corinthians 10:4).' See below Chapter 23, p. 442: '…the Lord sends his Great Angel Who has the name of God engraved upon him…' (comment on Exodus 14:19).

[47] Genesis 31:38-42.

[48] Philippians 3:7-8.

body and spirit have been guided by God is to dishonour them by not imitating their example, for the same pathway and footprints that led them to a blessed departure will lead you also.

Joseph given part of Reuben's inheritance

Now if Joseph had returned home empty-handed, he might have considered his visit had been disappointing, and have wondered if it had been a waste of time[49]. But there was no way his father would allow him to go away without a legacy, for he gave him the testament of an inheritance that remained with him his entire life. He gave Reuben's portion to Joseph;[50] by his birthright as the eldest son, Reuben ought to have received a double portion, but Jacob took it from him and gave it to Joseph. He did not give all the privileges of the birthright to Joseph, only the double portion, for we must understand that there were three special privileges that went with the birthright. First, the eldest inherited greater wealth than the others, for his inheritance was to be a double portion, while his brothers received only single portions. Although this was before the Law was given, it was confirmed in the Law (Deuteronomy 21:17). Second, the birthright also gave the eldest son rule and dominion over his father's other sons. Third, the role of priest in his father's house was bestowed upon the eldest; he was to be the teacher of the others to instruct them in the fear of God. However, Joseph was given the double portion, whereas the rule and dominion was passed over to Judah[51] and the priesthood to Levi;[52] consequently what was due by birthright to Reuben was divided between Joseph, Judah and Levi.

Reuben had forfeited his rights on account of his wicked action, for he had lain with his father's concubine, and so he deprived himself of the privileges that were his by virtue of being born the eldest. Reuben would never have suspected that his father had remembered his former sin, committed twenty-four or twenty-six years previously, especially since then he had done some good things such as saving Joseph from being killed.[53] He would never have expected his father to have kept in

[49] Bruce has, 'he micht haue fund falt with it'.

[50] Genesis 48:22; see also 49:4a, 'Unstable as water, you shall not have pre-eminence…'. Also compare 48:22 with the LXX of 49:26.

[51] Genesis 49:8c.

[52] Deuteronomy 10:8-9.

[53] Genesis 37:22, 29.

his mind what he had done so long ago, but it was the Spirit of God who brought it to mind in Jacob, for the Spirit says that when there is no repentance our sins are remembered. Every sin that we hold on to and will not repent of will bring shame upon us. Even if you think they will be overlooked and forgotten about, when it comes to the final crunch, if you have not repented of them, they will cover you with shame.

A final appeal

Then learn this lesson with which I conclude. Because God neither forgets our former sins nor rids our consciences of them, apart from the cleansing blood of Jesus Christ, may that truth constrain us to repent from the depths of our hearts, and to sorrow over our past sins even more than we once took pleasure in them. Therefore, each one of you examine your past lives, and see wherein you have offended God in your youth, and while there is still the opportunity, repent of your past. Then your conscience will be able to say to you, 'I clearly know that at one time I indulged in this particular sin, but I thank God that now just as clearly I know I have sorrowed over it, and I am certain of his mercy through Jesus Christ, for whose sake all my wrongdoings are buried.'

When you have this testimony, your conscience will be clear, and will remain with you to accompany you to that everlasting glory. May the Lord in his mercy bury my sins and yours, and bring us to crave his mercy now while we are here on earth, that on the Final Day we may be clothed with Christ's righteousness and holiness. May he give us grace to seek this in Christ's righteous mercy, while we still have time. To whom with the Father and the Holy Ghost be all honour, praise and glory, now and forever. Amen.

Chapter Eighteen

Hebrew Chapter 11 from the middle of verse 21

> [21] *Leaning on the end of his staf worschiped god.* [22] *By faith Josephe when he died maid mentioun of the depairting of the childrein of Israell and gave commandment of his bonis.*

Well-beloved in Jesus Christ, as you heard the last day, the apostle demonstrated how Jacob, the father of Joseph, had been a man of steadfast faith who had lived and died trusting in God's promises. The apostle proved this by selecting two particular outcomes of Jacob's works which showed clearly, as in a mirror, both the greatness and excellence of his faith. We saw in my last sermon how he dealt with the first outcome, as God gave me grace and as time allowed. It now remains for us to consider the second outcome whereby Jacob's faith was displayed to the world.

As you heard last time, the man being very aged, and already carrying the death of his body about with him, worn out as he was with great trials and afflicted by various maladies, it pleased the Lord who had used Jacob's ministry throughout his life, now that he was approaching his death, to lay upon him a new and final commission. It was at this point that God sent his Spirit into his heart in even greater measure than he had done throughout the patriarch's life, and through the Holy Spirit working mightily within him, instructed the old man as to the directions he should give to his sons. Equipped with this word from Almighty God, even though he no longer had physical strength to move his frail body, by the power of the Holy Spirit he was enabled to sit up and slide his legs over the side of his bed. As a gesture of reverence, he attempted to stand but as his legs could no longer take his weight, he remained seated on the edge of the bed. Leaning back on his bolster, he took hold of his staff in his right hand.[1]

Jacob prepares to deliver the commission he has been given

Sitting up as straight as he could, he began to utter the words of the commission he had been given, which concerned the will of the living God for each of his sons.[2] The posture he had adopted by God's enabling was the nearest he could get to show his reverence for God and his word. It was then, and still is, the custom of God's servants, prophets and ministers, who had been given a word to deliver from God, to show their reverence by standing on their feet; likewise, those to whom the word was addressed also stood as they listened.

We know that this was the custom because we find it recorded in several passages of Scripture. One such place is Numbers 23 where we find Balaam, the false prophet, coming to curse the people of God; but extraordinarily, against his intentions he was compelled to bless them; the Spirit of God came upon him with superior force, and caused his cankered and disobedient heart to yield to the divine purpose.[3] So the mighty power of the Spirit controlled the heart of Balaam, and returning from the presence of God he said, 'Rise, Balak, and hear; give ear to me: God is not man that he should lie…'.[4] These words verify my proposition that as a sign of reverence it was the custom to stand to hear the word of God.

Examples of standing to deliver and hear God's word

There are other examples of this such as in Judges 3:19-20. When Ehud came to slay Eglon king of Moab, finding him 'sitting alone in his cool roof chamber, he said to him, "I have a message from God for you". And he arose from his seat.' The king hearing that there was a message for him from God, even though he was not a believer but was a profane king, motivated by reverence, he rose from his throne and came near to hear Ehud. So this standing up has always been a sign of reverence.

[1] Genesis 47:31; 48:2; Hebrews 11:21.

[2] Genesis 49. For a full recent exposition of Genesis 49 and Jacob's distribution of the land between his sons, see *Joseph*, pp. 177-234.

[3] Numbers 24:2.

[4] Numbers 23:18.

Further, in 2 Kings 22 we read how the Book of the Law was found and was read to King Josiah. The king then gathered the elders and priests in the House of God and he stood and read in their hearing all the words of the Book of the Covenant; the people stood to listen.[5] Likewise, during the reign of Joash, we read how Zachariah was clothed with the Spirit of God, and stood above the people to deliver the Word of God to them.[6] Yet again in Nehemiah we read how Ezra stood on a wooden platform to read the Book of the Law, and as he opened it all the people stood.[7] I quote all these incidents so that you can see it was the custom to stand as a sign of reverence when the Word of God was declared to the people.

Back to Jacob. The old man was moved with this reverence, and having the voice of the Spirit of God within himself, he accordingly adjusted his physical posture as far as he was able by rising from his bed, sitting himself on it and using his staff to steady himself. This is recorded in Genesis 47:31. Also in 49:33 we read how after he had completed his final commission and ended his words to his sons, he drew up his feet into the bed and died.[8] He had adapted the reverent act of rising to speak God's word according to the frailty of his failing body.

After he had delivered his will and testament[9] and had given to each son the appropriate reproof or blessing, to conclude his commission and to mark the end of his earthly life he turned himself as best as he could towards the bedhead, and leaning upon the end of his staff, he bowed down to thank and worship the living God who had given him strength at that time to discharge his instructions to his sons. He also thanked the Lord for the increase of his grace upon his soul in this hour of greatest need. He thanked God as well for the evidence of his favour in causing Joseph to agree so readily to his request.[10] And so before he

[5] 2 Chronicles 34:31-32.

[6] 2 Chronicles 24:20.

[7] Nehemiah 8:4-5.

[8] See also the sermon's text, Hebrews 11:21. In his description of Jacob's movements, Bruce has apparently conflated these three references.

[9] Several times in this sermon Bruce uses the expression 'his letter will'. The usual older Scots term was 'settlement', whereas 'will' was an English term; but Bruce, after graduating with a Master's degree in St Andrews had studied Law at the Belgian College in Louvain, where he would have gained knowledge of English Law; hence his use of the term 'will'.

[10] The reference is to Genesis 47:29-31, when Joseph swore he would bury his father in Canaan and not in Egypt.

breathed his last, he ended his life by leaning upon his staff and worshipping God. This I take to be the meaning of the apostle.

An apparent difference between Genesis 47:31 and Hebrews 11:21

It is true that the words of our text differ from the original Hebrew as they are recorded in Genesis 47:31. Therefore I understand the apostle's form of words to be an explanation of the original; I mean our text in Hebrews 11:21 serves as an exposition. In Genesis it says that *he turned him toward the bedhead and worschiped*, that is, he gave thanks for the reasons I have just mentioned. In the original Hebrew (as the points are placed[11]) there is no mention of a staff that he was leaning upon; he simply says that he turned towards the bedhead. Therefore I take it that the apostle has added a word to elucidate the original, and to explain to us how it was that such a frail, sickly man was able to turn himself about; he needed all the help he could get to manipulate his dying body to make this move.

Even if at times there is a slight difference in the words, there is no difference in the meaning of the sentence. Whatever the Spirit of God says to Moses, and then says to Paul,[12] he does not contradict himself. In Genesis 47 the Spirit means that Jacob bowed down and worshipped. That is essentially the same as the meaning in our text of the old man leaning on his staff to bow down and worship; both the apostle and Moses bear witness to this worship.

However, neither of them mean that he worshipped or adored the head of his staff. Nor do they mean that he worshipped Joseph or Joseph's robe. Therefore, because the meaning of the Spirit is preserved, it does not behove us in curiosity to dispute over words or argue over syllables. It is true that the translators of the Septuagint use the same form of words as the apostle,[13] so it would appear that the seventy scholars used the original un-pointed[14] Hebrew text; had these translators

[11] In Hebrew the vowels are added under the consonants as small 'points' or symbols to aid the reader's understanding of the text.

[12] Bruce is assuming that Paul is the author of the Letter to the Hebrews.

[13] LXX for the final phrase of Genesis 47:31 has, καὶ προσεκύνησε Ισραηλ ἐπὶ τὸ ἄκρον τῆς ῥάβδου which is exactly the same as that of the apostle except that Hebrew 11:21 uses the name Ιακωβ. It would appear that the apostle is quoting from the LXX.

[14] See Note 9 above.

used the pointed Hebrew text, no doubt they would have rendered 'staff' as 'bedhead', for when the points are removed 'staff' can be read as 'bedhead'.

However, what I said a moment ago still stands: the form of words the apostle used is not to be discarded, for the true meaning intended by the Spirit of God is retained. These translators always kept the sense and meaning of the original author, and even though the actual words may vary, they are not misleading. On the other hand, if they were to introduce some meaning and exposition of their own devising that was contrary to the original wording, then they would be liars and false interpreters and their translation would have to be rejected. Whoever brings in a meaning of his own that the Spirit of God never intended, and interprets the author's words divergent to his meaning, clearly introduces lies and error instead of the truth. Therefore whenever the Greek departs from the sense and meaning of the Hebrew, or the Latin from the meaning of the original Greek, then such Latin and Greek mistranslations must be rejected, and we must have recourse to the correct meaning of the Spirit of God, as given to us in the original texts.

Mistranslation to allow adoration of relics

Why do I say all this? Firstly, because certain uneducated[15] interpreters and translators of the New Testament have perverted the meaning of these words that we have been considering, and have changed what God had said, as recorded in the original Greek. For the meaning they give is that when Jacob had finished speaking he then adored the head of his staff. Hence the meaning intended by the Spirit of God is wholly perverted. To depict Jacob adoring his staff's head instead of adoring his God is plainly a complete departure from what the words mean.

Those of you who wish to compare what the apostle and Moses wrote (as translated in the Septuagint) with how these ignorant translators render the words, will at once see that the preposition επι (it means 'upon' 'towards' or 'against') has been deliberately omitted, though it is needed to give the true meaning. So it is clear that the so-called

[15] Bruce's word is 'vulgar', but although it had the connotation of 'common' or 'vernacular speech', it also was used of elementary education in reading and writing in Scots and not in Latin; thus a *vulgar schole* meant an elementary school. (DSL 4.)

translator has not done his duty, for he has deprived the sentence of the Spirit of God's intended meaning.

I can only conclude that this omission has been made by the papists who had the custody of these books at that time with the purpose of legitimising the adoration of material things, or else so that they might give permission to bow down and worship before[16] created things. This interpretation implies that the Old Testament practice of falling down on one's face before the ark of the covenant, or before the tabernacle, or on the Mount, is still appropriate today.[17] Therefore they conclude that it is still right to fall down before created things and worship them. However, note firstly that there is a great difference between worshipping material objects on the one hand, and on the other hand falling down before an object such as the ark which represented the presence of God; that was not wrong. But if we worship some created object instead of the Creator, we do wrong, for that is idolatry.

Secondly, because it was right to worship when the cloud descended upon the tabernacle does not justify falling down before the crucifix, or before relics or other images. There was divine warrant for worshipping God before the tabernacle, but there is no warrant for worshipping before a crucifix, a relic or any other image; this kind of adoration is nothing more than idolatry. It is true that these practices that take place in popish churches took some time before they became accepted.

That did not happen immediately the first time it was done, nor even after a year. For those who first introduced images into the church were forbidden the adoration of them as can be seen in Gregory's Seventh Book.[18] Even if he consented to these objects being displayed in

[16] Bruce has 'to fall doun, at, besyde and befoir creaturis.'

[17] Exodus 33:10; 1 Samuel 5:3-4; 2 Samuel 6:5-11.

[18] Most probably Gregory the Great: 'For it is hence that Moses, coming from the wilderness, encounters the king of Egypt with authority, saying, *Thus saith the Lord God of the Hebrews, How long wilt thou refuse to humble thyself before Me? let My people go, that they may serve Me* [Exod. 10, 3]; and when Pharaoh, being driven hard by the plagues, said, *Go ye, sacrifice to your God in this land* [Exod. 8, 25]; he thereupon answered with increased authority, *It is not meet so to do; for we shall not sacrifice the abominations of the Egyptians to the Lord our God*... It is hence that when proud Ahab, being bowed down to the service of idols, ventured to upbraid Elijah, saying, *Art thou the man that troubleth Israel?* [1 Kings 18:17]; Elijah forthwith struck the foolishness of the king in his pride with the authoritativeness of a free rebuke, saying, *I have not troubled Israel, but thou and thy father's house,*

churches, he forbade the worship of them. But little by little over a period of time, the adoration of relics and images became accepted, until it was regarded as permissible to adore them with the measure of adoration that was held to be competent to each object. The papists even gave it a name, calling it 'dulia'.[19] This was very different from the adoration and honour that is proper to the living God.

Some time later, a new Pope[20] was appointed and he permitted worship that was due to God alone to be offered to relics and images. For as you may read in that book they call 'The Pontifical', it is laid down that the cross in their great procession with the emperor, pope, papal legate and cardinals,[21] ought to go in front of the emperor's sword, but on its right side. So you see that this gross idolatry they now practise in place of the true worship of the living God, was not introduced at once, but some time later. For the devil does not in an instant blind men's eyes, so that he causes them immediately to set up a stone statue[22] in place of the Creator. It is not possible for the devil to extinguish the natural light in us in one stroke, by persuading us to give to some created thing the adoration that is due to God alone. However, it is true that if I decide to listen to him and follow him, allowing him to confuse my mind, he will succeed in blinding me and turning into darkness the light that was formerly in me. I shall then end up robbing God of the honour and worship due to him by giving it to some creature.

---

in that ye have forsaken the commandments of the Lord, and have followed Baalim [ver. 18]. *Moralia in Job*, Book 7, [xxxv]. 53. Readers may be interested to know that Calvin wrote of Gregory I with great appreciation and approval, probably the only Pope he ever commended. See for example. *Inst*. IV.7.4.

[19] In Roman Catholic theology, 'dulia' is 'veneration and invocation given to saints'.

[20] Possibly Pope Leo III (Pope from 795 to 816). The 'Pontifical' mentioned in the next sentence would have been a papal decree, and the honour given to the emperor sounds very much like the gratitude due to Charlemagne by Pope Leo III. Protected from his enemies in Rome (partisans of the late Pope Adrian I) by Charlemagne, Leo had strengthened the emperor's position by crowning him Holy Roman Emperor and 'Augustus of the Romans'.

[21] Bruce's word is 'conveint' [those convened] meaning a gathered assembly; as well as cardinals, it may also have included lesser clerical officials.

[22] Bruce's word is 'stok' which had a wide variety of meanings ranging from log to stone pillar to a headless corpse! (DSL) It is possible that he used 'stok' intentionally in its most derogatory sense.

Warning against the spirit of error

The Lord can abandon people to their own devices, so that as the spirit of error blinds them they become increasingly apostate, until ultimately they are not ashamed in either their writings or their deeds to give to created beings the very honour that ought to be given to God. I find no pleasure in saying this, but I have to speak out so that we will beware of the devil and the manner in which he tries to enter[23] our thinking. It is easy enough to resist him when he first seeks an entrance, but it is not so easy to get rid of him once he has gained a foothold in our minds.

It is the same when we resist some vice and the temptation remains fresh and green in our hearts, before it has won over our wills. But once the temptation has conceived and given birth to our agreement, and all that is lacking is the opportunity, the moment when circumstances make the sin possible, then we will not rid ourselves of the danger as easily as when it originally was suggested to our minds. When we begin to commit the sin, both our souls and bodies become its slaves, and when such slavery could previously have been avoided by prayer, now it has become too late and we have become servants of sin. As Jesus says in John's Gospel, *he that commitis sin is the servand of sin.*[24]

Peter says, *of quhomsoevir man is ovircum he is his servand.*[25] But you are overcome by your lusts when you indulge their appetite for wickedness. For though you may have been free before, now you have become enslaved, and from this slavery there is no redemption, unless the efficacy of the blood of Christ is applied and the devil is cast out. Then your heart that had given place to the devil will be sanctified again. So I say, that just as it is with our fleshly, heinous sins that we commit against both body and soul, so it is with spiritual whoredom and idolatry. If we resist the devil when he begins to seek entrance[26] and we persevere in calling upon the Lord for grace, he will answer and enable

[23] Bruce's actual phrase is, 'be warr of the devil in the *entrie*'; he uses this word five times in the next couple of paragraphs to refer to the devil's stratagem of gradually beginning his temptations. Interestingly, Gregory also uses the same word in the same context: '…when the mind is lifted up at the very first step of its progress, and when it already exalts itself as on the ground of its virtuous attainments, it opens an *entrance* to the adversary…', *Moralia* Bk 7, [xvii] 20. See Note 18 above.

[24] John 8:34.

[25] 2 Peter 2:19, 'For whatever overcomes a person, to that he is enslaved.' (ESV)

[26] See Note 23 above.

us to eschew those spiritual errors. On the other hand, if we dally[27] with the devil's enticements, the result will be that we will start following the allurements of our fallen natures. For false religion appeals particularly to our human natures in that it involves our outward, bodily senses, and entangles them.

It is when we begin to give in to these corporal inducements that they lead us astray into such whoredom that the spirit of error has us in his grip, and it becomes no longer possible to believe the truth. When error finds a place in our hearts, it can only lead us into more error. However, when the Spirit of truth occupies a man's soul, he[28] will not suffer him to be taken in by lies and falsehood, but will increasingly confirm him in the truth so that he comes to realise he must believe it alone. Therefore, the crucial time is when the assault upon our souls is first initiated: at that point we must refuse to give ear to false doctrine, and shut our ears to the devil's voice. Because when you hear his suggestions, he will not at first entice you into offering adoration to created things, but then he will gradually draw you on into veneration of relics and images, until he causes you little by little to rob God of his honour. This is as far as I will go in opening up for you the meaning for today of Jacob leaning upon the head of his staff.

Constant thanksgiving is due to God

For your further instruction, I want briefly to mark here two other points. Regarding this holy man, the first is that he concluded all that he had said and done with thanksgiving to the living God. This had been his wont in all his various deliverances, as from time to time throughout his life he had experienced them: he praised and thanked God for all his benefits. Now in his final breath he will not neglect this duty, but by the outward posture of his body he would have his feelings acknowledge his gratitude to God. Thus at this crucial moment, just before he is about to yield up his spirit, in the presence of his sons he bows down and worships God.

This would be a most excellent lesson for us if only we could learn

[27] See Note 23 above. Bruce phrase here is, 'If thou give ear to him in the entrie…'. The fifth occurrence of 'entrie' in the next sentence was tautological and did not require inclusion in the translation.

[28] Clearly by 'the Spirit of truth' the Holy Spirit is meant, hence the masculine pronoun.

it; it would be an admirable example for us to follow, if in every circumstance we could offer praise and thanksgiving to God; for all of our of our lives—every moment, every hour, every day—are blessed with some special benefit from God. For if we were constantly thanking the living God, then as we had lived so should we die. Why are we unaccustomed to thank and praise the Lord? The reason is that our hearts are not touched with any feelings for his kindnesses, nor have we the eyes to see whence flow all his abundant blessings; because we are blind in our minds and our stony hearts are as hard as flint, we take for granted his infinite store of benefits and never bow low before him in worship. Our souls quickly swallow up the judgments of God without fear or reverence and his mercies without gratitude. We ignore both his judgments and his mercies without any reaction, either of fear for the one or gratitude for the other.

We remain unaffected because we have not taught ourselves to lift our eyes heavenward to God, and so we do not acknowledge that everything we have has come to us through his mercy. Whereas if we would learn constantly to look to heaven, we would acquaint ourselves with God's actions, and we would see how all that takes place flows from his gracious providence. Once we have recognised his love, no chastening of God would be visited upon us without our bowing before him; nor would there be any cross laid upon the Kirk that would not cause us to abase ourselves. Likewise, neither would there be any mercy bestowed upon the Kirk that would not bring tears to our eyes and melt our hearts in thankfulness.

What else can I say other than to exhort you to beseech God that he would banish the deadness, false security and stubbornness that is in the hearts of us all, and that in his mercy, since there has been some moving in our souls through his quickening Spirit, the Lord would touch us in some measure with the awareness of both his chastening and his mercies. Thus, being affected in this way, we may patiently accept his discipline whenever it alights upon us, and thank him that it has been applied to us. So may the Lord graciously work! Otherwise all this teaching and exhortation will most certainly serve nothing but to add to your sorrow in the day of his righteous judgment—unless, that is, this word becomes spirit and life to you. For unless his word becomes effectual in you, and you begin to live by it and practise it, it had been better that you had never heard the evangel preached. I beseech the living God that this word that I bring to you may be clothed in such power that it will be effective for my and your everlasting salvation. This far, then, for my first point.

Purifying ourselves in the hope of heaven

The other point I perceive regarding Jacob is this: I mark his great care and exceeding concern to wean his sons' hearts away from Egypt. Even though God's timetable[29] rendered him unable to have them leave the country at that time, for the hour of their deliverance had not yet approached, nevertheless he clearly displayed his desire for their ultimate departure. He wanted their hearts and minds to be separate from the lifestyle of the Egyptians, and so he exhorted them always to remember the land of Canaan, and in faith and expectation to depend upon the Lord until he gave them the opportunity to return there. The old man knew well the dangers of evil company and the perils of living among idolaters. He also knew the depravity of human nature, and how the greatest part of us remains immersed in corruption; he knew too that corruption loves corruption so that an evil environment will affect the best soul that ever lived.

Therefore, Jacob utters his profound concern regarding this, that his sons might beware of associating with idolaters and being influenced by their manner of living. He prays they may sanctify their hearts and minds, and associate themselves with their own people; even though they were daily bound to rub shoulders with idolaters, they should keep their own religion and in their hearts guard their form of worship, in order that they might retain the favour and smile of God upon them. Countries, whole nations and individual people know from experience how hard it is to live within an evil culture and not be contaminated by it. However well-disposed your soul might be, and even though to begin with you were grieved by their customs and talk, yet residing continually in the midst of evil company you are bound to become like them.

Suppose you begin by sorrowing over their filthy conversation, little by little you will become accustomed to it, and by the sheer force of depravity you will find yourself accepting what they say, and soon you

[29] Bruce has 'dispensation'.

yourself will become like those around you. Ultimately, you will enjoy whatever villainy they practise. Indeed, the more serious and modest a person you are, the longer you participate in evil company, the deeper their sinful attitudes will take root within you, and the harder it will be to extract them from your gentle and quiet nature. It will be even more difficult than removing these roots of evil from the most obstinate person on earth. Therefore of all evils on this planet, unsavoury company is the most dangerous of all.

Prayer needed against the evil company among courtiers

This is true for every member of our commonwealth, and that applies to us all whatever may be our status in this land. Here in our country we have experience of this in the bad influence of our nobles and lords. Some of us have experience of the dangers that have beset both our Kirk and the common folk on account of the evil company our king enjoys.[30] So we must crave of God that he would not only sanctify us so that we delight in good company and flee from evil, but especially when our temporal prosperity is so dependent upon the king's prosperity, that the Lord would so sanctify his heart by his Holy Spirit, that he will delight only in the companionship of those who set the will of God before their eyes.

There are many things done that we would prefer not to be done, and there are many things left undone that ought to have been done. However, the point is always this: on the one hand there appears to be nothing more powerful than godliness, and on the other hand nothing more powerful than wickedness; the same goes for evil company versus godly company. These are in opposition. So I leave Jacob and verse 21 and now turn to Joseph and verse 22 of our text.

Joseph lived and died in faith

Verse 22 reads, *By faith Josephe when he died maid mentioun of the depairting of the childrein of Israell and gave commandment of his bonis.* These words let us see that Joseph not only lived by faith in God, but also died in that faith and the religion of God. Even though his father loved him dearly and bestowed on him a great blessing, yet that blessing was not the cause of his salvation, nor the means of his justification.

[30] See Chapter 17, note 17 above.

Rather was it Joseph's personal faith that was instrumental in both his justification and salvation. After Jacob, therefore, the apostle brings in Joseph, giving him his place as seventh in the list of the men of faith.[31]

This is the man to whom the Lord gave a particular part of Reuben's birthright, for it pleased the Lord to displace Reuben who was the eldest, and to divide his portion among his brothers, though he gave Joseph a double share, for he had found favour in God's sight. This is the same man whom the Lord had sent down beforehand into Egypt, to provide for his Kirk in time of famine. This is also he who lived among idolaters for so many years in Pharaoh's court, yet as far as we know was in no way affected by the errors surrounding him.

Concerning Joseph's justifying faith

Thus the apostle tells us that he died in faith, as did his forebears before him. The apostle proves this with two conclusive[32] arguments. First, he brings before us the confession uttered by Joseph before he died: it was a prediction regarding the accomplishment of God's promise made to his ancestors and renewed to him. He foresaw this fulfilment of the promises as if he had actually seen them with his physical eyes, and gazed upon them. Therefore he was moved to assure his brothers of this, and to pass on to his sons this same assurance. This confession that issued in a prediction of their future deliverance is the apostle's first argument.

His second argument regarding the reality of Joseph's faith is set down at the end of our verse, where he issues the command to his brothers that when it pleased God to visit and deliver them so that he could bring them back home to the land of Canaan, they must remember about his bones. He instructed that they should be kept safe in a kist,[33] and taken with them back to the land of Canaan. So he gave them his remains to be a pledge and surety, as it were, that their deliverance by God would certainly come to pass, and his bones would

[31] Bruce simply states: 'Josephe and his place in the sevint roume'. He means that he is seventh coming after Abel, Enoch, Noah, Abraham, Isaac and Jacob in the apostle's parade of men of faith in Hebrews 11:4-22; 'roume' can mean 'a particular or allocated space' (DSL. 5).

[32] Bruce has 'by two infallibill argumentis'.

[33] Scots word still used today, meaning a large chest used for safe-keeping of things or personal belongings.

be retained as a guarantee. He was not asking them to convey his body to Canaan as was his father's body, rather his remains were to be kept in a tomb beside them to remind them of what he had said. Thus the apostle brings this second argument to demonstrate Joseph's faith to us, and to prove that he died in faith as did his ancestors.

This detail[34] regarding his last words lets us see how he died in faith, for it said of Joseph (as it was said of Jacob) that he spoke these words when he was on the point of death. He had said farewell to his position of honour and dignity, and bidden his kinsmen 'goodnight'. Now that his heart was stripped of all earthly and fleshly things, his mind and soul were about to be lifted up to heaven, and there issued from this godly man naught but holy feelings, holy thoughts and considerations. His heart being full of faith and of the Spirit, he spoke these words clearly to his brothers. So we see that what he said flowed from faith, and that the Holy Spirit was working in him at the hour of his departure.

Three points regarding justifying faith

Before I proceed any further, and in order that every detail of the verse may be conveyed to you with its own particular instruction, I also perceive here a little more regarding the nature of justifying faith. I mention three points.

First, when we are given, as it were, an eye in our minds, whereby we are enabled to see spiritual things yet to come such as the life everlasting, then faith is working belief in our hearts along with the assurance that we shall one day be partakers of heavenly things; when it pleases the Lord to call us from this life, we shall have the use and enjoyment of the eternal blessings. Not only does faith impart this guarantee to us and for us, but it also imparts the guarantee of these promises that will not come to fruition in our lifetime, but will be fulfilled during our children's lifetime for their benefit. It granted a surety in the hearts of the holy Fathers that even if these temporal promises were not to be fulfilled for them in their lifetime, yet they saw that the promises would become effective for their posterity in their lifetime. Thus the nature of faith is not only to give personal assurance to us, but also an assurance of the same things promised to our children.

Faith let the Fathers see these things, faith empowered them to

[34] Bruce's word is 'circumstance' on which see above, Chapter 17, Note 10.

believe these things and faith enabled them to rejoice and to exult at the sight and feeling of them, as if they had touched them with their hands and seen them with their own eyes. Therefore we can say that faith gives to men a foretaste of the sweetness of those benefits that the Lord has to bestow. Even though these holy men did not see these blessings with their physical eyes, by faith they rejoiced as if they had been spectators of their fulfilment.

The second thing I perceive is that all these Fathers, Abraham, Isaac, Jacob and Joseph died the same way, for they all died in faith. I also see that these holy men saw the same things that were to come upon their posterity. Not only did they foresee them, but each of them foretold them, and as they did so they themselves, as it were, felt them and rejoiced at the sight of them.

The third thing I perceive is that there was such harmony in these holy Fathers in their faith that not one of them is different from the others, but they conspire to speak with one voice, the son confirming the testimony of the father, and the father confirming the testimony of the son—all this by the mighty operation of the Holy Spirit wrought in them by God. He did this designedly so that the hearts of their posterity might be confirmed in the hope of these promises, when their descendants consider their father's testimony, that of their grandfather and that of their great-grandfather. This harmony in each of their testimonies assured them of their coming deliverance. Such uniformity served to work belief in the hearts of the succeeding generations, and maintained in them the hope of their ultimate fulfilment, even if the Lord did not perform his promises immediately.

Certainly, the Lord does not fulfil his promises as soon as he makes them, for usually there is an intervening period between the giving and performing of them. This deliberate delay is for our good, that in the meantime we might be occupied in his service.[35] If God immediately

[35] Bruce's word is 'worschip', but he will have been using the word in its basic sense of 'serving'. See, for example, the Second Commandment where English translations vary between rendering the Hebrew *'abodah* as 'serve' and 'worship' (Exodus 20:5): ESV opts for 'serve', NIV for 'worship'. I myself deplore the way in which today many churches regard 'worship' as singing, thus virtually stripping away the biblical meaning of worship as a surrender of oneself to the Almighty as his lifelong *servants*. Compare the third temptation and the answer Jesus gave to the tempter who asked him for his worship. The Hebraic parallelism in the allu-

fulfilled his promises, we would abuse them to the wantonness of our fleshly desires, whereas when he suspends their fulfilment, we are bound to be exercised in humble prayer and supplication. Yet if the Lord has promised then it is not wrong for us by prayer and tears to beg for him to act, as in faith and expectation we await his fulfilment. His delays do not mean he will not do as he has promised, but are intended to maintain in us true reverence and sobriety. In short, when we find the Lord has not immediately done what he has promised, let us keep on beseeching him to act while waiting patiently, for in due time he will certainly accomplish his word.

Concerning Joseph's death

Now I return to the record of Joseph's death as it is recorded at the end of the last chapter of Genesis.[36] When we carefully study these verses we will find they contain three points. First, we are told Joseph's age when it pleased the Lord to summon him from this life. Second, there is an account of Joseph's posterity that the Lord had given him prior to his final summons. Third, there is mention of his written will and testament, and his final words of parting to his brothers and his own family. They would first have been downcast to learn that his death was near, but he comforted them by the injunction he gave them.

Concerning Joseph's age

As to the first point concerning Joseph's age, we read that he was a hundred and ten years old when the Lord called him. He had been aged thirty when he entered Pharaoh's service, so he had been a courtier four score years. For all of those eighty years he had been held in such high esteem and dignity that there was no lord or nobleman in the country who could be compared to him. In all that time he retained the highest rank of being second only to the king, and he was held not only in his monarch's favour but also in the favour of God. Having lived in worldly honour, he died in worldly honour, having been loved both by his king and all the people. But more importantly, he had lived in the favour and esteem of the living God.

sion to Deuteronomy 6:13 is very explicit in its meaning: to 'worship' is to 'serve' in the sense of surrendering our whole beings—minds, hearts and spirits—to God as our only Lord and God.

[36] Genesis 50:22-26.

Joseph, however, had a blessing that his father never had in that he was loved by both his father and God. Jacob had certainly been blessed by God sufficiently for all his needs, but Isaac had loved his older brother Esau more than he loved his younger son Jacob. Thus Joseph had this additional blessing of being loved by Jacob his father as well as by his God. However, my main point is that during all those eighty years, there is no indication that Joseph was ever influenced by the godless environment, though he served an idolatrous king and lived in an idolatrous court. This was truly extraordinary, for we do not read of the like in either pagan or biblical history, that a man with a nature the same as ours and naturally no better than we are, should live so long in the midst of a profane society, and never be affected one way or another by his surroundings.

There is an instance in Genesis of Joseph twice swearing an oath such as an Egyptian would have sworn: *by the life of Pharao.*[37] We cannot be sure if this was wrong, for[38] it could well have been permissible, nevertheless it is the only fault we find in him. Otherwise, because he always conducted himself in such an exemplary manner, it must necessarily follow that this man, compared to all others, must have been wonderfully upheld and assisted. Out of question, had the Holy Spirit not possessed his heart and carried him through all he did, undoubtedly in some aspect or other of his living he would have been guilty of some notable defection. Thus it is evident that the Holy Spirit constantly guided all his conduct throughout his life.

Why should this have been so? It was not primarily for Joseph's own sake as for the cause of the Kirk of God; it was that he might be the maintainer and defender of the Kirk during the years of her great exile. This is why the Lord had him sent down to Egypt, and why he upheld him in his conduct so that he remained steadfast in his religion and lifestyle. It was because the Lord's ministry for him was to nourish and protect his Kirk that he did not fall away. Had he been left to his own devices, he would have shown himself to be like other men.

[37] Genesis 42:15, 16.

[38] I am tempted to insert here the phrase 'in the context in which he swore,' for his brothers were assuming he was an Egyptian and on this occasion he was deliberately behaving as such, not yet being ready to make himself known to them.

Another word regarding courtiers

Let us apply this point. Do courtiers retain their reputation, do they hope to avoid some foolish error so that their names will not end up being dishonoured? Then let them without delay show favour to the Kirk; no matter how humble and poor her members may be, let them show some affection for them. They must choose rather to offend the king of this country, rather than to offend the least of those who are sent by our Lord Jesus. They must not touch those who have been anointed by the precious oil of the Holy Spirit, for they are dear to the Lord. Would you prefer your worldly reputation rather than being held in honour with both God and man? Then put your hands to the maintenance and protection of the Kirk of God.

On the other hand, will courtiers follow the course along which their fallen natures carry them? Then let them be sure that they will not bear themselves as Joseph did, let them be sure that the time of their being in favour will be short, and let them also be sure that they will leave their reputations besmirched with ignominy. No, as truth is truth and God is God, they shall not escape the warning implicit in these words. For the Lord has such a concern for his glory in his servants and has such a particular love and affection for them, that he has not spared rulers who have banished them, and who have been so rash as to lay hands upon them. Much less will he spare men of inferior rank if by any means they trouble or dishonour his Kirk on earth. Would to God they had the mind of Joseph, and would to God they had the joy he had in recognising this; then they might be touched with some reverence, and so be in time to avoid that great judgment of God which he already has in his hand. For he is going to cut off those who neglect and show contempt for this our Kirk. All these things arise from the first point concerning Joseph's age.

God's preparation of Joseph

However, before we move on, there is one other thing to be considered. You yourselves may have read how unnaturally Joseph was treated by his brothers when he was sold at about the age of fourteen or fifteen. Then in Egypt, his time in Potiphar's house and in prison came to fourteen years, so he had this long period of trial and affliction. Yet it was the Lord who sent that trouble upon him to prepare him for a great work. For such trials do not come by chance nor, as we say, 'as a cosy garden walk,'[39] but they come from the living God, and are experienced by every member of the Kirk, as well as by the Kirk in general. The reason is that she and all her members may learn not to depend upon human strength, but upon the living God.

If you yourself encounter some kind of trial and seek God's mercy in the midst of it, there can be no doubt but that he is preparing you for some greater honour. I mean, if you are aware of his mercy mingling with the affliction that is laid upon you, be sure that God is calling you to experience what happened to Joseph, and is summoning you to some distinction both in this world and in the next. Therefore in times of trouble we must beware of murmuring against God, rather ought we to seek to discern the direction he is taking in sending this trial.

When you recognise that his purpose is for your good, then be patient and look for some experience of his favour. Then as you wait upon the pleasure of God you will find that, having endured the fourteen years of affliction, there will be four score years of honour awaiting you, as happened to Joseph. Of course after the time of honour in this life, there awaits everlasting honour in the life to come. Therefore learn to be patient and to look for the Lord's purpose, and be assured that he will ultimately reward you.

Now for all his wealth and honour, Joseph did not live as long as his father; Jacob lived thirty-seven years more than his son. Although Jacob attained a greater age than Joseph, his life was a continual fire-pan and furnace. When he came before Pharaoh and looked back over his life, he said that his years had been few and evil,[40] yet he was to live much longer than his son. In spite of Joseph's great wealth, honour and worldly fame, these privileges were not able to prolong his life by a single moment, for he was obliged to depart as soon as the Lord summoned him.

Then do not rely upon uncertain riches, neither upon their unstable honours, nor upon the fleeting affluence they can bring, as if these

[39] The whole clause is difficult: 'trubill cumis not begues or ala vole as we speak'. 'Begues' means 'random' and 'ala' a 'garden walk or path'; 'vole' is a variant of 'wole' meaning 'wool', but can also mean 'padding'; 'vole' sometimes is used with other words as a proverb (DSL 6).

[40] Genesis 47:9.

things might prolong your days. Do not lean upon them because if you do, your love for them will sever you from God, and being severed from him means also being severed from life both temporal and spiritual. For it is by the presence of God that I live this temporal life, and it is by the favour of my God that I live the spiritual life.

Through belief in Jesus Christ, I am assured that in whatever way my body dies the temporal death, my soul shall never die, but both body and soul shall live for ever. Thus it is by the presence and favour of God that I have the benefit of life both temporal and eternal. Because both my temporal and eternal life is in God, if I desert him I am heading for a temporal and eternal end that will be evil. If I keep close to God, I also keep this temporal life so long as is necessary, and thereafter I keep everlasting life.

What shall I say of our nobles who have become exhibitions of all wickedness and defection, vying with each other to see who can go furthest away from God? As well as losing eternal life, they are also forfeiting the temporal life as fast as they can. Therefore I keep waiting to see when they shall be made examples of the eternal wrath of God. Doubtless, unless they are visited by some extraordinary affliction in either body or soul,[41] you will all see them becoming spectacles of the divine wrath. You that are great men, if you would be sure of life both temporal and eternal, take heed to this and strive to have the assurance of the love and favour of God. Hold on to that, and you will have life both temporal and eternal; lose his love and favour, and you will lose both of the other. So live to God, and not to your lusts and pleasures. Thus far, then, concerning Joseph's age.

Concerning Joseph's posterity

Joseph had two sons, Ephraim and Manasseh. Somewhere in Scripture there is mention of more, but the word used is general and takes in friends and kinsmen,[42] therefore I take it he had only two sons. We come now to see the effect his blessing had on them.

He begins with Ephraim who had the chief blessing though he was

[41] He means 'some affliction sent by God to bring them to repentance'.

[42] The reference may be to Numbers 1:32, where Hebrew *bên* is variously translated 'sons' (AV), 'people' (ESV), 'tribal list' (NEB), 'tribe' (GNB), 'descendants' (JB).

the younger. We are told that before Joseph died he witnessed Ephraim's posterity increase to the third generation, so that Joseph had become a great-great-grandfather. He also saw how Manasseh was blessed, though in his case Joseph only became a grandfather. So before he died Joseph saw how effectual the blessing administered by Jacob had been, as he had pronounced it upon the younger and the elder sons; where more had been promised, more had been bestowed.

We learn, therefore, that the blessing of God is never in vain, and that whenever he blesses he gives good things. Let us then strive to receive his blessing, not so much in temporal things as in eternal blessings through the Spirit of sanctification. For when we are blessed by him in heart and mind, we shall be blessed for all eternity. God's blessings are always effectual. So much then for Joseph's posterity.

Concerning Joseph's will and testament

I come now to Joseph's death and to his will and testament.[43] At first he had saddened his brothers and his family when he pierced their hearts with his sorrowful words, but then he raised their spirits and comforted them. Finally, he gave them his last farewell and bade them 'goodnight'. As to his piercing of their hearts it was because he had said, 'My brothers and kinsmen, I am shortly to die, for I have been called upon and am no longer to remain here on earth; I have to depart and, blessed be God, I am ready to go.' What secret notice he had been given of his impending death we cannot say, but no doubt by some means or other, the Spirit of God had made him quite sure his time had come.

We know that when an old man becomes seriously ill he is aware he is more likely to die than to continue living, for advanced years are the forerunner and special messenger of death. Finding himself at this point, Joseph admonishes his sons and his family, and makes it clear to them that he is content to pass away. Even though he had lived surrounded by great wealth, affluence had not divorced his heart from his God. What then makes for a peaceful end and a joyful departure? Only being prepared and ready beforehand. If this man had not followed in his father's steps, meditated upon death in advance and laid the best and worst before himself, deciding in his heart what he must do, he would not have spoken these words so easily: *I am readie to die*.

[43] See Note 9 above.

Otherwise he would have departed from this world grudgingly, loath to leave behind his wealth and honour. But he leaves his brothers, his children, his wife and everything else without any regrets.

Everything rests on this: think seriously about your death now and prepare yourself for it, and then it will be welcome whenever it comes to you. It is when death comes upon a man unawares that it becomes the most bitter experience in this world. So learn this lesson from Joseph: the deeper the impression it makes upon your hearts, the better prepared will you be to lay aside your place and position here on earth. Yield your hearts to God and learn to have them looking upward to him, so when it shall please the Lord to call you, then you shall be ready.

But how can you be ready? I spoke of this in my previous sermon,[44] so I shall be much more brief now. No doubt every man's heart by nature of the desires within it is set upon carnal things, or upon the attractions of this world. If that is not so of someone, it can only be because the mighty God has worked within that person's heart, and caused him to be drawn by his love. How is it with your heart? Are you set upon carnal things, or upon filthy pleasures? Or do you find yourself fixated by the spoils[45] and trash of this world. If so, be sure that when approaching death begins to sever your heart from all that you love, it will be a painful separation, for no one departs willingly from the things he loves. Therefore, if I set my heart on this world and my love on carnal things, when I am charged to depart from them all, my heart is then bound to be grieved and sorrowful.

The right preparation for death

Here then is the right preparation for death. Before you die, bid this world farewell, and bid farewell also to all carnal attractions and worldly affections. For if your soul is willing to leave these things and in their place to drink in the love of God, then you will be ready to crave of God that in his infinite mercy he would season your heart by cleansing your soul. The proportion to which you once poured out your heart upon love of the earth and the riches of this world, will be the propor-

[44] See above Sermon 17, under the sub-heading, 'The Fourth Circumstance of Joseph's Visit' (pp. 305-308).

[45] 'Pelf' means 'spoils of battle', 'plundered goods', 'booty', or simply 'possessions' in a depreciatory sense. (DSL)

tion to which now your heart will be poured out upon the love of God. Without delay ask for this, and no doubt the Lord will grant it to you. So he will enable you to find comfort in your death as in your heart you repose upon his love. For who will be loath to go to the one that he loves? Then death shall be the most welcoming experience of your whole life.

You need to pray for God's strength that you may be willing to forsake the world and fleshly lusts. You also need to ask for his grace to sanctify your soul, to cleanse the power of your heart, and to lift your mind from this earth that you may raise it up to heaven. Oh, how bitter is death to those who live according to the flesh, and who have the love of the world embedded in their hearts. But oh, how sweet is death to those who love God before they come to die. This far, then, for Joseph's first words about his approaching departure.

Three points concerning Joseph's final words

Notice three points about what he said. First, no doubt it had pierced his family's hearts when he told them he was about to be taken from them. He had been their provider and defender, and because of him they had continued to be in the king's favour. No wonder his words cast them down, to discover that suddenly they would be bereft of the hope they had had in Joseph. Seeing that they had been so downcast at hearing of his impending departure, he began to comfort them, saying. 'Be assured that even if I must leave you, the living God will not leave you, but he will most certainly come and visit you.' He spoke to them, explaining what he meant: 'God will deliver you from this land and will give you back the land that he promised to your forebears.' He further explained, 'By the word "visit", as it is used in the Scriptures, is meant that the Lord who has chosen you as his people, will remain with you until the time when he comes to fulfil his promise.'

All these words he used to console their sorrowful hearts. A man whose heart is grieving because he has sustained some great loss and now sees no prospect of future happiness, is loath to be comforted. That is why Joseph was very insistent that the Lord would indeed continue with them. By the words he spoke he wanted them to catch a glimpse of the Jewel of Faith that was concealed in his soul.

Second, by these words he confirms the weak faith of those to whom he was speaking and does his best to strengthen and console them. Third, by putting a bridle on their troubled feelings he restrained them, lest they should tempt God by seeking their deliverance without his help; they must wait patiently for the timing of the living God when he should choose to visit them. 'Take care,' he was saying, 'that you do not tempt God by your impatience.' Our proverb is true when it says, 'A hasty man is never without woes'. Therefore, wait for the Lord's plan, and do not take a single step until he bids you, for his chosen day will most certainly come.

The danger of looking to human instruments rather than to God

Although there was some mitigation of their perturbation in Joseph's last will and testament, nothing he said could have been sufficient to console the hearts of these poor men, for unless the Holy Spirit had worked through his words, they would not have offered them any comfort at all. Our problem often is that we are so taken up with those through whom God is speaking, that we forget it is God who has sent them. Here is a case in point: at present we are looking to the king of France, but we are forgetting that it is God who may choose to use him;[46] thus we assume that if he as an instrument is withdrawn, our cause is lost, as if the Lord was restricted to only one means, and lacked any other instruments he could use.

The people of Israel were in that same frame of mind when Moses

[46] I can find no historical reference to the Scots looking to France for help at this time. It is possible, however, that Bruce is referring to King Henry IV, formerly King of Navarre. Though baptized a Catholic, he was raised as a Protestant by his mother Jeanne d'Albret, Queen of Navarre. As a Huguenot, Henry was involved in the French Wars of Religion, barely escaping assassination in the St Bartholonew's Day massacre. On the death in 1589 of Henry III of France, his brother-in-law and distant cousin, he was called to the French succession by the Salic law. For the first four years of his reign, he kept the Protestant faith (the only French king to do so), but in 1593 he found it prudent to abjure his Calvinism, but to his credit, he promulgated the Edict of Nantes (1598) which guaranteed religious liberties to Protestants, thereby effectively ending the Wars of Religion. However, the likelihood of Bruce referring to Henry IV of France is made probable in that when this sermon was preached (1591-92?), for the first time ever France would have had a Protestant king. See Chapter 19, note 16 below, and the sentence to which it refers, namely the anticpated relief of persecuted Protestants in France.

died: they thought there could never be anyone able to take his place. Yet see how the Lord who first raised up his servant Moses, then sent forth a man who fulfilled the leadership role as faithfully as Moses had done. He chose Joshua, endued him with his gifts and graces, and prospered him as well as he ever prospered Moses. Likewise, read the same in the Book of Judges. Are we not accustomed to assume that when the Lord removes some chosen instrument, he no longer has any care for the Kirk? Suppose an instrument fails, that does not mean God's work then fails. Often the Lord takes a good instrument from you, because you have misused him. For you do wrong to his servants if you give to them the honour that rightly belongs to God alone, thereby robbing him of his glory.

The reason why the Lord at times has withdrawn his grace from some of his servants is that you have elevated them above their proper station, and regarded them as the principal operatives in their ministry. There have been a number of outstanding ministers from whom grace has been temporally withdrawn, so that the world might see the difference between a man left to himself, and those who are furnished with God's grace. It is the difference between nature and grace: there is nothing but confusion in the one, while in the other is displayed holiness and divinity. Oftentimes, I say, it happens that when the Lord's servants are abused, he then permits them to be beset by encumbrances of their own making. Then his people say, 'We can see that as long as the Lord guided yon man he followed an upright course, but from the time his grace was withdrawn we recognised he was but a man.'

Therefore do not gaze upon the Lord's servants, but set your eyes on him who sent them forth. Be aware that if all his servants were removed from the Kirk in one single night, the Lord still has enough instruments to raise up and equip the Kirk the next morning without needing to take fourteen or fifteen years of preparation, as it took the king of Spain to fit out and equip his invading force.[47] The Lord can swiftly prepare an instrument for his use even if the man is a blockhead! So learn always to depend on God and never on the instrument, but only inasmuch as is appropriate, praise and glorify God for his work through his servant.

[47] The Armada of 1588.

Joseph's final words

We come now to Joseph's final words, and the injunction which is the last item in his will and testament: *Carie my bonis with yow, forget not my bonis.* He is commanding them not to transport his remains [to Canaan], but to lay them in a kist[48] within his tomb, until such time as they should return to their own land, when he bids them to take his bones with them. By these words it is evident that he has foreseen the long period of time that would intervene before the Lord would perform his promise, for there were one hundred and forty-four years between his words here and that future event. Without question, during those years his remains would all be eaten away, leaving only his bones.[49] When he spoke thus, he clearly saw with the eye of faith those many intervening years before his bones would be carried back to the Land.

Consider, then, Joseph's purpose in saying this. He had no intention of nurturing superstition, nor was he curious about what they would do otherwise with his bones. Neither did he consider the place of his burial of any great importance, for as every servant of God already is aware, no resting-place, however profane it might be, is able to inflict any harm upon the bodies of the Lord's saints. On the other hand, the remains of a wicked man without any faith can never benefit by being laid beneath a pulpit or a high altar. Joseph knew perfectly well that the location of the sepulchre brought no spiritual advantages with it. Sepulchres were introduced for the living that the remains of the departed might be laid to rest in a known place; they were never intended to benefit the dead.

Burial of the Lord's people today

Yet I have no doubt that the practice of burials helps to foster hope of the resurrection. You will never find anyone who dies in the faith of Jesus Christ being concerned over the location of his burial place; his concern will be that his soul will depart to heaven and that it will be committed to the hands of Jesus Christ. He will not want any outward pomp or a place to lie within a Kirk. Nowadays nobody wants to lie

[48] See Note 33 above.

[49] Bruce spoke truly here. See Chapter 6, note 6 above; also Chapter 4, note 4 above.

within a Kirk building, far less near to the pulpit,[50] other than those who never came into a Kirk during their lifetime. No! Joseph's concern in commanding his family to preserve his bones, and to carry them with them to Canaan, was to give them firm assurance of their ultimate deliverance.

There was however another reason why he asked them to carry his bones with them when they left Egypt, namely, to avoid any occasion of superstition. Had they left his bones behind them, when in the wilderness they remembered the meat, fish, onions and garlic, and murmured against Moses,[51] and wanted to use the Egyptian food as an excuse to return, Joseph's bones still in Egypt also would have served as an added reason for going back. Therefore, to avoid that kind of superstition, he commanded them to have his bones buried in the Land.

I repeat, we should not be concerned about where our bodies will lie, but rather should be concerned regarding our souls. Nevertheless, great care ought to be taken that the bodies of departed saints are handled with reverence, and laid among the remains of the faithful. As they have lived holy lives here on earth, so in hope of the resurrection their bodies ought to be respectfully buried among other people of faith. However, our chief concern must still be that our souls are commended to the care of Jesus Christ, that, as it pleased him to show them mercy during their lives, so now it will please him to show them mercy in their deaths. You will do well if you do this.

The oath

Very briefly, Joseph requests them to make an oath. His father had made him take an oath before his death,[52] and so he does the same. He knew that if they swore, they would keep their oath. His father had bowed in thanksgiving and worship when Joseph swore, for he knew he would honour his promise. See in what reverence oaths were held then, how highly in their religion they esteemed their promises, to such an extent that when they had sworn they would not break it for all the world's

[50] Ironically, Bruce's remains were buried at the foot of the original Larbert Kirk pulpit. See Chapter 6, note 6 above. However, his comment regarding tombs inside a church building was undoubtedly aimed at aristocratic families and their elaborate burial vaults.

[51] Numbers 11:4-6.

[52] Genesis 47:31.

possessions. Compare those times with our times, and see how swearing an oath has become a profanity. Now in civil actions in court, when a man takes his oath upon both his body and soul, he considers he has won his case. Thus what was once done with great religious devotion has now, through the passage of time, become the greatest profanity. This makes it plain that as the world grows in age, so it grows in wickedness. Therefore let us strive to draw ever nearer to God.

Joseph does not give his family the same instructions regarding his burial as his father had given him.[53] As no reason is given for this in the Scriptures, I will not speculate. But it would appear it was because they did not have the authority he had, but were poor men who could not afford to embalm him as he had done for his father.[54] Further, knowing the weakness of their faith, he knew that having his kist situated near them would cause them to bring back his words to their memories, and enable them to live in the hope of the fulfilment of the promise. I think this is why he discharged them from burying him as he had buried Jacob. 'Rather,' he said, 'when you return to the Holy Land, carry my bones with you.'

See, then, how mindful they were of that Promised Land, and how diligent they were to betake themselves back there. If they were so watchful of the pledge of their oath, how much more attentive ought we to be of that true Holy Land symbolised by Canaan. And if they were diligent about returning there, how much more diligent ought we to be to have both our bodies and souls conveyed to heaven, the true Promised Land! That can only be through the righteous merits of Christ, to whom with the Father and the Holy Ghost be all honour, praise and glory, now and for ever. Amen.

[53] Genesis 49:29-32.

[54] Genesis 50:2-3.

Chapter Nineteen

Hebrew Chapter 11 verse 23

> [23] *By faith Moses was hid three monethis of his Parentis, Because they saw he was ane proper chyld, nather feared they the kingis commandment.*

Well-beloved brethren in Jesus Christ, so far the apostle has introduced notable examples to demonstrate to us that never in this world has there ever been anyone who was justified before God, or was granted the sight of his merciful countenance, or attained entry to the glory of his kingdom, other than those who were declared righteous by faith alone. He proved this before the Flood in the persons of Abel and Enoch; he proved it during the Flood in the person of Noah; and after the Flood he proved it in the persons of Jacob and Joseph and their sons who went down into Egypt. He also mentioned other patriarchs. Now he moves on to speak of these patriarchs' families, those who had been born and bred in Egypt, citing in this verse two examples of persons raised there, who were also justified by faith, as had been their forebears.

The decay of faith in the third generation

Just as in our own times, the third generation of our people are not like our predecessors, so it was true of the third generation after Jacob and Joseph that they were not like their fathers; nor was the fourth generation that came out of Egypt at all like the patriarchs. The old men, who had had the knowledge of the living God and reverenced his word that caused his people to fear, had died. Then there had been Joseph who had put, as it were, the food into his people's mouths and had fostered them in their distress. But from the time that such good and holy men had departed this earthly life, the following generations fell away from God and from the religion and customs of their forefathers. Indeed, you can read in Ezekiel 20:7-8 how widespread and wicked was their backsliding. At the time the Lord sent his servant Moses to deliver them, there was scarcely anyone to be found who truly and sincerely worshipped God as their fathers had done.

Turn to Exodus 5:2-21 and read there how, when they saw neither Moses nor Aaron had been able to soften Pharaoh's heart and secure their deliverance, they arose in a fury against them. Then again they turned upon Moses and Aaron and, in spite of all the miraculous events that had occurred in Egypt, they declared that these two were even worse than any of the plagues; it had been the most unexpected and universal defection.[1] Yet notwithstanding this rebellion against him, the Lord did not withhold his hand (as you may read in the song recorded in Exodus 15), but came to them at his preferred and appointed time, as you may read in the passage to which I have alluded.[2]

This decay of faith in the Kirk will certainly continue right to the end of the age. Even though it will be widespread and cause universal confusion, yet the Lord will always preserve a remnant, even some 'on foot'[3] whom he will take up and greatly honour, and who in heart, soul and body will glorify him. The two greatest and most widespread defections were at the time of The Flood, and then later among the people of God when Jesus Christ came in the flesh. There were only eight elect souls who feared God at that first defection (and not all of those eight did so truly). At the time of the Incarnation, so great and almost universal was the defection in the visible Kirk that those who held the spiritual sword, drew that sword to attack Jesus Christ, the head of the Kirk, and banished him from their midst, excommunicating him.

[1] The reference is apparently to Exodus 14:11-12.

[2] The reference is clearly to Exodus 14: 24-25.

[3] I have translated Bruce's phrase quite literally: 'sum on fute'. It would appear that he is using this expression of men who are 'walking in express contrast to riding' (so DSL 2.b.). It is tempting to guess that there could be an unconscious reference to himself when he gave up his wealthy inheritance of Kinnaird, sent his horse to the fair and set off on foot to walk from Kinnaird House to St Andrews, there to study divinity under Andrew Melville. MacNicol, p.24.

The faithful remnant

Behold, and judge for yourselves! When the visible Kirk was in the grip of this heretical error and in the midst of such a great defection, even at that time it pleased the Lord to preserve some for himself, keeping them in step, namely Mary the mother of Jesus, Elizabeth the mother of John, Joseph and Simeon and a few others of similar lowly rank. But this is where the papists, of all men on earth, utter the greatest folly: they claim that the entire multitude belong to the visible Kirk. Yet here we see that the true face of the visible Kirk was reduced to just a few persons, whom the Lord himself had chosen.

There can be no doubt that there is another defection to come before the Lord returns; it has already begun and continues to grow, so that, as he himself has said in Luke 18:8, 'When the Son of Man comes, will he find faith on the earth?' Therefore, it is not great numbers that is the true and essential mark of the Kirk. Nevertheless, the defection has never been so great that the Lord has not reserved some to bear witness to him.

Seeing this final defection is continuing to increase—for the greater the light, the greater the rebellious contempt—we must crave of the Lord that for the sake of Christ he would include us in the number of those who have received his mercy extended to us, so that on that Day we will be able to share in the glory that has been purchased by his Son's death.

Rejected opportunities

There is one further point to be noted regarding these rebellious generations: the more opportunities they had to reform themselves and the more help they were given to nourish their faith, the more wicked and perverse they became. It did not matter how near the Lord drew to them to strengthen their faith through his Word and sacraments, they fell away and drew back from God even more. As we say, they drew the cat harrow[4] [but without any spiritual response], for if you examine the measures visited upon the second and third generations, compared to the scant help their predecessors had, you will find they were afforded far more opportunities than their fathers.

[4] To 'draw the cat harrow' is to go through a hard time and so 'to have a serious experience of strain'. (DSL 1[2])

For example, they had the promises of God given to their forebears, those promises being often reiterated; they even had God's solemn oaths confirming his promises; they also had the testimonies of the earlier generation, all of which were consistent in that each witness corroborated the other witnesses. Thus their consciences should have been fully assured of their ultimate deliverance. Furthermore, they had as a pledge Joseph's bones left with them, assuring them of the coming liberation.

The promise regarding four hundred years

They had also been given a definite number of years attached to the promise spoken by the mouth of God, as in Genesis 15:13. A certain number of generations had been set before them, so they could have calculated when the final issue of their deliverance would be accomplished. They could at first have counted from the persecution of Isaac by his brother Ishmael who mocked him when he was about five years old.[5] The apostle called this mocking 'persecution',[6] so we should count the four hundred years of affliction of Abraham's seed from Isaac's fifth year, according to God's word. Had they done this calculation they would have found a great many of these years were already past, so the time of their deliverance could not have been too far away. After Isaac's fifth year, Abraham lived another ninety years in Canaan, and after him Isaac lived another hundred and fifteen years, so these two hundred and five years were past while in Canaan.

Then Jacob went to Egypt and lived some years there and his son Joseph after him, totalling another hundred years. So now there were not all that many of the four hundred years remaining. But we must not forget the years before the birth of Isaac, for included in the four hundred years promised in Genesis 15 and up to Isaac's birth in Genesis 21 was a further thirty-three years when Abraham lived in Canaan. Therefore at least three hundred and thirty-eight of the four hundred years had now passed.

Remember that Abraham's seed were to be afflicted in a land that was not theirs, but this also applies to Canaan as well as to Egypt, even though the heritable title of Canaan pertained to them by the charter

[5] Genesis 21:8-10.

[6] Galatians 4:29.

given to Abraham. For as Stephen said, Canaan would still be regarded as a foreign land to them, as 'God gave him no inheritance in it, not even a foot's length'.[7] Three of the four generations had expired, and now the fourth generation was already upon them.

Therefore in every respect the people should have been constrained to believe that their deliverance would come soon, and so they should have stood fast in their religion. Had they done this, God would have afforded them more help in nourishing their faith, yet in circumstances when they could have persevered, they backslid ever further from him, and so their defection constantly grew worse. Alas, this has been the pattern in every generation since that time.

Contempt of God cannot go unpunished

You will not find any nation to whom God has been more beneficent in journeying with them, yet the nearer God drew to them by outward means, and the more opportunities he gave them of doing well, the further they fell away from him and the more rebellious they became towards his majesty. Likewise today, compare the zeal of our forefathers in times past when the light shone but faintly and there were few if any encouragements—compare those past times with the spiritual coldness that now reigns among us, who have great opportunities now the light is shining brightly, then you will see the same situation replicated today. It is true: the nearer God draws to us through Word and sacrament and by the increase of his means of grace, the further away we draw from God.

It is not possible that our contempt can pass unpunished by God. For as the apostle says, How can we escape if we neglect so great a salvation?[8] We have so many opportunities and abundant measures of grace generously offered to us, much less then shall we escape, if we arrogantly and contemptuously distain them. Therefore judgment upon our land cannot remain dormant. As God is the God who judged the people of Israel after he delivered them out of the land of bondage, so shall he judge our nation for the great contempt and rebellion that reigns throughout all the estates of our people, both great and small. What of the great men, whom you know to be ringleaders of iniquity,

[7] Acts 7:5.
[8] Hebrews 2:3.

trouble-making and wickedness? As today they are spectacles of contempt and profanation of the name of God, so will you shortly see them—unless the Lord works otherwise with them—as spectacles of his furious indignation and burning wrath.

In order to persuade you to change by beginning now to walk in another direction,[9] and not to complain against the merciful calling of God, I have insisted on outlining the years of the three generations. We do need to understand their meaning. What then was the apostle's purpose? Through him the Lord is showing us here that in every generation there were some who continued in the faith and religion of their predecessors.

Moses' parents

Therefore now the apostle brings us to the parents of Moses who were faithful, an example drawn from the generation that descended from the sons of the patriarchs. Their names are repeated several times in Scripture, once in Exodus 6:20, and then again in the Book of Numbers.[10] The father's name was Amram; he was the son of Kohath who was a son of Levi, so that Moses' father was a grandson of Jacob. Moses' mother's name was Jochebed, but we are told in Exodus 6:20 that she was his father's sister.

The marriages that took place among the Fathers would be too difficult a question to discuss just now, not least the union of Moses' parents between a nephew and his aunt. Even though there are some who want to justify such a practice, personally I regard it as wrong and not to be commended.[11] God forbid we should assume that everything the Fathers did was right, for although many of their actions were done with far better consciences than we have, yet not all their practices can be approved. In their day the Law had not yet been given, but not long after Amram's generation we find such issues dealt with in Leviticus 18.[12]

[9] Bruce's clause here is not easy to translate: 'To move yow to scowp, and fold your feit in tyme'; 'scowp' means 'to move in a different direction', and I have taken 'to fold your feit in time' as amplifying 'scowp'.

[10] Numbers 3:19; 26:58, 59.

[11] There is a relevant comment on this subject in an explanation of Cain's marriage to his sister. Leupold, pp. 214-215.

[12] Leviticus 18:12. 'You shall not uncover the nakedness of your father's sister; she is your father's relative.'

After such a union had been plainly forbidden, I have no doubt that Amram's descendants honoured this law. Because the Israelites lived within their own tribes, they were obliged to marry someone from among their relatives. It appears that Amram had had this same restriction and had to choose a wife from his own tribe. Nevertheless, I can only consider this to have been wrong, as shortly after this time the Law of God forbade it. In spite of that, the apostle regarded Moses' parents as being faithful, for he records, *By faith Moses was hid three monethis of his Parentis*. He was pointing to their actions in preserving their child as confirmation of their faith.

The faith of Moses' parents

So how was it that they showed their faith? Moses was born during a perilous time when they dare not acknowledge his birth, but in faith they preserved his life, keeping him hidden for three months. But then the rumour that they had a new-born baby must have begun to spread, so that they were unable to keep him concealed any longer. So they went through the motions of obeying the edict by wrapping up the child, putting him in a basket that had been lined with pitch and clay, and placing it in the water. They did not leave his cradle alone there, for his sister Miriam stayed near the water's edge to watch and see what God would do.

No doubt Moses' parents in doing this were depending upon the fatherly care and provision of the living God. They were assured in their consciences, either that God would provide for their child's safety in some extraordinary way, or else that he would show them what they must do meantime. Therefore their action of leaving the child there was neither from rashness nor fear, but was done wisely so that the tyrannous law might appear to have been satisfied. It was perfectly plain that what they did arose from faith issuing from the root of holiness, right from the day the child was born and then safely kept hidden.

We have the record of these events in the first and second chapters of the Book of Exodus, which was written by Moses himself regarding his birth. The old king whom Joseph had served, and who had protected his descendants, had died prior to all this, and Joseph himself was now dead. A new king had arisen who had known neither Joseph nor his people.[13] The king, seeing such a rapidly expanding multitude of aliens in his country, realised that they could soon match the population of his own subjects. He began to be afraid of them and so took counsel as to how he might control their growth and reduce their number. To begin with he sought to achieve his aim by crafty methods, but when he saw that scheme was ineffective, he resorted to cruelty and violence.

Pharaoh's attempts to suppress the Hebrew slaves

His crafty scheme consisted in a twofold measure. First, his plan was to lay heavy burdens and sore labour upon the backs of all the people, so he ordered them to make bricks by tramping clay. Second, he set ruthless task masters over them, to keep their necks bowed under the yoke, and to ensure they toiled incessantly. He thought that by these means he would so oppress the people that they would grow weary of living, and would be deprived of all the comforts and resources of life. That was his plan, and indeed he put it into practice and made the people begin to build his storehouses. However, the Lord prospered his people, even under their burdens, and he blessed them so that they grew even more in number and in other ways.

When the king of Egypt realised that his crafty scheme was not nearly as effective as he had planned, he wondered about some other way to get the number of these aliens reduced. He enquired about the Hebrew midwives, and had the two principal ones brought to him. Their names, recorded in Exodus 1:15, were Shiphrah and Puah. He told them that as soon as a male child was born they must kill him. By this means he thought he could gradually destroy these people. However, the two midwives feared God, and, being endued with faith, they recognised that as well as their duty to the king there was also their duty to God. Therefore they chose to obey God rather than to obey the king, to whom they gave a very clever excuse for letting the male babies live.

When the king saw that this plan had not worked either, he ended up breaking out into blatant cruelty, manifesting his brutality in an edict decreeing that his own people must seize every male child that

[13] It is possible that Joseph came to prominence during the Hyksos period of dominance; they had held sway in Egypt for many decades, until there was a resurgence of Egyptian nationalism and a return to the Fourteenth Dynasty. See *Joseph*, p. 79.

was born and cast it into the river. We must learn an incidental lesson here: when hypocrisy lurks in a man's heart, it is impossible for it not to burst forth sooner or later in an open display of cruelty. Thus it erupted from the tyrant when he issued his edict. It was at this very time that the baby Moses was born.

A grave peril for Moses' parents

Consider then these circumstances as to how dangerous and perilous it was for Moses' parents, Amram and Jochebed, to conceal their new-born child. No doubt they must have experienced a great conflict within themselves between hope and despair, and faith and doubt, causing them to be filled with self-pity. For they knew perfectly well of the inhuman cruelty that was in the Egyptian king's heart, that expressed itself in various ways, partly through his plans which had such an adverse effect on his subjects, and partly by the issuing of his edict which had affected their own neighbours. There was also the grave peril that they themselves faced, for they knew that the tyrant's cruelty could cost them their lives if they did not surrender their baby to be slain as the king had commanded. Little wonder then that they were apprehensive regarding their own lives and that of their son.

No doubt the devil, knowing their human weakness, tempted them to expose their little one to destruction, but the fear of God was in them and the faith lurking in their hearts prevailed. They could see that the edict was clearly against both the law of God and the law of nature. This command of the king was also against the promise of God made to their forefathers concerning the growth of Abraham's seed and their posterity. Considering all these things, the faith in their hearts wrought in them compassion for their child, that by all possible means they must hide him and so preserve his life. (I have deliberately delayed the timing of what happened to the child in order to show you how the outcome of their actions arose entirely from faith.)

Two lessons for today

I want to bring before you now two lessons arising from the initial part of the story. The first lesson is this: where faith has the word of God as its warrant, and has that solid foundation on which to lean, it disdains all the commands of men. Second, I also see that what we ourselves have experienced is by no means the first time that tyrants have plotted and taken weighty counsel against the Kirk. When our enemies plotted to destroy the Kirk but failed they have imposed heavy burdens upon us, bringing great misery and vexation to the Lord's people. We have first-hand experience of the Pope and the Council of Trent,[14] as well as the attempts made by Spain not so long ago.[15]

These experiences let us see that the treatment of the Kirk has always been the same. Likewise I see, whatever the schemes of our enemies or the direction which the devil is taking, that under these crosses, burdens and edicts the Lord always blesses his Kirk, nourishing and upholding her with inner, spiritual consolations, when all outward help is failing us. Look at the situation in France, where the Kirk that has so long suffered under the cross will soon be relieved;[16] also see in England and in our neighbouring country,[17] how the Kirks there, that have also been long under the cross, shall yet be relieved. As the Lord is Lord, he shall bring to naught every device of the enemy, and in spite of them bless his Kirk and at length relieve her and grant her liberty, that she may praise his name with wide open mouth.[18] Thus far concerning these lessons.

The faith of Moses' parents confirmed

We move on now to the outward thing that confirmed the faith of these parents, and motivated them to preserve and hold on to their child. (Note that I am not referring here to what it was that gave birth to their faith.) When they saw that their baby was clearly a special child, with

[14] The Council of Trent was held between 1545 and 1563 in Trent, northern Italy. A Council of the Roman Catholic Church, it was prompted by the Reformation, and has been described as the embodiment of the Counter-Reformation. Covering eighteen years, it was overseen by three successive Popes, Paul III, Julius III and Pius IV. Crucial doctrines discussed included *Tradition, Justification, The Sacraments and Veneration of Saints*, all of which were deliberately defined to contradict the reformed doctrines of grace.

[15] Bruce's word 'bygaine' is indeterminate and means 'in the past'. He makes explicit reference to the Spanish Armada in his sermons on Isaiah 38. Isa 38, p. 61; see also Chapter 18, Note 47 above.

[16] See Chapter 18, Note 46 above.

[17] Possibly a reference to Ireland.

[18] Possibly an allusion to Psalm 81:10b, 'Open thy mouth wide and I wil fill it' (Gen.B).

a bonny face and very lovely to look upon, no doubt the baby's beauty moved them all the more to pity and compassion. But if they had seen no further in the bairn than his outward comeliness, that would have been of little consequence, for everyone who looked at him would have seen the same thing and also been moved with compassion. It is not uncommon for neighbours to look at a baby and comment on how bonny he is. But with this child his parents saw more than just his beauty.

It is when the fires of persecution are burning that the Spirit is most alert. That is why these parents, inspired by the Holy Spirit, saw much more in their baby boy than any natural onlooker could have recognised. I do not doubt but that they saw grace hidden within the child's lovely face; they saw the marks and signs[19] of a latent excellence. They saw that in the coming years when he grew to maturity, he would become a great leader, and that the Lord would use him to undertake some notable ministry of immense importance. Being dimly aware of this and noting the evident signs[20] in the bairn's face, they were moved to work resolutely to preserve him.

The nature of the plans to save the baby Moses

Four reasons concurred within the parent's plan to save the boy. These reasons were partly natural and partly supernatural and spiritual. The first natural reason was one that is common to humanity: it was the deep affection we all have for a new-born child; because our children are from our flesh and blood, we cannot help but feel a deep affection for them. The second natural reason was the remarkable outward beauty of this baby. But more importantly, the third and principal reason was their[21] faith along with the assurance they had of the prom-

[19] Bruce twice here uses the unusual word 'taikin' which means 'an identifying characteristic', 'a sign', or 'a symbol' (DSL).

[20] See Note 19 above.

[21] From here on in this sermon, Bruce refers only to Amram, for he consistently uses the singular masculine pronouns 'he' and 'him'. As editor of the sermons, I will use either the plural pronouns 'they' and 'their' or, where appropriate, the feminine pronouns 'she' and 'her'. Bruce also represents the husband as preparing the basket and placing it in the river. However, Amram is only mentioned once in Exodus 2:1-10, in the first verse, otherwise the scheme is entirely attributed to Moses' mother. This is not to suggest that Moses' father was not entirely in agreement with all that his wife was doing. Towards the end of the sermon he refers to

ises of God. The fourth reason arose from their spiritual insight of what they perceived behind the physical comeliness of their child. The parents realised that God was going to use their son as an instrument in the deliverance of his Kirk. Thus, through their personal faith, they reposed upon the promises of God.

First, natural gifts may become special gifts

I mark another three points here. First I see that outward beauty and natural comeliness of form are graces and gifts from God. If they are rightly used they become special gifts and graces in anyone who has them. Read the biblical histories and you will find that almost all those whom Lord employed as his instruments in any great work, particularly in law-making and in governing the commonwealth, were ratified as God's servants by their natural gifts and graces and by their manners.

For example, in 1 Samuel 9 we read of the Lord choosing Saul who was herding donkeys, and stamping him, more than any other, with both gracious manners and through the comeliness of his person. He was taller than any of his people by a head. It had pleased the Lord to endow him with these outward physical adornments. No doubt Samuel himself was drawn to love him because of his appearance.

Again, it was said of David at his anointing that he was red-headed, had beautiful eyes and was handsome.[22] Similarly, we read in Daniel 1:4 that Daniel was a youth of good appearance, and the four noblemen that were fed along with him were more handsome than all the others who ate at the king's table (verse 15). So you see that all of these were stamped with outward graces. We see the same in Stephen who before he died was given by the Lord the beauty of an angel.[23]

All these examples let us see that outward looks and demeanour are gifts from God, provided they are not abused. It is those whom the Lord intends to employ in some notable work who are endowed with such graces, so that the world may see something in them that is not normally seen in others. However, we must not make too much of outward appearances, for they cannot communicate the salvific grace that leads to everlasting life. Therefore any who have a comely appearance

---

Jochebed twice, the first time implicitly and the second time explicitly.

[22] 1 Samuel 16:12.

[23] Acts 6:15.

should not be proud of it, but should rather look to the inward grace. For even though Saul was called to be a king, we cannot be certain that he was also called to the kingdom of heaven; though he had the outward graces, he lacked inward grace.

Therefore, although a person may have natural beauty as a generous gift of God, we must principally look for that spiritual grace that brings forgiveness of our sins and washes clean our consciences, making us members of the kingdom of heaven. When someone has both the outward and inward grace, then he is greatly adorned. But those who have the outward, but not the inward, are not in a good state, for the outward is often abused.

Second, by faith an inward hidden grace may be seen

The second thing that I perceive here is that when those who fear God look at their children and admire them, they see more than the child's outward comeliness, for by the Spirit of God they also see a hidden grace of which other onlookers may not be aware. Pharaoh's daughter could not have observed this, for no physical sight could recognise it, whereas the one who fears God, by faith will observe far more than those who only look with human eyes. Without question, the light of the Spirit of God must see much more than can normally be detected.

It was through this spiritual sight that Simeon, when he took the child Jesus in his arms, was able to acknowledge him to be the Redeemer and Saviour of the world.[24] Similarly, it was through this same spiritual insight that Mary and Martha, sisters of Lazarus, knelt at the Lord's feet and uttered their remarkable confession of faith.[25] Thomas, who at first could not believe, later, when enlightened by the Holy Spirit, said to Jesus, 'Now I see and acknowledge that you are my Lord and my God'.[26] Thus it was that by this same spiritual insight the father of Moses was able to see what the neighbours did not see with only human eyes; Amram had been endowed by the Spirit of God with far more than physical sight.

Then we too must strive to obtain even a little of this spiritual insight. For as by our normal vision and understanding we are able to

[24] Luke 2:25-34.
[25] John 11:20-25; 12:3-7.
[26] John 20:24-29.

observe earthly and temporal things, so labour to get the heavenly light whereby you may perceive heavenly things. Then you will be enabled to reach out for a portion of heaven itself. Just as God has blessed us with our natural wit so that we can live sensibly here below in this world, so crave of him that he would also give you heavenly insight to discern heavenly things. Pray for a heavenly understanding, that here on earth you may gain at least part of that heavenly inheritance laid up for us through the righteous merits of Christ. Thus far concerning mere outward sight.

Third, the action of Moses' parents was inspired by faith not fear

The third point is this: it is said at the end of the verse *they feared not the kingis command*, yet when we read the record in Exodus 2:3, the implication seems to be that it was on account of fear that she laid the baby in the river. For why else, other than because of fear of the king's edict, would they have placed the child there? My answer is that hiding the child in the river was not on account of fear, but was done wisely and in faith as the means of preserving the baby's life. This was their reason and it was completely successful. Had she put the child into the water through fear, or impetuosity, or in order to satisfy the king's edict, she would not have wrapped him up so warmly, but would have left him naked. But as we read in Exodus, he was concealed in a little basket that was waterproofed and so he was as warm and safe as if he had been on dry land. Moreover, she left his sister to watch over the basket, to see what God might do. Also, he was not left in the middle of the river, but among the reeds that grow near the water's edge.

We see now what the parents had in mind. Their plan was not to obey the edict, but to elude the edict, preserving their child by appearing to satisfy it. The basket was placed near the bank where the river flowed alongside the palace, doubtless because they were sure that someone from the court passing by would be used as the instrument of God to deliver the child. We know how folk love to see something unusual, and the parents had no doubt that when some courtiers went past and saw the little vessel floating in the water, they would have it brought to them. Then, when they saw the baby, his beauty would secure his preservation. This then was clearly their purpose, that in some extraordinary manner the Lord would save Moses.

Their faith did not fail them, because they were wholly dependent upon the provision of God. Therefore it was the Lord himself who caused Pharaoh's daughter to come to the river just at that time, and to see the basket and ask for it to be brought to her. When she saw the baby, she was moved with compassion, and she gave him to his sister. Later, she herself adopted the boy as her own son, and he was brought up in the court beside the king, there amongst his enemies. Pharaoh cared for him though he did not know he was raising a serpent, as it were. Thus far, then, for the story and this third point.

Five lessons for today

First, the wisdom of faith does not despise ordinary means

Now what must we notice here? This first thing that I gather is this: we will not find a person whose faith in God is steadfast, who will not also be wise. Real faith is always accompanied by wisdom, and wisdom with faith prevents a man from doing what is foolish or rash. Faith that is guided by wisdom does not despise the most mundane methods, but employs all legitimate and everyday means that the Law of God permits. It is not that faith is dependent upon such means, but rather that it leans upon the favour and blessing of God who prospers the means. For if the Lord withdraws his blessing, no matter how many means in this world you employ, they will prove to be ineffective, and will only produce a curse and blight upon you. Take heed then to be diligent in your calling, and do not neglect any means, however commonplace they may be, which the Lord has prescribed for us to obtain his favour. Do not depend on your own efforts and planning, but look for the blessing of God.

You must realise that without his blessing, however early you rise in the morning, or however late you sit up at night, you are bringing forth nothing but wind[27] that shall turn all your efforts into a cross laid upon you in chastisement. Those who commit the outcome to God will always put him first, for we cannot expect his blessing if we have not begun our enterprise by seeking his mind and will. If we begin without God in some venture, we cannot expect to end up with him. If in all

[27] An intentionally derogatory metaphor used in Scripture: see Job 6:26; Isaiah 41:29; Jeremiah 5:13.

conscience you have started with God and you are keeping close to him in what you are doing, you may be assured that he will bless you. But if you have begun without him, then stop what you have been doing and start all over again; then he will be with you and the outcome will be blessed. Take heed to this! Every man knows when the path he is taking is restricting him and his conscience is forbidding him. Therefore, in the name of God reform your ways. Faith, then, is wise when it does not despise ordinary means.

Second, depend wholly upon God

What is the second lesson? The next point you must mark is this: depend upon God! However great the danger and perils may be, however cruel the prince, however tyrannical the law—depend upon God. He has a storehouse of means—yea, an infinite storehouse of infinite means—to preserve his own people from the greatest perils that can overtake them in the world. The child who could not be safe in his father's house, the Lord made safe in his enemy's house, and he caused the one who should have been his murderer to become his provider and promoter.

Therefore, depend upon him who is able to promote religion by the enemies of religion.[28] He is able to manipulate and bend the will of a king, even though that king may be an enemy of the faith. Whenever princes do promote religion, it is because God does it through them by his providential care for his own people who serve him. Therefore, in full assurance depend upon God, and he will deliver you in the hour of greatest need, even if he uses his enemy to do so. He did not lack caves in which to hide his prophets.[29]

Third, distinguish between the laws of God and the laws of man

The third thing I mark here concerns both the midwives and the parents of Moses. Peter is another example of the extent to which the laws of man should be obeyed.[30] Learn then to distinguish between God and man, between his laws and their laws, for the faithful have observed this distinction, and have never neglected it in any generation. As long as the chief magistrate who has no superior (but the supreme Magistrate

[28] As in Philippians 1:15-18.

[29] 1 Kings 18:3-4.

[30] Acts 4:19.

is the living God), enacts some measure that is neither contrary to the Scriptures nor the law of God, in all conscience you must obey him.

But if it happens that the magistrate commands something that is clearly opposed to Scripture, and there is general agreement that what he is demanding is contrary to the law of God, then unquestionably you must obey the supreme Magistrate rather than the intermediate magistrate. I would rather forfeit my earthly inheritance,[31] than lose my heavenly and eternal inheritance. And if I should incur indignation for breaking some law, I would rather incur the indignation of him who has power only over my body, than incur the indignation of him who, after my body is slain, has power to cast my soul into hell. Therefore, carefully distinguish between these two.

It is not that I want you to question every single edict of the king, only when even the sun and moon can see that some edict is contrary to God's word! In such a case, our supreme Superior must be obeyed. Had those who have gone before us had the strength, courage and discretion to have distinguished between their office and duties to earthly kings on the one hand, and to God on the other hand, then atheism would not have been prevalent so long among us. For the cause of this godlessness and idolatry has been that when former kings drew up laws contrary to God and his word, there was no one who resisted. Never was there a single person to stand in the gap[32] and declare that it was wrong; they all compromised and subscribed to it, consequently this atheism and idolatrous worship came in with its appalling confusion.

Because none followed in the footsteps of the martyrs, these kings were not resisted. I know that it is easier to say all this here than it is actually to do it. Nevertheless, it is certainly true that we ought to resist unto blood[33] before we suffer the law of God and his word blatantly to be broken. It is also true that none of us can stand in our own strength, and that a man can only stand in God's cause through his strength. Therefore, it is the duty of all those of us who fear our weakness to seek God's strength to defend his cause. Because his cause can only be

[31] See Note 3 above.

[32] Ezekiel 22:30. 'And I soght for a man among them, that shulde make vp the hedge, & stand in the gap before me for the land, that I shulde not destroy it, bot I founde none' (GenB).

[33] Hebrews 12:4. Bruce's phrase is 'sweat vnto blude'.

defended through his strength, he will impart it to us if we ask him. Confess, then, your weakness to him and admit that you are afraid of the king and his law, because you might forfeit all your possessions as well as your wife. Show the Lord that unless he guards you by his might when you resist the king's law, you will not be able to stand firm, but will end up denying him and being ashamed of him.

If you crave the Lord's help in this way, I have no doubt that when the time comes for you to stand before the king, God will grant you to open your mouth and glorify him by gainsaying whatever edict contradicts his word. If need be, he will even enable you to glorify him right to the end by the rendering up of your life. You must therefore pray to him, because not one of us has the strength within himself to resist a king's edict, for we can achieve nothing notable in his work unless we receive his enabling from above.

Fourth, faith will always be attacked

The fourth thing that I mark is this: I perceive that faith will always be attacked. No one yet had faith without daily temptations. Yet the temptations can never be so great, nor the trials so dangerous and grievous, but a man's faith will stand firm and cause him ultimately to be victorious. Yea, the powers of hell that our Master called the 'yetts'[34] of hell, shall not prevail against faith. That is not to say that faith possesses strength in and of itself. In itself faith is weak, and in the best of us is mingled with incredulity, so where faith believes one hour, the next two hours faith is beset by doubts. Rather, faith relies upon the power of him to whom it looks and on him on whom it fixes its sight.

I am referring to Jesus Christ and his strength, for faith does not repose upon itself. Because it knows that it flows from Christ, faith goes to Christ and finds refuge in his wisdom and power. He measures his grace and it pleases him to impart exactly what is needed. If he gave to us the measure of grace that we ask, our natural corruption would abuse his bounty. That is why he lays upon us a cross and trials, and only gives us sufficient strength to uphold us.

Moreover, as you continue to look to Christ and depend on his grace, he will send upon you further strength when you least expect it. That is why faith stands fast in temptation, not by its own strength,

[34] See above, Ch. 15, Note 17.

but by the power of Christ Jesus. If it were possible for you to see into your soul that Jesus Christ is constantly there within you, you would understand the impossibility of him ever denying you or refusing to grant you what you should ask. Yet, on account of the corruption of our fallen natures, the power of our passions, like a spate of flood-water, sweeps us away from the duty we owe to God and his Son, and all that his light within us asks of us. This bearing us away from our duty causes us to fall and offend against God, and that produces in us an evil conscience that cannot believe, and so bereft of faith we obtain nothing. Because it is the raging of our inner corruption that has fouled our consciences, the only way that we can keep the sight of Christ before us is the mortification of our vile natures.

However, you must not imagine the evil that has been lurking in you has been slain once and for all. If you know what your calling is and what it means to walk in it faithfully, you will learn by experience the error of deciding to take some time off from the life of faith. Even if it has just been a very short break to please your body and mind, you will discover that during your time off, so to speak, you have ceased to be employed in the will and work of God. Now you have begun to be controlled by a corrupt compulsion, very different to the calling of God that previously you obeyed. In other words, the mortified corruption that you thought had been slain has gotten new strength, and those passions which seemed to have become like a tame lamb now rage like a tiger. Indeed, you will discover the fury of them like the roar of a lion ready to break forth from its previous restful composure.

Therefore, constantly mortify your fallen natures, so that by mortification you may be diligent in your calling. The one who will not accept the calling of serving God shall find himself a servant and instrument of the devil, and a slave to his fallen passions, dictated to by his evil master; all who forsake the Lord's service will find themselves bound to a cruel master. So take heed to this, and each one of you keep watch over your calling, he over his calling and she over hers.[35] Even though maintaining your calling is difficult and may bring hunger and poverty, you shall find rest in it and a clear conscience; you will lie down in quietness and rise without fear, and you shall be as content with your meagre portion as if you possessed all the riches of this world. So be

[35] See the concluding sentence of note 21 above.

steadfast and diligent in your calling. Crave of Christ Jesus the power to put to death the works of corruption, for prayer and the exercises[36] of our calling are the special means to keep us in his sight; for in his sight there is joy, comfort and strength to uphold us in all our perplexities.

Fifth, the faith of believers brings profit to others

The last thing I mark is this: the faith of Christians is not only profitable for themselves and their families, but is also profitable for their neighbours. Indeed, Amram's and Jochebed's[37] faith was profitable for the entire nation of the Jews. For it was through their faith that Moses, who became the means and instrument of their deliverance by God, was preserved. Thus faithful men and women are very necessary in families, cities and commonwealths; they bring blessing not only to their own souls and bodies, but also to their families and the towns of the country where they live. Indeed, the Lord has such a regard for faithful men that a few will hold back the destruction of their city; ten would have stayed the destruction of Sodom,[38] and five would have stayed the destruction of Jerusalem.[39]

Clearly, then, it is a matter of great importance to be faithful, and to have faithful men as your companions. As this is true on the one side, so on the other side it is perilous to have wicked men as your companions, for they carry about upon themselves a malediction and a curse. Nor can you be certain when it might light upon one of them, so if you are in a house with such a man, you cannot be sure whether the roof will fall upon you both. If you are in a field with him, how can you know whether or not he shall be the cause of your slaughter, for the devil is lurking within him. Therefore, as faithful men are noticed and chosen to serve in cities and families, wicked men are ignored and avoided, in case others are included in the curse upon them.

Because faith brings a blessing with it, but infidelity brings a blight and a curse, crave that you may be partakers of the faith that reforms the soul. This is the whole purpose of this chapter in Hebrews, and also

[36] By 'exercises' is possibly meant reading of Scripture, attendance at worship and at the Lord's Table.

[37] See note 21 above.

[38] Genesis 18:32.

[39] Jeremiah 5:1, though in this verse only one faithful man was needed for the city to be saved.

of all that I have said so far and what I have yet to say: it is that you may obtain the faith that can renew your hearts and minds. Therefore pray for your pastors who teach you, that they might have the Spirit to edify you in faith, that you may also grow in faith and convey God's blessing upon yourself and upon the company you keep. The Lord bless his word and his administering of it, so that faith may grow both in you and in me, and that only through the righteous merits of Jesus Christ, to whom with the Father and the Holy Ghost be all honour praise and glory, now and for ever. Amen.

Chapter Twenty

Hebrew Chapter 11 verses 24-26

[24] By faith Moses quhen he was cum to age, refuised to be called the sone of Pharaois dauchter. [25] And chuse rather to suffer adversitie with the people of god, then to enjoy the pleasuris of sine for a seasoune. [26] Esteiming the rebuikis of chryst greater richis then the treasuris of Egypt, for he hade respect to the recompence of the reward.

In the last example, well-beloved in Jesus Christ, the apostle brought before us the parents of Moses, who gave very clear proof of their faith during extremely hard and troubled times. As to the circumstances when they gave this evidence of their faithfulness, he told us that Moses was born during that period when the king of the land had decided to issue an edict ordering death by drowning of all the new-born baby boys: every male child had to be killed by being thrown into the river. The Spirit-inspired account tells us that Moses' parents demonstrated their faith by not fearing this cruel edict, but preserved their baby by concealing him. In short, we saw that the apostle considered this violation of the law by their disobedience to be the effect and proof of their faithfulness to God.

I particularly emphasised this so that you would understand that in certain cases, violating and disregarding some man-made edict, resulting in disobeying a magistrate, could be as much the consequence of a person's faith, as humbly keeping some other law set up by the same magistrate. So what does the apostle mean by stating that disobedience to a magistrate could be a notable effect of faith? The biblical text itself explains the meaning, for in Romans 13:1-7 we are commanded to obey the lawgivers, not on account of fear of their anger as for the sake of our consciences. So note carefully this rule. When I obey for conscience's sake, my obedience is the effect of faith; whereas when I disobey for conscience's sake, my disobedience is also the effect of faith.

The Word of God is the objective rule for conscience

However, as this principle is to be applied according to a person's ability to understand it, each must reflect on it according to his conscience. Therefore, in examining the nature of your obedience or disobedience to some law, you must not use unreliable criteria and so conceal the real truth regarding your conscience, but you must apply the objective rule regarding conscience, namely, the Word of God. Thus when your conscience and the Word of God concur, you will not fail to be aware of what amounts to disobedience. When you have an express warrant from the Word which gives you the warrant of your conscience, if you then disobey your conscience, your disobedience will not emanate from faith but from rebellion. I say, therefore, that it will be clear if disobedience to some edict is the genuine effect of a person's faith.

I mention this again alongside the doctrine that we drew from this same verse last Sunday.[1] The apostle referred to this, not only on account of the two midwives and Amram and Jochebed, but regarding Moses himself. He was concerned that we should be aware of the times in which this baby was born, the manner in which he was preserved and the education that he subsequently received.

Now in the verses I have just read he moves on to Moses' inclinations when he reached more mature years. He underlines very emphatically the choices that Moses made. Remember the emphasis he placed upon the outcome of Abraham's faith, when he opened up that theme for us. Similarly, now he has come to Moses, he also emphasises the outcome of his faith. For as before the Law was given Abraham was praiseworthy and one of the most notable men of whom we read in Scripture, so when the time had come for the Law to be given there was none to be compared to Moses who then lived under the Law. Therefore, quite rightly the apostle says far more in praise of Moses than he does of any of the others.

[1] See above, Chapter 19, pp. 353-354, on the midwives and especially under 'Two Lessons for Today'. In addition, Bruce's phrase is 'on the last day', which, rightly or wrongly, I have assumed would be a Sunday.

Moses was given the highest commendation

I could say many things in this man's commendation, yet briefly for now I will remark on the following points to be found in the Scriptures. First, as you have already heard, when this boy was born the Lord caused his face to show such grace that all who saw him loved him. It was this feature of the child that God chose to be the means of providing him with his education, for it was his beauty that allured Pharaoh's daughter. So he was trained in all the wisdom of the Egyptians in their schools, as Stephen tells us.[2] So before he left Egypt he had received the best education.

Stephen also adds that he was mighty in both word and deed. The Lord himself gave Moses greater praise than was ever given to any other man. The occasion was when dissension occurred between him and his brother and sister, Aaron and Miriam, who envied the honour and estimation in which he was held, saying, 'Why is he regarded so highly? Has God only spoken by him? Has he not spoken by us as well?' So the emulation he received was given in consequence of their grudge. It pleased the Lord to pronounce on the matter: he descended in a cloud, and summoned Aaron and Miriam. You can read the account of this in Numbers 12:1-9.

The Lord began by speaking in praise of Moses, saying that he was very meek, yea, the meekest man on all the earth. So spoke the Spirit of God. Then the Lord derided the envy of Aaron and Miriam, and went on to say, 'It is true that there are prophets of the Lord among you, but how do I make myself known to them? Only by a dream or a vision; I draw no nearer. But as for Moses, I speak to him much more intimately, mouth to mouth, not through a dark cloud; but I let him see the similitude of my face.' Therefore the Lord said, 'You have done evil when you spoke against my servant, even my servant Moses.'

This praise God gave to Moses in that chapter of Numbers. After Moses' burial and in the last chapter of Deuteronomy, the Spirit of God said that there had never arisen a prophet like Moses. He also said that never would there ever again be (apart from our great Prophet)

[2] Acts 7:22. Josephus expounds on Moses' exploits while he was still living as Pharaoh's daughter's son, claiming that as the general of the Egyptian army he defeated the Ethiopians in battle. Josephus Book II chapter 10. This account is probably apocryphal.

someone with whom God spoke face to face as he did with Moses. Nor would there ever be such a man as he who brought the people out of Egypt with a mighty hand.[3]

Moses was also a type of Jesus Christ

Moses was also a type of Jesus Christ in many ways. We see in the 3rd chapter of this epistle that a comparison is made between Jesus and Moses, for these two may be compared in various ways, but mainly in the following points. As Moses delivered the people out of their many years of slavery and bondage to Pharaoh, so Jesus Christ delivers us out of our spiritual slavery and captivity of the devil, in which we are bound by nature, having been conceived and born in sin. Christ is the Lamb of God who takes away the sin of the world by the shedding of his own blood. In Luke 16:31 our Master also says that if they will not hear Moses, they will not listen though a man should rise from the dead and come to them. In Hebrews 3:5 the apostle adds that Moses was a most faithful servant, yea, in all that concerned God's house. All this was said in praise of Moses.

Concerning him when he died, it is written that his eyes were undimmed and his strength was unabated; none of his outward senses had declined. Further, concerning his burial it is written that he was interred neither by angels nor by man, but by the hand of God himself.[4] Jude implies that the devil disputed with Michael over the body of Moses,[5] because he wanted to know where his burial place was. But the Lord had buried him with his own hands so that his bones could not be dug up and used as relics; God's purpose was to avoid the superstition that later was adopted by the world.

The Law was given through Moses, but grace came through Christ

When we consider his birth, education and burial, we see how the Lord took very particular care of this man Moses. Therefore, seeing that he was such an outstanding instrument, it is no wonder that the apostle should insist somewhat on his praise. There is a further point to be made. Briefly, Moses was the giver of the Law of Works, for, says John,

[3] Deuteronomy 34:10-12.

[4] Deuteronomy 34:5-7.

[5] Jude 9.

the law was given by Moses, but grace and truth came by Jesus Christ.[6] Compared to everyone else we read of, Moses lived most agreeably to the Law, to the extent that if anyone could ever have been justified by the Law of Works, it was him. But as the record of the apostle makes clear, Moses never made such a claim; indeed he fled from the righteousness of works, and sought the justification that comes through the blood of Jesus Christ and his righteousness.

Moses directed his descendants away from the righteousness of the Law and to Christ Jesus who is the end of the Law, as the apostle says in Romans 10:4. Again as the apostle says in the same epistle, God is the justifier of those who have faith in Jesus.[7] He is not the justifier of everyone, only of those who have faith in his blood. That is why the apostle insists on this in his exposition: he wants to persuade his fellow-Jews who gloried so much in Moses, that if they wanted to follow in his footsteps, it behoved them not to claim the righteousness of works, but rather to glory in Jesus Christ alone and lay hold of the righteousness that is only through faith in him.

The implication in these verses is that the apostle's main purpose is to direct the Jews to the righteousness that is through faith, and is freely given and comes to us from heaven. This is why here he emphasises the faith of Moses in the various examples of his deeds that he cites for us in these verses. There is no other way in all the world other than this, to show that a man has faith; that is why the apostle has insisted on maintaining his theme right through this entire chapter in Hebrews. James says in chapter 2 of his epistle that faith is shown by our works, thus our behaviour and our deeds are the evidence of our faith; indeed there is no other way under the sun to express our faith other than by our works.[8]

Three ways in which Moses' faith is seen

To prove that Moses was full of faith, the apostle brings before us the fruits that sprang from his faith and he mentions three things that demonstrate this. First he says that when Moses came to the age of maturity, when he had reached as high a position of importance and

[6] John 1:17.
[7] Romans 3:26.
[8] James 2:17-18.

honour as anyone could have ever have enjoyed, he voluntarily took a cross upon himself—a cross that he need not have taken. Second, as soon as he began to fulfil his calling (I count the killing of the Egyptian as his first attempt to fulfil his calling, and I shall make this clear from Acts 7:23-25), persecution arose. The king was angered by what he had done and when he was pursued he fled from the king's presence. Had he been humble and petitioned the king, he could well have been restored to favour and recovered his position in the court. But he chose banishment, and so the cross was laid upon him. This choice also clearly declares his faith and testifies to it. The third witness to his faith was his deliverance out of the trouble into which it had pleased the Lord to cast him. Reflect upon his various deliverances, and you will find that the Lord guided him through every difficulty and preserved him.

The cross that Moses chose to carry

At this time I am only going to speak about the first evidence of his faith, that is, the cross that Moses voluntarily took upon himself, for this is what underlies the three verses we have read. First of all, in verse 24 the nature of this cross is described. Second, the circumstance of time when he took the cross upon himself is dealt with verses 26 and 27. Third, the motivation and causes that inspired him to take upon himself this voluntary cross are noted and subjoined.

We return, then, to the 24th verse. It is recorded that it was when he came to years of maturity he refused to be called the son of Pharaoh's daughter. These words reveal the cross he chose to bear. At this time, he was considered to be a member of the royal family and the son of a king's daughter. Yet, notwithstanding the honour and dignity conferred upon him, he now refused this title with all the wealth and privileges that accompanied it, and chose rather to be called the offspring of Abraham, Isaac and Jacob. Thus he opted for his share of the blessing that had been promised to Abraham and his descendants, and turned his back upon the status and riches that pertained to a king's son and a member of the royal court. This was the cross that he himself chose to carry, for no one compelled him to take it up.

We do not find it explicitly spelled out in Exodus that he refused to be called the son of Pharaoh's daughter. It never says so, but it is clearly expressed both in his actions and his attitude that he turned his back upon this dignity. It was when he grew up that he discerned between good and evil, and found that the family of which he was a member was godless; even though it was a powerful family, he saw that the curse of God was upon it. On the other hand, he knew that the Kirk of God and its members—even though they were of lowly estate and god-fearing—stood in the favour and under the blessing of the living God.

Moreover, he was persuaded in his heart that the Lord had raised him up to deliver the Kirk at that time and to be its saviour. Stephen confirms this saying that when he slew the Egyptian, he thought his brethren would have known he had been appointed to be their prince, their judge and their deliverer.[9] The Holy Spirit had planted that conviction in his heart, and because he himself had no doubt about it, he assumed that his people would also have had no doubts about it either; yet at that time they rejected him.

Inspired by the inward calling implanted in his heart by the Spirit, he had left the court and gone to visit his kinsmen. When he found them being oppressed, he acted to help them by revenging the injuries inflicted on them by the Egyptian. In this way, he showed clearly that he too was a Hebrew, and by what he had done he renounced the honour that he had through being the son of the king's daughter. We read of no other renunciation he made of his high estate and dignity, but undoubtedly this action resulted from his faith and was inspired by the Holy Spirit.

The reason why he cast off his royal status, which was his through the Lord's merciful provision, could only have been that he realised this was the way to God's spiritual blessing, and to those eternal riches offered in the promises made to Abraham and his descendants. Realising that he had another calling, and because he saw that the blessing of God was reserved for his people, he chose the Kirk rather than the court, and so left the latter and joined himself to the former. This I take to be the explanation of the cross that Moses took voluntarily upon himself.

The dangers for those who covet high positions of state

Further to these observations, briefly, I mark the following. I see a man here who is anxious to leave the court in which he had a place that he

[9] Acts 7:25.

had not chosen for himself; he was now anxious to forsake its honour and wealth. Moreover, I see that his inclinations were very different from those men of our generation, who seek by every means possible to ingratiate themselves before the king, thinking to find happiness in gaining a higher status. Indeed, in order to achieve their ambition, they will use devilish and unworthy methods to obtain an audience with his majesty. Such inclinations could not be more different to those of Moses. If only they realised how untrustworthy[10] such a status is, they would not pursue it so greedily.

As long as we remain mortals, there is no lofty status that does not have its downward slides and pitfalls, especially for those who succeed in gaining a place in a monarch's favour. For only those who ascend to that pinnacle of their ambition are liable to a disastrous fall from their prince's grace. The higher a man rises, the further down he will drop, and when the painful crash comes, how hard it always is to rise up again! That can never happen to those of lowly standing. Of course, there are snares to entrap us all in whatever level of society we live. But those who move in the highest circles are most exposed to temptations that will lead them into sin. Therefore the great men and women in society must tread very warily.

It is true that there have been exceptions, for we read of just a few who have maintained their lofty status without losing the favour of God—Joseph for example. Therefore, lords and nobles should always be on their guard and live circumspectly. They must maintain a straight course, without ever be enticed by fleeting pleasures; nor should they compromise in order to please their prince, a snare into which all carnally-minded men can be drawn. Unless they watch over their integrity, they will meet with a miserable end.

It was essential that Moses bore all this in mind. Having lived in the court for forty years, he then withdrew to a happier and more honest position, and was able to live the whole of his life in the fear of God. His example should be pondered by all those who recognise that such integrity must be an important aspect of their happiness, and they would do well to withdraw from high positions of state into which they have ingratiated themselves.

[10] Bruce's word is 'slidderie', its basic meaning being 'slippery'.

Was Moses guilty of ingratitude towards his adoptive mother?

Further to Moses' departure from the court, it might appear that he sullied himself with ingratitude. Without doubt he had a huge debt of thanks to Pharaoh's daughter, for she had preserved him when by rights he ought to have been killed according to the edict. She had raised him and provided for him his education in Egyptian learning. She had adopted him as her own son, and she could not have advanced him to a higher status in the land. Yet he left her without even bidding her farewell. His action could be thought to have shown great ingratitude.

But alongside that we must consider his calling and the duty he owed to God. His departure from the court cannot be considered to have shown him to be ungrateful. Yes, we are bound to be thankful to others, but although our chief duty of gratitude is thankfulness to God, it is right to express our thanks to others within God's purposes for us and before him. Nevertheless, when the circumstances are such that we cannot give thanks both to others and to God at the same time, then our duty to thank God must come first. It is a source of sorrow when pleasing men conflicts with pleasing God, and even causes him displeasure. Yet, such is the persistence of men that, whether their cause is just or not, they want to have their own feelings satisfied.

Unhappy is the one who gives in to men's wishes, even when thereby they bring displeasure to God; they end up pleasing men but defiling their own consciences. Unless their requests are agreeable to the will of God, let them leave you with the answer they do not want to hear, otherwise you yourself will part from them with a bad conscience, because you will know full well that you have assented to what is wrong. So we must ensure that the duties we owe to others are compatible with the duty we owe to God. From what experience has taught me, and this is confirmed as we read the Scriptures, we never find anyone who ignored the displeasure of God by choosing to please a man, but God allowed that same man to bring sorrow to him who had offended God; indeed, the very man he sought to please became his executioner!

This manner of God's working—as you will learn from your own experience—teaches us that kings are thwarted most often by men they love the most. Therefore it would be an excellent lesson if men, especially great men, could learn always to begin with God, to love no others except those whom they love 'in the Lord'. Then the friends I love in Christ would not thereafter deliberately oppose me, or become my executioner.

Moses reaches the age of maturity

We turn now to consider the circumstance of the time when Moses embraced this cross: it was when he came to the age of maturity. If he had taken this cross upon himself when he was still a child, it could have been thought that he had acted in ignorance. Had he taken it on when he was still an immature youth and still being controlled by his feelings, it might have appeared that he had acted rashly and foolishly. But he took upon himself this cross when he reached the age of discretion, for as Stephen records, he was aged forty.[11] We see then that this steadfast resolution was taken in faith, and in the knowledge that he was choosing the better course. Had he not made this choice in faith, the apostle would not have attributed it to faith.

We have seen how the Lord constantly cared and provided for him, both at his birth and in his education. Now he watches over him as he reaches his adult years, graciously inclining him to obey his calling, and sending his Holy Spirit to bend his will, mortify his heart and illumine the darkness of his mind. That was how it came about that Moses recognised his effectual call and gladly responded by his obedience. Such is the care the Lord has for his vessels of honour, having appointed them for eternal distinction. Yes, he watches over every aspect of their lives, from infancy, through childhood and on into maturity. He endues his chosen servants with the mighty power of his Holy Spirit, to work obedience in them so that they may follow their calling. Thus far, then, for verse 24.

Moses' motivation for taking up his cross

We come now to verses 25 and 26 where we are given the motivation and reasons for Moses taking up this cross. As to the first motive, we are told in verse 25 that it was his own decision*[12] and choice that moved

[11] Acts 7:23.

[12] The three words I have translated as 'decision*' are marked with an asterisk (as they are further on). Bruce's word used three times is 'electioun', which can be used both in the passive voice, i.e., 'being chosen', or as in the active voice, i.e. 'a personal choice' (DSL). The context seems to imply a free personal choice, though Bruce's thought underlying his 'electioun' was undoubtedly that he was elected by

him. Before him were the two options, the first in the world and the second in the Kirk among the people of God. In the world, royalty awaited him along with the glory, honour and wealth that accompanies kingship. On the other hand, being numbered with the Lord's people would mean espousing poverty, accompanied by a cross that must be carried every day; along with this would be the ignominy of the world's contempt.

By the help of the Spirit of God, the choice he made was the one that the natural man would have considered to be the worse by far of the two options. Thus we see that his motivation was entirely his own decision*. He was free to choose as he wished, but he deliberately chose the Kirk, preferring it rather than the honour and affluence he would have enjoyed in the royal court.

Moses gladly rejected worldly glory and chose to suffer with God's people

First, Moses chose to suffer with God's people. So was his decision* a good one or not? To answer that question, I refer you to verse 26: *Esteiming the rebuikis of chryst greater richis then the treasuris of Egypt, for he hade respect to the recompence of the reward.* Here we see how worthy he was of great praise and commendation because, from being in a powerful and honourable position in this world and knowing that God's Kirk was poor and despised, Moses gladly and willingly rejected the former and embraced the latter, even though the Egyptians must have considered membership of the Kirk to be the most miserable of conditions.

Today we regard true friendship as standing up for someone who has been plunged into some distressing situation, for the true test of loyalty is how we react when someone is subjected to adversity. Thus it was that Moses gave testimony to his love for Jesus Christ and his Kirk, by not turning his back in her time of greatest affliction, but being willing to share the distress that had come upon her.[13] Thus he put his

God for the task before him.

[13] In these sentences, Bruce consistently uses the feminine pronouns 'her' and 'she' of the Kirk, according the reformed understanding of the Kirk as our 'mother'. As Calvin writes, 'I shall start, then, with the church, into whose bosom God is pleased to gather his sons… that they may be guided by her motherly care until they mature and at last reach the goal of faith.' *Inst.* IV.I.1, where also see Note 3 and Cyprian (*et al.*) cited: 'You cannot have God for your Father, unless you have

shoulders under the burden she was bearing as God gave him the grace to uphold her.

It is true that those who will not share in the trials and afflictions of the Kirk shall have no share in her peace and tranquillity. Likewise, those who are unwilling to suffer the poverty of Jesus Christ[14] will never reign with him in glory. It is not enough to see and acknowledge that Christ's Kirk is suffering most miserably, even if you withhold your hand and refuse to take any part in afflicting her. Rather is it incumbent upon you to put out your hand and come to her aid when she is in distress.

Ammon and Moab were punished by the living God, not because of any injury they inflicted upon his people, but because they withheld their assistance from them in their hour of need, refusing even to permit them to use the highway; they ought to have succoured them with bread and wine.[15] So it is not enough to hold up your hands and to refuse to injure the Kirk. Rather the living God demands of us that we use every means and facility that he has given to us for her relief, help and advancement.

An appeal to the nobility

I say all this deliberately, so that those of you who have the authority and opportunity to help the Kirk should not stand by impassively as she suffers, but should consider it one of the best actions that you could ever undertake to advance the cause and honour of her distressed members. We cannot doubt that if Moses himself was present among us at this time, his priority would be to identify with the Kirk in order to honour and help her. That is why I speak thus to you, my lords, that you may learn to choose to work for Jesus Christ rather than for any other cause in this world. I urge this upon you not only on account of the help you might bring to the Kirk, but so that when the Lord shall one day bring you to trial, your consciences may bear witness that, as best as you were able, you helped her in her mission; so shall you then be commended as having done her good. Can you see, therefore, that

the church for your mother.' Cyprian is implicitly quoted by Calvin here in his own text. Those who argue for God to be called 'mother' are (probably unintentionally) ascribing sexuality to God, who creates, but does not pro-create.

[14] Hebrews 13:12-13.

[15] Deuteronomy 23:3-6.

my desire is that when your hour comes, you will depart in peace. This is even more important than that the Kirk should be supported in these days of confusion. Therefore act now, and always make Jesus Christ and his Kirk your highest priority, so long as she survives within our land and commonwealth.

Sinful pleasures end in bitterness but the reproach of Christ leads to glory

The second point I mark regarding the right choice is this. On the one hand, I see the lot of the Kirk as she is now, and on the other hand, I see the lot of many who are not within the Kirk, but instead are in the very highest position of authority in the courts of various princes, enjoying all the luxuries of this world. The pleasures in which they indulge are the pleasures of sin, which only continue for a short time. Just as the cross that is presently laid upon the back of the Kirk will not always continue, no more will those pleasures in which the worldly indulge always continue.

Then what will be the final outcome of such pleasures of sin? No doubt it will be bitterness. And what will be the outcome of the Kirk's trials? Without doubt it will be peace and tranquillity. Likewise, what will be the outcome of her poverty? Most certainly it will be felicity and riches, for the end of all her reproach and false accusations can only be glory and honour. Contrast that, if you will, with the ignominious end of the godless!

It is evident, then, that the pleasures of sin ought to be eschewed, for, as it is implied here in these verses, they are deceitful and false. They are deceitful because though they appear to be genuine, they are not what they claim to be, for they are cloaked with a false enjoyment which not only cannot last, but ultimately will end in bitterness and eternal remorse. They are false because they have a taste which quickly disappears, for it too is deceitful. Genuine pleasure is not deceitful, but endures, whereas the pleasures of sin, though they briefly bring some enjoyment, soon evaporate, proving their falseness. The reason for this is not only on account of the essence of sin, but also stems from our depraved, fallen natures. For if our hearts and minds, souls and bodies, were not foully corrupted, we would be completely unable to find any pleasure in this world's sin.

Our fallen natures will never delight in holiness until they are washed and cleansed

What is carnal pleasure but desires and feelings that arise in us because they find assent from within our corrupt natures? There is nothing that agrees more with our natures than sin, which is why there is nothing that our natures find more delightful than sin. Until we are washed and cleansed from the guilt that sin has brought upon us, and until the eyes of our minds are enlightened so that we can recognise the ugliness of sin, and our hearts are sensitised to feel sin's bitterness, it is not possible that any single one of us can cease to delight in sin.

None of us is naturally able to find pleasure in heavenly and holy things, until in some measure we are made holy and spiritual. If our natures remain carnal and vile, will corruption ever find delight in purity, or could there ever be harmony between us and holiness? Therefore we need a clear insight into what sin really is, the disguises it can wear, the various personas it can adopt and the abominations of which it is capable. Then at last will our minds and hearts be ready to be purged and renewed by the mighty working of the Spirit of God.

The necessity of repentance

The apostle tells us that our hearts and minds are cleansed and renewed when we begin to repent of our offences against God. When repentance is genuine, it reaches into a man's heart, causing him to be touched with sorrow and remorse for the sins in which previously he took the greatest delight. And when a man's heart is so affected that he detests what he formerly loved, the Holy Spirit has begun to work holiness into his nature and is sanctifying his body and soul. Nor will he cease this work until that man becomes like the holy angels. So examine yourselves to see whether you take pleasure in sin or not. Scrutinise your hearts and minds.

Everyone conceived and born of natural seed is bound to have some personal idol, some particular sin to which he is addicted, as well as sins that are common to us all. When the evangel is preached, that personal idol and sin, peculiar to him, will rob his heart of any love for and pleasure in Christ. Your idol is identified by whatever you employ in the service of your soul and body. So think as to what sin it is that you are closely acquainted with, and what it was that you spent your energies on in your earlier years. Ask yourself what sin it is that you would find hardest to expel from your soul; that is the sin that carries deceitful pleasure with it, and allures you into continual indulgence of it.

Therefore your whole aim and effort should stand firm in the resolve to renounce your idol, and to yield your heart to be cleansed by the power that flows from the blood of Christ. Only then will you find this disposition within you is able to say, 'The thing I liked best before I now detest, and what my Master asked of me before I could not obey because I loved that particular sin. But now it is my slave and I am able to cast it behind me.' Those in whom this new disposition is wrought will experience the power that accompanies the gospel of Jesus Christ, and they will receive his eternal blessing upon their souls.

Therefore, my dear friends, take heed to yourselves, and each one of you understand that many momentary pleasures invariably end in eternal bitterness. If human tribunals and the stern countenances of mere mortals bring men low, creating in them fearful dread, how much more shall the tribunal of the Most High, the God of consuming fire, terrify them! I have no doubt that, unless in the here and now we have the testimony of a good conscience that we have not yielded to deceitful, sinful pleasures, when the Lord himself shall come, we shall call upon the hills and mountains to fall upon us, to hide us from the face of the Lamb.[16] For God shall come in a devouring fire to consume and destroy all evil, so that if there be sin in any of us, we must of necessity be devoured. But those in whom he finds that the blood of Christ has cleansed their soul and sanctified their heart, then, acknowledging Christ's blood, he will see them as being 'in him', and the righteousness and holiness of his Son shall plead effectually for them. Therefore here in this life choose faith in Jesus Christ! This is the substance of the whole evangel!

Consider this: those who refuse to repent after being warned but continue to despise the evangel proclaimed by the Lord's servant, as God is God, for them the torments of hell shall be doubled.[17] So lay your hand upon your heart, and do not refuse to turn from transient pleasures, but submit and take upon yourselves the cross of the Kirk.

[16] The allusion is to Revelation 6:15-17.

[17] Probably an allusion to Luke 12:47-48.

If you will not then, at the last, your heart will be grieved. Shun all fleshly gratification, and indulge only in those pleasures which at your departing will bring eternal peace to your conscience. This far, then, for our consideration of verse 25.

Moses' choice led to union with Christ

Moses' choice might have appeared to have come from an unhinged mind, for it may have seemed a foolish decision when he joined the company of poor slaves. Therefore in verse 26, the apostle declares that his choice flowed neither from folly nor rashness, but from wisdom, the best counsel and a steadfast resolve: *Esteiming the rebuikis of chryst greater richis then the treasuris of Egypt, for he hade respect to the recompence of the reward.*

For further verification, he describes his resolution in the clearest of terms. The taunts and mocking of the people of God and his Kirk are represented in Scripture as the reproach of Christ.[18] This is because there is a close union between Christ and his Kirk, closer even than union between our heads and the other parts of our bodies. Consequently, Christ considers an injury inflicted on any of his people is an injury inflicted upon himself, for we read in Hebrews 4 that he is affected[19] when his people are also affected.[20] This refers even to an injury done to lowliest of his members.

Regarding this close union, the Kirk here signifies his Head. Thus Moses considered that this reproach of Christ, and the ignominy in which his Kirk was held, to have been greater riches and advancement than all the treasures of Egypt. Having resolved accordingly, he held to his decision[21] and, as we have just seen, made his choice, even though it might have appeared that his choice was as foolish as any ever made. It is quite a thought that shame and contempt could have been greater riches than the wealth of Egypt!

The last part of verse 26, *for he hade respect to the recompence of the reward*, indicates that his decision* was holy and his resolve was wise, because they proceeded from faith. True wisdom is when the insight of faith leads to a firm resolve, and a man's choice is guided by faith. Faith

[18] Hebrews 13:13.

[19] His verb is 'twitchit', meaning 'touched with painful consequences'. (DSL)

[20] Hebrews 4:14. See also Luke 10:16; Acts 9:5; Colossians 1:24.

[21] See note 12 above.

was his counsellor regarding the path he should take, and it was by faith that he saw the rich recompense and its reward that would follow after the reproach of the Kirk. It was infinitely more to be desired than all the world's wealth and honour. Ignominy would be exchanged for everlasting glory, poverty for unending felicity, temporary trials for eternal joy!

An appeal to those who are spiritually blind

What choice was there? Can you not see that whoever chooses the eternal and ignores the temporal has made the best choice? When you realise that this resolve flowed from faith, there can be none of you who does not commend Moses' decision*. However, if you are not endowed with the insight with which he was endowed, it will not be possible for you to discern what he discerned. What spiritual eyes are able to see cannot be seen by natural sight, as the apostle says in 1 Corinthians 2:14-16. For what our natural sight cannot see are things spiritual and eternal, and they can only be seen through faith and by the eyes of the soul. Whoever remains blind in his soul and without faith can never perceive these things, therefore he can never resolve to choose these things. So without these spiritual eyes he wanders in darkness and makes his heaven here on earth, and whoever does that will never reach the heaven that is above.

Therefore, that you may make the right choice and resolution, seek to obtain spiritual eyes. Do not remain in darkness after you have been offered light in abundance. Have you not often heard these words sounding forth? Even if you have heard them spoken many times and by other voices, and even though you still neither perceive nor feel anything, should you not be moved to ponder upon them, and to realise that they refer to weighty matters? Even though you have neither spiritual eyes nor feelings, and you are unaware that the divine threats are to be avoided, and even though you neither believe in mercy nor in judgment, do you not ask yourself why you are so hard-hearted that you cannot find within yourself anything but natural abilities? Do you say that you have no feelings in your heart to persuade you of the reality of these things, or whether there is a heaven and a hell after this life? In short, you remain completely in the dark about all such matters.

Any of you who realise this is your condition, do not despair! It is not by accident or by chance that the Lord has brought you under the sound of his word, because this opportunity to hear the gospel is either to convert you, or else to warn you of your impending condemnation. Anyone completely lacking in spiritual insight, who randomly comes to hear the word of God, must ask the Lord for spiritual eyes; he gives generously to those who seek and multiplies what he gives, so that the one who has asked might continue to grow spiritually until he comes at length into everlasting life. So those of you who lack this disposition, I say again, do not despair! Rather seek his knowledge and assurance. For there are some who are still unconverted and in their old natures, yet they have been appointed to receive mercy when the Lord's time for them comes. Some of you may have reached the Lord's season of mercy today.

You who do have this disposition, be careful to nourish it; you who do not have it, diligently seek for it. It matters not whether you are in ecclesiastical or civil office, for I have no doubt that there are persons in both of these ranks who have never yet experienced the things of which I have been speaking. Therefore beseech God that what you have heard today may be of profit to you, and that in your souls you may feel and acknowledge that what has been said is true. Does not John say in chapter 3 of his Gospel that the greatest glory you can give to Christ is to say in your hearts that his message is true?[22] Therefore so strive that the Spirit of God may accomplish this in you, and then you will experience genuine joy.

A final admonition to believers

I have one final point to make and then I will finish. Seeing that Moses counted the reproach of Christ so dearly, let us also place our dignity in the reproach of Christ for his sake; similarly, let us also place our wealth in the poverty of Christ for his cause; more, let us place our rest and quietness in his cross. If for the cause of Christ the problems of our natural bodies increase, the peace and tranquillity in our hearts will also increase, and we will find the effects of our justification being enlarged within our souls. If it be for Jesus' sake, trials will be the Christian's honour, and shame will be his glory.

But if you bring some trial upon yourself, though you may weep over what you have done, do not despair, rather crave the peace that

[22] John 3:33-36a.

flows from the Lord's compassion. For with him is the peace that passes human understanding. The natural man cannot understand how peace can come to a troubled conscience and an indisposed soul. Yet when it pleases the Lord to awaken such a soul, then the fears that caused alarm will be pacified.

How else can we get the peace that takes away the burning fire that otherwise would consume us, other than by the power of the blood of Jesus Christ? If then you share in his kingdom, you must be willing to suffer with him; certainly such sufferings are but tokens of the coming eternal felicity and joy. So take care that any calling or status you may have is held only by God's favour. Unhappy am I if the status I have is incompatible with the burning holiness of God, for if that be so, then I have allowed my own heart to become my executioner. If by nature you do not want to give up your status—for our fallen natures do not want to turn their backs upon worldly wealth—then crave of the living God that he would sever you from everything that severs you from him.

If your heart and conscience are running headlong towards your destruction, then crave of God that he would subdue your will, and fashion your heart in such a way that at length you will be willing to give up the status and position of honour which you cannot retain with his favour and approval. Whatever you are unable to do willingly, crave the help of God that you may die with his blessing and mercy upon you. All of you pray that you may have grace to live and die in his peace, and then after your death to receive the crown of eternal glory. I beseech the Lord in his mercy to grant that crown to every one of us, and that through the righteous merits of Christ, to whom with the Father and the Holy Ghost be all honour, praise and glory, now and for ever. Amen.

Chapter Twenty-One

Hebrew Chapter 11 verses 26-27

> [26] *Esteiming the rebuikis of chryst greater richis then the treasuris of Egypt, for he hade respect to the recompence of the reward.* [27] *By faith he forsuik Egypt and feared not the fearcenes of the king, for he indurit as he that saw him who is invisible.*

Brethren and well-beloved in Jesus Christ, you have heard the particulars of Moses' birth, and how wonderfully it pleased the Lord to preserve him. You also heard a brief account of his education and the circumstances in which it pleased the Lord for him to be brought up. You heard, too, of Moses' feelings when he came to years of discretion, and of the calling to which he inclined his heart, for when he reached the age of forty it pleased the Lord to awaken him by stirring up his mind. God moved effectually in his heart showing him he must leave the court and embrace the vocation to which he had been appointed, even before he was born.

The two alternatives that had been before Moses

There was doubtless a great inward wrestling and debate within Moses at this time, because there lay before him two options, both extremely difficult choices. However, by the gracious assistance and mighty power of the Spirit of Jesus Christ, that great Angel,[1] Moses chose the better of the two, and so he changed direction by following his choice. On the one hand, his first choice had been the security he was already enjoying at that time, with the world at his feet, together with all its honour and glory, riches and wealth, pleasure and ease; all this had been laid

[1] Genesis 48:16. See Chapter 17, note 46 above.

out before his very eyes. On the other hand, there had been the second option: it was the promise of only poverty and wretchedness, and as long as he remained in this world he would see nothing but trials and vexation. It was up to him which of the two he preferred.

Had the choice been left to flesh and blood, unquestionably Moses would have chosen the honour and glory of this world. But being powerfully directed by the Holy Spirit, this servant of God took no heed of the temporal glamour before him, rather he thought deeply and saw the implications of the outward, glittering show. Through the insight granted to him by the Spirit of Jesus, he also caught sight of the implications of the present trials and ignominy, and saw that the second choice was of the cross of Christ, whose reproach and sorrows his members must of necessity be subject to while here on this earth. Therefore, says verse 25, *he chuse rather to suffer adversitie with the people of god, then to enjoy the pleasuris of sine for a seasoune*, and so he had turned his back upon the wealth and glory of the court. Because his heart was instructed by the Spirit, he esteemed the reproach of Christ and whatever that might involve to be greater glory, greater riches and greater advancement than all the honour and wealth of this world.

The chief reasons that caused him to make his choice were the promises of recompense and the sight of a great reward. The Spirit of God let him see that concealed beneath the present poverty were eternal and heavenly riches, and hidden under present ignominy was everlasting and infinite glory. The Spirit also revealed to him that, obscured by present pain and temporal discomfort, awaiting him would be perpetual rest, quietness and felicity. The same Spirit also let him see that the delights of the court's pleasures, and indeed anything that he could not have in good conscience, would invariably end in eternal remorse, vexation and torment. Likewise, the end of wealth and riches would be eternal bankruptcy of all spiritual graces, and the final outcome of temporal glory and honour would be the everlasting shame of God's wrath.

By faith Moses gladly chose the cross of Christ

Therefore, being enlightened by the instruction of the Holy Spirit, and realising that all temporal pleasures, delights and worldly gain were fleeting, outward show that could not endure, but seeing also that the present trials and sufferings of the Lord's people would lead to a happy and righteous end, Moses understood that the only possible choice was the second alternative. The Spirit of God enabled him to avoid what the world considered to be the least desirable option, and instead to take the cross of Christ upon his shoulders willingly, courageously and gladly. Thus he turned his back upon the court.

His voluntary choice is taken by the apostle to be an evidence of his faith. Undoubtedly, had he not been enlightened by this heavenly understanding and the faith which is imparted by the Spirit of Christ, flesh and blood alone could never have made the right choice. For who can choose what he cannot see, or who is able to assent to conditions that he cannot understand? That is how it is with the natural man, who is still in the spiritual darkness in which he was conceived and born, and does not have the insight to consider or grasp the spiritual graces that are being offered to him; without that insight it is impossible for him to make the right choice.

Only through the Spirit's illumination can we make the right choice

Therefore, seeing that spiritual things can only be discerned through the Spirit of God and of Jesus Christ (for who can know what is in God except his own Spirit?), it is impossible to grasp the spiritual realities that are in God unless we have some portion of his heavenly light. That is why I say that we must admit our guilty negligence and reprove our slothfulness, and must find fault with our rebelliousness that prevents us from seeking mercy for the sake of Jesus Christ. We forget to seek the Spirit's light which alone can illuminate our blind minds as they vainly grope in the darkness, unwilling either to accept Christ's light or to receive his admonition and chastening. We have neither sought nor sensed the infinite complexities of evil mysteries that lurk deep within us. Little wonder we do not seek Christ's light nor the good things that would then be offered to us.

As it has pleased the Lord outwardly through his word to offer Jesus Christ to us along with all the benefits he brings to those who seek him, so he would also prepare and sanctify our hearts to enable us to receive the gratuitous offer that he has been making to you for so long. Only then would you avoid his awesome wrath, for he desires that every one of us should have some awareness of it in our hearts, that we may grieve over the stubbornness and blindness of our sinful natures.

Without delay, therefore, take heed to the instruction of the verse that I have read and briefly expounded to you, that you may perceive and understand the light, wisdom and discernment that enable a man to assess rightly earthly and heavenly things together with personal values.

The Spirit's illumination and faith

Consider now what kind of light it must be that enables us firmly to make our choice and adhere to it.

The first benefit of the Spirit's illumination

We can only make the right choice if first our minds have been enlightened by faith, for unless the light of faith is shining in our souls we will be unable to distinguish between eternal heavenly things and transitory earthly things. For this world's deceitful pleasures soon will be taken from us; they are carnal and will entangle us in their snares and bring us to eternal death; it is faith that opens our eyes to this. On the other hand, faith enables us to see that the pleasures offered in heavenly things are both genuine and enduring, and the longer our hearts are set upon them, the greater becomes our enjoyment of delights that are permanent and everlasting.

The judgment of the natural man is unable to discern this difference, for such is the corruption in human nature since we fell away from God that our intelligence, which is the best part of us, has made us enemies of God. Consequently, we are not now able to judge correctly between one person or another, nor upon any other issues that come before us. Even those who are considered to be among the world's wisest men, such as the great philosophers, cannot reach the right conclusions regarding what constitutes virtue and what constitutes vice. As to understanding a man's character, they are swayed in their judgment by outward appearances, mistaking mere show and shadow for the things that matter. Their problem has been that they are bereft of the clear light of faith through which they might have been able to judge rightly. It is the same with you and me. Indeed, anyone who attempts to assess someone, but does not have the light of truth and faith, will be swayed by outward appearances in and of themselves, and will be unable to come to valid conclusions regarding that person, far less judge his beliefs and religion correctly. The crux of the matter is that outward show and shadows can deceive us all.

Therefore, seeing that right judgment proceeds from the Spirit of Jesus Christ and faith, should we not all seek to be spiritual? That means beseeching Christ that it would please him to mortify in our carnal natures all that is unclean, dispelling the darkness of our minds with his light, so that in all that concerns our salvation we may be able discern between what is best for us and what we must avoid. We have to pray—and I urge you to join me in this prayer—that we would earnestly seek this light and the spirit of grace, so that we may learn to assess people rightly and be granted insight into spiritual matters.

The second benefit of the Spirit's illumination

There is a second benefit of this inward sight: it enables us by faith to deny ourselves and all that our carnal natures hold dearest in this world.[2] Through the light of Jesus Christ and when faith works effectually, his Spirit gives us the strength to renounce and turn our backs upon what previously may have been most pleasing to us. That is how it was when Moses renounced the honour, wealth and luxuries of the court. Because we are all ambitious, we are attracted by what appears desirable to our fallen natures. Yet because Moses had the benefit of faith and the insight of Christ's Spirit, he willingly renounced all the pleasures and attractions of the court. When he left the king, his court with all its favours and departed from Egypt, Moses put behind him all those things upon which flesh and blood naturally depend; instead, by the benefit of faith he voluntarily took up the cross and followed Jesus Christ and his call.

Consider then this extraordinary benefit of faith. Those are said to deny themselves who renounce anything that withholds them from the presence of God in Christ Jesus. What is it then in your life that you cannot keep without offending God and displeasing Christ? If you do not renounce it and sever yourself from it, you have not yet enrolled in the school where you learn to deny yourself and embrace Jesus Christ. Certainly, those whose custom has been to engage constantly in something that displeases God and Jesus Christ, will find it extremely difficult when first confronted with the necessity of renouncing it, for they will not be able immediately to sever their corrupt natures from it.

[2] Bruce's phrase is 'quhat is deirest to [our] flesche and blude in the earth'.

If for some there is an initial desire to quit their evil practice, and they genuinely do want to break their sinful habit and rid themselves of it, that is because they now see that it is incompatible with the grace of Jesus Christ. They have realised that they cannot hold on to what is sinful and at the same time share in the mercy and favour of God, for that sin robs[3] them of the sense of his presence and of the joy and peace in their hearts and minds that is the Lord's gift to them. You may say, 'I will renounce the thing that robs me of that joy [and peace for which I long], and accept anything that is going to help my life, especially if it is going to enrich[4] it.'

Sometimes repentance may be gradual

Suppose a man cannot at first sever himself from everything that is carnal, if he resolves to deal with his sins little by little, and he constantly prays for strength, asking the Lord to impart more and yet more of his grace, also little by little, then, by the effectual working of his Holy Spirit, the Lord will enable him at length to make a complete break from his sinful past, and when it is all finally put behind him the eternal God will fully impart his blessing to him. If this applies to you, you are now almost ready to be blessed. Then take careful note. Without any doubt, this is both the first and the last lesson: learn to deny yourself, to take up the cross and to follow Jesus Christ. And if you can only do this little by little, be firm in your resolve, attend diligently to your ways, and understand how it is that you may yet have the blessing and presence of Jesus Christ.

Watch out for anything that will mar your testimony and hinder you and, recognising it, make a fresh resolution to be rid of it. For it is better to enter the kingdom of heaven naked than to be clothed with some sin that will cause you to drown in hell for ever. However, if you resolve to receive God's blessing but find your stubborn heart and will refuse to obey, then apply yourself to constant prayer that the Lord, who is far stronger than both you and the devil at work within you, will make your resolution effectual.

[3] Bruce's verb used twice in this paragraph is 'spuilyeis' which literally means 'plunder' in the sense of carrying off 'spoil'.

[4] Bruce's very homely and unexpected verb is 'wair' which means 'to spread dung on a field', presumably to increase its fecundity.

Is there someone who needs to apply this to himself? Knock on the door of your conscience, examine your possessions, how you came by them and why you kept them. Consider whether they have brought you peace and inner tranquillity, and whether with them you also have had the sight of the face of Christ. Then as you make your resolve, and so that your resolve may be effectual, continue to be instant in prayer to that end. Remember the promise that Christ makes in the gospels, that those who resolve [to carry the cross rather than indulge in carnal pleasures and] to quit anything for his name's sake, whether it be father or mother, possessions or inheritance, shall not only be rewarded in the world to come, but in this life also.[5] Yea, whatsoever you lose in order to gain Christ Jesus, this is his clear and faithful promise, and it can never fail in one single jot.

Do not let your hard heart and blind nature move you to incredulity. Believe Jesus Christ and you will be recompensed twice over. Can you not see this exemplified in the experience of Moses? No doubt, I suppose that in him we have the greatest example there is, for with his excellent education and scholarship, and being considered at this time as the king's son, in time he could well have become equal to Pharaoh himself; had he remained at court, he might even have risen to the very highest estate and succeeded the Egyptian ruler.[6] No other living person could have attained higher honour. Nevertheless, as we have seen, he renounced that dignity and all the privileges it would have brought to him. Yet when he could see no other prospect other than ignominy and poverty, the Lord so guided him that here on earth he called him into even greater honour than if had been a king.

Therefore take heed to Moses' experience of God's faithfulness to his promises, and may you be encouraged to resolve as he did, and to hold fast to your resolution to sever yourselves from everything that comes between you and the gracious presence of God in Christ Jesus. Keep in mind the way in which the Lord raised him up higher than any other ruler or prince, making him a god to Pharaoh, and a god ranks higher

[5] Mark 10:29-31.

[6] Josephus recounts an outstanding military campaign led by Moses against the Ethiopians, but he maintains that it was jealousy over his successes on the part of Pharaoh and subsequent plots to have him killed that caused to Moses to flee to Midian. Josephus, II, X, 1 & 2. Chapter 20, note 2 above.

than a king. Moses' presence ultimately struck such fear into Pharaoh that he trembled at the sight of him, so much so that he could not abide him.[7] I mention this only to let you see the faithful fulfilment of Jesus Christ's promise that there is no one who leaves house or family or children or lands for my sake who shall not receive as recompense a hundredfold in this life.[8] This lesson is hard indeed to put into practice, and I know no other way to do so than the one I have told you: when you make the choice before you, resolve also to be steadfast in prayer, that your resolution may be effectual.

The third benefit of the Spirit's illumination and faith

The third thing that I mark is this: Jesus Christ counts as his own all the crosses, injuries and trials that we sustain through no fault of our own, but for the cause of righteousness and for his sake. I mean he counts them as done to himself. Therefore the murmuring, malice, envy and troubles that Moses endured at the hands of his own people, are counted here as the reproach of Jesus Christ. He suffered similar rebukes from his kinsmen and countrymen during the time he was here upon earth in the flesh. Thus it is clear that Moses' suffering was an identification with Christ's own suffering. Yet Jesus Christ was exposed to the most shameful and bitter death through the wickedness of his own people. It was in a more limited way that Moses identified with Christ's reproach.

Christ counts his believers' sufferings as his own

Apply this to yourselves. Any rebukes that we suffer in the cause of righteousness, Christ counts as his. When Saul was pursuing the believers, the Lord asked him, 'Why are you persecuting me?'[9] Thus we see there is a direct union between the Head and the members, for the injuries done to the lowliest members affect the Head who himself feels them and counts them as his own injuries. This is deliberately implied by the apostle.[10]

There can be no doubt that he wanted to comfort the Jewish believers to whom he was writing, for they too were being subjected to

[7] Exodus 12:29-32; 33-36.

[8] See Note 5 above.

[9] Acts 9:5.

[10] Bruce is referring to the words 'the reproach of Christ' in his text at verse 26. See also Romans 8:17; 2 Corinthians 1:5; Colossians 1:24.

humiliation for their faith in Christ, and they were grieved that obdurate fellow-Jews were condemning and despising them for embracing Christ and his kingdom. He was pointing to the experience of Moses, whom they greatly honoured, so that they would patiently endure the cross and willingly accept the rebukes, recognising that it was an even greater privilege to be despised than it would have been to possess all this world's riches.

'Through many tribulations we must enter the kingdom of God'

If there had been some other way that could point a man to heaven and bring him into that eternal blessedness, rather than by the pathway of suffering and shame, no doubt our Prince and Captain, the author and finisher of our faith,[11] would have trodden it. But he did not choose some soft and easy path, the kind that flesh and blood would choose, but took a most bitter, difficult way that none of us could ever have trodden. Seeing that he who is our Lord has gone before us, who among us will not be content to follow him? Those who are unwilling to follow him, bearing the cross which Christ has specially prepared for them, are not worthy of the kingdom of heaven.

Therefore, seeing there never was, nor is, nor ever shall be a way to heaven other than through suffering, take earnest heed and do not let the present peace in our land deceive you, for it is inevitable that at some point we shall all face suffering. So ask for patience[12] while we experience the calm. For the soul who is so inclined towards evil that he is addicted to it, remains in servitude; such a person shall never endure when times of suffering come. On the other hand, those who have patience will experience its power to keep their souls secure, for their minds and hearts will enjoy perfect peace. It is not that patience inhibits discussion or logical thinking, but it does help us to make the right decisions.

However, the one who is still a slave to sin rages and breaks into a fury, even at times doing himself an injury, all for the want of patience; he was unprepared, not having mortified himself, nor ever having sought patience from the hand of Christ. That is why he is unable to

[11] Hebrews 12:2, 'Loking vnto Iesus the autor and finisher of our faith' (Gen.B).

[12] In this paragraph and the next, he mentions 'patience' eight times; the context suggests that he means 'quiet endurance'.

endure whatever trial or sorrow it has pleased Christ to visit upon him. Seeing then that patience is so necessary (for there is no better antidote to suffering), suffer we must, but without patience we will be unable to endure. Then, while you still have time, all of you seek patience, for after you have patiently borne the good will of your good God, his promises will be fulfilled and at the last you will find his everlasting comfort.

A misunderstanding about 'the recompense of the reward'

One other word is needed on this subject before we move on. It says in verse 26 that Moses saw the recompense of the reward.[13] Therefore the recompense of the reward was his objective in the fight; in the text the apostle regards it as the objective of faith. The papists seize on this, thinking that here they have gained an advantage when they hear that Scripture refers to a recompense or reward as the objective of faith. Briefly, I answer that there are two kinds of reward or recompense: there is a reward that is earned, and there is a promised reward that is undeserved. Those who argue that here is meant a reward that is earned and therefore deserved are utterly wrong, for the apostle says nothing here about deserving a reward. But those who take the second sense of a reward that is freely promised and gratuitously given, rightly understand that here the apostle means that the undeserved reward is the objective of faith. For we may be certain that what God has promised he will faithfully fulfil.

Why, then, has God promised a reward and recompense for all our sufferings and not for the good things that we do? Not for the worthiness of our deeds, nor for any merit that our works deserve, but only for Jesus Christ's sake. Because it was his love that drew us into this life of suffering, he has promised us a free reward, and freely will he fulfil his promise. Therefore, there is no deserving in us nor any merit in our works, only a gratuitous promise with a gratuitous reward. This is the nature of the reward towards which faith is directed. As to the works that we do, what are they? Anything that is good in them flows from

[13] Gen.B has, *he hade respect to the recompence of the rewaird*, however ESV has, 'he was looking to the reward'; therefore Bruce's interpretation here of *respect to* as 'the recompense of the rewards' agrees with the modern translation of the Greek text.

the Lord's own gift and grace, for who can have any goodness except it be given to him from the Father of lights?[14] Therefore when he rewards our works, he is crowning his own virtue and good grace. I say all this in order to inform your minds so that you may be able to understand aright this verse when you read it: it is a reward and recompense that we do not deserve, but it is freely promised and freely given.

The second cross laid upon Moses[15]

The apostle continues by bringing in another cross that Moses took on himself, whereby he also bore testimony of his faith in Jesus Christ. Yes, he had already voluntarily chosen a cross, but there was also a cross that was not his choice, but was laid upon him by someone else; it was just as necessary for him to carry this cross also, just as he had to carry the first. None of us must think that when we have finished carrying one cross, that is the end of it. We must learn from Moses' experience: the end of one cross marks the beginning of another cross. Therefore accept that we must not only suffer for one day, or even for one year, but for as long as we live. Just as our bodies need to be nourished with food, so since time began we must endure some cross or other. You deceive yourselves if you think this is not how it will be for you.

We are told in Exodus 2:11-15 how it happened that this other cross was laid upon Moses at this time. It came about as soon as it pleased the Lord to take him from the court and enlist him into his service and to the calling to which he had appointed him. When he visited his brethren, he found one of them being beaten by an Egyptian, and he saw the injury that had been done to his kinsman. He was now aware of his calling and of the commission and authority given to him by the God of heaven and affirmed in his own heart. Moses also assumed that his brothers had been made aware of his new powers to be their judge and deliverer. (Alas, he was to find otherwise!) He believed he was justified, according to his commission, in revenging the injury inflicted on his brother, and so he slew the Egyptian and went away.

[14] A clear allusion to James 1:17, 'Every good gift and every perfect gift is from above, coming down from the Father of lights with whom there is no variation or shadow due to change.' (ESV)

[15] This heading refers back to the first heading at the second paragraph of this chapter; Moses first cross had been his voluntary submission of himself to bear the reproach of Christ by identifying himself with his own people.

This deed could not remain a secret, but because kings always have long ears, Pharaoh soon heard that Moses had killed one of his subjects. Had the king known of Moses' calling, it is possible that he would have overlooked what he had done. But he considered Moses to be someone without any authority, and so he sought to take his life. Thereupon, considering his situation, Moses saw he must leave Egypt, and he was guided by the Spirit of God to go to the borders of Ethiopia, to an area known as Midian.[16] There he remained for forty years in that place to which God had banished him, until he was better prepared and sanctified to discharge his calling, than he had been when he first left the court. Then his own people had refused him and would not acknowledge his authority; they demanded of him, 'Who made you a prince and judge over us?' However, forty years later their pride and impiety had subsided, for they had been humbled and broken by the strokes upon their backs that it had pleased the Lord to inflict on them by the hand of Pharaoh.

It would have been perfectly clear (as by spiritual insight anyone would have perceived) that Moses could not instantly rid himself of the customs in which he had been raised in the court. He must have imbibed certain evils in which he had been obliged to indulge during the forty years he had lived in that environment. Because the Lord knew that he could not be purged overnight of the court customs, and therefore was not ready to carry the burden of such a weighty charge, nor to accept the responsibility and dangers of leading such volatile people, it pleased him to send his servant to a very hard school. This training included a banishment[17] that the Lord caused to continue for forty years, during which time he scoured out of him all the courtly

[16] This is a strange geographical confusion regarding the whereabouts of Midian, an area separated from Ethiopia by the Gulf of Aqaba, the Sinai peninsula and the Gulf of Suez. Granted that the whole topography of the Red Sea has undoubtedly changed over the centuries, it indicates how little was known in the 16th century about the Middle East. Nearly two hundred years after Bruce, John Brown (1722–87), who compiled the first known *Dictionary of the Bible*, first published in 1769, was reasonably accurate as to the location of Midian on the east side of the Red Sea. Brown, II, p. 161.

[17] Later in these sermons, Bruce will expound 'banishment' as one aspect of persecution. See Chapter 27 below, under the heading 'Faith exhibited through suffering', pp. 536-537.

manners of living. He pulled off him the fine clothes he had worn at the court, and scrubbed him clean of all the Egyptian ways that could have hindered the execution of his calling. In the meantime, the Lord humbled the people and bowed their wills. They had been proud when Moses had left them, but when he returned their arrogance was gone and they welcomed him. They were now ready to hear any words of comfort he brought when he spoke to them.

A great charge demands great preparation

Therefore mark carefully God's methods and his ways of proceeding. Observe first that there must be a great preparation before a great and weighty charge. Notice also that before an extraordinary deliverance there must first be an extraordinary humbling of his servant. God takes forty years in preparing and sanctifying the instrument upon whose shoulders God is going lay an unspeakably heavy burden, unsupportable in the estimation of flesh and blood. It is not that he does his work of preparation quickly, rather he uses the most mundane means, taking plenty of time, during which he blesses his servant as he sanctifies him.

Whoever would do a notable work either in the Kirk or in the commonwealth must first be thoroughly sanctified and equipped. On the other hand, only where there has been a severe lesson in humility will there be a great work of deliverance done. Thus the Hebrew people had been so greatly humbled and were now so deeply cast down that they wearied of living. I cannot deny that the majority remained exceedingly sinful and that their humiliation had not sanctified them in the slightest, for the Lord had not conjoined their woes with his sanctifying Spirit. However, they were so dejected that though previously they had refused to accept Moses, now they no longer disputed about accepting him.

We see, therefore, that it is the Lord who slays and it is he who bestows life, it is the Lord who casts down and it is he who raises up, it is the Lord who makes poor and it is he that makes rich, it is the Lord who brings a man low and it is he who mounts others up to a higher place. Accept all of these experiences as from the Lord's hands, and constantly pray that he would sanctify to you your trials or afflictions, for when he conjoins with them the grace of his Spirit, it will be to you a blessed humbling. The lower you are cast down, the higher will you be lifted up in his mercy.

I have already told you that the cross of Moses' departure from Egypt is here counted by the apostle to be a proof and demonstration of his faith. The reason I believe the reference here is to his first departure from Egypt to the land of Midian, is that in the verses immediately following, he speaks of the second departure when the people kept the Passover and then crossed the Red Sea, whereas in verse 27 he refers to Moses' first departure, and then in verses 28 and 29 he goes on to the second departure, that we might see both departures arose from faith in Jesus Christ. In Acts 7 Stephen confirms what I have been saying to you regarding Moses' first departure being by faith, for he plainly says that his brothers thrust him aside and would not let him fulfil the calling given to him by God. He also repeats the history of how he could not return to the court.[18]

Three reasons why we know Moses departed in faith

First, he departed through faith because he did not return to the court

I have already hinted that had he wanted to recover his position at the court and win back the favour of the king, his step-mother would doubtless have acted as his advocate, and would have had means and ways for him to regain his place. After all, the one who was considered to be his mother was Pharaoh's daughter, and she would have been able to have won a 'respite'[19] for her son. Thus, had his former estate suited him, he could well have returned to the court, but finding that his conscience and the court did not agree,[20] he was compelled to chose to leave, and since those to whom he was sent would not receive him, there could be no opportunity at that time to engage in his calling. Through the wisdom of faith and by the counsel of the Holy Spirit he had to await a more opportune time, until the Lord had humbled the people and he himself had been better prepared. He could not return

[18] Acts 7:25-29.

[19] Bruce's word 'respyte' is a legal term meaning 'a privilege, normally granted only under royal prerogative, entitling the grantee to have legal action against him postponed for a specified period' (DSL 3).

[20] Bruce himself, commenting later as to why at first he refused the invitation to be minister in St Giles, wrote, 'For well I knew the court and we could never agree'. MacNicol, p. 40, quoting Cald. iv, p. 637.

until it pleased the Lord to renew his commission and send him back to Egypt.

Second, he departed through faith because his departure was blessed

This part of the sacred record lets us see, therefore, that his decision to leave arose from the wisdom of faith. Added to that was the manner in which his journey was blessed, and the happy outcome granted to him after he departed with a good conscience. For any journey undertaken without being sanctioned by the mighty God, and without his express command, will neither prosper nor be blessed by him. When a journey is undertaken in obedience to God's counsel, then the Holy Spirit acts as our director.

This was the case with Moses, and so the outcome was wonderful blessing, for the Lord gave him favour with one of the great men of the country he reached, who bestowed on him the gift of his daughter as his wife. In addition, the Lord gave him the patience[21] to endure forty years of banishment. How else could he have borne such a wearisome experience had not the Lord nourished his heart with patience and hope, and in the expectation that his commission would be renewed? All these blessings could only have been the outcome of faith, and so we must conclude that his journey away from Egypt was made in faith.

Third, he departed through faith because he did not fear the king's anger

The third argument comes from the same verse, for the apostle's words testify that not only in leaving Egypt did he act in faith, but also in his faith he was not afraid of the king's anger, for his eye was constantly upon him who is invisible. Therefore, both with regard to his departure, and in not fearing the fury of the king, he kept before him the sight of the living God. The Lord was with him first, when he despised Pharaoh's wrath, and second when he left Egypt. Is anyone able to see him who is invisible other than by faith? It follows that Moses was motivated by faith. These two clear evidences of faith, therefore, prove that Moses resolved within himself to be a faithful servant of God and of Jesus Christ.

I must again emphasise both of these evidences. First, his faith is seen in his courageous execution of his calling in killing the Egyptian,

[21] See note 12 above.

notwithstanding the inevitable wrath of Pharaoh and the subsequent hot pursuit that was bound to follow. Second, his faith is also seen in his judicious departure, because on the one hand he was a hunted man, and on the other hand as yet he had no opportunity to fulfil his commission from God. Therefore, the Holy Spirit's counsel to him was to depart.

God forbid that we should assume that all departures are against a man's conscience and offensive to the Lord. But before I say more on this subject, it might appear that there is a contradiction within the biblical records. The apostle says that he was not afraid of the king, whereas Exodus states that when he heard that Pharaoh sought him to kill him, he fled.[22] How can these two statements be reconciled? By God's grace, I shall show that they are both true: yes, he did not fear the king's wrath, and yes, he fled from the king's face when through faith and the guidance of the Holy Spirit he departed from Egypt. Regarding him not being afraid of Pharaoh's anger, we need no further argument than his execution of the Egyptian taskmaster, for had he been afraid of the king he would never have killed one of his subjects. As to his flight, it was not through fear of Pharaoh's anger; I grant that the text says he was afraid,[23] but this fear was not excessive, for it did not dampen his faith.

It is impossible for any of us always to be able to avoid fear, but where such emotion is controlled by the Holy Spirit it will not harm us, but may well prove beneficial. It can alert a man, arousing him out of a false sense of security, so that he does not fail to see the danger he may be facing, so he can then prepare himself and look for a wise resolution of his situation. So it was with Moses, his fear did not choke the faith by which he saw him who is invisible. This same God was the author of his flight and sanctioned it. As he first commanded him to undertake his calling, now he commanded him to withdraw from it; as he gave him a warrant to embark upon it, so he also gave him the warrant to withdraw from it. Moses had a warrant from the Lord for living in Egypt, and the Lord gave him a warrant for leaving Egypt. So whenever we have a sound warrant from God and are challenged regarding what we are

[22] Exodus 2:14c-15.

[23] Exodus 2:14c: 'Then Moses feared and said, Certenly this thing is knowen' (GenB).

doing, our warrant will defend us.

I return, then, to this issue of departing, or fleeing, from a place.[24] We must not always condemn those who have to flee in certain situations, otherwise we will find ourselves condemning Jesus Christ. We could also find ourselves condemning some of his servants in the Old Testament, as well as the apostles in the New Testament. Nor was the Lord's command recorded in Matthew 10:23 intended only for the days of his ministry. We see Paul's flight in Acts 9:23-25, and how he was lowered over the city wall in a basket. Jesus fled, so did David, Elijah and many others.[25] The scattering of fleeing believers led to the planting of the gospel in many parts of the land.

The flight of heart and mind from the flock of God

There is another flight that we may not be aware of, and it is given little or no attention. It is the flight of the heart and mind from the flock of God. There is also a physical flight, when a man is compelled to tear himself away from his flock. The former kind of flight, the flight of heart and mind, though the pastor[26] may still be physically present

[24] The remaining 2000 words of this sermon are on 'flight'. According to James Melville's *Diary*, Bruce had been present at a gathering in Lawson's manse on the evening of the day when Andrew Melville had defied the Privy Council, and had refused to accept its jurisdiction over the Kirk. Melville had been condemned to incarceration in Blackness Castle, but late that evening he slipped through the city gates and within twenty hours was safely across the Border and into Berwick, thus avoiding imprisonment. Shortly after, when Parliament in 1584 had passed 'The Black Acts', the Edinburgh ministers, Lawson, Balcanqual and Pont had boldly protested against the Acts at Edinburgh's Mercat Cross, and orders were issued for their arrest. They too discreetly made their way to Berwick and safety. James Meville, Andrew Melville's nephew, was meantime filling his uncle's teaching position in St Andrews. A writ for his arrest was also issued, and reluctantly he crossed the Firth of Tay to Dundee, from where he escaped by sea to Berwick. Thus fleeing James' attempts to silence those whom he regarded as his opponents was an event well-known to Bruce's congregation. Hume Brown, Vol. 2, p. 152; MacNicol, p. 34. It so happened that about four years later Bruce himself had to flee from the wrath of the king who saw in Bruce the chief obstacle to his getting his own way in the Church; the year was 1596, and when James declared that before long he wanted Bruce's head, the minister of Edinburgh wisely slipped away on horseback and took temporary refuge in Yorkshire. Murray, p. 47.

[25] See, for example, 1 Samuel 22:1; 1 Kings 18:3-4; 19:1-3; Jeremiah 36:26; John 8:59

[26] Throughout this paragraph and the next, Bruce simply uses the noun 'man',

among his people, is always condemned and forbidden in the Scriptures of God. You may ask what I mean by this kind of flight. I am speaking of a pastor who neglects the various duties that have been imposed upon him when he was appointed. A pastor flees in heart and mind from his flock and their salvation when, for example, he sees false teachers and corrupt doctrine perverting his people's thinking, but fails to stand against it. When he fails to expose such teaching's sophistry and does not help his congregation to resist it, then he flees in his mind, and this is a most dangerous failure in his responsibilities.

Similarly, if a pastor sees his flock being cruelly and illegally oppressed by some tyrant, and does not make a stand against such unlawful behaviour, then he is guilty of this same kind of flight. Or if he sees his flock indulging in hypocrisy and trying to cover up and disguise their evil deeds, and if he does not determine to expose their sin by uncovering their masquerades, and by the grace of God show their wickedness in its true colours, he too is guilty of this disreputable flight. Or if his flock in some way defects from God by falling into some wrong practices and he fails to correct them and by admonishing them restore them, then he too is guilty of this flight. Thus we see that this kind of flight must always be condemned and the pastor guilty of it must be reproved.

Three reasons for permissible physical flight

As to physical flight, it may well be permissible if circumstances obviously make it necessary, that is, if the occasion, means and reason make it clear that a pastor must depart. (By the 'occasion' I mean the timing, by the 'means' I mean that it is done honourably, and by the 'reason' I mean the intended purpose.) When these circumstances are taken in consideration, then no doubt flight is permissible, and those concerned have as much warrant to depart as they originally had to stay.

As to the occasion or timing, I make three possible reasons. First, a man must flee when he is being pursued for his life, or when he is certain in his own conscience that he must flee, or when other honest and faithful men are quite sure that he must flee. I am not so sure

but the context makes is clear that he referring to ordained ministers, therefore I have translated each occurrence of 'man' as 'pastor' since he constantly calls the congregation 'the flock'.

about some impulsive decision, rather I think a pastor must be quite convinced in himself. Just say there is every reason a man ought to flee, but he himself is uncertain in his own conscience whether or not the reasons are sufficient, such doubting could be a fault on the part of the one who hesitates. But when someone is absolutely sure that he is about to be subjected to persecution, then it is permissible for that man to depart; such a flight is to be commended, just as Moses' departure was, for it was a clear evidence of his faith.

Secondly, when a pastor's flock are exhibiting rebellious folly, and refuse to hear the wholesome word of Christ preached, in such circumstances it is permissible for him to shake the dust from his feet and to leave them.[27] If there seems to be no hope of a change in the people, then he should depart and find some other place where he is able to preach freely. Thirdly, there is another circumstance when a pastor may depart. When a pastor is so impoverished that he does not have the necessities of life because the people refuse to support him in temporal things, then it is permissible for him to depart. These three reasons, then, are when fleeing is permissible: persecution, contempt for the word, and a flock's failure to provide temporal necessities.

The manner of a pastor's flight

What about the manner of a pastor's flight? First, he should take care that his departure is discreet and becoming, so that no godly ears should be offended by the account of it, and no gracious soul should be troubled when they hear of it. Never flee in a dishonest or uncouth manner. Second, as to the intentions of the one departing, he must not leave to go and live idly somewhere, for that would indicate that he did not act out of faith. Those who depart must go to preach in some other town or city, and so continue to exercise their calling. Nor should a man depart hoping to gain some advancement or financial gain.

Third, no one should ever depart looking for a quieter, safer life. Are we not under the protection of the living God in every aspect of our calling? Therefore always consider whether your reasons for leaving are praiseworthy, and its outcome will glorify God and advance the edification in faith of the Kirk of Jesus Christ. If these honourable aims are your motives, then your departure will be justified. Moses fled

[27] Luke 10:10-11.

for worthy reasons, and being assured in his conscience he departed discreetly; because these grounds and motives for his flight were trustworthy, it was sanctioned by God.

Lessons for those engaged in spiritual ministries

I shall now bring two or three other points to your attention before I conclude. The first is that we must learn from Moses' example that we are all placed in our particular callings, especially those in spiritual ministries. Therefore we must not be hindered or restrained from exercising our ministry, either by fear of man or of the king, or fear of danger or peril. When we are assured by the word of God that something is appropriate and well within the parameters of our commission, no matter what the consequences might be, we ought to proceed with it.

Second, from Moses' example we also learn when it is permissible to depart, and to conserve our energies until our situation is such that it is imperative for us to remain. Everyone of us must bear this in mind, if we do remain we must be assured that we have a genuine warrant from God, and that our eyes are fixed on him who is invisible. Therefore, remain in faith if remain you must, and depart in faith if depart you must.

Third, I perceive here what it is that enables a man to fulfil his ministry boldly, whether to remain with a warrant, or to depart wisely, but to be spiritual in all his decisions: it is by looking steadfastly upon him who is invisible, and keeping his eyes fixed upon the living God. For the Lord's presence imparts boldness, a sound and tranquil mind, and above all joy. For where the mighty Lord is present in the soul of any man, he takes away the spirit of fear and gives him the spirit of power, love and a sound mind; so the apostle says in 2 Timothy 1:7. For what can make a man bolder than the presence of God with him and the vision of him who is invisible?

It cannot be denied that those who turn aside to gape at material, transient things shall find that as soon as they set their minds on them, they will find themselves ensnared by them. Further, if it transpires that a preacher uses eloquent and well-spoken language, but his words do not flow from the spiritual vision of the living God, but merely from his own heart because he has been speaking in his own strength, moved by his own emotions and borne along by his inward agitations, then when he is challenged regarding what he has said he will find that he is lacking any authority. It is only through the inward working of the Holy Spirit in a preacher that he is able to fulfil his commission with boldness, and when he is challenged regarding the authenticity of his ministry he will be able courageously to defend his message.

It is only the wisdom of the Holy Spirit that assists a man so effectively that his initial calling is justified by the fruit of his ministry. Therefore, take careful note. This boldness does not flow from human authority, nor from any outward methods he may use, but it flows from the vision of the invisible God and the Holy Spirit's presence within the man. When we depend on God alone without any respect of persons, we are sufficiently equipped and defended. Your own heart will justify you and the living God who is greater than your heart shall justify you, and he will stand with you in the day of your trial, and will cause your accusers to be ashamed and you to be honoured. So let us learn to be at peace with God and to hold fast to our union with him, even though that will cause some to be displeased with us. Let us also learn to have God's approval of us, even though it causes us to be disapproved by any living person.

I want to assure you of this (and would to God I could fully persuade you of it, even if it was sometime in the future), that however grievously you might displease someone, the pain that may be caused to your bodies as a consequence cannot ever be compared with the hurt to your consciences should you displease God. But if the Lord shall suffer you to lapse into such a frame of mind that you strive to seek human approval rather than his approval, then the grief of your consciences shall be far more painful than the tortures that men have devised to inflict upon the human body. You will never rigidly follow their dictates if God by his Holy Spirit has shown you what it is to feel the wrath of his consuming fire, like some human monster breathing fire.[28] Unless a pastor be taught by the Holy Spirit to consider such things and he has been given some awareness of the wrath of God compared to the worst wrath of man, he will never faithfully fulfil his ministry.

[28] I hope I have understood Bruce correctly here; he appears to be likening the wrath of God to a fire-breathing dragon: 'except by his holie spirit he lat yow sie quhat it is to feill the wraith of ane consuming fyre, in respect of ane earthlie creaturis quhois braith is in his nosthirlis.'

Be certain, therefore, that this calling of ours will never be rightly exercised unless the living God sends forth pastors who will not preach their own ideas, but who will accept the burden of God's commission. Yea, the living God who sends a man forth with this burden will always be with him; he will not suffer him to withhold any part of the message that has been entrusted to him, for as he commissions him and sends him forth on his journey, he will be with him; he will give him a heart to obey and a mouth to speak the words that have been committed to him. Without such a divine commission, no ministry will achieve anything. Therefore, you who are teachers be sure that your calling has come from God, and be sure also that your calling dwells upon the mercy and grace of God in Jesus Christ. Having this assurance, you will know that God will watch over you by his Holy Spirit, that he will not suffer you to fail by withholding any part of his commission, but will enable you so to exercise your ministry that its end will justify its beginning.

The Lord grant us grace to crave this may be so, and the Lord grant grace that every one of us may faithfully fulfil our calling, so that we may have peace with God through Jesus Christ. And may we have clear consciences when it pleases the Lord to visit us in our earthly lives, or when by death he takes us from this life. The Lord grant this for the sake of Jesus Christ, to whom with the Father and the Holy Ghost be all honour, praise and glory for now and for ever. Amen.

Chapter Twenty-Two

Hebrew Chapter 11 verse 28

> [28] *By faith he ordeined the pasover and the effusioun of blude, least he that destroyed the first borne sould twitche them.*

From the time that the Lord in his mercy called his servant, working effectually in him so that he obeyed, his obedience continued unwaveringly. Moreover, there was constant significant evidence of his inward calling and faith in God. You have heard me telling you of this ever since we began to consider this man Moses. The first time we read of the Lord working in him was when he was still at court and about forty years of age. Then it pleased the Lord effectually to bring him into his kingdom and show to him the task he must undertake. As soon as he became aware of the Spirit of God indwelling him, he responded to his calling. He was not obdurate, nor did he maliciously resist the Holy Spirit, but realising that life at court could not agree with his office,[1] he left the court and prepared to embark upon his task.

Three evidences of Moses' faith

Although he was surrounded by immense wealth and every worldly pleasure and delight, notwithstanding it all, as soon as the Spirit of Jesus opened his eyes, he preferred the Lord's poverty and ignominy to all the riches, honour and dignity that he could have enjoyed had he remained at the court. He chose the affliction and adversity of Christ's people, eschewing the ease and leisure he would otherwise have enjoyed. Consider how very wisely he chose, even though his choice was contrary to human nature. It was because the Spirit of God had enlightened his

[1] See above Chapter 21, Note 20.

mind, imparting to him a spiritual insight that was by no means innate, but by which he now perceived that the reproach of Jesus Christ would ultimately find fulfilment in eternal and infinite glory. He could see that the affliction of the Lord's people would one day lead to perpetual rest. On the other hand, by the direction of the same Spirit he realised the pleasures of the court would end tragically in bitter remorse, and that all its wealth and glory would lead to everlasting shame.

The first evidence of his faith

By contrast, Moses' resolution led to a wise choice, for the light of the Spirit showed him that there was great gain in the cross of Christ, that is, eternal profit and honour. I have often told you, and I do not weary in repeating it, there can never be a wise choice unless the Spirit of God himself guide you to it. Unless he enlightens you, your end will be tragic, and you will learn too late that you have been a fool from the start.

This, then, was the first proof that Moses gave of his faith: his voluntary choice to take up the cross. Thus he left the court and went to visit his brethren. He found them being grievously and unjustly oppressed against all common humanity and conscience. Therefore, acting according to the authority and commission God had given him, of which he had the warrant in his own heart and conscience, he entered upon his calling to exercise his office as their leader. One aspect of his leadership was to act as a judge among his people, and, finding that the injury inflicted upon his fellow Hebrew deserved the sentence of death, he seized the offender and slew him, and so meted out justice for his brother.[2] He himself was quite assured that what he had done was in compliance with the calling that God had laid upon him.

The second evidence of his faith

Had Moses considered the king's wrath, no doubt the thought of Pharaoh's ferocity might have restrained him. Had he also considered his own position, no doubt the thought of the danger into which he was putting his own life might also have held him back. But he had set his eyes upon God alone and, as verse 27 tells us, *he indurit as he that saw him who is invisible*. Because of this, he set aside all difficulties

[2] Exodus 2:11-12.

and impediments, and fulfilled his commission boldly. This courageous execution of his calling I consider to be the second evidence of his faith, and it was a most notable effect of faith at that time.

The third evidence of his faith

When the king heard of the death of the Egyptian and how it had happened, he sought to take Moses' life. Learning that he was being hotly pursued on the one hand, and on the other hand realising that his brethren to whom he had been sent were refusing to acknowledge him, he saw that it was going to be impossible for him to execute his commission. Being caught between these two extremes, he was compelled to take counsel and consider what would be his best course of action. He had made a wise decision, and had now gone ahead and acted so fearlessly because—as the verse to which I have just referred says—*he indurit as he that saw him who is invisible.* It is as if the apostle is saying, 'In his dilemma, he conducted himself well for he was never deprived of the living God's presence, but always kept before him the vision of him who is invisible.'

Now no one can retain that vision other than through faith. Therefore, his departure and flight from Egypt arose from faith and by the authorisation of the one whom by faith he saw, for the God whose Spirit was now within him and had bade him enter upon his calling. This same God now bade him to desist for the present and wait for a more opportune time. Thus the third evidence of his faith was his wise departure from Egypt.

Moses' years in exile

Moses fled to the land of Midian, which lay along the border of Ethiopia.[3] During the years of his banishment, we read only good of him, for there is nothing in the sacred record that suggests he ever forgot God's calling. Moreover, he remained true to his faith and worship of the one true God. The names that he gave his two sons who were born in the land of Midian bore testimony to the steadfast faith in his heart.[4] Thus it is clear that he did not deviate from his religion, but knew

[3] See Chapter 21, Note 16 above.

[4] 'The name of one was Gershom (for he said, "I have been a sojourner in a foreign land"), and the name of the other, Eliezer (for he said, "The God of my father was my help, and delivered me from the sword of Pharaoh")' Exodus 18:3-4.

that one day he must return to his calling. We may be certain that for a long time the Lord tested this man's patience,[5] for consider how he was kept in banishment for forty years, the same length of time that he had resided in the Egyptian court. After a demanding education in the court when he was young and throughout his adolescence, now in his mature years the Lord sent him to a far more exacting school, for his instruction in the wilderness was gruelling and difficult.

Moses re-commissioned

God purposely did this, for the office to be laid upon him was going to be exceedingly difficult and weighty. Great callings and difficult charges necessitate great preparation, and those who must submit[6] to them must be well instructed, sanctified and prepared, otherwise they will finish with shame a task they embarked upon with too light a heart. However, in spite of these years of arduous nurture, the Lord gave him patience so that he might continue in the constant hope that his commission would yet be renewed.

Accordingly, after forty years his expectation proved not to have been in vain, for it pleased the Lord to re-embark him upon his calling so that he could fulfil his responsibilities towards his brethren.

Even though at this point Moses did at first raise some objections, he was not obstinate but obeyed the Lord and returned to Egypt. During all those years that he was absent from Egypt, the faith that he had had before his first departure had not been lying idle, for now it bore fruit and became greatly effective during the months up to the exodus, producing far mightier results than ever it had done before he had first fled. We see Moses travailing with the Pharaoh for the deliverance and freedom of the people. Even though he found only hardness in the king, together with proud boasting and cruel threatening, God's servant continued to speak with him and to warn him of the impending harm that would be visited upon him if he did not render obedience to the Lord. However, the king constantly met him with evil answers. Indeed, the longer God's servant dealt with him, the more furious the enraged king became, until at length, when he was at the height of his

[5] See Chapter 21, Note 12 above.

[6] The verb is 'underly' (used twice) and means 'to submit to some discipline that inevitably will be unpleasant and arduous' (DSL).

anger along with all his subjects around him, the Lord enjoined his servant to initiate this sacrament.

The Passover

God had appointed the Passover to be observed by the Hebrews, who at the same time, incidentally, were also raging against Moses. He had prescribed to his servant the way in which the Passover had to be observed. On the day appointed, all householders and the heads of every family must have prepared a year-old lamb that was without any blemish, whole and fair. Each lamb had to be killed and its blood sprinkled on the lintels and the doorposts of each house, so that the homes of the Hebrews would be distinguished from those of the Egyptians. Verse 28 tells us why this must be done: *least he that destroyed the first borne sould twitche them.* When the destroying angel was sent forth at the Lord's command, as it moved across the land it would pass over the houses whose doors had the Lord's marks on them, and would only execute its commission on those that did not have the Lord's mark. This was the instruction given to Moses who then passed it on to the people.

Faith requires obedience

Now the grounds of Moses' faith must be apparent to you: in every sacrament there is both a command and a promise; the command demands our obedience and the promise requires our faith. What God commands is not only to be believed, it also requires obedience; what God promises is not about something we must do ourselves, rather his promise is to be embraced by faith. This applies to all his promises: he sets them before us to be believed, for they are given to be objectives of our faith, and faith is the only means we have of taking hold of God's promises.

All sacraments of necessity must consist of a command and a promise. The command in the Passover was that at midnight the lamb must be sacrificed and its blood sprinkled over the door. The promise of God, given through his servant, was that when the destroying angel was moving across the land to execute righteous judgment on the Egyptians, it would pass over the Lord's people, and so the plague would not touch them.

Blood was to be the sign and token of the promise

I repeat: self-evidently this promise demanded faith, and anyone who did not receive it in faith was treating God as if he was a liar, whereas all who put their seal upon, and subscribed to his promise, thereby attesting their belief in him, counted him to be God in truth. No doubt Moses himself set a good example to all the people, in that by his action he led them in both obedience and faith. It was he who received the promise directly out of the mouth of God and believed that the Lord would cause his angel to do exactly what had been promised. The Lord will have confirmed his word to Moses in order that his faith would be all the stronger. 'This will be the sign and token that I will honour my word,' says the Lord to him. 'Daub the lamb's blood in three strokes over your door, one stroke across the lintel and the other strokes down each of the two doorposts. This blood will be my own mark, and I will command the angel to pass over every home which bears it, for this mark will testify to the faith of that household that they believed my promise.'

We see, therefore, that the sacrament is joined to the promise in order to confirm it, and to strengthen the faith of Moses and the people. As I have said, Moses led them in embracing God's word and in obeying his command. Therefore he is worthy of commendation on two counts, first because he expressed in his own person the outcome of justifying faith, but second on account of the fidelity and diligence that he took in fulfilling his calling. Consider what pains he would have taken to persuade a stiff-necked and rebellious people, and so the Lord honoured his care and blessed his faithfulness at that time, for the people submitted to God's ordinance, their obedience now flowing from faith.

We may be sure that the marks of blood on their doorposts and lintels bore witness to all, that they too had by faith embraced the Lord's promise, and so had obeyed by performing the ceremonial Passover. We may also be sure that if the destroying angel found a home that did not have the distinguishing marks in blood on its door, he would not have spared that household from the plague as he did not spare the Egyptians. But finding those distinguishing marks, which were symbols of the Lord's own mark on both body and soul, the angel spared them.

Before I move on, I want to remark that, just as Moses was

praiseworthy both for the faith exhibited in his own person and for the faithful execution of his office, you will not find a faithful office-bearer whoever he might happen to be, who is not also faithful in his person. It is impossible that someone who is false towards God will be true towards either men or women. Thus a genuinely faithful office-bearer will also be faithful towards God.[7]

The occasion of the appointment of the Passover

The occasion that moved the Lord to institute and appoint his Passover was without doubt the arrogant obduracy of the rebellious king. His sinful intransigence not only brought judgment upon himself and his people, but also caused God to extend his mercy and blessing upon his chosen flock. These two go together: the punishment of the wicked and the deliverance of the Kirk. To give you some insight into the sacred record, these events came about after the Lord had repeatedly warned Pharaoh through his servant Moses. (This was the Pharaoh who had not known Joseph.[8]) Plague after plague had accompanied each warning.

Mark this carefully: God never steals up on a person unawares, for he always forewarns before ever his hand strikes. That was how it was with Pharaoh—warning after warning until the final plague was inflicted upon the king himself. No warnings or plagues had moved the tyrant to render obedience to God, rather the sterner the warning and

[7] In Bruce's hand-written sermon script, the previous two paragraphs may appear at first to be full of circumlocution and tautology; this is true of large tracts of all his sermons. See remarks of T.F. Torrance in his Introduction to his translation of *The Mystery of the Lord's Supper*: 'I have taken the liberty of frequently shortening clauses and sentences when the exposition seemed needlessly repetitious, at least according to modern standards.' (Quoted in my Introduction to my translation of Bruce's sermons on Isaiah 38. Isa. p. xiii.) But on closer examination, it could be that his style has been influenced by Aristotelian syllogistic reasoning. It is sometimes possible to identify a major premise, followed by a minor premise, followed by the conclusion; then another syllogism follows to argue for the negative of the first syllogism. While it cannot be said that Bruce thought in syllogisms, this style of logic seems to me to be often reflected in his arguments. One example will suffice from this present paragraph: (major premise) An office-bearer must be faithful towards God; (minor premise) An office-bearer must be faithful in himself; (conclusion) A person faithful in himself will also be faithful towards God. For the sake of contemporary readers, I have not retained the syllogistic form.

[8] Exodus 1:8.

the more pestilent the plague, the greater had been Pharaoh's rebellion and the harder his heart had become. The first nine plagues having only resulted in ever greater obduracy, the tenth plague was to be the severest and most dangerous of all.

So take note of the way in which God works. The only thing in any man or woman that angers God is sin; indeed, there is nothing else in any of his creatures that displeases him. The more we increase in sin, the more is God's wrath increased, and the greater his wrath the greater will be his judgment. We see clearly this principle being worked out in the case of Pharaoh: as his contempt grew so the plagues grew in their severity, and when the king's contempt for God reached its peak, the final plague was then poured down upon him and his people.

Carefully note again the sequence of events. First, God sent Moses to warn the king that at a certain hour of a certain night he was going to send his destroying angel throughout the land, and without exception every firstborn of both man and beast in Egypt would be struck down without mercy. The plague would begin with Pharaoh's own household, and then would spread across the whole land until every single household had been stricken. This final warning to the king fell on deaf ears, its only effect being to raise him to a height of fury against Moses, ordering him out of the court and telling him he would never again be admitted. 'Take care never to see my face again, for if you do you will die,' he said. It is implied that Moses himself left the court in anger, for he said, 'As you say! I will not see your face again!'[9] Unwittingly, the king had prophesied, for never again did he see the face of Moses.

The Passover was a confirmation of divine grace

The divine judgment was now at hand, and so the Lord prepared for the gracious assurance of his people and the confirmation of their hearts. As he had warned the king of dire consequences, so now he sent Moses to comfort his people and to promise them they would be preserved. In the meantime, he appointed the Passover as a sacrament to be celebrated, using the blood as a pledge of the people's safety. Thus while he threatened the tyrant with fearful consequences, he confirmed the hearts of his own and appointed the sacrament for their further instruction. Therefore it is clear that prior to their deliverance he instituted

[9] Exodus 10:28-29.

this sacrament of the Passover with more regulations than the people had ever been accustomed to use up to that time.

Involved in that sacrament were certain temporary regulations, in that they were concerned with the manner of their deliverance that was to come about immediately after the sacrament had been celebrated; thereafter, these temporary regulations would cease. I refer to the blood being sprinkled upon the lintels and doorposts of their houses, for that instruction was solely as a sign to the destroying angel to pass over their homes. Similarly, the way in which they were to partake of the roast lamb was a temporary regulation; they were to eat standing with their shoes on, their staffs in their hands, and the skirts of their robes hoisted up and tucked into their belts; it was to be eaten in haste with them ready to begin their journey. Because this all signified the passing over of the destroying angel, they would have needed to have remained inside their homes all that night. None of these temporary regulations for that first Passover were used thereafter.

Teaching arising from the Passover regarding the contrite heart

Having spelled all this out for you, I must now ask you to attend to the doctrine and instruction that arises from this sacrament, that was instituted at the time when God's judgment was poured down upon the wicked hearts of the rebellious, while his mercy and blessing were extended to his own people. Enshrined here is an enduring principle. There is not a single plague that falls upon either soul or body, either in this life or in the hereafter, that is not occasioned by a hard heart. Out of every plague that is experienced, or that we read of, there is none so great as the plague of a hard heart. An evil and stubborn heart is the greatest plague because we are born with it, and that is true of every one of us. I reckon a hard heart to be the greatest of plagues because it lacks all feeling and spiritual senses. Do you not see that a hard heart within the body is such an evil as to be the greatest disease of all? It robs us of all sense and feeling, so much so that the only course of action is for it to be cut it out.[10] So it is with the soul: if action is not taken

[10] Bruce's words referring to the remedy for a hard heart are, 'There is no remead bot af cuting'. The allusion is most probably to Matthew 5:30, 'If your right hand causes you to sin, cut it off…' but the clause ends up being a mixed metaphor, as the heart obviously cannot be cut off! However, he explains his meaning in the next paragraph when he says that 'the Spirit must cast the heart down… and to

quickly to deal with the heart, its obduracy will increase, rendering the soul helpless, deprived of all sense and feeling, to such an extent that nothing remains for it other than to be cut off for ever from the mercy and sight of the living God.

The heart is considered to be hard because it withholds from us the sense and feeling of sin and the depth of misery that lies within us. Of course such sense and feelings could never originate from either our hearts or our fallen natures, but only from the work of Jesus Christ. His Spirit must move in our hard hearts to open our eyes to our sins, to fill us with remorse and sorrow that we have been so stubborn as to have committed them. The initial effect of the Spirit's work is to make us afraid when we realise we have become slaves to sin, because in healing the heart and so bringing us home into the kingdom of Jesus Christ, the Spirit must first cast the heart down. Only then will the heart recognise its misery and tremble before the divine justice, only then will it sorrow over the sin that has brought it under condemnation.

It is for this reason that the apostle in Romans 8:15 speaks of *the Spirit of bondage to feare*. When we are sufficiently humbled, the same Spirit raises up the heart that was cast down, and to heal its wounds the Spirit distils in the heart some drops of mercy and grace, bringing the assurance that in Jesus Christ there is deep compassion and loving consolation. The heart that had come near to despair and had been ready to abandon the struggle, now opens its mouth and cries the name that previously it had not dared to utter—'Father'![11]

I have dwelt on this only to let you see that the awareness of our miserable state and the assurance of mercy do not flow from our natural heart in its fallen state. For by nature our hearts are hard, void of all sense and feeling, either of our unhappy condition or of the mercy of God. This is why the natural heart is permanently presumptuous. The papists therefore remain in their fallen condition, presumptuously proud of their own merits. By contrast, the truly Christian heart has become meek and lowly, looking only for mercy, for it has had experience of its natural depravity. Pagan and atheist hearts are likewise presumptuously proud of their own abilities, because the Holy Spirit has not as yet given them the true insight into themselves, nor the

heal its wounds the Spirit distills in the hearts drops of mercy and grace'.

[11] Romans 8:15 again.

awareness of their helpless condition.

It stands to reason, therefore, that the happiest and most blessed condition anyone can experience in this world is when it has pleased the Lord to make us constantly aware of our spiritual poverty. For as a hardened heart will always be an offence to God, so a broken and contrite heart is what he most desires in us. Read for yourselves Psalm 51:17, where it says, *a broken & a contrite heart, o God, thou wilt not despise*; a contrite spirit is ever acceptable to him. Look also at Ephesians 2:10, where we are told that we must be made anew: *For we are his workemanship, created in Christ Iesus vnto gude works, which God hathe ordeined that we shulde walke in them.* So unless we are created anew it is not possible that we can enter the kingdom of heaven. This is expounded in John 3:5, *Except that a man be borne of water and the Spirit, he cannot enter into the kingdome of God.* So our hearts are not born again or created anew unless they have been broken and bruised, beaten down into powder until they lose their natural fallen condition. For whatever is ground to powder has lost its original condition.

This then is the heart that Christ reforms and remakes, this is the heart that is his workmanship, and this is the heart that shall enjoy the kingdom of heaven. On the other hand, a heart that is persistently hard is the cause of afflictions visited upon it by God; these afflictions lead ultimately to the destruction of both body and soul. What a contrast this is to the broken heart that now knows its true condition and its need of mercy and grace! This is the heart that is in the hands of God who is shaping and refining it so that at length he will take it to heaven.

So do not be complacent if you have no sense of sin, and are not touched either inwardly or outwardly by guilt, but sleep at night without any worries. No, those who have the sense and feeling of their deceitfulness and spiritual poverty, they are blessed because they know their rest and peace are to be found in God's mercy. For the Lord has ordained that here on earth we must live in the shadow of his mercy, and then hereafter in the light of eternal felicity and glory. Therefore do not complain that you must constantly be asking for the Lord's merciful forgiveness, and seeking the peace of Christ that passes all understanding.[12]

I have dealt with this subject at some length, as it is crucial for our

[12] Philippians 4:7.

daily living. These truths have to be constantly hammered in![13] For this contrition and brokenness of heart is the only thing that will benefit our souls. Without it, we are left to everlasting condemnation. Therefore ever crave the awareness of your sinfulness and the assurance of God's mercy. Thus far, then, for the occasion of the Passover.

The equity of God's judgment

We come now to the judgment which struck the firstborn of both man and beast. We must mark here what I shall call 'the equity of the divine judgment', for it applies across the whole world and also to each one of us. I will explain what equity of judgment means. Ever since we first began to consider this man Moses and his birth, you heard of the cruelty of the king's edict, and how he targeted every male child born to the Hebrew people. The edict ordered the baby boys to be seized and thrown into the river.

This was a judgment inflicted upon the Hebrews by God, partly on account of their rebellion against him and also because of the apostasy into which they had fallen. It was therefore a just punishment, for scarcely any were found among the people who were still faithful to God; only a few remained faithful such as poor Amram and Johebed. However, the action was also inflicted partly by the king whose heart had been stirred up by the devil to mete out this unspeakable cruelty upon innocent children.

Now, perceive how the Lord deals with Pharaoh, by inflicting upon him the same atrocity that he had inflicted on others. However, not only did he return to him what he had done to others, but he added 'an extra'[14] to the judgment, for he threw it into the king's lap along with a bonnet (as we say)! For judgment was not only visited upon the first-born male children, but also upon the females, and also on the beasts into the bargain![15] It is the same whenever God is dealing with the wicked. Because they have not only inflicted evil upon another,

[13] Compare this statement with Ecclesiastes 12:11. 'The words of the wise are like goads, and like nails firmly fixed are the collected sayings.' (ESV) His verb is 'dung' meaning 'beaten' or 'struck with heavy blows' (DSL); it was used earlier when he spoke of the heart 'being beaten down into powder'.

[14] Bruce's word is 'ane vantage' which means 'something free added on to make up what we call "a baker's dozen"'—an extra, so to speak. (DSL 3.b).

[15] Exodus 12:29-30.

but have also offended the one who is clothed with infinite majesty, he returns to them 'an extra', so to speak, over and above their wicked actions.

Mark this principle of equity of judgment. The punishment visited upon Pharaoh is according to the measure he visited upon the Kirk. See how wicked men abuse the Kirk! God will mete out to them what they have done to his Kirk. However, this is not only true of cruel men who afflict us, it also pertains to every one of us. There is not a single person whom the Lord has appointed for the glory of his Kirk who has not had experience of this equity in his dealings. This applies to our personal sins. For however it is that we offend the living God and provoke his holy majesty to anger, whether it be by a sinful word from my mouth, or by some sinful thing I do, in whatever way I offend God he will offend me.[16]

Every sin is a transgression of God's law and so incurs a punishment. That is why every sin brings with it bitter remorse. It may begin with deceitful flattery that confuses your judgment, stirring up conceit in you; but it will also lead to the same bitter remorse. Therefore God's method will not be to send some plague upon you, but to use your own deviations and fabrications, for he employs the sins that offend him to offend us.

The Lord's chastening of his people

Pay heed to this by examining your life, and you will find that the sins with which you have offended God now cause you pain and anguish in the same measure that they formerly brought you pleasure. Therefore learn to recognise the deceitfulness of sin so that you may weigh it against sin's consequences, and thus learn to flee from it. However, when the Lord is dealing with his own people he does not add on 'the extra' to his judgment. Rather he tempers and mitigates it, so that we may be chastened as his strokes sting us for what we have done. In his mercy he does not prolong his punishment [or 'chastening'] but mod-

[16] Bruce is doubtless alluding here to 1 Corinthians 3:17, 'If anyone destroys God's temple, God will destroy him.' Hodge comments, 'The verb φθειω means "to bring into a worse state". The passage may therefore be rendered, "If any man injure the temple of God, him will God injure".' *Comm. in loc.* Findlay suggests that the verb φθειω should be understood as meaning 'corrupt morally, deprave or desecrate'. Comm. in loc.

erates it and soon concludes it, otherwise we would give up the battle. As to the reprobate, his punishment of them always has 'the extra'[17] added to it, for their desertion is so serious they never recover from it.

I say again, we must all take heed to our lives. Even if there are sins that lurk within you but have never yet come to your knowledge, and even though you cannot think of any as you turn these things over in your minds, do not conclude that means there are no sins there beneath the surface. For as the Lord is Lord, and as his word that I speak to you is true, ultimately you will come to understand what I am saying in your own experience. You will indeed find unsavoury things lurking within you, offering you deceitful pleasures. Either you must hate them before you die and reject them so that you will escape eternal regret, or else you will begin to indulge in them only to find that you are disappointed with them both now and forever.

You ought therefore to reflect on the painful regrets your conscience has felt, but also keep alive your sanctified memories, so that you will loathe the former and cherish the latter. Then you will continue to seek the Lord's mercy in the assurance it will be granted, for whoever resolved in his heart to do better has been enabled to mend his ways. But if you neglect to do that, remember that dire punishment awaits you, and it will be even greater because, having been forewarned and admonished, you refused to ask for mercy. In addition, take time to reflect on the pain your consciences will suffer over the rest of your lives, increasingly torturing your hearts. Yet that will be as nothing compared to the anguish when an endless troupe of sins parade before you as you are confronted with the wrath of God on the final Day of Revelation!

The reason why the final judgment is called the Day of Revelation is that on that day all will be revealed. However secret your sins have been, they will then be completely unmasked. How much greater will be the hideous sight of them, and how much more intense the unbearable anguish, when at the present time the thought of one single sin can cause you to despair. 'O Lord, in your mercy touch each of us, I pray!' It is impossible that words alone can move us, only he in his mercy can do that, causing us to search our consciences and reflect with genuine grief

[17] See Note 14 above.

on our sins that have offended him. May we thus avoid that revelation in eternity, where concealment of our sins is impossible. Hell chiefly involves two things: the unending presence of sin and the perpetual awareness of the wrath of God; from them the only escape can be a conscience full of remorse and a cry to God for mercy, for whoever calls on the name of the Lord shall be saved.[18] This far on our need for mercy.

The long-suffering nature of God's judgments

The second thing I note regarding God's judgment is this. As well as acting with equity and noting the manner in which God worked, I see that he did not begin with his most severe judgment, for then the offender would have been immediately lost forever. Rather, his dealings proceeded little by little, before he brought upon Pharaoh his final, heaviest punishment. Thus he began with the first plague, followed by the next until all nine plagues had been visited upon him.[19] God's purpose in delaying the last most devastating plague was to give the king the opportunity to repent, had that been possible.

See how each plague was mitigated and then ended to see whether the hardness of his heart would thaw, and there would be his conversion and turning to God. But the Lord could see that his gentle dealings were doing no good, and so ultimately he had no alternative other than pour down upon the king his furious wrath. That final plague was surely full of divine indignation and brought upon Pharaoh terrible anguish. Even the souls of those who survived thus far and who had witnessed God's earlier judgments, were also ultimately visited with plagues, troubles and woes, as Psalm 78 recounts.

We learn therefore that the Lord never begins his judgment with the heaviest punishments. These initial actions were said to be only 'the finger of God'.[20] Whenever the Lord begins by gently laying his hand lightly upon a people, if they treat his dealings with contempt he brings down upon them a slightly heavier punishment, until finally they are overthrown by God's very hottest wrath and indignation. As this is true

[18] Romans 10:13.

[19] See K. A. Kitchen's article on the first nine plagues as a complete ecological cycle in IBD, Vol. 3, pp. 1234-1236.He comments '... the plagues demonstrate the divine use of the created order to achieve his ends.'

[20] Exodus 8:19.

of nations, so it is also true of individuals. There is not a single person who treats with contempt the admonition that the Lord is pleased to visit upon him, who does not consequently bring upon himself a slightly heavier admonition; contempt of that will bring the heaviest judgment of all, until at last both body and soul will be overthrown in the heat of God's wrath.

A warning to the ungodly nobility

Why do I tell you this? I want to bring before you the terrible spectacle that is to be made of our lords, those whom we refer to as our nobility. (This also applies to every stratum of society in our land, for none will escape it.) I perceive that chiefly 'the extra'[21] is hanging over the nobles. As anyone with eyes to see will have already realised, God has been dealing with our nobility for several years now, even as he dealt with Pharaoh to bring him to obedience; he repeatedly inflicted upon him plague after plague, visitation after visitation, to see if he would turn and be converted. Is anyone here ignorant of what has been happening among us? If it were not that I am reluctant to name names, I could tell you who they are upon whom the Lord has sent plague after plague, yet apparently without any effect. Indeed, these men have become even harder and have returned to the same quagmire from which they have offended God. Indeed, their wallowing in wickedness has even increased.

Can there be any doubt, seeing that our God is the living God and his justice remains unchanged, that these men shall be made spectacles of his wrath? Can there be any question but that the same anger and heaviest judgment poured out upon those who were living in Moses' day, shall also soon be poured out upon them? Is this not why the Lord has now taken from them all grace and understanding, so that you and I might see that the days of his wrath are imminent? The onlookers in this land will acknowledge that it could not have been otherwise, for these lords have been given many warnings and their contempt has been very great. Now the living God is teaching his people to fear and reverence his name.

Would to God this could be prevented! But they have made a mockery of good behaviour, and have foully apostatised in their religion.

[21] See note 14 above.

Therefore the only way of escape for them would be for the Lord so to afflict them with sorrow upon sorrow, his Spirit working through their anguish, that the hardness of their hearts might be softened. Yet perhaps that is now no longer possible. Alas, terrible is the judgment that awaits them, and not only them, for it also awaits many others of lower estates in our land. For there are none who are not guilty of unyieldingness; they are so miserable in their sins that they appear unaware of their pitiful condition.

Blessed is the hard heart that recognises its obduracy, and happy are those who are distressed as they accuse their own consciences, for that is the condition that causes them to run to Jesus Christ to plead for his mercy. But where there is no longer any trace of remorse, then that terrible fire is already burning in their souls—it is called Satan's fire in a man's body—and the divine wrath for them is unavoidable. Therefore, always crave that you may be touched with the sense of those sins whereby you have offended God, and being so touched crave also that the Lord would bruise your hearts, and then grant you everlasting peace, that hereafter you may dwell with him for ever. Certainly it is lamentable to see the state our country, and if my heart was not hard as I speak of these things, fountains of tears would distil from the eyes of everyone of us that recognises our tragic state.

God's judgments reflect his mercy, power and justice

The final point I mark regarding God's judgment is this: the Lord is like unto himself, that is, he is true in mercy, power and justice. He is true in his mercy for he fulfilled his promise to his people that the judgment of the final plague would not touch them, and, yes, he did keep his promise. He is true in his power by which he destroyed the one who rebelled against him. And who dare challenge him when he reveals that power? He is true in his justice when he punishes sin by sin, and a king's hard heart with a hard judgment.

It is not very material[22] to try to describe the kind of angel that executed the final judgment, whether it was a good or an evil angel. For it is certain (if this satisfies the curiosity of some of you) that in pouring out his judgments the lord sometimes uses a good angel, and

[22] 'Materiall': in Scholastic theology means, 'Consisting of the elements or factors which together make up or go to produce a state of affairs.' (DSL)

sometimes an evil angel. But usually when he executes his justice upon reprobate and wicked persons, we find that he uses the service of good angels.

God can employ both good and evil angels

When God executed his judgment upon Sodom, he used the services of good angels, for we read that the Lord himself was one of the three angels who visited Abraham, and he was the one who put his arms around Lot.[23] Again, the slaughter of Sennacherib's host was doubtless done by a good angel.[24] The visitation of a pestilence upon the people after David's sin was undoubtedly executed by a good angel, for David then raised an altar at the place where the angel had appeared.[25] The judgment meted out upon Herod when he took upon himself the honour due to the living God and was eaten by worms, as we read in Acts 12:21-23, must also have been done by a good angel. All this evidence inclines me to think that it was also a good angel who was the instrument of God's judgment upon the rebellious and faithless Egyptians.

Certainly Psalm 78:49 appears to imply that, as well as his wrath, anger and indignation, God sent an evil angel to judge the Egyptians. Yet even though this is the Bible's translation,[26] the original properly allows an alternative interpretation that his angel was the messenger of ill events.[27] The angel is called 'evil' not so much in respect of his character as of the effects of his visitation. It was not that the angel was wicked in the way the devil and his angels are wicked. Therefore I conclude that in verse 49 a good angel is referred to, not least because it is stated that it was the Lord who let loose his anger upon them.

On the other hand, it is true that the Lord also uses the service of evil angels to punish men. For example, we read in 1 Samuel 16:23 that

[23] Genesis 18:1, 10, 17, 20; Bruce's verb 'hals' means to put one's arms around another's neck: see Genesis 19:10 for the allusion.

[24] 2 Kings 19:35.

[25] 2 Samuel 24:15-19.

[26] Geneva Bible of 1562.

[27] Psalm 78:49 in the Geneva Bible reads, 'He cast vpon them the fiercenes of his anger, indignatioun and wraith, and vexation by the sending out of euil Angels.' ESV translates, 'He let loose on them his burning anger, wrath, indignation, and distress, a company of destroying angels.'

after the good spirit from God departed from Saul, an evil spirit from the Lord entered into him and troubled him. So the very spirits which are the Lord's executioners are available to him to punish men as it so pleases him. Furthermore, we read in 2 Corinthians 12:7 that a messenger from Satan troubled Paul. I do not think that was the same as his thorn in the flesh, but rather that this messenger from Satan aggravated the thorn in his flesh that had been given him. Thus I take it that Paul had his own trial in being visited by such an evil power.

No, do not think it strange that the devil is never entirely cast out of even the best of men as long as they live. He remains to some extent in every man and woman, rekindling their corruption, and casting up vile emotions and thoughts. I grant that the Spirit of Christ occupies the other part of the soul, for he is casting up holy emotions and thoughts, and he is far stronger in his support and power to subdue our inner corruption than the power of the devil is to stir it up.[28]

Therefore, even though the apostle was more afflicted in this way than we are, and even though the devil retains a foothold in us, we have to thank God that Satan neither controls nor dominates us, neither has he any authority over us. This we must attribute to the grace of God, and not to any merit of our own. So I say, yes, the great apostle had his own inner corruption, even though it was more mortified than any other man we read of. We too have our own inner corruption with an evil spirit seeking to stir it up within us; however, it is sufficient for us to know we have the grace of God, as the Lord said to Paul when he complained about these things, 'My grace is sufficient for you'. So as the apostle was content with the grace and merciful compassion of Jesus Christ, let us also be content with it, for when we seek his grace the Lord will grant it. I have said all this so that you will understand that God can use the ministry of both evil and good spirits, both to chasten his own and to punish the rebellious. Thus far, then, for the Lord's judgment.

[28] Ninety years later, John Bunyan would echo the same thought in one of the lessons in Interpreter's House, where an evil man (the devil) kept trying to extinguish a fire in a grate by pouring water on it, while on the other side of the wall a gracious man (Christ) kept pouring oil on the fire to revive it and keep it burning brightly.

The Passover as a sacrament

As far as the sacrament is concerned, as you are already familiar with its meaning, I will not repeat it, other than to mention something I have not yet told you. I will say a little more about this next Lord's Day.[29] Regarding the Passover, first, I find the people praiseworthy in that they did not despise the Lord's ordinance or his sacrament, but accepted it. Indeed, in their wholehearted embracing of it they gave evidence of their faith; in this they are worthy of praise and commendation. Second, their faith, which was evident on account of its effects, was not trusting in the outward, visible sacrament—that is, it was not directed to the blood that was sprinkled on their doors—but of necessity their faith was dependent upon the word of God, both on the promises he made and on him who made those promises. As they leaned upon God and his word, they were convinced they could trust him. In both of these two points, they were worthy of praise. (That is not to say that every single person was faithful in that hour, but certainly the majority of them were.)

And now for your instruction, learn not to despise the sacraments of Jesus Christ whenever you are admitted to partake of them. Take heed lest you bypass them lightly and say, 'I have a complaint against myself in my conscience, so I cannot partake of the sacrament.' That would be the quickest way to cut yourself off from the body of Jesus Christ. If your conscience is troubled, then do what you must to be washed clean of all that stains you, and confess before God and men that you have put it from you, and attend the sacrament. Do not disdain it. For those who disdain Christ's sacrament disdain God, and he does not hold as guiltless those who take his name in vain. To despise the sacrament is to despise yourself. Therefore, as often as the opportunity to partake is afforded you, do not neglect or bypass it.

A second point for your instruction is this: when you draw near to the Table, do not gaze upon the outward symbols, looking at the bread and wine as if they were gods. Use the outward symbols to convey to you what they signify, that is the body and blood of Jesus Christ, for they point you to the Person of him who is the Mediator between God and man. Upon him fix and repose your faith, and then the sacrament

[29] Bruce does not say 'next Lord's Day', but only 'the nixt day'. I am assuming that these expositions were given in the kirk on the Lord's Day.

will fulfil its purpose, and you shall leave with your faith stronger than when you came. So much, then, for the lawful use of the sacrament.

The original Passover compared with Christ our Passover Lamb

Regarding the Passover, we should note that when it was first prescribed the people had their particular Passover before they had received the Law. After the Law had been given, the people had their own Passover with particular regulations regarding the blood, and this ordinance continued until the advent of our Passover Lamb and his blood. You see, therefore, that we who are under grace have our own Passover, our own Lamb and his own blood. The previous Passover lambs represented our Lamb, and their Passover represented our Passover; thus the blood they sprinkled represented the blood of Jesus Christ, which speaks better things to us. For as it is well expressed in Hebrews 10:4, it was impossible for the blood of a beast, whether a cow or an ox, to take away sin. Indeed, is it possible for anything physical on earth to enter a man's soul in cleansing power? Even natural reason would be unwilling to accept that!

Therefore while it was impossible for the blood of beasts to cleanse the souls of these godly men, nevertheless that blood represented to them a spiritual, heavenly blood, the blood of God and the blood of Jesus Christ, through which the souls of every woman and man can be cleansed. Likewise, the Hebrew people's Passover lamb represented the Lamb of God who takes away the judgment of God; the 'passing over' of the angel at that time of temporal danger represented our spiritual passing over from death to life, from the slavery of sin to our liberty and freedom in Jesus Christ. Similarly, as their Passover lamb had to be without any blemish, so our Lamb is spotless and undefiled, in that sense distinct from sinners, and even higher than the heavens. Seeing, then, that we have our own Passover Lamb (as the apostle says in 1 Corinthians 5[30]), and this Lamb has already been sacrificed for us, and seeing also that his blood is far better than the blood of beasts, and is available to us to penetrate into our consciences and hearts making them even cleaner than they were before they were defiled with filthiness, let us

[30] 1 Corinthians 5:7-8: 'For Christ, our Passover lamb, has been sacrificed. Let us therefore celebrate the festival, not with the old leaven, the leaven of malice and evil, but with the unleavened bread of sincerity and truth.' ESV

hold fast both to this Lamb and to his blood and its power.

The application

However, it was not sufficient for the people at that first Passover just to look to the blood of the lamb they had sacrificed; they must also sprinkle the blood upon the lintels and doorposts of their houses, for when they had done this they were assured that the angel of death would pass over them. In the same way, it is not enough simply to say that the blood of Christ will cleanse our souls, nor is it enough to know that his blood is a blessing[31] that will heal your diseases. No, it is not enough to look to Christ's blood from afar, so to speak, for we must apply his blood by sprinkling it upon the lintels and doorposts of our souls (if I may put it that way). I mean we must apply it to our bruised consciences and wounded souls, for it is the application of Jesus' blood that will bring us to see that we have passed from death to life. Undeserving and unworthy as we are, we will then have the assurance that we have been saved.

Yea, often against my expectation the Lord has poured his grace upon me, imparting the virtue of his blood to cleanse my soul and relieve my fainting conscience. Where before there had been nothing in me but grief, molestation, anguish and vexation of spirit because of the awareness of my sin, now I dare to repose upon the pledge of my salvation in Christ Jesus who came to save me. Yet before, so sharp were the accusations of my conscience that I dare not trust him nor rest upon his promises.

We see, then, that we have a Lamb of our own, a Passover of our own, sacred blood of our own, and we also can be assured that his blood when applied to our souls will cleanse us. Since this blood may be freely offered and is now available, how could I never speak of it, and so leave you unhealed? Alas for the one who knows that this blood is freely available but refuses to apply it to his sick soul! Therefore, while the opportunity is afforded you, learn to accept it and to apply it to your consciences and souls. Then you will be able to declare that by its virtue you have passed from death to life. You will say, 'I have been overwhelmed to find in my heart the mercy and peace that passes all

[31] The verb used, 'sane' (or 'sain') can mean to bless with the sign of the cross over a person (DSL).

understanding, I am experiencing the joy and assurance that is the first instalment and guarantee[32] of that life to come!'

May the Lord himself apply the blood of Jesus Christ to every one of your souls, and by the power of his blood may he wash away from all your consciences every stain and guilt, and that through the merits of Christ, to whom with the Father and the Holy Ghost be all honour, praise and glory now and forever more. Amen.

[32] Bruce's word is 'ernest' as in the Geneva Bible, Ephesians 1:14; (see also AV).

Chapter Twenty-Three

Hebrew Chapter 11 verses 29-30

> [29] *By faith they passed threuch the red sea as by dry land quhen the Egyptians they assayit they war droined.* [30] *By faith the wallis of Jericho fell doun efter they war compased sevin dayis.*

Brethren and well-beloved in Christ Jesus, you have heard many things spoken in praise of the faith and deeds of Moses, that most worthy servant of God. The longer he lived and the older he grew, he progressed from grace to grace, until by God's gracious mercy he completed his course in joy. The nearer this holy man drew to his end, the more living was his faith and the more excellent were his works, giving us ever greater proof of the vitality of the spirit within him. You have learned of those works that pertained to him personally, and you also have been told of some of his works that were shared with others.

By a 'shared work of faith' I mean a faith such as that exercised through the observance of the Passover, for the people followed Moses' good example of faith by reverently obeying the command of the living God. We studied this when we met together last time. However, the chief praise of the faith exercised in that sacred celebration of the Passover belongs to Moses, in that first he embraced God's promise, personally obeying the instructions the Lord gave him, and so encouraging the people also to obey along with him.

The Faith of Moses and the people in crossing the Red Sea

In the first of the two verses that I have just read to you, the apostle highlights for us another effect of Moses' faith, similar to that exercised in the observance of the Passover, in that this act of faith was also shared by the people, who therefore were worthy of the same praise as was due to Moses. The apostle sets it before us: by faith, he says, 'The people boldly passed through the Red Sea as if they had been walking on dry land.' Their pursuing enemies, no doubt following the example of the people, thronged after them. But those waters that spared the people did not spare their pursuers, but swept back upon them and sucked them into the womb of the sea.

The apostle affirms that this passage of the people through the Red Sea came from no source other than their faith. To demonstrate this we must turn to the sacred record of this event, because either the crossing of the Sea proceeded from faith, or else the Sea was crossed by some natural means or by human ingenuity. But since it is clear the Sea could be crossed neither by natural nor by human means, this event must have occurred supernaturally.

No one would normally walk straight into such obvious danger, without nature offering some means of survival. But these people were proceeding straight into the bosom of the sea, with waves heaped up on either side of them. Therefore their crossing was done solely through a faith that did not depend upon either human cleverness or some act of nature to aid them. No, where nature could do nothing, the eye of faith found help in the living God. When nature said it was impossible, faith made it possible to pass through the midst of the sea.

Obedience led the people into grave danger

To illustrate this even more clearly, we must turn to the biblical record in Exodus 14. This event came after the people had been brought out of the temporal bondage of slavery through the blood of the sacrificial lamb that had been offered. The Lord then commanded Moses to lead the people to the Red Sea, and to set up camp on the shore (v. 2). Always ready to follow the Lord's commands, Moses obeyed and did not follow a more obvious route, but led them as he was instructed into a place that obviously presented danger and peril, with no possible means of escape. For any of you who want to know about the situation they were in, you can see on a map of that area that they were now cornered, with impassable rocks and hills on both their right and left sides. Further, they have their cruel foe with his entire army in hot pursuit (14:9). In whichever direction they looked, they were surrounded, and neither man nor angel could help them.

Seeing the danger they were now in, they began to turn on Moses, cursing him and raging against him. They asked, 'Were there not burial places for us in the land of Egypt, and would it not have been better for us to have died there rather than in this wilderness? What folly and madness has it been to bring us away from our servitude to the Egyptians?' (14:11-12.) So obvious and desperate was the danger they were in, that they could scarcely be restrained from seizing hold of Moses. However, the Lord's servant did not waver in this situation, but partly by exhortation he quieted them, and partly by assurance and consolation he withstood their anger. Then he made time to meet with God, and by supplication and agonizing in prayer he drew down the message of the living God, and so found relief.

The waters divide

The Lord asked him, 'Why are you crying out to me like this? Take your rod, go down to the sea and command the elements thus: the waters must divide themselves and the firm ground that is beneath them will appear as the waves part. They will stand like walls, piled up on each side, and they will remain like that until all the people have safely crossed over.' So Moses obeyed God and it came about just as the Lord had said: the waters parted and remained where they had gone back, and the people saw that there was a pathway for them.

But who among them would dare to step out on to that dry passage? Had their faith not inspired them because of all that God had recently wrought on their behalf, not one of them would have ventured to walk forward into the midst of the sea. Might not that force of nature that caused these waters to form a wall on either side of them unexpectedly permit the waves to recoil upon the people, as would happen when the Egyptians attempted to follow them?

So had they looked to natural powers and human reasoning, none of them would have ventured forth to begin the crossing. Thus it was only their faith that persuaded them not to depend upon any phenomenon of nature, but rather to look to the God of nature and to trust his word and promise to preserve them. He would hold back the waters as they fixed their eyes upon him and upon the Great Angel whom they could see going before them.

Protected by the Great Angel

However, when their enemies began to catch up with them, the Angel in the cloud moved from leading them and came at the rear of the people and at the vanguard of their pursuers, thus interposing between those fleeing and those pursuing, so that at the Lord's command the Great Angel protected them, standing between them and their foes (14:19). At the same time, the cloud that gave guiding light to the host of the Lord's people, enveloped their enemies in darkness. Therefore, although it was still daytime, Pharaoh's battalions could not even see those whom they were pursuing.

Realizing that the Angel and the cloud were protecting them, the people who had previously been complaining and quarrelling were now reassured and fully persuaded in their consciences, and their faith was reawakened to believe that the God who had shown such love for them would bring them safely through the waters across to dry land. Thus it was by means of the visible signs of God's presence that, with a strengthened faith, they boldly passed in between the walls of waters of the Red Sea. By contrast, their enemies, assuming that what was possible for poor slaves would also be possible for them, rashly followed them. But the elemental powers that had held back the waters for the Lord's people now withdrew, and the waves recoiled over them and swallowed up the Egyptians into the depths of the sea. This I take to be a summary of what is recorded in Exodus 14.

Five Lessons from the crossing of the Sea

This historical record before us sheds light on our subject, so we cannot move on without noting the lessons for us contained in it. They will provide us with instruction if we apply them to ourselves.

First, God sometimes leads us into danger

The first point is that God by his own holy hand sometimes leads his people into great dangers and perils. He may bring them into situations in which they will see that there is no help to be found from either men or angels. Then their only recourse can be to cast their eyes up to heaven, waiting for him to act, and looking to him alone for help as they steadfastly depend upon him. This is what he deliberately does from time to time, so that all the praise for his Kirk's preservation may be ascribed to him, the living God, by both his people and the onlookers.

For such is the corruption of our natures and the malice in our hearts, that whenever he employs some instrument to bring about his Kirk's deliverance, we end up robbing God of his glory. We attribute to those he has used much of the praise due to him. On the other hand, when the Lord works so wonderfully that he uses no human instruments, but accomplishes his deliverance simply by his own finger, then we are compelled to render to him all the praise and glory.

Hannah confesses in her song and prayer that it is God alone who can bring to the gates of hell and raise up again from there.[1] She was referring to the living, whom the Lord can bring low and then raise up, for he can bring men right to the portals of Sheol and then back again to the yetts[2] of heaven. Therefore, whenever the Lord brings us into some danger to soul or body (for without doubt we are always in some danger), it is our duty to turn our eyes from natural or human means, and earnestly seek a sight of the throne of grace. We must turn from every hindrance that is within our hearts, so that we may be able to see the face of Jesus Christ, in whom there is always an abundance of comfort and help in the hour of the greatest extremity that we can meet in this world. Though this is our duty, we often forget, and when we are exposed to some danger we run to someone or other for help, or in our despair we turn to this or that cause.

Second, God at times overturns nature to protect his people

The second point I mark is this, such is the concern and deep love he has for his Kirk, rather than letting her perish or be handed over into the clutches of the devil and her enemies, he will turn upside down the order of nature and the laws of the earth and skies, in order to succour and bring her aid in the hour of her extremity. He will silence the elements and will transform the sea into dry land, that she may escape and be delivered. Therefore seek the Lord while he may be found, and when you do find him hold fast to him, for then when you face danger you will never despair.

[1] 1 Samuel 2:6. 'The Lord killeth and maketh aliue: he bringeth down to the graue and raiseth vp.' GenB

[2] See above, Chapter 15, note 17.

Third, the Lord sends his Great Angel to interpose

The third point I see here is that the Lord sends his Great Angel, who has the name of God engraved upon him. But there is no angel who can be called God other than the Son of God. In his determinate counsel the Lord sends his Great Angel to interpose between the Kirk and her enemies, for it belongs to the office of Jesus Christ to stand between his people and their opponents, so that they will have no power to hurt them.

If only we had the eyes to see it, ever since the world began Christ has been the protector of his Kirk in her hour of peril. Had our past experiences in our unhappy country moved us, we would have seen that Christ Jesus has always stepped in between the Kirk and the multitude of those who were set against his cause, but because we were blind to his intervention, the Lord has been deprived of the praise due to him. Indeed, it could be on account of our lack of spiritual insight that we may end up being delivered into the hands of those who hate us. On the other hand, if we diligently seek godly discernment and hearts that will thank the Lord for his intervention, then he will send his Great Angel to preserve us from our foes and bring their devices to nothing.

Fourth, God is inclined to mercy, pity and compassion

I also perceive here that in God there is a wonderful inclination to mercy, pity and compassion, notwithstanding the people's opposition to Moses, and their grumbling and cursing against him. For the Lord spared them, forgave and blessed them, and then opened up a passageway for them so that by faith they could cross the Red Sea. Nevertheless, we must not abuse his pity and compassion, but as he is ready to receive us, so we must be ready to meet him with thankfulness. However, if we do persist in abusing his mercy (there are times when all of us do), we shall find that ultimately his mercy will turn into bitter judgment, and God shall have no other option than to let us learn what it is like to face an angry judge.

Fifth, the attitude of the Lord's people has often angered God

The last lesson here is that as well as these things that I observe in God, I also observe in his people an ill disposition, for at times it has been their practice to murmur, grumble and quarrel when some disaster threatens or some vexation unexpectedly comes upon them. This kind of attitude in his people has always angered the living God, and when it has persisted it has been the cause of the subjugation of their cities, commonwealths and nations. Even though the Lord spared them on those and many other occasions, there came a time when many of them were not spared.

You may have read in Numbers 16 of the notorious sedition instigated by Korah, Dathan and Abiram. There was another sedition by the people against Moses and Aaron, a consequence of which was that only two of the people born in Egypt actually entered the Land of Promise.[3] Therefore it is incumbent on us all in the hour of calamity to clothe ourselves in great patience, to look to the working of God and his instruments, and not to come to rash judgments. Further, it is the duty of the magistrate so to conduct himself in his calling as he must answer to God; in the event of any complaints being made against him, he must have a warrant in his conscience for his actions, otherwise the Lord who knows the secrets of men's hearts will reveal the truth to his servants for their approbation.

The necessity of prayer

We may be sure that God's servant Moses was convinced in his heart and resolute in his conscience that the Lord would open up the way to rescue his people, for he had already told him before ever he brought them to the shores of the sea that he would glorify himself in his judgment upon Pharaoh.[4] Therefore, even though Moses was firmly convinced in his conscience that God would not fail them, nevertheless his faith was not idle nor was he complacent, for he earnestly sought God's face and made fervent supplications to Jesus Christ, using every possible means, as if he had never been assured that they would be delivered. We must learn, then, not to ignore the Lord's intentions of what he is about to do, nor must we be lulled into a sense of security because we are quite certain that God is going to come to our aid. No, rather use the appointed means of grace, and when you see the Lord acting on your behalf in compassion and mercy, even more must you offer thanks to him. We have an example of this in the person of Moses.

[3] Numbers 14, esp. verses 20-24, 30.

[4] Exodus 14:4

Lessons from the impiety of Pharaoh

Next, I mark certain other points regarding Pharaoh and his people. I see in them the recompense and outcome of obdurate impiety and irredeemable stubbornness. Their punishment was the destruction of soul and body, for Pharaoh only ever made one good decision, after which he broke his word.[5] Indeed, he was compelled to let the people go, and then they were hardly away when he changed his mind and reverted to his continual rebellion against God and his chosen people. Thus having filled up the cup of the Lord's wrath, he and his army were swallowed up by the watery elements in an extraordinary manner. So we see the final recompense of men's perverse impiety.

Such impiety displays an inflexible obduracy against God on the part of those who take pleasure in provoking his wrath. If outward physical judgments upon the body and inward spiritual judgments upon the soul had taught this unhappy man and changed him enough to reverence God and turn to him, there would never have been the judgments visited upon any man's soul as those visited upon him. Yet neither physical judgments upon his body nor spiritual judgments upon his soul could bring him to turn to God to seek mercy from his hands, therefore he died in his obstinate impiety. He died with his heart still as obstinate as ever because he had perversely aroused the ire and indignation of God.

The corruption of many nobles

Pharaoh's death ought to cause us to lament and deplore our human condition that mars us during the course of our earthly lives, for it can never be changed either by prayer, supplication or by any visitation upon our souls or bodies. We have men in our country, chiefly of the highest rank, who are engaged in malicious acts against God, having loosed the bridle to all kinds of fleshly filth and wicked oppression. They have inverted the order of nature, turning it upside down. Such is the state of their consciences that nothing that is wholesome pleases them, for they only find pleasure in things that are displeasing to God, indeed, anything that pleases God displeases them.

So depraved have their consciences become, that it is evident God has cast them off as reprobates, a condition from which it is almost

[5] Exodus 8:28-32.

impossible to recover. When a man has lost both his wits and his conscience so that only evil deeds and scurrilous company please him, and he only enjoys watching wickedness, then most certainly that man's heart has become thoroughly depraved, and he daily grows more opposed to what is acceptable to civilized society. We are all bound to abhor such people, for when they draw others into their company, society is contaminated and there can be neither commonwealth nor Kirk.

The reason why we should abhor and shun such men is that there may be some in their company who may by our attitude become ashamed, and so be moved to reflect upon their ways; their consciences may be awakened to the evil in their lives, and who can tell but that the Lord is able to renew the hearts even of those who for a time were reprobate.[6] The flood of mercy purchased by Jesus Christ is able to transform and recover them. But as long as our King tolerates them and the Kirk fails to censure them, and no one shuns and abhors them, they will continue headlong in their wickedness, and we will all be guilty of their blood.[7] Therefore, it becomes every single one of us, whatever our estate or standing, to ostracize them, and it becomes the Kirk to censure them, not in order to lose them but rather to win them back. Likewise, it behoves the King to act severely towards them, not to lose his subjects but to win them, so that none of us will be guilty of their blood. If they perish, they will not only perish in their impiety, but they will draw others after them.

None can deny that, as there is a God in heaven and truth in his Word, before many of you die you will witness the destruction of these men who have replaced virtue with vice. They will become examples of the everlasting judgments of God, witnessed by all the world as spectacles upon whom his finger has been laid in his divine retribution of their obdurate impiety. However there is something we may do: we may seek to win some of them by prayer, beseeching the Lord to visit them with his choice of affliction, that he may sanctify his chosen trial, and so make them objects of his workmanship into new creations, that after this life they may be partakers in the life to come.

[6] In the light of what is said in Chapter 24, Note 7 below, it can only be that here Bruce refers to some who appeared to others to be reprobate, but in fact were not.

[7] There may be an allusion here to Ezekiel 33:1-9.

I am fully aware, through my own experience and from the faithful reports of reputable men who are to be believed, of the conversations of many of our nobles and how they are defiling this city. They find delight in pursuing their own carnal lusts and contaminate every house they enter. It is indeed astonishing that the earth puts up with them and does not spew them out. What is more, some of them are men whom the Lord wrought well with in past days, and they gave every impression of being genuine Christians. Yet these same men, of whom we once had great expectations, have now fallen away.

I am not going to name any of them. Perhaps they will hear reports of what I am now saying, and if some apply my words to themselves the Lord may draw them out of their shameful behaviour. No doubt some of those who confessed themselves to be true Christians have now fallen into shameful ways. We all know who these men are, we will all witness how those of persistent impiety meet their end.

Our need for the Holy Spirit's sanctifying power

There is one other necessary point I must make before I move on. It is something that we ought to apply to ourselves since the Lord has dealt gently with us in exercising our faith. We need to ask him that it would please him to implant in us the power of his Holy Spirit so there may be no hardness of heart remaining in us, and that his work in us would soften us, that when it pleases him to chap on us to depart from this world we may go on to that better life. Except we crave from him inward sanctification, all our temporal crosses and trials will be of no avail. May the Lord in his mercy grant us the spirit of prayer to beseech this from him. Be assured that we will all die in our sins unless he does his work in us by his Holy Spirit to cleanse our souls and enlighten our minds.

The Red Sea a type of baptism

Now regarding the crossing of the Red Sea, it is certainly a type of our baptism, for the various ceremonies performed by the Fathers were types of ceremonies that also apply to us. In each of the ceremonies is some special blessing[8] if we can accept it for ourselves. In 1 Corinthi-

[8] Bruce's word is 'comfort'; its original meaning of a strengthening presence is intended here.

ans 10:1-3 the apostle points out that this passing through the Red Sea prefigures our baptism. As in our baptism the symbol of water and the word concur with the invisible grace, so these three elements—water, the word and grace—also concurred in the people's passing through the Red Sea. In baptism we pass from death to life, from the kingdom of darkness to the realms of light, from the power of Satan to the kingdom of Jesus Christ. All this is symbolised in the physical passing of the people through the sea.

In baptism the word of grace is contained in the promise, which for the people crossing the Sea was the promise of their preservation. Therefore grace was included for them, and now in our baptism grace is also included, so that even though the practice of their baptism was different to ours, the visible grace remains the same. Seeing the actual performance of the people's baptism had an inward spiritual significance, let us take the order of the events involved their deliverance and apply them to ourselves, and thereby benefit from them.

In baptism we must renounce our sinful past

First, we see that the people departed from Egypt, renouncing their life there and leaving it behind them. Similarly, it behoves us to leave our old lives by renouncing our sinful affections and passions along with the cares of this world and the tyranny of the devil, the prince of this world. It also behoves us to remember the baptismal promise made in our names, that we should renounce the devil, the lusts of the flesh and the pride of life, and that we should mortify our sinful natures. It behoves us to stand by that promise and to seek for spiritual power from Jesus Christ. We need his help to slay the enemies of our souls and to hold down the burdens of the world as often as they arise, and also to withstand the tempter when he assails us.

Our baptism calls us to look to the future

Second, as the people when they went out of Egypt kept their eyes upon the Lord and his power as he led them, so it behoves us whose names have been given to Jesus Christ to look upwards to heaven, and to remember his blessed words that lead us onwards and upwards. But just say your carnal hearts prevent you from doing this and the cares of this world weigh you down. Then let the Lord himself stir you up afresh. Each one of you must remember once each day that there is a place of rest if only you will embrace it, whereas if you refuse his resting place there remains a place of pain. So with the memory of these things, even if only once each day, lift up your hearts to crave godly eyes that you may be granted a glimpse of both heaven and hell, so that you might embrace the one, but eschew the other.

Perhaps you should learn to remember these things each night before you go to your bed, or else when you rise each morning, you should ask God that he would help you to remember heaven and keep the vision of it before you. Ask him too to grant you a foretaste of heaven in your souls, for then you will be willing to go there, for without question when the Lord gives us a foretaste and vision of a sweeter life, we shall be ready to depart with joy. If we have never sought the Lord for a sight of the far better life in heaven then, at our departure, our souls will be troubled and anxious as to what lies beyond death.

The Christian life is beset by trials

When the people had crossed the Red Sea, before them lay the wilderness, and as the entire record tells us, it was a time of continuous temptation on account of some complaint or other. From this we learn that from the moment we come out of our mother's womb into this life here on earth, we are in the equivalent of a wilderness with its constant trials and vexations of soul and body right to the end of life's journey. Therefore we must all expect troubles while we are in the wilderness of this world,[9] where each assault upon us will prove greater than the previous one. Unless we realise this, these visitations upon us will catch us unawares, and we could end up losing both body and soul.

If we do not forget that in our journey through this spiritual desert we will often be sorely tried, then we will be watchful and alert, and we will be content to endure this condition into which the Lord has placed us. May the Lord in his mercy grant this. The people who escaped from Egypt found themselves severely tempted, and because they yielded to their temptations, they all perished.[10] Nevertheless, we do not need to give in as they did. We cannot avoid being tempted,

[9] Bruce's phrase predates by nearly 90 years the opening words of John Bunyan's *Pilgrim's Progress* (1678): 'As I walked through the wilderness of this world…'.

[10] 1 Corinthians 10:5.

but you must beware of giving place to the devil. Take care to resist him, no matter what kind of temptation he assails you with, for we are not all tempted in the same way. No, he knows the various inclinations of each one of us and by what vice we may be enticed. The devil also knows where our defences are weakest and where to target his assault. Moreover, he knows exactly in what way we will be most easily deceived, and so he sets before us the temptations by which we will be allured and snared.

The evil subtlety of Satan

If we are unaware of his devices and of our personal fleshly weaknesses, we could be overcome by the devil and fall in the hour of temptation, for each of us has a fatal weakness whereby we can too easily be deceived. Even our consciences can fail us in some particular sin. What I mean is this. Yes, our consciences will warn us regarding almost every snare, but in one secret sin to which in the past I was enslaved, for I loved it and always yielded to its enticements, I silenced my conscience when the tempter offered it to me again, and I found myself willing to depart from my God.

Therefore, examine yourselves! Search your hearts to uncover the one thing that is your idol in which you delight, and to which your whole soul longs to yield. Renounce it! Turn your back upon it! Even though it tortures you day and night, resist it, crave grace to rid yourself of it, so that little by little at length your conscience will be able to say, 'I thank God that what I once loved, now through the power that flows from Christ Jesus, I abhor it! What was once a tyrant controlling me is now my slave, and my conscience that was formerly silent over it now alerts me and is cleared.'

Therefore, I repeat: each one of us has some beloved sin over which our consciences are silent. We must learn to be watchful and alert, and we must examine our hearts and put our consciences on trial. Examine that secret idol by putting it under the scrutiny of the law of God, and you will find it is condemned. Either you must separate yourself from it, or else you will go to hell in company with it. Pray constantly that the Lord would enable you to see and recognize it as an idol. Ask him to let you taste the bitterness of it, for though you are aware it is contrary to God, in creeps the deceit of the false pleasure it gives, and so you keep longing after it. Know that you will find no peace of mind until you tear it out of your soul. Thus far for the lessons from the wilderness trials. I shall be more brief in my next point.

Joshua's faith

The apostle moves on and comes to Joshua. He shows us how this holy man who succeeded Moses accomplished all he did by faith, as Moses had done before him. However he begins with a work in which Joshua's faith acted along with the rest of the people. It was the first great work done in the land of Canaan, and demonstrated clearly that it was accomplished through faith. The apostle wants us to be assured of Joshua's faith when he says, *By faith the wallis of Jericho fell doun.*

When Joshua and the people went to the city walls, they were unanimously persuaded in their consciences that God would keep his promise. They walked round the walls as God had instructed them, carrying the ark with them, because they trusted God's word. Nor did he disappoint them, for just as he had said, the walls fell down. The manner in which it happened was astonishing, yet they believed God and looked to him, and so by faith the walls collapsed. This is a brief summary.

Without faith it is impossible to please God

It is clear this victory occurred through faith, for God would not have rewarded his people if they had distrusted him. It stands to reason that if someone distrusts us we would not be able to help them. Likewise, no more can God help the person who regards his word as false, for refusing to believe God is the same as attributing falsehood to him. On the other hand, when someone sincerely believes God's word, then he ascribes truth to him, and such trust pleases God more than anything else[11] as we read in John 3.[12]

Had the people not believed, it would not have been possible that such notable work could have been attributed to their faith and declared in their favour. Indeed, all such notable works that have been recorded since this world began have been attributed to trust in God. So that you may become familiar with the way in which the walls fell, I

[11] Bruce's phrase is 'aboue all thingis'.
[12] John 3:33-36.

must now recount to you the manner in which it happened.

The fall of Jericho

The Lord had assured Joshua that he would succeed in capturing the city. First, he commanded him to arm all his men of war, so that they must be got ready to lead the march around the walls. Next, the priests must bring the ark and be ready to fall into their place behind the armed men. However, immediately in front of the ark must be seven priests each holding a ram's horn; the horns would be sounded in front of the ark. Finally, the whole host of the people must bring up the rear, silently marching behind the priests with the ark.

This procession was then instructed to encompass the city walls once each day for six successive days. On the seventh day, however, the procession must be in place early in the morning, for they were to march round the walls seven times, and on completing the seventh march, the seven priests were to blow a loud, long blast on the rams' horns, while the whole host (the first six days they had been totally silent), at the same time as trumpets sounded, were to give a loud shout. At the sound of that shout and the blast of the trumpets, the Lord would reach down from heaven and in the most extraordinary way would cause the walls to collapse completely.

Once the walls had been flattened, the people were to take the city, execute its king and destroy the whole place, man and beast; they were to spare only Rahab the harlot, along with her family and possessions. Her preservation was granted to her on account of her faith. Also to be preserved were the gold and silver which was to be melted down and consecrated to the Lord's service. Because this was the first city captured in Canaan, the gold and silver were to treated as 'first fruits'.[13] No gold or silver metals must be taken by anyone, though one man disobeyed that injunction and was punished for it. This then was the way in which the city of Jericho was captured.

As to the city of Jericho, it was in the territory allotted to the tribe of Benjamin and was one of Canaan's most famous cities, second only to Jerusalem. It was situated in a plain and its borders stretched to ten miles in breadth and twenty miles in length. The records tell us that its soil was among the most fertile on earth, and plane trees, roses and

[13] Exodus 23:19.

flowers replete with nectar grew there, so there was an abundance of honey. The famous historian, Josephus, tells us it was one of the most flourishing cities in the land, surrounded by such high, stout walls that no siege engine had been invented that was able to breach them.[14] Jericho became famous because it was where the Lord called on Zacchaeus (Luke 19). In the previous chapter of Luke, we learn that this city also achieved fame through the restoring of a blind man's sight there. I say all this to let you see that Jericho was a strongly defended city, more so than any other settlement in that country.

God uses the weak to overcome the strong

However, the point I want to make concerns the means the Lord used in overcoming those strong walls. He used men of war silently marching round the city and the seven rams horns trumpeting out a blast. Could such means ever conquer any city? Would they not have seemed ridiculous in the eyes of natural man, serving no useful purpose whatsoever? Yet the Lord in his wisdom devised that strategy, and he put his blessing on them to accomplish his plans.

Why did he use such an unlikely method? He deliberately used these means so that we would learn that what is weakest in this world is able to overcome what appears to be strongest, and what seems to be foolish can confound the wisest. He does this so that his power might shine forth from the weakest, then all the glory will be given to him and not to the means or persons he uses.[15] Contemptible instruments and base means! This is done on the one hand for God's honour, but on the other hand it is done for our benefit, that we should be satisfied to know we are under God's command.

Therefore, let us not look to our own abilities, nor should we enter into curious disputations questioning how can this be. Has the Lord commanded you? Then obey, for it is as easy for him to use a few as to use many. It is also easy for him to use the weakest things in the earth to overcome the strongest. Thus we who are weak must learn obedience

[14] I can find no such description of Jericho in Josephus' account of the fall of the city (V.1:2-7), though he does recount that when the Romans plundered the city, they found it full of good things and provisioned their forces from its abundant stores. *Josephus* XIV.15:3.

[15] The allusion is to 1 Corinthians 1:27-29.

so that God may have all the glory. This far, then, for God's part in the conquest.

What about the inhabitants of the city? They had the strong walls they had built, and they depended upon their stout doors, looking to the strength of their city gates and the height of their defences. They believed that their fortifications would keep out their assailants. They thought that the Hebrews' God would not be able to climb over their city's walls, and certainly the attackers could never scale them. No siege weapon men had invented could breach them. So what was the outcome for the city's inhabitants? Their end was disaster, for the walls on which they depended fell flat.

Four further lessons

What are our lessons then? First, everyone who has trusted in himself, and every city and commonwealth that had relied upon its own strength ultimately has perished. As God's people prevailed when they looked to him alone and not at the city's fortifications that seemed to defy them, so those foolish inhabitants perished who did not look to the Lord God, but depended upon their own defences and on things of this world. So let us take heed and beware of abusing God's good gifts to us; by all means enjoy and honour them, always remembering that natural wisdom is one of his good gifts. Be careful not to abuse his gifts by using them to engage in ungodly affairs, for then you will be fighting against God himself. Beware of turning any of his gifts into your own personal god, for that happens when you trust to something instead of trusting in him. Some think to escape through riches, others through friends, yet others through the influence of the court and familiarity with the king.

Never abuse God's gifts

Second, whenever such means are abused, the Lord can descend with some extraordinary action and make wealth melt away like the snow, and a man's honourable estate to fade like a flower. Mighty walls were laid flat as by the blast of an earthquake, and so he can take from a man the king's favour, reducing him to misery. The lesson is this. If God has endowed you with good gifts, use them as a means of drawing yourself to him, for then you will keep close to him and he will preserve you despite the circumstances in this world that might come upon you. However, if you turn one of his good gifts into your god, then he will cause that same good gift to become a veritable devil to you. Therefore do not put your confidence in yourself, but trust in the Lord alone.

All things possible through faith

Third, I see in the persons of God's people that all things are possible to those who believe. There is nothing impossible for nature that is not possible for faith; as our Master says in Matthew 21:21, if our hearts are sufficiently strong in faith we would be able to command a mountain to cast itself into the sea. Therefore, all is possible for faith when it does not look for second causes, but only to God for whom everything is possible.

Certainly, since the beginning of the world you will not find any great work done in defiance of human expectation, that did not flow from faith. For example, Sarah aged four score years conceived and bore a child because she believed; the people crossed through the midst of the sea because they believed; the walls of Jericho fell down because they believed and the virgin conceived because she believed. Thus all the extraordinary works that the Lord has wrought for the children of men have flowed from this fountain of faith.

There was never among the Lord's people any warrior who effectively besieged and captured a town, or fought valiantly on the battlefield, who was not a man of faith. When one of Israel's leaders acting justly conquered a town, faith was of far more value to him than all the strategies or engines of war that had ever been invented. Consider Jonathan whose faith in Jesus Christ inspired him to undertake a most hazardous venture that would not have been possible for any man without faith. We read of it in 1 Samuel 14. He made an assault upon a band of Philistines and took with him only his armour-bearer, because he was convinced that the Lord would enable his action to succeed. What did he say to his armour-bearer? 'Nothing can hinder the Lord from saving by many or by few.' In this assurance he made a perilous ascent, and at the top of the crag the Lord gave him a sign that he would deliver the band of Philistines into his hand, and according as he trusted and believed, success was granted to him.

Thus there is never in Scripture any who did valiantly in battle who did not go forth with faith in Jesus Christ. For faith is the secret of a good conscience, and a good conscience is far better than any Jack,[16] better indeed than all the armour in this world. We find another example of this in 2 Chronicles 20:20 when Jehoshaphat assured his people that if they trusted in God and believed his prophets, the victory would be theirs. So when it comes to battle, faith is far better than any amount of armour. Without faith, strong walls will not protect you, neither will all your clever strategies save you. Without faith and the blessing of God, all your efforts will lead to disarray and defeat. Therefore, even though you may have wealth and honour, make certain that you have it with faith and the blessing of God, that he may protect you, for trusting in men will prove futile.[17]

Wait for the Lord's time

Fourth, the last thing I mark here is this. We must patiently endure in our trials and wait for the Lord's time, and not act in haste. For if these people had been impatient they might have said after they had marched round the walls of Jericho once, then twice and then a third time, 'We are exhausted with all this endless walking, this is getting us nowhere.' Yet in faith they patiently waited for the Lord's time, for at length he will always come and deliver those who wait upon him. Therefore, do not be over-hasty, for it is one of the proper uses of the Lord's benefits to wait for his time to act.

I have one final point to make and then I shall end. We have seen how this city was destroyed with such a fearful destruction that it

[16] The expression 'any Jack' was the equivalent in the 16th century of what today would be 'any Tom, Dick or Harry'.

[17] Twenty-first-century readers should bear in mind that about three years before Bruce preached this sermon, Scotland and England had trembled at the thought of the mighty Spanish Armada that was being made ready to attack and conquer both countries. On 6 August 1588 (the day the Armada anchored off Calais) on the instructions of the Kirk's Assembly, Bruce had called the nation to prayer and fasting (Shaw 860), and so his comments in this paragraph would have been listened to with immense respect. Nor was the defeat of the Armada in 1588 the end of the believers' anxiety as the infamous conspiracy of 'The Blanks' plot in late 1592 made clear. https://en.wikipedia.org/wiki/Spanish_blanks_plot. However, if the date of January 1591 suggested above in Ch.17, Note 17 is accurate, The Blanks conspiracy would not have yet occurred, though the threat of a renewed Spanish invasion would still have been very much alive.

makes us tremble to think of it. God's purpose in utterly wiping out Jericho was to make its ruins a sign and monument to his immense wrath against its inhabitants, and indeed against all sin and sinners. It was done also as a warning to us, and that the ruins might serve to remind us on the one hand of his casting down of this world's rebellion against him, and on the other hand as a memorial to his singular mercy towards his own. Yet this is not my main point here.

The curse upon Jericho

There was a particular curse I have not yet mentioned that Joshua pronounced over the ruins of Jericho after its destruction was complete.[18] Because this curse was quite unique I need to enlarge upon it. After the city had been burnt to the ground, God commanded a curse would be upon any man who began to rebuild it, for if he laid new foundations it would cost him the life of his eldest son. If he then continued to rebuild, it would cost him the life of his second son and so on. If he persisted in rebuilding the city, as soon as he had completed the work, it would cost him his youngest son's life. The message of the curse was clear: whoever set out to rebuild this city would have his progeny cut off entirely, so that there would be none of his family left to stand and piss against its walls.[19]

We can calculate the date of the Jericho's destruction as over one thousand years before Christ.[20] It was rebuilt in the reign of Ahab who married Jezebel; he was the king who exceeded in his wickedness all his predecessors. It was while he ruled in Judah that a man of Bethel called Hiel obtained Ahab's permission to rebuild the city. The account of this can be found in 1 Kings 16:34, that is, in the final verse of the chapter. As soon as he began work on the foundations, his eldest son died according to the curse. Nevertheless, this unfortunate man continued rebuilding the city, and as the work proceeded one after another his sons died. So he kept losing his progeny. Yet he would not learn the lesson. At length he completed the work, and then his youngest son

[18] Joshua 6:26-27.

[19] Bruce takes this expression from 1 Samuel 25:22; the AV translates the Hebrew phrase literally, exactly as does Bruce's Geneva Bible: 'any that pisseth against the wall'. The ESV translation of the same Hebrew phrase indicates what the expression means, that is, a 'man': 'so much as one male'.

[20] Bruce's date is the year 2,493, presumably calculated from OT genealogies.

died. The names of his eldest and youngest sons are recorded in that verse.

This rebuilding of Jericho was completed about seven hundred years after the curse was put upon the city by Joshua at God's command. Therefore, notwithstanding the great period of time between the city's destruction and its rebuilding by Hiel, the curse of God remained as true and fresh as if it had only just been pronounced. Thus we see there is neither passage of time nor distance of place that is able to weaken God's curse, for on whatever it has been placed, there it will continue. If we judge this according to human reasoning, it seems utterly bizarre. As Hiel starts to build, the Lord begins to demolish his family, and as he persisted in rebuilding what God had destroyed, the Lord pulled down his 'building' in the sense of his progeny. While he was busy working, God was working too! So the Lord met like with like, so to speak.

It is true that there is no mention of Hiel himself coming under the curse, yet that made the curse more bitter because now he must live to see each of his sons dying, one after the other. In a sense he himself died a kind of death as each son was taken from him, and of course at length he also died. Therefore this kind of curse that takes away a man's entire posterity before he himself dies is most dangerous. Yet in the purposes of God, he so dealt with this man as to make him a warning to all. We read of Julian the Apostate[21] who in spite of what God's plans were, gave an order to the Jews to rebuild their temple, and they set to and began re-laying the foundations. But a curse of God pronounced by his prophet stopped the work and turned the project and the entire country to be a spectacle to this very day of God's intense indignation. Even in our own day, during this past century the Turks have attempted to build a temple in Palestine, yet the curse of God has prevented the work. So we see that there is no lapse of time or distance of place that can erode God's curse. It strikes upon a man, a people or a city as he has appointed it to strike.

[21] Julian was the last of the non-Christian Roman Emperors, ruling from AD 361 to 363. His rejection of the Christianity imposed on him in his youth, and his promotion of Neo-platonic Hellenism in its place caused him to be remembered as Julian the Apostate by the church. Gibbon, Ch. 23.

The curse of ill-gotten gains

This is the one point I want to make so that you may take careful note as to where the curse lies and where it does not lie. Too often men take no heed to this, but attend only to increasing their wealth, disregarding both the blessing and the curse of God. They assume that multiplying their possessions will make them rich when, underlying all they attempt, is a secret curse conjoined with their amassing of ever more wealth, for meanwhile an unseen canker is corroding their goods and eating up their houses—timber and stonework, as it were. On the other hand, if only men would pay diligent heed to the blessing of God, and possess only what they may have with his blessing, the Lord would make them rich. Unless we take heed to ourselves, therefore, in the end it will become apparent that the curse which fell upon Hiel, will also fall upon us and our posterity.

We should all be aware that none has experience of the same scourge[22] as others, yet nevertheless everyone of us has known in his life some scourge or other. Therefore identify what you may have with God's blessing, and what you may not have. The rule for any increase in your possessions is that it must only be achieved with a continued good conscience; then you will know the blessing of God is given with that increase. But if you find that you do not have his blessing, meaning your increase in wealth is not within his purposes for you, then renounce your wealth, give it away, otherwise that silent canker shall not only devour you, but also everything that you have.

The natural, unspiritual man will not understand this, but the living God shall cause you to find that it is true through your experience of his hand upon your body, unless you part with anything you have gained without his blessing. For it is only the blessing of God that makes rich. I know the earthly heart will cling to this world, for the carnal mind cannot sever itself from the world; there is little that can be done about such men. However, I pray to the living God that he will work so effectively in each of you before it is too late and you bring his curse upon yourselves and your posterity.

[22] Bruce continues to use the word 'curs' but the context would seem to be better understood by the synonym 'scourge'.

Preserve a good conscience

I pray that before it is too late you will part with anything you have that cannot be enjoyed with his blessing and a good conscience. Therefore, from your hearts beseech God that you may be fully resolved and say, 'I see that I cannot hold on to this thing in all conscience, so may the Lord part me from it.' Then the blessing of God may make you rich, unless it is not his will that you have great possessions. And if you are unable to part with something you know you ought not to have, pray that the living God would not let you gain anything that you should not have, unless it be according to his good will. Otherwise, pray that you may find contentment. But whether or not you are content, pray that he would enable you to give up anything that keeps you from his blessing. So may you ever seek eternal life, and prefer his heavenly heritage to every worldly heritage.

May experience teach you that the mouth that has given you this word is blessed, but far more blessed was the Spirit that wrought obedience in the one who spoke it. I close urging you again to part from everything that parts you from God, and I pray for you that he will enable you to do this. The Lord in his mercy so grant to each of you that, trusting upon the blessing of God here, you may be partakers in his everlasting kingdom in the hereafter, and that through the righteous merits of Christ, to whom with the Father and the Holy Ghost be all honour, praise and glory both now and for ever. Amen.

Chapter Twenty-Four

Hebrews Chapter 11 verse 31

31 By faith the harlot Rachab perischit not with them who obeyit not when sche receavit the spyis peaceablie.

We have already heard, brethren and well-beloved in Jesus Christ, how the walls of Jericho fell down and the city was overthrown. We considered carefully these means, the 'siege engines' and armaments[1] he employed to demolish the thick, high walls of that well-defended city. We also saw how weak and contemptible these means were. First, he urged the people to believe so that they would go forth in faith. Second, he commanded the priests to sound blasts upon their trumpets. Third, he commanded them to have the ark present with them as they encircled the walls. These were his 'siege engines' and it was by these means that the walls collapsed and the city was taken.

We are engaged in spiritual warfare

What more can I say about this? There is one further point I did not previously mention. Remember the apostle's words that the armaments of the Lord's warfare are not corporal, that is, not carnal, nor do they appeal to our outward senses, for there is no outward attraction or beauty in the means he uses, rather his weapons are spiritual.[2] However contemptible they may appear to be, they are accompanied by an invincible strength and endued with spiritual and heavenly power. So mighty are they that not only are they able to oppose the highest bul-

[1] Clearly, he is speaking figuratively when he uses the words 'ingynis' and 'armour'.

[2] 2 Corinthians 10:4. 'For the weapons of our warefare are not carnal, but mightie through God to cast doun holdes' (GenB).

wark and strongest tribes that rise up against the Lord, but they are also able to strike down the most haughty spirits and ingenious strategies on earth that dare venture to raise themselves against the living God. Therefore it is by such means that this world will be overthrown along with the walls of Rome and Babylon. Indeed, unless such means are used to undermine both Satan and the antichrist, do not expect any disruption of either of them, for their kingdom cannot be opposed unless three means are applied.

All three means must be used

If we are to subvert the kingdom of darkness we must apply the same means. First, we must use faith, the faith that depends upon the power of God and on the omnipotent authority that resides unseen in the word of Jesus Christ. This is the first of the special means we have been given to use for the overthrow of Satan's kingdom. It must be in faith that we pray, 'Thy kingdom come,' for God's kingdom opposes all evil. This prayer is heard and its petition is wrought effectually as our faith leans upon Christ's invincible power. Yea, prayer in faith is a most effective and powerful means of subverting the kingdom of antichrist.

The second means is the blast of the trumpet, which denotes the evangel being proclaimed throughout the world, for it is through its proclamation that faith is engendered and begotten in the hearts of those who hear. Without the trumpet sound it is impossible for the devil's kingdom to be confounded. Thus the trumpet blast is the 'siege-engine' that batters the kingdom of evil, by which we mean the sound of the evangel proclaimed with authority and power.[3]

The third means and 'engine' that must be employed to subvert the kingdom of darkness is the presence of the ark. The ark of god, so to speak, must be present in the heart of the preacher and in the hearts of the hearers, otherwise the trumpet blast will avail us nothing. What I mean is that Jesus Christ must be in the preacher's heart, that is, he must be endued with the Holy Spirit, and likewise those who are listening must be possessed by Christ's Spirit, otherwise it will be impossible for the kingdom of antichrist to be defeated. For if the word that we preach does not enter your hearts and move you to renounce your evil

[3] Commenting on Joshua 6:16, Calvin states that the sounding of the rams' horns spoke of the authority of God. *Comm. in loc.*

practice of idolatry and turn to Jesus Christ, that dark kingdom will never be subverted among us. No, this can only be accomplished by the presence amongst us of the ark of God—I mean by the effectual working of the Spirit of Christ.

The importance of the three means concurring

Therefore, these three means must concur—faith, the effectual preaching of the word and the inward presence of God's Spirit in the preacher's heart. In short, when God is present, without doubt the devil and antichrist are cast out. That is why the preacher should be sanctified before he blows the trumpet, and why the hearers should be sanctified before they hear the trumpet's sound. Of what use or profit can this teaching be if it lacks the authority and power to move the hearers, to break down and to raise up, to demolish and to plant?[4] If the word does not carry any power or authority, what use is it?

Or how can it be possible for the preacher to move and persuade you, unless he himself is moved and persuaded in his own heart by the same Holy Spirit? Yet moved he will not be except he be sanctified, and has taken time to present himself before the throne and majesty of God. Unless by the mercy of God life has been breathed into his message, he speaks in vain and without any effect, for his words will not achieve anything.

Therefore, it is essential that whoever blows the trumpet must daily spend time before God and so be constantly sanctified. It is also necessary that you who are hearers of the word should prepare yourselves by prayer to drink in all that you hear. For you should not come here to sleep or for ostentation and to put on a show, though that is why some of you come. Yet whoever comes will either receive the declaration of absolution, or else the declaration of everlasting condemnation. Take heed to yourselves that you do not come here to sleep, which would be to mock God to his face, for then, unless you repent, you will hear the sentence that one day will be pronounced against you. Therefore, you must sanctify yourselves and continue instant in prayer for the Spirit of Jesus Christ to be present. Would to God that it would please his divine majesty that both in preacher and hearers the effectual power of his Spirit to subvert the kingdom of Satan will be among us, now and

[4] The allusion is probably to Jeremiah 1:9-10.

always!

Overview of the theme of Hebrews

Before we consider the example that I have just read to you, because it concerns a foreigner who had no part in the covenant of mercy but was a Canaanite and a stranger to the commonwealth of Israel, I need to begin by reminding you of the grounds on which this doctrine wholly depends. We must recall that before ever the apostle began the eleventh chapter of this epistle, his reason for writing was to demonstrate to his fellow Jews that true religion and worship of God was founded upon faith and innocence. These marks of the right worship of God were the whole scope of his first ten chapters: faith by which men's hearts are renewed, and innocence which is verified by their reformation. Because it is not possible that an unclean heart can offer clean service to the living God, pure religion and righteous worship[5] acceptable to God can only proceed from faith. As to innocence, it is the fruit of faith and makes clear what faith has wrought inwardly in a man's heart and soul. Therefore all true religion emanates only from true faith.

That this principle and foundation is correct, the apostle then makes clear in the eleventh chapter of his epistle, as he presents to us successive examples from the beginning of human history up to this day, for there is nothing more appropriate to demonstrate a point of doctrine than some examples. The various examples he cites show clearly that no one was ever justified before God or shared in heaven's glory after his departure but those in whose heart faith had been implanted by the Lord's mercy and grace; the same applies to all those whose works were good and whom God held in high honour during their earthly lives. These examples prove the validity of the three means we have been considering.

Two objections to the principle of faith

Against this doctrine two objections have been made, which could arouse doubts in the hearts of penitent sinners, but he anticipates them both by bringing in this particular example as an explanation and answer. The first objection is this. It could be said that out of the

[5] The parallelism in this sentence reminds readers Bruce understood 'service' and 'worship' in Scripture are synonymous.

list of examples he has given, everyone cited in this chapter was an outstanding person who was beyond reproach in the eyes of the world. The second objection is that they all had been born and raised within the visible Kirk and belonged to families of noble and faithful predecessors to whom the covenant promise of God had been given. Therefore, it could be argued that as far as their justification was concerned, the Lord had taken into account more than simply their faith; indeed, he had had respect for their personal qualities, their place in society and also their notable families within his Kirk. These doubts might have been raised, for both of them could have appeared to be valid objections.

Certainly, it is true that since the beginning of this eleventh chapter we have not been told of any notorious sinner or wicked persons who had been justified by faith. Nor have we had an example of any profane character born and raised outside of the Kirk, who was a stranger to the commonwealth of Israel, and to whom the promises of God had not been made. It becomes clear, therefore, how these possible objections could be made and doubts raised as to whether there had ever been anyone genuinely justified by faith alone.

Can you see then why the apostle wisely forestalls this objection, and lets us see that faith is able to justify the worst of notorious sinners, born outside of the Kirk of God and begotten of aliens to the covenantal promises? The example he gives is of someone of whom all these things are true, for this person in our text was outside the Kirk and was counted as an abominable sinner before God. Incidentally, the point he is making would apply also to those outside the Kirk and commonwealth of Israel, but who were regarded by the world as having good reputations, though they were not righteous in the eyes of God.

The objections refuted

However, the apostle's point is now fortified: come to God in faith, and whatever your past may have been, you will be justified. Why otherwise does the Spirit of God quote this person and record what she had been, specifically calling her a prostitute? Was this done to upbraid her, or to cast up her past in her face, when she was now a penitent sinner? Certainly not, for the Spirit of the living God would never treat someone maliciously in that manner. We could expect that from human beings who can be spiteful, but never from the Spirit of God. How could it ever be possible for God to do such a thing when we heard in the Psalm that was read to us this morning that he does not impute our sins to us.[6] No, he never upbraids us for sins that he has forgiven, and borne witness in our hearts and consciences that we have been cleansed. Therefore the case given us in verse 31 is not to condemn this woman, but is given to us for the encouragement and instruction of all sinners in every generation right to the end of the age.

Would to God that every one of you was touched with the sense and awareness of your own sins, and that you, along with me, and I along with you, might know and feel in our hearts the consolation of hearing such a doctrine. Otherwise, the hard heart rejects all comfort, and the opinionated person, though sick, refuses all medicine. Therefore unless the Lord works in us even more effectually, we are bound to perish. This woman, infamous and notorious prostitute that she was in the eyes of men, recognised that she was immensely indebted to the Lord, and we also may consider her greatly obliged to the mercy of God far beyond her deserving. Whoever reads about her will come to this same conclusion.

The depth of our indebtedness

Yet now, assuming that you believe her to have been indebted, will you consider along with me the extent to which you also are indebted, for indeed you may be far more indebted to God than you think she was. Yes, she was justified, her sins were all forgiven, and in body and soul she received eternal salvation. But there is this footnote in the register of God's Book, for the record of her shameful past remains inscribed there for ever. Are we then not even more beholden to the Lord than she was? If you examined closely your past life, ruminating on all the wrongs you have done, how would it be with you if the Lord had kept a record of you the way he kept a record of her?

In all conscience, what would we say if a footnote regarding our shameful past was added at the bottom of the page of each of our records? Notwithstanding that the Lord has justified you, he has also covered your shame, not exposing your disgrace for all the world to see, nor has he left a record of it to be kept for ever in his Book. Therefore,

[6] The allusion may be to Psalm 32 and in particular to verse 2: *Blessed is the man, vnto whome the Lord imputeth not inquitie.'* (GenB)

if Rahab was indebted to him, are you and I not even more indebted to him? What is our opinion of shame? We consider public shame to be worst that can be inflicted on us. Yet the Lord not only hides our shame from view, but he bestows eternal salvation upon us.

I ask you again, are we not indebted to God even more than Rahab was? Surely therefore we have to lament the deadness and false security in our hearts. For myself, I know that I am not sufficiently stirred up by the consideration of this inestimable benefit, for I am not moved by enough depth of emotion to be able by this doctrine to arouse gratitude within you, when it is so precious and comforting. If we are not truly grateful, we should confess our ingratitude and earnestly beseech the Lord that his living Spirit may move within us and touch our hearts with the awareness of the benefit offered to us. We should pray that, with our souls, hearts and minds and every part of our beings, we will praise him for saving us, covering our shame and granting to us the hope of a better life after this. Yet, because we ourselves live in an ungrateful world and generation, we too could share the unhappy experience of gross ingratitude.

No sins can ever outweigh the mercy of God

As to the teaching that arises from this example, it can be summed up very simply. In the unregenerate man there is no sin however heinous it might be, nor any multitude of sins however many they may be, that can withhold from him the mercy of God from that moment when he is called to the truth through the preaching of the word. For it would fare ill for us if the devil, the corruption of our fallen natures and the satanic wickedness welling up within us, could outweigh the mercy of God. Therefore, this example of Rahab teaches us that no amount of vile wickedness, however immense it might be, is able to withhold God's mercy from those to whom he extends his mercy. (Yet whom he so wills he hardens.[7]) On the other hand, there are no commendable qualities in the unregenerate man, nor any natural excellences, even

[7] This seems to be the first time in these sermons on Hebrews 11 that Bruce refers to Paul's assertion, 'So then [God] has mercy on whomever he wills, and he hardens whomever he wills' (Romans 9:18). Calvin comments on this verse, 'Do you see then how Paul attributes both to God's decision alone?' *Inst.* III. 22, 11. Calvin explains 'reprobation' more fully in III. 23, 1 & 7. Bruce again states this doctrine of 'reprobation' in the next paragraph. But see Chapter 23, Note 6 above.

though they shine and gleam like stars illuminating the world, but the Lord attributes to them not a whit of value. No, whatever those qualities may be and even though they have the appearance of virtues, in the Lord's eyes they are filthy rags,[8] for until they are cleansed by faith they remain an abhorrence to the living God. Thus the example of this woman is given to us for our comfort and for the consolation of all penitent sinners.

When we consider the definition of the Kirk that is the bride of Christ, we realise that she is nothing more than a company of penitent sinners. So do not fete the supposedly just man, for neither the law nor the evangel was given to just men, as the apostle states in 1 Timothy 1,[9] rather was it given to those in whom are the seeds of all the abominations on the earth. I am not speaking of those abominations that erupt in the deeds of the knaves, traitors and wastrels of this world, but of the seeds that are in your hearts and mine, for I am referring to the restraining hand that keeps you from disgraceful actions such as theirs. That restraint is not inherent in your natures, but emanates from the grace and mercy of God through which he has saved you, but leaves other men to run with loose reins headlong towards eternal perdition.[10] Thus, I say, the entire Kirk is nothing more than a company of penitent sinners, who must repent not merely for one day, or even for a whole year, but for all the days and years of their lives. This far, then, for our general consideration of the woman in our text.

Three points for our instruction

In order that you may fully grasp the substance of our text, I will put before you three points for your consideration. First we must consider the circumstance of both the place where the people of the city perished and also the kind of persons they were; also how it was that this prostitute was saved, and how she was kept safe. Second, what it was that

[8] The allusion will be to Isaiah 64:6, 'filthy cloutes' (GenB), 'filthy rags' (AV, NKJV), 'polluted garment' (ESV).

[9] 1 Timothy 1:9, 11 '... the law is not giuen vnto a righteous man, bot vnto the lawles and disobedient, to the vnholy, and to the prophane, to murtherers of fathers and mothers, to manslayers... according to the glorious Gospel of the blessed God, which is committed vnto me.' (GenB)

[10] Apparently an allusion to the second function of the Commandments to restrain evil men. *Inst.* II.7.10.

saved her, and how it was that salvation was granted to her. Thirdly, we have to note the tokens and fruits by which she herself declared that she would be saved. Indeed, she assured her family, as well as let the spies know, that she believed she would be safe.

First, the nature of the city where Rahab lived

First, then, we have to inquire regarding the place where she remained safe but where the townspeople perished. As you already heard in the last sermon, the place was Jericho, a town situated in the fertile plain of Moab, the most renowned town of all others in that country, apart from one other.[11] It was famous for a precious balm that grew in that area, the like of which was not be to be found anywhere else in the land. Jericho was also the first city that the Lord overcame on this side of Jordan, and being the first it was offered as a first fruits sacrifice in his honour.[12] You heard how this place was more or less totally destroyed, for neither old nor young, male nor female, were spared other than the prostitute and her family. The place was burned to the ground, its walls having collapsed, so that only heaps of rubble remained as a testimony to the depths of its sins.

This destruction came in fulfilment of God's promise that he would delay his divine visitation upon the land until the iniquities of its inhabitants had reached their completion.[13] Therefore the devastation of the remains of Jericho bore witness to the fact that her sins had now attained their fullness. No doubt the Lord used such a terrible execution of his will to strike fear (as indeed it did) in the hearts of neighbouring towns, and also that they might realise the wrath of God had been justly kindled against them. Then perhaps they would be constrained to surrender to the Lord's people, and begin to live in obedience to his divine majesty.[14] So by this example of the fate of Jericho, God first displayed his wrath as in a mirror, but then also issued an awesome warning to onlookers as they beheld the piles of rubble and carcases that had once been a flourishing city.

[11] The more illustrious city than Jericho would undoubtedly have been Jerusalem.

[12] See also Deuteronomy 13:12-16.

[13] Genesis 15:16.

[14] On the surrounding Canaanite towns being witnesses to God's actions see Joshua 7:9.

It was in this same city that Rahab lived, and her nationality is recorded as being Canaanite, as those were who had perished.[15] As to her name, she is described as being a prostitute, that is a woman who gave her body to be abused for financial gain. However, the word 'prostitute' can also occasionally be translated as an 'inn-keeper' who provided food and drink. Some argue that using the word 'prostitute' does an injustice to Rahab and her descendants, for it is repeated several times in the Scriptures.[16] According to the flesh, Jesus Christ was descended from her in that she was married to David's great-great grandfather Salmon, whose son by her was Boaz, and his son by Ruth was Obed, and his son was Jesse who was David's father. Therefore the Jews reject the word 'prostitute' and prefer 'inn-keeper'.[17] However, those familiar with the Hebrew language will know that the proper translation is in fact 'prostitute', with all its shameful associations, and that the alternative word 'inn-keeper' is seldom used. Why then should we choose 'inn-keeper' to honour men, rather than keep to the proper meaning of 'prostitute' in order to honour God (as we shall shortly see)?[18]

Therefore, should we honour men or should we honour God? No, let us use the accepted designation of 'prostitute', for it was not considered so shameful in her culture. Moreover, since Christ was not ashamed that according to the flesh he was descended from her as Matthew indicates, how can anyone consider that calling her a prostitute is an insult? To the contrary, the glory of God shines forth from this designation, for as the apostle has written, where sin abounded, grace abounded even more![19] The more abominable she may appear to us, the more do we see the mercy and grace of God displayed. And so why

[15] The biblical evidence that Rahab was a Canaanite is in the first person plural pronouns in Joshua 2:8-11 where she implies that she is one of the native inhabitants of Jericho; also see also 6:23b where we are told that after their rescue from the doomed city she and her relatives were 'put outside the camp of Israel', yet in 25b she is now described as living 'in Israel to this day'. Perhaps in the weeks between 23b and 25b there were ceremonial purifications in order that she might be no longer regarded as profane, but could be admitted to life among the chosen people of God.

[16] Joshua 2:1; 6:17, 22, 25; Hebrews 11:31; James 2:25.

[17] This was the view of Josephus, v. 1.2.

[18] Calvin makes the same point in discussing the two possible meanings of the Hebrew word *zanah*, harlot.

[19] The allusion is to Romans 5:20.

on account of this woman's reputation should God's honour and the consolation offered to sinners be suppressed?

Therefore, do not think it inappropriate to give her the title of prostitute, for as Christ said, unless you mend your ways and change your thinking, tax collectors and prostitutes, debauched men and bankrupts, will go into the kingdom of God before you, and shall no doubt sit at the right hand of Jesus Christ.[20] How could this be when without repentance it is not possible for anyone to enter heaven? Certainly the kind of people Christ spoke of were obviously in need of repentance and faith. Their own consciences and awareness of their personal shame and public disgrace would tell them that they will never find inner peace until they repent and earnestly seek faith.

On the other hand, many of us live with high opinions of ourselves, and we consider that we are fortunate that we are not like them in that our secret vices are not public the way theirs are. Thus we delude ourselves. Yet those who are disreputable are compelled to hasten to repentance, lest the yetts[21] of heaven should be closed in their faces. You should not be surprised that the Master says in Matthew 21 that tax collectors, prostitutes and fraudulent money changers will enter the kingdom of heaven before you, unless you make greater haste to repent than you are presently doing. Repentance does not grow in your garden, neither is it to be found in your fallen natures; it is the gift of God and comes through hearing his word. Therefore, you who have not yet discovered it, seek it from God. Have you not yet grieved over your sins? Then turn to the Lord and pray for this gift, for unless you repent, it is not possible that any of you can ever be absolved from the sins in which you have grovelled.

Those of you who have already received the gift of repentance, continue to cherish it.[22] Those of you who do not yet have this gift, seek it while you still have the opportunity, for time is precious and you can never tell when the Lord will come and chap on your door, nor how

[20] The allusion is to Matthew 21:31-32.

[21] See above, Chapter 15, Note 17.

[22] Bruce has already said earlier in this sermon, 'Thus, I say, the entire Kirk is nothing more than a company of penitent sinners, who must repent not merely for one day, or even for a whole year, but for all the days and years of their lives.' Now he says that repentance must be jealously guarded and cherished for daily use.

soon it will be before he commands your soul to depart from this world. That is why you must carefully examine your spiritual condition, and earnestly seek repentance. This applies to all of us. We must enquire whether or not we share the same faith of this prostitute. Moreover, in your personal examination of your condition, take care not to be too indulgent with yourselves so that you find nothing amiss in your lives; of all the tests we must apply in this life, to test ourselves too leniently would be the most foolish thing we could do. It can only be an accurate test when faults are found, and when you do find those faults, be assiduous in dealing with them. For if your self-examination is genuine, you will most certainly find many faults. It follows that each exercise in scrutinising your lives will afford you a fresh opportunity to seek mercy and grace, because you will always be reminded of your sinfulness, and so will cease to depend upon your own merits.

I am not insisting that Rahab was still a practising prostitute when the spies visited her, even though previously that had been her manner of living. It is probable that when the spies came she had repented of her prostitution, for although her new faith was confirmed by the visit of the spies, it would appear that true faith had already been born in her before they arrived. A similar case would be the occasion recorded in Mark 14:3 when Jesus lodged in the house of Simon the leper. When the Lord was with him it is clear he no longer had leprosy. He had had it previously, but Jesus had cleansed him. It would appear, then, that the woman is called a prostitute, not because she was still earning her living that way, but for this one single point of instruction: we are being warned that unless we repent the likes of her will enter the kingdom of heaven and be seated at Christ's right hand before us.

Second, how salvation was granted to Rahab

We must now consider the means of this woman's salvation, and how she came by these means. Also, why her neighbours were destroyed. As to Rahab, we are told quite clearly that she was saved from destruction by her faith in God and in Jesus Christ. As to why her neighbours perished, their destruction was the fruit of their unbelief, resulting in disobedience and rebellion. She was saved through faith, they were lost through unbelief. It was faith that brought about this division between them and her, and her and them. Both she and her neighbours were one in nature and sinfulness, but when faith came in, a distinction was made, and for her it was a blessed separation from them. Being left to their fallen natures they died, she being taken up by grace was saved. This same separation and distinction is made today between believers and the world. Unless we too are taken up, called and drawn out of the world by faith, we must perish with the world. As faith severed from Jericho then, so now faith must sever us from this world.

So how did Rahab come by this faith when she was a stranger to the commonwealth of Israel? Although the Law of God had not been given to her or her people, nor had the Word of God been transmitted to them, nevertheless she attained to faith. She herself confesses that it was by hearing the Word of God (as the apostle says in Romans 10:17). It was not that she heard God's Word being preached, for no prophet had been sent to her generation. Rather she states that she heard of the fame of how God's people had been delivered from Egypt and of the wonderful works the Lord had wrought there. So she says to the spies, 'I have heard of your deliverance and the way in which the Egyptians were afflicted by God, and I have also heard of what happened to the two kings of the Amorites beyond the river, Sihon and Og.[23] As soon as we all heard of these things, the whole town was afraid and courage left us. Then I saw that the Lord would deliver this city into your hands, and after that the whole land.'[24]

This was her confession. It was by hearing that she came to faith, not by hearing some messenger that had been sent, but by hearing the accounts of the miracles and works of God. Just as the engendering and begetting of faith in ordinary times belongs primarily to the hearing of the preaching of the word, so in extraordinary times when the word is not being preached, hearing the word through truthful reports is able to engender and work faith in the hearts of those who hear it, and by grace to use it well. That was how this poor woman came to her faith in the Lord God. As for the rest of the citizens of Jericho who were born with hard hearts, as indeed Rahab also had been, what they heard cowered and frightened them to such an extent that there was neither heart nor

[23] Numbers 21:21-27, 31-35.

[24] Joshua 2:8-11.

hand left in king or people. The very hearing of what God had wrought did not have the blessed effect on them that it had on her, for though like them she was terrified, unlike them she believed.

Her faith was quite remarkable, for she had never received the promise, and usually it was God's promise that was the object of faith. Because she was alien to the commonwealth of Israel, the divine promise of mercy did not appertain to her, yet she fled to God to seek his mercy. She was not struck dumb like the other inhabitants of the city. She found a means of escape from the impending judgment simply through the faith in her soul, undoubtedly planted there by the mighty Spirit of Jesus Christ. For it was not possible that such a notorious woman, who was fully aware of her sinfulness, would have been able or even dared to believe, had not the Spirit of God come down and relieved her conscience, and then calmed her fears with his peace that passes all understanding, enabling her to trust his mercy. As she was occupied in hearing outwardly of the Lord's works, he was meanwhile occupied inwardly in creating faith in her heart, a faith that enabled her to depend wholly upon him, in spite of her being an idolatrous Canaanite and not a member of God's chosen people.

By contrast, unbelief caused her fellow-citizens to depend upon their own resources such as their high walls and stout portals, in other words, to entrust themselves to themselves. While faith preserved Rahab by enabling her to depend upon God, false confidence deceived the rest of the inhabitants and so they perished. It is far better to stand firm upon solid ground, to make your anchor secure, and to be certain of a way of escape in the hour of crisis,[25] but for those who depend upon themselves there never is a reliable way of escape. Again, those who do not depend upon themselves but on the mercy of God in Christ Jesus, can be certain that there is a stronghold for them in times of trouble, and they will find mercy meeting their need in greater abundance than they ever expected.

Lessons for us

So what is there here for us to learn? There is just one further thing to note before I leave this second point. It is that in faith there is both a strong power and an amazing virtue in that by faith the yetts of heaven

[25] Bruce occasionally mixes his metaphors without a blush!

are thrown open to the greatest sinners in the world, however dire their condition or sins might be. For example, the tax collector who has faith cannot be kept out. Have you not read the parable in Luke 15 of the debauched, destitute son; entrance to heaven was not withheld from him for he came in faith. Mary Magdalene of whom we read in Luke 7:36-39, she by reason of her faith was not debarred. The jailor in Acts 16 who had his sword in his hand ready to slay himself, on account of his faith was not debarred either. Therefore faith pays no heed to a person's status or to any qualities he may have or lack, but wherever there is genuine faith the door into the kingdom of heaven is open. Faith also bestows upon you the power to become a child of God. When others around you are children of the devil, faith grants to you the privilege of sonship. And if you are a child of God, then you must be an heir of God, and consequently a fellow-heir with Jesus Christ. Thus far, then, with my second point.

Thirdly, the tokens and fruits of her salvation

The third and final point was the four tokens and fruits by which she declared herself to be saved. Although these are not all set down in our text, we can read about them in Joshua 2, where there is one very notable token that testifies to her faith which the apostle does record for us. First, she received the men whom Joshua had sent to spy out the city along with the surrounding country and its people, and she treated them honourably, peaceably and lovingly, even though she realised they were enemies of her king and all his citizens. Her attitude towards them arose from her further confidence, in that her faith caused her to hazard her life and risk her king's wrath as well as the anger of the entire region. Her faith is also seen in her reaction when word got out that she had received the spies, even though they deliberately went to her dwelling because it was in an disreputable area of the city where brothels were to be found. The reason why the spies chose to lodge there was the obscure location of her house,[26] not at all for the same reasons why lustful men visited her.

The second evidence of her faith arises from the king's actions when he heard about the spies, and sent some of his men to find them so he could interrogate them. The searchers reached her dwelling before she had been able to send the spies on their way, but she would not betray

[26] Calvin also makes this point. *Comm. in loc.*

them or hand them over to the king's men. She had hidden the spies on the roof and covered them with stalks of flax. When the searchers asked her about them she lied cunningly, admitting they had called on her, but saying they had already left. She said that if they pursued them, they should be able to make up on them before they reached the ford at the River Jordan. The king's men promptly set off in pursuit of the spies. Clearly she acted in faith, for had the spies been discovered in her house she would have lost her life and all her possessions.

There is a third evidence of her faith, for we read that in her own words she confessed to the spies that she was quite certain that the God of the Hebrews would deliver Jericho into the hands of his people, on account of the sins of the city and its people. Since she knew that it was their sins that would be their downfall, no doubt she herself was full of remorse for her own sins. She then went even further, for she acknowledged that there was no other god in heaven or earth like unto their God in his power and majesty. 'We have heard,' she said, 'of the singular deeds and wonderful miracles that your God did when he brought you out of the land of Egypt, and what he did to our neighbouring two kings on the other side of the Jordan. Therefore it would be sheer folly for our people to put their trust in strong gates and high walls, and I can see that our king has already been delivered into your hands.'

Here, surely, is evidence of a great faith, and no doubt if the king of Jericho with his council and nobles had resolved as wisely as she did, their city and lives would have been preserved. But by means of the faith that they lacked, this woman made the right choice, and while her faith was not shared by the king and his people, she saved herself and her family. How often I have heard that there cannot be a wise resolution without faith, for this woman's intelligence, on account of her faith, surpassed the intelligence of all the people of Jericho, including the king himself.

There is a fourth aspect of her faith that bears witness to her conviction that God was at work. She says to the spies that she needed them to make a promise to her: *Now therefore, I pray you, sweare vnto me by the Lord, that as I haue shewed you mercie, ye wil also shewe mercie vnto my fathers hous.*[27] She goes on to speak of the victory as if it was already won, and, not content with a verbal assurance, so she enters into a firm

[27] Joshua 2:12 (GenB).

indenture with the spies, demanding they make an oath, not swearing by some pagan god, but by the great Lord God of Israel.

In short, what has been wrought in this woman is quite wonderful, for everything about her speaks of a strong faith, notwithstanding that no promise of God had been given to her, for the covenant of mercy had not yet been given to the Gentiles, and membership of the Kirk at that time was restricted to a relatively small company of people. Was it not amazing that when she had not received the divine promise, she still believed boldly and hoped with such assurance to receive mercy on the day of visitation? As I have already said, this was all done by the mighty work and operation of the Holy Spirit.

The Lord did not leave her faith unrewarded, for when the city's walls were brought down and Jericho was destroyed, he put it into Joshua's mind to save both her and her family. So God rewarded her for the honour she showed towards him, saving her and all her kindred, her father, mother, brothers and sisters. He accepted her into the bosom of the Kirk, and he counted her as an Israelite. He did her the further honour of making her one of the forebears of his own Son, one of those of whom Jesus Christ was born according to the flesh. This was all bestowed on the woman of little means because she had such a strong faith in God's mercy and power.

Lessons from the tokens of her salvation

Now is there anything from all of this that we should note? Yes, but first we have to learn what our duty is when we hear of God's mighty works being wrought in other places, as well as when we see them here before our own eyes. We must learn from this poor Canaanite woman that we must not be complacent when we witness what God is doing, either in his dealing with ourselves or with our neighbours. Rather must we profit from them, and as she ceased to depend upon herself and cast herself upon the Lord, so let us do the same.

Certainly, as we take heed to ourselves regarding this, and learn to look carefully at what God is doing in our land and in our neighbouring country, we will realise that we are not able to obtain the grace that was granted to Rahab. For even though it appears on the surface that things here are calm (some even flatter themselves on the state of our nation), nevertheless all is far from well. Widespread among us is the inner corruption of men's hearts manifesting itself as a lack of integrity at every level of society, to say nothing of the complaints and outcries of the poor against the abuse of justice. Many have complete freedom to do wrong, and even commit murder with impunity. All this convinces me, and should also convince you, that a heavy cloud of wrath hangs over our land, so that we can expect severe judgment to be poured out soon upon this city.

Furthermore, should the fires of persecution in France[28] that are likely to consume the heart of that nation be something that we merely glance at complacently? And should the same fires burning in Flanders[29] also be an idle spectacle to us? Could we look indifferently upon these trials, even contemptuously disregarding them, assuming meanwhile that we will always have the evangel without needing to shed our blood as they are doing? Will we always have a glorious and peaceable evangel, while those who deserve peace far more than us never enjoy it? No, it is certain that heavy judgment will come upon our land, so we must observe the daily events that are tokens of it. Let us learn from this woman who so greatly benefited by hearing of what God was doing, and let us likewise benefit from observing his hand at work within our nation.

Next, learn how to eschew the judgment of God in the same way as Rahab eschewed his judgment through profiting by what she heard. The only way for us to escape the divine visitation is through faith in Jesus Christ, for all who have that faith will be kept secure. Indeed, God himself shall perish (if that were possible!) before those shall perish who trust in him and are resolved to be true to him. It is only by faith in Jesus Christ that we can escape in the hour of calamity. This nectar of

[28] Probably a reference to the French Wars of Religion, a prolonged period of war and popular unrest between Roman Catholics and Huguenots (Calvinist Protestants) in the Kingdom of France between 1562 and 1598. It is estimated that three million people perished in this period from violence, famine, or disease. However, see Ch.28, Note 2 below.

[29] During the time Bruce was preaching these sermons, the Duke of Parma, appointed governor of Flanders by Philip II of Spain, was capturing town after town, causing a flood of Protestant refugees which resulted in the population of many towns being halved. When Ghent, Bruges, Brussels and Antwerp fell the flow of refugees became a flood, while the population of northern cities such as Amsterdam, Haarlem and Leiden doubled. The persecution of the Calvinists continued until 1648 and the Treaty of Munster.

faith[30] is very precious, for even if a man possesses the whole world, he cannot find acceptance before God other than through faith. Therefore, now while you still have time, seek faith!

No one can find faith through making themselves holy or good; it is faith that bestows holiness upon us, enabling us to become the kind of people we cannot be by our own efforts. Therefore we should all earnestly seek this jewel of faith without which there can be no change in the condition of souls since we were formed in our mothers' wombs.[31] Once you have received the gift of faith, Jude tells us that it will never be taken from you.[32] What is given is constantly being renewed, so even though for a time our faith is crushed and defiled by sin, the Lord will renew and restore it in his own time.[33] Therefore, for Christ's sake continue to seek this jewel of faith that transforms the soul, and imparts the wisdom that knows how to escape the awesome judgment in the day of calamity.

The account of the fall is Jericho is an allegory

My concluding point is that all these things are figures of events that were still to come.[34] The apostle says in 1 Corinthians 10:1-6 that everything that happened to the Fathers were figures of what we in truth and deed must experience here and now. Although I myself take no delight in allegories, for they can be difficult and tricky to deal with, where the case for them is clear in God's Book there is no doubt that that we can profit and learn from them.

Tucked away in this historical account are allegories which have lessons for us, which I shall shortly explain to you. The main one is

[30] Bruce's phrase is 'liquor of faith'. DSL defines 'liquor' as 'fluid or liquid in general'; the context suggests that Bruce's metaphor has the meaning of faith being an 'elixir' or 'life-giving drink', hence my translation 'nectar of faith'.

[31] Psalm 51:5; Romans 5:12.

[32] Jude 1: '... to them which are called and sanctified of God the Father, and reserued to Jesus Christ.' (GenB) See verse 24.

[33] Isaiah 42:3.

[34] For the first time in these sermons on Hebrews 11, Bruce is about to allegorize in a manner I have never found in Calvin. In Bruce's sermons on Isaiah 38, I found no comparable allegorizing. (Isa.38) Bruce himself is aware of the controversial nature of this kind of interpretation of Scripture. He says allegories are 'difficult and tricky'—his word is 'kittill' meaning 'sensitive, touchy, difficult to deal with' (DSL).

Rahab and her family who represent for us the Kirk of God. As she and her relatives were saved by faith, so the Kirk is comprised of both Jews and Gentiles who have faith. Jericho foreshadows the world, and her king foreshadows the prince of this world, that is the devil. The king's execution represents, in God's appointed time, the devil being thrown into that bottomless pit in which he will perish for ever.[35]

Further, Rahab and her family live in Jericho in the same way as the Kirk dwells in the midst of the wicked. The spies calling on her represent for us the messengers of Jesus Christ. These messengers are instruments of her salvation, but they put the city on trial; although Christ's messengers are the instruments of the Kirk's salvation, they are also instruments of the destruction of the world. Rahab and her family are in the same deadly danger as they were in the former state of their futile lives; the Kirk and her messengers also live surrounded by constant hazards. Rahab and the spies are preserved by contemptible and weak means; the Lord also preserves his Kirk by weak means so that the glory of their salvation may redound to him alone. Rahab received the promise of the spies sent by Joshua; the Kirk receives the promised mercy sent from God the Father of Jesus Christ. Rahab marks her house with a red cord so that it will be recognised; Jesus Christ has stamped his own mark on his Kirk to indicate that she is his own, for he has joined his sacraments to his word so that his people may be distinguished from the rest of the world. No one was safe in Jericho except those in Rahab's house; likewise none are safe other than those who are the Kirk of God, for there is salvation in none other than in Jesus Christ, as we are told in Acts 4:12. Those who are outside the Kirk seek their salvation in other means than in Christ, though there are some who come to him, but continue to rely on other means as well as on him, and so are not wholly trusting him; only those who depend upon him alone will be saved. Only those who cast all their hopes and faith upon Christ are genuine members of his Kirk.

There is just one other point I must make, and then I finish. Because no one can be safe unless he is in Christ, and no one can be in Christ

[35] Revelation 20:1-3, 7-10. Bruce is not quite accurate here, as 'the ancient serpent who is the devil' is confined to the bottomless pit for a thousand years, and then after an indeterminate period of limited freedom, is cast for ever into the lake of fire and sulphur.

unless he has faith, there is no religion other than through faith, nor is there any right worship of God apart from faith. Therefore no one can be grafted into Christ Jesus other than through faith. All of you should examine yourselves as to whether or not you stand in the faith of Jesus Christ, and those who are willing to do this will find in yourselves many faults along with errors and infidelity. Nor should any of you assume that this self-examination should take place for just one day, or even for one year; no, it must continue for all the days and years of your lives. Even though you hammer down the head of some vicious sin in which you once indulged, I deny that you will ever kill it outright. I grant that you may abstain from it for a time and be deeply penitent over it, but the root and stump of it will remain in your heart, and then some time in the future it will sprout and bud again.

Therefore, let none of you ever think you have secured yourself against your besetting sin, assuming that the battle has been won for the rest of your lives. That cannot be, for though that root and stump may be dormant in your heart, sooner or later it will send forth shoots and rise up to confront you, and it will overcome you unless you stand firm against it. So we all have a constant struggle against the harassments of evil to which we were formerly inclined. That is why each of us must carefully try ourselves and fight, yes fight, right to the end of our days. We must crave strength from God and depend constantly upon his mercy, for all who do that will be kept secure. So pray for eyes that will search within yourselves, and beseech the Lord that by his mercy you will be able to stand firm in the faith, that you may live and die in that faith. And that can only be through the righteous merits of Christ, to whom with the Father and the Holy Ghost be all honour, praise and glory for now and evermore. Amen.

Chapter Twenty-Five

Hebrew Chapter 11 verse 32

---

32 And quhat sall I say more? For the tyme wold be schort for me to tell of Gedione, Barac and Sampsone, and of Jephte, also of Dauid and Samuell, and of the propheiteis.

Well-beloved brethren in Jesus Christ, you have already heard me saying that Rahab was justified by faith, certainly not by her prostitution, that most abominable and evil of all occupations. In spite of her past harlotry, God was able to declare her justified. You also heard that faith, this gift of God, cannot achieve anything through someone's own natural goodness or sanctity, however highly esteemed that person might be by the society in which he lives, for in God's sight no one is counted as holy, upright or just until he has faith. Thus, it is only faith in Jesus Christ that enables anyone to be reckoned as holy, thereby initiating a life of righteousness that will never be perfected as long as we are in this world. For prior to faith there is no holiness or righteousness in our carnal natures.

You also heard how the special consequences and effects of her faith were evidenced by the manner in which she received the spies whom Joshua had sent. The apostle records that she received them peaceably, that is, she not only welcomed them but also gave them hospitality and devised the means of preserving their lives. He also tells us that this excellent work, done for the living God, was the most special mark of her faith. Regarding the rest of what I said about Rahab I must leave to your memories, and return to two other points that I did not have time to deal with.

Was Rahab right to betray her own people?

The first is the question as to whether this woman did right in not seeking to help her own people, but instead protecting the spies who had come to check out the weaknesses of her town. Assuming that she did well in receiving the spies, the second question is whether she was right to support them by telling lies. We need to examine both these points before we go on to consider the verse that I have just read to you.

As to the first point, if we judge her by the attitude of the king of that town and his laws, and if we had questioned her neighbours, we would have found they all believed that she did not do the right thing. For why should she betray her king and country in order to preserve the lives of men who were obviously their enemies? In betraying her people, surely she was being a traitor to them all. Nevertheless, what she did was regarded as a special act of faith that was to be commended as a deed justifying her before God.

Therefore, we must conclude that faith cannot be assessed by measuring it against the laws of men, but rather by the will, laws and counsels of God. We must humbly contrast human laws with the divine laws, and only reverence the laws of men in so far as they reflect the image of God and are in agreement with his will. Rahab recognised what the will of God was, as you heard last Sunday[1] in her confession. She knew very well that the iniquity of her people had reached its zenith, and therefore that the Lord was about to strike, for her king was obdurate and her people could not be reformed.

We cannot deny that had she been able by her labours to have reclaimed both her king and his people by persuading them to yield to God and pledge obedience to him, then certainly she would have been wrong to betray them. But being convinced (as she acknowledged in her confession) that her people's hearts were hardened against God, and that their sin had reached its fullness, she made provision both for herself and many of her family whose lives could be saved by the grace of God. For faith never sides with wicked and obstinate men who are destitute of any reverence for God, but invariably prefers to join with those who do fear and reverence him.

[1] Bruce has 'the last day'.

To express this in terms we use today, faith invariably prefers those of our own religion who share our faith in their worship of God, rather than the practices of papists, even if they are near blood-relatives to us. That is not to say we do not cease to try to win them over, yet when they remain intransigent, we cannot ever prefer our own flesh and blood to those with whom we are united in the Spirit. Therefore there is a lesson here for you who are in positions of authority. You should not side with stubborn papists, however closely they may be related to you, rather you should support those to whom you are bound by the Spirit of God. In this way you will be saved, whereas if you take the part of others who do not share your religion, you too will perish along with them. Thus we see that Rahab acted rightly, because what may appear to be treasonous before a human tribunal, may well be highly commended before God's tribunal.

Were Rahab's lies permissible?

The second question was whether she was right to support the spies by her lies. She spoke falsely when she told the searchers that they were no longer with her but had left to return to the river crossing, and if they hurried after them, said she, they would catch up with them before they reached the ford. I cannot hold that such falsehood was right, even though some may think it was a permissible lie because no one was hurt by it. No, she did not speak the truth and, because God is always true, the lies she told were not compatible with his divine nature. So in this Rahab failed and what she said betrayed the weakness of her sinfulness.

It is true that the Lord overlooked it and even rewarded her preservation of the spies by including her in the genealogy of his own incarnate Son, Jesus Christ. But that reward was not for the falsehoods spoken in the weakness of her flesh, but for her faithful service in preserving his servants and believing that there was sufficient mercy in the Lord to save her, even though she had been a profane prostitute. In short, her lies were wrong and reflected the weakness of all our fallen natures, which even the best of God's servants share with her right to the end of their lives.

The faith of three judges[2]

I now proceed to consider with you the text I read this morning, for here in verse 32 the apostle concludes the first section of the chapter and sums up what he has been saying concerning this subject of justification by referring to many examples from the Fathers. Now he sets down several names of those whom he is about to describe; some were judges, some were kings and some were prophets—these will be the remaining ones he will choose to consider. Of course, there are many others who could have been mentioned, but he is forced to leave them and he tells us why. Were he to describe them all with every detail as to how they were justified by faith, he would run out of time and space, though never out of matter! But what he has said so far of each of these Fathers would be true of all the rest, and it will remain true until the end of time, for out of every single person who is justified, not one of them will gain for himself any part of the portion of God's glory—their justification will always be by faith alone.

The scandal of unjust judges

Regarding judges, kings and priests, he points out that all may have a place in heaven, but only on the condition that they are men of faith. He implies that if a judge is corrupt and perverts judgment, either by accepting a bribe or being deferential to men of importance, he cannot be a faithful man. Judges, he says, are deputizing for God, for judgment is the Lord's, therefore if they hope to have a place in heaven they must judge righteously. Therefore they must be faithful to the law, and as their knowledge of the law increases, so the righteousness of their judgments must also increase.

However, if any judge allows himself to be deflected from the merits of a case, and gives more weight to the standing or status of a person, he is turning judgment on its head. Unless such a judge is granted the grace of repentance and turns away from such unfaithfulness, be sure he will never be included in the company of faithful men nor be given entrance to the kingdom of heaven. Today there is much complaining and a great outcry against the corruption of certain judges. I know that one party in a case will often complain, therefore I could not possibly comment on whether or not an injustice has been done.

[2] He will only deal with Gideon, Barak and Samson in this sermon.

Nevertheless, you who are judges must pay heed to this, and I am bound to warn you that if you have been guilty of giving an unjust verdict, whether by showing deference to some person of importance or else through your acceptance a bribe, you are answerable to God for your corrupt judgment, and without question he will avenge it. It cannot be doubted that, just as certainly as you now hear me with your own ears, such judges will be made spectacles of the Lord's everlasting judgments, for by ignoring the right procedures they have abused the very name and character of God. Indeed, the Lord's honour always stands upon the integrity of judgment, but by corruption his name is besmirched.

This is the fountain that ought to purge the rest of the judiciary throughout our country, for if there is contamination in the fountain, how could we expect to find purity among other judges? If each in his own station will not take heed to this and obey, then no doubt the purging of the judiciary will come from the Lord of heaven, until each can say in his own conscience, 'I have kept myself pure and I am innocent in this matter'. Let each of you judges who are present today be able to have this testimony, for then you will witness the Lord purging the rest. So each of you be faithful in both your living and your office, for there are places reserved in the kingdom of heaven for faithful officers of the law.

The message of the Book of Judges

The apostle sets before us the names of four judges taken from the Bible book of that name, Judges. They are Gideon, Barak, Samson and Jephthah. We find the record of each as follows: Barak in chapters 4 and 5, Gideon in chapters 6, 7 and 8, Jephthah in chapters 11 and 12, and finally Samson in chapters 14, 15 and 16. In the history of these four judges we have the image, as it were, of the entire book of Judges. As we read the whole book and the record of other judges in it, the Spirit of God gives us understanding and enables us to see that this entire book contains general notes and observations which I find very relevant for the Kirk and the people of God today, so that we may learn to apply these lessons for our benefit and comfort.

The first general point: God's people's infidelities

First, I perceive that throughout this whole book the people of God have constantly conducted themselves in a manner true to their fallen natures, always continuing in the same way without any real change in their behaviour. Similarly, I perceive that God likewise has invariably conducted himself in a manner true to his divine nature, in that his goodness towards his people has never changed. Read the book for yourselves and you will discover that his people's conduct consists in defection after defection, fall after fall, and always the final fall and defection have been the worst. Indeed, the entire book is the record of seven major defections from God. As often as the nation was set up standing on firm ground, they could never maintain their stance, but were so wobbly that they constantly fell back into the same filthy quagmire.

As for God, I see that as often as his people fell he raised them up and again established them firmly on their feet, so to speak, delivering them out of their afflictions and the dangers into which they had cast themselves. Just as there was no end to their falls and calamities, leaving them unable to maintain their stance as a nation, so on God's part there were never so many offences and disasters that they prevented his kindly nature from receiving them back. Nor could their defections hold back his compassion from his miserable and declining people.

The depth of the Lord's compassion and mercy was so great that should a man of the world try to understand what could move God to act in such a way, according to his natural assessment he would be at a loss to comprehend it. Would not any normal person soon tire of constantly lifting up people who never stopped falling over? Whatever could you see in such people that would ever be worthy of such a majestic God? What could move him to persist in his mercy so long, continuing to restore those who were determined to keep on rebelling against him? There is nothing under the heavens, either in the air or on the earth, that could move him to such constant compassion, other than his own purpose and resolve.

We have that resolution concerning his chosen people, Jacob (or Israel), set down in many places in the Scriptures, notably in Isaiah 48:4. Mark that verse for there we see what it is that at times still moves God to such pity and compassion towards us. In verse 4 the Lord was speaking to people who were then his only Kirk, for his Kirk at that time was restricted to the family of Abraham. In effect he is saying, 'I foresaw and foreknew from before the beginning of time that you who are now my chosen people would have obdurate hearts, necks with sinews of iron and foreheads of brass.' And in verse 5 he says that from of old and even before it happened, he knew that they would sin and transgress grievously against himself.

Notwithstanding that he knew all this would be their habitual behaviour, he resolved to save them and made this his avowed purpose and promise. Thus he says, 'I will keep this promise and for my name's sake and my glory I will restrain my wrath, withholding it lest I should destroy you.' What then do you think it is that motivates the Lord? It would be a devilish thought to assume it is something desirable in you, for there is nothing whatsoever in flesh and blood to move him. No, there was nothing in his Kirk, in Jacob or in Israel, that could ever move the Lord to pity, for in his people there was only fall after fall and defection after defection.

We see, then, that the Lord was moved only by his gracious resolve and purpose to save such as he would choose out of the decadent, perishing race of Adam. That was why he did not reject Israel on account of her iniquities, or turn away from her because of her transgressions. That false prophet Balaam (even though he was a renegade), uttered a remarkable prophecy concerning Christ and his Kirk. We read of it in Numbers 23:23 where we find God inspiring him to say that there was no enchantment in Jacob, nor transgression in Israel.[3] It is as if the Lord was saying that there was no lack of defection in Israel, for she was the same as Moab who abounded in iniquities, yet see what God has wrought—for although in Israel there were just as heinous sins as in the rest of humanity, the Lord had resolved to pass over them in pardon and mercy. Thus we see it is only through his free forgiveness that sinners are saved.

Blessed, then, are those who are included in the company of Jacob, and belong to his people Israel, for then there can be no wickedness or multitude of sins that can exclude you from his mercy. Nevertheless, if

[3] Numbers 23:23, 'For there is no sorcerie in Iaakob, nor soothsaying in Israel: according this time it shal be said of Iaakob and Israel, What hathe God wroght?' (GenB).

you are not included in Jacob (I mean included in the company of the Lord's people), even if you are endowed with all the finest qualities in human nature, and deserve the greatest of praise and adulation from men, your natural graces can never purchase for you mercy from the hand of God. Therefore, draw near and enter into the body of the Kirk, and become a member of the company of those who are justified by the blood of Jesus Christ. The only society on earth that relies wholly upon Christ is the Kirk, therefore come and become part of those whose salvation and eternal safety is in him. This my first general point regarding the Book of Judges.

Second general point: God grants repentant hearts to those who seek him

The second general point that I mark is this. I perceive that the Lord has a certain way of working in that he periodically raises up his people, stands them upon their feet, as it were, having delivered them from the perils and dangers into which they had cast themselves. Read the chapters in Judges and you will see this pattern repeated regularly. He does not deliver them as long as they are 'asleep', for before he can deliver them he first must arouse them out of their spiritual stupor and false sense of security. So how does he awaken them? He must grant them the grace of repentance with the sense and feeling of their rebellion, and hearts to seek grace and help from his hands.

Only through repentance do we have access to the countenance of God and entrance into the kingdom of heaven. That is why John the Baptist cried, 'Repent, repent, for the kingdom of God is at hand!'[4] It was as if he was saying that the only entrance into the kingdom of heaven was through repentance. Have you become repentant? Are you truly heart-sorry for your sins? Then you can be sure of his deliverance, for salvation will never be withheld from a truly penitent sinner.

On the other hand, persistence in sin will incur the wrath of God, for only repentance can turn away his anger from both a man and a nation. That is why John the Baptist says to the Sadducees and Pharisees in Matthew 3:7, 'O generation of vipers, who has taught you to flee from the wrath to come?' For there is no way to escape God's wrath except by repenting unfeignedly and cleaving to him. This the pattern of God's dealings with his people as recorded in the Book of Judges:

[4] Matthew 3:2=Mark 1:4=Luke 3:3.

he awakens his people from whence they have fallen before delivering them.

Repentance

As to repentance, it is a gift of God, for it is not born in our breasts, nor does it grow in our stomachs, neither can we have it hidden up our sleeves to shake it out whenever we choose. Rather it comes from heaven, for it is wrought by the power and virtue of the blood of Jesus Christ in men's souls and consciences. It is that blood-bought virtue that must flow into us to cleanse the stains on a guilty conscience, and to pluck out the scorpion's stings that cause such bitter remorse. Only then is peace and quietness imparted to our hearts. By repentance we are delivered from bondage, says the apostle in 2 Timothy 2:25-26: 'Repentance leads to knowledge of the truth, that we may escape from the snare of the devil.' Without repentance no man is safe either now or at his departing.

Now there is a great need of repentance in us, yea, even in the best of us. O that God would move within each of us by his Holy Spirit, for we all need to repent over something. In his mercy may he begin his work within our hearts. It is entirely our own fault that has caused the Lord to withdraw his Spirit from us, for we have continually been stubborn and rebellious. Regarding the reason for repentance among us, there was never seen a greater need than there is in our country today. Alas, it is appalling to see the fires that are being kindled among us.

Even though our country may appear to be in a state of calm tranquillity, yet when we look closer it is apparent that every man has his hand on his sword, ready to plunge it into the breast of his neighbour. The facts bear witness that the Word of God has not been implanted deeply among us, nor has his Spirit worked effectually in our people's hearts, for all have gone astray. Because his Word has brought forth little or no fruit among us, we are either barren or else the paltry fruit in the best of us is fragile, imperfect and marred by our corruption. All of us ought to pray, 'Lord, except you show us mercy and grant us repentance for our sins, there can be no place for us in your kingdom.' I pray that the Lord will grant grace and mercy to everyone here today, that we all may seek his gift of repentance for the sake of Jesus Christ. I beseech him also that, like the necessity for those Sadducees and Pharisees, we may learn to flee not only from the present impending wrath, but also from the wrath to come.[5]

The third general point: first affliction, then conviction, then consolation

The third general point that I mark is this. I perceive that the Lord, in awakening his stubborn people, first brings them to conviction of their sin with a feeling of remorse. It is then that they cry to him for mercy and grace, whereupon he comforts them by bringing his word to them. We find throughout the whole book that he produces this remorse through their afflictions. It is the Lord himself who lays this rod of affliction across their backs, until at length they say in their consciences, 'We have turned aside from God, we have forsaken his religion and our worship of him, and because of our neglect he has brought this affliction upon us'.

So God hands them over to some enemy or other, who ploughs furrows across the back of his Kirk, until at length he has brought them to the realisation of their backsliding from him over seven, ten or even sometimes twenty years. He never lets them rest until by means of affliction and troubles he has wrought in their hearts a deep sense of their miserable state. So by severe chastening he brings them to conviction of their sin, and then by his word he comforts them. So what good does the word do them before they experienced the affliction? None whatsoever! It is as good as dead, for it works nothing in the hearts of those who have not been brought low by some cross or other. Yet, whoever has his heart cast down and has been humbled by some daily cross he must bear, now has his eyes opened and his heart softened to hear the Word of God. So we see then the manner of God's working: first affliction, then conviction and finally the consolation of his word.

May the Lord touch all your hearts in time, that this nature the Lord has given to us should no longer be abused as it has been in the past, but that being effectually touched by him we may yet, while there is still time, drink in comfort from his word. For as long as there is no awareness of our miserable state or our need of his mercy, the word is but a dead letter without any power to awaken our hearts. Therefore crave that the Lord would concur through the inward ministry of his Spirit, so that you may feel your need of his word's consolation, and

[5] Matthew 3:7-10.

may discover what a comforting jewel it can be to you through its offer of his mercy and grace. This far, then, for the three general points that I have perceived in reading through the whole Book of the Judges.

Gideon

As I now come to the particulars, I will follow the order as the apostle has written it down. Although Barak comes first in Judges, Gideon is the first to be named in our text, so by God's grace we shall begin by considering him. All four of these judges have in common both their faith and their weaknesses. Therefore as with the other three, Gideon gives clear evidence of his faith in certain things, but also of his weakness in other things.

The evidence for Gideon's faith

He first showed his faith in his obedience to the Lord's call to him through the ministry of his holy angel. Even though he initially raised difficulties, yet he was not obstinate but did end up obeying the command the Lord had given him. His obedience was clearly a fruit or an effect springing up from the root of his faith.

The second way in which Gideon's faith was evidenced was that as soon as the Lord called him he did the deed that he knew would be pleasing to the Lord, for he immediately destroyed the altar to Baal and the Asherah[6] beside it. He was constrained to do this during the night because he knew that he would endanger himself and stir up the anger of the local people who no doubt would try to stop him. Notwithstanding this, he chose rather to obey God rather than to please men, for he trusted God so to bless his actions that the civil peace would not be disturbed for too long. Even though at first Gideon's neighbours were angry with him and his father, the Lord did preserve the peace, for he has the hearts of all men in his hands. Therefore, after these pagan abominations had been destroyed, good relationships between Gideon and his neighbours were restored.

There are two points to note here. First, the wrath of God and the fires of his judgment will always come upon that country where idolatry is not punished but is fostered. Second, even if God's punishment

[6] In Judges 6:28, Geneva Bible calls the Asherah 'a groue' (grove), but Bruce calls it 'a bus' (bush).

at first seems to disturb the civil peace (as it often appears to do when any offender is judged), yet harmony will soon be restored. Therefore, if you have his warrant in your conscience that some action is pleasing to God and agreeable to his will, you may be sure that God will bless your deed by maintaining peace, and settling men's hearts according to your expectations.

Therefore let no one tolerate idolaters under the pretence of keeping the peace, especially those who have been excommunicated, for that is the quickest way to become an enemy of God, and then you will drink from the same cup of his wrath as the unrighteous must drink. Although we have only a few who have been excommunicated, they are well protected and their supposed incarceration[7] is no incarceration at all, neither is their punishment genuine punishment but simply an opportunity to re-offend, so their sentence turns out to be a farce.

The point is this: to appease God's displeasure and to demonstrate that you have genuinely experienced his mercy and are ready to please him by doing what lies within your jurisdiction, ensure that either men obey God or else are banished from our land to some place where they may freely practice their idolatry. Clearly it is most shameful in this our reformed country to hear of men who refuse to practise our lawful religion in these times of peace. Such behaviour should not be permitted to continue, for it is a slur on our king's counsellors who govern our country.[8]

Therefore I admonish you, my lord, as one of the king's special counsellors,[9] that you put your hand to this to ensure that those to whom

[7] Bruce's word is 'ward' which can either mean 'a place of confinement' or 'a judicial sentence' (DSL ward[1], ward[2]); the context would suggest that 'a judicial sentence' is the meaning, as in the next paragraph Bruce speaks of counsellors who fraternize with them in hawking and hunting; also 'their supposed incarceration is not incarceration at all.'

[8] It is significant that Bruce advocates banishment of Catholics to a land where they could 'freely practise their idolatry', rather than the horrific executions practiced by Mary I and her sister Elizabeth I. For example, on November 22 in 1592, about the time Bruce was preaching these sermons, for the crime of being a Catholic, priest William Harrington was hanged until not quite dead, then disemboweled while still alive, then beheaded. He was only one Catholic martyr of many others. Mary I is reckoned to have hanged or beheaded about 300 Protestant martyrs.

[9] Bruce appears to be directing his remarks to one particular aristocrat in the

I am referring will either conform to this country's religion, or else be banished from our land. It is not that I hate these men as persons, for I would rather win them over. But as long as they remain obdurate, all of us should abhor what they stand for. Yet how can nobles and other great men abhor these men's idolatrous practices when they go hawking and hunting with them, as well as eating and drinking, as if they had not been proclaimed outlaws by the horn of Jesus Christ,[10] and as if there was no Christ in the heavens to be avenged on the contempt shown to him. Therefore, my lord, if you would have Christ's favour and his peace imparted to you in your last hour here on earth, attend to this matter in a lawful manner. For I assure you that the Lord himself will be avenged for this scurrilous contempt upon his person.

The second effect of his faith, therefore, was evidenced in the casting down of the altar and the idol, for this was most commendable. That is why later on the Lord prospered him in his battle against the nation's enemies, when with only three hundred men he routed an innumerable army. So whoever will be zealous in God's work will be honoured by him, and whoever honours God, as God is God, he will be honoured before men. For the Lord has all men's hearts in his hands. The means by which we offend him will be the means by which he will offend us.[11]

Gideon's feeling of inadequacy was evidence of his weakness

Gideon indeed showed his faith in casting down the altar and its idol, but he also showed his weakness. For when we see how long it took him to continue with his calling, we also see his weakness as he raised many obstacles to be overcome before he could be persuaded to obey God fully. His problems did not arise from unbelief, for when he asked for a sign he would never have followed the Lord's instructions if he had not believed what he told him to do. All the miracles in this world can never engender faith, and without faith no one obeys the Lord.

congregation, possibly sitting in a prominent seat in one of the galleries. I am grateful to Stephen Preston, Heritage & Culture Coordinator of St Giles Cathedral, for the following information: 'Because St Giles' was subdivided rather "hastily" into four parish churches in 1562-3 (Howard 1995, 177), and galleries had to be inserted (Spicer 2003, 34), some accidental damage may have occurred in the process, necessitating the replacement of windows or panels.'

[10] A horn was used to proclaim an outlaw, three blasts being blown by the king's messenger. (DSL 2c)

[11] 1 Corinthians 3:17.

Miracles were never intended to produce faith, only to confirm it and establish what God has already begun.

We conclude, then, that when Gideon asked for a sign he was neither displaying unbelief nor showing contempt towards the heavenly messenger, rather was he displaying a certain weakness, because he was conscious of his lack of the gifts needed for the task. That was why when he requested the confirmation of a sign, the Lord granted it. He went on to ask for other signs and the Lord responded, not only to confirm this poor man in his faith, but also because he wanted him to realise that he was the same God who had brought his people out of Egypt. Gideon must know that just as his hand was powerful then, so it was still as powerful now. The Lord doubled the miraculous signs[12] he gave him to let him see that there was no lack of strength in God, only lack of faith in him and the people. If only he and his people would believe, he would act as marvellously as he had done before.

So let us return to the account of the angel coming to him in the form of a man holding a staff in his hand, and saying to Gideon, 'The Lord is with you, O man of valour!'[13] Though he was only a poor man busy threshing his father's corn, the angel called him a man of valour, not for what he was then but for what the Lord was going to make him. He would endue him with great courage, and so he addressed him as having the qualities which he would infuse into him. Gideon replied to him, 'How could God be with us when we are so oppressed and held in such thraldom? Yes, our father has told us of many past miracles, but we have never witnessed any.'

His answer betrays that he doubts that the Lord would work again the kind of wonders that he had performed in the past. That was why the Lord then more than doubled the miraculous signs, both to confirm his faith and to assure him that he was the same God who had delivered his people from Egypt. His power was undiminished.

Gideon's weakness is also shown in his terror of God

Second, we see his weakness in that from the time he saw that the angel in human form was none other than the mighty God, he could not prevent himself from trembling with fear and crying out, 'Alas my Lord

[12] Judges 6:36-40.
[13] Judges 6:12.

and my God, I am now bound to die for I have seen thee face to face!' Thus we see his fragility displayed in his uncontrollable quaking with terror. If a reassuring and quiet appearance of God such as revealing himself in a bush or in the form of a man should strike such fear in a poor man's heart, what effect would his appearance have if he came in his great majesty as a blazing fire? Would we all fear that we would be consumed by the flames? Therefore we must enquire as to the reason of this fear and trembling that, when he reveals himself so gently in human form, we should shrink away in fear and cry out in despair. The cause cannot be in God, nor in these human bodies of flesh and blood that we carry about with us.

First, as God, he is a quickening Spirit, comforting in himself and the God of consolation. Therefore he must quicken his creatures and comfort them when they seek him, for each of us is his workmanship, and if you and I were simply his creations and nothing more, the sight of him could only bring us consolation. Further, if these bodies in which we are clothed was an impediment preventing us from being able to endure the sight of God, then Adam would not have enjoyed fellowship with him before the Fall. But the truth is that originally before the Fall, Adam did enjoy God's presence and was overjoyed at the sight of him. Therefore these bodies of ours cannot be the cause of our fear in his presence.

There is another point to consider. Jesus Christ took flesh and blood upon himself and has joined his person to a human body in a substantial union. He would never have done that if flesh and blood had been an impediment preventing him from enjoying his Father's presence. Therefore the fault is neither in God, nor in our human bodies, but in the sin that has defiled both our bodies and souls, permeating all the faculties of our entire beings. Take from me all of my sin, leaving only in my soul and body what God himself has created, and then it would not be possible for God to hate his work of creation. For sin is not a creation of God, but is a forgery of the devil, and a product of man consenting to Satan.

Therefore it is sin that the Lord hates and that causes our consciences to quake and our souls to tremble, preventing us from being able to endure the majesty of the presence of the living God. For as soon as God presents himself to us, our consciences condemn us and we become so aware of his spotless holiness and his hatred of any impurity, that we know his divine majesty cannot abide even the stain of wickedness. This is so certain that every man's conscience bears witness to it. Knowing that sin defiles and debars us for ever from the sight of God's face, should you not seek his strength and power to cleanse your consciences and renew your natures? Previously your hearts were inclined away from him, but oh that they may now be inclined towards him in order to please him! Only if the Lord in his mercy does this work of grace in you will your corrupt and evil nature be reformed. This far, then, for Gideon.

Barak

As for Barak, I shall be much shorter with him. Like Gideon, he gave evidence of his faith, but also his weaknesses were apparent. We see his faith in that, although his call came to him through one of the weaker vessels,[14] he obeyed. Not only was his faith proven through his obedience to God in response to the ministry of Deborah, but it was also vividly demonstrated in his valiant and courageous victory over an enemy who came against him with nine hundred iron chariots led by Sisera, the commander of the army of Jabin, king of Canaan. Added to that was the song of praise he and the woman sang before the sun went down on the evening of their great victory. You can read their song in Judges 5.

Barak's faith evidenced in his obedience and song of praise

Note how Barak and the woman praised God for the victory. In all that was accomplished that day, a genuine, living faith was displayed, but chiefly in that without delay as soon the outcome of the battle was apparent, they gave the glory to God. Fie! Too often you and I must be ashamed that we delay so long in praising God when he grants us some notable success. There is hardly anyone whose heart is inwardly moved to thank him. Why should this be so? Because our hearts are not touched with the awareness that it is God who has been at work, and so we are unthankful. Whereas if we had the same awareness in our hearts that Deborah and Barak had of seeing the mighty hand of the Lord

[14] 1 Peter 3:7. 'Ye husands … giuing honour vnto the woman, as vnto the weaker vessel.' (GenB; See also NKJV.)

preserving his people, we would not only thank him one day, but often we would praise him in our hearts while kneeling before him.

Hearts that have no sense of the Lord's benefits will not ever give thanks either to God or man, whereas the hearts that have been touched and become aware of his blessings will gladly express their thankfulness. On the other hand, when there is no sense of gratitude in us and no praise to God, men are left to perish, for our words have not come from our hearts. This is why I always praise Barak because before the sunset he sang his praise to God. You would never delay or procrastinate your praise to God if your hearts and mouths were inspired by a real sense of gratitude, for you would run straight to the Lord to thank him.

Barak's need to have the prophetess at his side in the battle

However, Barak also showed his weakness in that he refused to go into battle unless the woman went with him. That was his condition—the prophetess had to be at his side! The Lord then made it clear to him that because of his weakness in this and his lack of courage, part of the honour of the victory would go to a woman. Had he gone alone, all the honour would have been given to him, but because he had been unwilling to render simple obedience to his calling, he would suffer this shame that Sisera would be given by the Lord into a woman's hand.[15] Because there may be times when the weakness of our faith causes promotion and advancement to be withheld from us, we should crave of God the strengthening of our faith that whatever it is the Lord asks of us, we may obey him willingly. This far for Barak.

Samson

Now I shall speak of Samson and leave Jephthah to another time. As with Gideon and Barak, there is evidence of both his faith and his failings. As to his faith, it is evidenced by his extraordinary feats of strength which are recorded. In all of them he acted in faith because we read that as he did each of them he was inspired by the Spirit of God who came upon him. Since the Holy Spirit was the author, we cannot doubt that they flowed from faith. However, there is another reason why we know his deeds were done through faith.

[15] Judges 4:9, 20-22.

Samson's faith seen in his acknowledgement of God's power

After that extraordinary slaughter of one thousand Philistines using only the jawbone of an ass, being overcome with thirst, he prayed and committed himself to God saying, 'O Lord, you have granted this deliverance by the hand of your servant,' thus acknowledging that his mighty deeds were not accomplished by his own strength but by the omnipotent power of God. They had all been put into his hand, as it were, for he was merely the Lord's instrument and servant, and all he was able to do was for the glory of God and the deliverance of his people. Then the Lord opened a hollow place and Samson found water there and was revived as he drank. Therefore this third notable deed that is recorded was done out of zeal for God, and clearly demonstrates his faith.

Samson's weakness was in deserting his calling for a woman

We now consider his weakness, for it can be discerned throughout the account of his exploits. Would to God it had only been weakness, but alas it was worse, for it was foul defection. He was so carried away by bodily lust, as the record tells us, that it was impossible to hold him back when he was ensnared by sexual desire and deserted his calling. So his first failure was his desertion of his calling, and his second was his failure to discharge that calling.

His third failure was that he was blind to the deception of the whore he lived with, even though the Lord repeatedly warned him. This third failure not only led to his own physical injury, but ultimately cost him his life. He never heeded the Lord's warnings because he was blinded and overcome by his lust. Because he could not rid himself of it, he ended up becoming a shameful spectacle of God's judgment.

The first lesson from Samson's defection

From this account of Samson that I have summarised, I want to make several points to enable us to learn how to eschew the wrath of God. First, we see from his failure that whoever chooses to serve his own lustful desires rather than give obedience to God's calling, the Lord will take from him his gracious gifts, bestowed on him so he could discharge his calling. Not everyone's temptation arises from physical lust, for each of has his own particular weakness; nevertheless, in whatever way we defect from him and disobey his calling, ultimately shame will be heaped upon us and we will become spectacles of his judgment.

Therefore be warned! No one should prefer his own desires to God's service, for as God is God, he will not allow us to continue mocking him! I say this deliberately for those who share my own calling to preach the word, but who out of some carnal desire consider leaving the place of their appointment. Those who depart for whatever reason without the Lord's direction, undoubtedly will lose the gifts he has given, without which their ministry cannot be discharged. A man may well sound out the word, but it will have neither power nor authority, because he has chosen his own desires to the appointment given him by the living God.

Second lesson: God's patience cannot be taken for granted

Second, I perceive here in God a wonderful patience and beneficence, for he does not remove from a man his gifts as soon as he falls for the first time. Samson fell once, twice and thrice, but each time God renewed his gifts. Likewise, the Lord does not take away a man's gifts even after several falls and warnings, but if he persists in preferring his own way to God's service in the place of his calling, then ultimately the Lord will take his gifts from him. Yes, he is a patient God, for he will not suddenly strike that man down, but will repeatedly warn him. It is only when no admonition has been heeded that God will withdraw his blessing and gifts from that man, so that he is left to become a slave to the carnal affection he has chosen in preference to God's appointment; then for that man there will be no return to his calling.

Therefore it is best to resist our errant desires right from the start. If you are not able to withstand their power when they only knock at the door of your soul, so to speak, how much less will you be able to withstand them once they have brought your body as well as your soul under subjection! He that is not able to refuse the intruder when he only has one foot in the door, will scarcely be able to eject him when has taken over the whole dwelling. What I mean is that if you resist what is only in your thoughts, then you have withstood the temptation before it has reached fulfilment. For once you have yielded, as James says, desire gives birth to sin,[16] and the slave obeys only his master. What might have be rejected on the threshold, will take over as master

[16] James 1:14-15.

of the house if we invite it in.

Also Peter says that whatever overcomes a man, to that he becomes a slave.[17] He means that if sin overcomes both body and soul, we become sin's slave. It is very hard for a man to be delivered from this slavery. That is why the advantage must be seized before sin gains entrance, for that is the crucial moment; may the Lord give you grace to resist at that point. Be assured that when you resist the devil he will flee from you.[18] So much for the second point that I mark.

Third lesson: a stern warning to those in authority

The third thing is this. When men refuse to be restored, in his righteous judgment the Lord gives them over to these same desires. They neither keep his knowledge, nor do they love him any longer in their souls. They are then given over to their passions and that is the severest of judgments, for then a man is no longer in charge of himself, having become the slave of that upon which he has set his heart. If he sets his heart on a man, he becomes the slave of that man; if he sets his heart upon a woman, he becomes the slave of that woman. It is a most fearful and dreadful thing when God causes the one on whom we set our affections to become our master, especially when it happens to great men and to princes. For example, if a prince fixes his affections on someone or other, according to this judgment of God, that person will control what laws the prince enacts, and then the whole country could be made to suffer.[19]

Clearly, our great men need discretion as to whom they associate with. They should choose those who have good qualities and virtues, and avoid any who would be completely untrustworthy on account of their corrupt behaviour. It would be most grievous for this judgment of God to fall on our men of high rank, for it would make them the pawns of their own counsellors who would allow them to run loose. Dictated to by their own passions, they would be carried here and there, and would end up being shamed as slaves of others. For we see Samson, his eyes gouged out, being a slave of those who ought to have been his

[17] 2 Peter 2:19.

[18] James 4:7.

[19] This is possibly an intentional hint that Bruce considered King James's injudicious relationships were adversely affecting his royal responsibilities.

servants. There he is, a prisoner in the land of the Philistines, dying at their hands.

So you see men, especially princes, must distrust their errant desires, and constantly be wary of them. For if at the start they allow themselves to be swayed by their personal desires, their end will be disgrace and they will be dictated to by the very thing they indulged themselves in. Such an outcome would be the judgment of God, for when a man will not serve God in his calling, he will cause him to serve a far worse master. In spite of a man choosing to take pleasure where he desires, the sweetness of it can turn to bitterness, indeed to awful bitterness, for by continuing in self-indulgence is the fastest way to be bereft of the Spirit of Christ. Once a man has lost Jesus Christ, it is always hard to find him again. Even though that man searches for him for the rest of his life, he may never succeed in recovering him. Therefore, I say again, resist the tempter before ever he crosses your threshold, and you will find comfort and profit in your escape.

God's gift of faith is never revoked

As to Samson, we read of his great fall, yet God forbid we should think he fell from the mercy of God. Notwithstanding his shameful disgrace, this man recovered and was granted repentance from the hand of God. Indeed, in our text he takes his place among the saints. How can this be? Here the apostle tells us he was full of faith, and the faith on which he stood was solid ground. For I am certain that faith is one of God's gifts that he never revokes. To whom faith is given, it is given for ever. That is why Jude says that those who are called are kept for Jesus Christ, and he is able to keep us and present us to God.[20] The faith once given to the saints will not be revoked but will remain in the soul for ever, because soul and body are justified for ever.

You ask how it was possible, then, that Samson fell so many times. When he fell the sparks of faith lay covered up, almost smothered by his corruption. Although the Lord permitted his passions to run loose for a time, allowing his body to become a slave to his lust, he did not extinguish those faint sparks of faith, permitting them for a time to be repressed by his desires. Then, when it pleased the Lord, he breathed new life into those sparks, rekindling them and causing them to glow

[20] Jude 1, 24.

brightly in the glory of unfeigned repentance.

In the same way, these great men who have cast off his grace will be made spectacles to the world, as happened to Samson, because like him they must be humbled. The Lord would have us all bowing low and admitting, 'Lord, apart from your grace, we cannot even think a good thought, let alone do a good deed.' So even though Samson's faith was almost smothered and covered over for a time by the strength of his corrupt passion, yet, as we read at the end of Judges 16, it revived and he was granted the gift of repentance as his prayer in verse 28 makes clear when he was about to die.

Did Samson take his own life?

There is, however, an objection that might seem to gainsay this. It would appear from the biblical record that Samson actually killed himself, therefore he could not truly have been a man of faith. We may be persuaded by this argument that whoever is the means of his own death has actually taken his own life. But there is an assumption here that I will answer, by asking whether he really did die by his own hand. First, I deny that it was his own deed that caused his death. It is a fallacy to make such a claim, even though he was the instrument of it. To be accurate, the deed should be attributed to the principal cause, and not to the instrument. But Samson himself was not the principal cause, therefore, properly speaking, the deed was not his.

Secondly, though he was the instrument of the deed, he was commanded by God to revenge the injuries that the Philistines had inflicted upon his people. What God commands us to do, whatever our vocation may be, pertains to his work and not to ours. In the same way your regeneration is not my work, even though I am God's appointed means of it; it is entirely his work. Thirdly, Samson was not acting as a private individual, for it is not permissible for any private individual to engage in killing other people. Rather he was acting as a magistrate and a judge for he judged Israel for twenty years, and the actions of a magistrate are not his personal deeds, but those of his office. Therefore, because he was not the principal cause of the deed, but only the instrument, it was not his deed, for he did not kill himself, but died in the execution of his office.

Do you want to know, therefore, when it can properly be said that a man has taken his own life? It is when he himself believes that there is nothing left to live for, and, because he thinks his soul would fare better outside his body, in desperation he kills himself. King Saul is properly said to have ended his own life because he deliberately fell on his sword. On the other hand, those who have God's glory as their motive, do not kill themselves even though their actions lead to their deaths. That is how it was with Samson. Because the strength he had lost by his disgraceful defection from God was restored to him by the Spirit of God, that is convincing evidence that he died discharging his calling.

Did the apostle Paul take his own life when he went to Jerusalem? Read about his journey when he left Greece for Macedonia, where there was a plot to take his life. Then when he left Macedonia for Caesarea, Agabus prophesied his arrest if he went to Jerusalem.[21] But Paul went on courageously, showing himself not only willing to be in chains for Christ's sake but also to die, yet God forbid that we should ever say he took his own life. The soldier who risks death in a fierce conflict by fighting in the frontline of the battle, would never be said to have killed himself, and similarly a soldier who volunteers to scale the walls of a besieged city cannot be accused of committing suicide.

Conclusion

It is time for me to conclude. Samson, then, is free from this stain on his reputation, for he recovered the faith that had been almost extinguished by his corruption, having had it rekindled and restored to him. Therefore, those who give themselves over to their corrupt desires may again receive God's mercy. However, it may be that the Lord does not grant his mercy to some who have sold themselves over to the sins of this world, so do not assume that Samson's experience grants you immunity from divine judgment. Nevertheless, these three judges we have considered are cited lest those who have plunged themselves into self-indulgence should despair.

Yet it must be said that any who abuse these three examples by persisting, even after many warnings, in acting against their consciences and knowledge of the truth, thereby deliberately pouring contempt on God's mercy, may never be reclaimed. Therefore, even though there is consolation for us in the accounts of these three judges, let us not abuse

[21] Acts 20:3; 21:10-14.

mercy on account of the wantonness of our fleshly lusts, but rather beseech the Lord that we may never become public spectacles of his wrath. We must ask him to give us grace to resist temptation while it is still on our thresholds, so that we may firmly shut the door on our lusts and so avoid falling victim to the slavery of sin.

In closing, I perceive that there is no wholly reliable history in this world, other than in the Bible. For in setting down the fine qualities of great men, it never conceals their faults, even though they may be judges, prophets or princes. Thus we learn that in Scripture there is no bias, yet in the world historians tend to show partiality. Only the Holy Spirit is a true and faithful historian, thus only the Bible contains wholly authentic accounts of men's lives. The Lord then grant all of us grace that we may learn from and embrace his truth, so that we may be free from just condemnation. That can only be through the righteous merits of Christ, to whom with the Father and the Holy Ghost be all honour, praise and glory, both now and forevermore. Amen.

Chapter Twenty-Six

Hebrew Chapter 11 at the midst of the 32 verse

[32] … *and of Jephte also of Dauid, and Samuell, and of the propheitis etc.*

Brethren and well-beloved in Jesus Christ, you have already heard how the apostle is now hastening to conclude his lengthy introduction to the subject of faith, and so now he refers to all the prophets, naming only David and Samuel. He will mention the deeds of the faithful in general, and their sufferings in particular. I spoke last time of the three different categories of person cited in verse 32. Some were judges, others were kings and yet others were prophets. We thought about three of the faithful judges, Gideon, Barak and Samson, but did not have sufficient time to consider Jephthah, the fourth judge the apostle named.

You may remember what you heard about Samson, but I could have said more. Even though this judge was raised up to be a notable instrument of God among his people, endowed with singular and rare gifts and graces, nevertheless he allowed his heart to be carried away by 'an enemy' within his domestic life. What I mean is that he was so corrupted by his own foolish lusts that neither warnings nor reproofs were able to restore him to his senses. Ultimately he was completely under the control of his physical desires, and consequently he was deprived of his gifts and forsook his vocation as a judge. The final outcome was that he became a public spectacle of disgraceful ignominy before men, angels and indeed the whole world. That was as far as we went concerning Samson, the third of the first three judges. Yet, notwithstanding his shameful fall from grace, he was pardoned by the infinite mercy of God and life everlasting was granted to him.

The danger of becoming a spiritual castaway

A lesson that I constantly seek to inculcate into your minds and drive into your very hearts is that in spite of Samson's unique gifts, because he increasingly indulged his burning, passionate lusts, not only was he exposed to open shame and infamy but he also lost his gifts and calling. All of us must learn from his experience, whatever age we may be. Are you an older person? Then learn to flee from the temptations that come with advanced years, for they can be almost as dangerous as those to which younger people are exposed. Are you still young? Then learn to flee from the lusts of youth,[1] for in our earlier years our passions can rage furiously. But whatever your age, you will have various sinful desires that can prove to be a burden on your hearts. If you do not resist them, they will take control of you and dominate both your body and soul.

Therefore before that happens, strive to retain your physical and spiritual purity, keeping yourselves as instruments[2] of holiness. Why? Because it is the Spirit of sanctification who has been appointed by the Lord to guard you in your holy calling.[3] If you lose your Guardian, you will also lose your calling and the gifts whereby you administer that calling. So guard the One who guards you, possess your soul in holiness, and retain that portion of sanctification that has been granted you. It is only the Spirit who can sustain you in your calling so that you retain his gifts, keeping them fresh and green as though they had only just been bestowed upon you.[4]

We read in 2 Timothy 1:14 that the apostle urged Timothy, being a young man, to guard the pledge he had been given, in other words to

[1] 2 Timothy 2:22.

[2] Bruce's word is 'veschellis', that is, 'vessels'; see 2 Timothy 2:21, 'If anyone cleanses himself from what is dishonourable, he will be a vessel for honourable use, set apart as holy, useful to the master of the house, ready for every good work.' See also Chapter 2, note 3 above.

[3] It appears very likely that Bruce is now particularly addressing ministers who may have been present, as well as addressing his congregation more generally.

[4] Here is one of Bruce's typical homely metaphors, picturing the gifts of the Spirit as the gardener's produce just brought into the kitchen from the castle's vegetable plot. (He had spent his earlier years in Airth Castle with its abundant gardens.)

watch over the gifts given to him by the indwelling Holy Spirit. It was as if he was saying that unless Timothy guarded and fostered the Spirit of holiness within him, he would inevitably lose both his calling and its gifts. So you see the Spirit of sanctification is not imparted to us merely for one hour on the Sabbath, nor for one day, nor even for just one year, but for every single hour and day of our lives. It is absolutely true, indeed, it reaches far beyond the measure of truth, that if you lose holiness in your soul, you will also lose the holy and precious gifts of God.

It is impossible for the Holy Spirit to remain in a soul that is consistently defiled. We are not defiled by outward physical dirt, but by whatever carnal affections we set our hearts upon. When you seek to resist wrong desires but find that you cannot rid yourself of them straightaway, beseech God for patience that you might at least stand firm against them.[5] For those who can remain standing also continue to believe, and those who believe are in a state of grace. Stand then in the battle, for you are fighters, and as fighters you will be crowned. But if you give in and allow your desires to rule over you, they will tyrannize you. Because the root of evil lurks deep within us, I must often repeat this essential lesson so that all of you take it to heart, for if we are not aware of the root of sin within but tolerate it, it will prevail over you and despoil you of the gifts that are essential to your calling.

This then is the vital lesson from the life of Samson who was caught unawares and fell into folly, becoming the slave of his passions. Remember his shame as he was made a public spectacle of ignominy by his enemies. They brought him from his prison to amuse the crowds as they jeered, scoffed and mocked him.[6] It was the Lord who took from him his extraordinary strength, and so handed him over to his foes. They gouged out his eyes and set him to work grinding at the prison mill. And so he became the star attraction to make them merry at their most solemn day of celebration in honour of Dagon, for when the crowds saw him they praised their god. No doubt that pierced him to the heart. After they had eaten their fill, many of them went up on to the flat roof to watch Samson being abused, as the Scriptures record.

However, it pleased the Lord to take pity on the grief of this

[5] In Ephesians 6:10-14, the apostle four times urges believers 'to stand'! Bruce's next two sentences suggest that these verses were in his mind.

[6] Judges 16:21-31.

miserable man. This is the way he works, for he brings a man low, permitting him to suffer until he becomes aware of the misery in which he has landed himself. The Lord then gave him the spirit of prayer, and by the Spirit stirring within him he poured out his complaint to God as he laid his request before him. Samson now beseeched the Lord to let him be avenged on his enemies for one last time. Remember that they were not just Samson's enemies, but the enemies of God and his people.

Wickedness ultimately destroys itself

The Lord heard his prayer and answered by restoring to him his extraordinary strength, though it appears he even gave him greater strength than he had had before. The result was that quite suddenly, when his tormentors least expected it, having been taken by the young man who was minding him to the two pillars that supported the entire structure, Samson took hold of them and heaved so that they collapsed bringing down the whole building in which the crowds had gathered. Thus on the day when he died, Samson slew more Philistines and their lords than he had slain during his lifetime.

The principle of God overturning unrighteous mockery by using it to destroy his enemies is worked out here, for those who mocked Samson and derided his misery were slain by him. What they thought provided them with their most amusing entertainment turned out to be the means of their destruction. Yet it was not Samson who judged them, it was the Lord who destroyed them by using the object of their evil pleasure and mockery as his instrument.

The lesson for us today is this. The very things in which the wicked find their greatest amusement are used by God as the means of their eternal destruction. On the other hand, events which appear to bring to naught the labours of his servants, the Lord, who is the wisest of strategists, uses these same events to strengthen his servants and advance the Kirk of Jesus Christ. Cast your eye across biblical history and you will see that scoffing, mocking and opposition of God's servants never went unpunished, rather those who taunt and deride invariably die in shame. Therefore it must be our study always to remain in the favour and good grace of our God.

Be sure of this: however dangerous a situation may seem to be, both in our judgment and in the judgment of others, when we stand within

God's favour he will turn that situation to our advantage and comfort, as well as to the advancement of his Kirk. However, if we lose his favour, then however great our advancement may appear to be in the world's estimation, it will bring eternal loss upon us. It is therefore obvious that the one thing to be preferred before every worldly profit is for a man steadfastly to keep himself in the favour of his God. Moreover, the only way to achieve this is by maintaining a clear conscience and living in the knowledge of God; otherwise in your hour of greatest need you will not find God at hand to help you. Take heed, then, that you are not deceived by the devil, nor beguiled away from God's favour by your own sinful desires.

The deaths of believers and unbelievers are different

The last thing I mark in Samson is this. It is true that he died along with the Philistines, ostensibly in the same way they died and by drinking of the same cup that they drank. Yet even though they shared the same death, his enemies did not have the same God, nor did they share with him the Lord's divine grace and mercy. They knew nothing of faith in Jesus Christ, nor of the promises of God. We cannot doubt that Samson's soul was received immediately into the kingdom of heaven, whereas the Philistines' souls were delivered into the place of torment.

Therefore we have to learn not to judge by outward appearances a person's happiness or unhappiness, his blessedness or profanity. Neither must we judge God's acceptance or rejection of a man by the Lord's outward dealings with him. For being hung on gallows, or burned at the stake, or incarcerated in prison are all experienced both by good men and evildoers, both by those who are in God's favour and those who are not in his favour. However, the causes of a man's suffering are often very different and may well arise from either their faith or their unbelief. If they undergo trials and tribulation on account of their faith, you will see that they are suffering as innocent men, and faith along with innocence always carries with it the favour and presence of God.

Jephthah

We come now to Jephthah. As with the first three judges, we must consider both this man's faith and his weakness. We find the account of him in the book of Judges chapter 11. He derived his title, Jephthah the Gileadite, from his father whose name was Gilead, which was also the name of the area where they lived. As to his mother, we are not given her name, but we are told that she was a prostitute, a common whore. The implication of Jephthah not being born of either his father's wife or concubine is that he was illegitimate, in other words, a bastard. In those days concubines were regarded as having the status of a wife and therefore their children were considered lawful and had their portion of the inheritance in Israel. You may read of this law in Deuteronomy 23.[7] The reason for disinheriting a son born of a prostitute was no doubt in order to discourage the vice of prostitution.

Grace for one who had been rejected by men

However, the sons of Gilead were not content with the severity of this law, but going beyond its statute they banished their illegitimate brother entirely from the country. Even though the custom was to debar such an offspring from all the normal family privileges of inheritance, contrary to normal practice they took the extraordinary measure of dispatching Jephthah off to another land called Tob. Even though this man was now excluded from all possibility of worldly honour, it pleased the Lord to give him the blessing that derives from heaven, for God who gave the law to his people is himself greater than the law, and he chose to give the outcast both grace and honour. We see, therefore, that those who are in the same situation as Jephthah who have been rejected and scorned, when they make God their refuge and help, there is grace, favour and honour to be found from his hands when there is none from their fellowmen. God gave grace and honour to Jephthah. So much then for the man himself.

We come now to his faith which can be seen in the way he conducted himself with great wisdom, for I consider true integrity and genuine manhood to be entirely the product of faith. When he was called to govern a neighbouring province (he was never the king in that area, only its chief officer), he did not neglect his dependence upon God or his personal responsibilities towards the people, but acted wisely in a difficult situation that arose.

[7] This may be implied in Deuteronomy 23:7-8. See also 2 Samuel 5:13-16; 19:5; 20:3.

There was powerful ruler whom we are told in Judges 11 was the king both of the Ammonites and the Moabites. He threatened to invade Israelite territory.[8] Jephthah acted with great discretion, for he first sent an ambassador to enquire as to the nature of the grievance that had arisen. He wanted to know the reason for the threatened invasion, and whether or not there could be a peaceful solution to the Ammonite king's anger.

Jephthah's wisdom

When the ambassador returned empty-handed, Jephthah again showed his wisdom in that he sent his messengers again to reason with the king, refusing to accept that the only alternative would be to take up arms. Thus he laid down the principle that force of arms should always be the very last resort of any prince. He saw that declaration of war should never be the only solution to a disagreement. This principle ought not only to hold good for the great and powerful, but should also apply to those of lower rank and also to men of the meanest estate. For it is easier to get into a quarrel than it is to get out of it; it is easier to start a fight than to stop it. It is possible (we often see this in our land) for the most humble worker to initiate a bitter feud that can persist, as happens in other countries, and not even the king offers a resolution of the quarrel, even though, alas, he has the authority to do so. So I highly commend Jephthah's wisdom in seeking to solve the issue by reason[9] and by law, before even considering resorting to force of arms.

This suggests that there is a ridiculous folly pervading our land, for the devil in hell could not have bewitched men's hearts with greater madness such as we see rampant among us at this time. For men of all ranks in society, from the highest to the lowest, seem to consider it an insult and shame if their disagreements are resolved by the intervention of friends or by reasoned arguments. Unless they take matters into their own hands, bypassing the local magistrate, and revenging their private quarrels, they consider their honour has been besmirched forever in shame. The notion has spread through our country that to resolve some grievance through a magistrate applying the law constitutes an insult to their family's name. This attitude has come about through contempt of

[8] Judges 10:17-18.

[9] As the word 'reason is used here and in the next several paragraphs, its meaning is 'behaviour that is conformity with what is good or right.' (DSL 7)

our magistrates. Yet if there was among us respect for the law administered by a magistrate and fear of the sword in his hand, then men would not immediately act to avenge themselves of presumed wrongs. What else is the reason for their rash boldness other than their view that they are above the law?

An exhortation to magistrates

Would that all magistrates strictly applied the law, irrespective of the rank of the persons involved, for then no doubt by the power of the Spirit of the living God, the proper execution of the law would engender respect for it. Where the law is not properly executed, the magistrate earns contempt for himself. Two possible outcomes follow from what I have said: either the magistrates and [the king's] council enforce the law on those who despise it, or else it will be the magistrates' misfortune that those who rebel against it will rob him of his office, honour and status, and then those who ought to be serving him will become his masters. I know perfectly well that some magistrates perjure themselves by laying all the blame on their council, while the council for its part quietly, though not publicly, puts the blame on the magistrate; however, neither are without fault.

When it comes to our King, in my opinion the blame lies mostly with his council. Nevertheless, their excuses will be futile before God's tribunal, for in truth when the council robs him of his crown, as it were, they are despoiling both the Kirk and the commonwealth. They do not care when they see him shamed before God and the people. If they had some compassion for him they would give their lives for him, rather than see contempt for his authority go unpunished. Thus because they have no consideration for him, far less respect for his royal status, they will stand by idly while he runs headlong into the wrath of God that burns so fiercely it cannot be quenched.

The dispute between the Ammonite king and Israel

I return to the issue that Jephthah dealt with so wisely. First he sent an ambassador to discuss the apparent quarrel. Then when he learned of the reasons, he sent a second ambassadorial commission to explain to the Ammonite king Israel's rights and titles to the lands in dispute. He was seeking if at all possible to resolve the matter by reasoning and through lawful means. In response to the first visit of the ambassador, the Ammonite king alleged that when the Israelites had come out of Egypt, having passed through the desert and reached the River Arnon, they entered his land and occupied the range of hills lying between the Arnon and Jabbok rivers, bounded by the Jordan on one side and the Arabah on the other side. 'Now,' said the king, 'restore my land and I will let you depart in peace.' That was the ground of the Ammonite king's grievance.

If what the king had said had been true he would have had a just complaint, and if a reasoned case against his claim had not been made, he would have been justified in seizing the land by force of arms. But it was quite certain that he was speaking falsely, even though he was a king. Jephthah's ambassador would have been able to inform him straightaway that it was untrue that the Israelites had taken any land from either the Ammonites or Moabites. Indeed, the Scriptures recorded that the Lord strictly forbade the Israelites from molesting in any way the Moabites, Ammonites and Edomites, even though these nations refused to allow Israel to pass peaceably through their territories. Nor did Israel retaliate when Edom and Moab refused to grant them right of passage through their lands.[10] The Lord had told them that he had given Mount Seir to their brother Esau as a possession, and Ar to Moab who were descendants of Lot. Therefore not a single foot's breadth of these lands would be given to Israel.

Now since it was the Lord who had said this, it was quite certain that the Ammonite king was not speaking the truth in claiming that Israel's territory belonged to him. It was true that certain lands had once belonged to Moab, for the Moabites had driven out the ancient tribes that once had rightfully occupied them. Consequently they now held the city called Arnon, so named as it stood on the banks of the River Arnon, though it had become known as Ar. The King of the Amorites then comes into the picture, for the River Arnon marked the boundary between his territory and that of the Moabites. He had done the same as Moab and dispossessed the ancient peoples of their rightful land, and had occupied it for some time without any intervention from other tribes.

When the children of Israel arrived, finding the Amorites in

[10] Deuteronomy 2:4-9; Numbers 20:14-21.

possession of this territory, they paused their journey and set up camp at the River Arnon. However, when Edom, Moab and Ammon all refused permission for the Israelites to pass through their lands, they journeyed round each territory on their way to Canaan where they occupied lands by fighting to win back what was justly theirs. It follows therefore that the allegations made by the King of the Ammonites were wholly false.

A warning to advocates

Here I pause to mark this point. When kings or powerful men decide to shoot at some target or other, something they decide to do off their own bat,[11] they take no account whatsoever of God's will or of the lack of integrity in their plans. All they consider is what means they can employ to get their hands on what they want, whether or not their actions are lawful; truth is of no consequence to them. Nor do they expect anyone to challenge what they are doing, far less reprove them. Often in the past this has been the attitude of kings and powerful men. Therefore Jephthah's allegation against the king of the Ammonites was fully justified.[12]

If this is the way in which many kings and those who hold power are accustomed to act, you who are advocates must not be surprised if at the bar in court you have to accuse them of duplicity. The lesson I would draw from this is that there should be no words spoken by you in this life without your bearing in mind the life that is to come. Therefore, however cunningly your client may brief you, you must never knowingly allege in court facts which you know to be false. If in your own conscience you believe something to be untrue, do not use it in evidence. I know that some magistrates can be taken in by false information, but an advocate who uses evidence he knows to be false will one day have to stand before God's tribunal.

Last Lord's Day[13] I warned the judges not to pervert their judgments knowingly. So now I warn you also never to use evidence that you know is false. Your evidence must always be just, so that you may remain on the pathway to heaven; otherwise be certain that by seeking to advance

[11] Bruce's phrase is, 'schutte at anie butt or wold be at their purpose quhilk they lay doun'.

[12] Judges 11:27-28. '... you do me wrong by making war on me.'

[13] I am assuming the sermons were preached on the Lord's Day. Bruce simply has 'I adverteised the judgis the last day...'.

yourselves on earth you will forfeit heaven. The judges are not present today, but the part they play in this issue is hugely important, and the widespread complaints throughout our land must indicate there have been miscarriages of justice. I admonished them to some extent last week, for I dare not neglect my commission,[14] and I only addressed them to correct them for their benefit. I am ever mindful that I must deliver myself from their blood,[15] and, if it is at all possible, turn them to God. I only say what is in accordance with my commission, not from malice but out of love. If necessity did not constrain me, I would never take it upon myself to admonish them, but because the matter is so urgent, I have admonished them and will continue to do. If I was in full possession of the facts concerning some municipal case corruptly administered, I would publicly reprove what had been done.

Let them be assured (I am not referring to our king whom I always reverence in God), that I stand in awe of none of them, but I dare to reprove them to their faces. In fulfilling my commission, I have no regard for either their hostility or their favour, and they will find that, as the words I speak are accompanied with power, the one who utters them also has the power to strike down[16] whoever exalts himself against God. Therefore ensure that you profit by these admonitions, and do not be foolish enough to show up your stupidity by complaining. If you do and it comes to my notice, be sure that I will let you know. The Lord forbid that his word be not clothed with his power. May no man ever minister in this place who does not have the courage to admonish in the name of God. The Lord forbid that he should forget (how could God ever forget!) to accompany his word with power, that those who exalt themselves against him may be struck down. So reverence the Word of God, and if you perceive that it is spoken in love, then reverence its message and his minister who delivers it.

The second ambassadorial commission

I return now to my subject. The king of Ammon puts forward a false case. After the ambassador and his companions had reported to Jeph-

[14] The word Bruce frequently uses regarding ministers' divine commission is 'warrand'.

[15] The allusion is to Ezekiel 33:1-6.

[16] Bruce's verb is 'ding' which means 'to strike with heavy blows'. (DSL)

thah on their first visit, he decided to send them back with the commission to explain fully the rights of the Israelites in occupying the land in question, and to show that the king's quarrel with them was baseless. Of course, before he set out his people's rights to the territory, Jephthah made it clear that the Ammonite king's claims were completely false. He stated that Israel had taken no land from Moab or Ammon, and that the record of how the Israelites acted when they departed from Egypt was still fresh in people's memories. It had been public knowledge that they had journeyed around the borders of both Moab and Ammon, and therefore could not have occupied their land. The charge that God had given them was also well known: they had not to molest or fight with Edom, Moab and Ammon, and his people had been warned against disobeying their God's command. Therefore the Ammonite king could not have any cause for complaining against Israel.

The first ground for Israel's occupation of the disputed lands

Jephthah's message went on to explain that his people had full rights to the land they now occupied. He gave a full account with three grounds for this assertion. His first ground was the rights of a just battle for, by a universally accepted law, land ought only to be occupied if it had been justly won. He made it clear what he meant. When the Israelites reached the River Arnon, they had sent messengers to the Ammonite king asking for permission to pass through his realm on their way to their own country. The king at that time, Sihon by name, not only refused, as did the other neighbouring kings, but he deployed all the weaponry and men at arms he had, not to protect his own land or defend his borders (had that been his intention he would not have been at fault), but to attack the Israelites. He crossed his own border and encamped his forces at Jahaz from where he launched his assault. Israel defended herself, and by the universally accepted law of nations, what fell to them from the battle was justly held, for they won the land by defence and not by attack. Therefore that territory became theirs by right.

Sihon was within his rights refusing to permit the Israelites to pass through his land, for there can never be any surety or promise that provides adequate warrant for a king to allow another nation's forces to march through his land. Men too easily break their word over far less important matters than the opportunity unexpectedly to seize another prince's land. No, Sihon's mistake was not to refuse the Israelites right of passage, but to march across his own borders and attack them. His unwarranted offensive demonstrated his own stupidity and rashness, and so the Lord had turned back upon him the folly of his heart, and in so doing gave his people permission to meet Sihon in battle.

Thereby God was not only visiting upon him his past sins and those of his people, but also his stubborn folly in his attitude both towards the Lord and his people. His aggression came in spite of all the great works of which he had heard, how the Lord had manifested himself in defending his people while they were in Egypt and since they had departed from there. Therefore Israel held by a title deed the lands in dispute, awarded to them through a just war.

The second ground for Israel's entitlement to their lands

The second ground arose from the gift and nature of God himself. He who has the authority to set everything in its proper order had given these lands to his people, therefore they belonged to them. Then Jephthah used a similitude, comparing their idol Chemosh to the Lord God of Israel. 'If Chemosh,' he said, 'gave you a portion of land, would you not possess it, and would you not think his gift entitled you to that land? For whatever men regard as coming from a god, they believe that they can own it with a good conscience.' Then Jephthah went on to say that the Israelites owned the land in question because it was given to them as a gift and by the disposition of their God. Therefore they occupied it by right and with a good conscience.

The third ground of the land belonging to Israel

The third ground of Israel's occupancy of the disputed land was taken from the right conferred by the prescription of time.[17] Jephthah's ambassador said to the Ammonite king, 'We have been in peaceable possession of this portion of land from Arnon to Jabbok for the space of three hundred years, never once having been challenged up until this very day by any of your forebears.' The implication, of course, was that the opportunity for a legal challenge to their possession of the land

[17] The Prescription of Time was a legal term meaning 'the time after the expiry of which the right to challenge possession of something or some territory lapses'.

had long since lapsed. The ambassador gave a round number that was approximately correct, give or take ten or twenty years either way. In fact, the time since Israel took the land was probably just less than three hundred years.

The ambassador made a further point. He said, 'If any man had had power to question our occupancy of this territory it was Balak the son of Zippor, king of Moab, who would then have recovered it from us. Balak warred against us in various ways, but he never contested our right to this land. You will not find in your own nation's chronicles, or in the register of our own history, that this was ever an issue with him, for he knew we gained the land through a just war. If Balak had had any entitlement to the land, he would have taken it up with us. Since he did not contest it, much less have you the right to contest it. Are you wiser and better than Balak? You are not nearly as wise as he was. He summoned a prophet to curse the Lord's people, thinking that by some unusual means he would overcome them.[18] Indeed, though he fought with us, he kept within his own borders. Further, even if you consider your nation had a rightful claim on the territory, you have lost it by your centuries of silence.'

This, then, is a summary of the three arguments upon which Jephthah grounded the right of the Israelites to the disputed portion of land. Regarding his third argument, I see the wisdom of Jephthah in putting it last, because it is not invariably conclusive. His first argument was that their title deeds to the land were sound according to the law of nations: they had won the land by a just battle when they were forced to defend themselves. His second argument was that by the gift and nature of God they were given possession of the land, consequently they occupied it through a valid entitlement and with a clear conscience.

To add to these first two arguments, thirdly, he introduced the Prescription of Time. I do not want to expand further on this argument, because although it holds true in civil matters, it cannot have a place in the realm of holy things and the worship of God. All these objects used in worship are consecrated to God, not to man, therefore this third argument cannot be prescribed against the worship or truth of God. Tertullian asserted that no antiquity can ever prescribe against

[18] Numbers 22-24.

religion.[19]

The Ammonite king replied in uncompromising terms, but the sum was that he would not listen to the ambassador and his entourage, even though they had faithfully passed on Jephthah's message. Rather he chose to run wilfully towards his own destruction. So in addition to his infidelity, we also note his obstinacy.

What, then, were the consequences of all this? The messengers returned from the king and advised Jephthah to prepare for an invasion. For his part, Jephthah recognized that reason and justice had been rejected, and he turned to God, calling upon him who judges righteously to decide between the people of Israel and the people of Ammon. Thereupon Jephthah prepared for war, but did not wait for the Ammonites to cross Israel's borders, but took the initiative by entering their territory, where he fought them and subdued them, capturing twenty cities.

Three lessons from Jephthah's wise actions

From all that we have heard of these events, I want to underline several points. First we should note carefully how a man, or even a king, can refuse sound reason[20] and helpful admonition when they are offered. To do this is to antagonise God himself who is able at the last to overthrow both body and soul. So let us learn to listen to reason and practise impartiality, and let us be willing to accept the rebuke, otherwise we make the impartial administration of the law our enemy.

Second, I also note here that there was never anyone who initially refused to listen to reason, but when the time came that he needed it he found it was too late. So accept wise counsel when it is offered and do not treat anyone with contempt. Rather remember that God can enable the lowliest man whom you disdain to overthrow you.

The third point I note is that whoever chooses to declare war in

[19] Paraphrased from Tertullian's *De Virginibus Velandis* 1: 'This observance is exacted by truth, on which no one can impose prescription—no space of times, no influence of persons, no privilege of regions. For these, for the most part, are the sources whence, from some ignorance or simplicity, custom finds its beginning; and then it is successionally confirmed into an usage, and thus is maintained in opposition to truth. But our Lord Christ has surnamed Himself Truth, not Custom.' I am indebted to Prof. Mark Eliot for this footnote.

[20] See note 9 above.

order to resolve a quarrel by force of arms must be fully convinced that his cause is righteous and for his part conflict is justified. He must also be convinced that in all conscience he has God on his side. When this is true, then in the ensuing conflict he will prove strong and firm. When your conscience is clear, it does not matter whether you live or die, for then either death or life is gain for you.[21] On the other hand, unjustified quarrels make for a bad conscience, and that enfeebles a man, causing him both a miserable life and a miserable death. In short, before ever you choose to contest a case, be certain your cause is sound, and that your mind and conscience testify to you that you mean well. Thus far, then, for Jephthah's faith.

Jephthah's rash vow

Now I shall say a little about his weakness, but I will have to continue our consideration of this on the next Lord's Day.[22] Jephthah shows both his weakness and rashness in the vow that he made. He was so carried away by his desire for victory that to ensure he won the battle he did not bother about the kind of vow he took, nor what he vowed; he spoke without thinking! No doubt his intention had always been to please God, but see what happens when there is a lack of wisdom and understanding, even when his desire was to please the Lord. When we do not bridle our guile with knowledge so that what we say pleases God, then our words become abhorrent to him. The kind of guile that is bereft of understanding will embark upon actions that nullify all our service to God. So, being obsessed with succeeding in the battle, and lacking real knowledge of God (for at this time the Israelites had little spiritual insight, for the Lord had not awakened them from their spiritual torpor), he made an indiscreet vow, hardly noticing what he was saying.

When we consider the implications of his vow, we see that wisdom was lacking and it did not constitute right service to God. He said, 'Lord, if you will grant me victory in this battle, whatever I shall first meet coming out of my door when I return home in peace, I shall dedicate to you and offer up as sacrifice.' How rash are the terms of such

[21] This clause anticipates the words of Philippians 1:21 chiselled on Bruce's gravestone: 'Christvs vita et in morte lvcrum'.

[22] See Note 13 above.

a promise! It might have been a dog or a cat or some unclean animal that the Lord had forbidden to be used as a sacrifice, and we might try to excuse him if that was what he hoped would happen. But then he might have been met by some man or woman, and that too would have shown his rashness, for human sacrifice was also unacceptable to God. This was why God ordained that every firstborn son had to be redeemed by the acceptable sacrifice of some clean animal.[23] So whether he meant men or beasts, the terms of his vow were ill-conceived.

When he returned home fully aware of what he had vowed, as soon as he saw his daughter coming to greet him he at once began to tear his clothes and beat his breast, so that everyone knew he bitterly regretted his vow. No vow which a man immediately laments can ever be a right offering of service to God, so that Jephthah's bitter regret is an indisputable indication of his rashness. So much for the general consideration of his weakness.

As Jephthah erred in making his vow, so he erred the second time when he came to perform it. Thus he erred twice over, once in speaking rashly and then a second time in wickedly fulfilling the vow. We find that Herod did the same when he promised the girl who danced that he would give her whatever she asked for, and she then asked for the head of John the Baptist. Herod took no heed to the justice of what he must now do, for he thought a king's duty was never to break a promise, so he gave her the man's head. Like Jephthah, he erred in making such a promise, then he erred a second time in honouring his promise.[24] On the other hand, though David vowed rashly that every man who served Nabal would be killed, he was wise when Nabal's wife Abigail acted with great discretion and dissuaded him, for he then overturned his vow and broke it.[25]

Alas, we are told that Jephthah performed his vow. Whether he offered her as a sacrifice, or else put her into confinement for the rest of her life, what he did was wrong. If it was the latter, and he consecrated her to God as a perpetual virgin, what kind of faith led to that action? For whatever is not done in faith is not righteous service for God. How could her virginity be a gift to God, and what sort of warrant had he

[23] Exodus 34:20b.
[24] Mark 6:21-28.
[25] 1 Samuel 25:23-25.

that God would accept that kind of offering? Make of it what you will, there was great fault in what he did, for it arose from his rashness and weakness. And what of the joy that he got from his victory? Was it not then seasoned with a bitter sauce?

What can we say about all this? None of us are free from weaknesses, for even the faith of the most godly is mingled with human frailty. In every godly man there are two sins—for foul thoughts issue in foul actions. Yet alongside those are holy thoughts and sanctified actions, both of which flow from faith. There is no one perfect here on earth, and that applies to our faith as well, for our faith is always imperfect. That is why we are urged to pray constantly that God would increase our faith. Even though faith cannot ever be perfect, if it is genuine faith, then its life will be manifested in love, and it is this life flowing from our faith that justifies us.

Therefore, we are so to strive that our faith may be genuine and its life will then be shown through works of love. We must flee from all that displeases God, and embrace what we know will please him. This surely is how we will be able to resist the sin and corruption that lurks within us all as long as we are here on earth.

May we all have this testimony in our consciences, so that we are able to say that even though we are tainted by corruption, we have not given way to it. At our end such a testimony will bring us honour, glory and joy. For when you and I resist sin, even though it is present as a vital force within our souls, it will not stain our consciences with guilt. It is only when we give way to sin, and indulge ourselves in some wrong, that our consciences are troubled. Therefore, although there is the root of sin in our lives here, our lives on earth are to be the means of conveying us towards the life to come. I beseech God that he will enable everyone of you to be partakers of that eternal life, and that can only be through the merits of Christ, to whom with the Father and the Holy Ghost be all honour, praise and glory now and for ever. Amen.

Chapter Twenty-Seven

Hebrew Chapter 11 verses 33-37

> 33 *Which throuch faith subdewit kingdomis, wroucht richteousnes*
> *obteinit the promeis* 34 *stoped the mouthis of lyonis, quenchit the*
> *violence of fyrre, escaipit the edge of the sword, of waik war maid*
> *strong, waxit valiant in battell, turned to flicht the armeis of the*
> *aliantis.* 35 *The women receaved thair dead raised to lyfe, vtheris also*
> *war rackit and would not be delywered, that they micht receave a*
> *better resurrectioune.* 36 *And vtheris haue bene tryit by mockingis*
> *and scourgeingis. Yea morovir by bondis and prissonmentis,* 37 *they*
> *war stonit they waer hewis a sunder, they war tempted, they war*
> *slaine with the sword, they wandered vp and doun in scheip skinnis*
> *and goat skinis, being destitude and tormented.*

The last time that we occupied this place, well-beloved in Jesus Christ, those of you who were present may remember that we spoke of Jephthah, the fourth of the judges cited by the apostle in verse 32. It would appear, therefore, that we should now go on to think about David and Samuel and the prophets. But it is not necessary that we should speak of David's faith by expounding his repentance, for it is sufficient to say that the whole Bible sets him apart on account of all that he was able to accomplish. Similarly, we do not need to speak of Samuel, a man who from his birth was consecrated and sanctified for the service of God, for his works also bear abundant witness to his faith. The same goes for the prophets, for all their writings and works testify to the sincerity of the faith. Therefore, to save time we will not speak of them at this time.

Now in the verses that we have just read, the apostle is hurrying on to conclude this eleventh chapter and his discourse on faith. Therefore, in the interests of brevity he no longer names those to whom is referring, as he has done up to this point, but mentions only the results of their works of faith. Thus he describes them not by their names but by their lives and deeds. So far the apostle's method in showing how these persons were justified by faith has been to name them first, then to recount what they have done. But now he will only recount what these others have done in order that we may see their deeds were accomplished through their faith, and that it was through faith they were justified.

Faith evidenced in both deeds and suffering

The apostle brings before us two kinds of results that flowed from the fountain of faith. First were the notable deeds and singular actions through which these faithful believers gave evidence of the strength of their faith. Second were sufferings and torments that bore testimony to the efficacy and power of the faith of these faithful men and women. Therefore, because the constancy and valour of faith is not only seen in deeds but also in suffering, he concludes this chapter with a catalogue of these two evidences of faith that proceeded from prophets, kings and judges. However, before he comes to this, he records in general three other things.

First, he mentions their conduct after it had pleased the Lord to call them, that is, what throughout their whole lives they strived and longed for most of all.[1] Second, he touches on the fountain from which this conduct and these longings flowed. Third, he indicates the results of these issues that their behaviour purchased and obtained from the merciful hand of God. After making these three general points, he takes us to the sacred record and sets down in more detail the actions by which the fruits and greatness of their faith were evidenced. He expresses the manner of their conduct in these words: *Which throuch faith subdewit kingdomis, wroucht richtiousnes*. These two phrases are making two general points.

Subduing kingdoms

In the first of these regarding their conduct he says that they *subdewit kingdomis*. We can take this literally, for it is absolutely true that some

[1] Bruce's phrase is 'to quhat studeis they wer addictit.'

of the judges, kings and prophets overcame kingdoms. He is referring to those kingdoms which had been earlier promised to Abraham, Isaac and Jacob and had been given to the Israelites by the grace of God. There had been several kingdoms lying within the bounds of Canaan, and these were conquered by valiant men. Moses, Joshua and David are all recorded as winning kingdoms. So when we understand this phrase literally, it is quite true that various faithful men subdued kingdoms.

However, if we take this phrase figuratively, we find that it contains great instruction, and to interpret it in this way is quite in accordance with the nature of Scripture. In the Bible, the word 'kingdom' often refers to where we presently live here on earth, for in this world great wickedness is to be found. There is no greater evil than the devil's kingdom of darkness, for here on earth many kings and their kingdoms remain as slaves to the darkness in which they were conceived and born, and these kings are instruments of Satan, fighting to do his will. So when we take this word *kingdomis* as the realm of the greatest evils in our world, its meaning in the verse will also be that faithful men dedicated themselves to opposing that manifestation of wickedness that dared to rise up to oppose the Lord God. Thus, in saying that they *subdewit kingdomis*, the apostle tells us that they hated all sin and valiantly devoted themselves to fighting against the power of Satan, and by their faith they succeeded in overthrowing the influence of the kingdom of darkness.

Enforcing justice

The second point regarding their conduct consists in this: they *wroucht richteousnes*.[2] He means that they occupied themselves in whatever pertained to their calling and vocation, that is, they engaged in what was honest, holy and godly, things that made for harmony and unity with their brethren. As they hated and opposed evil, so they loved and sought to promote what was good; as they overcame and punished evil, so they rewarded and encouraged godliness and virtue. This then was the way these faithful men of old lived, for all their efforts and longings were that evil should be abhorred, whereas what was good should be

[2] ESV translates as 'enforced justice'; Bruce is therefore correct in understanding the phrase as 'punishing evil and rewarding good'.

cherished and loved. If they were magistrates, they punished[3] misdeeds and all that was wicked, yet they were so inclined to love goodness that they rewarded it.

Those today who do not share these same inclinations cannot be men of faith. Unless this transformation of attitude has been wrought in the heart and affections, so that in some measure at least men abhor what is wrong and love what is good, in vain they boast that they have faith, because without faith no one can genuinely be upright or a true office-bearer. It is these two dispositions of character, abhorrence of evil and love of good, that mark out a man as blessed and like Christ his Master. For when we hate what God hates and love what he loves, we are at one with him, and if we are at one with him then we are partakers of his nature and his Holy Spirit.[4]

There cannot be peace and reconciliation with God apart from the intervention of his own Spirit, therefore when my attitude towards good and evil are in agreement with God, it lets the world see that God and I agree, and that I am at one with him in heart and spirit, and therefore I am a partaker of his nature. It is this attitude and outlook that makes a man in his Presbytery examination[5] a happy man. For the greatest happiness to be counted is being at one with God. Thus sharing the Lord's attitudes marks out a man, office-bearer or magistrate as faithful. It is from such a godly attitude and outlook that true justice and religion emanate. For unless you hate evil how can you punish it, and except evil be punished how can justice be maintained unless you act as a faithful magistrate? All depends upon love for God and for

[3] No doubt Bruce's conception of punishment was purely retribution—'an eye for an eye'. The contemporary emphasis on the curative element of punishment would probably not have been an intended factor, though protection of society from dangerous persons may well have been.

[4] This is another example of Bruce's oft repeated syllogistic form of reasoning: I love God's nature and love what God loves; and hate what he hates; therefore I am at one with God. He continues in the same vein in the next sentence. (See also Chapter 22, Note 7 above.)

In love and in hate I am at one with God.
Therefore if I am at one with God I partake of his nature.

[5] Bruce's word is 'privie' and refers to a meeting of a presbytery at which each member was examined separately and questions put to his fellow-presbyters as to his way of conducting himself both in his church duties and in his private life. (DSL 1.)

godly men, for only out of these attitudes can come both justice and genuine religion.

The failure of magistrates

When a magistrate neither hates evil nor loves godliness, it is not possible that the commonwealth can be in a healthy state. For as so many men nowadays are evil in their inclinations with their hearts addicted to some sort of wickedness, our country is bound to be inundated with crime. That is why there is no recourse or help for upright citizens, since there is no one with a sword in his hand to punish or deter evildoers. And when godly attitudes are absent not only in the lower ranks of magistrates but also in the higher ranks, the outcome can only be bleak for the administration of the nation; law and order is bound to collapse.

All this causes me to wonder whether our commonwealth will decay, and whether the disorder, long expected, will cause widespread chaos. We have been constantly warning that such lawlessness rampant among us will end up degrading and humiliating us. Widespread confusion will overtake us sooner than we might think, unless God puts into the hearts of our magistrates the right kind of attitudes towards good and evil, which alone can restore law and order among us.

Our king needs to change his attitude towards good and evil

This time and place are not appropriate for him to hear this exhortation, but it will be sufficient if this teaching is passed on to him.[6] If he was present among us he might see that his own attitudes to good and evil need to be changed. He needs to crave of God that these righteous attitudes might be bestowed upon him. It is also necessary that you who are present today, while you have the opportunity at this time, should also beseech God in his mercy so to multiply upon him the spirit of government, that from the fountain of that same spirit, justice and true religion may flow. For on these two pillars alone—justice and true religion—stands the commonweal. (Without them, we can bid farewell to our nation's wellbeing!). If these two things abounded in him, the Lord could well through him bring us the enjoyment of wonderful blessing, and cause him to be considered a prince of justice and

[6] It is clear that in both this paragraph and the one following that Bruce is referring to King James.

true religion, acknowledged not only by his subjects, but also throughout other nations.

No doubt it is our own sins that are responsible for this negligence in the prince's person, and no doubt it will also be our sins that will soon bring upon us this chaos that has long been looming over us. It may be, however, the Lord in his mercy may pour down upon us the spirit of repentance, as he has done in past times, and touch us with a far greater sense of remorse than we have at this present time. Just now, I think, both pastors and people are asleep, for at the present time there is hardly anyone touched with the awareness and feeling of the miserable state of our country.

A call to self-examination

So as we depart from the subject of our magistrates, each one of you for your own instruction must remember that you must abhor evil to some extent, and likewise love good to an equal extent. So examine your hearts to enquire what is the good that you love and what is the evil that you hate. Ask yourselves this question, 'Is there the inclination in me to hate what is good, and to cherish what is evil? If that is not so, am I still a child of the devil?'

Then ask yourself also, 'Is there such a disposition in my heart that I can truthfully say I love God and those who are godly, and I yearn for that godliness in others?' Can I say that God has given me a measure of hatred of all that is wicked? For when there is even a little abhorrence of sin, then there is within you a godly hatred of evil. If you cannot answer these two questions affirmatively, you may be sure that God has never entered your life. Then it will not matter though you have all the outward, temporal gifts in this world, indeed as many gifts as the devil himself has, unless your attitude changes these gifts will benefit you no more than they benefit the devil. For there is no created being that can rival him in gifts and knowledge, wisdom and strategy, yet because he does not have that righteous disposition of his affections towards good and evil, he remains for ever the devil and the originator of all wickedness.

Spiritual warfare in the hearts of believers

Do not think it is sufficient merely to know what you ought to love and what you ought to hate, unless, that is, you are ready and willing in your heart to love the good and hate the evil. It is over this that the battle is fought in our secret hearts. Of course there is no battle at all within the hearts of those whose inclinations are set upon evil. However, in those whose hearts are torn between good and evil, one side set on ill, and the other side set on good, in them the battle is raging between the new man and the old man. In believers the new man is urging them towards the good and to follow their calling, and the old is urging them back towards the ill and to follow their sinful desires.

Except you resist evil and oppose evil with all your strength, do you think you will be able to *subdewit kingdomis*, when you yourself are not yet a 'king', or do you imagine that you will be the victor in winning others, when you have not made a conquest of yourself? Examine yourselves! Is there in you a genuine hatred of what is evil? It goes without saying that in the heart where there is that spiritual hatred of evil, opposition to it will arise, and there will be wrestling and conflict against it. Then if you are engaged in this conflict, you are indwelt by the Spirit, for there is no battle other than by his power.

If you have the Spirit then you have his life also, for the Spirit himself is life, and where this life has once been given, the Lord shall never take it away. So the only battle for us is against evil, and we continue to stand firm as long as we are engaged in that warfare. This spiritual wrestling (as the apostle says[7]) is clear evidence of the Spirit's presence, and it also shows that we have been endued with faith, for there can be no resistance against evil other than through faith, and there is no vigour within us to engage in this battle other than by virtue of the Spirit's presence within us.

But are there some of you and your hearts feel no remorse, neither do you have any sense of opposition or revulsion towards evil? You are stone cold regarding this spiritual battle. Then, as you were conceived and born in spiritual death, you still remain in that state of spiritual death. For the human life we got from our parents is not spiritual life, for we are all born subject to physical death and, following that, to an eternal death of both body and soul. Therefore, if the only life you have is this physical life and there is no spark in you of spiritual life, it would have been better for you never to have heard these words that proclaim

[7] Ephesians 6:12. See also Galatians 5:16-25.

and expound eternal life. So take heed and ask yourselves whether there is in your hearts the desire to abhor all that is wrong, and whether you do long to resist and fight against it, until ultimately you overcome it. If not, not only will you have listened today in vain, but what you have heard will add weight to the just sentence of your condemnation, and being present here today will have contributed not one whit to your salvation.

As you leave this place, take this exhortation away with you: 'I have now heard that hatred of all evil is the mark of a man of faith. I know that my desires yearn for what is wrong. Then either I must deal with my wayward desires, otherwise (as he who spoke assured me according to God's Word), I am bound to be condemned forever. Therefore, in my heart I must turn away from all evil, and though my will is stubborn I will subdue it, and though my desires are very strong I will stop them in their course. I will avoid all the occasions and activities that stir up this licentiousness in me, and I will earnestly beseech the Lord to increase in me the spirit of sanctification, that I may learn to hate those things I have loved.' Make this your resolution, for if you do not you will be condemned and will perish for ever. Moreover, your condemnation will be all the more severe because these truths have been told you, and you refused to obey them.

These faithful men were not justified by works

The apostle tells us that, because these holy men of whom he is writing hated evil and loved what is good, they *wroucht richteousnes*. Does that mean that they were justified by their works? The papists conclude that they were, but their conclusion is quite wrong, for they have taken no account of the phrase, *throuch faith*, the apostle's antecedent, and so have neglected what we might call 'the master-sinew'.[8] Just as a strong sinew or tendon connects the bone to the muscle, likewise it is faith that connects a man to righteous works. But the papists have ignored that. The text does not simply say that these men *wroucht richteousnes*, but that *throuch faith they wroucht richteousnes*. It is this antecedent, *throuch faith*, that they have omitted. If they had said (as does the text)

[8] John Donne uses a similar metaphor in his 4th Meditation, 'Medicusque vocatur' in a work dedicated to Prince Charles, in gratitude for kindness shown to him by his 'Royall Father', James I, in 1624. *Donne*, p. 19.

that righteousness was wrought through faith, they and I would be in full agreement, but by neglecting this spiritual tendon they have reached a false conclusion.

The believer's imperfect righteousness[9]

There was never yet anyone declared righteous before God on account of his works. Nevertheless, there is a righteousness arising from works that is accredited to us in this life. There can be no doubt that after the Spirit of sanctification has been bestowed on a man, the measure of his sanctification will thereafter be the measure of his righteous conduct, and as his sanctification increases so also will the manifestation of the righteousness of his works also increase. For it cannot be denied that as our sanctification grows, a measure of righteousness is bestowed upon us, that we might live holy and upright lives in this world.

Yet this righteousness is not able to justify us before God, because right up to the time when we are about to die it remains imperfect and is still only in its rudimentary stages. However, could something we have that is imperfect justify us before a perfect God? There is no righteousness in any man that is able to justify him before his infinite majesty. Therefore it is absolutely necessary that the holiest human being must have recourse to him who is both Man and God, which is why his righteousness is called 'the righteousness of God', for only the righteousness of God is able to satisfy God. Unless we are partakers of his righteousness, it is impossible that we should ever be justified before him.

The two requirements for perfect justification

How, then, can I become a partaker in his righteousness, and how will I

[9] Calvin states that when through the free remission of our sins we are accounted as righteous, 'through [God's] Holy Spirit he dwells in us and by his power the lusts of our flesh are each day more and more mortified; we are indeed sanctified… with our hearts formed to obedience to the law… But even while by the leading of the Holy Spirit we walk in the ways of the Lord, to keep us from forgetting ourselves and becoming puffed up, traces of our *imperfection* remain to give us occasion for humility.' Further,' he says, 'while [the saints] examine themselves before God, the purity of their own conscience brings them some comfort and confidence.' *Inst.* III.XIV.9, 18. (¶ 18 has the heading, *The sight of good works, however, can strengthen faith.*) In ¶ 19, he quotes Proverbs 14:26, 'In the fear of the Lord one has strong confidence.'

ever be declared righteous before him when it is impossible for anyone to be acquitted before his tribunal who is not already clothed in his righteousness? To understand this, take heed, so that you may learn that there are two requirements for anyone to be justified before God. First, there is something needed that is missing in you, and another thing required that is not at present in you. I shall make this clearer.

In order for you to be justified before God, something which is present in you needs to be absent, and something which is absent in you needs to be present. Yes, it is sin that is present in us all, for it is rooted in our fallen natures and dwells within us as long as we live, but we must crave that it might be absent. Just as sin's absence in us must be craved, what is absent—the righteousness of God—must also be craved that it might be present. Now this is very tricky, to make what is present absent, and what is absent present! Yet the Lord of heaven who is wonderful in his ways of working, has found the means of counting absent what is actually present, and then declaring that the thing that is absent has become present.

He has done this by the free remission of sin, that is, sin which is undoubtedly present, to be counted as absent, *quoad*[10] condemnation, thus cancelling out our condemnation. Again, we are told that the righteousness of Christ (that is, the righteousness of God) is the end of the law, for, says the apostle, 'Christ is the end of the law for righteousness to all who believe'.[11] It is true that this perfect righteousness which is only present in Jesus Christ for it is inherent in him, could only be made ours by inhesion,[12] as it can never in actuality be present physically in us. Impossible as that might seem, the Lord has created a way whereby this same perfect righteousness may be granted to us, counted as ours and grows in us to such an effect as if it was blooming and bearing fruit in our natures. So the first requirement is fulfilled in that sin is absent by free forgiveness, and the second requirement is fulfilled by gratuitous imputation. These are the two seeds of perfect justification.

[10] *Quoad*, a legal term used in the written pleadings of an action to indicate the point beyond which the defender makes no further admission of the pursuer's allegations.

[11] Romans 10:4. τελος, 'termination' in the sense of a temporal end, but also 'fulfilment' as in Luke 22:37. Grimm-Thayer.

[12] 'Inhesion' in a legal context is used either of qualities that exist in someone, or of rights that are vested in someone.

Now here comes a question. You may ask, 'These two seeds are indeed very good but how can I be sure they are mine, so that I know my sin shall never rise up against me either in this world or in the world to come, nor bring me into confusion and condemnation? Also, how can I be sure that the righteousness of Christ has been freely imputed to me, and that there is nothing lacking in my perfect justification?' I answer that just as he freely forgives our sins and imputes to us the righteousness of Jesus Christ, at the same time God imparts faith to our hearts, and increases that faith, so that we may have the assurance of our forgiveness and justification. So there you have the three aspects of our perfect justification: the two seeds, free forgiveness and free justification plus a true living faith that grasps hold of these two seeds. If you are not justified before God in this way, you have no firm ground on which to stand.

The benefits of our imperfect righteousness[13]

There may be times when your conscience is assaulted by the memory of all your past sins and the prospect of God's wrath looms before you, then your only stance and recourse must be to flee to Jesus Christ, the righteous one, in whom is God's promise of forgiveness and justifying grace to all who believe. As for this as yet imperfect righteousness of ours, of what use is it? Its actions and outworking are given as a pledge and guarantee[14] that Christ's perfect righteousness already pertains to us, for without that guarantee our consciences would not be able to accept that his righteousness had already been counted as ours.

On the other hand, if your conduct began to fall far short of God's commands to you, so that you had ceased to live in the manner to which he has called you, then your conscience would no longer be assured of your forgiveness and the free imputation of Christ's righteousness. This is because when a man constantly engages in evil-doing, his conscience is clouded by fear and vexation as he turns away from God as if he was his enemy. When that happens he loses his hold on faith, without which he can have no assurance of forgiveness and justification.

That is why we are given this imperfect righteousness that our

[13] See Note 9 above, but also see (as quoted in Note 9) *Inst.* III. XIV. 18.

[14] Ephesians 1:14, '… the promised Holy Spirit, who is the guarantee of our inheritance until we acquire possession of it.' (ESV)

consciences may be kept in tune with peace and serenity; then when we are provoked by our inner corruption or tempted by the devil, by faith we flee to Christ to seek his grace. Although this imperfect righteousness is given to us as a pledge of our justification, and to afford us peace of conscience, by no means are we in any sense justified by works that proceed from our godly conduct. No, it is only by the works that come from our Saviour that we have assurance through a living faith. Thus far for the second point.

Two further benefits through faith

Having dealt with the apostle's two general points,[15] a third point arises, namely the fountain that is touched upon by the apostle's words *throuch faith*. First, it is as if he said that all their strivings and yearning did not spring from the fountain of their natures. Hatred of evil is not a work of the natural man, for the Fall has produced only children of wrath and slaves of the devil. We read in 2 Timothy 2:24-26 that the pastor is exhorted to be meek and longsuffering towards all men in the hope that the Lord would grant them repentance, that they may escape from the snare of the devil, for they have been captured by him to do his will. Also in Ephesians 2:3 we read that humanity is described as 'children of wrath'. Therefore, our fallen natures do not produce in us this hatred of evil, but rather the contrary that we should indulge ourselves in evil. Likewise in Colossians 1:21 we read that by nature all men's hearts are bent[16] on doing evil.

Therefore, this alteration in our inclinations to hate evil does not spring from the fountain of our fallen natures, but from grace and faith. Even though a man has attained to the highest honour this world affords and possesses every luxury there is, without this grace all his prestige and wealth avail him nothing. So crave this grace without which you are graceless! Even though you possess very little, if you have grace you are sure of God's favour, upon which rests all our felicity. Pray, then, for this grace that you may be able to some extent at least to abhor evil, and if you are a magistrate to punish evil-doers and cause

[15] See above: 1. They subdued kingdoms, 2. They wrought righteousness.

[16] The clauses referred to in Colossians 1:21 are translated by ESV as 'you were alienated and hostile in mind, doing evil deeds,' but in Geneva Bible are translated as 'you were in timis past strangers and enemies, because your minds wer set in euil workes'.

good men and godliness to flourish.

Second, I bid you observe that faith is within a man's heart; it is not an attribute of his importance, status or power. Faith enables you to see what you did not see before, and to understand things of which you were once ignorant. From within your heart it causes you to love what formerly you did not love, and to hate what you did not hate. So genuine faith can actually alter our affections, which is quite wonderful, for to accomplish such a change is something human nature itself cannot do.

Further, what I mean is this: faith enlightens our minds to give us a clear understanding as to what we should do, and what we should leave undone. Not only does it guide us by our knowledge of what is right, but in some measure it enables us to desist from evil by giving us a love for all that pertains to what is good. How does a man experience heavenly joy? Only by love, for God is love. So do you have this love for God and have you his nature so that as a believer you may enter his rest?

It is through love for God that we may partake of his nature, and consequently, because we now abhor what is wicked and corrupt, we seek to eschew it. It is this change in a man's affections that make him blessed, for abhorrence of the devil makes us avoid him, and the love of God in our hearts makes us partakers of his nature and his kingdom. Therefore, when a man's affections have never been changed, he has never experienced justifying faith. Our Master has foretold that the days are coming when faith will scarcely be present on the earth.[17] Indeed, justifying faith has always been scarce on the earth, as men's deeds testify.

But Christ our Master meant more than justifying faith. He meant that even the understanding men have in common with the devil shall be smothered and extinguished by a flood of wickedness, so much so that there will hardly be anyone who knows there is a God and godliness, or a devil and devilry. Such a time is already near, for today many doubt the existence of Satan, and if a man doubts the devil exists he will soon also doubt whether there is a God. This causes me to suspect that our habitual evildoings have blocked all knowledge out of men's minds, and consequently we have become even more degenerate than

[17] Luke 18:8b.

unregenerate human beings.[18] For pagans are not so blind that they do not follow the light that is innate within them.[19] But our generation, by despising both the natural light within us as well as the heavenly light given to us, has been cast into a deep darkness by the just judgment of God.[20] That is why faith has already become so scarce that men doubt the existence of both God and the devil. This is why I think that the end and consummation of the world is close at hand.

Particular experiences of God's mercy for those who have faith

A third point is this. Those who were resolved to do God's will received his promise. Now here I am not referring to that general promise of eternal life that was given to all the faithful, but rather to the particular promises of the Lord's favour towards those who were depending wholly upon him and walking in obedience according to their calling. These people had particular experiences of God's mercy. When they were in dire extremities and in urgent need of divine intervention, they found the Lord was present with them. The apostle is thinking, for example, of Daniel in the lions' den and of the three men who were thrown into a fiery furnace. As he had promised Daniel, the Lord was with him, and so too the fury of the flames was quenched, though not for those who cast them into the furnace.[21] Also Hezekiah, when he knew he was in the final throes of death, was restored to life by the Lord's power.[22] So we find that there is no one who waits upon the Lord as his servant and faithfully follows his calling, who in his extremity will not find proof of God's favour towards him.

If you put your trust in men, you will find they are nowhere to be found when you most need them. For what tends to happen with so-called friends is that they keep up their acquaintance with you so as long as you are of some use to them, but when they think they no longer need you, they cast you off. Whereas our gracious God is of a completely contrary nature: in our hour of greatest need, he is our

[18] His thinking here is probably derived from Romans 1:18-23.

[19] John 1:4-5

[20] Romans 1:24, 'Therefore God gave them up...', though Bruce does not pursue Paul's thought at this point, but is rather seeking to amplify his allusion to Luke 18:8b. See Note 17 above.

[21] Daniel 3:8-30; 6:16-24.

[22] Isaiah 38:1-5 = 2 Kings 20:1-6.

most faithful friend. Those who serve the living God will never be in need here on earth, nor shall they lack honour in the world to come. What! Do you hope for honour both here and there? If you wait upon the Lord in your hour of greatest need you may be sure of both, for he will be there with you, and when you are alone the Spirit of God will comfort you.

This kind of doctrine ought to be accompanied by exhortation, but unless my heart is awakened by the spirit of exhortation, I am unable to exhort you, and you are unable to accept it. It is true, none of you are young in years, but I would that you truly knew what God is, and also what is his calling, for there is not one of you who does not have some calling or other, assuming you are serving the Lord in which ever station or rank in life he has given you. Therefore, if you think back you may remember some experience you had when his mercy and favour was particularly shown to you.

Have you learned true gratitude?

What ought such experiences to have taught you? Did they teach you to anger God? Or did they teach you to follow your own desires and affections? Or did they even teach you to serve the devil? Of course not! Then if you complain against him, you are of all people in this world most ungrateful, for not only has he withheld from you his judgments, but also you have experienced mercies you did not deserve. Where will all this end for you who have neglected his kindnesses? In your final hours your conscience will accuse you before God's just tribunal. For when you rebel against God's truth, and with obdurate hearts refuse to benefit from his mercies, your consciences will finally cry out, 'Fie upon my slavery to my passions! For now I see there is no longer mercy left for me!' With other such howls of despair will you meet your end.

Therefore, do not only record in a notebook—as I do—these special experiences of God's mercy and favour towards you, but also write them in your hearts, that they may be pledges of his unchanging love for you. Serve and love him, for in your hour of greatest need he will be with you. Honour him and he will honour you,[23] serve him and he will reward you, for the more you are devoted to his honour and service, the more you will be honoured both here and now and finally in heaven.

[23] 1 Samuel 2:30.

Faith exhibited through suffering

As to all the other deeds recorded in the verses of our text, I have said enough about them and will not speak of each one individually. Just as the faith of these men was exhibited in their actions, so it is also shown in their sufferings. For a person's valour is not only seen when he is fit, healthy and thriving, but also when he is burdened with illness and distress. Therefore the apostle records for us their sufferings which bore witness to their faith as well as their courageous actions accomplished when they themselves were prospering.

While it pleased the Lord to lay many kinds of sufferings upon his servants, they can be considered under three headings: first, suffering prior to their deaths; second, death itself; third, various kinds of banishment.

The first, suffering prior to death, can be subdivided into three kinds of trial. It pleased the Lord to let them be tried by torture, second by mocking, scoffing and slander which is as spiteful a trial as any, and third by imprisonment, bonds and scourging.

Under the second heading of death itself, there are various ways in which death could be inflicted: one, by the sword, another, by stoning as we read of Naboth,[24] or a third, by being sawn asunder as we read of Isaiah, not in Holy Scripture but in Jerome, one of the early Fathers.[25] As to the other two means of executing faithful men, the common experience of many martyrs bear witness to them. So it pleased the

[24] 1 Kings 21:1-14.

[25] Allusions in rabbinic literature to Isaiah contain various expansions, elaborations and inferences that go beyond what is presented in the text of the Bible itself. For example, in the Talmud we read that Rabbi Simeon ben Azzai found in Jerusalem an account in which it was written that King Manasseh killed Isaiah: "King Manasseh said to Isaiah, 'Moses, thy master, said, "There shall no man see God and live." Exod. 33:20; but thou hast said, "I saw the Lord seated upon his throne".' Isa. 6:1; and went on to point out other contradictions—as between Deut. 4:7 and Isa. 40:6; between Exod. 33:26 and 2 Kings 20:6. Isaiah thought: 'I know that he will not accept my explanations; why should I increase his guilt?' He then uttered the Unpronounceable Name, a cedar-tree opened, and Isaiah disappeared within it. Then King Manasseh ordered the cedar to be sawn asunder, and when the saw reached his mouth Isaiah died; thus was he punished for having said, 'I dwell in the midst of a people of unclean lips.' (Yeb.49b)." It became a generally received opinion of the ancient Christian writers, that Isaiah was sawn asunder. Among those who refer to such a death are Justin Martyr, Origen, Athanasius and many others. In Jerome, alluded to here by Bruce, reference to Isaiah's cruel death occurs in *Isaiah*, fol. 101, and *Matthew*, Homil. 26. fol. 51.

Lord to show forth the steadfast faithfulness of his servants by their being subjected to various kinds of death.

Under the third heading of sufferings, it pleased him to make their faith apparent through undergoing banishment. Here I take banishment to refer to flight to escape persecution, and not the kind of flight arising from a personal decision.[26] There are two categories of flight, the first being from city to city or from man to man, as our Master mentions in Matthew 10:23, saying, that when we are persecuted in one town we must flee to the next. However, there is a second kind of banishment much more dangerous, when on account of their enemies men do not live in towns, but are compelled to flee to the mountains to hide in dens and caves of the earth along with wild animals. He combines with these two forms of banishment the loss of basic necessities such as clothing, for they went about wearing skins of sheep and goats. They were also in want of food, for he says they were destitute and afflicted. So by these extraordinary banishments these believers bore witness to their faith.

What causes their heavenly Father to lay these sufferings upon his servants? There were two reasons. First, it was that they might receive a better resurrection (verse 35), and second, he withdrew them from the world of men because they were not worthy of them (verse 38). By 'a better resurrection' he means 'a better deliverance', but not from the sentence of absolution passed by some earthly judge. It was not that the Lord was angry or displeased with them, nor that he took pleasure in their sufferings, rather it was on account of the infinite love that he bore for his own children. He purposed to make their souls partakers of the resurrection of the just, and of that heavenly and highest felicity. This is what is meant by 'a better resurrection'. It pleased him to allow them to suffer under the unjust sentence of an earthly judge, so that they might become partakers of the gracious sentence of the heavenly Judge.

The Kirk's privations today

The teaching that arises from all this may be expressed in the following way. It is indeed true that the Lord chastens his Kirk by various afflictions, banishments and martyrdoms. And when men consider from the human point of view the effect on the Kirk of her sufferings, they

[26] See Chapter 21, Notes 17, 24 above.

conclude that she will not survive. They say, 'Half of her members have been slain and the rest have been banished, therefore the evangel has failed.' However, on the contrary, what men think is the Kirk's final humiliation and the overthrow of the evangel, the Lord by these same afflictions brings honour to his servants, progress to his Kirk and the advancement of the gospel. The apostle affirms this same principle in Philippians 1 where he writes that through his sufferings the gospel has been advanced.[27] Thus the suffering of the saints, though ignominious in the world's eyes, are but the saints' honours, for they are decorated by them more than by any earthly pearl or jewel.

Therefore we see that afflictions are invariably profitable as far as the Kirk of God is concerned and also profitable to men, but only faithful men; they are certainly not profitable to the wicked of this world. These benefits for the Kirk do not come from the nature of her sufferings, but from God's mercy that accompanies them. This is because when we are afflicted God's mercy imparts his favour, which is why the cross itself is not the cause of honour, but the mercy of God that accompanies the cross. The Lord's chastening does me far more good than if I was left to run loose as men of the world do. So if God ever afflicts you in some way, ask him to do so in mercy, and also that your affliction may be accompanied by the presence of his Holy Spirit, so that you may know it comes from a loving Father and not from an angry judge.

Have you had experience of his mercy in your afflictions? They will bring you honour, for the cross always brings honour to the faithful and thus benefits the Kirk. Therefore do not let the Christ's Kirk attempt to cast off the cross, rather kiss and embrace the cross for it is sanctified by the cross of Jesus Christ. The lot and cavil[28] of the Kirk always underlies the cross, for without it there cannot be any Kirk. If you have no experience of this, you cannot be truly a child of God, for all the descriptions and images we are given of the Kirk invariably depict her bearing a cross that brings affliction which God uses in her preparation to be a virgin bride on that great Day. Sometimes she is pictured as a boat tossed between wind and rocks, other times like a woman in

[27] Philippians 1:12, also verses 12-18.

[28] A lot and cavil were used in the assignment of shares in merchandise; the cavil was a small round piece of wood used to determine the lot. Here the meaning will be the nature of the portion of the affliction allotted by the Lord for his church.

danger of being devoured, yet other times as a bush in danger of being consumed, or like a besieged city whose walls are about to be breached, and else as a woman in travail.

Study all the various biblical metaphors of the Kirk and you will not find one of her without a cross to bear. Therefore the sufferings of those described in our text are as notable testimonies to their faith as are their outstanding deeds. Wisely, then, the apostle places their afflictions alongside their deeds, for he wants us to know that a valiant man is as distinguished by his sufferings as he is by great actions. By the various examples that the apostle gives us, he lets us see that the Lord does not necessarily deliver by saving our lives, for he can deliver by death as well as by preserving this temporal life. Nor will he always deliver from the lion's mouth or the fury of the flames, for he may permit both to strike. But be sure of this, whatever afflictions he chooses for us, he always will deliver. Nevertheless, however he works, he invariably imparts contentment to us, and if you are content you have all you need.[29] So do not try to tie him down to some particular way of dealing with you, only ask for his peace in your heart.

As you see some of the saints suffering, you will witness the cruelty of this world as it devises various punishments and tortures to execute God's servants. You will be witnessing how superstitious and idolatrous worshippers can act, for such mercilessness is the mark of false religion. When you find a religion practising cruelty, you will know it is from the devil and flows out of hell and human corruption, for it is a godless world that delights in such viciousness.[30]

Conclusion

My final point is this. In our hours of greatest extremity, where should we be looking? We must have our eyes fixed on this better resurrection. Even though the tyrants offered them their freedom, and they could have obtained it by renouncing the truth, these men refused mere temporal deliverance, for the prospect and expectation of a better deliver-

[29] 1 Timothy 6:6.

[30] Almost certainly a reference to the torturing, hanging, beheading and disembowelling of Protestants by Queen Mary, and Catholics by Queen Elizabeth, some 300 by the former, and several dozen by the latter; the implication must also surely be that in Bruce's opinion both the Roman and English churches were therefore in error.

ance made them despise the world. Therefore, let us in every extremity keep our eyes fixed on that eternal life that has been promised. Begin now to nourish and cherish that hope, and let the prospect of it grow, lest the blessed hope fade in your minds and be forgotten. The way to avoid this is to keep a good conscience by taking care not to do wrong knowingly.

Therefore, in daily pursuing your calling, stay within the bounds of your conscience, and constantly pray for sufficient grace to reach the life you hope for. Yearn for the conviction and vision of that life, for whenever the devil or the world targets your conscience, that vision shall comfort and uphold you with joy. Maintain your course with ever greater determination, and however difficult your trials may be, the Lord will always be at your side.

May the Lord in his mercy work all these things into our hearts, and make us earnest suitors[31] in time of need, that in our darkest hour we might find strength through these truths. May the Lord in his mercy grant this to us for the sake of Jesus Christ his Son, to whom with the Father and the Holy Ghost be all honour, praise and glory for now and ever. Amen.

---

[31] The word suitor ('sutter' in Scots) was a legal term for one chosen to act on someone else's behalf; it came to refer to someone who requested or asked to obtain some benefit. (DSL 1 & 3a.)

Chapter Twenty-Eight

Hebrew Chapter 11 verses 38-40

> [38] *Whom the world was not worthie of; They wandered in wildernes and mountainis, and dennis and cavis of the earth.* [39] *And these all throw faith obteined gude reporte and receavit not the promis.* [40] *God provyding ane better thing for ws that they without ws sould not be maid perfect.*

Well-beloved in Jesus Christ, there are only two ways whereby men and women may show forth and declare the faith that is within them. We either declare our faith by our deeds and works, or else we declare it by suffering patiently for the sake of righteousness and for Jesus Christ and his cause. Right from the beginning of this chapter, and now as he reaches his conclusion, the apostle portrays the faithful in these two ways: first, each person makes his faith known to the world by his deeds and his works, but secondly, as he draws this subject to a close he introduces us to a multiplicity of sufferings by which the faith of his servants in every past generation had been known. (This also applies to future generations.) For valour, fortitude and strength do not only reveal a man's character in the heat of battle or in the performance of noble deeds, but also in prayer, illness and the endurance of pain and torments, all for the sake of Jesus Christ and his righteousness.

In this respect, the apostle has let us see that the faithful in past times were subjected to three kinds of sufferings. There were tortures and inquisitions, there were cruel and gruesome deaths, and there were different kinds of banishment. The first of these fell into to three categories, trials by torture or various kinds of torment, trials by mocking, taunting and scoffing, and trials by imprisonment, bonds and scourging.

Next he set before us three kinds of death, stoning, being sawn asunder, and execution by the sword. Then there were two kinds of banishment, flight (for I regard flight from persecution as a form of banishment) from one city to another city where fellowship could be had with likeminded brethren, and flight away from all human contact in order to seek refuge in mountains and caves or in dens and holes of the earth. Thus he let us see how men and women of faith in former times had been subjected to such crosses and trials that bore witness to the strength of their faith in steadfast and patient suffering inflicted upon them by their torturers.

The lessons for us from such sufferings I shall not repeat. I have already entrusted them to your memories. Therefore we now proceed to consider briefly what remains in the three verses I have just read to you.

In verse 38 we are given the reason why the Lord withdrew these holy men from the earth. It was because the world was not worthy of them: *whom the world was not worthie of.* In the next verse, we have the final conclusion of his theme in this chapter with its entire catalogue of all these persons, whether they are named, or simply referred to by their sufferings and their deeds: *these all throw faith obteined gude reporte*; they were justified by faith in the promise. The promise in which they trusted was that Jesus Christ was to be manifested in the flesh, and their faith was in him even though he had not yet come, for they themselves *receavit not the promis.* Finally, in verse 40 we are given the reason why throughout their generations Christ was not manifested in the flesh with our humanity, as had been promised to the Fathers: *God provyding ane better thing for ws that they without ws sould not be maid perfect.* I take this to be a summary of these three final verses, for they divide themselves naturally into these three themes.

Why some escaped a cruel death but others died

Before we begin to consider the reason why the Lord withdrew his servants from cities, commonwealths or nations, and the means that he used either banishment, death or other kinds of persecution, we need to remind ourselves very particularly of the effects and working of this faith by which alone a man is declared righteous before God. For last time we saw in verses 33 and 34 it was by faith that these holy men subdued kingdoms, wrought justice, stopped the mouths of lions, quenched the violence of fire, escaped the edge of the sword and out of weakness were made strong. But then the apostle went on to say that by faith some were consumed by the fire, or devoured by lions or slain by the sword.[1] So how can we reconcile these two seemingly contradictory statements on the effect and working of faith?

The first observation

The contrast is that the first category of valiant men by faith escaped temporal death, inflicted either by lions, fire or sword, whereas the second category who submitted to various kinds of temporal death died but also in faith. The former were delivered temporally, the latter were not delivered temporally, yet both acted in faith. What then do we learn from this? We learn that faith does not always bring a temporal deliverance, nor is a temporal deliverance ever promised, so no one can claim from God what his word has not guaranteed.

However, what God has promised and what we can experience by faith, even if we are not going to be saved from a temporal death, nevertheless is that if death is threatened he will ensure that the outcome for us will redound to his glory and our encouragement. Therefore, we must always live within his will and purposes. For if the Lord knows that temporal deliverance will work more effectively for his glory, for your reassurance and for the edification of his Kirk than would your deliverance by temporal death, then he will grant you temporal deliverance.

On the other hand, if the Lord knows that temporal death will not only lead to your eternal deliverance, but will also promote his glory and grant you everlasting consolation more than would mere temporal deliverance, then submit to his will and accept the outcome that it has pleased him to choose for you. For it is sufficient for us to know that whether we live or die, we are at peace, for we may be quite sure that faith invariably brings us peace. If the Lord has ordained that you die, then he will grant you a contented heart, and you will be glad to leave this world rather than continue to live in it. Should it be his will for me to continue living here longer, then I will be content to serve him

[1] Clearly, Bruce is using preacher's license to paraphrase the following verses from 35b to 37 in order to bring out the paradox of the contrast between men of faith who were delivered and men of faith who apparently were not delivered.

longer, and offer him better service than I have given so far. Therefore, we cannot necessarily expect a temporal deliverance at the hands of God, or that faith will invariably produce a temporal deliverance from the hands of men. Nonetheless, faith will always yield a deliverance, whether it be by life or death, that will be most for God's glory and our eternal consolation. This my first observation.

The second observation

My second observation arises regarding the question as to how the sufferings of holy men were counted as the effect of their faith. It is evident that patient endurance is not always the result of faith, for if it was then the majority of the wicked would also be men of faith. There are plenty of examples of such endurance in all the history books. You who are older have witnessed that just as evil men can proudly walk upon this earth on their two feet, so they are also able to accept the court's verdict of condemnation as patiently as do men of faith. It does not matter what tortures are devised or to what inquisition they are subjected, you will hardly perceive any difference between the faithful and the faithless. Thus it is obvious that patience in suffering is not always the fruit of the faith of faithful men. Yea, there are other men who will patiently suffer the consequences of the most heinous crimes, their own consciences knowing full well how wicked they have been. Even though their consciences, the law and the prosecutor declare that they are suffering justly, yet, supported by Satan and his devilish power over their human flesh and blood (which is just the same as ours), they patiently endure any kind of gruesome death decreed by the court, rather than confess to their wickedness.

There are other kinds of felon who suffer quite justly for equally heinous crimes, yet their consciences will not admit that their deeds were scandalous, but sincerely believe in their hearts and consciences that the verdict imposed on them was unlawful and absurd, beyond all reason and wit. I give you an example. All of you must have heard of the person who killed the Prince of Orleans, and doubtless some of you have also heard of the pain he endured before he himself died, paying for his heinous act. You will have heard, too, of his patient endurance of his torture (for that nation is ingenious in inventing devices of torment), but in his suffering he showed no signs whatsoever of impatience or annoyance, although it was certain that his was a most heinous crime. Yet I think his conscience was not affected by his deed because he had been informed by the priests in Spain that his deed would be an offering of good service to God. Thus his conscience not being troubled in any way, he was unmoved in his suffering and remained steadfast.[2]

Therefore I conclude that there are two kinds of endurance of those who have committed wicked deeds. There are those who will patiently endure torture even though they know their consciences are accusing them, and there are others who endure without any pangs of conscience whatsoever, even though it is absolutely certain that their actions have been evil. My point is this, calm endurance of pain does not invariably mean that the sufferer has faith, for there is a distinct difference between the reaction to pain by men of faith on the one hand, and evildoers on the other hand. The former endure patiently because they have a sure and certain hope of their final deliverance with the joy of eternal life, whereas the latter do not have this true hope and therefore are destitute of genuine patience in their suffering.

I can give you a token of the truth of this that is incomprehensible to a wicked man of this world. Genuine spiritual patience is always accompanied with a profound joy that we are counted worthy of being like Christ in suffering with him here, in order that we might reign with

[2] The reference is to the assassination of Henri III of France in 1589. Prof. Jane Dawson helpfully commented to me that she considered 'it was significant that Bruce used the title "the prince of Orlians" rather than "King of France," possibly to downplay that this was an act of regicide.' The assassin, Friar Jacques Clement, was apparently killed immediately after the deed, committed because King Henri III had made an alliance with the Protestant Henri de Navarre, and the Treaty of Nemours (1589) had stipulated that all Calvinists had six months to choose between abjuration and exile. (The wider background was the fierce persecution in France of the Huguenots.) The assassin's body was thrown from the window of the room where the deed had been done, and some of the visual prints of the period show his corpse being pulled apart by four horses, the French punishment for regicide. Bruce's assumption that Clement suffered torture 'with no signs of impatience or annoyance' suggests he was relying on stories about the murder circulating at the time in both France and Scotland. The view of Spanish theologians that the assassination of those acting against the Roman Catholic faith was justified would have meant that Clement sincerely believed his conscience was clear, but of course Bruce and his congregation would have held that Jacques Clement was misguided because Roman Catholicism was by no means 'a good cause'.

him hence. This joy, peace and tranquillity in the heart is the mark and token of true patience, for it establishes such peace in the mind that it causes the sufferer's voice and gestures to display such serenity that a foretaste of heaven can be seen in his face.[3] But although the courage and calmness of some who endure intense suffering is undoubtedly counterfeit, this heavenly likeness glimpsed in the face of a genuinely godly sufferer cannot be counterfeit. Therefore, this is the mark that distinguishes the godly and faithful sufferers from the suffering of the ungodly, many of whom have shown outstanding courage and steadfastness, but have never themselves known or shown the joy and heavenly consolation of the godly.

Therefore the constant joy, created by the Holy Spirit to inspire patient endurance and righteous hope, is the distinguishing mark of the sufferings of the faithful. This is a most important point, for the profane of this world know nothing of the peace of mind and inward strengthening encouragement of God's Spirit; it cannot be counterfeited by the devil, for he is incapable of imparting it, which is why wicked men cannot ever experience it. Only the kingdom of Christ stands firm in the Spirit's joy and tranquillity of mind, for wherever his Spirit is present there will always be contentment and consolation.

You have read in the final verses of Hebrews 10 that the apostle wrote to his fellow countrymen to remind them of how they had joyfully accepted the plundering of their property and confiscation of all they owned. Why? Because they knew they had far better eternal possessions laid up for them in the heavens.[4] So this genuine joy of the Holy Spirit that is always conjoined with patient endurance cannot ever be experienced by any evil person of this world, whether man or woman.

To sum up this second observation, it is not sufficient only to suffer, but our trials must be borne with steadfast patience. I am not speaking about us putting up with all the slight and light daily troubles we may meet. That is not the kind of endurance we are considering. Rather

[3] Perhaps an allusion to Stephen, the first Christian martyr: 'And gazing at him, all who sat in the council saw that his face was like the face of an angel.' (Acts 6:15; 7:54-60.) Bruce would have known well of the deaths of Patrick Hamilton (1527), George Wishart (1546) and Walter Myln (1558), all burned at the stake in St Andrews. All died calmly and in serene faith as did Stephen.

[4] Hebrews 10:34.

it is the patient endurance that is inspired by the blessed hope of our ultimate eternal deliverance, for it is this endurance that is inseparable from the joy and consolation of the Holy Spirit. Wherever there is patient rejoicing in suffering, there can be no doubt that such suffering flows from faith.

The third observation

The third thing I mark is this. I perceive that the faithful, even though they are not subjected to these kinds of sufferings, crosses, trials or calamities, nevertheless will experience something or other. Those who are not tortured may be mocked or despised, others who are not mocked may end up being imprisoned after being beaten, and those who do not experience any of these may yet end up being killed, some of them by one kind of death and others of them by a different form of execution.[5] My point is that although faithful men and women were not subjected to every form of suffering, not one of them could be exempt from some trial or other, for all had to carry their own particular cross and endure the suffering fashioned and appointed for them, whatever its length, breadth or height,[6] in full measure.

There are none chosen for the kingdom of heaven who do not have their cross to bear, not just for a single day, but for as long as they live upon this earth. Even though this is a well-known doctrine, it is one that you here today never really take to heart or keep in mind. For as soon as you ride out one storm, there is another one already bearing down upon you. And when you have seen off one trial, you are apt to relax and be off your guard, so that you are not prepared for the next assault. The Word of God and Christ himself in all four Gospels command us to take up our cross daily, and either follow him bearing the cross, or else desert him.[7] Those who do not obey the voice of Christ saying, 'Take up your cross and follow me,' shall be compelled to obey his other command, 'Depart from me you workers of iniquity!'[8] Therefore, choose now the daily battle and cross, and stake your future on the

[5] Common in 15th and 16th century Britain, as well as death by beheading, were hanging, burning at the stake, disemboweling or slow death by torture.

[6] Bruce occasionally indulges in mixed metaphors!

[7] Matthew 10:38; 16:24; Mark 8:34; Luke 9:23; and by implication John 15:18-21.

[8] Matthew 7:23.

outcome of the first being the beginning of your trials.

It does not matter where we look, there is no other alternative to daily trials. Look up, or below, or look around you or beneath you, look inside or outside—look, yes look!—and you will see that there is no other option, but only a great abundance of trials, molestation and vexation. They will not have to be endured only by you, but also by our whole nation. For ever since the time that I was able to perceive and discern these things, I never saw greater stores of impending tribulations, or reasons for them, than I see today. That is why all of us must be forewarned to prepare ourselves to endure the cross that the Lord has prepared for us to carry.

Indeed, I already see as clear as the sun shining upon us this morning that the Lord of heaven is mightily at work uncovering our impiety, and delivering into our human hands gracious opportunities to do something about it. But I see also negligence among the great men, and little or no fidelity among the lower ranks of office-bearers and magistrates. Consequently, unless God from his heaven perform some extraordinary work by stirring up men's hearts and openly exposing these things, I fear we can only expect a terrible confusion. Judge for yourselves as to whether any good can come from this.

Therefore, unless these gracious opportunities for repentance that the Lord is granting us are used to the full, so that innocence may be recognised and wickedness be punished, I fully expect that we shall live to regret the confusion which will envelop us. This is why I am warning you all to prepare for trouble, and the cross we will have to bear. This applies to all, from the highest to the lowest, from prince to people, and from priests[9] to people, for we all justly deserve such troubles on account of our ill practices. Unless by these gentle chastisements and

[9] A surprising use of the word 'preist' (priest), as after the Reformation, the designation 'priest' generally referred exclusively to Catholic clergy. Could the reference and context then be deliberately directed towards toleration by King James and other dignitaries of the practice of Catholicism in certain areas of the country, and among certain aristocratic families such as Huntly and Errol? For example, when it came to light in 1589 that these two earls, along with others, were intriguing with Spain, they were briefly only imprisoned, for James soon released them. Though hard pressed by the Presbyterian preachers, the king refused to gratify the Kirk by dealing firmly these Catholic earls. His calculated leniency caused him years of trouble.

kindly corrections, some order is restored among us, we will perish along with the rest of the world.

Therefore let every one of us be prepared to take up our cross willingly. Crave contented hearts and resolute minds and souls, that are disposed patiently to accept the will of God. May all of you be able to say, 'I shall welcome whatever the Lord may send and appoint for me, and here on earth I am ready to endure it patiently.'

If however you are not prepared for it, crave of him that you may be willing, so that your will and his will may agree. For by doing the Lord's will and abiding within it, you may be able to bear witness to his comfort in your trials, and be assured of his enduring promise of eternal salvation. Take into your consideration, that even if it seems that there is no cross or trial for you, nevertheless it is impossible that any of us can avoid some cross or other, for even your own children and wife can become the very cross you imagine you do not have.

For my own part, my own emotions, cogitations and perturbations can be my cross, should I think I lack one. So it simply is not possible to avoid a cross, no matter what your station in life might be. Moreover, the cross is the only way to life everlasting, for had Christ seen some better means, or a more expedient pathway for us to tread on our way to heaven, he would not have constantly reiterated this lesson as often as he has done: 'Take up your cross and follow me!' If he who is our heavenly Prince and the King's only Son had known of an easier route, would not he himself have taken it? But he has left us his word and his example, showing that the way of the cross is the entrance to the kingdom of heaven. So let each of us take that way gladly as we follow him.

It will be of no help to you if you take up the cross grudgingly. Why grumble and complain? That will bring no mitigation of the pain. No! The more you murmur, the greater the pain will become. So crave contentment of the Lord that you may be enabled to bear your cross willingly, for then you will be granted patience and that will keep your heart in peace. Remember that peace in your heart is sure evidence of your eternal salvation. For the kingdom of heaven is marked by quietness of spirit, and Christ himself dwells in those who have a quiet and meek spirit, because it is in a calm and tranquil mind that the living God takes up his residence. Therefore, since there is no other way to heaven than by the cross, let us embrace it patiently, willingly and without complaining, resolved to be content to accept and abide by the Lord's will for us, whatever it may be. This then is the third lesson.

To sum up, every man shall not have to submit to the same kind of cross as others, for appointed for us all is our particular cross, made exactly for us in its length, breadth and height. Through bearing it we become conformed to Christ in his humility, for it stands to reason that those who are not like Christ in his humility will never be like him in his glory. Those who are not like him in enduring affliction will not be like him in his eternal peace, rest, joy and heavenly glory. His earthly humanity is the image we must bear in this life, so that in the hereafter we may be like him in his glory and joy, for in heaven the consolation of his face shall bathe us in overflowing gladness.

Although the afflictions we endure will continue as long as we live here on earth, they are profitable for us in conveying to us his grace. Those who are reluctant to submit to their cross must nevertheless carry it in spite of their unwillingness. On the other hand, the wicked who seek to avoid it, shall find themselves oppressed by even greater troubles. Seeing that bearing the cross we must, the more willingly we do so, the greater will become our patience in enduring it.

Remember, then, these three observations. First, faith does not always yield a temporal deliverance, but it does lead to an eternal deliverance. Second, endurance in suffering may be counterfeit, but only joy in suffering can flow from faith. Third, all afflictions are not the same, for each person has his own particular cross to bear, appointed specially for him.

Why God withdrew his light from the world

Why did God withdraw from this world the lights that illuminated its darkness? In verse 38 the apostle tells us: *whom the world was not worthie of.* The Lord did allow his servants to remain in the world and live among its people, as long as to a certain extent they were respected and their ministry was reverenced. While the people acknowledged his servants' commission was in the name of God and Jesus Christ, he permitted them to live on earth. But when the time came that people cast off any semblance of reverence for his servants and their ministry, in righteous justice God withdrew them from this unworthy world. Note this very carefully, for as soon as his servants were taken from some part of the world, that place was destined for destruction.

You can take this to be an inevitable consequence and token of divine judgment. For as soon as the Lord withdraws wise men who fear him, good servants who carry the burden of their commission in both Kirk and State, faithfully fulfilling their calling in the power of the Spirit, then chaos spreads across that land and it is doomed for destruction by fire or some other catastrophe. The reason is that God only preserves a country for the sake of his Kirk, and once the Kirk militant is withdrawn, that place is committed to the flames.[10] The Lord preserves his Kirk in this world for he has appointed her to show forth his glory and honour, and it is on account of her presence here that our land is not destroyed. His Kirk is found in one place after another, wherever he directs it to bear witness to him, and for her sake that place is preserved.

Whenever God withdraws his servants chaos descends

Take note and observe how from the four corners of the world, wherever and whenever he withdraws his evangel, his ministers and his servants, that place is destined to be destroyed. You will see this from the far west and to the far east beyond Judea and from the furthermost parts of Asia. As often as he removes his word from each place, destruction follows as wars and fighting break out, and fires spread that are not quenched. This causes me to expect confusion in a land very near to us, for there I see wise men being withdrawn, men endowed with the Spirit's power in their ministry; they are either departing from that country or else they are being brutally treated.[11] This is why I am antic-

[10] Bruce may well have in mind the destruction of the cities of the plain after Lot and his two daughters had been withdrawn from Sodom by the two angels. See Abraham's prayer in Genesis 18:22-33 that the cities be spared for the sake of ten righteous, and the account of the two cities' destruction in Genesis 19:23-29. See also 2 Peter 2:1-10, where both Noah and Lot, in Bruce's thinking, could well be depicted as representatives of the Church militant: 'Noah, a herald of righteousness' and 'righteous Lot, greatly distressed by the sensual conduct of the wicked… tormenting his righteous soul over their lawless deeds' (verses 5 and 7).

[11] It might be assumed that the reference here is to France where the Huguenots had been persecuted for decades. During a period of intense violence that became known as the Wars of Religion, on August 24, 1572 the massacre in Paris on St Bartholomew's Day saw the deaths of almost all the leading Protestants in the city, and further slaughter continued throughout France as Protestants were killed in their thousands. (https://www.britannica.com/topic/Huguenot) See also

ipating that confusion will descend on that land. It is the unworthiness of cities, countries, kingdoms and commonwealths that causes the removal of good and godly men from them. *Whom the world was not worthie of*, writes the apostle.

Regarding our own land, unworthy as we are, it does not appear that we have yet reached the lowest depths of worthlessness, though we are moving in that direction. Yet because some of our godly men are spared and not withdrawn, even though there are not many of them, I do not anticipate we will be smitten with an unexpected state of chaos. But undoubtedly if the Lord withdrew even a few of his servants to the extent that our unworthiness deserves, we could expect a terrible confusion to envelop our whole nation. Therefore, it is our duty to forestall that grievous judgment wherewith the Lord threatens our land, and which our sins justly deserve at his hand. It behoves us to humble ourselves in order to assuage his wrath, although if every rank in our commonwealth turns to him but his judgment falls upon us nonetheless, be sure that you will see the head[12] struck down and the members smitten, as sudden confusion quickly descends upon one and all. I can see how inevitable that would be.

Pray for our king

This looseness among us makes it abundantly clear that few, if any, give respect to God. Even among his subjects there is not even reverence for our king. This persuades me that if this state of affairs continues, the Lord will act in some way that will cause us all to quake and tremble. Therefore, it belongs to all of us, while we still have the opportunity and time, to beseech the Lord to preserve our prince, in whom there are so many good graces, and through whom the Lord has already wrought great things and will continue to work in the future. Yet without doubt our sins are to blame for the state of our nation. Therefore we must also crave God's pardon for our sins, and beseech him to multiply the graces of government upon our prince's person. Then he might be a blessing

Note 2 above. However, against Bruce's reference being to France, see Chapter 18, note 46 & Chapter 19, note 16 above and passage referred to. Perhaps, therefore, it is more likely that the reference is to Flanders. See Chapter 24, note 29 above.

[12] By 'head' does Bruce mean the king? In the light of the following paragraph, probably he does.

to us, and we might become a credit to him. However, if things continue as they are, doubtless our security shall be taken out of our hands. So much, then, for the unworthiness of cities and nations as the reason why the Lord removes from them men that are good and wise, and who have a concern for the wellbeing of their land. But I must move on.

God's thinking is contrary to ours

If you question men of the world, you will find that they consider those who serve God as unworthy of their company. However, God has a very different opinion, for he considers the whole world to be unworthy of the company of the lowliest of his servants. Consider how contrary to God's thinking are the thoughts of men, for they regard his servants as poor because outwardly they are in a humble state, destitute of all the trappings of affluence and grandeur. However, God's thinking is that for all their outward magnificence and pomp, worldly men are unworthy to be in the presence of his servants or to receive their words of comfort.

Why should this be so? It is because God's servants enjoy peace and glory in their consciences, of which the world knows nothing, for this glory is not intended to shine forth upon the world. If this was the hour for their inner glory to be made manifest, it would far surpass the world's glittering grandeur, but his servants' glory is reserved for that final day of eternal glory. Then those qualities that are presently concealed within their poor bodies and hearts shall burst forth to the confusion of those who have so despised them, to the honour and advancement of his servants who have cherished and nourished them.

Christ's coming promised since the creation

In the next verse, he concludes his treatise on faith by saying that all these men obtained a good report through faith in the promise that is in Christ Jesus, even though he had not yet come in the flesh. In saying, *these all throw faith obteined gude reporte*, he means that this great company of the Fathers were accounted as righteous and made partakers in that heavenly kingdom through faith in him who was still to come, though he was not yet manifested in human flesh. You must understand that even though Christ's incarnation, his coming down to take upon himself our flesh in the virgin's womb, was delayed for more than four thousand years, nonetheless it is certain that his coming was promised from the beginning of the world. Indeed, from the beginning of creation he was pledged for the whole elect, to be, as it were, their cautioner and guaranteed security.[13] It is true that although it was not until these latter times[14] he came in our flesh and paid our debt, yet in the former times he had already pledged himself to take our debt upon himself, for it was understood by the Fathers that he was the Lamb slain from the foundation of the world.[15]

As soon as man fell in Eden, he offered himself, for it was at once said, 'Thy seed shall tread upon the serpent's head'.[16] Thus the apostle says that by his death Jesus Christ overcame the devil who was the prince of death,[17] meaning that he trod down the serpent's head. Therefore, it was by his death and resurrection that he made complete payment and gave full satisfaction for all the debts of the elect of God, right from the beginning of time and until the end of the world. Even though that debt was not paid until these latter times, yet in the former times he had already pledged himself to pay it, and so, by taking our debt upon himself, he completely freed us from it. By his offering of himself once and for all,[18] the virtue of his payment reached from the world's beginning right to its end.

In respect that right from the beginning he took upon himself our debt, at the same time he pledged himself to die for us, which is why the apostle states that he was slain from the beginning of time. That is how from the very first of the Fathers, our forebears were counted as

[13] Bruce has, 'became debitor soveritie and cautioner for them.' In Scots law, a cautioner was one who becomes bound as a surety for another, for the performance of any obligation or contract contained in a deed.

[14] A theme now dwelt upon in the remainder of the sermon is the contrast between 'the former days/times' and 'the last days/times'. The NT writers frequently refer to the period between the ascension of Christ and his Second Coming as 'the last days' or 'last times', as the 'parousia' was understood to be constantly imminent. Hence the era prior to the incarnation was 'the former days or times'. See John 11:24; 2 Timothy 3:1; Hebrews 1:2; 1 Peter 1:5, 20; 2 Peter 3:3, *et al.*

[15] Revelation 13:8 (AV), also GenB, RV, NKJV. However, RSV, NIV and ESV have [whose] 'names have been written before the foundation of the world in the book of life of the Lamb that was slain'.

[16] Genesis 3:15.

[17] The allusion is to Hebrews 2:14.

[18] Hebrews 9:26; 10:14.

free from their sins, for Christ Jesus had already, in effect, taken their sins upon himself. Although they had been set free from their sins, Christ was not yet free from them, for he remained their debtor until he finally discharged the debt in these latter times, that is, in our times when he died in our nature, was raised in our nature, ascended in our nature, and now in our nature sits at the right hand of the Father. Thus our godly forefathers were free from their debts because they had laid their sins on Jesus Christ, although he himself had not yet paid their debt. On the other hand, we living in the latter times are free because now Christ has died and given satisfaction for our debts.

To sum up, mark well that the power of Christ's death reaches back to the beginning of time, but also reaches forward to the end of the age. Mark, too, that this debt is our sin, for he took all our sins upon himself, not to affect in any way his sinless nature so that he became sinful in the same way as we are, for our sins that he bore did not defile his body or heart in the way they defile us. He did not take upon himself our sins by adhesion but by imputation, so that our sins would be laid to his charge because he willingly submitted himself to that burden and the consequences of bearing it. Thus his spotless nature endured the pain of our punishment laid upon him, so that his righteousness could be imputed to us. This does not mean we ourselves are made righteous, but that we are counted as righteous by imputation. In this way he became our cautioner[19] and the guarantor of our eternal security by paying the full price on our behalf.

Christ has paid all our debts

However, also note that when Christ took this office upon himself he was not poor, for when a poor man appears in court as a cautioner he mocks the prosecutor, for he has not the wherewithal to fulfil such an office. No, Christ was not poor, but was rich enough not only to cover our entire debt charged to him, but debts a thousand times greater, for the virtue of his Godhead was infinite and could never be exhausted. Thus when he took upon himself our debt he was rich beyond all measure and because his store of grace and strength could bear the weight of our burden, our debt was paid and we were granted full exemption. Therefore, what Christ has already paid God will never be put to our

[19] See note 13 above.

charge.

This complete immunity from all our debts is ours by faith, therefore crave for an increase in your faith, and ask the Lord to grant you a confident quietness in your consciences, and ask him also to enable you to continue in well-doing, lest you are tempted to turn aside from him. For becoming involved in ill-doing will disturb your consciences, and a troubled conscience cannot repose in faith upon Jesus Christ, but will flee from him as if he were at enmity with you, as from one who is condemning you. On the other hand, when we maintain ourselves in well-doing and our consciences are quietly at rest, we can approach the Lord in confidence and say to him, 'I have cast my debts upon you, knowing that you have already paid them for me, and so because I believe I know I am secure.'

Unless we live uprightly we cannot truly believe in Jesus Christ, for upright living imparts peace to the conscience, and a conscience that is at peace is the means of strengthening our faith. For it is only through faith that we are assured Christ has died for us and that by virtue of his death we are on our way to the kingdom of heaven. Therefore, guard your conduct, live circumspectly, do not turn aside from God, but constantly increase in godliness so that your conscience will be always clear and at peace within you. Then your faith will flourish, and by that faith you will be counted righteous before God.

The Fathers' strong faith rebukes our weak faith

The point is this. The apostle wants to amplify the faith of the Fathers, for notwithstanding Christ had not yet been manifested in the former times, they had such a strong faith in him, that for him and his cause they endured any torture that could be inflicted upon them. Thus in recounting this to us he magnifies their faith, because even though they had not seen him in the flesh, they were willing to suffer so greatly for him. Surely this must convict and condemn us who have seen him in the flesh, delivered over to death, resurrected and ascended, and yet our faith is far weaker than theirs. Indeed, compared to them we are less willing to suffer on his account the loss of our possessions, let alone pain inflicted upon us.

Considering all this, it is patently obvious that so often, when much spiritual food has been offered to our people, they have declined to accept it. For there was never a nation that had as great an opportunity to be fed spiritually in Jesus Christ as we now have, yet no country has ever been so lacking in spiritual growth as ours is today, for the present state of our society plainly displays our evil living. So many chances to be fed with an abundance of spiritual nourishment have brought little or no spiritual growth, and this can only be the reason that we are so contemptuous of the offer of God's grace. For no matter how often it is offered to the people, they do not want it.

Therefore, begin to take stock of your ways, and strive to grow in your faith, for the evidence of spiritual growth is seen in the increase of faith and godly living. Whoever flees from vice and carnal lusts, and embraces rather the love of God and godliness, is showing signs of real spiritual growth. Absolutely everyone of us will be justly condemned by the example of the Fathers, unless we seek mercy for our past negligence. Nevertheless, be sure that if God renews our hearts and causes us in some measure at least to give some evidence of spiritual growth, then here in this life we may be sure of our ultimate inheritance in heaven.

Why Christ's incarnation was delayed

The final point is this. In this last verse, the apostle tells us why Christ was not manifested in our Fathers' days: they *receavit not the promis*. It was because the Lord of heaven made some other provision by appointing Christ to be exhibited in the flesh for us in these latter times. He determined he should come in our times so that we could have faith in him as one already made manifest, while the Fathers had faith in him not yet made manifest; thus both they and we are saved through our faith in him. So why did God appoint things in this way? It was that at the end of this age we might be perfected at the same time as the Fathers are made perfect.

Let me put it like this. Those who died from the beginning of creation such as Adam and Eve, even though they are separated from us by four or five thousand years, together with us they will be glorified in both body and soul as we enter heaven. I grant you that they are already perfected in their souls, and so their transformation has already been started, for their souls now rest and have fulfilment before the face of the Lamb. But as to their bodies, they still lie in their graves, sleeping as they await the blast of the trumpet, which is called in 1 Thessalonians 4:16

'the trumpet of God'. When his trumpet sounds, both they and we shall be wakened and shall rise to be perfected together. That then is the reason why God has appointed Christ to be exhibited in these latter days, that we and they in our bodies may enter heaven together. His purpose is to bring his earthly creation to completion by perfecting all his elect at the same time, even though the departed souls of the faithful of former times are already in heaven.

I do not want to persist in stating this, except that the Papists come in at this point with their teaching,[20] so I will simply refer you to some other places in Scripture where you may read the evidence for yourselves that the souls of the faithful are already resting in heaven before the face of Lamb. You need have no doubts about this biblical teaching. Heaven is described in Luke 16[21] as the place of rest, for the soul of Lazarus immediately after his death was carried there into the bosom of Abraham. There is no place of rest other than in heaven, and it is this same heaven which is already present in our souls. All who believe enter into this rest,[22] and the more this rest grows in your souls, the more of heaven you have within you. It was to this place that the soul of Lazarus was immediately carried after his departure.

Again, in a notable exposition in Luke 20,[23] Jesus says [verse 38] that God is not the God of the dead but of the living, for Abraham, Isaac and Jacob lived before Moses and their souls were then with the Lord, and therefore they could only have been in heaven. Further, in Revelation 6:9 we read that the departed souls of the elect were resting under the altar, and in chapter 15:2 we read that those who had conquered the beast stood in heaven beside the glassy sea with the harps of God, and sang the song of the Lamb whose face they saw. There are many other references such as these. But I thought it appropriate to show you some Scriptural evidence on which to ground your faith, that when you die,

[20] Bruce is referring to the Roman Catholic's teaching on purgatory. In Roman Catholic theology, purgatory is an intermediate state after physical death in which some of those ultimately destined for heaven must first 'undergo purification, so as to achieve the holiness necessary to enter the joy of heaven,' holding that 'certain offenses can be forgiven in this age, but certain others in the age to come.' (Catechism of the Catholic Church, www.vatican.va.)

[21] Luke 16:22.

[22] Hebrews 3:9-11.

[23] Luke 20:27-40, where the Sadducees asked about the Resurrection.

your souls depart immediately to God who gave it, as Solomon says in Ecclesiastes.[24]

Therefore, without any shadow of a doubt, the souls of the Fathers have begun to be perfected ahead of us, in that already they have entered that place of rest. As to their bodies, they still lie in their graves until the time comes for the trumpet of God to awaken both them and us, so that together we shall be gathered into our eternal abode. So you see why it was that the Lord delayed the manifestation of Christ in the flesh until these latter days. For even though their being made perfect has been begun, without us it will not be completed so that both they and we may be perfected together.

However, just suppose that Christ had not been appointed to be exhibited in these latter times, but had been manifested in the flesh in the former times, then it would not have been possible for us to be made perfect with them, because the former times would have been, in effect, the latter times. But because his manifestation in the flesh was appointed to have taken place in our times, by faith in him we shall be made perfect in company with the faithful who lived in the former times. Thus the apostle says, *God provyding ane better thing for ws that they without ws sould not be maid perfect.* This 'better thing' was the manifestation of Christ in the flesh in our times. For the Fathers only had the promise, but we know that its fulfilment is better than the promise. Therefore the difference between the promise of Christ in the flesh and its fulfilment is the same difference as the difference between them and us. And again it is undeniable that the fulfilment of the promise must produce in us an even greater measure of faith, providing that we are faithful. Therefore, what God appointed is something better for us.

The Lord in his mercy grant that we may reflect wisely upon our calling, for we now live in these times of better things. So may we find the effect of them working within ourselves. May we daily grow increasingly better, and more and more in our consciences apply the mercy that is freely offered in his death and passion, that it may be a balm for our wounded consciences. The Lord in his mercy work these things in us all and effectively and powerfully touch you with the assurance of all that you have heard. And this for the sake of Jesus Christ his

[24] Ecclesiastes 12:7.

Son, to whom with the Father and the Holy Ghost be all glory, praise and honour for now and evermore. Amen.

Appendix I

The Date of the Sermons

There are several hints in his sermons which enable us to estimate the approximate year(s) when they were preached. The first is in Sermon 9 where his subject is Sarah's conception. Having stated that the gift of Isaac had been obtained by 'the prayer of faith', he went on to say that 'those who yearn for a similar blessing ought to have recourse to the spiritual power of faith and prayer, so that what nature by its normal means has denied them may be procured and obtained'. He then states that when 'the natural means is not blessed for princes, for whom an heir is important, by faith and prayer they may obtain what nature has refused'. He next says, 'This particular exhortation, because it concerns our king, I shall leave until I next have the opportunity of speaking to him' (p. 147).

We know that before Queen Anne gave birth to Henry Frederick on 19 February 1594, she had miscarried several times. Therefore the sermon must have been preached before the summer of 1593 when it would have been public knowledge that she was expecting a child. James had married Anne at the Old Bishop's Palace in Oslo on 23 November 1589. Therefore we can safely assume that the sermon would not have been preached any earlier than late 1590, by which time she probably had had her first pregnancy and miscarriage. This narrows down the time-frame for the ninth sermons to between late 1590 and early 1593. The first eight sermons could have been earlier.

The next rather dubious hint is found in Sermon 17. Here is the full quotation:

> Think of those men who caused trouble in our streets this past week. Had they been indwelt with the fear of God, even with

> respect for men, would they have treated the king as they did, having no more regard for him than if he had been a private citizen who had no authority? How does such a thing happen? It came about partly because the king himself has been too familiar with them and so has deprived himself of his unique status, and partly because these courtiers have been educated so poorly, and have not been nurtured in the fear of God (p. 302).

I have trawled through scores of pages of Calderwood, covering the period 1589 to 1593, looking for any possible reference to some scandalous event witnessed by the public, and have come across only one account of a fracas that took place publicly on the Edinburgh High Street. It was on 7 January 1591, when a sword fight broke out involving the Duke of Lennox and Lord Hume against the Laird of Logie. The king fled the scene and took refuge in a skinner's booth. The full account is quoted in note 17 of Sermon 17. I have said this was hardly a reliable piece of evidence. Prof. Jane Dawson assured me this would not have been an unusual occurrence, and certainly Hewison comments that the king could be seen at times 'scuttling down shady alleys out of street brawls'. But this incident is surely worth bearing in mind.

A further piece of evidence is to be found in Sermon 14 where he speaks of some Assembly project that had been embarked upon inadvisedly, without humbly seeking God's mind and will. It had apparently failed as the outcome a year later made clear. I am suggesting that the reference could have been to a 'Book of Policy' that was agreed by the Assembly in August 1590. In the next Assembly, July 1591, a fine of 40 shillings was ordered to be imposed on the many Presbyteries that had ignored the previous Assembly's injunction (p. 239, note 10). The sermon could have been preached after the 1590 Assembly and before the 1591 Assembly, as it would have already become clear that most of the Kirk was cocking a snoop at the injunction.

The final pieces of evidence are references Bruce makes to France. They all concern the relief from persecution that the French Protestants had been granted, for in 1589 the Calvinist Henry of Navarre had succeeded the Catholic Henry III as King Henry IV. During the first four years of his reign from 1589 to 1593, it appears that the savage persecution of the Huguenots had ceased. (See p. 342, note 46.) In Sermon 19, Bruce again comments on the French Protestants: 'Look at the situation in France, where the Kirk that has so long suffered under the cross, shall yet be relieved' (p. 358). Although Henry IV abjured his Calvinistic stance in 1593 (doubtless to save himself from assassination), he did promulgate the Edict of Nantes in 1598, which guaranteed religious liberties to Protestants, thereby ending the Wars of Religion. The reference on page 549 (see note 2) to the assassination of Henry III of France in 1589, suggests an early slot for the Hebrews sermons in Henry IV's four years as France's first Protestant king. This fairly firm evidence confirms a time frame for the twenty-eight sermons of between 1590 and 1592.

Appendix II

The Apostate Earls

The Earls of Huntly, Errol and Angus are most certainly indirectly referred to by Bruce in various of his sermons on Hebrews 11. Hence this brief summary of godless men with whom the king feasted, hunted and whom he repeatedly protected from the just penalty of the law. It will not be difficult for those who read Bruce's sermons on Hebrews 11 to realise that there are frequently repeated references to powerful men who were greatly troubling the land.

George Gordon, 1st Marquess and 6th earl of Huntly, (*c.* 1563–1636), was a Roman Catholic conspirator who provoked personal wars in sixteenth-century Scotland. Son of the 5th earl (George Gordon), he was educated in France as a Roman Catholic. Although he signed the Presbyterian Confession of Faith in 1588, he was soon engaging in plots for a Spanish invasion of Scotland. Elizabeth I discovered this and sent on to James some of Huntly's treasonable correspondence with the Spanish authorities. However, James pardoned him. Huntly thereupon raised a rebellion in the north of Scotland, but was obliged to submit and, after a short, nominal imprisonment in Blackness Castle, was again set at liberty.

Within three years he was the prime instigator in a plot against his hereditary enemy, the Earl of Moray. He set fire to Moray's castle at Donibristle in Fife on Feb. 7, 1592, and he is said to have taken part in stabbing the Protestant earl to death. This outrage brought down upon Huntly the wrath of his enemies, who ravaged his lands, yet James himself treated him leniently. Some have alleged that the king was the secret instigator of the murder.

In December of the same year there occurred the plot of the

'Spanish Blanks'. Andrew Knox, Minister of Paisley, acting upon information supplied by an English agent in Scotland, was sent to arrest George Kerr, who was about to sail to Spain from Cumbrae in the Firth of Clyde, carrying with him incriminating correspondence. He was arrested and taken to Edinburgh along with the 'blank' documents, which were found along with other letters in a chest on Kerr's boat. The 'blanks' were signed by several members of the Catholic nobility of Scotland, but left blank to be filled in.

Kerr was examined by the Privy Council on 2 January 1593. Under torture, he said that the blanks were to be filled in by Crichton, to request a Spanish invasion on England, to be launched by an army that would land on the west coast of Scotland, and would be augmented by forces to be raised by the Catholic earls. Damagingly for James, Kerr was also alleged to be carrying a copy of a document by the king on the possible advantages to him in accepting Spanish help. In fact *Spanish State Papers* (Vol. IV, 603), reveal that James had a secret understanding with the earls, which was why in spite of the clamour from the Kirk, he sought to shield them from the penalty of the law.[1]

Three prominent Catholic Earls were found to be implicated: George Gordon, Earl of Huntly, Francis Hay, Earl of Errol and William Douglas, Earl of Angus. Although Huntly and Errol were ordered to appear on 5 February to explain themselves, they both travelled north with no intention of attending the hearing. However, when eight months later they confronted James some miles south of Edinburgh, their spurious explanation of the 'Blanks' was that they were only concerned with support of the Jesuits in Scotland.

In spite of the persistent outcry from the Presbyterian Ministers, James refused to take any action against these powerful Earls. A full account of the Kirk's strictures issued against 'the apostate lords' (four of whom were named along with three Jesuits), was recorded in the Assembly's minutes of May 1594. A severe reprimand was issued to the populace and ministers of Perth for receiving them, and the rest of the country were forbidden to 'furnish them meat, drink, house, nor harbourage'. As well as the Blanks, the strictures cited 'the treasonable fire raising and burning of the place of Donibristle, and the murder of

[1] Hume Brown, Vol. II, p. 169.

the late James, Earl of Moray.'[1] Two years later during the Assembly in Edinburgh in March, the king's failure to punish Huntly for the 'odious murder' of the Earl of Moray was minuted as again condemned by the Kirk.[2]

In the summer of 1594, Huntly joined the earls of Errol and Bothwell in an open rebellion. The earls gained a victory in October over Argyll's troops at Glenlivet, but when James himself rode to Aberdeen with an army, the earls slipped away into the northern mountains. However, Huntly's castle of Strathbogie, and Errol's house at Slaines were blown up by James; thereupon Huntly left Scotland in March 1595. The next year he returned secretly, submitted to the kirk, and was restored to his estates.

During the Assembly held in Dundee in 1598, the Presbyteries of Dundee and Arbroath were enjoined to summon the Countesses of Huntly, Sutherland and Caithness to subscribe to the Confession of Faith, 'under pain of excommunication'.[3] However, the Assembly minutes of 1599 recorded that the Earls of Huntly and Errol were [welcomed to] Edinburgh, an act of the king deliberately calculated as 'a hard dealing with the ministers of Edinburgh to break them.'[4] In another insult to the Kirk and unwise display of James' own desire for ascendancy Huntly was created a Marquis in April 1599, and soon after, with the Duke of Lennox, was appointed lieutenant of the north.

Doubts, however, as to the genuineness of Huntly's abjuration of Catholicism continued from time to time to trouble the kirk. He was excommunicated in 1608 and warded in Stirling Castle until late in 1610, when he again signed the Confession of Faith. After the accession of Charles I in 1625 Huntly lost much of his influence at court. For yet another minor private war he was imprisoned in Edinburgh Castle in 1635. The following year he died, declaring himself to be a Roman Catholic.

[1] Shaw, pp. 966-70.
[2] Shaw, p. 1032.
[3] Shaw, p. 1134.
[4] Shaw, p. 1156.

Appendix III

Anne Askew

Anne Askew was born *c.* 1520 in Lincolnshire. A noblewoman and a daughter of Sir William Askew, she was well-educated. She was affected by the Protestant ideas that her brothers, who were students at Cambridge, would talk about when they came home to visit. However, when there were widespread protests against Henry VIII's break with Rome and Dissolution of the Monasteries (The Pilgrimage of Grace 1537), Anne saw the protestors attack her home and seize her brothers. It is thought this violence influenced her against the old religion.

Anne was forced to marry Thomas Kyme, but it was not a happy union. Kyme was traditional in his religious views and Anne had come to hold evangelical views. She spent the early days of her marriage with her sister Jane, whose Protestant husband, George St Paul, was friends with Charles Brandon, Duke of Suffolk, and his wife Catherine, all of whom were supporters of religious reform. From 1538-1543 the law allowed public access to the English Bible in churches, and those of Protestant leanings took the opportunity to conduct Bible readings and share their evangelical views.

In 1543 Henry passed an act which prevented all women (and men below the rank of gentlemen) from reading the Bible. However, this did not prevent people like Anne from sharing their views and preaching because they had memorised scripture. In fact, this law made Anne even more determined to share her Bible knowledge with those who were deprived from reading the Bible themselves. Kyme, a traditional Catholic, could not cope with his strong-minded wife, so, advised by his local priests, he ejected her from his home. Anne petitioned for divorce, but, being denied by the local court, she headed to London where she was convinced that she would get her divorce.

'Anne revered Henry for freeing his people from the evil of popery. She was certain the king, who had himself disposed of several unworthy spouses, would allow a godly woman to be free of her unbelieving husband.'

While in London, Anne was introduced to Hugh Latimer (Bishop of Worcester), Nicholas Shaxton (Bishop of Salisbury) and Dr Edward Crome. These men were not only high profile Protestants, they were also connected to Henry's new queen, Catherine Parr. Anne flourished with the support of such friends and the climate of reform in London and 'quickly, exuberantly, she became one of London's most famous and beloved gospellers, her beauty and high rank marking her as the "Fair Gospeller".'

However, Anne was making enemies. Bishop Stephen Gardiner, a Catholic Conservative, was looking to discredit the new queen, Catherine Parr, and deal with Protestant climate that seemed to surround her. He saw Anne Askew as a heretic who was stirring up the populace. She was also linked to the Duchess of Suffolk, who was a good friend of the Queen. Perhaps Anne could be used to bring down the Queen.

Anne's refusal to return to her husband was just the 'weapon' Gardiner needed. Although she had been arrested again in March 1546 and again released, Gardiner summoned her to London to order her to return to her husband and used this opportunity to question Anne on her religious beliefs.

'Anne no longer attempted to evade admitting her own beliefs. She treated transubstantiation as a joke. Of course Jesus has said he was the bread of the Eucharist. He had also said he was the door to salvation—did that mean he was present in any door a priest chose to bless? She was courting martyrdom and on June 18 she was condemned to die at the stake.'[1]

She was then moved to the tower of London to await execution. But Gardiner was determined to extract from Anne evidence that Catherine Parr and her close friend Catherine Willoughby, the Duchess of Suffolk, had links to the 'sect' of evangelical Protestants. He saw Anne as a means of seriously compromising those in high estate. Therefore Anne was put in the rack.

[1] Lindsey, p. 195.

The Lieutenant of the Tower was appalled, for the rack was only used to extract confessions of guilt, and Anne had already been sentenced to death. He hastened to convey a message to the king, and secured an order for the racking to be stopped immediately. However, in the meantime, Gardiner's henchman Wriothesley had pressed on with the torture to such an extreme that Anne was then no longer able to stand, far less walk. Yet she had refused to yield any information whatsoever to her tormentors.

As she awaited death in the Tower, she wrote a full account of her arrest, interrogation and racking and gave the manuscripts to her maid who, having smuggled them out of the Tower, passed them on to some German merchants who in turn gave them to the exiled Protestant Bishop Bale. He passed them on his friend John Foxe, who included them in a fuller account of this courageous woman.

As well as being known for her gospel preaching and death at the stake, Anne Askew is also famed for being the only recorded woman to have been tortured in the Tower of London. Thus, on the 16th July 1546, Anne Askew, John Lascelles and two other Protestants were burned at the stake at Smithfield. Anne had to be carried to the stake on a chair because of her injuries from racking, and the stake itself also had a seat fixed to it to support her broken body.

At the last minute, Wriothesley forced his way through the crowd to offer pardon to the four if they would recant. Anne answered for them all, crying out loudly that she 'came not hither to deny my Lord and Master'. The torch was lit and the four died quickly, thanks to a friend who had thrown gunpowder into the flames. A fortuitous thunderstorm, breaking out suddenly, added to the legend that grew to surround the death of the Fair Gospeller: the 18th century ecclesiastical historian John Strype tells us that the thunder, 'seemed to the people to be the voice of God, or the voice of an angel'.

Anne Askew was just 25 years old when she died but her short life had been courageous and significant. In an age where women had no voice or opinions of their own, she was an outspoken preacher and died for her faith, remaining true to her friends and her Lord. She is reputed to have written the following poem while in Newgate prison. Were these the words to which Bruce referred at the beginning of his fourth sermon, 'A British poet has written at some length in praise and commendation of faith, this precious jewel of a genuine, living faith'? Perhaps, but alas we cannot know for certain. Almost certainly, Bruce would have known of Lady Anne Askew's courageous faith and her faithful stand for the truth.

> Like as the armed knight appointed to the field,
> With this world will I fight, and Faith shall be my shield.
>
> Faith is that weapon strong, which will not fail at need.
> My foes, therefore, among, therewith will I proceed.
>
> As it is had in strength and force of Christes way
> It will prevail at length, though all the devils say nay.
>
> Faith in the fathers old obtained rightwisness
> Which make me very bold to fear no world's distress.
>
> I now rejoice in heart, and Hope bid me do so,
> For Christ will take my part and ease me of my woe.
>
> Thou saist, Lord, whoso knock, to them wilt thou attend.
> Undo, therefore, the lock and thy strong power send.
>
> More enmyes now I have, than hairs upon my head.
> Let them not me deprave, but fight thou in my stead.
>
> On thee my care I cast, for all their cruel spight
> I set not by their haste, for thou art my delight.
>
> I am not she that list my anchor to let fall,
> For every drizzling mist my ship substancial.
>
> Not oft use I to wright, in prose nor yet in rime,
> Yet will I shew one sight, that I saw in my time.
>
> I saw a rial throne, where Justice should have sit
> But in her stead was one, Of moody cruel wit.
>
> Absorpt was rightwisness, as of the raging flood
> Sathan in his excess suct up the guiltless blood.
>
> Then thought I, Jesus Lord, when thou shalt judge us all,
> Hard is it to record on these men what will fall.
>
> Yet Lord, I thee desire or that they do to me
> Let them not taste the hire Of their iniquity.

For fuller accounts of Lady Anne Askey, see *ODNB*, Vol. 2, pp. 709-11; *Divorced, Beheaded, Survived: A Feminist Reinterpretation of the Wives of Henry VIII*, Karen Lindsey (Addison-Wesley, Reading, MA, USA, 1995), pp. 190-97; *Foxe's Book of Martyrs*, (Religious Tract & Book Soc., Edin. 1883).

Appendix IV

King James' Account of the Murder of the Earl of Gowrie

(*This is James' own account which Robert Bruce could not accept as truthful. Therefore he declined to assure his congregation that King James had no involvement in the murder of the Earl of Gowrie and his brother. It was his refusal that was the reason why he was exiled to France by the king. It was engrossed in the General Assembly's minutes of March 1601.*[1])

On Tuesday last, Alexander Ruthven [master of Gowrie,] came to Falkland to his majesty, and found him at his pastimes, and desired him to go to St Johnstone, so he led from Falkland to Perth as a most innocent lamb, from his palace to the slaughter house. There he got his dinner, a cold dinner, yea, a very cold dinner, as they know, who were there.

After dinner, Alexander Ruthven led his majesty up a turnpike, and through a passage, the door whereof; so soon as they had entered in, shut to with a lock; then through a gallery, whose door also was locked; through a chamber, and the door thereof locked also; and, last of all, brought him to a room scarcely six foot broad, and six foot wide, and the door thereof he locked also; in which there was standing an armed man with a drawn dagger in his hand to have done this filthy deed, the most unnatural, and contrary to that duty we owe to princes. Then Alexander covered his head, and said, 'I am sure, your heart accuses you now. You were the death of my father, and here is a dagger to be avenged on you for that death.'

[1] Shaw, pp. 1227-30.

Now judge you, good people, what danger your David was in, when, as an innocent lamb, he was enclosed between two hungry lions thirsting for his blood, and four locks between him and his friends and servants; so that they might neither hear, nor harken to him. This was his danger. But what sort of delivery did he get? It was wholly miraculous, altogether to be ascribed to God, and no part to man. And, among many that occurred, I shall point out to you five or six circumstances, which you will all call and acknowledge to be miraculous.

And, first, his majesty standing between two armed men, without any kind of armour, having nothing on, but his hunting horn about his neck, when he, at his entry , should have been astonished at the sight of an armed man to take his life; yet, on the contrary part, this man was so astonished at his sight, that he might neither move foot nor hand. Was not this miraculous?

But yet further, when Alexander had taken him by the throat, and had held the dagger to his breast, not two inches from it, so that there was scarcely two inches between his death and his life; yet even then, by his gracious, Christian and most loving words, he overcame the traitor.

His words were these, 'Mr Alexander, consider, that you are a Christian; and further, that hitherto you have been trained up in the principles and grounds of Christianity. And then consider how you were brought up in the school, which sent forth many noble and holy youths, the college of Edinburgh, under Mr Robert Rollock, that holy man, and most worthy of all good memory, who could never have taught you to put hands on your prince. And last of all, Mr, suppose you take my life, neither you, nor your brother, will be king after me yea, the subjects of Scotland will root you out, and all your name.'

The words so moved the heart of the traitor, that he began to enter into making conditions with the king, and made him swear, (which he also did,) that all these things should be forgotten, and that after he should ever be favourable to him and his brother. And so he went forth to his brother, from whom he received commission to dispatch him hastily.

He then coming up again, brings a pair of silk garters in his hand; after he had locked the door, said, 'Traitor, thou must die: and therefore lay thy hands together, that I may bind thee.' To the intent, no doubt, that, he being bound, they might have strangled him, and cast him into a cave, or pit, which they had prepared for that use; that, no blood being found, his friends might miss him without suspicion, and not know where to seek him. Now here is the third miracle.

The king answered the traitor, 'I was born a free prince. I have lived hitherto a free prince. I shall never die bound.'

With this, each of them gripped each other's throat. While in wrestling the king overcame, and got him under him. Now, is not this miraculous? Will any consider it, the master of Gowrie, an able young man in comparison to the king, I am sure, had strength double, yea, and threefold greater than the king; and yet is overcome, and cast under. When they were thus wrestling, up came John Ramsay [notary] by the black turnpike; and, at the king's command, gave the master a death stroke. Now yet a miracle.

My lord, being in the close, when he heard that the master was slain, he had so bewitched the hearts of the people of Perth, by the counterfeited virtues he had begun to make himself known amongst them, that if he had cried, 'My brother is murdered,' that same people would have sacked the same whole house but yet so the Lord directed by His providence, that he came up the stair immediately with eight with him. And mark, how that same word, which they had prepared to be a word for the keeping close of their knavery, God used to be a means for the preservation of the prince: for they had appointed this for their watchword, 'The king is gone to the Inch.' Which words, his servants hearing, ran about to meet his majesty in the Inch; and going by the window, where the king and the master were wrestling, they heard the king's screeches and cries, which had made such impressions on their hearts, that, so long as they live, will never go put of them; and are here sitting to bear witness to it. The cry was, 'Treason, fy, help, earl Mar, I am murdered.'

The king's servants hearing the cries, presently came up to this black turnpike. Now yet a miracle. Into the chamber with the king are only four, two lads, and two men; and one of them mutilated. My lord, a man well exercised in arms, came up with eight with him, And, at the first, called up all these four in a nook; and never rests until John Ramsay chanced to cry, 'Fy upon the cruel traitor. Hast thou not done evil enough? Thou hast gotten the king's life; and would thou have ours?' At which speeches, he drew back a little and in going back he got the stroke whereof he died.

This is the very truth of the act, which I have received not by the king's majesty; but by him, who should have been the doer of the deed. He is living yet; he is not slain; a man well enough known to this town, Andrew Henderson [of Lawton,] chamberlain to my lord Gowrie. This day I received a letter from him, subscribed by his own hand. Any man, that would see it, come to me, and see, if they can recognise his handwriting for their satisfaction. The tenor of the letter is this.

'It is of truth, that, on Tuesday last, I was commanded by my lord of Gowrie to ride with his brother to Falkland from where he sent me back again, to tell my lord, that the king was coming, and to bid prepare for his coming. My lord commanded me to put on my secret, and my plate sleeves, and to await on the master, and do whatever he bade me.

At the master's alighting, I went to him, and told him of my lord's command, which I had received. He took me with him up a turnpike, through a passage, a gallery, and a chamber, and locked me into the room that goes off the chamber. At which doing, I began to grow afraid, and suspected some evil against the king; and then I took to my knees to pray, that it would please his majesty never to suffer me to be employed in such a deed; and while I was sitting on my knees, Mr Alexander came with the king in his hand.'

The rest of his narration differs in almost nothing from this which you have heard according to the king's information.

Appendix V

Bruce's Scots Language

Originally derived from West Germanic and Anglo-Frisian, Scots Leid or Lallans, as it was known, was the language of much of Scotland for nearly five centuries. The region in which it was spoken was not large, Gaelic being the language of Galloway and the Highlands. But from the Borders to the Rivers Clyde and Forth, and northwards to the East of Scotland, Braid Scots was the common language.

During the reign of King James IV (1488-1513), Braid Scots had reached its zenith. The monarch was wealthy and refined, speaking several European languages as well as his own. European visitors to the court heard poets reciting their verses in Scots in the king's presence. However, with the Battle of Flodden in 1513, when James IV was killed and the Scots were decisively defeated by Henry VIII's army, the slow decline began of both Scottish power and the Scots language.

In 1560 came the Reformation with its Geneva Bible, along with the influence of correspondence in English to and from the Reformers. Finally, the union of the crowns in 1603 brought James VI to the English throne. The consequent change in the Court's spoken language, together with the influence of Shakespeare and Ben Jonson, ultimately replaced the Braid Scots with Elizabethan English.

This change was by no means rapid throughout Scotland. The normal needs of life retained Scots words in the common speech of both people and nobility. The language in which Bruce preached was typical of a Scots dialect spoken in the closing decades of the 16th century; it was partially English but retained many characteristic of Braid Scots in its everyday terminology. Therefore, in my work of translating Bruce's sermons, I was constantly thrown back upon the invaluable

Dictionary of the Scots Language. As my work proceeded, I built up a glossary of scores of words that are no longer known or used today, but which were used constantly by Bruce in his preaching.

Those who are familiar with Bruce's sixteen sermons, republished in 1843 by the Wodrow Society and edited by William Cunningham, should note that they are not in Bruce's original spoken dialect, but have been translated into mid-nineteenth century English. By contrast, the present translation is direct from the 16th century language of the Minister of Edinburgh.

Appendix V will give readers the opportunity first to transliterate a few pages into the English alphabet and then to translate them. They are just four of the 340 pages of Bruce's sermon scripts on Hebrews 11, and have been reproduced in Appendix V by kind permission of New College Library, Edinburgh.

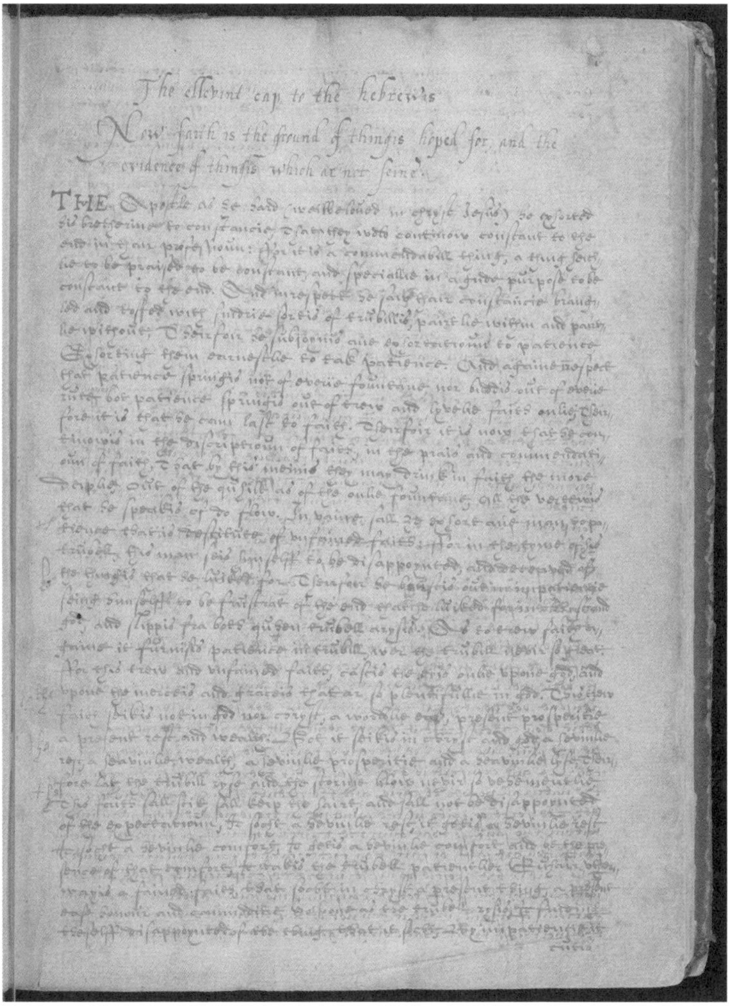
The ellevint cap. to the hebrewis

Now faith is the ground of thingis hoped for, and the evidence of thingis which ar not seine.

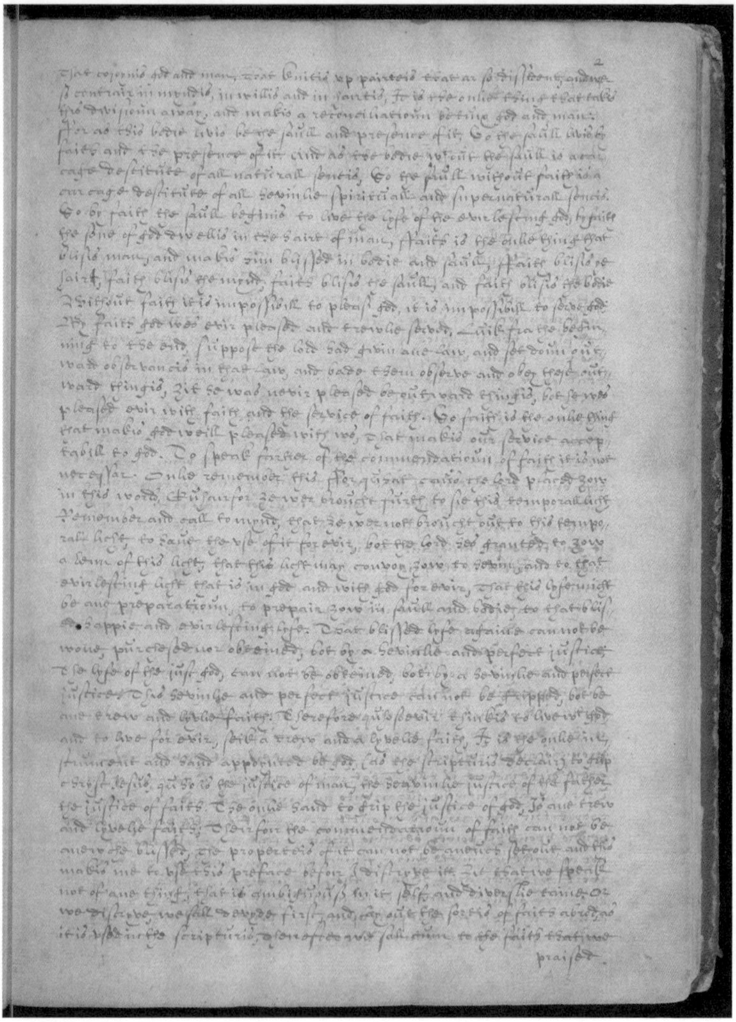

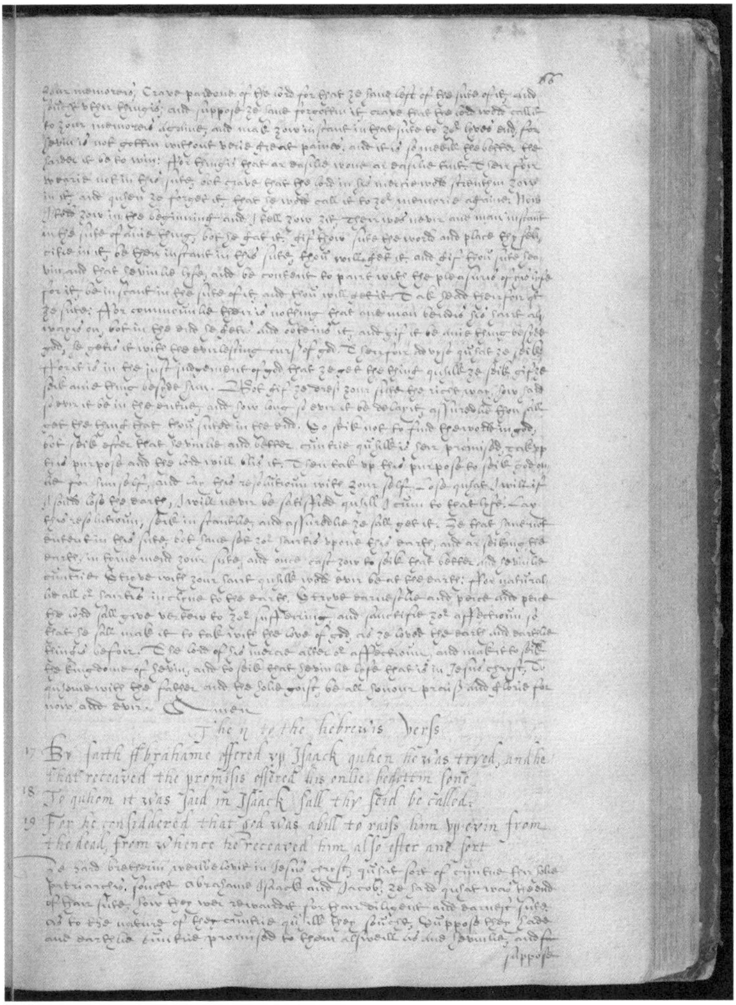

The 11 to the hebrewis verss

17 By faith Abrahame offered vp Isaack quhen he was tryed, and he
that receaved the promisis offered his onlie begottin sone
18 To quhom it was said in Isaack sall thy seid be called.
19 For he considdered that god was abill to raiss him vp evin from
the dead, from whence he receaved him also efter ane sort

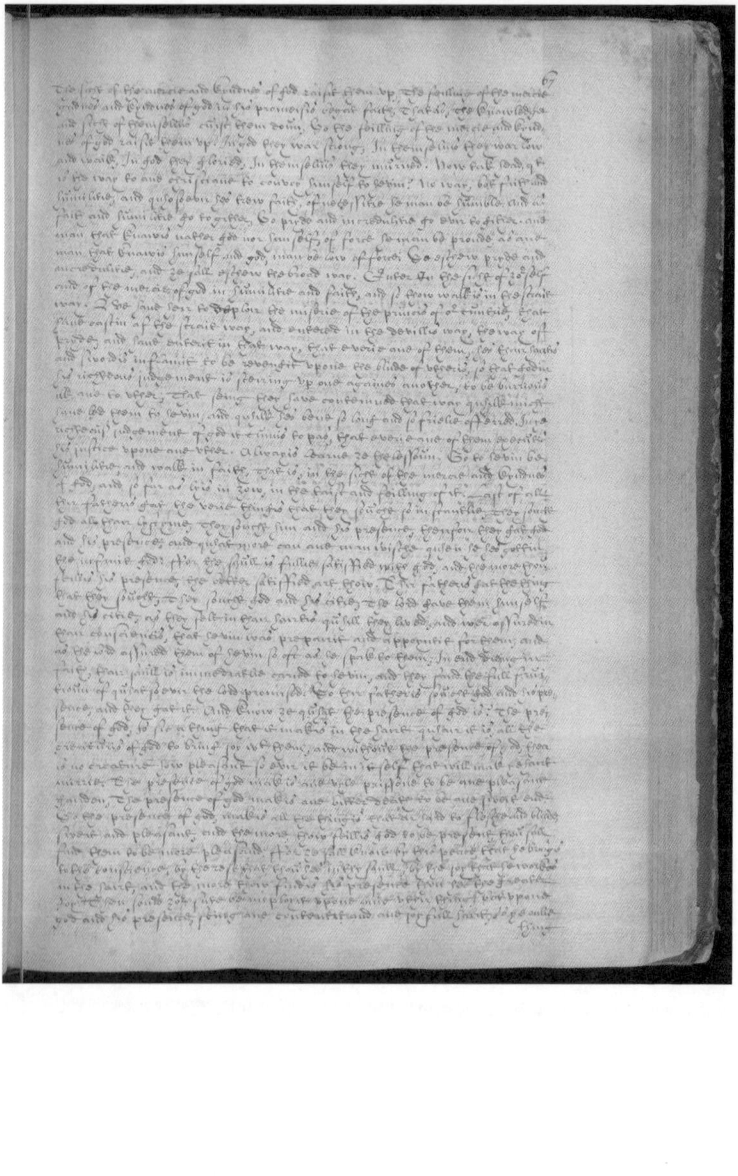

Index

Personae

Events

Subjects

Scripture Index

Genesis

Luke

John

Acts

Romans

1 Corinthians

2 Corinthians

Galatians

Ephesians

Philippians